International Business

International Business

SHAD MORRIS
Brigham Young University

JAMES OLDROYD
Brigham Young University

WILEY

EDITORIAL DIRECTOR	Michael McDonald
EXECUTIVE EDITOR	Lisé Johnson
SENIOR MARKETING MANAGER	Anita Osborne
PROJECT MANAGER	Jennifer Manias
PRODUCT DESIGNER	Wendy Ashenburg
EDITORIAL ASSISTANT	Alden Farrar
SENIOR CONTENT MANAGER	Dorothy Sinclair
SENIOR PRODUCTION EDITOR	Sandra Rigby
SENIOR DESIGNER	Wendy Lai
SENIOR PHOTO EDITOR	Billy Ray

This book was typeset in 9.5/12.5 Source Sans Pro Regular at SPi Global and printed and bound by Courier/Kendallville. The cover was printed by Courier/Kendallville.

This book is printed on acid free paper. ∞

Founded in 1807, John Wiley & Sons, Inc. has been a valued source of knowledge and understanding for more than 200 years, helping people around the world meet their needs and fulfill their aspirations. Our company is built on a foundation of principles that include responsibility to the communities we serve and where we live and work. In 2008, we launched a Corporate Citizenship Initiative, a global effort to address the environmental, social, economic, and ethical challenges we face in our business. Among the issues we are addressing are carbon impact, paper specifications and procurement, ethical conduct within our business and among our vendors, and community and charitable support. For more information, please visit our website: www.wiley.com/go/citizenship.

ISBN 978-1-119-43361-3

Library of Congress Cataloging-in-Publication Data

Names: Morris, Shad, author. | Oldroyd, James, author.
Title: International business / By Shad Morris, Brigham Young University,
James Oldroyd, Brigham Young University.
Description: Hoboken, NJ : John Wiley & Sons, Inc., [2019] | Includes
bibliographical references and index. |
Identifiers: LCCN 2018012495 (print) | LCCN 2018013325 (ebook) | ISBN
9781119433613 (epub) | ISBN 1119433614 (epub) | ISBN 9781119244851 (pdf)
| ISBN 1119244854 (pdf) | ISBN
Subjects: LCSH: International business enterprises. | International trade. |
International finance. | International economic relations.
Classification: LCC HD2755.5 (ebook) | LCC HD2755.5 .M673 2019 (print) | DDC
658/.049—dc23
LC record available at https://lccn.loc.gov/2018012495

The inside back cover will contain printing identification and country of origin if omitted from this page. In addition, if the ISBN on the back cover differs from the ISBN on this page, the one on the back cover is correct.

Printed in the United States of America.

V057381_060518

About the Authors

Photo courtesy Shad Morris

SHAD MORRIS is the Georgia White Fellow and Associate Professor of International Business at the Marriott School of Business, Brigham Young University. He received his Ph.D. from Cornell University. He has spent over seven years of his adult life outside the United States, living in countries like China, India, South Korea, Bulgaria, Serbia and Denmark. In addition, Professor Morris conducts research and consults in many emerging markets within Asia, Latin America and Africa. He has been a visiting professor at the Indian School of Business, China Europe International Business School and the Copenhagen Business School. He has been a Fulbright Scholar and is a Research Fellow at Cambridge University. He has also received numerous awards for his international research, including one of the top research awards from the Academy of Management.

Professor Morris serves as a Council Member for the Global Management Center Board of Directors and has held leadership roles within the Strategic Management Society. Prior to becoming an academic, he worked for the World Bank, for Management Systems International, and for Alcoa. He speaks Bulgarian and has working knowledge of Serbo-Croatian.

Photo courtesy James Oldroyd

JAMES OLDROYD is the Ford Motor/Richard Cook Associate Professor of Strategy at the Marriott School of Business, Brigham Young University. He received his Ph.D. from the Kellogg School of Management at Northwestern University. He was an assistant professor of management at SKK-GSB in Seoul, South Korea for five years and an assistant professor of international business at The Ohio State University for three years.

Professor Oldroyd's research explores the intersection of networks and knowledge flows. This work has been published in outlets such as the *Academy of Management Review*, *Organization Science* and *Harvard Business Review*.

He teaches courses on strategy, strategy implementation, international business, and negotiations to undergraduates, MBAs, and executives. In addition, to teaching at SKK, OSU, and BYU, he has taught at the Indian School of Business and the University of North Carolina. He is actively involved in delivering custom leadership training courses for numerous companies including Samsung, Doosan, SK, Quintiles, and InsideSales. He speaks Lao and Thai.

Preface

Welcome to *International Business (IB)—a cutting-edge platform* for learning about international business. Interactive, modular, and innovative, this easy-to-use textbook answers two key questions:

1. **What does today's global market look like?**
2. **How do businesses succeed within the global market?**

Interactive

International Business meets your students where they live and learn with digital resources such as white-board animations and seamlessly embedded videos. Interactive resources illustrate content for students while deepening their understanding, focusing their attention, and significantly shortening readings. In fact, this text is ½ to ¾ the length of most international business textbooks—with even richer content.

Each chapter is accompanied by at least one innovative animation to bring content to life. The animations also allow you to flip your classroom and assign the animations for students to view before coming to class. Research shows that student recall increases by more than 15% when material is presented with animations versus a typical lecture presentation.

Modular

The international business environment changes quickly, and your credibility with students relies largely on how current your information and cases are. Because *International Business* is designed in a modular fashion, we can update it as needed, providing you with a seamlessly current version every time you teach. You will always have the most up-to-date content of any international business text, and when you step in front of each class, you'll be armed with current cases and examples. *International Business* provides short video and written cases integrated with each chapter, eliminating the expense and hassle of assigning both a textbook and an expensive course packet.

Innovative

International Business innovates by providing vital information not found in any other IB textbook. We introduce essential topics your students are concerned about, such as global sustainability, poverty, technology, innovation, and leadership. These issues put international business growth in real-life context and vastly increase student engagement. For example, in the simulation called Poverty Trap students are acquainted with the conditions of entrenched poverty that often exclude groups from participating fully in the economy. Who knows what innovative solutions your students will come up with?

Another innovation is our simplified framework, PEST. By organizing the daunting complexity of most IB textbooks, *International Business* helps students see how each fact they acquire relates to the whole, increasing comprehension and applicability. The acronym PEST stands for four factors that influence successful decisions in international business.

1. Political
2. Economic
3. Sociocultural
4. Technological

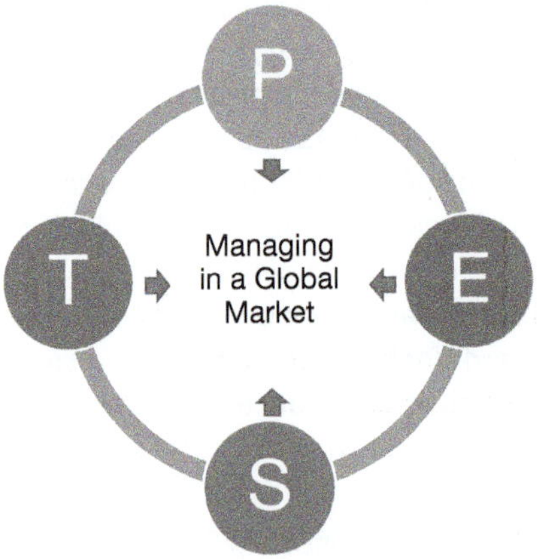

But don't just take our word for it. See what some of your colleagues have said. We've bolded the highlights.

> *Congratulations. This book appears to be* ***setting the tone*** *for a new wave of IB books. An innovative book that goes much deeper into a number of salient topics that are frequently covered in IB courses.* ***Colorful examples and graphics that will keep students (and faculty) entertained and engaged.*** *Excellent coverage of financial, currency and exchange concepts. Solid graphics. I like the current and planned video and website links.*
>
> *Christopher Robertson, Northeastern University*

You've done a nice job looking at key concepts and how they relate to each of the chapters. Also, your ***pedagogy is spot on for the typical college student*** *(layout of chapter spiced with videos, short cases, and quizzes to test learning).*

Chip Baumgardner, Pennsylvania College of Technology

A new book, up-to-date, that includes many of the issues that global businesses are facing today. ***Well organized and easy to follow***

Masud Chand, Wichita State University

Relevant, well-written, well-organized and with ***materials that will quickly draw students in.***

Andrea Smith-Hunter, Siena College

New topics in IB were covered and explained very well with useful examples. The use of ***current examples and topics*** *were the biggest strengths in the adoption decision.*

Prakesh Dheeriya, California State University, Dominguez Hills

None of the textbooks cover poverty in this detail *and the chapter on technology is followed by innovation, which is very logical.*

Anthony Pantaleon, Baruch College

An ***outstanding*** *introductory International Business text. One that could be used in a community college or in a four-year institution.*

-Larry Devan, Frederick Community College

Great coverage of material. Good current examples. ***Easy way to bring a complicated subject to beginners.***

John Michaels, California University of Pennsylvania

The textbook appears to add some elements that are ***reflective of the current business environment, particularly along the social and technological dimensions.***

Dan Himelstein, University of California, Berkeley

You can believe us, too. We've taught this innovative content on multiple continents to thousands of students, and are convinced that using *International Business* will dramatically increase your students' satisfaction and learning. Not only are the content and product features cutting-edge, they'll cut your preparation and evaluation time significantly. As you use this platform, remember that just because you're having fun doesn't mean that they're not learning!

Content and Organization

Part One: Globalization and Tools

Starting with debate is always engaging to students. IB's first chapter introduces the current debates about globalization and its future role. Chapter 2 focuses on why companies still want to do business in a global environment and teaches them the PEST tool to effectively analyze the global market.

1. Globalization
2. Analytical Tools for International Business

Part Two: Analyzing the Global Market

The ten chapters of part two (half the book!) demonstrate the nature of today's global market and teach students to critically analyze *any* country environment. Chapters are divided into subsections based on the PEST analysis. By analyzing political, economic, socio-cultural and technological factors, students can effectively assess the current opportunities and threats in different countries' markets.

Politics

3. Political Systems
4. Legal Environment

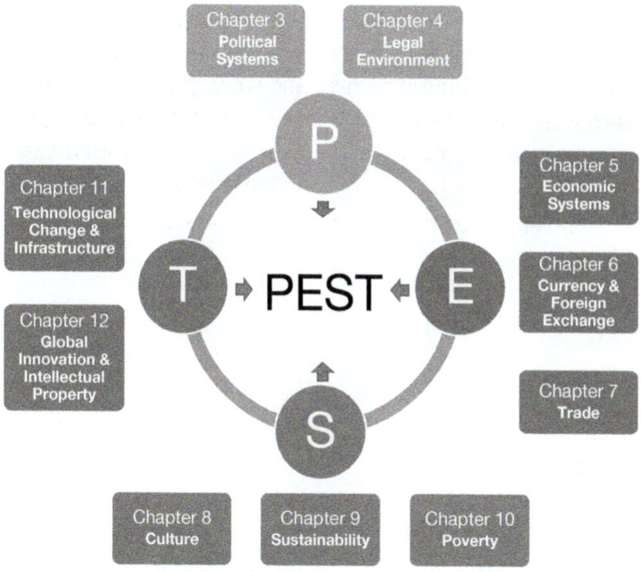

Economics

5. Economic Systems

6. Currency and Foreign Exchange

7. Trade

Socioculture

8. Culture

9. Sustainability

10. Poverty

Technology

11. Technological Change and Infrastructure

12. Global Innovation and Intellectual Property

Part Three: Managing the Global Market

The remaining eight chapters of the book focus on how businesses can succeed in a complex foreign market. These chapters help students understand how and when to enter a new market, what their international strategy should be, how to structure the organization, and how to manage and lead the different functions of the organization to ensure successful internationalization.

13. Country Selection and Entry Modes

14. International Strategy

15. Organizational Structures

16. Global Leadership

The final chapters in the textbook address four core functional parts of a business and how they can be managed to improve international businesses.

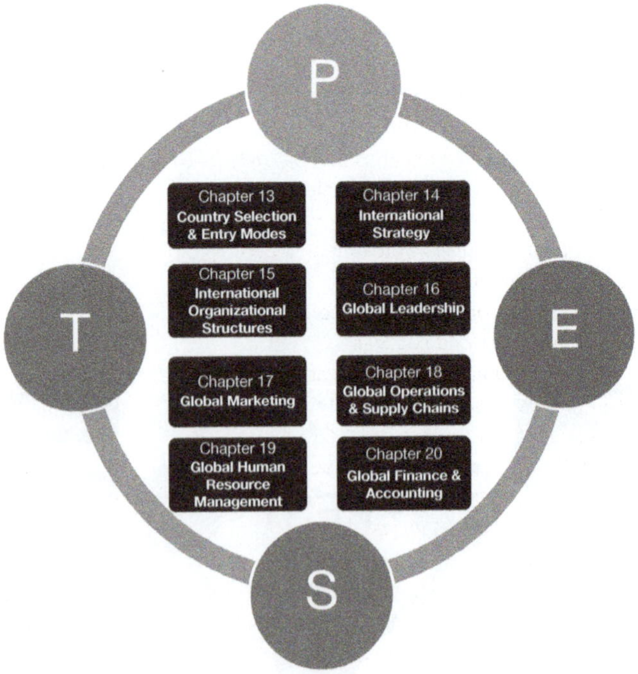

17. Global Marketing

18. Operations and Supply Chain Management

19. Global Human Resource Management

20. Global Finance and Accounting

Teaching and Learning Resources

The *International Business* Companion Site (www.wiley.com/college/morris) includes myriad tools and resources for instructors and students.

The Instructor's Manual offers helpful teaching ideas, including advice on course development, sample assignments, and recommended activities. It also offers chapter-by-chapter text highlights, learning objectives, lecture outlines, class exercises, lecture notes, and tips on using cases.

The Comprehensive Test Bank includes multiple-choice, short answer, and essay questions that vary in degree of difficulty. In addition to being tagged for learning objective and difficulty level, the questions are tagged with Bloom's Taxonomy categories and AACSB guidelines. The *Respondus Test Bank* allows instructors to modify and add questions to the master bank and to customize their exams.

Robust PowerPoint Presentation Slides consist of a series of slides for each chapter that incorporate key points from the text and include text illustrations as appropriate.

Practice Quizzes with questions of varying levels of difficulty help students evaluate their progress through each chapter. They are accessed on the student portion of the *IB* companion site.

Management Weekly Updates emailed to you every Monday, spark classroom debate around current events that apply to your business course topics. These relevant news articles and videos are tagged to your textbook and complemented by discussion questions. http://wileyibupdates.com/.

WileyPLUS

WileyPLUS is an innovative, research-based, online environment for effective teaching and learning. Students learn and prepare for class while identifying their strengths and nurturing core skills. A personalized study guide is created for each student as they interact with you, the course content, and their peers. Students using WileyPLUS become invested in their learning experience, make deeper connections to the material, and use their time more efficiently.

WileyPLUS is class tested and ready-to-go for instructors. As an instructor using *WileyPLUS*, you'll be able to easily

- Organize learning activities
- Manage student collaboration
- Customize your course by adding special materials
- Guide students by assigning specific content
- Set up and monitor group learning
- Assess student engagement
- Gain immediate insights to help inform teaching

Special visual reports in WileyPLUS will allow you to

- Help identify problem areas in student learning
- Focus your attention and resources
- See exactly where students are struggling
- Create early interventions

Acknowledgments

International Business is a dynamic team project. We'd like to acknowledge the work of key team members.

We've tested the content and received feedback from students in schools in the United States and around the world. Their push-back and insights have made this a relevant and student-friendly text.

- Ohio State University
- University of North Carolina
- Cornell University
- Northwestern University
- Brigham Young University
- Indian School of Business
- China Europe International Business School
- Sungkyunkwan University
- Copenhagen Business School

Student research assistants Emily Burton, Tyler Hatch, Adriel Johnson, Derek Kirchhoefer, and Mallory Stack have stood out among their peers in insight and helpfulness.

Professionals—leaders of international businesses, management development program participants, business recruiters, and our colleagues—have given us invaluable context and feedback. In particular, we would like to express our appreciation to Jonathan Wood and Bruce Money, directors of the Whitmore Global Management Center at the Marriott School of Business. We would also like to thank Jonathon Richards and Lisa Thomas for their helpful insights, research and editorial support. They are wonderful partners.

Team members at Wiley have been key to developing this text and the seamlessly integrated material that makes navigating it easy. Thanks to Executive Editor Lisé Johnson; Project Manager Jennifer Manias; Freelance Development Editor, Elisa Adams; Product Designers, Rebecca Costantini and Wendy Ashenberg; and Marketing Manager, Anita Osborne for helping us bring such a massive undertaking to fruition. Their professionalism has enriched our content and our own lives. Their patience with us as we moved through the process has been inspiring.

We are extremely grateful to our families. Our oldest daughters Susan Oldroyd and Bailey Morris are students themselves. They have made sure our test questions are relevant and that our stories are student-relatable. Our wives Mindi Morris and Kim Oldroyd—who have contributed in so many ways to this product—are always sources of invaluable guidance and assistance. Their continued enthusiasm and support has made a difficult process more pleasant and rewarding. Our families' many contributions to this publication, and to our lives, fill our hearts with gratitude.

Finally, thanks to the numerous reviewers who have contributed valuable time and feedback. They have been so thoroughly involved in producing this product that we consider them part of the team:

Bamidele Adekunle, University of Guelph; Ryerson University
Mohammad Ali, University of Maryland Eastern Shore
Hussein Alzyoud, Athabasca University
Winston Awadzi, Delaware State University
Kiran Awate, Ohio State University
Anastasia Bailey, The Ohio State University
Chip Baumgardner, Penn College
Patricia Beckenholdt, University of Maryland, University College
Mamoun Benmamoun, Saint Louis University
Ed Bruning, University of Manitoba
Paul Buffa, Missouri Baptist University
Lana Carnes, Eastern Kentucky University
Masud Chand, Wichita State University
Alexander Chen, University of Central Arkansas
Frank F. Cotae, Mount Royal University
Sheng Deng, Brock University
Harry Derderian, Eastern Michigan University
Larry Devan, Frederick Community College
Ratan Dheer, Florida Atlantic University
Prakesh Dheeriya, California State University, Dominguez Hills
Keith Dickinson, The University of Texas at Dallas
Frank DuBois, American University
David Estelle, Indiana University East
Frank Ferrara, Northern Virginia Community College
John Finley, Columbus State University
Wing Fok, Loyola University, New Orleans
Animesh Ghoshal, DePaul University
Debbie Gilliard, Metropolitan State University of Denver
Connie Golden, Lakeland Community College
Joseph Goldman, University of Minnesota
Trina Hamilton, University at Buffalo (SUNY)
Laura Hart, Barry University
Dan Himelstein, University of California, Berkeley
Julie Huang, Rio Hondo College
Sara Jackson, University of the Incarnate Word
Stephen Jaros, Southern University
Douglas Johansen, Jacksonville University
Ali Kara, Penn State University, York
Raihan Khan, SUNY Oswego
Rajat Khanna, Tulane University
Jan Klakurka, University of Toronto
Michael Kuryla, SUNY Broome Community College
Ann Langlois, Palm Beach Atlantic University
Gary Lefort, American International College
John Lipinski, Middle Tennessee State University
John Manley, Iona College
David McCalman, University of Central Arkansas
Mantha Mehallis, Florida Atlantic University
John Michaels, California University of Pennsylvania

Athanasios Mihalakas, SUNY Brockport
Steven Moff, Pennsylvania College of Technology
Dovel Myers, Shawnee State University
Lilac Nachum, Baruch College
Nabil Nahra, Montclair State University
Maydelin Nunez Noguez, Mount Royal University
Sam Okoroafo, University of Toledo
Anthony Pantaleon, Baruch College
Daewoo Park, Xavier University
Panagiotis Petratos, California State University, Stanislaus
Herve Queneau, Brooklyn College
Mahesh Raisinghani, Texas Woman's University
William Rapp, New Jersey Institute of Technology
Christopher Robertson, Northeastern University
Carlene Rose, Lakes Region Community College
Rajib Sanyal, Ball State University
Raj Shea, California State University, Eastbay
Mark Sheehan, Bunker Hill Community College
Thomas Shirley, San Jose State University
Pradip Shukla, Chapman University
Harold Simpkins, Concordia University
Alexander Smith, Oklahoma City University
Andrea Smith-Hunter, Siena College
Joseph Stern, New Jersey City University
Charles Stevens, Lehigh University
Linda Stockton, McMaster University
Vasyl Taras, University of North Carolina at Greensboro
John Thanopoulos, University of Piraeus
Erin Thomas, Mira Costa College
Halia Valladares, Mount Royal University
Joyce Wang, The University of Texas at Dallas
Michael Woods, Indiana University East
Bi-Juan Zhong, Baruch College
Anatoly Zhuplev, Loyola Marymount University

Brief Contents

Contents

CHAPTER 1

Globalization

Tribune Broadcasting – Elaine Ruiz/ Getty Images; NewsHour Productions-2010/10 MR ED/E/Getty Images

Introduction

Globalization has many advantages. As countries trade and do business with one another, they make products and services cheaper, and they increase the rate of development for lifesaving devices, medicines, and technologies that improve living conditions. These collaborations also make those improvements more readily available to the greater world population.

However, globalization also has its disadvantages. The spread of new technologies and foreign investments may increase levels of socioeconomic inequality. Some people also fear that increased globalization will reduce or limit their quality of life because it enables employers to eliminate jobs in developed countries and relocate them to foreign locations where labor is cheaper, or to exploit the lax regulatory and environmental policies in less developed countries.

LEARNING OBJECTIVES

After you explore this chapter you will be able to:

1. **Identify** the causes and consequences of globalization
2. **Discuss** the "flat world, round world" debate
3. **Explain** the roles of the organizations that regulate global markets
4. **Describe** a road map for doing business in a global market

1.1 What Is Globalization?

LEARNING OBJECTIVE

Identify the causes and consequences of globalization.

The phrase "the pen is mightier than the sword" tells us that discussion and dialogue are more powerful tools for change than violence and war. It was coined in the 1800s[1]—the same era in which countries began to assert their independence from the world-spanning empires in order to become independent, sovereign nations.[2] **Sovereign nations** are countries that

sovereign nations countries that govern themselves rather than being controlled by a foreign power

govern themselves rather than being controlled by a foreign power. One obvious example of gaining sovereignty during this time period was the American colonies declaring independence from the British Empire in 1776. This shift toward sovereignty allowed for increased trade and business between countries with strong cultural and political differences.

globalization the evolution of an integrated and interdependent world economy

Today we are in the midst of another great shift: toward globalization. **Globalization** is the evolution of an integrated and interdependent world economy. It builds on the principle of sovereignty to strengthen the relationships that connect us. Free trade agreements, broadband networks, communication technologies, and global express shipping are all major innovations that connect us to each other and to everyone else around the world. Globalization influences almost every aspect of your life, from the foods you buy to the clothes you wear to the places you work. Even the subjects you study in school are affected by the changing global marketplace. How global are you? Complete the **Global Exposure Activity** to find out.

Events in countries worldwide now have long-reaching, long-lasting effects—even for people who never visit those countries. For example, the changing economies of four nations in particular have profoundly affected the global economy and the way business is done today. In the past 30 years or so, events in Brazil, Russia, India, and China, often referred to as the "BRICs," have made some dramatic marks on the world. For instance:

- In Brazil, after years of stifling inflation and closed markets, the central government introduced in 1994 the *Plano Real* (Real Plan), meant to break the inflationary cycle. Part of the solution was to link the Brazilian currency, the real, to the U.S. dollar, limiting the inflation rate in Brazil to that in the United States. As a result, money in Brazil stabilized, and people began to trust in their currency once again. This shift in economic policy successfully reduced inflation and almost instantaneously created 25 million new consumers among the poor, who now had some means to spend.[3] Such policy reforms helped set the rules for global markets.
- In Russia, dramatic growth emerged from increased global commerce as the government opened trade in the early 1990s. Both internal and external competition increased during this period. This dramatic shift began as the Berlin Wall separating East from West Germany was literally torn down as people in the streets removed the 30-year-old barrier. It meant the end of state-controlled, closed markets and the beginning of open trade between Eastern and Western Europe, paving the way for the European Union of today.
- By the end of 1990, India was in a serious economic crisis and near bankruptcy. Up to that point, Indian currency, the rupee, was inconvertible (unable to be exchanged for foreign currency) because money exchangers wouldn't take the risk of being stuck with rupees that they couldn't use. At the same time, high tariffs and import licensing fees prevented most foreign goods from entering the Indian market. In 1991, however, India's democratic government began major reforms to increase market development and allow for trade of goods and services with other countries.[4] These policies increased domestic efficiencies and opened foreign trade.
- During the 1990s, China also began free-market reforms. In 1989 citizens engaged in several weeks of demonstrations in Beijing's Tiananmen Square to demand more economic freedom. Chinese troops eventually fired on civilians and ended the demonstrations; however, the international backlash from the event pushed the Chinese Communist party to consider economic reforms. As a result, in 1990 stock markets opened in Shanghai and Shenzhen, and in 1992 the Chinese government endorsed a "socialist market economy" as the goal of reform.[5] This reform would lead to what is now one of the most powerful market-based economies in the world.

These examples illustrate the unprecedented changes occurring on the world stage during the 1990s: the collapse of the Soviet Union and the opening of Indian, Brazilian, and Chinese markets, as well as other markets in countries such as Indonesia and South Africa. Today, companies around the globe are able to sell goods and services in nearly every market. For instance, a company headquartered in the United States may sell goods and services to all but a handful of countries, such as North Korea (sanctions are in place to curb North Korea's nuclear ambitions). With recent efforts to allow trade with countries like Cuba and Iran, global trade options continue to grow.[6] Thanks to globalization, companies have unprecedented access to billions of potential customers.

Globalization of Markets

Broadly defined, a *market* is a virtual or physical setting where people exchange goods and services. For a market to succeed, however, it needs a set of rules. For example, a rule could be that individuals are allowed to own property. Another could establish penalties for breaking contracts. To have any effect, rules must be enforced by some power or authority. Typically, governments fill this role. A major difficulty in globalization is that governments already have their hands full trying to enforce the rules within their own borders. Creating global markets that span national boundaries—so-called globalized markets—is even more complicated, but the benefits often outweigh the difficulties.

A **globalized market** is a large market created by combining separate national markets. For example, each nation in the European Union (EU) has a separate national market. A primary motive for establishing the EU was to create a broad marketplace that allows the free flow of goods and services across the countries of Europe. As a citizen of a member state in the EU, a person living in Italy is not limited to buying an Italian-made motorcycle such as a Ducati or Benelli, as in **Figure 1.1**, for instance. The agreements that form the foundation of the EU mean the person could easily get a German-made BMW motorcycle, without paying the extra fees or taxes that are traditionally attached to the purchase of a foreign product.

globalized market a large market created by combining separate national markets

In other words, globalization makes it easier to buy and sell internationally. In turn, this ease of exchange means that preferences and tastes across the world start to converge. The global spread of products such as Coca-Cola, McDonald's hamburgers, Apple iPhones, Honda Accords, Microsoft Windows, IKEA bookshelves, and Disney movies are a few examples of **global convergence**. Global convergence represents the spread of common preferences across national borders. Companies benefit from convergence because it decreases the amount of localization required to sell their products; therefore, they often instigate convergence. For example, when Chinese manufacturers experienced a surge in local consumption, they turned to Africa to help source many of the natural elements, such as copper and cobalt, needed to build their products. These Chinese companies started to invest heavily in Africa, helping build roads and other infrastructure to ensure they could efficiently extract the resources. In fact, a seemingly unrelated investment made by the Chinese government has been the building of Confucius Institutes, or institutes that focus on teaching Confucian ideology, often located on university campuses, as shown in **Figure 1.2**.

global convergence the spread of common preferences across national borders

While we were in Dar es Salaam, Tanzania, in 2017, we spoke with the dean of the business school at the University of Dar es Salaam, who pointed out the Chinese government's generous gift of a new library and Confucius Institute. While the gift was welcome, the dean mentioned that its intent was to shift Tanzanian culture toward Chinese culture, as it would create a greater convergence, whereby Tanzanian preferences would become more similar to Chinese preferences. This convergence is not new to Africa; it also took place during colonialism, when similar "gifts" given by the British, French, and Americans helped move Africa away from its traditional cultures and toward Western culture and greater global convergence.[7] To put this in perspective, China plans to build 1,000 Confucius Institutes throughout the world by 2020, all with the intent to increase awareness of China and Chinese ideologies.[8]

The Confucius Institutes from China may improve brand recognition, decrease the perceived foreignness of Chinese goods, and increase perceptions of the

Jerome Delay/AP Images

FIGURE 1.1 **Buying in a global market** When the British actor Ewan McGregor was considering buying a motorcycle for his epic 20,000-mile journey, he finally settled on the German-made BMW over a British brand, a transaction possible only in a globalized market for bikes.

FIGURE 1.2 **Chinese culture in Africa** Chinese Confucius Institutes are given as gifts from the Chinese government to top universities in Africa and act to promote Chinese culture on the international scene.

quality of Chinese business and consumer goods sold in Africa, such as Huawei telephones. However, despite the brand recognition of Chinese goods, consumer products are actually less globalized than industrial products. *Consumer products* serve individuals in large, diverse communities across the world, and the cultural and economic differences between these communities make consumer products slow to spread. *Industrial products*, on the other hand, serve the production and other needs of massive companies and conglomerates in manufacturing, mining, utilities, agriculture, and power generation. For example, markets for the mining industry offer materials such as oil, copper, and aluminum. These materials are *commodities*, meaning they function basically the same way no matter where they are mined, so companies can source them from nearly anywhere in the world with the same end result.

When Boeing makes a new 787 Dreamliner passenger plane, for instance, the company sources the necessary materials from wherever it can find the right quality for a good deal—with little respect for the country of origin. For example, Boeing could get its aluminum from Rio Tinto of Australia or UC Rusal of Russia. That same plane, once finished, could serve in a fleet for a U.S. airline, a French airline, or a Chinese airline. IKEA has been known to sell one Billy bookcase every 10 seconds somewhere in the world.[9] Not only does that take a lot of wood sourced from the timber industries in a number of different countries, but it also means many people across the world have similar tastes in bookshelves—convergence inspired by globalization.

Within global markets, the same firms often compete with one another in nation after nation. In Korea and China, the Samsung Galaxy is more popular than the Apple iPhone.[10] In other countries, such as the United States and Canada, iPhones are sold more often than the Galaxy.[11] Some other big rivalries include Boeing (based in the United States) versus Airbus (based in France) for airplanes, John Deere (United States) versus Mahindra (India) for tractors, Cemex (Mexico) versus Holcim (Switzerland) for cement, Vodafone (United Kingdom) versus Nippon Telegraph and Telephone (Japan) for telecommunications, and Huawei (China) versus Cisco (United States) for networking routers. Rivalries force firms to stay current and can also push smaller players out of the market. For example, Pepsi and Coke often dominate small, local soft drink brands because of their massive size and aggressive marketing campaigns. Some rivalries get contentious, such as that between Cisco and Huawei, and the companies may use their respective home governments to accuse the rival firm of spying and espionage.[12] Such activities can make it more difficult for a foreign company to compete in a rival's home market, inhibiting the full globalization of markets.

Globalization of Production

Production refers to the process of manufacturing or providing any good or service—from the assembly of a computer to the financial services delivered by a credit card company to the creation of this textbook. Production of a product or service requires different component parts, skill sets, or information. These components, also known as **factors of production**, can be classified as land, labor, or capital. The **globalization of production** refers to sourcing land, labor, and capital from different nations rather than obtaining everything locally. By globally sourcing their production factors, companies can take advantage of national differences in cost and quality. The search for deals on production factors across geographic boundaries is known as **arbitrage**.[13] Arbitrage treats differences across nations as opportunities—not constraints—and encourages sourcing goods and services from locations that can best supply them.

factors of production the component parts, skill sets, or information required to produce a product or service, usually classified as land, labor, or capital

globalization of production the sourcing of land, labor, and capital from different nations rather than obtaining everything locally

arbitrage the search for deals on production factors across geographic boundaries

Consider Walmart as an example of the power of globalizing production. Thanks to the globalization of markets, Walmart has more than 6,000 stores outside the United States[14]. The combined operating income from these stores is estimated to be nearly half the amount the company makes in its domestic U.S. market. While Walmart does not disclose the extent to which it practices arbitrage, estimates suggest that its savings from sourcing low-cost goods and services from places like China are larger than the operating income generated by all 6,000 stores operating internationally.[15] This means that by having its vendors source the production of goods to low-cost producers in different foreign markets, Walmart saves more money per year, on average, than it makes by selling products back into those markets. While the globalization of markets provides some benefits for Walmart, its globalization of production is far more beneficial.[16]

As part of its rationale for outsourcing so much of its production, Walmart states that it is simply finding suppliers that are the best in the world at what they do. For example, China has developed a manufacturing industry known for quickly producing low-cost, high-quality products. Companies that outsource in the countries that can produce most effectively and efficiently are able to reduce costs and increase the quality of their products. This allows them to pass savings and quality improvements on to customers and potentially beat out competitors.

Globalization of production is not limited to manufacturing. Many service sectors also engage in global sourcing. For example, if you have x-rays taken at a local hospital, they may be sent to a foreign country and diagnosed by a doctor there faster and at a much lower cost than at your local hospital. Medical tourism has been increasing and allows people to individually outsource their health care. If you are looking for cutting-edge medical technology, such as using the CyberKnife to perform the most difficult surgeries, then you would fly to the United States. If you want implant surgery, costs are lower in Costa Rica. If you need to be diagnosed and treated quickly, then India is becoming a popular destination for medical tourists.[17]

Nowhere is outsourcing more prevalent than in India. If you drive along the outskirts of Hyderabad or Bangalore, India, you are likely to see large, multibillion-dollar buildings housing thousands of employees from companies such as IBM, Wells-Fargo, Microsoft, and Citibank. Many of these companies have set up operations in India to take advantage of the services of excellent software engineers and back-office managers who demand much lower wages than their European or North American counterparts.

Lower wage-related expenses are not the only advantage of globalizing production. Companies that work with global suppliers and employees are also usually exposed to a wide range of new and innovative perspectives. Such exposure allows companies to tap into top talent and ideas from all over the world, thereby helping them reduce production costs, improve product quality, and find new sources of revenue. The company HireVue tries to help other companies tap into a globalized workforce. Headquartered in the United States, HireVue's video interview technology makes it just as easy for someone in Nairobi, Kenya, as it is for someone in New York City to interview for a job in Manhattan. Combining data analytics with online video interviewing, where people respond to a series of questions, record themselves, and send it into the company, HireVue is helping companies like Hilton Inc. and Carnival Corporation hire thousands of performers, chefs, and service workers from all over the world. Go online and watch the **HireVue Video** to get a better understanding of what HireVue does to help companies connect with people all over the world.

WileyPLUS

See Video: HireVue Helps Companies Connect

1.2 The Flat World, Round World Globalization Debate

LEARNING OBJECTIVE

Discuss the "flat world, round world" debate.

The search for bigger markets, lower costs, and greater innovation has led to globalization, but these goals are not the only explanations for the trend. Rather, at the same time, the economically powerful countries of the world were making policy changes to encourage businesses to globalize and information technology was undergoing a colossal shift that made global coordination easier. For example, in 1927 it cost over $250 to make a ten-minute, coast-to-coast call in the United States[18]; by 1980 it cost about $7.50 to place the same ten-minute call. However, the advent of the Internet in the early 1990s ushered in a wave of opportunities—from email to digital video conferencing—to send large amounts of data instantaneously and spread ideas and knowledge with the click of a mouse. Internet technologies have driven the cost of international communication to nearly zero.

The second effect of the Internet on globalization was to initiate a boom in Internet companies, which triggered billion-dollar investments in fiber-optic telecommunications cables connecting countries all over the world. As a result of those investments, to name just one example, the Indian information technology company Infosys—founded in Pune, India, in 1981—was able to communicate with and provide on-demand services to large Western companies, in effect eliminating geographic barriers. The Internet took people-to-people connectivity to a new level. This connectivity, combined with the BRICs opening to global trade, enabled traditionally local businesses—such as software developers, marketing agencies, and accountancies—to reach a global audience.

The author Thomas Friedman termed the globalization of markets the advent of the "flat world."[19] The flat world is a world with free access to markets, few barriers to competition, and consistent enforcement of regulations. Geographic distance is essentially irrelevant, individuals are able to compete head-to-head with large global companies, and those in poor countries with limited infrastructure are able to compete with people in rich, well-developed countries. For example, a 22-year-old in Cambodia, Kenya, Colombia, or anywhere else now has access to all the information, tools, online courses, and software she needs to gain skills and provide solutions to customers anywhere in the world—that is, she does so in a perfectly flat world.

We don't live in a perfectly flat world, however. The other side of the flat world argument—the "round world" argument—insists that the world is not as connected as we might think. For instance, the few cities that dominate international financial markets—Frankfurt, Hong Kong, London, New York, Singapore—represent the peak of global integration. Most of the world's other cities are much more connected at the local level than they are to any other domestic city, and more connected domestically than to any foreign city. For that reason, most business is still done in home markets.

Of the amount of money firms make through direct investing, less than 10 percent is generated by investing overseas, meaning more than 90 percent of all business investments are domestic. As shown in **Figure 1.3**, the balance between foreign and domestic sources of investment hovers around 10 percent for most economic activities in the United States. Fewer than 10 percent of the calls made in the United States are to people outside the United States. Only 3 percent of people immigrate to the country. Other activities such as management research, direct investment, charitable giving, granting of patents, and portfolio investment all hover around 10 percent. Even trade, as a percentage of a country's productive output, reaches only about 20 percent once we adjust for certain kinds of double counting. These data enable us to estimate that, for most U.S. markets, the **10% presumption** holds: Only about 10 percent of activity is conducted globally; the remaining 90 percent is domestic.[20]

10% presumption the presumption that ten percent of activity is conducted globally, with ninety percent being domestic

Many businesses have discovered, to their dismay, that access to foreign markets isn't enough. Efficient distribution, locally desirable goods and services, and effective marketing require expertise in each foreign market. The experience of Metro Cash & Carry, a large German wholesaler similar to Costco in the United States, illustrates this point well. Metro successfully expanded from Germany to other parts of Western and Eastern Europe, learning and adapting along the way. When it came time to enter China, company executives knew they'd have to make some changes, but they thought their basic formula for success would work in China just as it had everywhere else. To their credit, they got a lot right. However, management had to figure out how to work with the local political and economic players in any given location

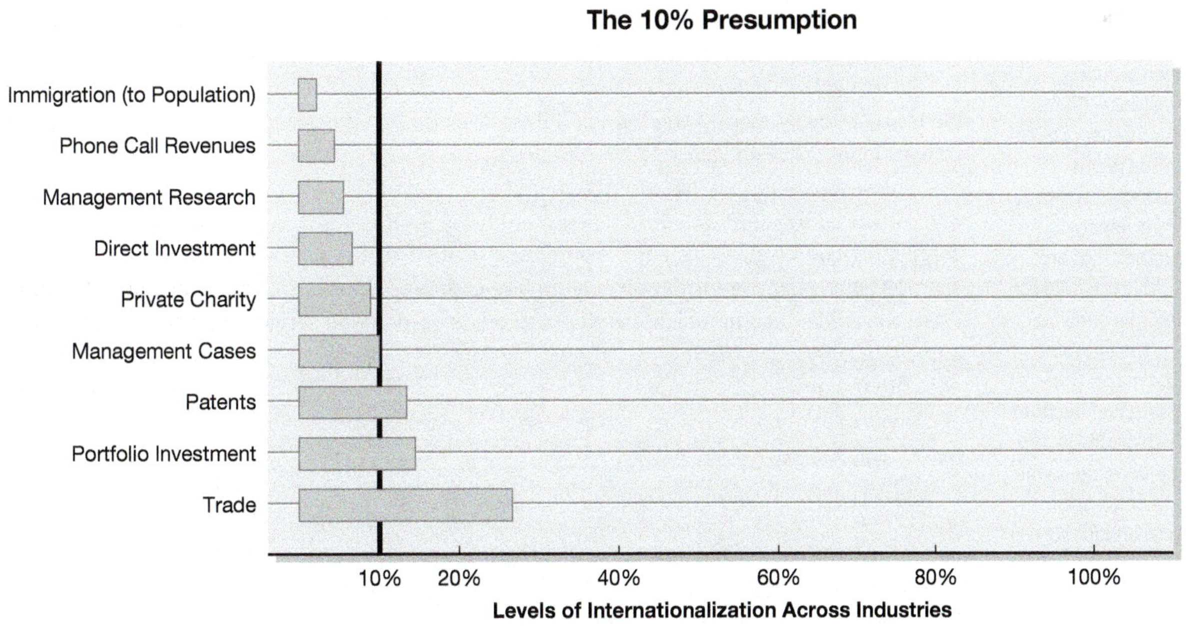

FIGURE 1.3 **Test your assumptions about globalization** The indicator bars are set at 100 percent, but we all know that much of our economic activity is domestic and not international. **Source:** Adapted from Pankaj Ghemawat, "Differences Across Countries: The CAGE Distance Framework," in *Redefining Global Strategy: Crossing Borders in a World Where Differences Still Matter* (Brighton, MA: Harvard Business Review Press, 2007), 40–64.

in China. This took months for each site, and lessons learned in one location often didn't apply to others. In addition, Metro managers were familiar with large, formal competitors, but in China they encountered a greater variety of rivals, ranging from informal street vendors to the government itself. And many consumers preferred to buy live or freshly butchered animals instead of packaged goods. As a result of these learning experiences, it took the company 14 years to break even after entering China.

Differences between countries are often more pronounced than any similarities, and those differences mean that what works in one place has no guarantee of success in another. **Figure 1.4** indicates the similarities of industry profitability between countries.[21]

Both Sides of the Coin

Some see globalization as a good thing. According to Amartya Sen, a Nobel Prize–winning economist, globalization "has enriched the world scientifically and culturally, and benefited many people economically as well."[22] The United Nations has even declared that the forces of globalization may have the power to eradicate poverty in the 21st century.[23] As countries trade and do business with one another, they make products and services cheaper—often making life-saving devices, medicines, and technologies more readily available to the greater world population.

Others disagree. Another Nobel Prize–winning economist, Joseph Stiglitz, argues that globalization perpetuates inequality throughout the world. Indeed, new technologies and the

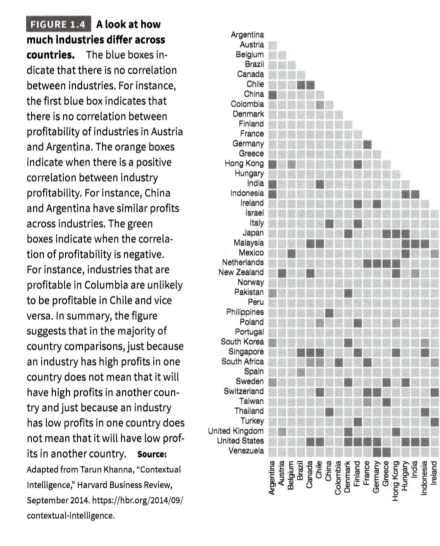

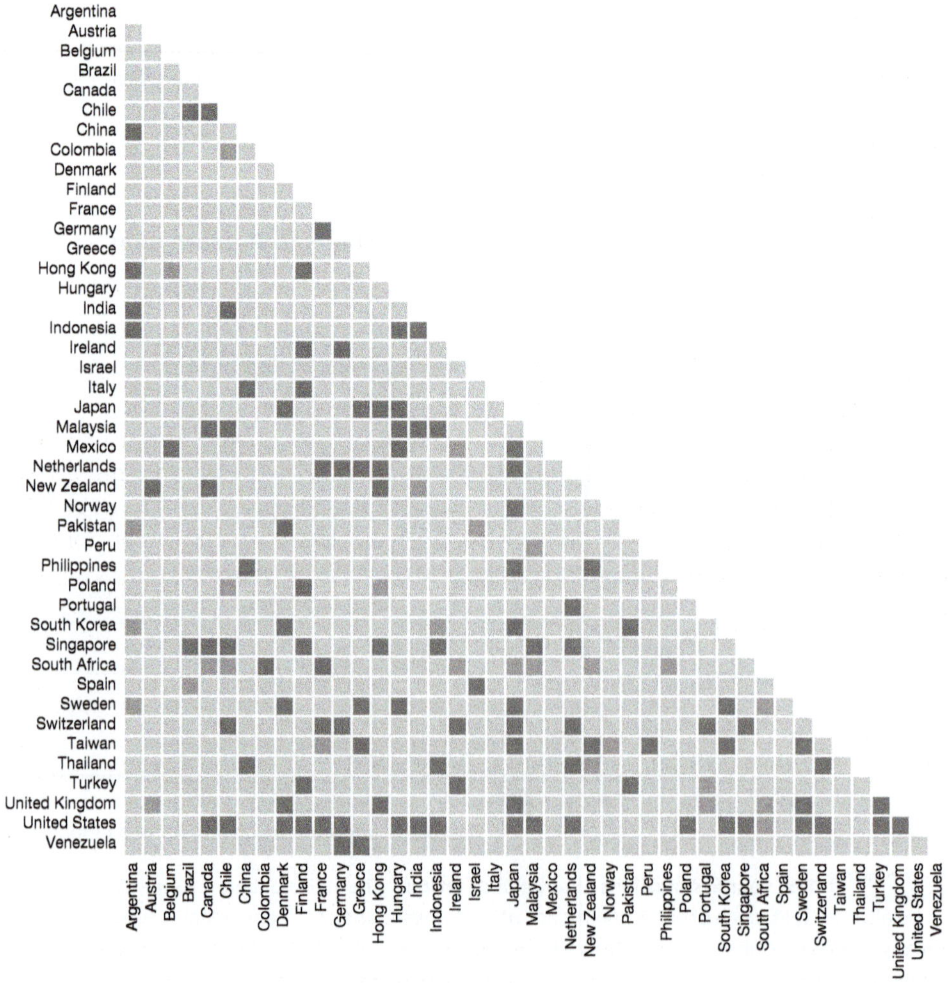

FIGURE 1.4 A look at how much industries differ across countries. The blue boxes indicate that there is no correlation between industries. For instance, the first blue box indicates that there is no correlation between profitability of industries in Austria and Argentina. The orange boxes indicate when there is a positive correlation between industry profitability. For instance, China and Argentina have similar profits across industries. The green boxes indicate when the correlation of profitability is negative. For instance, industries that are profitable in Columbia are unlikely to be profitable in Chile and vice versa. In summary, the figure suggests that in the majority of country comparisons, just because an industry has high profits in one country does not mean that it will have high profits in another country and just because an industry has low profits in one country does not mean that it will have low profits in another country. **Source:** Adapted from Tarun Khanna, "Contextual Intelligence," Harvard Business Review, September 2014. https://hbr.org/2014/09/contextual-intelligence.

investment of foreign capital in developing countries may actually increase levels of inequality.[24] For example, the introduction of heavy farm machinery allows richer farmers or companies to cultivate larger plots of land, consolidating the farming sector and pushing smaller farmers from their land and livelihood. The introduction of technology and investment capital allows a country to create more food and more wealth as a whole, but it creates greater inequalities between the very few rich farmers and the rest, who cannot afford to compete.

Globalization may also have detrimental effects on developed markets. Many people fear it makes it too easy for employers to move jobs to cheaper locations. In France, for example, only 22 percent of the population sees globalization as a "good thing."[25] They tend to take the round-world view of the debate by pointing out their desire to maintain their cultural distinctiveness. In the United States, President Donald Trump and many Americans agree with this cultural sentiment: "We must protect our borders from the ravages of other countries making our products, stealing our companies and destroying our jobs. Protection will lead to great prosperity and strength."[26]

1.3 Governing Globalization

LEARNING OBJECTIVE

Explain the roles of the organizations that regulate global markets.

A number of different organizations worldwide establish and enforce guidelines governing the interactions of individuals, businesses, and governments in a globalized world. These bodies are called **multilateral organizations** because they are funded and managed by representatives from multiple governments or organizations. The most influential are the World Trade Organization, The International Monetary Fund, The World Bank, the United Nations, the G20, and The World Economic Forum.

multilateral organizations organizations formed between three or more nations to work on issues that relate to their joint interests

The **World Trade Organization (WTO)** (www.wto.org/) came about as a result of negotiations in the 1990s. Its purpose is to ensure that international trade runs freely and fairly between countries, and that member nations impose the minimal number of restrictions on each other. To be accepted as a member of the WTO, a country must first ratify the WTO regulations in its own parliament or governing body. The WTO then monitors and coordinates trade across member countries, making sure they are trading according to the regulations.[27] For example, if Bolivia decides to restrict the number of flamenco dresses Spain sells into the country, Spain can file a complaint alleging that Bolivia has breached one of the agreed-upon trade rules. If the ensuing investigation by the WTO shows that Bolivia has indeed violated the rules, it will require Bolivia to pay for the damage caused or risk losing its status as a member. As of 2017, the WTO had 164 member countries, as shown in **Figure 1.5**, which together account for more than 99 percent of the world's trade. This gives the WTO significant influence in promoting free trade across countries.

World Trade Organization (WTO) a multilateral organization designed to foster the rules of trade between nations

In addition to mediating trade disputes, the WTO audits national trade policies, oversees trade agreements, helps developing countries create trade policy, and cooperates with other global groups like the International Monetary Fund and the World Bank. Countries that are members of the WTO are required to uphold the multilateral trading system—a system designed to allow for trade without discrimination, for the gradual reduction of trade barriers, and for increased stability.

International Monetary Fund (IMF) a multilateral organization designed to standardize global financial relations and exchange rates

The **International Monetary Fund (IMF)** (www.imf.org) and the **World Bank** (www.worldbank.org/) were both created by representatives of 44 nations, who met at Bretton Woods, New Hampshire, in 1944, shortly before the end of World War II. The IMF was established to rescue countries from financial crises like the one that brought Hitler to power in Germany and paved the way for World War II. The World Bank was set up with similar intentions, but now

World Bank a multilateral organization designed to provide financing, advice, and research to developing nations to aid their economic advancement

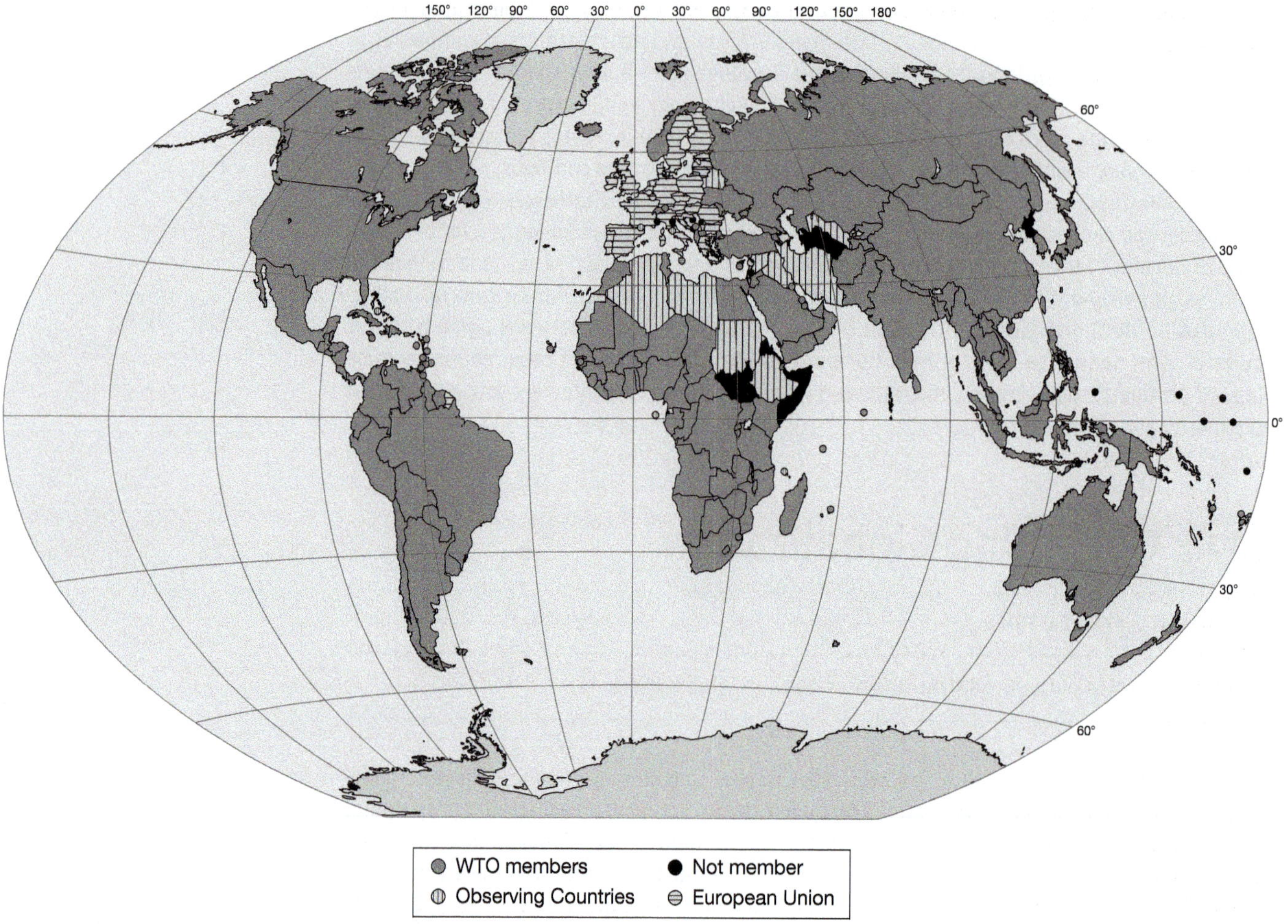

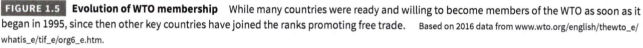

FIGURE 1.5 Evolution of WTO membership While many countries were ready and willing to become members of the WTO as soon as it began in 1995, since then other key countries have joined the ranks promoting free trade. Based on 2016 data from www.wto.org/english/thewto_e/whatis_e/tif_e/org6_e.htm.

it focuses more on preventing war by promoting economic development in poor countries. The World Bank provides heavily subsidized loans to poor governments in an effort to help them build infrastructure such as roads, the private sector, and public utilities.

The IMF is often considered a "lender of last resort" to nations whose economies are in trouble and whose currencies are losing value. For example, the Asian financial crisis of 1997 started when the baht (Thailand's currency) lost significant value and the government lost all its currency reserves. This crisis created a panic in Malaysia and Indonesia that later swept through other parts of Asia and eventually South Korea. The IMF served as the lender of last resort and offered a $54 billion loan to South Korea. At the time, this was the largest bailout loan in the history of the world. Luckily, the loan helped many of the countries affected by the crisis regain public confidence and rebuild strong economies.

United Nations (UN) a multilateral organization designed to increase economic and political cooperation among member countries

The **United Nations (UN)** (www.un.org/) was established in 1945 as a way to get countries to resolve their differences through diplomacy, with the goal of maintaining and promoting global peace. When a country becomes a member of the UN, it agrees to accept the obligations of the UN Charter—an international treaty that guides proper dialogue and discussion to resolve issues affecting multiple countries. Today the UN comprises over 190 member countries. The UN consists of five different sister organizations, or organs: the General Assembly, the Security Council, the Economic and Social Council, the Secretariat, and the International Court of Justice. Four are located in the main UN headquarters in New York City, whereas the International Court of Justice is located in The Hague, the Netherlands. The General Assembly is the main assembly and meets during yearly sessions to discuss issues and vote on resolutions. Each member country has one vote. Resolutions agreed upon by the General Assembly are not binding, although a member country's reputation can be marred if it goes against a UN resolution.

Issues on which the General Assembly might make recommendations include peace and security, human rights, economic development, and humanitarian assistance. For instance, in 2015 the UN had 16 different peacekeeping operations employing over 106,000 troops and police. The largest group was in the Democratic Republic of the Congo, with the goal to help stabilize the country amid political infighting. The UN's central mandate, however, is to increase the standard of living and reinforce human rights throughout the world—two issues central to successful globalization.

The **G20** (www.g20.org/) was established in 1999 and consists of finance ministers and central bank governors of the 19 largest economies in the world, plus representatives from the European Union and the European Central Bank. The G20 operates without a permanent secretariat or staff. The group's chair rotates annually among the members and is responsible for hosting the annual summit. For example, when Russia's finance minister presided over the group in 2013, Russia also hosted the eighth annual summit in Saint Petersburg.

G20 an international forum for governments from 20 major economies to discuss policy issues related to international financial stability

While the G20 finance ministers have met annually since 1999, the first annual summit for country leaders took place in 2008 in Washington, DC. The G20 head-of-government summits were started in order to respond to the growing role of key emerging countries and to ensure they were adequately included in the global economic governance and coordination across nations. The summits aim to coordinate financial and monetary policies to respond to financial crises. For example, from 2008 to 2010 the G20 became the channel through which the major countries coordinated policy in an attempt to stem the financial crisis that started in the United States.

The **World Economic Forum (WEF)** (www.weforum.com) was not set up by different governments. Instead of being funded by countries, this organization is funded by over 1,000 member *companies*, typically multinational corporations with more than $5 billion in revenue. Despite its foundation in business, the WEF shares many objectives with global groups such as the G20, World Bank, and WTO. Each year, WEF members gather in the Swiss mountain resort of Davos. The forum consists of approximately 2,500 top business leaders, international political leaders, thought leaders, and journalists, with the goal of improving the state of the world through public-private cooperation.[28] Sections of the organization also come together six to eight times a year in locations around the world to discuss both global and regional issues. In addition to these meetings, the WEF produces research reports about issues related to gender equality, geopolitics, the future of the Internet, global talent gaps, global financial systems, and other business-related topics.

World Economic Forum (WEF) an independent non-profit organization designed to improve global economic and social conditions

A prominent criticism of the WEF is that the Davos meetings are just groups of the global elite, wealthy people (predominantly men) who "have little need for national loyalty, view national boundaries as obstacles that thankfully are vanishing, and see national governments as residues of the past whose only useful function is to facilitate the elite's global operations."[29] Some critics have argued that such elitist positions are not representative of the majority of the world's population, and that the elitist, "Davos man" mentality does little to represent the interests of the general populace. The Peruvian economist Hernando de Soto Polar (known for his work on business and property rights) refers to this "Davos man" as someone who is internationally connected but part of such an elite group that he is out of touch with his own people. Their isolation may even foster a tendency to be oblivious to the fates of their fellow citizens.[30]

Global Business School Network is another nonprofit organization not founded by governments but rather funded by multiple business schools worldwide. Among other things, the network provides advisory services to business schools in the developing world, helps train corporations and nongovernmental organizations such as the Red Cross and Save the Children, and measures the results and impacts of management training programs.[31] Today's emerging countries—like Russia, China, India, and Brazil—are in need of entrepreneurs and qualified managers to navigate the complex problems of health care, agribusiness, education, and job creation. Education of local management, as offered by the Global Business School Network, helps stimulate the growth of local leaders who are capable of generating success in their individual spheres of expertise.

Global Business School Network an independent non-profit organization designed to improve access to locally relevant management education, creating long-term impact on development

1.4 Managing Globalization

LEARNING OBJECTIVE

Describe a road map for doing business in a global market.

Research indicates that globalization can be a powerful tool for increasing prosperity, but companies engaged in international business still face many challenges. Since the 2008 financial crisis, international trade in merchandise has increased significantly, but trade in services has been stagnant. Financial markets are actually becoming less globalized as investors keep more of their funds in their home markets. And sentiment in developed countries such as the United States and Europe has recently turned more strongly against globalization, in favor of nationalization. Still, the level of international communication has gone up in some areas, leading to a wide range of globalization levels.

As a result, some countries are more globalized than others. For example, the top-ranked global country, the Netherlands, is almost 150 times more globally connected than the bottom-ranked country, Syria. At the regional level, Europe is the world's most globalized region. The region of East Asia and the Pacific ranks second overall and second in trade.[32] Being globalized is in some ways a benefit, but a lack of globalization isn't always a bad thing when doing business internationally. For example, developed countries offer high levels of stability, have many rich consumers, and tend to be more globalized. On the other hand, poorer countries typically have less political and economic stability, but they offer growth and arbitrage opportunities.

Emerging Markets

emerging markets countries moving toward economic policies of open trade and free markets

Emerging market economies have driven most of the recent growth in globalization. **Emerging markets** are countries moving toward open-trade and free-market policies. The list varies, but around 130 countries are currently considered emerging markets.[33] Three common factors help identify an emerging market. The first is political policies that encourage (at least to some extent) free trade, private ownership, and foreign investment. The second factor is a "catching-up" level of growth. For example, advanced economies or developed markets experience average economic growth of around 2 percent/year; to be emerging, markets should have at least double that amount (4 percent/year or more). The third factor is an intermediate income level among citizens. Thanks to these three factors, emerging markets present high-potential locations for growth because they represent largely untapped markets with high levels of economic activity.[34]

As **Figure 1.6** shows, when we compare the combined productive outputs (that is, goods and services) of emerging markets with developed markets, the former surpassed the latter

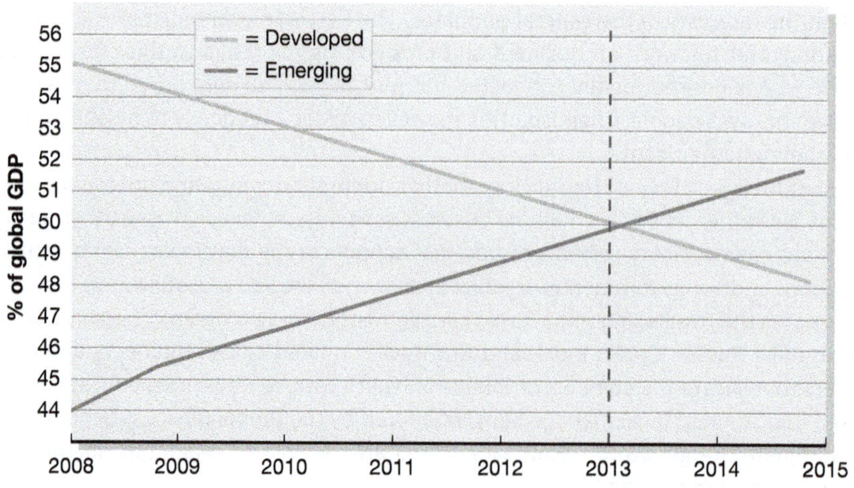

FIGURE 1.6 Emerging and developed markets' shares of global production Adapted from Patrick Hyek, "Six Global Trends Shaping the Business World: Rapid Technology Innovation Creates a Smart, Mobile World," *EY Client Portal*. https://wewanttolearn.files.wordpress.com/2013/02/six-global-trends-shaping-the-business-world-rapid-technology-innovation-creates-a-smart-mobile-world-ernst-young-global.pdf (accessed May 3, 2017).

between 2013 and 2014. The BRIC nations (Brazil, Russia, India and China) were responsible for most of this growth. Their primary attraction for businesses is population size; together, these countries represent more than one-third of the world's population—a vast market for products and services. For example, a key factor in Germany's strong economy is the volume of its sales to China and India. In addition, these countries represent markets that have made significant strides in opening to free trade since the 1990s. Finally, they have reasonably stable governments, ensuring that foreign companies can invest within the countries with some confidence their investments will be protected.

Multinational Corporations

The companies best positioned to take advantage of growth in emerging markets are often those that already have a presence in multiple countries. A **multinational corporation (MNC)** is any company with operations in more than one country. MNCs are typically large companies with strong brands. For example, six of the world's seven most recognized brands worldwide are all products of U.S. multinational corporations—Apple, Microsoft, Google, IBM, McDonalds, and General Electric.[35] Managing their operations effectively and integrating their activities to achieve global advantage is a challenge for the leadership of these companies. They have extensive facilities and staff in various countries. Coca-Cola, for example, actually employs more people outside the United States than in it.

multinational corporation (MNC) a company with operations in more than one country

While these huge companies are the most recognizable, they are not the most common. The majority of multinationals are actually smaller companies, often with operations in only one or two countries beyond their home market. Global trends such as political reform and technological innovation have made it easier for these smaller companies to operate as **micro-multinational corporations**. These represent global companies with lower staffing costs, greater access to talent and expertise, and a wider choice of markets than they might find at home. They are able to capitalize on speed and agility while still communicating and coordinating across borders using low-cost (or free) products such as Skype for conference calls, Dropbox for sharing files, LinkedIn for finding talent, PayPal for making transactions, and eBay and Amazon for sales. In fact, even individuals working out of their homes can now be multinational businesses. Thanks to globalization and the ease of becoming a multinational, the United States and other developed countries no longer dominate the global market the way they once did.

micro-multinational corporations small, web-wired start-ups that are using social media to recruit the best talent from around the world and leverage it for immediate innovation and impact

The number of non-U.S.-based multinationals is a growing force. From the end of World War II in 1945 until the 1970s, U.S. firms dominated global business, generating two-thirds of all foreign business investments throughout the world. In 1973, 48.5 percent of the world's 260 largest multinationals were U.S. companies. The United Kingdom was in second place at that time, with 18.8 percent. For comparison, Japan then had only 3.5 percent.[36]

Since that time, the United States' monopoly on multinational companies has contracted. Though still significant, the United States now houses just over one-quarter of the world's largest multinationals, whereas China is home to 12.5 percent of them. MNCs are now found throughout the world, as companies from Europe, Japan, and China have taken advantage of globalization. A global top-ten list from the year 2000 would have shown that five of the top ten companies were located in the United States—General Motors, Walmart, Exxon, Ford, and General Electric. Four of the others were Japanese—Mitsui, Mitsubishi, Toyota, and Itochu. The 10th, DaimlerChrysler, was from Germany.

In 2016, five of the top ten companies were still headquartered in the United States (Berkshire Hathaway, JPMorgan Chase, Wells Fargo, Apple, ExxonMobile). However, the three largest were from China (ICBC, China Construction Bank, and Agricultural Bank of China; Bank of China was number 6), and only one of the top ten—Toyota—was from Japan.[37] Many of these companies generate more revenue annually than the gross domestic product of some small nations. Consequently, these MNCs can significantly affect factors like the pace of fossil fuel extraction, the spread of consumerism, and even the quality of education.

MNCs from emerging markets are slowly becoming a recognizable force in the global market. In fact, some companies from emerging markets are at the top of their industry, surpassing many of their older U.S. and European rivals. Cemex, a Mexican company, is one of the largest cement producers in the world, with operations in more than 50 countries. Another formidable company is Alibaba.com, a Chinese e-commerce company, which handles more business than any other e-commerce company in the world. Its initial public offering was the largest in history to date; it raised $25 billion in 2014. (Facebook was second largest, raising $16 billion in 2012.)

A major competitive advantage for MNCs from emerging markets is the rapid growth they experience in their home markets. Because consumption is rising so quickly, emerging-market MNCs have no choice but to ramp up capacity to meet demand. Using the latest technologies, these companies are able to match and surpass the efforts of larger, more established firms from other countries. Competing with foreign multinationals from the beginning means they can come close to matching the experience of their established competition in far less time, learning from the mistakes of companies that have gone before them.[38]

Still, MNCs from emerging markets don't have it easy. Some are successful, but many struggle outside their home markets. Often, though, so do their foreign competitors. This means that local competition in emerging-market economies is more complicated than managers typically expect, and neither developed-market nor emerging-market multinationals have all the answers.

Investing in these markets is worth the effort. For example, these economies are expected to account for 53 percent of world economic growth until 2018. The world economy is projected to grow faster until 2018 than it did in the preceding four decades. To harness that growth, managers of companies from developed countries need to make sure they have the skills and abilities to effectively manage in emerging markets.[39] As the global environment fills up with MNCs from all over the world, managers are facing increased pressure to understand the global context in which they operate. Managing an overseas office as if it were a separate company attached only by a common brand and finances is no longer sufficient.

The road to doing business in a global market starts with understanding the ways international business differs from domestic business. To help you recognize and effectively analyze these differences, in the next several chapters we discuss the role of political systems, economic environments, social and cultural settings, and technological advances, and their effects on business. We introduce the PEST—political, economic, social, and technological—framework to help you identify threats and opportunities that come from these important factors.

In Chapter 2, we will explain how companies identify and respond to the PEST factors. We'll explore how companies might examine these factors to decide whether to enter a new market, and the strategies they use to join and operate within the global market. Then we will examine the different forms companies assume in order to compete in a global environment—international, multidomestic, global, and transnational. In many respects, these organizational forms influence the kinds of managerial and strategic issues a company faces. Finally, we'll highlight how aspects of logistics, operations, finance, marketing, and human resource management are all influenced by the PEST factors, and how these different business functions adapt in a global environment.

Summary and Case

Summary

LEARNING OBJECTIVE 1.1 Identify the causes and consequences of globalization.

The collapse of the Soviet Union and the opening of India, Brazil, China, and other markets in the 1990s brought significant social, economic, and political changes. Now, companies around the globe are able to sell goods and services in nearly any market, leading to a more integrated and interdependent globalized world economy. The ease of buying and selling internationally is leading to a convergence of preferences and tastes across the world.

LEARNING OBJECTIVE 1.2 Discuss the "flat world, round world" debate.

The Internet made it easier for small companies and companies in poor countries to compete with traditional global giants. People can share information instantaneously and connect across national borders at essentially no cost, thanks to fiber-optic telecommunications cables. Despite these shifts, however, global trade still accounts for only about 20 percent of all economic activity.

LEARNING OBJECTIVE 1.3 Explain the roles of the organizations that regulate global markets.

The World Trade Organization, International Monetary Fund, United Nations, G20, and World Bank are multilateral organizations intended to help countries, companies, and people interact more effectively and peacefully in a globalized world. These quasi-governmental organizations do much to encourage economic and political cooperation, but they aren't enough on their own. Companies, nonprofit organizations, and universities also play a critical role in improving global economic cooperation and health.

LEARNING OBJECTIVE 1.4 Describe a road map for doing business in a global market.

Any type of company buying or selling outside its home market is engaged in international business. The number of MNCs from emerging markets have been increasing in the past decade. Emerging markets are untapped opportunities for growth and are estimated to produce over half of world economic growth between now and 2018.

Case

Siri, Where Were You Made?

When Apple first began making Macintosh computers, Apple CEO Steve Jobs bragged that it was a machine "made in America." Today, however, the effects of a globalized economy have changed things, and Apple has turned to foreign manufacturing. Ask Siri, Apple's famous personal assistant program on the iOS operating system, where the iPhone was made or where it was manufactured. Siri's usually quick, accurate, and sometimes whimsical responses are absent as the iOS clearly tries to avoid the question. It may tell you it was designed in California, but it won't tell you it was manufactured in China. It certainly won't admit it is really a mixture of parts and labor from all over the world.

The iPhone is made of hundreds of components, more than 90 percent of which are manufactured outside the United States. For instance, the rare metals come from Africa and Asia, chip sets from Europe, display panels from Japan and Korea, and advanced semiconductors from Germany. The final assembly is done in China by Apple's major subcontractor, the Taiwanese MNC Foxconn. In fact, of the $179 it costs to produce an iPhone, 34 percent goes to Japan, 17 percent to Germany, 13 percent to South Korea, only 6 percent to the United States, and 4 percent from China. So, even though the iPhone was designed in California and manufactured in China, only 10 percent of its labor and components come from these two countries.[40] Globalization played a major role in increasing the iPhone's quality for the price.[41] Indeed, turning to those outside a domestic geographic domain can account for roughly one-quarter of successful innovations within companies today.[42]

That said, outsourcing to emerging markets can have drawbacks. Problems such as poor working conditions tolerated by its subcontractors—low pay, long hours, unsafe factories—have plagued Apple's decision to source products from different markets and move manufacturing overseas. Those are not the kinds of problems a brand-conscious company like Apple wants people talking about. In addition, many argue that because only 6 percent of the cost of the iPhone goes to the United States, Apple has actually moved many jobs out of the country. Had all the components and labor been sourced at home, Apple could have created jobs and helped U.S. families and the economy. However, when compared with the allure of maintaining crucial supplier relationships, low labor costs, and fast delivery of new products, problems like these tend to take a back seat.[43]

Case Discussion Questions

1. Do the benefits outweigh the drawbacks of Apple outsourcing the assembly and production of most of its products to foreign countries? What may be some future costs and implications of this decision? What are some current implications?
2. How can Apple deal with ethical questions regarding its subcontractors' operations and the working conditions of their employees?
3. Should Apple's decision to outsource set an example for other MNCs in the United States? Explain your reasoning.

Endnotes

[1]Allison Gee, "Who first said 'The pen is mightier than the sword'?" BBC News, January 9, 2015. http://www.bbc.com/news/magazine-30729480.

[2]Andreas Wimmer, Yuval Feinstein, "The rise of the nation-state across the world, 1816 to 2001," *American Sociological Review* 75, no. 5 (2015): 764–790.

[3]Guillermo A. Calvo, Carlos A. Végh, "Inflation stabilization and BOP crises in developing countries," in John Taylor and Michael Woodford, eds., *Handbook of Macroeconomics*, vol. 1 (Amsterdam: North Holland, 1999), 1531–1614; Richard Lim, "Brazil's Battle Against Inflation," *Sounds and Colours*, June 20, 2011. http://soundsandcolours.com/articles/brazil/brazil-battle-against-inflation-8189/.

[4]Bernard Weinraub, "Economic Crisis Forcing Once Self-Reliant India to Seek Aid" *New York Times*, June 29, 1991. http://www.nytimes.com/1991/06/29/world/economic-crisis-forcing-once-self-reliant-india-to-seek-aid.html.

[5]"China Economic Reform Timeline" *Center for Strategic and International Studies*. https://www.csis.org/regions/asia/china (accessed May 3, 2017).

[6]"When the Sanctions Come Off: Foreign Businesses Eye New Frontiers. But Many Obstacles Lie in Their Way." *Economist*, July 25, 2015. http://www.economist.com/news/business/21659738-foreign-businesses-eye-new-frontiers-many-obstacles-lie-their-way-when-sanctions.

[7]Personal conversation with U.O.L. Mbamba, Dean of the University of Dar Es Salaam Business School, July 2016.

[8]"How China's Confucius Centres Affect African Culture," *New African Magazine*, May 21, 2015.

[9]Lara Parker, "19 Things you Never Knew About Ikea," *BuzzFeed*, June 11, 2014. http://www.buzzfeed.com/laraparker/things-you-never-knew-about-ikea#aib6al

[10]Counterpoint Editor, "Top 10 Handsets in October" *Counterpoint Technology Market Research*. http://www.counterpointresearch.com/top-10-handsets-in-october (accessed May 3, 2017).

[11]Chuck Jones, "Samsung Galaxy S III and Apple iPhone 5 Smartphone Web Traffic Neck to Neck. iPhones Overall Generate 2x the Traffic of Samsung's Smartphones," *Forbes,* February 20, 2013. http://www.forbes.com/sites/chuckjones/2013/02/20/samsung-galaxy-s-iii-and-apple-iphone-5-smartphone-web-traffic-neck-to-neck-iphones-overall-generate-2x-the-traffic-of-samsungs-smartphones/.

[12]Cecilia Kang, "Huawei's U.S. Competitors Among Those Pushing for Scrutiny of Chinese Tech Firm," *Washington Post*, October 10, 2012. http://www.washingtonpost.com/business/technology/huaweis-us-competitors-among-those-pushing-for-scrutiny-of-chinese-tech-firm/2012/10/10/b84d8d16-1256-11e2-a16b-2c110031514a_story.html.

[13]Pankaj Ghemawat, *Redefining Global Strategy: Crossing Borders in a World Where Differences Still Matter* (Brighton, MA: Harvard Business Review Press, 2007).

[14]Our locations. Walmart website. http://corporate.walmart.com/our-story/our-business/locations/ (accessed Sept 15, 2015).

[15]Pankaj Ghemawat, "Arbitrage Strategies." http://www.ghemawat.com/management/files/academicresources/arbitragrefeb2012.pdf (accessed April 30, 2017).

[16]Niall McCarthy, "Walmart's Wealth of Worldwide Outlets," Statista, June 28, 2013. http://www.statista.com/chart/1230/walmarts-wealth-of-worldwide-outlets/.

[17]Fan Fan Wang, "Merck's Keytruda Finds Fast Entry into China via Medical-Tourism Push," *Wall Street Journal*, September 23, 2016; "Medical Tourism: The 7 Top Destinations in the World During 2016," *TornosNews*, October 10, 2016. http://www.tornosnews.gr/en/tourism-businesses/thematic-tourism/19256-medical-tourism-the-7-top-destinations-in-the-world-during-2016.html.

[18]Tracy Waldon, James Lande, "Reference Book of Rates Price Indices and Household Expenditures for Telephone Service," Federal Communications Commission, March 1997. http://transition.fcc.gov/Bureaus/Common_Carrier/Reports/FCC-State_Link/IAD/ref97.pdf.

[19]Thomas L. Freidman, *The World Is Flat: A Brief History of the Twenty-first Century* (New York: Farrar, Straus and Giroux, 2005).

[20]Pankaj Ghemawat, "From International Business to Intranational Business," in Laszlo Tihanyi, Elitsa R. Banalieva, Timothy M. Devinney, and Torben Pedersen, eds, *Emerging Economies and Multinational Enterprises*, Advances in International Management, Vol. 28 (Bingley, UK: Emerald Group Publishing, 2015), 5–28; Pankaj Ghemawat, "Why the World Isn't Flat," *Foreign Policy*, April 2007. http://www.foreignpolicy.com/articles/2007/02/14/why_the_world_isnt_flat?page=0,0.

[21]Tarun Khanna, "Contextual Intelligence" *Harvard Business Review*, September 2014. https://hbr.org/2014/09/contextual-intelligence.

[22]C.R., "When Did Globalisation Start?" *Economist*, September 23, 2013. http://www.economist.com/blogs/freeexchange/2013/09/economic-history-1.

[23]C.R., "When Did Globalisation Start?"

[24]C.R., "When Did Globalisation Start?"

[25]C.R., "When Did Globalisation Start?"

[26]Martin Wolf, "Donald Trump and Xi Jinping's battle over globalization," *Financial Times*, January 24, 2017.

[27]Julian E. Gaspar, Antonio Arreola-Risa, Leonard Bierman, Richard T. Hise, James W. Kolari, L. Murphy Smith, *Introduction to Global Business: Understanding the International Environment & Global Business Functions* (Ohio: South-Wester, Cengage Learning, 2014), 13.

[28]World Economic Forum website. http://www.weforum.org/world-economic-forum (accessed May 1, 2017).

[29]Stan Alcorn, "The True Biography of 'Davos Man,'" *Marketplace*, January 21, 2015; Timothy Garton Ash, "Davos Man's Death Wish," *Guardian*, February 3, 2005.

[30]Hernando de Soto Polar, *The Mystery of Capital: Why Capitalism Triumphs in the West and Fails Everywhere Else* (New York: Basic Books, 2003).

[31]Global Business School Network website. http://www.gbsnonline.org/ (accessed May 1, 2017).

[32]Pankaj Ghemawat, Steven Altman. "DHL Global Connectedness Index 2014: Analyzing Global Flows and Their Power to Increase Prosperity," *IESE Monograph,* March 11, 2014.

[33]"World Economic Outlook: New Setbacks, Further Policy Action Needed,," International Monetary Fund, July 16, 2012. http://www.imf.org/external/pubs/ft/weo/2012/update/02/index.htm.

[34]Julien Vercueil, "Les pays émergents. Brésil - Russie - Inde - Chine . . . Mutations économiques et nouveaux défis" (Emerging Countries. Brazil - Russia - India - China . . . Economic change and new challenges), 3rd edition (Paris: Bréal, 2012).

[35]Kurt Badenhausen, ed., "The World's Most Valuable Brands," *Forbes,* 2016. https://www.forbes.com/powerful-brands/list/#tab:rank (Accessed May 3, 2017).

[36]United Nations Conference on Trade and Development (UNCTAD), World Investment Report 2014. Investing in the SDGs: An Action Plan (New York: United Nations, 2014). http://unctad.org/en/Publications Library/wir2014_en.pdf.

[37]"The World's Biggest Public Companies," 2016 ranking. *Forbes*. https://www.forbes.com/global2000/list/.

[38]Shad Morris, Daniel Chng, Jian Han, James Oldroyd. "Innovation Capabilities in China: Talents, Behaviors, and Processes." Working Paper, 2017.

[39]Penjaj Ghemawat, Depth Index of Globalization 2013. http://www.ghemawat.com/dig/.

[40]Andrew Batson, "Not Really 'Made in China': The iPhone's Complex Supply Chain Highlights Problems With Trade Statistics," *Wall Street Journal*, December 15, 2010.

[41]Morris, Shad S., Bijuan Zhong, and Mona Makhija. "Going the distance: The pros and cons of expanding employees' global knowledge reach." *Journal of International Business Studies* 46, no. 5 (2015): 552–573.

[42]Ibid.

[43]Christopher Minasians, "Where Are the iPhone, iPad and Mac Designed, Made and Assembled? A Comprehensive Breakdown of Apple's Product Supply Chain," *MacWorld Magazine*, April 18, 2016; Gu Huini, "Human Costs Are Built into iPad in China," *New York Times*, January 26, 2012; C. Duhigg, K. Bradsher, "How U.S Lost Out on iPhone Work," *New York Times*, January 22, 2012; Jordan Kahn, "Apple Takes Credit for Over Half a Million U.S. Jobs," 9to5Mac.com, March 2, 2012. http://9to5mac.com/2012/03/02/apple-takes-credit-for-514000-u-s-jobs/.

Analytical Tools for International Business

Bronek Kaminski/Getty Images; primeimages/ Getty Images; Easy Company/Getty Images

Introduction

Globalization creates complications for international businesses that do not exist for domestic businesses. The inability to manage and overcome these complications may lead companies to fail in international markets. If doing business is so much more challenging internationally than at home, why would a company want to go abroad in the first place? Several reasons exist. For example, doing business internationally can help increase sales. It can also help a company develop new resources and knowledge it might not be able to obtain domestically. Finally it may help companies limit, or at least diversify, risk. But to succeed, companies need to understand the management activities that will bring about increased sales, new learning, or reduced risk. And these activities will be embedded in a political, economic, sociocultural, and technological climate that largely determines what actions are relevant and useful, and how managers should initiate them.

While increasing sales and learning and reducing company risk are good reasons to do business internationally, they do not help businesses manage the complications that come with going abroad. Because each country possesses unique political policies, economic situations, social and cultural norms, and technological capacities, businesses need to understand relevant external factors in each country in order to successfully handle these complications. Once they understand these factors, managers can capitalize on the positive elements of the external environment and minimize the negative ones. These efforts make it more likely the company will reach its international objectives.

LEARNING OBJECTIVES

After you explore this chapter you will be able to:

1. **Explain** why companies engage in international business
2. **Describe** how managers can effectively analyze external factors in order to identify international threats and opportunities
3. **Discuss** how companies can adapt their management practices to operate in a global context

2.1 Why International Business?

LEARNING OBJECTIVE

Explain why companies engage in international business.

WileyPLUS

See Video: Why International Business

Have you ever noticed that much of what you buy wasn't made in the country where you live? The shirt you're wearing right now was probably made in Bangladesh, Vietnam, Indonesia, or China. You might know where the company reflected by the brand name is headquartered, but it is unlikely to be in one of those countries. As another example, the cologne or perfume you wear was probably sold by a U.S. or European company. But even if it was made with real ambergris (sperm whale vomit, one of the most expensive perfume ingredients available), it probably was not made in the same country where the company selling it is headquartered. In fact, most companies today manufacture their products in a country or countries other than where they have their headquarters. This is one of the most common strategies in international business.

International business varies from domestic business in several ways. First, it necessarily places greater emphasis on differences between countries. When a company begins doing business internationally, it has to consider all the assumptions and culture-specific knowledge it's been taking for granted up to that point and realize that they may no longer apply.

When a company conducts business in the United States, many *external factors* (see **Figure 2.1**) are consistent across companies and even industries. One of these is a judicial system that is generally fair and expedient if, for example, someone copies a patented product or reneges on a contract. In this instance, the injured company reasonably assumes it can take the offender to court. Another factor companies rely on is that the government will not come along and take their property without warning or justification. Companies also assume their customers and suppliers speak the same language, and that everyone understands the norms of business.

In an international setting, in contrast, these assumptions not only don't necessarily apply but also can cause serious problems if business managers rely on them. Differences between countries mean managers can't take for granted the same things they do at home, and those who are better able to identify and respond to local nuances tend to be the global winners. Companies that cannot adapt will eventually flounder, at the mercy of either a local or foreign competitor that better understands the local market or a foreign government whose regulations the company has failed to follow.

Knowing how to *manage activities* (see Figure 2.1) when differences arise is key to successfully engaging in international business. This knowledge becomes ever more critical as international business comes to represent a large and increasing portion of the world's

FIGURE 2.1 **Factors in international business**

business growth. Global events and competition affect almost all companies, large and small, regardless of industry, so managers who want to succeed should recognize that the best way to do business domestically may not be the best way to do business internationally. In fact, a history of success at home may mean little for your ability to succeed in business internationally.

We turn now to the three major *objectives* (see Figure 2.1) that motivate companies to engage in international business: (1) to increase sales, (2) to acquire new resources and knowledge, and (3) to reduce the risk of being exposed to a given market.

Increased Sales

A company's sales depend primarily on the desire and ability of consumers to buy the company's goods or services. If companies believe they can persuade people in a different country to buy their products or services, then setting up operations in that country has the potential to boost their overall sales. An additional benefit of increased sales from abroad is that they may enable a company to reduce its per-unit costs by covering its fixed costs (such as research and development [R&D] costs) over a larger number of sales. For example, Apple spent about $150 million on R&D to develop the iPhone.[1] The company therefore needed to sell a lot of iPhones to recoup this development cost. If it sold only 10 phones, it would need to charge $15 million each just to recover the R&D investment. On the other hand, if it could sell 150 million phones, the R&D expense would be only $1 per phone and consequently allow for a higher profit margin. It's no wonder that Apple has been very anxious to expand the iPhone into foreign markets and increase sales volume.

Many of the world's largest companies sell more of their products in foreign markets than they do in their home markets. For example, Nestlé, the Swiss food products company, sells more goods outside Europe than it does within Europe.[2] The Chinese company DJI is the world leader in camera drones. DJI began in 2006 with an idea Frank Wang had when his village got its first remote-control helicopter. Frank remembers, "It was too hard to control and I thought, 'There has to be a better RC helicopter out there.'" After tinkering around for years, he finally decided to build camera drones for serious hobbyists and professional camera crews (**Figure 2.2**). His idea took off, but not in China. "The real market for drone cameras," Frank says, "is in the United States." From the beginning, DJI has sold more of its drones in the

Jim Olive/Polaris/Newscom

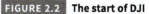

FIGURE 2.2 **The start of DJI**

United States than in its domestic market of China, and the United States is by far its largest market.[3] DJI now uses 3-dimensional printing to develop additional pieces to attach to existing drones to allow them to do other things, like operate as a search and rescue drone. With 3-dimensional printing technology, DJI can rapidly customize drones for local needs on the other side of the world.[4]

To more rapidly increase sales, many firms elect to go international from the outset or early on, upending the pattern of first succeeding in the domestic market and then moving abroad. Firms that internationalize from the outset or quickly after founding are called **born global** firms.

These rapidly internationalizing firms are becoming more and more common. In fact, 20 percent of firms in Europe and half of the firms in Romania, Belgium, and Denmark are born global firms.[5] In 2009, Markus Persson of Sweden founded Mojang AB to help develop his idea for the video game Minecraft. Mojang was international from the outset and eventually became a global phenomenon. Due to its success, Microsoft purchased the company and all its intellectually property in 2014 for $2.5 billion dollars.[6] In moving to global markets, both born global firms and more traditional firms are able to dramatically increase the size of their markets.

New Resources

Not only can a company sell to people in foreign countries; it may also gain specific types of resources from foreign sources that it might not be able to get in its home country, such as new knowledge about how to do something; minerals or other natural resources that cannot be found in the home country; lower costs for labor, equipment, or land; and higher-quality goods and services. In fact, most companies don't go abroad looking for just one of these resources, but for many or all of them. For example, when BMW set up production operations in South Africa, not only was it able to reduce labor and utility costs, but it also had closer and cheaper access to iron ore for use in its cars.

Today, many companies learn a great deal by going to foreign countries, and what they learn is not trivial. For example, many of the world's major automobile companies have design shops or partnerships in Italy because of its reputation for sleek and stylish car designs, such as Ferrari and Lamborghini. Even though Bugatti cars are manufactured in Germany, the company's founder, Ettore Bugatti, was born and raised in Milan, Italy, and the company is currently headquartered in France (**Figure 2.3**).

Until 2005, the U.S. company General Electric (GE) had one central R&D center in New York. Since that time, it has built four other R&D centers around the world—in Munich, Shanghai, Bangalore, and Rio de Janeiro. GE decided that it needed to tap into different countries for new and insightful ideas—ideas that could not come if it limited itself to scientists from just one country. An example of the benefits of this approach is the new Vscan ultrasound machine. It was designed at the Shanghai R&D center in response to a need among rural Chinese doctors. But the idea turned out to be valuable not only for China but also for GE's home market in the United States and in other countries around the world as well.

Bernard Menigault/Contributor/Getty Images

FIGURE 2.3 The reputation of Bugatti The Bugatti Veyron was designed and developed by Volkswagen and manufactured by Bugatti Automobiles S.A.S. in France. As the world's fastest production car, it has a top speed of 267 miles per hour. It costs a mere $1.7 million.

Reduced Risk

Companies that operate in just one country can be very successful and profitable, especially when that country has a strong economy. However, they face a disproportionate risk of loss when things go bad. During economic expansion, sales can increase quickly, but during a recession, they grow more slowly or even decline, and nothing is available to offset the loss. These economic shifts are inevitable and, like a pendulum, often swing back and forth. They can also make being restricted to the domestic market a feast-or-famine operation and can cripple some businesses.

Sometimes a downturn in one country, however, can be a growth period in another. For example, during the Great Recession of 2007–2009, many U.S. companies flipped their sales: Rather than selling the majority of their products at home, where the economy had weakened and spending was down, they switched their focus to emerging markets such as the BRIC nations—Brazil, Russia, India, and China—and other countries where demand remained strong. Some companies were able to replace their dependence on U.S. sales by increasing the sale of products and services in these emerging markets. However, the pendulum is swinging again. With the economic slowdowns in China, India, and Brazil, and the growth of the U.S. market in 2017, some of these sales have shifted back as U.S. consumers have become more willing and able to spend again.[7]

Operating in multiple countries can thus minimize the impact of economic swings an individual company may experience over the years. When sales are down in one country, the firm can focus on increasing sales in another.

Similarly, by diversifying the places where its products are made, a company can soften the impact of price increases or supply shortages that may occur in any one country. For example, history's fourth-largest tsunami struck Japan in March 2011, causing $300 billion of damage, but Japanese companies weren't the only ones hurt. Many foreign companies relied heavily on Japanese plants to manufacture parts for their products. One such company, General Motors, had to temporarily shut down its truck plant in Louisiana for lack of Japanese-made parts, costing the company millions of dollars in lost production at a facility half a world away.[8] Diversifying the locations of suppliers and manufacturing plants can help to avoid this type of scenario.

Operating in multiple countries also reduces risk by helping a company stay competitive. If a company's competitors go abroad, they can gain advantages such as those discussed earlier, making them better equipped to operate in the home market, too. In comparison, a domestic company may limit itself by staying put, forgoing access to cheaper and better resources and to opportunities to gain a foothold abroad. For example, when Coca-Cola decided to go abroad in the 1920s (see **Figure 2.4**), Pepsi knew it had to follow in order to make sure Coke didn't capture the foreign global soft-drink market. This led to an all-out cola war as each company tried to beat the other into new markets, with lasting effects. Today, Coke and Pepsi are two of the most globalized companies in the world. In fact, the cola war was so effective that some countries such as Pakistan can now be considered Pepsi countries, whereas others such as Kenya are Coke countries.[9,10]

Some countries, such as Denmark, are trying to detach themselves from the cola wars altogether as they implement a war on products with high sugar content that can lead to diabetes. In fact, the World Health Organization suggested that all world governments introduce a 20 to 50 percent "soda tax" to fight against obesity and type 2 diabetes.[11] As a result, Coke and Pepsi have started introducing more health-conscious options to their product line. These "wars" show that companies not only need to worry about risks from competing companies but also risks from governments.

Reducing risk, gaining access to resources, and increasing sales are important benefits of taking business abroad. Yet, to obtain any of these objectives, a company must understand the external factors in the particular foreign market and then effectively manage the situation. What does a company need to think about as it considers doing business internationally? In the next section we answer this question and show you how companies can more effectively assess the threats and opportunities they face in a global setting.

TENGKU BAHAR/Staff/Getty Images

FIGURE 2.4 **Buying the world a Coke** Coca-Cola was one of the first U.S. companies to enter the Chinese and Indian markets.

2.2 External Environment

LEARNING OBJECTIVE

Describe how managers can effectively analyze external factors to identify international threats and opportunities.

Because each country has different political policies, economic situations, social and cultural norms, and technological capacities, companies devote a lot of time and money to addressing the complications that arise when operating in multiple countries. For example, Mary Kay, a company that sells cosmetics, encourages managers from its headquarters to visit foreign markets at least twice a year.[12] These visits help ensure that operations and policies are consistent across the globe and allow leaders to learn from local managers about ways to modify and improve existing operations.

External factors such as economics, politics, and culture affect a company's modes of operation as well as the objectives it will be able to achieve. To manage these objectives and determine appropriate modes of operation, companies turn to a tool called "PEST analysis." *PEST* stands for the **p**olitical, **e**conomic, **s**ociocultural, and **t**echnological aspects of the business environment (**Figure 2.5**). A PEST analysis examines these factors in order to gain insights about the company's environment. Let's explore these four factors in depth.

WileyPLUS

See Video: **PEST Analysis, Part 1**

Political Factors

political factors external factors including labor laws, property rights, and patent processes

economic factors external factors including the strength or weakness of markets, stability of trade cycles, specific industry conditions, customer preferences, and government's economic policies

First, companies assess **political factors** by examining a country's labor laws, property rights, and patent process. For example, when the Ohio-based welding company Lincoln Electric started operations in Brazil, it was not able offer its yearly bonus program based on performance because in Brazil any bonuses paid for two consecutive years become a legal entitlement.[13]

In many countries, particularly in Africa, property rights are poorly protected by governments. Whoever has the political power or authority can seize others' property with few or no legal repercussions. In other places, civil unrest has led to poor enforcement of property rights, including intellectual property rights. As a result, companies have less incentive to locate factories or other investments in those countries. For instance, investment in and output of agricultural production in Zimbabwe have declined dramatically as a result of land seizures under President Robert Mugabe. These seizures began in 2000, when Mugabe's government orchestrated a large-scale redistribution of farms to his supporters. This action is considered to be largely responsible for halving the country's agricultural output and scaring off foreign investors.[14]

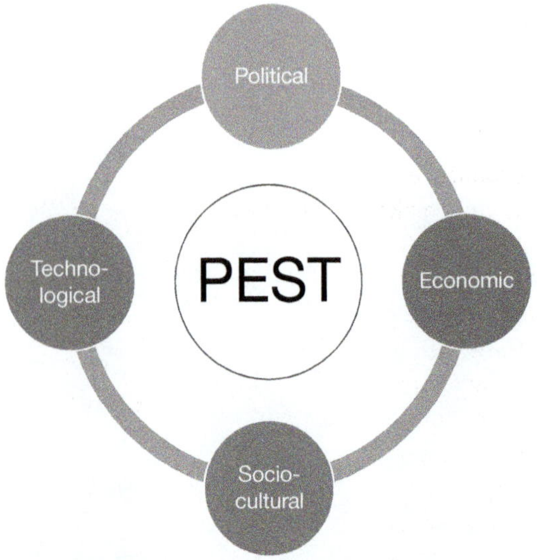

FIGURE 2.5 **Factors in the PEST analysis** A PEST analysis guides users to consider four factors that may affect the risks and rewards of international business in a given country.

Economic Factors

Economic factors consist of the strength or weakness of a market, the stability of trade cycles, specific industry conditions and related changes, customer preferences, and the government's economic policies. These conditions can be measured in several ways. Other economic influences are multilateral efforts to increase global economic interactions, such as the activities of the World Trade Organization (WTO). As a result, countries are continually negotiating free-trade agreements with each other in the hope of increasing their economic activity and power.

For example, since China joined the WTO in 2001, its economy has grown dramatically, drastically altering its political and trading relationships with many nations. In a strange twist of fate, Xi Jingping, the leader of the communist world and China's president, has taken to defending free trade and globalization, whereas Donald Trump, leader of the free world and America's president, has taken to attacking them.[15]

China's population of 1.3 billion represents a massive and rapidly growing consumer market for global companies. Today, more cars are sold in China than in Europe.[16] Fueling this trend are big multinational corporations that are expanding into the country, although many smaller firms are heading to China as well. "It's not so much that [companies] want to go East," said one international human resources staffing consultant. "They feel that they have no choice. They must be in China . . . even if the old high growth rates are not what they used to be. It's not a question of if, but a question of how."[17] China isn't the only country that companies are clambering over each other to get into, either; India's economy is also growing very quickly, as is Mexico and those of other emerging markets.[18]

Sociocultural Factors

A country's **sociocultural factors** also have important implications when it comes to a company's decision about when and how to do business there. Sociocultural factors include the method and style of communication, major and minor religions, common values and ideologies, educational standards, and social structure. For instance, because of language similarities and low labor costs, many U.S. companies have found India to be an attractive place to locate their facilities, particularly those focused on communication, such as call centers and software development companies. Eastern Europe has also begun to attract interest because citizens there are often well educated and speak fluent English. Similarly, the U.S. military's long-term stay in Panama developed a bilingual workforce that already understands the U.S. work culture. Now that the Panama Canal has been expanded to accommodate new, larger freight ships, the United States is looking to take advantage of these close ties to and cultural similarities in the workforce there.[19]

sociocultural factors external factors including method and style of communications, religions, values and ideologies, education standards, and social structure

Managers stand a better chance of understanding the culture of a **host country**—a country in which an international business operates—by recognizing and accommodating different ideologies, religious beliefs, communication styles, education systems, and social structures. Even in countries that have close linguistic or cultural links, management practices are often dramatically different. For example, night shifts may be taboo. Employers might be expected to provide employees with meals while at work and transportation between home and work. In most of the Islamic Middle East, it is completely acceptable to ask coworkers very personal questions about their children, especially their sons, but never about their wives.[20]

host country a country in which an international business operates

Technological Factors

Related to a country's sociocultural norms, the level of technology available in a country also influences the threats and opportunities foreign companies face. **Technological factors** make up the technological infrastructure in a country and include such things as intellectual infrastructure, such as investments in universities and research, and physical infrastructure—for example, investments in manufacturing equipment, information systems, and technology platforms, and consumer access to Internet technology. Because of the increased emphasis on and quality of manufacturing technologies in many countries, the number of manufacturing jobs is decreasing. Companies are increasingly turning to sophisticated machinery to produce the same amount of product using fewer workers—a common trend with products like cars, clothes, and computers—and it is spreading to other segments of industry.

technological factors external factors pertaining to the technological infrastructure in a country, including intellectual infrastructure and investments, information systems, manufacturing equipment, and consumer access to technology

In less developed countries, manufacturing has traditionally been a stronger sector because the low cost of labor; even in these markets, however, labor-saving technology is becoming more affordable and accessible. Consider, for instance, a textile factory in Vietnam. It is now often more cost-effective for the factory to purchase high-tech threading equipment to spin cotton into thread than to hire hundreds of people to spin the cotton by hand, even when the average wage for such employees is less than $100 a month.

While advances in technology have pushed employment out of manufacturing and toward more service-oriented jobs, information systems and technology platforms have also increased the rate at which these services can be traded across countries. Along with the creation of the WTO, 1995 also signaled the beginning of the Internet era. America Online (AOL) went public in 1995, marking the beginning of integrated technology platforms and instantaneous global sharing. **Integrated technology platforms** are common operating systems, such as Microsoft Windows 10, that can be used across multiple computers connected through the Internet. When work platforms are standardized across locations, work becomes less specific to particular companies or countries.

integrated technology platforms common operating systems that can be used across multiple computers connected through the Internet

In today's era, workers have become empowered to compete without the need of a large company. For example, many websites such as Guru.com have helped develop an online marketplace where individuals can offer various services and compete for business throughout the world—without needing the affiliation of a multinational company or brand. If you are interested in developing a new website for your company, for example, you can go online and select from various individuals offering the specific services you need—whether they be in Manila, Mumbai, Manhattan, or Munich.

In sum, the PEST factors affect the risks and opportunities of doing business in different countries and change the way companies manage their international operations in those markets. By shifting and adapting to compensate for differences in these factors across countries, companies can more effectively increase international sales, acquire valuable resources and knowledge, and reduce risk.

WileyPLUS

See Video: PEST Analysis, Part 2

Conducting a PEST Analysis

You alone don't have much control over the external factors your company faces, but that only makes it more urgent for you to understand what they are so you can take advantage of the opportunities they present while steering clear of the threats. A PEST analysis is the best way to get a picture of the competitive landscape in a country. It entails scanning different contextual environments to understand long-term trends and how they might affect your business. As a manager, you can use PEST analyses to (1) spot possible business opportunities and identify potential threats, (2) implement appropriate practices from local cultures while avoiding problematic ones, and (3) break free of old assumptions about how managers should run organizations.

To conduct a PEST analysis, first identify the specific environmental factors you need to consider and assess. **Figure 2.6** lists some potential factors to get you started.

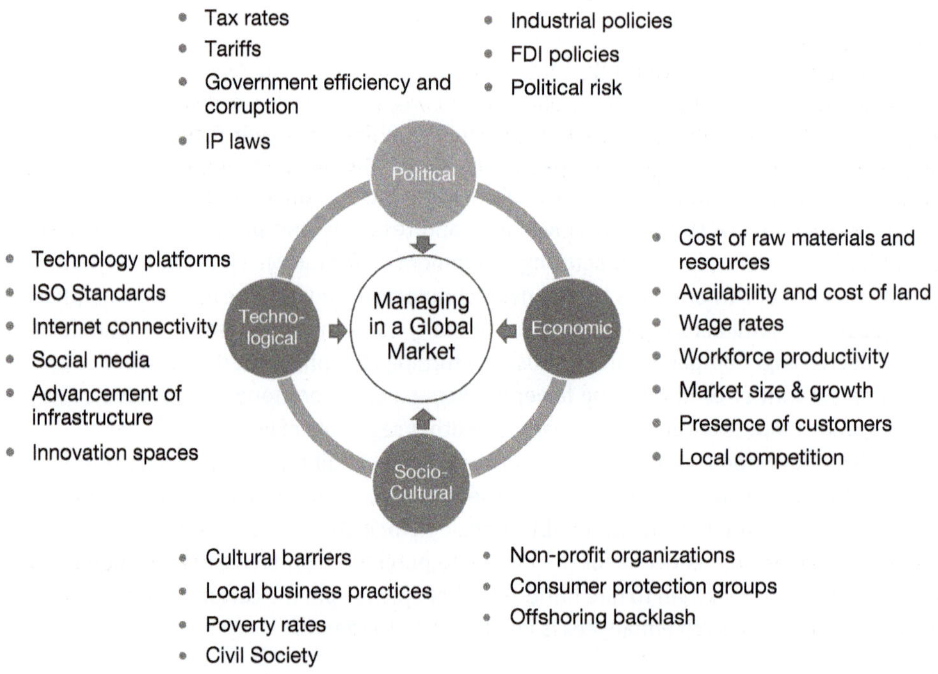

FIGURE 2.6 Factors commonly used in a PEST analysis FDI, foreign direct investment; IP, intellectual property; ISO, International Organization for Standardization.

Next, assess how these factors affect your company's international operations, as shown in the **PEST analysis tool**. To do this, we have provided an analytical tool to help you make this assessment. This tool can be expanded to include other factors as you explore PEST, but for now it will provide you with everything you need to quantify how attractive a country might be for your business. Based on these PEST factors and the way your company conducts its international operations, you can develop appropriate practices in the right locations and for the appropriate contexts.

PEST analysis tool a spreadsheet that allows you to quantify the different PEST threats and opportunities to determine which countries are most attractive

For now, remember that engaging in international business requires much more than simply identifying threats and opportunities presented by the external environment. It also requires making changes to a company's internal management activities, from the way it strategizes and enters the business environment in a new country to the way it leads and structures its international operations. Identifying threats and opportunities gives the company a roadmap, but that map is useful only if the people in charge of steering the company align its management practices to move in the intended direction.

2.3 Internal Environment

LEARNING OBJECTIVE

Discuss how companies can adapt their management practices to operate in a global context.

Companies need to consider several internal management factors as they decide to do business internationally: the mode of entry into new countries, the overall strategy or reason for entering the country, the company's organizational structure, and its leadership capabilities. Using a careful PEST analysis, companies can examine the attractiveness of a foreign market. An equally important second step, however, is determining how to enter a new market most effectively; companies need to adapt their strategy, reconsider their structure, and reinforce a strong global mind-set among leadership. While using PEST to choose a market is important, history shows that trying to do business internationally without adapting internal management activities is likely a mistake. Most competent managers across the globe would agree that creating a coherent strategy, determining an appropriate mode of entry, properly organizing the business, and motivating talent are universally important factors in success. At the same time, different views about how best to build, strategize, organize, and motivate and develop people quickly emerge across countries.

For example, many people still believe the best practices for manufacturing merchandise are universally applicable and only need to be tweaked in order to fit local conditions. In reality, however, manufacturing practices often require radical changes. The practices themselves are not faulty. Rather, everything surrounding them—the political, economic, social, and technological factors—changes their effectiveness in a given environment[21] (**Figure 2.7**). Unless managers understand the interplay between the external context and the internal management practices, the failure rate for an international business will be high, and achieving the opportunity for global growth will likely remain difficult.

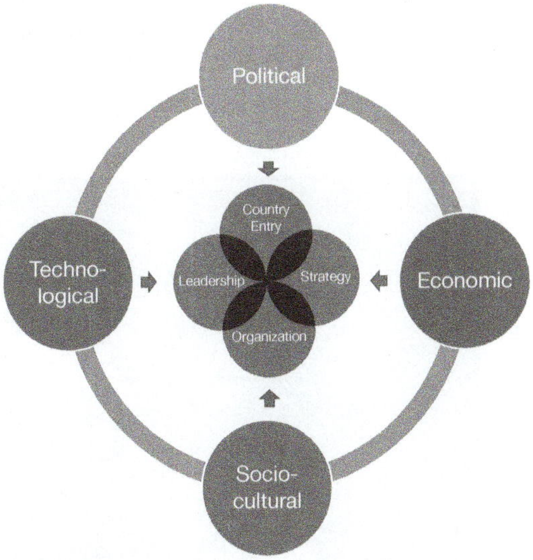

FIGURE 2.7 Key global management practices Engaging in international business requires firms not only to choose markets carefully, with the help of a PEST analysis, but also to create and align internal management practices that successfully build and execute strategy.

Country Entry

Once a company decides to enter a foreign market, one of its first management decisions is choosing the best method for entering that market. In general, firms can use one of six different modes: exporting/importing, turnkey projects, licensing, franchising, establishing joint ventures, or setting up a new, wholly owned subsidiary. We briefly consider each below.

exporting sending goods or services out of a company's home country

importing purchasing goods or services from another country to be sold in a company's home market

Exporting and Importing. Exporting and importing are the most popular modes of international business, especially among smaller companies. **Exporting** is the act of sending goods or services out of a company's home country. It does not entail the costs and complications of opening additional locations or expanding internationally. Exporting companies can increase sales with minimal increases in costs, especially thanks to the ease of access provided through the Internet.

Importing consists of purchasing goods or services from another country to be sold in a company's home market. The lifestyle apparel company Black Clover purchases some of its products from manufacturers in China. These products are considered exports for China and imports for Black Clover. Even though Black Clover sells its products in the United States, this relatively simple importing strategy makes Black Clover an international company (**Figure 2.8**).

turnkey projects A project ready for immediate use, especially a project in which a company already in a particular country builds a building, plant, or machine for a foreign company

Turnkey Projects. A **turnkey project** is one that is ready for immediate use—like a car, all a consumer needs to do is "turn the key" to get started. In the case of international business, a turnkey project is one in which a company already operating in a particular country builds a building, plant, or machine for a foreign company. Foreign companies often turn to local contractors to construct facilities because local builders understand local requirements. Once the project has been completed, it is turned over to the foreign company, which moves in to make use of the project. Until then, however, the sole responsibility for it rests with the local company—another advantage for the foreign firm.

licensing permission to use another company's trademarks, patents, copyrights, or expertise

royalties payments from the licensee to the licenser consisting of a percentage of what is earned from selling such products and services

franchising permission to use another company's trademarks, patents, copyrights and expertise according to a strict template setting out the way it does business

Licensing. A third way to enter a foreign market is through licensing. When one company allows another to use its trademarks, patents, copyrights, or expertise, the two companies typically enter into a **licensing** agreement. In return for allowing the second, sometimes foreign, company to use its intellectual property, the licensing company receives earnings called **royalties**, or a percentage of what is earned from the sale of such products or services. For example, Nike pays Ohio State University a royalty on all sales of athletic gear with Ohio State University's logo.[22] Similarly, Lucasfilm and its new owner, Disney, have licensed the Star Wars brand for fees of more than $30 billion to companies that market products as diverse as oranges and toys[23] (**Figure 2.9**). While licensing can reduce risk, it can also result in lost opportunities for parent companies. For instance, in 2016 the value of Nintendo shares soared as the Pokémon GO mobile game became immensely popular around the world. However, when investors realized that Niantic Labs had in fact developed the game and paid a licensing fee to Nintendo, Nintendo shares plummeted nearly 18 percent in one day. While Nintendo still benefited from Pokémon GO, it certainly lost an opportunity because it had only licensed and not developed the game.[24]

David Hahn/Icon Sportswire CID/David Hahn/Icon Sportswire/Newscom

FIGURE 2.8 **Is Black Clover international?** Black Clover imports to the United States apparel manufactured in China.

Franchising. **Franchising** is similar to licensing, but it requires a much higher level of commitment from the two parties. The *franchiser* is the owning, or parent, company. It allows another company, the *franchisee*, to use its trademarks, patents, and copyrights, as in a licensing situation, but only according to a strict template outlining the way it does business. The franchiser may also assist the franchisee in running the business on an ongoing basis. As with licensing, the franchisee pays a royalty in return for using the franchiser's intellectual property and receiving managerial support; this royalty can be a set fee or a percentage of the franchisee's revenues.

Manufacturing companies usually choose licensing agreements, whereas service companies are often franchises. McDonald's is probably the best-known example of the franchise model. Although it owns one of the most recognizable brands in the world, the company owns only about 6,200 of its 36,000 locations worldwide; franchisees own and operate the rest.[25] In fact, if you've ever eaten at a McDonald's in a foreign country, it was most likely owned by a local person or company, not by McDonald's. However, you likely noticed the uniformity in quality and design between that foreign site and those back home; this uniformity is because of the strict template that all McDonald's franchisees must follow. Of course, franchisees are typically happy to step in line, because this is one business model that has proven successful all over the world.

JOSH EDELSON/Stringer/Getty Images

FIGURE 2.9 **Disney licensing** Disney licenses its Star Wars brand to producers of products as diverse as toys, clothing, and even oranges.

Joint Venture. When two or more companies jointly own a third, separate company, they are engaged in a **joint venture**. As an example, in 2014 the British luxury car manufacturers Jaguar and Land Rover entered a joint venture with the Chinese company Chery Automobiles[26] (**Figure 2.10**). The new company they created is known as Chery Jaguar Land Rover Automobile Company. The purpose of the joint venture is to develop a line of luxury automobiles that specifically targets the needs of Chinese consumers. Because all risk in such situations is solely the responsibility of the joint venture company, this form of business can reduce the risks of not knowing the local market while also ensuring that neither of the two original companies is directly harmed by failure.

joint venture a separate company jointly owned by two or more other companies

subsidiary a "child" company to parent company; the parent company owns 100% of the subsidiary's operations

Wholly Owned Subsidiary. A **subsidiary** is like a child company to a parent company, which owns 100 percent of the operations of the subsidiary. When a company decides to go abroad with a wholly owned subsidiary, it can set up that subsidiary in two ways. First, the parent firm can build new plants or offices and then hire employees when it enters the market. This is known as a *greenfield venture*, using the analogy of breaking ground in an empty field. The second option is to buy an established company in the foreign country. In this case the building is already there and the organization has the employees necessary for operations. Acquiring an existing foreign company is much easier than building from scratch, but it comes with problems of its own. Most of these relate to the difficulty of integrating the subsidiary's existing culture with that of the parent company, rather than building the culture from the beginning. In some cases, these cultural differences can cause the venture to fail. However, many companies choose to take the risk in order to begin operations immediately. For example, when Amazon wanted to move into the British market, it acquired a British rival, Book Depository.[27] As a result, Amazon was able to move into the United Kingdom immediately through a wholly owned subsidiary.

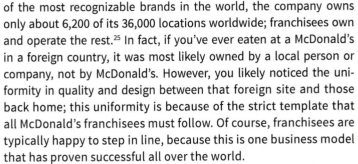

REUTERS/Alamy Stock Photo

FIGURE 2.10 **Jaguar, Land Rover, and Chery** This joint venture inaugurates the first manufacturing facility for Jaguar Land Rover outside the United Kingdom.

Strategy

In addition to the mode of entry into a country, companies need to develop a strategy for their international operations. One of the key objectives of any international strategy is to help companies manage the wide differences that exist across countries and regions. Recognizing these differences through a PEST analysis is the critical first step, but there's more to the process. The company must then use the analysis to formulate a strategic plan for managing the opportunities and threats it uncovers.

Strategic planning for international business requires that companies first identify their specific objectives for international expansion. Do they want to increase growth in the foreign market? Do they want to mitigate risk? Do they want to increase innovation or access to foreign resources? It's possible to achieve all these things, but companies need to prioritize their objectives or risk failing by attempting too many things simultaneously. Once the company identifies and prioritizes its objectives, it must consider how to respond to the local needs of the foreign market while also standardizing operations as much as possible in order to increase efficiencies.

For example, the Irish clothing company Zara has developed a strong strategy around global efficiency by locating most of its designers in Spain and then manufacturing the clothes there as well.[28] This strategy enables Zara to respond quickly to changes in styles and to move fashions from the runways of Paris and Milan to retail stores all over the world much more quickly than competitors can.[29] Its global efficiency is a powerful competitive advantage, but it also means Zara may have difficulty being locally responsive. Zara does some things to adapt its products to local customers, most of which revolve around color and can be changed quickly.

Organization

Once a company has figured out its international strategy, structuring the global organization around that strategy is the next critical management activity. When doing business internationally, organizations need to consider how they are structured both vertically and horizontally. **Vertical structuring** determines where in a hierarchy the decisions about the company are made. For example, does the CEO at the company headquarters make all the decisions, or is each country responsible for its own decisions? International firms must often balance the tension between flexibility, allowing local managers at lower levels of the organization to have decision power, and efficiency, having centralized decision makers and operations.

vertical structuring determines where in a hierarchy a company's decisions are made

horizontal structuring reflects the way the company subdivides itself

Horizontal structuring reflects the way a company decides to subdivide itself. Because running a large organization with only one decision maker is impossible, companies organize subunits and then choose how decisions are delegated among them. One common practice is to base subunits on specific geographic locations. For example, some international businesses have in each country a separate division with its own decision-making power. Or a division may consist of an entire region of the world whose manager makes all major decisions and the managers in given countries of that region make minor decisions. Other companies are divided into subunits based on function, such as finance, marketing, information technology, human resources, and operations. Still others subdivide according to their various business missions, customers, or products. For example, some of IBM's divisions are Global Technology Services, Global Business Services, Systems and Technology, Software, and Global Financing.[30] Each is responsible for its own business activities worldwide, and decisions are made to manage the individual product families at a global level.

Leadership

Good leadership is—and has always been—a top priority for global companies. In survey after survey, CEOs say one of the most important factors for internal management in a global environment is good leadership.[31] Global leaders must have different competencies than domestic leaders. A recent study suggests that more than 75 percent of executives think their organizations need to develop global leadership skills, but less than 10 percent are effectively doing so.[32]

Many skills and capabilities contribute to the general success of global leaders, but four specific competencies are critical: a strong corporate vision, functional excellence, industry expertise, and market savvy. A *strong corporate vision* is a larger understanding of the global company and its mission and values, including how different localities can contribute strengths to compensate for one another's weaknesses. *Functional excellence* is the ability to work across different functions (such as finance, marketing, information technology) to ensure corporate-level operations work in different countries. *Industry expertise* means understanding where the industry is going in the future, who the key players and competitors are, and how the company might lead that industry. Finally, *market savvy* represents a deep understanding of local context and customer needs, and the ability to cultivate that knowledge in new contexts and locations.

In summary, for a company to lead in today's global environment, its managers must understand the threats and opportunities in its external environment and then be able to adapt managerial activities to meet these external factors and achieve the firm's specific objectives.

Summary and Case

Summary

LEARNING OBJECTIVE 2.1 Explain why companies engage in international business.

Companies engage in international business to increase sales, obtain new resources and knowledge, and to reduce risk by minimizing the effect of economic swings of individual countries.

LEARNING OBJECTIVE 2.2 Describe how managers can effectively analyze external factors to identify international threats and opportunities.

Going abroad exposes companies to at least four categories of risks and opportunities: political, economic, technological, and social (also known as "PEST" factors). A successful analysis of PEST factors can change the way companies manage their international operations. By compensating for these factors, companies can increase international sales, reduce risk, and acquire valuable resources and knowledge.

LEARNING OBJECTIVE 2.3 Discuss how companies can adapt their management practices to operate in a global context.

Analysis of the external environment is only the first step in achieving success internationally. Companies must also look internally, choosing an appropriate entry strategy such as exporting and importing, turnkey projects, licensing, franchising, joint ventures, or wholly owned subsidiaries. They also need to develop and properly execute an international strategy to manage the different PEST factors, then structure the global organization around that strategy using a vertical or horizontal structure. To operate in a global context, firms should also attract leaders who are competent in the four areas of strong corporate vision, functional excellence, industry expertise, and market savvy.

Case

Toyota for the World

Few companies can match Toyota's success in and domination of the international scene. The Japanese company stands as one of the world's largest carmakers, with sales exceeding 10 million new vehicles since 2013.[33] Toyota has managed not only to penetrate nearly every major global market but also to be actively involved in directing a large portion of its sales efforts to emerging markets. To learn where this success came from, let's rewind.

Toyota was founded in 1937 as a small company with Kiichiro Toyoda as its president. The auto industry began booming that year as World War II erupted, and by the end of the next half-century, the company had used multiple strategies to expand into all major international markets.

Toyota's Expansion Abroad

Before targeting the international market, Toyota first focused its attention on the national level. After building a solid base at home in Japan, the company expanded to South America. Its first batch of exported cars went to Brazil in 1952 after the company received an order for 100 units of Model FXL large trucks.[34] This was a pivotal moment for Toyota to gain market share abroad. Like the rest of South America, Brazil was plagued by poorly developed and maintained roads, scaring off many large automobile companies at the time. Toyota saw this as an opportunity and marketed its Land Cruiser (4WD) as a vehicle adept at navigating the poor road infrastructure of the country.

By establishing a "first-mover advantage" in Brazil—that is, by being the first company to market a product before any competition moved in—Toyota was able to differentiate its product and gain success. Leveraging that success, the company was then able to export to other markets in Latin America and South America, such as Puerto Rico, Venezuela, Costa Rica, and Colombia. During the 1950s, Toyota also began exporting to Thailand, China, and the Middle East. Toyota specifically delayed exporting to Europe at that time because the region was known as the world's most sophisticated automobile market, with strong German, French, and Italian car makers.[35] Eventually, though, Toyota did start exporting to Europe (Denmark) and Africa (Ethiopia) in the late 1950s.[36]

In the 1980s, after establishing a solid presence abroad, Toyota was ready to expand to the United States. The company faced import restrictions implemented by the U.S. Congress, however, and the only way to circumvent them was to start building cars in the United States. Therefore it became crucial to find a U.S. partner to form a joint venture and to help Toyota understand and work with U.S. workers, rather than just produce cars in Japan and export them to the United States. Conveniently for Toyota, General Motors was struggling to compete with the reliable, inexpensive cars produced by Toyota and its Japanese competitors, making a joint venture a mutually beneficial path for both companies. Toyota got the expertise it needed in worker relations and operations in the United States, while General Motors got firsthand experience building reliable, inexpensive cars. Thus, by 1998, Toyota had used various entry strategies to build a network of 150 distributors in 25 countries, with 34 overseas subsidiaries and affiliates.[37]

Toyota Today

Toyota has continued to form joint ventures and partnerships with other firms, with the aim of improving and releasing more competitive cars. For instance, Toyota and Tesla partnered to make electric cars in 2010,[38] and in 2012, Toyota and BMW announced their intentions to work together on a jointly developed sports car.[39] Toyota and Mazda, former rivals, recently entered a long-term partnership to focus on developing new technologies to improve safety and fuel efficiency.[40] Strategic partnerships like these have become more appealing and more common as the costs of ensuring safety and meeting emissions standards have risen. Partnering allows rival companies to spread research costs over a broader base.

Case Discussion Questions

1. Why did Toyota export its products first, instead of establishing a wholly owned subsidiary?
2. Toyota initially hesitated to enter the European and U.S. markets. Do you think this was a good strategic decision? Why or why not?
3. What are some potential drawbacks Toyota should consider before forming partnerships and joint ventures—especially with rival automakers?

Endnotes

[1]Tim Worstall, "Developing Obamacare's Health Care Exchanges Has Cost More Than Apple's Original iPhone," *Forbes*, October 17, 2013.

[2]"Coca-Cola Company," Statista. https://www.statista.com/topics/1392/coca-cola-company/ (accessed May 2, 2017).

[3]Personal interview with representatives from and site visit to DJI in Shenzhen, China, by Shad Morris and James Oldroyd, December 2015.

[4]Tyler Koslow, "3D Printed Exoskeleton Attachment Transforms DJI Phantom 4 into Search and Rescue Drone," 3D Design, October 13, 2016. https://3dprint.com/152433/dji-search-and-rescue-drone/

[5]Cavusgil, S. Tamer, and Gary Knight. "The born global firm: An entrepreneurial and capabilities perspective on early and rapid internationalization." *Journal of International Business Studies* 46.1 (2015): 3–16.

[6]Klint Finely. "With Minecraft acquisition, Microsoft reveals its desperation." *Wired*. September 15, 2014. https://www.wired.com/2014/09/microsoft-minecraft-mobile/

[7]Neil Irwin, "The Big Question for the U.S. Economy: How Much Room Is There to Grow?" *New York Times*, February 24, 2017; Josh Boak, "US Retail Sales up 0.6 pct., but Signs of Caution Emerge," Associated Press, October 14, 2016.

[8]Steve Lohr, "Stress Test for the Global Supply Chain," *New York Times*, March 19, 2011.

[9]Euromonitor Research, "In Battle for Pakistani Youth, Coca-Cola Gains Share by Cultivating Local Stars," Euromonitor International, September 19, 2014. http://blog.euromonitor.com/2014/09/in-battle-for-pakistani-youth-coca-cola-gains-share-by-cultivating-local-stars.html.

[10]"Coca-Cola in Brazil: Global Events and Energy Drinks Could Drive Growth," *Forbes*, March 12, 2014.

[11]Karan Kaplan, "World Health Officials Want Super-Size Tax on Soda and Sugary Drinks, But Are Countries Ready to Swallow That?" *Los Angeles Times*, October 12, 2016.

[12]Personal interview with six Mary Kay managers, December 2016.

[13]Jordan I. Siegel and Barbara Zepp Larson, "Labor Market Institutions and Global Strategic Adaptation: Evidence from Lincoln Electric," *Management Science* 55, no. 9 (2009): 1527–46.

[14]Martin Plaut, "Are Zimbabwe's New Farmers Winning, 10 Years on?" BBC News, December 1, 2011. www.bbc.com/news/world-africa-15919538.

[15]Larry Elliott and Graeme Wearden, "Xi Jinping Signals China Will Champion Free Trade if Trump Builds Barriers," *Guardian*, January 17, 2017.

[16]Kenneth Rapoza, "China Vehicle Sales Beat Europe and U.S. Again," *Forbes*, January 10, 2013. www.forbes.com/sites/kenrapoza/2013/01/10/china-vehicle-sales-beat-europe-and-u-s-again/#2417491d2e68.

[17]Scott Snell, George Bohlander and Shad Morris, "*Managing Human Resources*," Cengage Learning, 2016.

[18]Joe Myers, "Which Are the World's Fastest-Growing Economies?" World Economic Forum, April 18, 2016. www.weforum.org/agenda/2016/04/worlds-fastest-growing-economies/.

[19]"The Panama Canal Expansion: Changes Beyond the Waterway," Knowledge@Wharton, June 3, 2016. http://knowledge.wharton.upenn.edu/article/panama-canal-expansion-changes-beyond-waterway/; Steven Mufson, "An Expanded Panama Canal Opens for Giant Ships," *Washington Post*, June 26, 2016.

[20]S. Vollmer, "How to Mind Your Manners in the Middle East: CPAs Who Do Business in the Region Need to Know the Cultural Rules," *Journal of Accountancy* 219, no. 1 (2015): 42; Ruchika Tulshyan, "Quirkiest Cultural Practices from Around the World," *Forbes*, March 18, 2010.

[21]Tarun Khanna, "Contextual Intelligence," *Harvard Business Review*, September 1, 2014. https://hbr.org/2014/09/contextual-intelligence.

[22]Kayla Byler, "Just Doing It: Ohio State, Nike Extend $46 Million, Brand-building Agreements," *Lantern*, December 13, 2013.

[23]Wallace Witkowski, "Disney Must Fight the 'Dark Side' of Star Wars Licensing," MarketWatch, December 18, 2016. http://www.marketwatch.com/story/disney-must-fight-the-dark-side-of-star-wars-licensing-2015-12-15.

[24]Charles Riley, "Nintendo Shares Plummet 18% after Pokemon Go Reality Check," CNN, July 25, 2016. http://money.cnn.com/2016/07/25/investing/nintendo-shares-pokemon-go/.

[25]Investor Relations: Company Overview—Company Profile. McDonald's website. www.aboutmcdonalds.com/mcd/investors/company_profile .html (accessed April 23, 2016).

[26]Li Fusheng and Li Fangfang, "Chery Jaguar Land Rover Changshu plant fully operational. Chinadaily," ChinaDaily USA, October 27, 2014. http://usa.chinadaily.com.cn/business/2014-10/27/content_18809722.htm; Angela Monaghan, "Jaguar Land Rover Seals Chinese Joint Venture," *Telegraph*, November 18, 2012.

[27]"Amazon Steps up Battle for Britain with Book Depository but Stock Should Be $200," July 27, 2011. www.forbes.com/sites/greatspeculations/2011/07/27/amazon-steps-up-battle-for-britain-with-book-depository-but-stock-should-be-200acquisition/#6081b13a1877; Zoe Wood, "Booksellers Fear 'Stranglehold' as Amazon Snaps up British Rival The Book Depository," *Guardian*, July 5, 2011.

[28]Clara Lu, "Zara Supply Chain Analysis – The Secret Behind Zara's Retail Success," *Trade Gecko*, December 4, 2014.

[29]Susan Berfield and Manuel Baigorri, "Zara's Fast-Fashion Edge," Bloomberg Business, November 14, 2013. www.bloomberg.com/bw/articles/2013-11-14/2014-outlook-zaras-fashion-supply-chain-edge.

[30]IBM Annual Report 2014. www.ibm.com/investor/att/pdf/IBM_Annual_Report_2014.pdf. See in particular pages 28–31.

[31]"Redefining Competition: Insights from The Global C-suite Study," IBM, 2016. http://www-01.ibm.com/common/ssi/cgi-bin/ssialias?subtype=XB&infotype=PM&htmlfid=GBE03719USEN&attachment=GBE03719USEN.PDF&cm_mc_uid=36788419335514540780823&cm_mc_sid_50200000=1454423499

[32]Pankaj Ghemawat, "Developing Global Leaders: Companies Must Cultivate Leaders for Global Markets. Dispelling Five Common Myths about Globalization Is a Good Place to Start," *McKinsey Quarterly*, June 2012. http://www.mckinsey.com/global-themes/leadership/developing-global-leaders.

[33]Yoshio Takahashi, "Toyota Output Sets Industry Record," *Wall Street Journal*, January 29, 2014. www.wsj.com/articles/SB10001424052702304428004579350030132963254.

[34]"Case Study of Toyota: International Entry Strategies," MBA Knowledge Base. www.mbaknol.com/management-case-studies/case-study-of-toyota-international-entry-strategies/ (accessed June 17, 2015).

[35]"Case Study of Toyota."

[36]"Southern Africa," Toyota Global website. www.toyota-global.com/company/history_of_toyota/75years/data/automotive_business/sales/activity/africa/index.html (accessed September 12, 2016).

[37]"Case Study of Toyota."

[38]Pui-Wing Tam and Jim Carlton, "Toyota and Tesla Partnering to Make Electric Cars," *Wall Street Journal*, May 21, 2010. www.wsj.com/articles/SB10001424052748703559004575257041321957772.

[39]Bob Sorokanich, "That BMW-Toyota Sports Car Is Still Happening, Both Companies Confirm," *Road and Track*, November 6, 2014. www.roadandtrack.com/new-cars/videos/a6372/that-bmw-toyota-sports-car-is-still-happening-both-companies-confirm/.

[40]Associated Press, "Toyota and Mazda form 'Long-Term' Partnership," *Detroit Free Press*, May 13, 2015. www.freep.com/story/money/business/2015/05/13/toyota-mazda-long-term-partnership-merger-consolidation/27225579/.

CHAPTER 3

Political Systems

ersen_cira/Getty Images

Introduction

Politics is more than just the candidates and campaigns we see on television. Understanding the political system of a country is a key element in understanding how to conduct business successfully within that country's borders. Wise political decisions by a country's leaders can improve the climate for international business, whereas poor ones can hamper opportunities. For instance, the government of India has proposed to standardize the different tax structures among its states, which are currently all different, to help companies more easily conduct business there.

A political system consists of the principles, laws, and procedures relating to a particular form of government. It influences a country's economic policies and laws, and the degree of freedom within the country. International businesses need to thoroughly understand the political systems of the countries with which they do business in order to make strategic operational decisions there and evaluate opportunities for new undertakings.

LEARNING OBJECTIVES

After you explore this chapter you will be able to

1. **Contrast** democratic and autocratic, and individual and collective political ideologies
2. **Outline** the types of political risks inherent in conducting international business
3. **Describe** some measures of political freedom and the consequences of freedom for international business
4. **Discuss** the levels of governmental involvement in business

3.1 The Political Spectrum

LEARNING OBJECTIVE

Contrast democratic and autocratic, and individual and collective political ideologies.

political ideology a set of principles, ideas, and doctrines used to organize and administer social order

political systems the principles, laws, and procedures relating to a particular form of government

A **political ideology** is a set of principles, ideas, and doctrines used to organize and administer social order. Political ideologies are manifest through different **political systems** and form the basis for why political systems organize the way they do. Political systems directly affect the opportunities available to international businesses and also interact to influence the economic, sociocultural, and technological climate in a given country, which in turn can affect global opportunities. For instance, by establishing trade and economic policies that align with their vision for governance, political leaders can affect economic profits; the degree of the country's participation in international economic systems, such as trading blocs; and the means by which businesses provide goods and services to citizens. For example, China's policies on currency, trade, and investment led that country to nearly two decades of rapid economic growth, though it has slowed in recent years.

Political systems tend to be shaped not only by the political ideologies that support the system but also by the cultural and religious values, history, and economic system of the country. For example, South Korea's democracy is a result of U.S. political influence following the Korean War, coupled with the opening of the economy and culture to outside influences.[1] While political systems differ, the past hundred years have been characterized by tensions along two dimensions of political systems: their degree of individualism versus collectivism, and their focus on democratic versus autocratic ideals.

Individualism

The concept of **individualism** gives preference to individual freedoms, liberties, and rights. The origins of individualism stem from Aristotle, and the concept was refined by British philosophers such as David Hume (1711–1776) and Adam Smith (1723–1790), then further developed by the modern economists Milton Friedman (1912–2006) and Friedrich von Hayek (1899–1992). Individualism puts the rights of the individual above the rights of the group, as long as the individual's rights do not impinge upon the rights of others. Those supporting individualism often argue that allowing individuals to own property and determine how to use the property is the best way to benefit society. Because the goals of individuals and society are often aligned, and because individuals are most likely to know what is in their own best interest, individualists argue, an individual pursuing his or her own self-interest most effectively promotes the good of society as well. Countries like Canada, New Zealand, and the United Kingdom are governed by individualistic philosophy. Extreme individualists, called **anarchists**, believe that all government or organization of society should exist only on a voluntary basis and that individuals should govern themselves. Anarchy seeks to liberate individuals from any system of control.

individualism a concept that gives preference to individual freedoms, liberties, and rights

anarchists extreme individualists who believe that all government or organization of society should exist only voluntarily and that individuals should govern themselves

Collectivism

In contrast to individualism, **collectivism** is the belief that people should prioritize the good of society above the advancement of the individual. The origins of collectivism can be traced to the philosopher Plato, who argued that the good of the individual should be sacrificed for the good of the whole. Karl Marx (1818–1883), a philosopher and author of *The Communist Manifesto*, refined this argument, believing that if individuals own the means of production, they will use those means to accumulate wealth and deprive workers of their fair share of the value they create. Marx thus argued that the state should own the means of production in order to fully compensate workers for their efforts. By collectively owning assets, allocating resources, and driving production, the collective could focus on improving the welfare of all members of society. Countries such as China, Japan, and Brazil have a collectivist political orientation.

collectivism the belief that people should prioritize the good of society above the advancement of the individual

Democratic Political Systems

A **democracy** is a political system characterized by citizen participation in the political process. Democracies are typically associated with cultures that value individualism, but social democracy uses democracy to achieve socialist outcomes. In its most basic form, "democracy" means that each eligible citizen has the opportunity to influence policy through a direct voting process. Because it would be cumbersome for every eligible citizen to vote on every issue, most

democracy a political system characterized by citizen participation in the political process

representative democracies a system of government in which citizens elect representatives to public office who hold ultimate sovereignty and form a government to implement the will of the people who elected them

presidential democracies a system of government in which a constitution outlines the separation of political power into branches, the president (executive branch) is most often elected directly in a presidential vote

parliamentary democracies a system of government in which a constitution outlines the separation of political power into branches, the ministers are chosen by the parliament (legislative branch)

social democracies a socialist or collective system of government achieved by democratic elections

democracies are **representative democracies**, in which citizens elect representatives to public office, and those representatives hold ultimate sovereignty and form a government to implement the will of the people who elected them. If the people are unsatisfied with their representative, they can replace him or her in the next election cycle.

Republics such as South Korea and the United States are examples of **presidential democracies**. Here, a constitution outlines the separation of political power into branches, such as executive, judicial, and legislative. The president (part of the executive branch) is most often elected directly in a presidential vote. **Parliamentary democracies** are similar to presidential democracies except rather than electing executive officers through a common vote, parliament or the legislative branch chooses ministers who run the government. The United Kingdom and India are parliamentary democracies. **Social democracies** are a socialist or collective system of government achieved by democratic elections. Social democracies use elections to determine who should govern, but the focus of government is promoting egalitarianism and regulating opportunistic individual behavior, rather than protecting individual property. Norway, Sweden, and Singapore are examples of social democracies.

Abraham Lincoln, the 16th president of the United States, summarized the idea of democracy by calling it "government of the people, by the people, for the people."[2] Democracies are usually built on a foundation of individual rights—such as freedom of speech, freedom of information, and voting rights—coupled with restrictions on political power: term limits, an independent judicial system, and relative governmental transparency achieved through the sharing of information. These structural features of democracy help ensure that decision-making power stays in the hands of the people, rather than being consolidated within a much smaller political class. As of 2015, of the 195 recognized countries in the world, 125 were classified as some form of democracy.[3]

Although democracy is most often associated with individualism, many successful democracies do not give cultural preference to the needs of individuals. For instance, the Japanese have a high degree of individual freedom, yet their culture values group collaboration and collective accomplishment more than individual success.

Autocratic Political Systems

authoritarian a political system characterized by concentrated power in the hands of a leader or small group of leaders with centralized power who are not constitutionally responsible to citizens for their actions

Though many democracies have collectivist values, collectivism is more often associated with governments that exert more centralized control over society. An **authoritarian** government is a political system that concentrates, or centralizes, power in the hands of a leader or a small group of leaders who are not constitutionally responsible to citizens for their actions.[4] History has seen many types of authoritarian governments, and they still exist in many forms today. Monarchs, emperors, and dictators are all examples of authoritarian leaders. Authoritarian leaders may have inherited power (like King Louis XVI of France, guillotined during the French Revolution, and the current King Abdullah II of Jordan), seized it by force (like Napoleon Bonaparte of France or Saddam Hussein of Iraq), been selected by an elite group (such as General Secretary Mikhail Gorbachev of the former Soviet Union), or used their authority to expand control after being elected (like dictators Adolf Hitler of Nazi Germany, Benito Mussolini of fascist Italy, and Ferdinand Marcos, the former president of the Philippines).

Most authoritarian leaders come to power by committing human rights violations, eroding civil and political liberties, and controlling the economy and media. For instance, the military government that seized power in Argentina in the 1970s was accused of kidnapping and killing thousands of its own citizens. Constitutional rule was restored in 1983, but the mothers of those who were murdered have protested in the Plaza de Mayo in Buenos Aires, Argentina, every Thursday for 35 years.[5]

Citizens of authoritarian societies have fewer individual freedoms than those in democratic societies. For example, by definition, citizens don't have the freedom to elect the leader of their country, to vote for or against policies and laws, or to replace unsatisfactory government officials. But that doesn't mean all authoritarian states are led by despots bent on suppressing all opposition among the citizenry. Some authoritarian monarchs or dictators are popular among their citizens. For instance, King Abdullah II and his wife, Queen Rania, of Jordan are very popular (see **Figure 3.1**), as is Vladimir Putin of Russia, who is said to enjoy nearly a 90 percent approval rating, though it is difficult to measure approval of authoritarian leaders independently because they have the power to punish opposition—and often do so.[6]

While authoritarian leaders have unchallenged political control over a country, many facets of society may remain uncontrolled by the authoritarian state, such as religion, ideology, and the economy. **Totalitarianism** is an extreme form of an autocratic political system in which the government regulates every aspect of public and private life. Totalitarian regimes may be communist, theocratic, or a dictatorship, but they all maintain absolute control over government, military, law, media, social organizations, education, religion, and the economy. They often use a combination of terror tactics and propaganda to control the ways people think and feel. In the Soviet Union, for example, from the 1920s until its collapse in 1991, the communist political party controlled all aspects of human society within its borders. Today, North Korea is an example of a totalitarian state. Kim Jong-Un, the country's supreme leader, has total control over all aspects of life in North Korea.

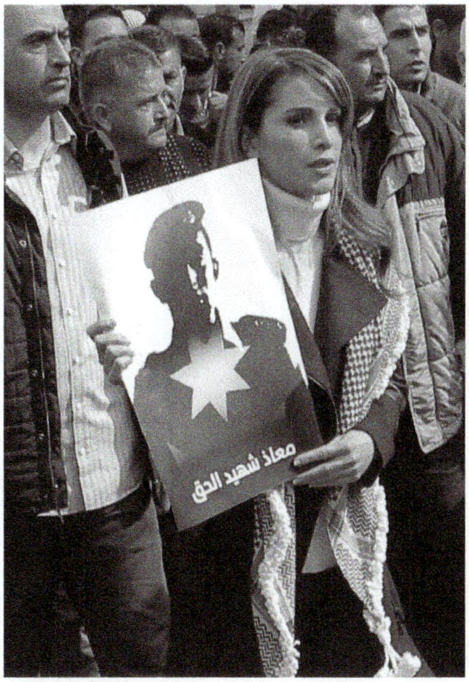

AFP/Getty Images

FIGURE 3.1 **Queen Rania** joins thousands as they take to the streets of Annan to show their support for Jordan's vow to destroy ISIS.

Iran, Saudi Arabia, Oman, Yemen, Sudan, Somalia, and Mauritania are all examples of countries ruled by a theocratic government. **Theocratic government** is a form of totalitarian autocratic government in which leaders rule by a mandate from God by interpreting religious law. In Vatican City, Christian commandments determine the law, whereas in Muslim states, Sharia law forms the basis of government.

In the Persian Gulf, many ultraorthodox Sunni Muslims joined together in 1999 to establish the Islamic State of Iraq and Syria (ISIS). The goal of this organization is to create a theocratic state, known as a caliphate, to govern all of Arabia. (A "caliph" is a political and religious leader who is a successor to the prophet Muhammad.) ISIS has been labeled a terrorist group by many governments because of murders and the destruction of others' religious sites. To ISIS, these actions are necessary to purge the world of heretical influences.[7] Nations ruled by theocracies often limit the political and religious freedoms of others.

totalitarianism an extreme form of autocratic political system in which the government regulates every aspect of public and private life

theocratic government a form of totalitarian government in which leaders rules by a mandate from God by interpreting religious law

ISIS and other organizations are often termed **terrorist organizations**. Terrorist organizations seek to establish rule and obtain power by means of terrorist activities such as suicide bombings, public executions, threats, intimidation, and other acts of violence. The U.S. Department of State maintains a list of foreign terrorist organizations, which includes groups such as Boko Haram operating in Nigeria, Cameroon, Niger, and Chad; the Revolutionary Armed Forces of Columbia (FARC) operating in Columbia; and HAMAS operating in the Gaza Strip and Palestine. In the United States, it is against the law for organizations to conduct any business with any organization on the State Department's terror watch list.

terrorist organizations a political group that uses unlawful violence and intimidation as a weapon to achieve its goals

Terrorist organizations gain followers by radicalizing individuals to a form of **extremism**. Extremism is defined as holding extreme political or religious views. Many terrorist attacks have been carried out by individuals who were radicalized either by visiting and living with terrorist groups, such as the estimated 20,000 foreign fighters who have traveled to Syria and Iraq to fight with extremist groups,[8] or merely by watching extreme content online.[9] U.S., European, and Chinese officials have made it a priority to counter the spread of extremism.[10]

extremism holding extreme political or religious views

Communism and Socialism

The communist and socialist political systems evolved out of the inequality inherent in individualistic systems. Karl Marx argued that capitalist individualistic systems would create dramatic inequality between the relatively few rich capitalists who owned the means of production and the thousands of poor workers they employed. In turn, this inequality would open the door to a widespread worker revolution. The outcome of the revolution, Marx argued, would be a political system called **communism**, in which the workers collectively owned the factors of production and appropriated the production outputs—goods and services—to be allocated to workers based on their needs.[11] Countries such as China, Laos, and Cuba are communist states, though they

communism a political system characterized by collective ownership of the factors of production and allocation of goods and services to workers according to their needs, argue for revolutionary means to establish a communal society

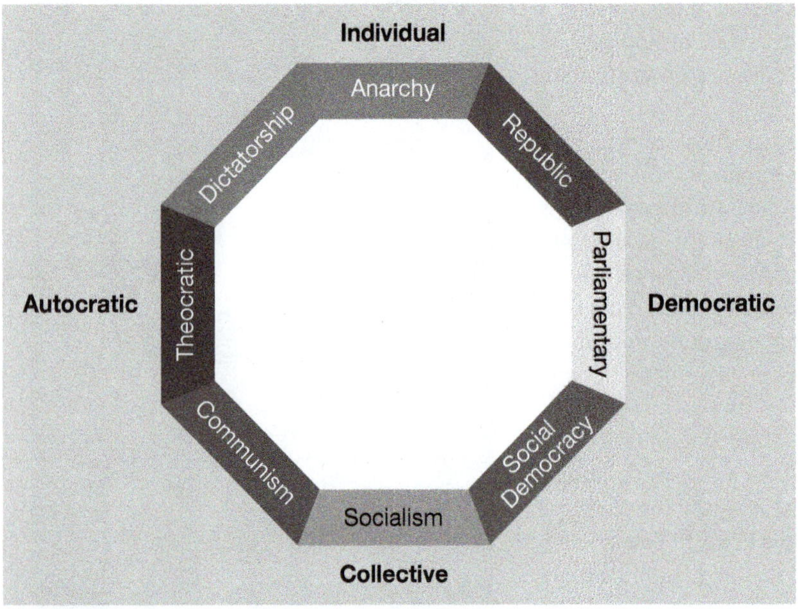

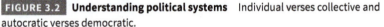

FIGURE 3.2 Understanding political systems Individual verses collective and autocratic verses democratic.

often operate governments that differ markedly from Marx's vision of communism.

Socialism argues for a collective form of government in which the means of production and the distribution of production are owned collectively by the community as a whole. Unlike communists, however, socialists argue for a peaceful rather than a revolutionary means to establish a communal society. India and Vietnam are examples of successful socialist states, whereas the socialist state of Venezuela has recently been less successful in fueling economic growth and providing a high standard of living for its citizens.

Categorizing Political Systems

In identifying a political system, two tensions are important: individual verses collective, and autocratic verses democratic. Dictatorships, anarchies, and republics tend toward individualism, whereas communism, socialism, and social democracies tend toward collectivism. Communism, theocracies, and dictatorships are autocratic, whereas republics, parliaments, and social democracies represent a democratic form of government (see **Figure 3.2**).

socialism a collective form of government in which the means of production and the distribution of production are owned collectively by the community as a whole

Mixed Political Systems

We talk in general terms about individual versus collective and democratic versus autocratic systems, but in reality, most countries actually adopt a political system that mixes elements. For instance, the United States is considered a democratic political system preserving individual rights, but in industries such as agriculture and military equipment, the government is more autocratic and imposes strict controls limiting foreign ownership, investment, and even sales. During the U.S. presidential election campaign of 2016, Bernie Sanders, a senator from Vermont and a Democratic presidential candidate who supported socialist ideas such as higher minimum wages, more regulations for corporations, and a larger welfare system, was widely popular, in particular among young voters.[12]

By contrast, China, known for its strict collectivist autocratic political system, has gradually instituted an increasing number of free-market policies. The economy in China is called a socialist market model and mixes a state-owned sector with a private sector. In the 1990s, China initiated a move away from communism by privatizing or selling many of its **state-owned enterprises (SOEs)** to private companies. An SOE is a legal entity created by a government or a representative to engage directly in commercial activities on behalf of the government. It is different from other government agencies in that an SOE is often intended to make a profit rather than meet non-financial aims, such as providing social services. In the 1990s many of the Chinese SOEs that remained owned by the government were restructured in an attempt to improve the efficiency of the organizations. Today, after a wave of privatization and restructuring, SOEs in China are fewer in number but tend to be very large, clustered primarily in sectors of strategic importance to the economy, such as mining, energy, transportation, utilities, banking, and telecommunication. **Privatization** occurs when a government either transfers or sells ownership of a certain property or industry, giving over its own control to the private (nongovernment) sector.

state-owned enterprises a legal entity created by a government or a representative to engage directly in commercial activities on behalf of the government

privatization transfer or sale of ownership of a certain property or industry by a government to the private (nongovernment) sector

While mainland China is a mixed market largely controlled by the state, Hong Kong is China's democratic experiment. Although now officially under the rule of Beijing, Hong Kong has retained some of the autonomy it enjoyed during its 100 years of British rule. When the United Kingdom's lease on the island expired and Hong Kong returned to China in 1997, the Chinese government left the city mostly autonomous, allowing it to run its own financial affairs—including customs, tax and trade rules, and currency (the Hong Kong dollar, pegged to the U.S. dollar), though with oversight from Beijing. In fact, in 2017, Hong Kong remained the world's freest economy for the 24th consecutive year. China frequently uses Hong Kong's capitalist economic model as both a testing ground for political experiments for the mainland and a significant source of foreign investment.[13]

Because most countries' economies have politically sensitive sectors, international businesses must have a deep understanding of the political environment in the countries in which they do business. For instance, in Japan, rice is more than a food commodity; perfect rice is a national passion. In fact, Zojirushi Corporation, a Japanese home appliance company, sells a rice cooker that costs the equivalent of $1,500 and relies on artificial intelligence to learn from past batches how to cook the perfect rice. If you want to flatter your dinner host in Japan, you can comment on how shiny and fragrant their rice is. Rice farmers also make up one of the strongest unions and largest voting blocs in Japan, with enormous political influence. The Japanese government therefore not only subsidizes rice farmers but also protects the rice farming industry by imposing strict limits on imports that would compete with homegrown crops.[14] Any foreign company seeking to sell rice in Japan must fight an uphill battle.

3.2 Political Risks

LEARNING OBJECTIVE

Outline the types of political risks inherent in conducting international business.

Perhaps the most important reason for understanding the political environment in international business is the need to gauge accurately the level of political risk inherent in a country. **Political risk** is the risk that political conditions in a host country might change, negatively affecting foreign businesses. For instance, YPF is the largest oil company in Argentina. It was jointly owned by Repsol (a Spanish oil company that owned 57.43 percent), Petersen Energia (a private company owning 25.46 percent), public shareholders (who owned 17.09 percent), and the government of Argentina (owning 0.02 percent). In 2012, however, the Argentinian government passed a law that unilaterally gave it 51 percent ownership of the company, shrinking Repsol's share to 6.43 percent. Repsol, backed by the Spanish government, sued for $10 billion in damages. It was ultimately awarded a judgment of $5 billion dollars to be paid by the Government of Argentina, but the company had no way to reclaim its ownership share in (or future profits from) YPF.[15]

political risk the risk that political conditions in a host country might change, negatively affecting foreign businesses

Political risk can result from the actions of a government *and* of nongovernmental organizations. In fact, a fair amount of risk stems from the actions of nongovernment players, including environmental groups, ordinary citizens, and even terrorists and extremists. Complications foreign companies face—such as loss of profits, inability to achieve strategic objectives, operational challenges due to currency and trade restrictions, and even **expropriation**, or a government's seizure of assets as a result of political action—make it essential for managers to both understand and assess the level of political risk in a country before opening operations, and then continuing to monitor that risk over time. Two primary categories of political risk exist: macro and micro.

expropriation a government's seizure of assets as a result of political action

Macro Political Risk

Macro political risk refers to adverse political actions that affect *all* foreign investments and operations in a host country. Examples include expropriation (also called nationalization), the imposition of currency and trade controls, changes in tax and labor laws, regulatory restrictions, war, terrorism, and insurrection.

macro political risk adverse political actions that affect *all* foreign investments and operations in a host country

The problem with expropriation is that corrupt governments can seize private property for their own benefit or purposes under the false claim that the action is in the "public interest." Property owners are often reimbursed at far less than fair market value—if at all. For example, when Fidel Castro's regime took power in Cuba in 1959, hundreds of millions of dollars' worth of U.S.-owned assets were expropriated, leaving owners with no recourse and no option to recover the value of those assets. Companies often avoid doing business altogether in countries where there exists significant danger of expropriation.

currency and trade controls government action to regulate the amount of currency and goods that can be traded or purchased; includes tariffs and taxes, export/import volumes, restrictions on licenses and permits, restrictions on currency exchange, fixed exchange rates, and bans on using foreign currency within the country

Another form of macro political risk involves the **currency and trade controls** countries put in place to regulate the amounts of currency and goods that can be traded or purchased. Examples of trade controls include tariffs and taxes, export/import volumes, and restrictions on licenses and permits. Common currency controls include bans on holding or using foreign currency within the country, restrictions on currency exchange, fixed exchange rates, and restrictions on the volume of currency that can be imported or exported. Currency and trade policies are most often used to restrict foreign competition in certain product categories, to protect the development of local business, or to respond to the political decisions or policies of other countries.

A frequent and unintended result of stringent currency and trade controls is the development of a black market where devalued currency or restricted goods are traded. Venezuela is a country with high macro political risk and severe currency and trade controls. In June 2016 it experienced the sharpest inflation rate worldwide at that time. In response, the government set price controls on basic goods and necessities; however, these prices were often below the cost required to manufacture the goods. The government also set a fixed currency exchange of 6.3 bolivars per U.S. dollar, well below the black-market rate of 1,000 bolivars per U.S. dollar.[16] As a result, black-market trading was rampant, and many foreign companies were forced out of business in the country. Buying necessities became so difficult and expensive that a common joke was that there "is no toilet paper in Venezuela."[17] The price controls set by the Venezuelan government affected all entities operating in the country, an example of macro political risk.

While Venezuela is an extreme example, not all macro political risks occur in developing nations. Even international businesses looking at the U.S. market face political risk. For instance, President Donald Trump's proposed wall between the United States and Mexico increases the political risk for Mexican firms operating in the United States and is likely to result in decreased trade with and investment by Mexican firms. Similarly, Trump's calls to place a 45 percent tariff on Chinese imports would have serious political and economic ramifications.[18]

Micro Political Risk

micro political risks the possibility of adverse political actions that affect only a specific sector, firm, or project

Whereas macro political risks affect all foreign investments and operations, **micro political risks** affect only a specific sector, firm, or project. Examples of micro political risks include corruption, prejudicial actions, contract breaches, political protest, and specific regulations. For instance, starting in 2002 a conglomerate of foreign companies and domestic energy firms made plans to construct a hydroelectric power plant in Brazil. However, the project faced widespread protests led by local environmental groups. The conglomerate, supported by the U.S.-operated firm Alcoa, agreed to increase the compensation for those being relocated and to take measures to minimize environmental waste and damage. These concessions increased the cost of constructing the plant but enabled construction of the dam to begin. In April 2016, however, development was again suspended over protests of indigenous peoples who did not want to be removed from their lands[19] (see **Figure 3.3**). Because the protests targeted Alcoa and its partners *specifically*, this is an example of micro political risk. Micro political risk in on the rise in many nations, as nationalistic policies such as closed immigration by a newly elected right-wing party in Denmark and Indonesia's limits on technology trade that have left Apple out of the market by requiring domestic sources be incorporated into goods become increasingly common.[20]

Adenilson Nunes/CON/Contributor/Getty Images

FIGURE 3.3 **Micro political risk for Alcoa** Indigenous protest in front of authorities during the seventh day of occupation of a hydroelectric plant

Direct and Indirect Effects of Political Risk

Political risk can have both direct and indirect effects on businesses operating in a host nation. Direct effects result from political actions that target or regulate a specific entity. Indirect effects are those experienced by any business that is not the specific target of a political action. In other words, indirect political risk is similar to collateral damage.

We often associate political risk with its direct effect and identify the risk at a national level. We look at risk this way because these effects are the most apparent. As an example, consider Disney's recent problems in Venezuela. In 2015 Disney reported a loss of $143 million as a result of the effects of Venezuela's deepening economic and political crisis. In particular, the devaluation of Venezuela's currency, the bolivar, had a significant effect.

Under normal circumstances, Disney would be able to minimize its losses by selling any Venezuelan currency it had and buying dollars at the Venezuelan government's official foreign currency exchange rate of 6.3 bolivars per U.S. dollar. In an effort to limit the size of cash outflows from the country, however, the Venezuelan government introduced two alternative exchange rates, called SICAD 1 and SICAD 2. As you might guess, both rates are significantly higher than any Disney had used through 2013. SICAD 1 was 12 bolivars per dollar (almost double the 6.3 rate used before), and SICAD 2 was 50 to 1—nearly 8 times the previous exchange rate. Even more challenging for Disney, the Venezuelan government declared the majority of Disney's monetary assets—valued at roughly 1.7 billion bolivars—ineligible for exchange at the more attractive SICAD 1 rate. With this political act, the government effectively cut the value of Disney's monetary assets in Venezuela by over 50 percent. Disney isn't alone in swallowing significant losses in Venezuela. According to a 2015 Reuters report, at least 40 other S&P 500 organizations will be forced to take billions of dollars in similar write-downs.[21]

In comparison to direct effects, the indirect effects of political risk are often more difficult to predict and prepare for. Political stability in the Middle East has recently decreased markedly as a result of the democratic uprisings known as the Arab Spring. For now, the revolutionary wave of mass protests that swept through many countries has paused while people focus on the armed conflicts and civil wars that have arisen as a result. The Middle East remains politically unstable.

Antony Jones/Contributor/Getty Images

FIGURE 3.4 **Deserted Sharm El Sheik Resort** Hotels are having to close as tourists are choosing to go to other vacation destinations because of political instability in the area.

While the hostilities are directed at governments, not businesses, the indirect effects for businesses are far-ranging. For example, the hotel and tourism industries have taken a huge blow. Occupancy rates have plummeted as travelers have chosen to delay visiting because of the political instability. Unrest has also led to an increase in terrorist activity, further reducing international travel to these countries. Bookings for major international hotel chains in Egypt's Red Sea resorts dropped nearly 50 percent from 2015 to 2016[22] (see **Figure 3.4**).

However, political instability in one country can present opportunities for neighboring nations. For instance, hotel occupancy has increased in both Turkey and Dubai as tourists who might otherwise have gone to destinations like Cairo or Damascus are now traveling to nations perceived as safer, helping them rebound as popular business destinations.[23]

The Constant Challenge of Managing Political Risk

The environments in which businesses operate aren't static. At any moment, the political landscape of a country may change, and even the soundest business decisions can be undermined in an instant. While complete elimination of political risk is impossible, several solutions exist to help international businesses make informed and calculated decisions—and to protect their foreign interests. Firms are hit hardest when they aren't prepared for and ready to shift with the changing tides.

Before establishing new operations in a county, most firms begin with a risk analysis. Firms can conduct this on their own or hire a consulting firm that specializes in such analysis. Based on this analysis, global leaders can make a more informed decision regarding which countries to enter and which countries to avoid. However, the prospect of doing business in an area might hold such potential that a company decides to enter the country despite its high political risk.

In these cases, companies can attempt to prepare for potential problems by negotiating some form of contract with the host country to establish an avenue of recourse in case something happens to disrupt the company's operations. The biggest caution here is that enforcing legal agreements in some countries, especially in the wake of political disruption, is often more trouble than it's worth because foreign businesses are unlikely to prevail against a host country's government. In the event of a revolution, a new government can simply refuse to honor the actions of the past regime. In consequence, and because the U.S. legal system is stable and well developed, many international contracts specify that U.S. courts will adjudicate any contract breaches. For instance, when Repsol—the Spanish oil company—sued Argentina, it did so in the U.S. court.

Most companies also purchase risk insurance intended to safeguard their interests in politically at-risk countries. Such insurance protects companies against adverse events in the host country. The higher the political risk in a given country or industry, and the more risks are insured, the greater the cost of buying a plan. The disadvantage of buying political-risk insurance is that there is no guarantee the company will receive immediate compensation following an adverse event. As with any insurance plan, certain underlying conditions must be satisfied before a company can collect, and some events aren't covered at all.

Ultimately, no solution completely protects international businesses against political risk. The best a company can do is to minimize political risk by performing due diligence in order to be aware of political risks before deciding to enter a country, then taking the necessary steps to manage against potentially adverse situations.

3.3 Measures of Political Freedom

LEARNING OBJECTIVE

Describe some measures of political freedom and the consequences of freedom for international business.

In measuring the political climate of countries, organizations often focus on the level of political freedom in the country. Freedom is a highly valued quality in the United States and many other nations. Because of that social conditioning, we often speak of freedom as a moral issue, defining it as something all people inherently deserve. For instance, when Thomas Jefferson penned the U.S. Declaration of Independence in 1776, he posited that all people are created equal and that each person has a right to life, liberty, and the individual pursuit of happiness.[24] In 1945 the United Nations adopted a similar view in its charter, arguing that all people have inherent, or universal, rights.[25] Many people throughout the world share this belief and strive to promote the spread of freedom because they believe it is a basic human right that everyone deserves.

Of course, international businesses are significantly affected by the level of political freedom in a country. It can have important implications for economic growth and prosperity, and can shrink or expand the opportunities available to international businesses. Historical data demonstrate a significant positive relationship between political freedom and economic growth, for instance. In political systems that value individual freedom, businesses can benefit from factors such as limited government interference; the effectiveness of law; the support for **property rights**, or the rights of companies and individuals to own resources such as land, equipment, and mineral rights; freedom to trade; and business-friendly regulations. Countries that have more freedoms tend to be wealthier and have more opportunities than do those with fewer freedoms.

property rights the rights of companies and individuals to own resources, make decisions about how to use it, and reap the returns or losses of business activities

The Freedom House and Heritage Foundation Measures

Many organizations throughout the world collect data and compile reports about the level of freedom in different countries. One of the best known is Freedom House, a nongovernmental, U.S.-based watchdog and advocacy organization for democracy founded in 1941. Since 1973, Freedom House has used a seven-point scale to rank nations across the world on their promotion of human rights, civil liberties, rule of law, elections, and religious freedom. Although the scores are somewhat subjective, the data provide a useful yardstick for governments and

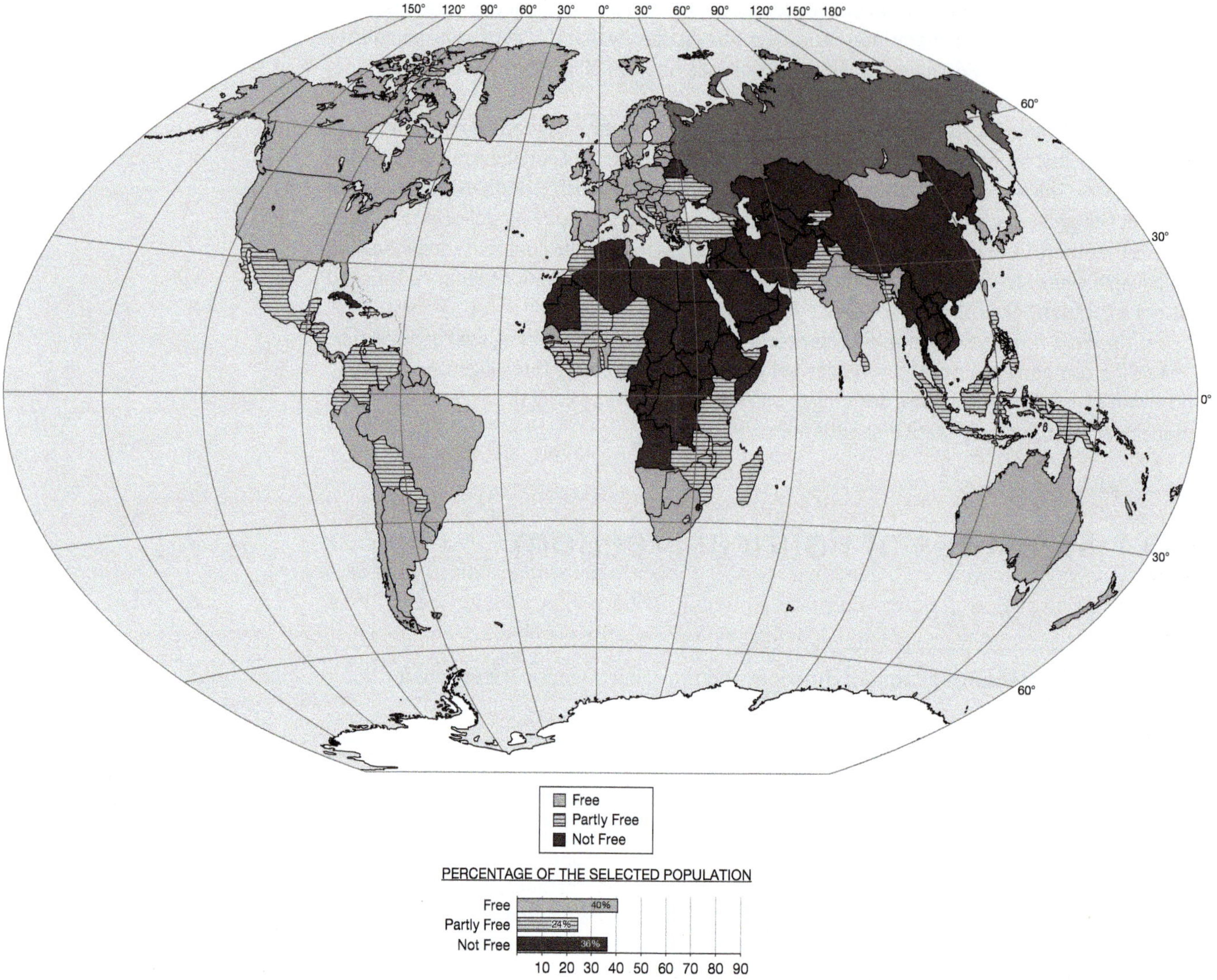

FIGURE 3.5 **Global map of freedom** Freedom is measured based on human rights, civil society, freedom of expression, freedom of the Internet, rule of law, elections, religious freedom, and lesbian-gay-bisexual-transgender rights.

businesses around the world. As **Figure 3.5** indicates, countries are categorized as free, partly free, and not free.

The Heritage Foundation, a conservative public policy think tank founded in 1973, also constructs a freedom index to rank economic freedom within individual nations. The Heritage Foundation measures variables such as the rule of law, limitations on government, the degree of regulatory efficiency, and the openness of a country's markets to domestic and international competition (see **Table 3.1**).

TABLE 3.1 **Heritage Foundation Economic Freedom Index.**

The Heritage Foundation uses the rule of law, extent of government, regulations, and openness of markets to assess the level of freedom in each country.

Rule of Law	Limited Government	Regulatory Efficiency	Open Markets
Property rights	Fiscal freedom	Business freedom	Trade freedom
Freedom from corruption	Government spending	Labor freedom	Investment freedom
		Monetary freedom	Financial freedom

Implications of Political Freedom for International Business

A country's internal laws can affect foreign firms' ability to own and use property and resources in that country, establish limitations on business income, govern the sale of property, and determine the extent to which the government may interfere in business processes. A country may also establish laws and regulations in support of businesses but then have trouble enforcing them. Politically unstable countries may not be able to protect private property against conflict, corruption, or economic collapse. Some governments—like Venezuela—have a history of taking private property,[26] which makes the country less attractive to multinational corporations. Some examples of the foreign assets seized by Venezuela's former president Hugo Chavez include at least five oil and gas expropriations totaling more than $30 billion, three agricultural companies include Cargill, mining firms, and heavy industry.[27] When President Chavez seized three gold mines from a Canadian firm Rusoro Mining Ltd. in 2011, the company sought compensation in an international arbitration court. In 2016, the court ordered Venezuela to pay the firm $1.2 billion for its losses.[28]

International businesses are also affected by the indirect consequences of political freedoms. For example, customers in relatively free markets are likely to have more discretionary income, longer life expectancy, and more leisure time in which to spend income. On average, freer countries have greater gross domestic product (GDP) (see **Figure 3.6**). However, they are also more likely to be discriminating in their choices because they have a wider range of options. Companies selling to them may have a larger potential market yet also face more selective customers and heightened competitive pressures. These are all reasons a thorough understanding of the level of freedom helps a multinational company create profitable country strategies, form positive relationships with local governments, and avoid costly mistakes.

Recent Political Trends That Affect Multinational Corporations

In addition to mapping out the political climate before entering a country, companies need to keep in mind that the global political landscape is constantly changing. At times, countries may shift toward a democracy, whereas at others they may move toward autocracy. At any given moment, some countries are improving their business climate and others are becoming more hostile.

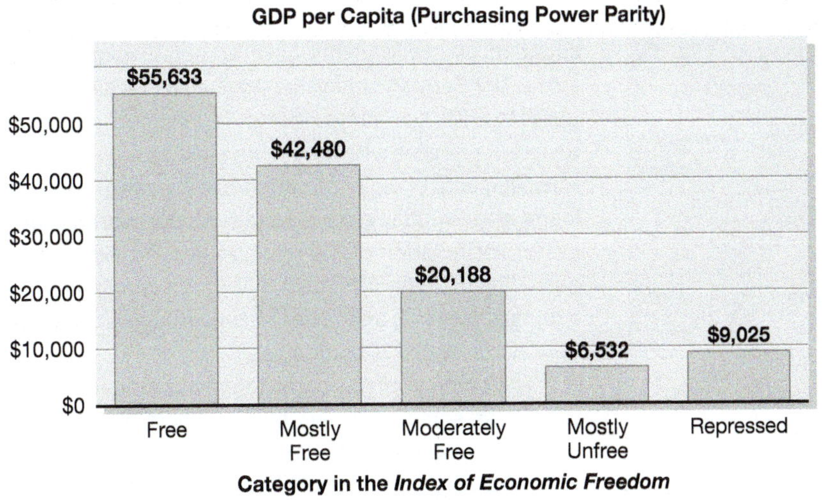

FIGURE 3.6 Economic freedom and GDP per capita in 2015 Those countries that are rated free have the highest GDP per capita, and as the level of freedom in a country drops, the GDP per capita also drops. **Source:** http://www.cato.org/blog/continuing-us-decline-economic-freedom-world-index

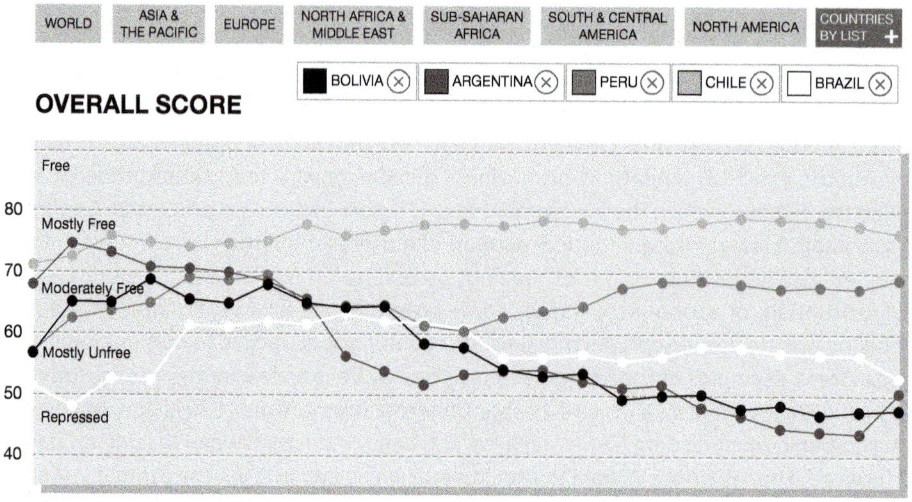

FIGURE 3.7 **Heritage Measure of Freedom for Select South American Countries from 1995 to 2017** **Source:** http://www.heritage.org/index/visualize.

For example, according to the Heritage Measures of Freedom (see **Figure 3.7**), the world is a freer place in 2017 than it was in 1995, but the gains have been slow and not spread equally. As Figure 3.6 demonstrates, South and Central America have seen few changes overall. Increased freedoms in Argentina and Peru have been largely offset in the region by retrenchment in Chile and Brazil.

Perhaps the three most significant political events of the past decade have been the refugee crisis; Brexit, or Britain's planned withdrawal from the European Union; and the Middle East uprisings known as the Arab Spring.

The Refugee Crisis. Few would argue that 2015 was a year of record humanitarian need. About 3.2 million people sought asylum, 40.8 million were displaced in their own countries, and 1.3 million fled to Europe—all world records.[29] In addition, 21.3 million refugees were fleeing wars around the world, a staggering number. In total, in 2015, 65.3 million people were displaced from their homes. Syria, Afghanistan, Iraq, and Nigeria accounted for 63 percent of all refugees in 2016; 30 percent originated from Syria alone, where more than 4.5 million people have fled their homes in the wake of civil war.[30] Most have gone to neighboring countries including Turkey, Lebanon, and Jordan, and about 10 percent have sought safety in Europe, particularly in Germany, Sweden, and Serbia. **Figure 3.8** shows the number of Syrian refugees (dark purple) and number of Syrian refugee asylum applications (dark green) for each country.

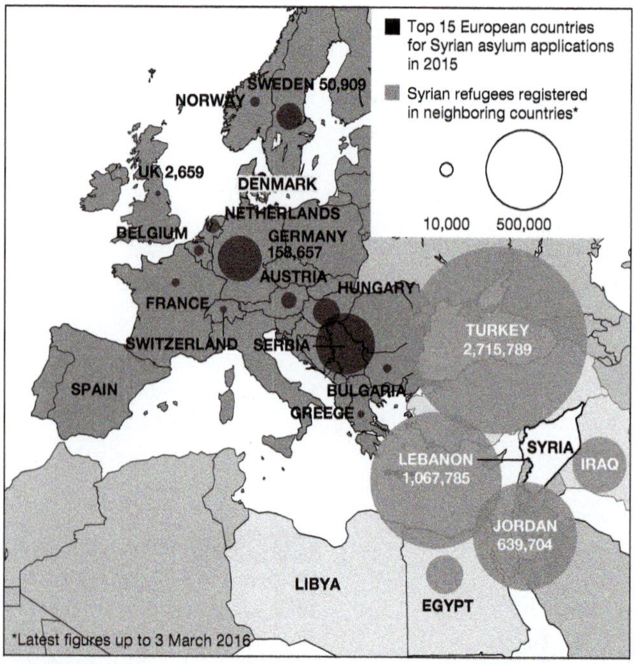

FIGURE 3.8 **Syrian refugees** Many Syrians have fled to neighboring countries, and many others have sought refuge in Europe.
Source: "Syria: The Story of the Conflict," BBC News, March 11, 2016. http://www.bbc.com/news/world-middle-east-26116868.

The human and economic costs of the war are staggering. In addition to the displaced, a quarter of a million Syrians have died in the war. The United Nations said it needed over $3 billion to help with humanitarian efforts in 2016.[31]

In Europe, the refugee crisis has led to a difficult political situation as governments have accepted refugees in fits and stops. The German chancellor Angela Merkel allowed many refugees to enter Germany under an "open door" policy that seeks to accept refugees with a *Willkommenskultur* (welcome culture). However, acts of violence committed by asylum seekers in Cologne and Wurzburg have wilted support for accepting refugees.[32] Assimilation of the refugees into the economy has also been difficult. Only 7 percent of German companies have hired a refugee to work, and fewer than 60 refugees are employed in Germany's largest 30 companies.[33]

The political effects of the refugee crisis have spilled across Europe as some countries blame others for not doing their fair share. The European Commission established a plan that allocated 160,000 refuges to each country in a quota scheme.

However, the quota system is facing challenges because some countries are resistant and because the refugees have a strong preference to settle in Germany and Sweden rather than in Slovenia, Romania, and Bulgaria. In an effort to enforce the plan, the Commission has announced a €250,000 penalty for each refugee not accepted.[34] A backlash against the influx of refugees in many countries has also created a rise in right-wing political groups. For instance, in Sweden, Austria, and Greece, political parties focused on an ethno-nationalist sentiment and promoting anti-immigration policies have gained significant political power.[35]

Brexit. Compounding the challenges of the refugee crisis in Europe is Great Britain's plan to exit the European Union. This action has the potential to dramatically reshape the political and economic landscapes of Europe and of the United Kingdom. The future ramifications of Brexit are still unknown, and the process will be slow. When the vote to stay or go was tallied, however, and the result was to go, among immediate results were the resignation of Prime Minister David Cameron and the appointment of Theresa May to replace him, and the drop in value of the British pound to a 30-year low. May has suggested that another result could be a decrease in the number of immigrants allowed into the United Kingdom, from over 300,000 a year to fewer than 100,000.[36] Another likely event is a second referendum on whether Scotland will leave the United Kingdom. Scotts overwhelmingly voted to stay in the European Union but will be dragged out of it if they remain in the United Kingdom. Scotland's First Minister Nicola Sturgeon has said the referendum is now "highly likely."[37]

International businesses are likely to be significantly affected by the exit. It will probably be more difficult for the British to move money, people, and products across Europe, and London's position as a world financial center may be threatened as well. "As long as the U.K. remains in the EU, the [financial] industry can do business anywhere on the continent and move employees around without worrying about visas, and the banking business is widely populated by people from other places," noted NPR's Jim Zarroli in July 2016. Whatever the results for Britain may be, that Brexit will affect global business in the short- and long-term future is certain.

The Arab Spring. The widespread political protests now known as the Arab Spring were a precursor to the refugee crisis and an event with global implications. The Arab Spring began in Tunisia in January 2011, when Mohamed Bouazizi, a 26-year old fruit cart vendor, set himself on fire in protest after police confiscated his street-cart and demanded a bribe for its return. The demonstrations following Bouazizi's death quickly grew in number and intensity, forcing the Tunisian president Zine El Abidine Ben Ali out of office in less than a month. The success of the uprising prompted similar protests across the Middle East and North Africa.

Millions of citizens rose up against their respective governments and demanded an end to governmental corruption and an increase in personal freedoms. The governments of Libya, Egypt, and Yemen fell to the protests and introduced political uncertainty in their countries. For instance, the Egyptian president Hosni Mubarak resigned in 2011 after 30 years of rule, but the new government was also seen as autocratic and was ousted in a coup just two years later. As of 2017, Abdel Fattah el-Sisi is the president of Egypt.

Unlike the governments in Libya, Egypt, and Yemen, the Syrian government resisted the protests resulting from the Arab Spring, which plunged the country into a long and violent civil war, still unresolved as this is written. Some nations, such as Morocco, have actually become more autocratic in response. In these countries, leaders have cracked down on free speech in a preemptive attempt to keep the protesters from organizing within the country.[38] As a result of all the conflicts—particularly in Syria—thousands of people have been killed and hundreds of thousands have fled their homes as refugees to seek shelter across Europe and elsewhere.

International businesses have been enormously challenged by the Arab Spring. For instance, tourism in Egypt, previously a mainstay of the economy at 12 percent of GDP in 2011, dropped to half that amount since the uprisings and fell still further following terrorist attacks on two commercial flights. "The 'volatile geopolitical backdrop' was causing some customers to postpone booking their holidays."[39] This reduction in travel and tourism not only cut into Egypt's GDP but also reduced the flow of foreign currency into the country, making it harder for the government to pay its foreign obligations. Saudi Arabia, the United Arab Emirates, and Kuwait have stepped in and together provided Egypt with nearly $20 billion in an effort to stabilize the country and prevent further spread of the demonstrations.[40] Across the region, the business environment is extremely uncertain, and global businesses have been increasingly hesitant to invest in these markets.

3.4 Government's Involvement in Business

LEARNING OBJECTIVE

Discuss the levels of government involvement in business.

Some governments don't stop at simply setting laws and regulations to govern business; instead they become directly engaged in operating businesses. For instance, the government of Saudi Arabia owns the world's most valuable company: Saudi Aramco. This company has assets in the neighborhood of 260 billion barrels of oil[41] and nearly 300 trillion cubic feet of natural gas reserves—including the yield of the world's largest oil field—and is estimated to be worth between \$2 and \$10 trillion.[42] Aramco is an SOE.

A government can be involved in business at several different levels, including full ownership, partial ownership, state supported, and state investment, as shown in **Table 3.2.**

Any government's level of involvement in business can change over time, creating or eliminating opportunities for international businesses. As discussed earlier in the chapter, the success of SOEs in China has largely been built on the protections they receive from the government, such as actions that keep competitors out of the country and create artificial demand. As a result, many experts fear China is actually supporting some number of "zombie" companies—businesses that should be dead but have been kept alive by government intervention. The zombie SOEs could be dragging down growth and increasing debt even while they seem to be profitable. For instance, Cosco (China Overseas Shipping Company) ordered \$1.5 billion worth of new container ships in 2015 despite China's overcapacity in shipping and a decrease in global trade. The orders were funded by the government to keep people building the ships employed.[43]

SOEs operate alongside private firms in China. However, given the competitive pressures the private firms face and the rigorous management practices they adopt as a result, their financial returns are nearly double those of the SOEs.[44]

TABLE 3.2 Different levels of government involvement in business

State Owned Enterprises	Partial State Owned Enterprise	State Supported	State Investor (Sovereign wealth fund)
Example: Saudi Aramco. Saudi Arabia's oil company. • State owns and operates the business • Goal is to make a profit • Profits are returned to the government	Example: Shanghai Disney. Joint venture between Walt Disney (43% ownership) and three companies owned by the Shanghai government (57% ownership). • State has partial ownership of the company • State may or may not have direct control • Part of the profits are given to the state	Example: Tesla. Tesla has received nearly \$5 billion in government incentives, grants, tax breaks, discounted loans, and environmental credits. • State backs a company either by guaranteeing loans or directly providing resources • State provide incentives, grants, tax breaks, subsidies • State does not have direct control • State often does not get direct payment rather it gets indirect benefits from job creation and growth	Example: Temasek Holdings Private Limited. Government of Singapore's investment company. Owns a portfolio of investments worth nearly \$200 billion. • State buys stocks or bonds in private companies • Fund returns the proceeds to the government • Government reinvests or spends the proceeds

When Governments Relax Their Policies

One major way a government can change its involvement in an industry is through privatization. This is the primary process by which countries with a command economy change to a market economy. In command economies, production is determined by the government. A government that owns and profits from firms in industries such as oil, steel, and agriculture can sell or give the SOEs to private individuals or companies, which then provide the goods or services instead of the government and also receive the income.

The level of privatization within a country matters to multinational corporations because it determines how much capital they can privately own and benefit from in a given market. British Petroleum, or BP, is a British oil and gas company that operates in dozens of countries around the world. Oil is a lucrative business, but BP, like all companies, must tailor its strategy to fit the requirements of each country in which it operates. For example, because the United States has a privatized oil market, BP has the freedom to operate across all phases of the oil industry in the United States and can sell its refined product directly to U.S. consumers. However, in Saudi Arabia—the largest oil producer in the world—the government has control over the oil industry and regulates the export of petroleum in order to influence global oil prices.[45] As a result, the state-owned oil company Saudi Aramco controls the domestic market.[46] Saudi Arabia's SOE-controlled market allows for only a low level of privatization, so Saudi branches of BP[47] and other foreign oil companies do not have much freedom there.

Privatization within a country can sometimes affect international businesses in markets outside the country. Emirates airline, the world's fourth-largest airline, is owned by the government of United Arab Emirates, which invested roughly $10 million dollars to start it.[48] This state-owned airline competes directly with privately owned companies like British Airways, Delta, and United Airlines. The private carriers have argued that they are losing business because Emirates is receiving ongoing government subsidies that enable it to offer rates below operating costs. As evidence, they show that when Emirates and other state-sponsored carriers from the region have entered a U.S. flight route, U.S. carriers have lost nearly 10 percent of that route's market share.[49] U.S.-based airlines have argued that these SOE carriers violate the U.S. State Department's guidelines for fair airline competition in U.S. skies by receiving at least $42 billion in subsidies from their respective governments. Emirates has denied the accusation.[50]

Another way in which governments affect international business is through their policies about property rights. These laws determine who can own property within a country and how income from that property can be used or distributed. The discussion of property rights usually includes two aspects: first, the laws regarding property ownership and usage, and second, the ability or willingness of a government to protect and enforce private property ownership.

A final way in which governments influence the conduct of international business is through the level of regulation or deregulation they enforce. **Deregulation** is the process of removing government regulations, oversight, and involvement from an industry. For instance, air travel was a regulated industry in the United States from 1938 to 1978. During that period, the government decided the number of airlines that could operate, the routes they could fly, and the prices they could charge. With the Airline Deregulation Act of 1978, the United States began the process of removing government control over air travel. Airlines reconfigured routes and equipment, increasing capacity utilization. The hub-and-spoke model was invented to consolidate travel through high-traffic "hubs," enabling airlines to fly closer to capacity and therefore reduce fares. Prices have actually decreased over time as a result of airlines having the freedom to innovate in both routes and pricing. Lower prices and increased capacity have made air travel more accessible to the general public. The number of passengers who fly in a year has more than doubled since 1978. Moreover, Ryanair, Southwest, and JetBlue—low-cost carriers that have disrupted the traditional legacy carriers—are further reducing the cost of air travel. Markets freed through deregulation typically enable more competition, give incentives for improving service and reducing costs, promote innovation, and ultimately result in lower costs and more options for the consumer.[51]

deregulation the process of removing government regulations, oversight, and involvement from an industry

Summary and Case

Summary

LEARNING OBJECTIVE 3.1 Contrast democratic and autocratic, and individual and collective political ideologies.

Market-based systems generally align with democratic governments and encourage private ownership and control of assets. Command-based systems tend to align with authoritarian governments and encourage government-run planning and ownership. While governments typically lean more toward one system or the other, most economies are actually mixed systems in which the market controls some aspects of the market and the government controls others.

LEARNING OBJECTIVE 3.2 Outline the types of political risks inherent in conducting international business.

Macro political risk affects all companies in a country, whereas micro political risk affects a specific company, industry, or project. Potential strategies for minimizing political risk include conducting a political risk analysis, negotiating a contract with the host country for recourse should the business face government interference, and buying political risk insurance. Ultimately, businesses have no perfect defense, and the best they can do is to remain well informed of the political dangers of a country and make decisions accordingly.

LEARNING OBJECTIVE 3.3 Describe some measures of political freedom and the consequences of freedom for international business.

When entering foreign markets, companies need to assess the level of freedom in those markets. Measures of freedom include the extent of personal property rights, rule of law, and the level of governmental regulation. These measures correlate, in turn, with increased levels of wealth, which typically indicate better business opportunities. Businesses are also freer, making the business environment more stable and predictable in politically more stable countries.

LEARNING OBJECTIVE 3.4 Discuss the levels of governmental involvement in business.

Some governments intervene more directly in the operation of business than by simply passing laws and regulation. In some cases, governments with extensive control of their economy will relax that control and shift from a command system to a market system through privatization, property rights, and deregulation. In privatization, a government transfers (sells) ownership of an SOE to private stakeholders. The adoption or expansion of property rights enables international businesses to control more resources in a market. Last, deregulation relaxes government involvement in an industry, opening it to free-market pressures of supply and demand.

Case Study

Micro Political Risk and the Fast-Food Industry in Korea

Despite technically still being at war with North Korea, South Korea enjoys relatively low political risk. The two-decade-old democracy functions well, laws are clear, and enforcement is fair. Local and global businesses are thriving. If asked to rate South Korea's level of political risk, many suggest it is 2 or 3 on a 10-point scale, with 1 being minimal risk. However, while the general risk is low, the specific risk for the fast-food industry is much higher.

The Korean Pizza Craze

Yong-jin Chung, the president of Shinsegae, a leading retailer in South Korea, had recently launched a super-supreme pizza at E-mart, a discount retail business unit of Shinsegae. Yong-jin was pleased to learn that consumers responded well to the recent launch of Super-supreme pizza. Over 6,000 pizzas were sold at one location during the first month. On average, E-mart locations were selling between 300 and 400 pizzas per day.

Consumers were elated with the quality of the inexpensive pizza and even stated that quality and taste of the Super-supreme pizza was comparable to that of the high-end large franchises. They mentioned that they can trust the product quality because a large company handled the pizza. Shinsegae went to great lengths to introduce this economical pizza. The pizza is 45 centimeters in diameter and costs just 11,500 KRW, equivalent to about US$10. Shinsegae adopted a firewood cooking method to enrich the flavor of the pizza, whereas other competitors used conventional ovens. This firewood method of cooking did have one large disadvantage: controlling the heat is more challenging, and therefore limited production to fewer than 400 pizzas per day.

While being pleased with the very successful results of the recent launch of its new pizza, Shinsegae remarked that it was not profitable business considering direct costs alone accounted for nearly 80 percent of revenue, yet Shinsegae stressed its desire to *serve* customers with inexpensive but tasty pizza. To cut costs, they did not take orders over the phone or provide delivery, and the company only offered three types of pizza.

To competitors, the Super-supreme pizza seemed invincible. It is a customer's dream: inexpensive, large, and delicious. As evidence of this disruptive product, one competitor in the pizza industry confessed to a reporter, "To make such a large pizza we would need to use three times more ingredients than that of our regular pizza. We cannot do that at such a low price without losing money. Shinsegae can produce it because they are such a gigantic player (that can handle a great deal of food ingredients)."

The Pizza Industry before E-mart

Pizza was first introduced into Korea in 1985 by the U.S. chain Pizza Hut, and the industry expanded rapidly. Four main franchises—two Korean, Mr. Pizza and Pizza E-tang, and two from the United States, Domino's Pizza and Pizza Hut—held the majority of market share with over 1,400 stores at the end of 2012. Mr. Pizza focuses on delivering fresh pizzas that use crab, shrimp, or other locally preferred ingredients. Other pizza companies have also localized their menus to the Korean market, including items such as beef barbeque, sweet potato, and even pumpkin pizza. Because of premium ingredients, differentiated menus, and spending on advertisement, big players sell expensive pizzas.

In addition to big franchisers, a host of mom-and-pop pizza stores can be found in nearly every alley of Korea. Many owners start their business after their retirement or after being fired from a job. With limited capital and experience, they are unable to come up with the $400,000 that is required to open a Pizza Hut franchise in Korea. Rather, they focus on low-cost pizza and sell a wide range of pizzas priced between $5 and $14.

The Beginning of the Controversy

E-mart's Super-supreme pizza was an instant hit with consumers. It was not uncommon to see a long line stretching around the store as people queued for up to two hours at some stores. According to the Korean Fair Trade Commission (KFTC)[52], Super-supreme pizza was ranked fourth in the market at the end of 2011, after just one year of business.

However, the success of the pizza ignited an unexpected controversy. Antagonists began complaining that it is unfair for a large corporation to compete with small pizza stores. These critics argued that these small stores were competing with E-mart on an uneven field because their hands were tied in terms of pricing as a result of fees paid to the franchise, which made it too costly to compete.

E-mart in turned argued that the goal of the Super-supreme pizza is not as a vehicle to make money for the owners, but rather a way to *share* profits with consumers.[53] They alleged that about 80 percent of the pizza's price is made up of food material cost and the margins are very small.

The argument between the big stores and mom-and-pop stores became a national controversy. With the instant success of E-mart's pizza, however, some people worried that the large stores had launched an assault on the mom-and-pop competition and that stores like E-mart could potentially monopolize the Korean market and increase prices once they forced small stores and chains out of business.[54] On the other hand, the large stores blamed franchisers for exploiting franchisees with high fees, which were eventually passed on to consumers and adversely inflated prices.[55]

Small pizza store owners complained that E-mart unfairly deprived them of their income source. Many mom-and-pop stores are small because these businesses do not require intensive capital investment or much expertise. So many small mom-and-pop pizza stores exist that it is impossible to accurately estimate the number.

The Fire Returns to Pizza

National controversy and pressure from senators led the KFTC to investigate the Super-supreme pizza business. However, E-mart refused to halt their pizza business, with a comment that their pizza has limited impacts on small businesses.[56]

On October 2, 2012, the KFTC released a report stating that it would impose a fine of $3.7 million on Shinsegae and its affiliate, E-mart, for illegally lowering transfer prices from Shinsegae producers to E-mart. In addition, the KFTC insisted that the sales of mom-and-pop stores plunged by 34 percent during the period, while Shinsegae was enjoying soaring revenue as its sales skyrocketed by 514 percent in 2011 compared with 2010 figures.

A Host of New Political Regulations

About six months before announcing the fine against Shinsegae, the KFTC had intervened in the market and created new regulations that set a distance limit, against which it would approve new launches of a franchisee. The law limited bakeries such as Paris Baguette owned by Dunkin Donuts, coffee shops such as Starbucks, and pizza shops such as Pizza Hut to open a new store within 500 meters of an existing franchise.[57] Moreover, new regulations on operating hours of retailers went into effect in April 2012 in an effort to preserve the business of small grocery shops.[58] The law imposed a mandatory closing of 115 large retailers and 334 super markets two weekend days a month. Moreover, in February 2013, the National Commission of Corporation Partnership designated 16 industries, including bakery and dining, as those in which only small businesses are allowed to compete. A 2 percent growth-limit rule was placed on large companies, which banned them from opening new branches comprising more than 2 percent of the number of stores at the end of the prior year. Paris Baguette, one of the leading bakery companies, argued that this policy would only stifle organic growth and make life worse for everyone: consumers who want to enjoy high-quality bread at low prices, bakers who seek jobs, and retirees who want to start a franchise.

Case Discussion Questions

1. What is the level of general political risk in Korea?
2. What is the level of micro political risk for the fast-food industry, in particular, pizza restaurants?
3. What implications does this have for international businesses such as Dunkin Donuts and Pizza Hut?

Endnotes

[1]Korean History and Political Geography. Center for Global Education. http://asiasociety.org/education/korean-history-and-political-geography (accessed September 19, 2016).

[2]Abraham Lincoln, "The Gettysburg Address," November 19, 1863. Abraham Lincoln Online, Speeches & Writings. www.abrahamlincolnonline.org/lincoln/speeches/gettysburg.htm (accessed February 2, 2016).

[3]Arch Puddington and Tyler Roylance, "Overview Essay: Anxious Dictators, Wavering Democracies," (Freedom in the World 2016), Freedom House. https://freedomhouse.org/report/freedom-world-2016/overview-essay-anxious-dictators-wavering-democracies (accessed September 6, 2016).

[4]Thomas Ambrosio, *Authoritarian Backlash: Russian Resistance to Democratization in the Former Soviet Union* (New York: Routledge, 2016).

[5]Vladimir Hernandez, "Argentine Mothers Mark 35 Years Marching for Justice," *BBC Mundo*, April 29, 2012. http://www.bbc.com/news/world-latin-america-17847134.

[6]EuroNews. "Queen Rania of Jordan Joins Protestors on the Streets of Amman," *EuroNews*, June 2, 2015. www.euronews.com/2015/02/06/queen-rania-of-jordan-joins-protesters-on-the-streets-of-amman/; "Vladimir Unbound: Russia's President Is Impervious to the Woes That Afflict Normal Leaders," *Economist*, January 30, 2016. www.economist.com/news/europe/21689626-russias-president-impervious-woes-afflict-normal-leaders-vladimir-unbound.

[7]Loren Thompson, "What If ISIS Wins?" *Forbes*, January 21, 2015. www.forbes.com/sites/lorenthompson/2015/01/21/what-if-isis-wins/#706226406644.

[8]Brittney Lenard, "The Local Fight Against Global Extremism," *Huffington Post*, August 20, 2015. www.huffingtonpost.com/young-professionals-in-foreign-policy/the-local-fight-against-g_b_8016394.html.

[9]Joseph Rago, "How Algorithms Can Help Beat Islamic State," *Wall Street Journal*, March 11, 2017. www.wsj.com/articles/how-algorithms-can-help-beat-islamic-state-1489187064.

[10]Gerry Shih, "Officials Warn of Global Religious Extremism Threat to China," Associated Press, March 13, 2017. http://abcnews.go.com/; Julia Edwards Ainsley, Dustin Volz, and Kristina Cooke, "Exclusive: Trump to Focus Counter-extremism Program Solely on Islam—Sources," Reuters, February 2, 2017. www.reuters.com/article/us-usa-trump-extremists-program-exclusiv-idUSKBN15G5VO.

[11]Karl Marx and David McLellan, *Karl Marx: Selected Writings*, 2nd ed. (New York: Oxford University Press, 2000). Karl Marx originally envisioned that communist governments would start through revolution and rely on authoritarian regimes to ensure the effective transition from the state to the people. After this transition, decisions would be made collectively and democratically. However, this goes counter to all prevailing communist models, as some centralized body (the party or decision council) needs absolute authority to ensure goods are equally distributed.

[12]Cathleen Decker, "Bernie Sanders and Hillary Clinton in a Tight Race in California as the Campaign Batters Her Popularity," *LA Times*, June 2, 2016. www.latimes.com/politics/la-pol-ca-latimes-presidential-primary-poll-20160602-snap-story.html.

[13]www.heritage.org/index/ (accessed May 3, 2017); He Fan, "The Long March to the Mixed Economy in China," Business Spectator, February 10, 2015. www.theaustralian.com.au/business/business-spectator/the-long-march-to-the-mixed-economy-in-china/news-story/7b031617dfab297b155b300ff3b59aad; Charlotte Alfred, "This Is Why Hong Kong Looks So Different from the Rest of China," Huffington Post, October 2, 2014. www.huffingtonpost.com/2014/10/02/hong-kong-china-differences_n_5916444.html.

[14]Leo Lewis, "Japan: End of the Rice Age," *Financial Times*, September 21, 2015. www.ft.com/intl/cms/s/0/f4db3b26-6045-11e5-a28b-50226830d644.html#axzz46C4NJdEb.

[15]"Argentina to Pay Repsol With Bonds for YPF Nationalization," April 25, 2014. http://www.americasquarterly.org/content/argentina-pay-repsol-ypf-nationalization (Accessed May 3, 2017).

[16]Anatoly Kurmanaev, "Venezuela to Overhaul Currency Controls Soon, Minister Says," *Wall Street Journal*, February 3, 2016. www.wsj.com/articles/venezuela-to-overhaul-currency-controls-soon-minister-says-1454548180.

[17]Moisés Naím and Francisco Toro, "Venezuela Is Falling Apart," *Atlantic*, May 12, 2016. www.theatlantic.com/international/archive/2016/05/venezuela-is-falling-apart/481755/.

[18]"Trump Presidency Rated Among Top 10 Global Risks: EIU," BBC News, March 17, 2016. www.bbc.com/news/business-35828747.

[19]Bruce Douglas, "Brazil Amazon Dam Project Suspended Over Concerns for Indigenous People," *Guardian*, April 22, 2016. www.theguardian.com/world/2016/apr/22/brazil-amazon-dam-project-suspended-indigenous-munduruku-sao-luiz-do-tapajos.

[20]Vas Panagiotopoulos, "Meet Denmark's New Anti-Islam, Anti-Immigration, Anti-Tax Party," Politico, February 14, 2017; Nationalism Handicaps iPhone in Indonesia," iAfrica.com, October 24, 2016. http://technology.iafrica.com/news/1038640.html.

[21]Steve Symington, "You'll Never Guess How Disney Just Lost $143 Million (Hint: It Wasn't a Movie)," The Motley Fool, March 1, 2015. www.fool.com/investing/general/2015/03/01/youll-never-guess-how-disney-just-lost-143-million.aspx.

[22]Kat Romero and Felicity Thistlethwaite, "Lost City of Sharm El Sheikh: Egypt's Tourist Hotspots are GHOST TOWNS Amid Terror Fear," *Express*, April 5, 2016. www.express.co.uk/travel/articles/623040/terror-chaos-Egypt-tourism-figures-drop-holiday-pictures.

[23]Sara Hamdan, "Arab Spring Unrest Helps Life Dubai Hotel Business," *New York Times*, April 12, 2012. www.nytimes.com/2012/04/12/world/middleeast/arab-spring-unrest-helps-lift-dubai-hotel-business.html.

[24]Thomas Jefferson, "Declaration of Independence," in *Founding America: Documents from the Revolution to the Bill of Rights*, edited by George Stade, 136–41 (New York: Barnes & Noble, 2006).

[25]United Nations General Assembly, *Universal Declaration of Human Rights* (Geneva: United Nations, 1948).

[26]"Factbox: Venezuela's Nationalizations under Chavez," Reuters, October 7, 2012. http://www.reuters.com/article/us-venezuela-election-nationalizations-idUSBRE89701X20121008

[27]Ibid.

[28]"Tribunal Orders Venezuela to Pay Rusoro Mining More Than US$1.2 Billion for Taking Over Company's Gold Mines," *Canadian Press*, August 23, 2016. http://business.financialpost.com/news/mining/tribunal-orders-venezuela-to-pay-rusoro-mining-more-than-us1-2-billion-for-taking-over-companys-gold-mines.

[29]Phillip Connor, "Number of Refugees to Europe Surges to Record 1.3 Million in 2015," Pew Research Center, August 2, 2016. www.pew-global.org/2016/08/02/number-of-refugees-to-europe-surges-to-record-1-3-million-in-2015/.

[30]"Syria: The Story of the Conflict," BBC News, March 11, 2016. www.bbc.com/news/world-middle-east-26116868.

[31]"Syria: The Story of the Conflict."

[32]Konstantin Richter, "A Refugee With an Axe, and Germany's Open Door Could Be Slammed Shut," *Guardian*, July 21, 2016. www.theguardian.com/commentisfree/2016/jul/21/refugee-axe-germany-train-open-door-migration.

[33]Yvonne Muther, "Despite Early Optimism, German Companies Hire Few Refugees," NPR Parallels, August 28, 2016. http://www.npr.org/sections/parallels/2016/08/28/489510068/despite-early-optimism-german-companies-hire-few-refugees.

[34]Matthew Holeshouse, "EU to Fine Countries 'Hundreds of Millions of Pounds' for Refusing to Take Refugees," *Telegraph*, May 3, 2016. www.telegraph.co.uk/news/2016/05/03/eu-to-fine-countries-that-refuse-refugee-quota/.

[35]Nick Robins-Early, "How the Refugee Crisis Is Fueling the Rise of Europe's Right," *Huffington Post*, October 28, 2015. www.huffingtonpost.com/entry/europe-right-wing-refugees_us_562e9e64e4b06317990f1922.

[36]Alex Hunt and Brian Wheeler, "Brexit: All You Need to Know About the UK Leaving the EU," *BBC News*, September 1, 2016. www.bbc.com/news/uk-politics-32810887.

[37]Hunt and Wheeler, "Brexit."

[38]Hicham Alaoui, "March of Arab Spring on Pause: Authoritarianism has Retrenched in the Middle East With New Strategies to Extend Control," YaleGlobal Online, May 10, 2016. http://yaleglobal.yale.edu/content/march-arab-spring-pause.

[39] Soo Kim, "Egypt's Tourism Industry Is Dealt Another Blow," *Telegraph*, May 19, 2016. http://www.telegraph.co.uk/travel/destinations/africa/egypt/articles/will-egypt-tourism-industry-ever-recover-egyptair-crash/.

[40] Omar Mawji, "Saudi Arabia Comes to the Rescue of the Egyptian Economy," Geopolitical Monitor, April 25, 2016. www.geopoliticalmonitor.com/saudi-arabia-comes-to-the-rescue-of-the-egyptian-economy/.

[41]Alenna Petroff, "7 Crazy Numbers About the World's Largest Oil Company," CNN Money, May 11, 2016. http://money.cnn.com/2016/05/10/news/companies/saudi-arabia-aramco-oil-ipo/.

[42]Anjli Raval, David Sheppard, and Neil Hume, "Saudi Aramco Prepares to Publish Its Accounts for First Time," *Financial Times*, October 6, 2016. www.ft.com/content/b4c92832-8af0-11e6-8aa5-f79f5696c731; Kevin Baxter and Summer Said, "Could Saudi Aramco Be Worth 20 Times Exxon?" *Wall Street Journal*, January 8, 2016. www.wsj.com/articles/saudi-aramco-confirms-ipo-study-1452254819.

[43]Gabriel Wildau, "China's State-Owned Zombie Economy," *Financial Times*, February 29, 2016. www.ft.com/intl/cms/s/0/253d7eb0-ca6c-11e5-84df-70594b99fc47.html#axzz497XbZBO6.

[44]"State-owned Enterprises: Fixing China Inc," *Economist*, August 30, 2014. www.economist.com/news/china/21614240-reform-state-companies-back-agenda-fixing-china-inc.

[45]Baxter and Said, "Could Saudi Aramco Be Worth 20 Times Exxon?"

[46]"Key Facts and Figures," Saudi Aramco website. www.saudiaramco.com/en/home/about/key-facts-and-figures.html (accessed November 1, 2016).

[47] "BP in Saudi Arabia," BP Global website. www.bp.com/en/global/corporate/about-bp/bp-worldwide/bp-in-saudi-arabia.html (accessed November 1, 2016).

[48]Mitchell Bingemann, "Emirates Airline Boss Tim Clark Says US Carriers Out to Destroy Rivals," *Australian*, October 14, 2016. www.theaustralian.com.au/business/aviation/emirates-airline-boss-tim-clark-says-us-carriers-out-to-destroy-rivals/news-story/8e042a537b538fb017499b0013da6ef7.

[49]Ted Reed, "Gulf Carriers Continue to Take Traffic from American, Delta and United," TheStreet, January 27, 2016 www.thestreet.com/story/13437676/1/gulf-carriers-continue-to-take-traffic-from-american-delta-and-united.html (accessed April 18, 2016).

[50]Micah Maidenberg, "Group Cries Foul Over Gulf Carriers' Impact at O'Hare," *Crain's Chicago Business*, January 28, 2016. www.chicagobusiness.com/article/20160128/NEWS10/160129816/group-cries-foul-over-gulf-carriers-impact-at-ohare (accessed April 18, 2016).

[51]Fred L. Smith Jr. and Braden Cox, "Airline Deregulation," *Concise Encyclopedia of Economics*. www.econlib.org/library/Enc/AirlineDeregulation.html (accessed May 16, 2016).

[52]Kang Hyun-kyung. "Consumer Watchdogs Silent Over Lotte Chicken." *Korea Times*. December 20, 2010. http://www.koreatimes.co.kr/www/common/printpreview.asp?categoryCode=116&newsIdx=78304

[53]Kim Tae-jong. "Shinsegae Slapped with Big Fine." *Korean Times*. October 3, 2012. http://www.koreatimes.co.kr/www/news/biz/2012/10/123_121380.html

[54]Choe Sang-Hyun. "South Koreans Resist Hypermarkets' Intrusion on Small Businesses." *The New York Times*. October 3, 2012. http://www.nytimes.com/2012/10/04/business/global/battling-the-retail-goliaths-in-south-korea.html

[55]Cho Jin-seo. "Small Eateries Cry Foul, but Discount Store Chain Says It's Fair Game." *Korea Times*. December 12, 2010. http://www.koreatimes.co.kr/www/news/biz/2010/12/123_77887.html

[56]Lotte Tonggan. "Chicken Pulling Out, E-Mart Pizza Next? Is Pizza Different from Chicken?" *International BNT News*. http://bntnews.hankyung.com/apps/news?popup=0&nid=05&c1=05&c2=05&c3=00&nkey=201012131706113&mode=sub_view, accessed May 4, 2017.

[57]Joon Jin-Seob. "FTC Franchise Tyranny Braking. Same Bakery 500 Meter Prohibition." *SBC CNBC News*. April 9, 2012. http://sbscnbc.sbs.co.kr/read.jsp?pmArticleId=10000428983

[58]Park Si-Soo. "Chicken, Pizza Franchise Stores to Be Banned from Opening Near Existing Outlets." *Korean Times*. July 5, 2012. http://www.koreatimes.co.kr/www/news/biz/2012/07/123_114543.html

CHAPTER **4**

The Legal Environment

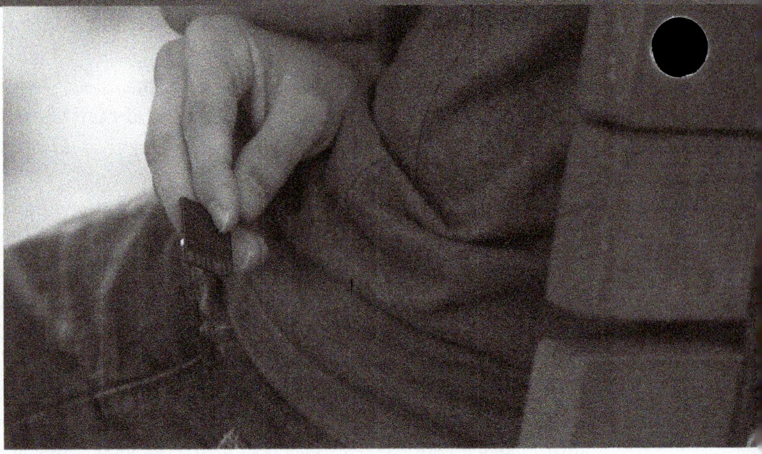
Discovery FootageSource/Getty Images

Introduction

Facebook, Google, and Amazon, technology giants in the West, have all been daunted by the complex and ever-changing regulations imposed on tech companies by the Chinese government. Each has finally given up the attempt to do business in China, and the ride-sharing service Uber recently did too, opting instead to allow its Chinese rival to buy its operations there. A practical result of China's challenging legal system seems to be the creation of two separate Internets: one in China, and another in the rest of the world.[1]

Companies must pay careful attention to the legal and ethical environments in which they operate and also must comply with international as well as national and local laws. For instance, bribes are illegal in many countries, though at the same time they may be considered customary in some of the same countries—or laws prohibiting them may not be strictly enforced.

LEARNING OBJECTIVES

After you explore this chapter you will be able to:

1. **Describe** different types of legal systems
2. **Explain** the ways in which crime and corruption affect international business
3. **Describe** the difference between illegal and unethical conduct
4. **Identify** key laws that govern international business

4.1 Differing Legal Systems

LEARNING OBJECTIVE

Describe different types of legal systems.

In ancient Egypt, from about 3000 BC to 30 BC, the pharaoh was considered a living god, the supreme judge and lawmaker whose decrees, coupled with decisions in prior cases, determined legal outcomes.[2] In ancient Mesopotamia, around 1750 BC, the dynastic ruler Hammurabi outlined more than 275 specific laws, mostly dealing with contracts, trade, and property rights, and the punishments associated with breaking them.[3] Partial copies of the Code of Hammurabi still exist today.

Ancient Egyptian law and the Code of Hammurabi are examples of the **rule of the individual**. Under such rule, one individual is the ultimate authority and has discretion to set and enforce laws. Today, some countries continue to operate under the rule of the individual. In North Korea, Kim Jong-un has acted as the "supreme leader" since the 2011 death of his father, who held the title before him. Using his absolute power, Kim has replaced the advisors appointed by his father with his own.

rule of the individual rule of governing whereby one individual is the ultimate authority and has discretion to set and enforce laws

In some cases the removal of a leader has been public and violent. For example, in 2015 Kim had his defense minister Hyon Yong-chol executed by antiaircraft fire in front of an audience of hundreds because Kim was upset at Hyon for falling asleep in his presence, talking back to him, and failing to carry out his instructions.[4] How could Kim do this? He is the "First Secretary of the Worker's Party of Korea," the "Marshal of the Democratic People's Republic of Korea," the "First Chairman of the National Defense Commission," and the "Supreme Commander of the Korean People's Army."[5] In other words, he is the giver and the enforcer of law in North Korea.

The Rule of Law

In contrast to the rule of the individual, the **rule of law** suggests that all individuals—regardless of rank, status, or office—are subject to the law. Nations that operate under the rule of law create laws and enforce them publicly and transparently. These laws govern politics and commercial transactions, and punish crime; they are based on fairness and justice as these concepts are understood by the people being governed. A key principle of the rule of law is that justice is blind (**Figure 4.1**), meaning that it is indifferent to the status of any who violate the law.

rule of law rule of governing whereby all individuals are accountable to well-defined and established laws that are fairly enforced

Under the rule of law, celebrities such as actor Bill Cosby,[6] business leaders such as Chipotle's marketing chief Mark Crumpacker,[7] and political leaders such as four of the last seven governors of Illinois (Rob Blagojeich, impeached for selling a U.S. Senate seat; George Ryan, convicted of racketeering; Dan Walker, jailed for bank fraud; and Otto Kerner, jailed for bribery[8]) all must abide by the same laws or face the same consequences as the rest of the population.

The rule of law typically supports individual liberties, democracy, and economic prosperity.[9] It also promotes international business in three ways. First, it reduces transactional risks, such as fraud, negligence, and bad debts, associated with international transactions. The 2017–2018 G20 Anti-Corruption Action Plan encourages all G20 member countries to ensure that their national legal systems strictly enforce international transaction contracts. The plan also calls for mutual legal assistance among countries to ensure fraud, negligence, and bad debts are pursued by all countries involved.[10] For instance, if a Tanzanian construction company did not deliver on a contract it made with the British company Vodafone, then according to the G20 Action Plan, both the Tanzanian legal system and the British legal system should work together to ensure that Vodafone is able to recover its losses.

Rocky Lee/EPN EPN/Newscom

FIGURE 4.1 **Justice** Justice, portrayed here before the Court of Final Appeal in Hong Kong, is blindfolded and holds the sword of truth in one hand and the balance of scales in the other.

Second, the rule of law puts a check on governmental power. A classic World Bank report established a clear link between strong legal regimes and economic development. It stated that "the judiciary [is] in a unique position to support sustainable development by holding the other two branches accountable for their decisions and underpinning the credibility of the overall business and political environment."[11] For example, Brazilian courts are holding lawmakers accountable and digging through a far-reaching scandal implicating Petrobras, the state-owned oil company that accounts for roughly 10 percent of the nation's economic output, and many of Brazil's top political officials. The courts are investigating allegations that politicians and government workers embezzled about $3 billion from the company. The scandal involves at least 50 politicians from six different political parties. While painful, the court's holding the state oil company and politicians accountable for their actions also holds the government accountable, and the outcome of the case will likely influence the Brazilian business environment for years to come.[12] To date, prosecutors have recovered nearly $2 billion of bribe money from bank accounts of officials and politicians in 36 countries.[13]

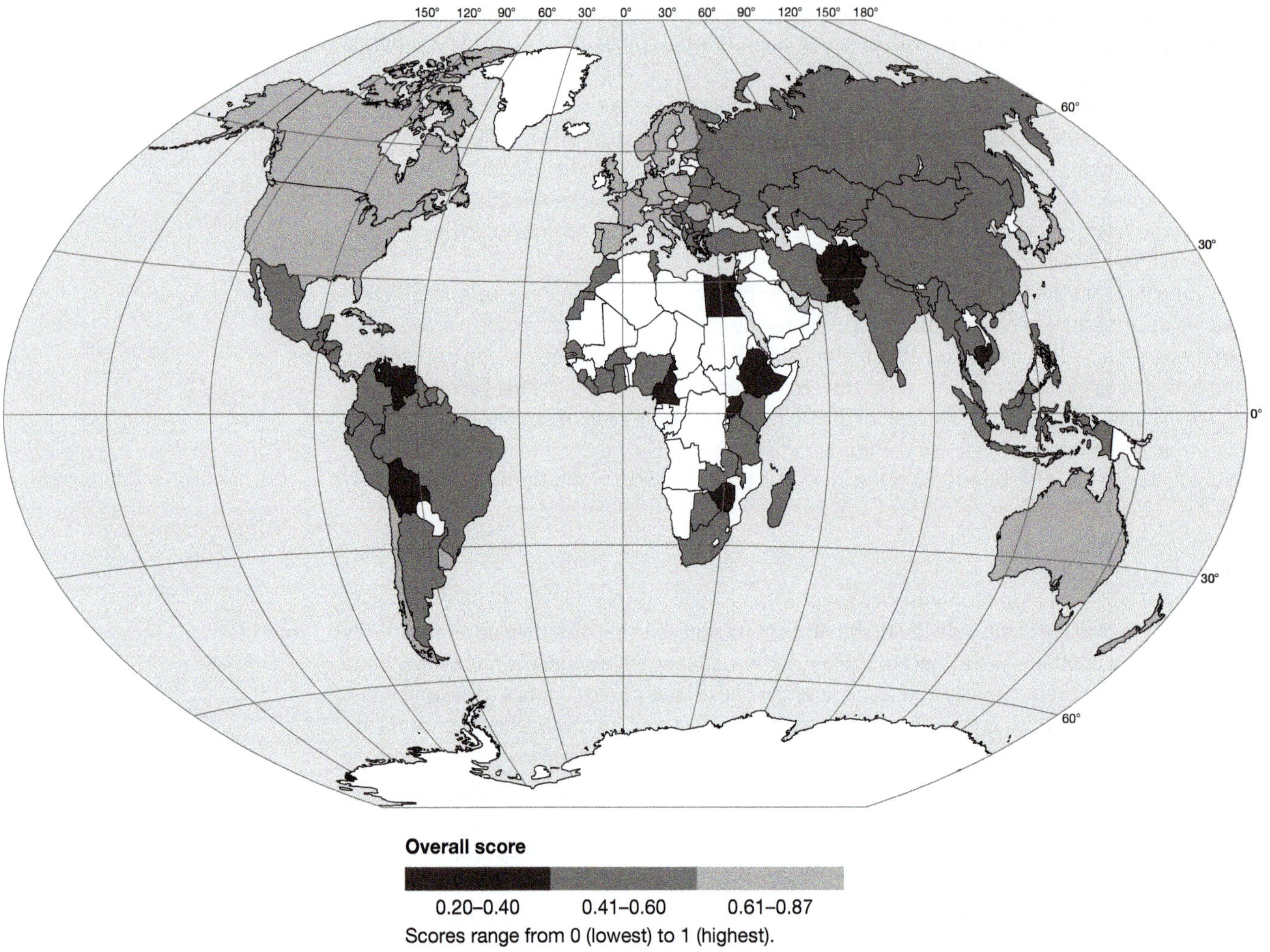

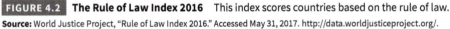

FIGURE 4.2 **The Rule of Law Index 2016** This index scores countries based on the rule of law.
Source: World Justice Project, "Rule of Law Index 2016." Accessed May 31, 2017. http://data.worldjusticeproject.org/.

Third, the rule of law codifies and clarifies business property rights and builds institutions such as courts, public records offices, and patent offices that protect those rights. In countries where such legal safeguards are lacking, international businesses face the risk of having their overseas property and goods confiscated at the whim of a politician, making them reluctant to invest there.[14]

The World Justice Project surveys over 2,500 judicial experts globally and compiles a report that indicates to what extent each country follows the rule of law. The report measures legal aspects such as regulatory enforcement, civil justice, and criminal justice, as well as measures of corruption, governmental restraint, and fundamental rights. In 2016 Denmark, Norway, and Finland received the highest scores, whereas Afghanistan, Cambodia, and Venezuela received the lowest scores, as shown in **Figure 4.2**.

Three Different Levels of Law

constitutional law laws that set the bounds of government and governmental procedures

criminal law laws and punishments that regulate social conduct and provide personal, property, and human rights protections

Many types of legal systems exist; these comprise the procedures, institutions, and routines used to interpret and enforce the law. Most include laws at three different levels. **Constitutional law** sets the bounds of government and governmental procedures, including creating the authorities that establish laws. **Criminal law** describes laws and punishments that regulate social conduct, including personal protections from actions such as assault, battery, kidnapping, murder, and robbery; property protections from actions such as arson, blackmail, burglary, fraud, and theft; and basic human rights protections against crimes like slavery, human trafficking, torture, and massacre. **Commercial law**—with which we are most concerned in this chapter—specifies the rights and duties of individuals in their business dealings, the way in which businesses are created and organized, and the manner in which business is transacted, including governance of contracts, property rights, and trade.

commercial law laws specifying the rights and duties of individuals in their business dealings, how businesses are created and organized, and how business is transacted

Types of Legal Systems

Legal systems vary across countries but often take one of five distinct types, depending on whether they are governed mostly by customary, theocratic, common, or civil law, or a combination of these (see **Figure 4.3**).

Customary law is derived from long-standing experience and practice, based on collective wisdom and shared philosophy. It is the form of law used in developing countries such as Mongolia, Mozambique, Somalia, and Indonesia, and in many indigenous communities. Customary law sets the boundaries and rights that define community members' relationships to each other. For instance, government has little presence in Somalia. Instead, Xeer, a form of tribal law that developed over 1,400 years ago, serves as the primary source of law.[15]

customary law laws derived from experience, practice, collective wisdom, and shared philosophy to set the boundaries and rights that define relationships between community members

Under Xeer, tribal elders representing the accused and the accuser act together to administer the law. If a case cannot be solved by the two elders, it is escalated to include others. If multiple tribes are involved in a crime, multiple elders engage in mediation to seek a satisfactory decision. A clan acts as a buffer, protecting members against harmful acts by other clans. The clan of the

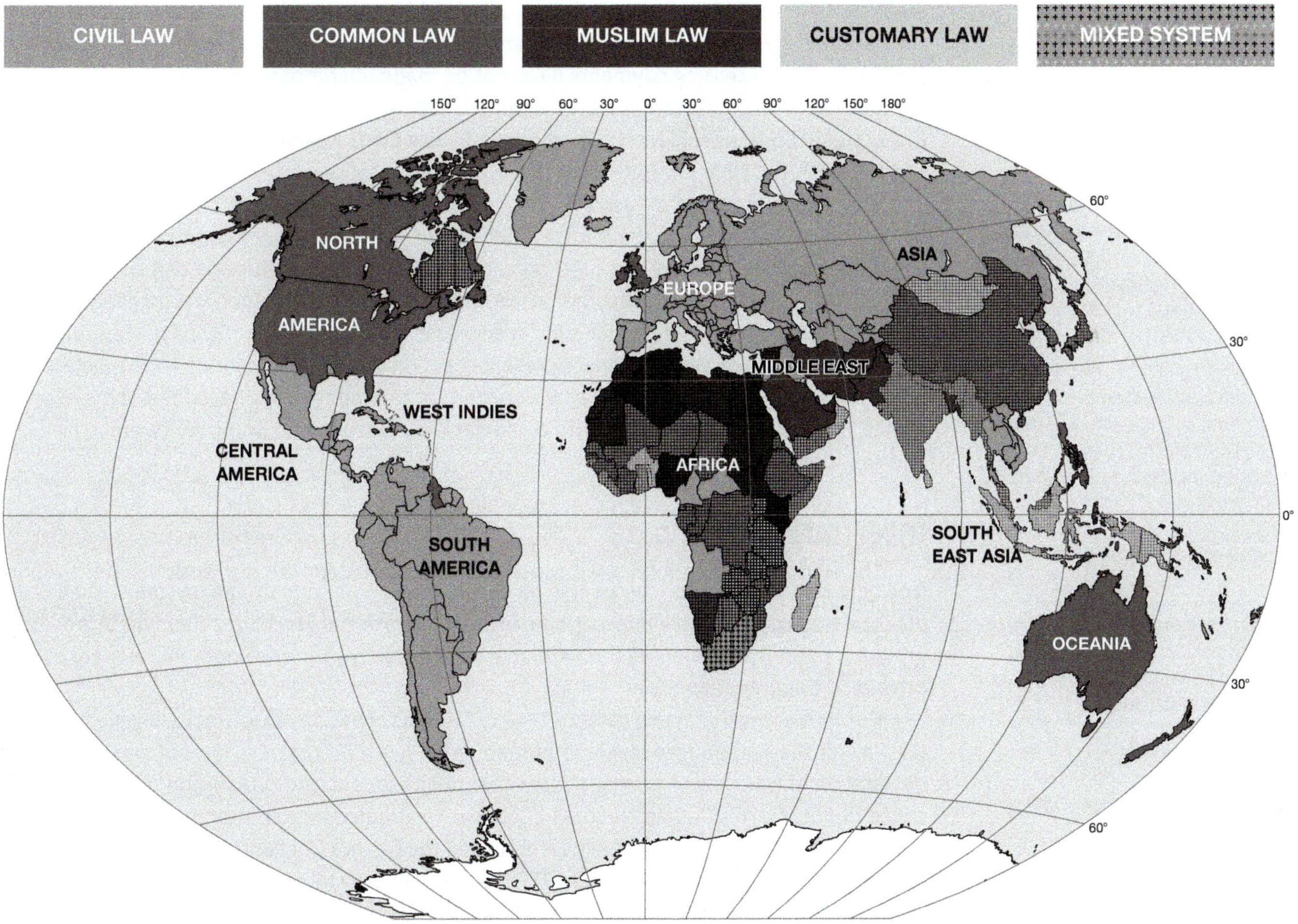

FIGURE 4.3 **Legal Systems of the World** North America and Australia operate under common law; South America, Europe, and North Asia operate under civil law; India, China, and much of Africa mix customary law with civil law or common law; and the Middle East and North Africa mix religious law with other forms of law. **Source:** JuriGlobe: World Legal Systems Research Group, University of Ottowa. www.juriglobe.ca/eng/ Accessed May 31, 2017.

offending individual ensures that he or she makes restitution; otherwise, the clan will step in and right the wrong.[16] If someone becomes a repeat offender, the clan will cast the person out.[17]

theocratic law a system of law that relies on religious doctrine and belief

Theocratic law is a system of law that relies on religious doctrine and belief. This type of system dominates countries in the Middle East and North Africa. Countries such as Saudi Arabia operate fully under theocratic law, whereas Turkey, Algeria, and Iran offer a mix of theocratic law and other forms. Theocratic law is adjudicated by religious leaders. Islamic law—or Shari'a—is based on the Qur'an, the religious text of Islam; the "Hadiths," or the opinions of Muhammad; and the writings of other Islamic scholars. Shari'a is a broad set of laws that govern crime, politics, contracts, and religious observances.

For instance, the law forbids charging interest, calling it an exploitive practice. Instead, Shari'a offers two alternatives. In the first, those financing a business can act as a capital partner, taking a stock in the business venture and earning a return or loss based on the results of the venture. In the second, lenders can purchase goods a business needs to buy and then can sell those goods to the business at an agreed-upon markup. Beehive, a novel loan maker based in Dubai, offers peer-to-peer lending that is Shari'a-compliant.[18] Beehive uses contracts to buy commodities at the Dubai Multi-Commodities Center and then resells these at specified prices. In this way, Beehive has financed more than $4 billion in Shari'a-compliant loans.

common law a legal system in which judges interpret law and set precedent for subsequent interpretation and usage

Common law is a legal system in which judges interpret law and set precedent for subsequent interpretation and usage. The United Kingdom, United States, and Australia are examples of countries that rely on common law. Judges in this system rule on cases by relying on the legal code and *stare decisis*—the idea that they "stand on decided cases" and are bound by these earlier precedents. For instance, in the United States, Marvel Entertainment licensed from inventor Stephen Kimble the right to produce and sell a Spider-Man toy that can shoot foam string to simulate spider webs. The license had no end date, but Marvel later discovered a 1964 Supreme Court ruling that licensing payments need not be made after a product's patent had expired.[19] Kimble's patent expired in 2010, Marvel stopped making payments to him, and he sued. In 2015, the Supreme Court upheld the 1964 ruling. As Justice Elena Kagan noted, "What we decide, we can undecide. But *stare decisis* teaches that we should exercise that authority sparingly."[20]

civil law a system of law that provides a comprehensive code of written law that judges translate into legal principles and regulatory statutes

Civil law is a system of law with ancient Roman origins and is found across continental Europe, South America, and the former USSR. It provides a comprehensive code of written law, and judges translate the law into legal principles and regulatory statues. In civil law, judges are bound not by earlier rulings as in common law, but by a written constitution and detailed statutory code that is always binding (earlier judicial decisions are not binding).[21] By relying on rules that are known in advance, civil law aims to prevent litigation and promote confidence in transactions.

mixed legal systems a legal system that combines two or more of the following types of law: customary, theocratic, common, or civil law

Mixed legal systems combine two or more of the frameworks described above. For instance, India unites common law with customary law. Canada and South Africa blend civil law and common law.

International Law

international laws laws agreed on by nations; these laws are binding on nations and supersede their national laws

Not only do international companies face differences in national legal systems, they must also understand applicable international laws. **International laws** are agreed on by and bind groups of nations, superseding their national laws. Three types of international laws are public, private, and supranational law.

public international law laws that govern interactions of nation-states

Public international law governs the interactions of nation-states, including war, criminal law, law of the sea, refugee law, and human rights law. For instance, laws of war govern the declaration of war, acts of surrender, treatment of prisoners, and prohibition of weapons that cause unnecessary suffering, such as chemical weapons. Modern international laws of war stem from a series of international treaties called the Geneva Conventions, established in 1864 and revised in 1906, 1929, 1949, and 1977.[22] More than 145 states are party to most of the provisions. Some of the Geneva Convention laws are that civilians should not be targeted in war; sick or wounded soldiers should be humanely treated and not be tortured, injured, or experimented on; and a record of the dead and wounded should be kept and shared with the other side of the conflict (log in to WileyPLUS to watch a video outlining the Geneva Convention). The Convention also established the International Committee of the Red Cross and the Red Crescent as the agency enforcing the laws it established.

Similarly, the **law of the sea** allows countries to seize and prosecute pirates (**Figure 4.4**) who commit crimes in international waters. However, acting under the law of the sea isn't always straightforward. Dealing with captured pirates, for example, is difficult. The registry or national flag of the pirated vessel, the nationality of any of the victims or crew, the nationality of the on-scene warship, and, in some cases, the identity of nearby coastal and port states can all be valid bases for assigning jurisdiction. It can take weeks or months to sort out the logistic and legal issues of any prosecution.[23] Prosecuting pirates in Western courts is difficult because the costs of organizing and transporting pirates, witnesses, and evidence can be daunting. Moreover, if the prosecution fails, the pirates sometimes claim asylum, which compounds the issue.[24]

PJF Military Collection/Alamy Stock Photo

FIGURE 4.4 **Pirates** Private security professionals on commercial boats do not usually carry guns, but they may have other deterrents such as water cannons to prevent pirates from boarding the ship.

In contrast to public international law, **private international law** establishes legal jurisdiction and procedures for people and organizations, including businesses. For instance, a law governing international trusts of deceased persons, known as the Hague Convention on the Law Applicable to Trusts and Their Recognition, allows trusts to be recognized as separate from individual assets and permits trustees to be appointed and to administer and dispose of trust assets across national boundaries.[25]

law of the sea law that allows countries to seize and prosecute pirates who commit crimes in international waters

private international law laws that establish international legal jurisdiction and procedures for people and organizations

Several countries have adopted the United Nations Convention on Contracts for the International Sale of Goods (CISG). This convention spells out the four basic elements of contract law for the sale of goods across national borders: jurisdiction, or where to hear a case; which country's laws will apply in the event of a dispute; what resolution techniques will be used, such as a legal process or arbitration; and what enforcement means are allowed. These contracts thus define both the obligations of buyers and sellers and the rules and remedies not otherwise stipulated by contract.[26] While CISG covers many transactions, most multinational companies explicitly state in their contracts which country's legal jurisdiction and system will apply if a conflict occurs between the parties. For instance, some companies may prefer a country unaffiliated with either party so a neutral judgment can be reached; others may choose arbitration rather than litigation to settle disputes.

Arbitration is the process of reaching a binding decision by an arbitrator (a third party) outside the courts. Arbitration is increasingly popular by companies around the world because it is seen as more predictable, more neutral, more confidential, more final, more expert, and more enforceable (the United States and 137 countries have agreed to uphold the outcomes of arbitration).[27]

arbitration the process of reaching a binding decision through an arbitrator (a third party) outside the courts

Some business dealings are not covered by a contract, such as purchasing a foreign manufactured good. In this case, jurisdiction may be established by the law of the place where the injury occurred, the victim's residence, the principle place of business of the manufacturer, or the place where the product was purchased.[28] In Europe, the 1972 Hague Convention prioritized the order in determining jurisdiction: the place of injury, then the residency of the victim, followed by the manufacturer's principle place of business.[29] In the absence of a contract, however, it is not always easy to decide which court and legal code apply. For instance, the U.S. Supreme Court recently decided that 22 residents of Argentina could not sue the German auto maker Daimler in California for actions it took supporting the kidnapping, detaining, torturing, and killing of citizens in Argentina's civil war of 1976–1983. The reason was that the California court had no jurisdiction over events that took place entirely outside the United States.[30]

While international law is important for international business, a significant limitation is that international law most often imposes obligations on nations rather than on companies. For instance, the Convention Concerning Forced or Compulsory Labour of 1930 outlaws the use of forced labor. However, the pact is binding only on nations that are members of the International Labour Organization (ILO) and that ratified the Convention; they are obligated to enforce the law against companies inside their borders. So, campaigns to end forced labor in countries that are not members of the ILO, such as Uzbekistan, Thailand, and Myanmar, can focus only on the government and not on the multinational companies that may be using forced labor there.[31]

supranational law international law that limits the rights of sovereign governments

The third form of international law is **supranational law**, which limits the rights of sovereign governments. For instance, when the European Union (EU) ratified the Treaty of Lisbon in 2007, it adopted laws governing the movement of goods, persons, and services; the movement of capital; and the creation of a customs union, a unified industrial policy, and a common currency.[32] New laws are enacted by the European Parliament together with the Council (a group that represents the governments of the 28 EU member states). These laws bind the member countries into the world's largest common market. EU law has the same standing as national law, granting rights to and placing obligations on the authorities in each member country as well as individuals and businesses. Authorities in each country implement EU legislation in national law and are responsible for enforcing it and guaranteeing citizens' rights under these laws.[33]

Similarly, human rights in Europe are governed by EU laws such as the European Convention on Human Rights and the Charter of Fundamental Rights of the European Union. Laws that protect life, liberty, equity, worker's rights, suffrage, and justice are addressed in the charter and are common across the EU. These laws supersede national laws of member states and are enforced by the European Court of Justice. While most members of the EU have adopted the human rights laws, exceptions exist—Poland, for example, preferred to retain its own domestic laws.

Other examples of supranational laws include a "Safe Harbor 2.0" agreement and the International Criminal Court. The Safe Harbor agreement establishes laws for consumer-data transfer between the United States and the EU, outlining what data companies can legally transfer across boundaries.[34] The International Criminal Court was established in 1998 when 120 nations adopted the Rome Statute as a legal basis.[35] Its responsibility is to try defendants accused of war crimes and crimes against humanity. To date, individuals from the Democratic Republic of the Congo, Uganda, the Central African Republic, Darfur, and Libya have all been tried by the Court. The former vice president of the Democratic Republic of the Congo was found guilty of rape, murder, pillage, and crimes against humanity.[36]

The Effect of the Enforcement of Laws on International Business

With so many different legal systems and country-specific variants in effect, it can be challenging to understand how international laws will affect specific international businesses. For instance, the ride-hailing company Uber has faced a litany of legal challenges in its global expansion. At one point France banned the company's operations, the United Kingdom required Uber to pay a minimum wage, and Singapore forced the company to buy cars and rent them out to drivers.[37] The company has faced numerous lawsuits by governments, drivers, and customers around the globe.[38]

Another way global regulations affect international business is through laws governing foreign ownership and operations of businesses. For instance, many emerging-market economies like China and India have strict regulations on foreign ownership of domestic businesses. While China's emerging middle class is a large and attractive market for many foreign firms, according to the U.S. Department of State China also has "a legal and regulatory framework that provides the government with discretion to promote investment in specific regions or industries it wishes to develop, and to restrict foreign investment deemed not to be in its national interest or that would compete with state-sanctioned monopolies or other favored domestic firms."[39]

China publishes a comprehensive catalogue that outlines which of its industries encourage, restrict, or prohibit foreign investment. The regulations are detailed; for example, according to a U.S. State Department report:

> *In the oil and natural gas exploration and development industry, foreign investment is required to take the form of equity joint ventures and cooperative joint ventures. In the*

accounting and auditing sectors, the Chief Partner of a firm must be a Chinese national. In higher education and pre-school, foreign investment is only permitted in the form of cooperative joint ventures led by a Chinese partner. In some sectors, the foreign shareholder's proportion of the investment may not exceed a certain percentage. For example, foreign stakes are limited to: 50% in value-added telecom services (excepting e-commerce), 49% in basic telecom enterprises, 50% in life insurance firms, 49% in security investment fund management companies.[40]

Similar laws apply in India. For example, foreign companies can own only up to 49 percent of a company in many industries, such as insurance, and foreign investments in India require approval by the Foreign Investment Promotion Board, along with a host of other local and national approvals. Foreign companies are also prohibited from investing in or owning property other than property directly used in their business. This ensures that companies are majority-owned by an Indian partner.[41]

While it is difficult for multinational companies to establish businesses in foreign countries, it is also challenging for them to obtain and enforce contracts across borders. For instance, India is the second-slowest country in issuing a construction permit. This means it takes on average 42 separate procedures to obtain a construction permit in India, compared with 12.1 procedures in high-income member countries of the Organisation for Economic Co-operation and Development (OECD). The cost of obtaining permits in India accounts for as much as 25 percent of the total costs of construction, compared with a mere 1.6 percent in OECD high-income countries.[42] While accessing electricity, registering property, trading across borders and enforcing contracts improved in India from 2016 to 2017, the country is still ranked near the bottom of the list at 130 of 190 countries (see **Figure 4.5**).

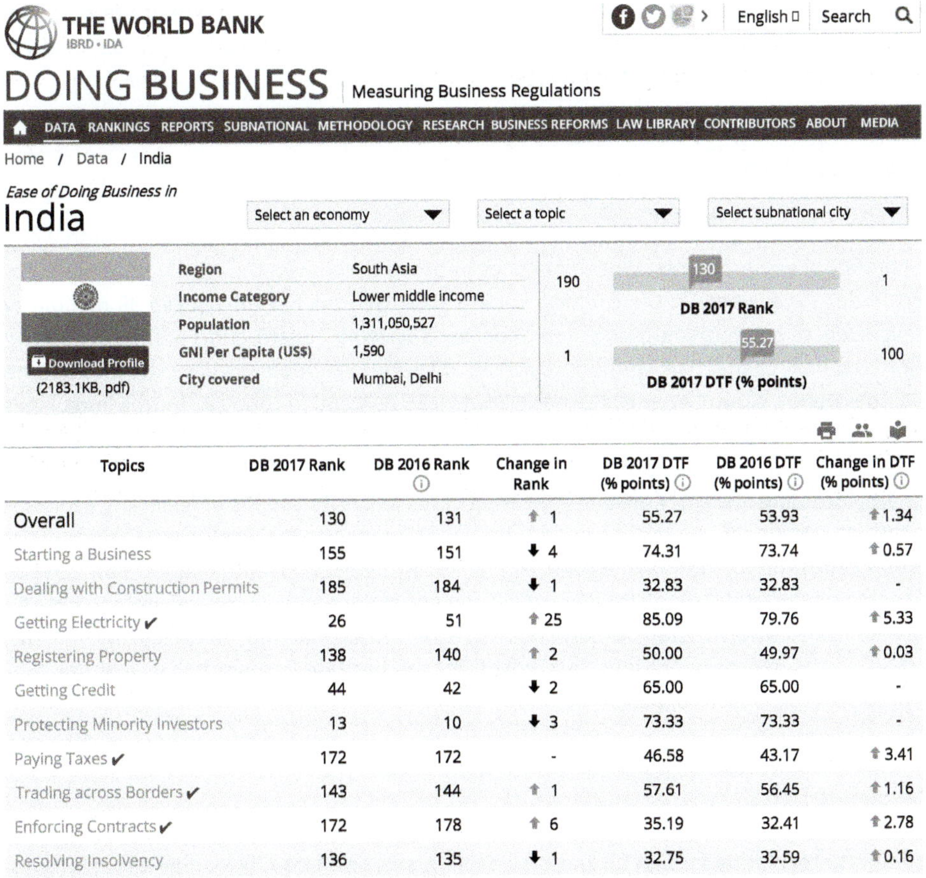
THE WORLD BANK
IBRD • IDA
English Search
DOING BUSINESS Measuring Business Regulations
DATA RANKINGS REPORTS SUBNATIONAL METHODOLOGY RESEARCH BUSINESS REFORMS LAW LIBRARY CONTRIBUTORS ABOUT MEDIA
Home / Data / India
Ease of Doing Business in
India
Select an economy | Select a topic | Select subnational city

Region	South Asia
Income Category	Lower middle income
Population	1,311,050,527
GNI Per Capita (US$)	1,590
City covered	Mumbai, Delhi

Download Profile (2183.1KB, pdf)

190 — 130 — 1
DB 2017 Rank
1 — 55.27 — 100
DB 2017 DTF (% points)

Topics	DB 2017 Rank	DB 2016 Rank	Change in Rank	DB 2017 DTF (% points)	DB 2016 DTF (% points)	Change in DTF (% points)
Overall	130	131	↑ 1	55.27	53.93	↑ 1.34
Starting a Business	155	151	↓ 4	74.31	73.74	↑ 0.57
Dealing with Construction Permits	185	184	↓ 1	32.83	32.83	-
Getting Electricity ✔	26	51	↑ 25	85.09	79.76	↑ 5.33
Registering Property	138	140	↑ 2	50.00	49.97	↑ 0.03
Getting Credit	44	42	↓ 2	65.00	65.00	-
Protecting Minority Investors	13	10	↓ 3	73.33	73.33	-
Paying Taxes ✔	172	172	-	46.58	43.17	↑ 3.41
Trading across Borders ✔	143	144	↑ 1	57.61	56.45	↑ 1.16
Enforcing Contracts ✔	172	178	↑ 6	35.19	32.41	↑ 2.78
Resolving Insolvency	136	135	↓ 1	32.75	32.59	↑ 0.16

FIGURE 4.5 **Doing Business (DB) report for India, 2017 vs. 2016** India is slowly reforming its legal system to make it easier to start a business and get electricity. **Source:** "Doing Business: Ease of Doing Business in India," World Bank. www.doingbusiness.org/data/exploreeconomies/india/. Accessed May 31, 2017.

Enforcing a contract in India can be equally difficult. A U.S. State Department report stated that it "takes nearly four years on average to resolve a commercial dispute in India, the third longest average rate in the world." Indian courts are backlogged with an estimated 30 million cases. The system is so slow that when judgments are reached against an Indian firm, the firm will sometimes just file a lawsuit in domestic courts "to delay paying the arbitral award." In one instance, a case is still pending after being filed in 1983.[43]

The World Bank's "Ease of Doing Business Annual Report" outlines many of the legal difficulties an international firm starting or operating a business may face by ranking the regulatory environment in 189 countries each year. The report compares countries on the challenges of completing 36 tasks, such as obtaining construction permits, getting electricity, registering property, getting credit, paying taxes, and enforcing contracts. For instance, New Zealand is ranked the second-easiest country in which to do business, behind Singapore. In New Zealand it takes just one process to start a business, and that process takes, on average, half a day.[44]

4.2 Common Legal Issues for International Business

LEARNING OBJECTIVE

Explain the ways in which crime and corruption affect international business.

One of the primary ways in which laws matter for international business is that, in general, there is a high correlation between efficient, effective regulation and the wealth of a nation. Those countries with easy-to-understand, easy-to-enforce regulations tend to be wealthy, whereas countries with complicated rules tend to be poor.

Increasing Wealth through Regulatory Changes

Over the past 12 years, Europe and Central Asia have made the most progress in simplifying their regulatory environments. When countries improve their laws, they likely open up more opportunities for business in the country. For instance, Georgia has introduced 39 regulatory reforms, such as establishing a one-stop shop for obtaining construction permits, reducing fees for electrical connection, and improving its dispute-resolution system.[45] Over the same period, the country's output per capita has grown by 66 percent. In contrast, Eritrea languishes at last place on the Ease of Doing Business Report. It takes 13 procedures and 84 days to start a business there, and on a scale of 1 to 18, the country scores just 2.5 on the quality of its judicial processes, including measures around allocating cases to courts and the efficiency of proceedings, case management, court automation, and alternative dispute resolution. The country's gross domestic product (GDP) average growth rate of 4.72 percent over the period from 1991 to 2014 came about partly through foreign aid; 50 percent of the population receives food aid and foreign remittances that account for 32 percent of GDP. Eritrea is looking for foreign investment, particularly in its mining operations, but most firms are hesitant to enter because of the difficulty of conducting business there.[46]

Product Liability

In addition to regulating foreign business ownership and operation, laws may affect international businesses even when the companies are merely engaged in importing and exporting products. For instance, many countries place product safety restrictions on the goods and services of foreign firms.

Genetically modified organisms (GMOs) are plants that have been genetically modified to make them resistant to insects, drought, or herbicides. In the EU, China, and India, GMOs have historically been banned because of fears that modifications make the food unsafe. These restrictions have eased recently, but strict labeling requirements are in force. In addition, 19 nations have opted to ban or partially ban the growing of GMO crops and continue to keep GMO crops out.[47] While Europe mostly remains hostile toward GMOs, other countries, such as Brazil, use them in abundance. According to Reuters, "Corn yields in Brazil, where GMOs are widely planted, have risen 60 percent in the past decade, versus a growth of only 11 percent and 20 percent in China and India that bar the cultivation of GMO food crops."[48]

While manufacturers are generally held accountable, even online retailers can face backlash from product defects. For example, several months after the initial surge in the popularity of hover boards, several cases of exploding hover boards were reported. The cause was the use of lithium-ion batteries, especially low-quality batteries, which eventually led the U.S. Consumer Product Safety Commission to classify all hover boards as unsafe. The U.S. government also sent out official notices to retailers, manufacturers, and importers about possible enforcement actions if safety standards were not met. Amazon.com, the Seattle-based online retailer, responded by offering refunds to anyone who purchased hover boards on its site.[49] That report effectively ended sales of imported hover boards in the United States.

Many international companies proactively manage product-safety liability concerns. For instance, the Danish toymaker LEGO decided to build factories in Mexico, Hungary, and Denmark, where it had extensive control over operations. Because of its desire to maintain strict quality controls and ensure product excellence, it has only recently warmed to the idea of manufacturing its products in China.[50]

Property Rights and Intellectual Property

Another reason that laws influence international business is that countries differ in the degree to which they allow companies and individuals to own resources such as land, equipment, and mineral rights. It is incumbent on international businesses to determine their property rights in any given country. For instance, in the United States, land owners control the mineral rights to any resources under their soil. In Botswana, the federal government owns all mineral rights regardless of who owns the land.[51] In Zimbabwe, President Robert Mugabe instituted a policy of property-rights redistribution that took land from large farmers and gave it to poorer farmers. The intent was to redistribute wealth across the country, but many studies indicate that it has resulted in lower agricultural yields instead. Some whose property rights were violated have sought restitution, but few have received any compensation, and now the government is taking land from anyone who opposes the ruling party.[52] Property rights may be difficult to enforce in some countries that keep poor records. For instance, owners of 17 properties in Telum, a beautiful beach town in Mexico, were recently driven out by court order. Most of them were foreigners trying to run hotel businesses in Mexico. While all had legally purchased the land, there were conflicting property deeds and ownership records. The government sided with local owners and expropriated the property from the foreign owners.[53]

Intellectual property rights are a particular type of property rights. Many economies across the globe are shifting away from agriculture and manufacturing and toward the development of Internet businesses and software and service industries. As a result, rights over the creative works of individuals, companies, and countries are often a source of competitive advantage for the company. According to the World Intellectual Property Organization, an organization established in 1990 in Switzerland to help creators obtain legal protection for their work, **intellectual property (IP)** is any creation of the human mind.[54]

intellectual property (IP) any creation of the human mind

For example, the Walt Disney Company spent more than 11 years negotiating with China to obtain the necessary permissions to build a new theme park in Shanghai, shown in **Figure 4.6**. Even as far back as 1999, negotiations stalled while both sides addressed significant complications on many levels, from financial and creative to logistical and technological. One of the

VCG/Getty Images

FIGURE 4.6 **Disney Shanghai** The park boasts the longest parade route of any Disney park in the world. Could this be a new "Long March" for the Communist Party of China?

notable problems was how Disney and China would determine property rights, including both ownership of the park and protection of Disney's private property, including IP such as the themes and characters from its animated children's films.

Ultimately a joint venture was created between Disney and the state-controlled Shanghai Shendi Group. Disney owns 43 percent of the venture and Shanghai Shendi, 57 percent. To safeguard its IP in a country notorious for counterfeits and poor enforcement of IP protections, Disney insisted that China improve its IP protection practices before an agreement could be made. In response, China granted special trademark protection to Disney, and Chinese authorities agreed to carry out a year-long campaign to eradicate Disney counterfeits as part of a wider effort to improve its reputation for safeguarding IP.[55] The trademark protection agreement also designates a 2.7-square mile area around the Shanghai amusement park as a "Disney trademark key protected area," with extra enforcement.[56] Ultimately, Disney's biggest bargaining chip in protecting its property rights lies in the fact that both the Shanghai municipal government and the Chinese central government recognize that the park's success means increased income and tourism for them both.[57] The park opened in the summer of 2016 and has been a boom for the economy—it even started driving up property prices in the city of Shanghai.[58]

4.3 Illegal Versus Unethical Conduct

LEARNING OBJECTIVE

Describe the difference between illegal and unethical conduct.

International businesses often face a dilemma: actions they may take may be legal, but also unethical. For instance, in many countries it is legal to employee children as young as 14 years old, but global businesses may consider these actions unethical and create policies that forbid their practice. Understanding this dilemma requires understanding the difference between legality and ethicality.

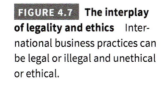

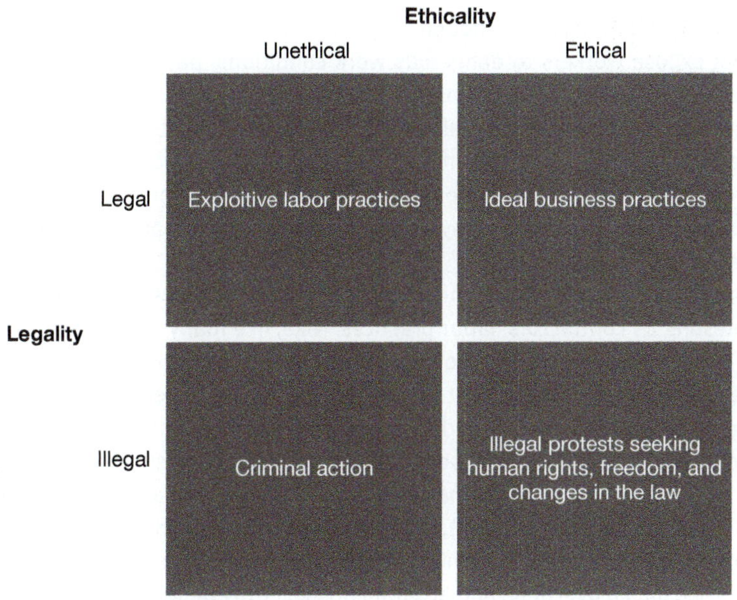

Ethicality
Unethical
Ethical
Legal
Exploitive labor practices
Ideal business practices
Legality
Illegal
Criminal action
Illegal protests seeking human rights, freedom, and changes in the law

FIGURE 4.7 The interplay of legality and ethics International business practices can be legal or illegal and unethical or ethical.

Ethics

ethics the moral principles of right and wrong that guide personal and organizational decision making

Ethics are the moral principles of right and wrong that guide personal and organizational decision making. These judgments of right and wrong are independent of what is legal or illegal. **Figure 4.7** shows that some actions are illegal and unethical, some are ethical and legal, but others may be legal but not ethical, or unethical but legal. For instance, a country may not have a law prohibiting child labor, long work hours, or low wages, but an international business may determine that such practices are unethical. Other actions may be illegal but deemed ethical. For instance, the protest of Ethiopian runner Feyisa Lilesa during the 2016 Olympics in Brazil against the human rights abuses and discrimination directed at his Oromo tribe were seen by many around the world as an ethical and peaceful resistance to government, but the government, which has killed more than 1,000 tribespeople, considers such action illegal.[59] Some practices, such as criminal actions, may be both unethical and illegal. Ideally, business practices should be both legal and ethical. Common ethical issues facing international businesses arise in the areas of employment practices, environmental practices, and human rights.

International Business and a Reactive versus Proactive Response to Ethical Dilemmas

International businesses may face social pressures to respond in certain ways to the many ethical dilemmas they face. These social pressures come from stakeholders such as customers, investors, employees, and governments. International businesses can be reactionary to these pressures, or they can take a more proactive approach to social pressures. Firms that are reactive seek to build capabilities that let them quickly respond to social pressures and engage in actions that attempt to minimize the damage to the firm. On the other hand, more proactive firms seek to build capabilities that build a reputation for ethical conduct. Actions by proactive firms seek to maximize their reputation. Some of the tools that proactive firms use to increase their reputation as highly ethical companies include engaging in corporate social responsibility (CSR) initiatives, such as Patagonia's efforts to "cause no unnecessary [environmental] harm,"[60] IKEA's funding of the Save the Children Foundation in India,[61] and Peet's Coffee's efforts in establishing and using direct trade coffee, where they work with farmers to ensure high quality and increased productivity.[62]

Employment Practices. Though legal in many countries, certain employment practices that expose workers to dangerous work conditions, pay wages below subsistence levels, and treat employees without dignity are considered unethical. Such unethical behaviors, though not illegal, can be detrimental to both employees and to employers alike. Some international businesses are proactive in their approach toward ethical situations, establishing strong guidelines to direct global actions toward employees, communities, and customers. Other organizations focus more on staying within the legal limits and have less concern for ethical issues.

For example, in 1997, Nike was stunned as college students across the United States began actively protesting its contractors' labor practices. Nike, like many companies, outsources its production to suppliers around the world, with the goal of reducing its costs. The strategy is, of course, perfectly legal, but at that time it was increasingly seen as unethical. Thanks to outsourcing, Nike had become the world's largest athletic shoe maker, but the strategy was beginning to backfire as students and other customers held Nike responsible for the appalling conditions in the factories. Allegations of abuse included low wages (14 cents an hour in Indonesia—less than minimum wage), poor living conditions; and even physical abuse.[63] In 1998, a low point for Nike, CEO Phil Knight noted, "The Nike product has become synonymous with slave wages, forced overtime, and arbitrary abuse. I truly believe the American consumer doesn't want to buy products made under abusive conditions."[64] As a result, the company became actively involved with suppliers to improve conditions. By 2005, Nike became the first company in its industry to audit its factories, publish a complete list of its suppliers, and even publish findings of wrongdoing. Through its continued efforts, Nike went from being perceived as an unethical company preying on poor factory workers to a company that is actively engaged in establishing international standards of business ethics. As of 2017, Nike stood as the 12th most admired company in the world, joining the ranks of companies such as Starbucks and Walt Disney.[65]

Environmental Practices. Environmental practices can improve the way in which a business consumes resources and disposes of waste. Many organizations are now turning to *sustainable* methods, meaning practices that reduce waste, such as responsible packaging and eliminating the use of plastic bags; that recycle metal, glass, plastics, and electronics; and that cut greenhouse gas emissions, such as by using solar or wind power instead of fossil fuels.

Some international companies are actively engaged in sustainable business practices that are both legal and ethical. For instance, Google uses power from renewable energy sources, employs 200 goats to keep the grass around its Mountain View, California, campus mowed, and hosts free sustainable-cooking seminars for its employees.[66]

Volkswagen's image as an environmentally responsible firm was tarnished when it was shown to have illegally and unethically installed a piece of software code that falsely reported reduced emissions in 11 million of its diesel cars around the world. The direct costs of the scandal, in addition to extra pollution introduced into the air, include fines of as much as $18 billion imposed by governments—such as the Environmental Protection Agency in the United States—and the loss of market share and over $17 billion in the firm's market value.[67] The company was also charged with fixing the problem and bringing the cars into compliance with emission standards. In the meantime, Volkswagen's reputation had been seriously marred.

Human Rights. Human rights are rights that belong to every person. In 1948, the United Nations published the *Universal Declaration of Human Rights*, including the rights of freedom, life, liberty, and security.[68] No one shall be held in slavery or tortured, all individuals stand equally before the law and are innocent until proven guilty, and all have the right to education and many other rights. International businesses may face challenges with respect to human rights because many countries deny them to their citizens.

For instance, as the United States now softens the sanctions placed on Cuba, many protesters are concerned that U.S. companies will return to Cuba without holding the Cuban government accountable for its many human rights violations.[69] The island state operates under a repressive totalitarian government that denies its citizens the right to protest.

In another example, Thai fishing boats—unregistered with any government and operating in the international waters of the South China Sea—have routinely used slave labor to catch fish sold to U.S. companies for pet food and animal feed. Laborers come from poor neighboring countries like Cambodia and Myanmar, lured by the promise of employment, but upon arrival they are enslaved, tortured, and forced to work for years with no payment. They have no chance for escape because the boats stay in international waters, off-loading their catch onto other boats and receiving supplies while at sea.[70] In response, many international companies are seeking full transparency by allowing customers to see sourcing details throughout the supply chain. For instance, Walmart requires all suppliers to list all their facilities and designate a company representative to ensure compliance with laws and standards, and provides workers access to anonymous means of reporting abuse directly to Walmart.[71]

4.4 Important International Laws

LEARNING OBJECTIVE

Identify key laws that govern international business.

International businesses face a number of laws that influence how they can opperate in global markets, affecting everything from the way they finance operations to the way they hire employees and share customer data across country borders. Understanding these laws and their implications for international business is challenging, if not critical. While many laws exist, we introduce here a few that have a substantial impact on international businesses.

The Foreign Corrupt Practices Act

Before 1977, it was common practice for global companies to bribe foreign officials. The intent was to persuade decision makers to purchase the company's products or help tip the scales in winning a key contract. Companies kept massive amounts of cash in "slush funds" in order to make such payments off the books. In 1973, the United States became embroiled in the Watergate scandal, uncovered in June 1972 when five men hired by the Republican Committee to Reelect the President were arrested while breaking into the Washington headquarters of the Democratic National Committee.[72] The investigation widened even as the Committee and the Nixon administration attempted to cover up the extent of the conspiracy. Investigators found "massive illegal campaign contributions" had been made to President Nixon's 1972 campaign. As one consequence of the investigations, the Director of the Securities and Exchange Commission (SEC) began a systematic investigation of company slush funds.

These off-the-books accounts were illegal for public U.S. companies, and in return for lighter punishments, companies were asked to disclose any foreign bribes they had paid. According to a report by PBS's *Frontline* program, "In total more than 500 companies stepped forward, including more than 100 listed on the Fortune 500. At least $300 million in questionable payments came to light."[73] In 1976 Lockheed Corporation admitted to Congress that it had paid more than $24 million in bribes to officials in at least 15 countries. The company argued that such payments were "consistent with practices engaged in by numerous other companies abroad" and that stopping them would put the company at a competitive disadvantage.[74]

While these events were unfolding, the SEC was investigating the potential consequences of outlawing such actions. Despite the resistance of many U.S. firms, the SEC concluded that "little if any business would be lost if US firms were to stop these practices."[75] As a result, President Jimmy Carter signed the Foreign Corrupt Practices Act (FCPA) into law on December 19, 1977.

This law, the first of its kind, made it illegal to pay foreign government officials for their assistance in obtaining or retaining business. The U.S. Department of Justice details the law, noting

> *The anti-bribery provisions of the FCPA prohibit the willful use of the mails or any means of instrumentality of interstate commerce corruptly in furtherance of any offer, payment, promise to pay, or authorization of the payment of money or anything of value to any person, while knowing that all or a portion of such money or thing of value will be offered, given or promised, directly or indirectly, to a foreign official to influence the foreign official in his or her official capacity, induce the foreign official to do or omit to do an act in violation of his or her lawful duty, or to secure any improper advantage in order to assist in obtaining or retaining business for or with, or directing business to, any person.*[76]

facilitation payments payments made to speed up the actions that government officials are already bound to perform

While the FCPA bans payments to win contracts or business, it does not ban **facilitation payments**. These payments are made to speed up the actions that government officials are already bound to perform. For instance, it is legal for a foreign firm to provide payment to Indian officials to quickly obtain necessary permits or licenses.

In 1988, the FCPA was expanded to cover foreign companies that operate in or have securities (stocks or bonds) listed in the United States. Since most multinational companies have securities listed in a U.S. stock market, the law now applies to companies in most countries of the world.

One of the biggest cases involving the FCPA was the Siemens bribery scandal, in which it was discovered that Siemens, a German engineering and electronics company, had paid bribes totaling between $40 and $50 million a year to win foreign contracts in Argentina, China, Nigeria, Iraq, and other countries. Siemens agreed to pay fines of $1.6 billion to U.S. and European governments and to stop paying bribes.[77] Actions by the U.S. government in 2016–2017 with regard to the FCPA are listed in **Figure 4.8**.

In 1997, 20 years after the United States passed the FCPA, the OECD adopted an antibribery convention that made it illegal for any of its member countries to bribe a foreign official. Before the convention, Britain, France, and Germany, among others, had tax laws that not only allowed bribery, but allowed it to be written off as a business expense, reducing the company's tax bill. With the OECD members on board, the fight against public corruption has been gaining legal muscle. In 2010, the United Kingdom passed the Bribery Act. This act mirrors the FCPA but adds provisions that outlaw facilitation payments, making it the most stringent foreign antibribery law.[78]

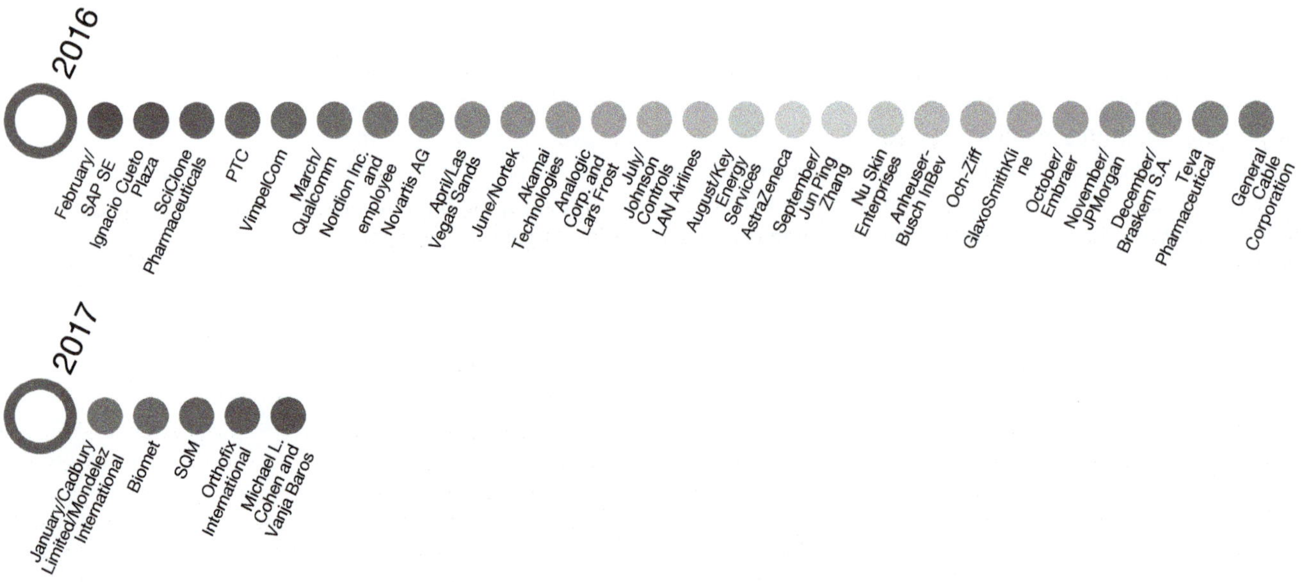

FIGURE 4.8 **SEC enforcement actions: FCPA cases** Actions taken by the SEC from 2016 to date.

Source: "SEC Enforcement Actions: FCPA Cases," U.S. Securities and Exchange Commission. www.sec.gov/spotlight/fcpa/fcpa-cases.shtml.

e-Commerce and Data Privacy

While global laws governing e-commerce and data sharing across countries are not established, regulations in the United States, China, and the European Union, among others have a significant impact on global e-businesses and data sharing, particularly regarding customers between global business units spread across the globe. For instance, e-commerce in the United States is governed by the Federal Trade Commission (FTC). The FTC regulates all forms of online advertising, data collection, and sales, and imposes penalties for companies making false claims or violating customers' rights. For example, in 2016, the FTC imposed a $950,000 fine against the Indian mobile advertising company InMobi for collecting location information on customers without their consent, and required the firm to delete all the data they gathered.[79] More recently, the United States Congress introduced legislation that would require companies to share personal Internet activities with third parties. This would allow Internet service providers to track customers' location, financial, health, and browsing data without consent.[80] Similarly, China is putting in place a host of regulations and taxes that aim to govern its citizens many transactions on foreign electronic marketplaces. It is estimated that one in five transactions in China happens on a foreign e-commerce platform.[81] The regulations increase inspections of incoming goods and aim to ensure both the health and safety of consumers and that the value-added taxes on foreign goods, which often amount to 70 percent, have been collected.

Global companies are also facing increased pressure to ensure that customers' data privacy is maintained. For instance, in October 2016, the European Union established the General Data Protection Regulation. This regulation identifies who is accountable for data security and details what data flows are allowed between EU member states and those outside the zone. In the crosshairs is WhatsApp and its global parent, Facebook. When Facebook bought WhatsApp in 2014, it asked WhatsApp to share customer information with Facebook. However, EU regulators asked the firm to stop sharing data with Facebook because the approval to share data was not in the original user agreement.[82] The regulation requires that personal data remain in the European Union unless the country or territory "ensures an adequate level of protection for the rights and freedoms of data subjects in relation to the processing of personal data."[83] Many countries have similar regulations limiting the flow of information between countries and requiring data about its nationals to be stored within the country.[84]

Summary and Case

Summary

LEARNING OBJECTIVE 4.1 Describe different types of legal systems.

Both the rule of law and the rule of the individual operate under the framework of a legal system that is divided into three types of law: constitutional law, criminal law, and commercial law. At the national level these three types of law take one of five distinct forms: customary law, theocratic law, common law, civil law, or mixed legal systems. Firms must also be aware of the different standards in countries regarding product liability, property rights, and intellectual property. Last, international companies also need to understand and navigate international laws.

LEARNING OBJECTIVE 4.2 Explain the ways in which crime and corruption affect international business.

The level of crime and corruption in a country can affect an international business. Crime can take two forms: individual crimes and the abuse of public office, or corruption. Corruption generally creates more lasting effects on international businesses than individual criminal activities. Corruption can include acts of bribery, embezzlement, and nepotism, the hiring of family members.

LEARNING OBJECTIVE 4.3 Describe the difference between illegal and unethical conduct.

Unlawful activity is determined by the different legal systems of individual countries. Unethical activity is determined by the moral principles of right and wrong an organization embraces. At times, unlawful activities may be deemed ethical, whereas lawful activities are considered unethical. Decisions about employment, environmental, and human rights practices can create ethical dilemmas that affect the growth and reputation of international companies.

LEARNING OBJECTIVE 4.4 Identify key laws that govern international business.

The Foreign Corrupt Practices Act (FCPA) of 1977 forbids payments to foreign government officials for the purpose of obtaining or retaining business. The FTC regulates all forms of online advertising, data collection, and sales, and imposes penalties for companies making false claims or violating customer's rights. Governments like the European Union are also passing laws to help ensure accountability for data security.

Case Study

Can Korean Entertainment Content Companies Compete with Pirates?

In the past 15 years the popularity of South Korean culture, especially its TV dramas, has been increasing so rapidly that it is often called *Hallyu*, or the "Korean Wave."[85] Korean dramas have become a global product. People from Saudi Arabia are watching the South Korean TV show "Person who gives happiness" from their living room couches, and U.S. viewers get excited for each new episode of the South Korean show "Boys over flowers." The show "Descendants of the Sun," which debuted in 2016, has been viewed more than 2 billion times in China. The speed and scope of South Korea's ascent was so rapid it was unimaginable just a few years ago. Yet, now the world's entertainment eye is often squarely focused on South Korea. A recent article in the *Financial Times* reported that exports of South Korean cultural products exceeded a record of $5.3 billion in 2014 and has grown at a rate in excess of 13 percent since 2010.[86]

However, the majority of international viewers who watch South Korean content online are assumed to be watching free of charge, through illegal online distributors. Websites such as mysoju.in and a host of others provide an easy way to find and view illegally acquired South Korean content. These sites do not host the content directly, but rather link international online viewers to illegally provided and often low-quality media, while enjoying advertising profits on the back of this stolen content.

Although the major South Korean network content producers and providers such as MBC, KBS, SBS work feverishly to eliminate sources of illegal online content, these efforts are like fighting the famed Hydra with its many heads.[87] When a link to a show is broken or a website is taken down, a host of others emerge in its place. Content producers have struggled to monetize their content abroad, working against significant roadblocks including online viewers' ease of accessing free content and the difficulty in taking legal actions against elusive illegal websites, often housed in foreign countries.

The strategic question for South Korean content providers is, Is there a way to successfully compete with free?

Learning Lessons from History

History often demonstrates that once a product has become available free, it is difficult to return to a direct-payment business model. In other words, a pay-per-view solution is unlikely to successfully compete with free content. To leverage their assets, South Korean content providers are likely to embrace the concept of free. In doing so, rather than selling content to users, they need to adopt a different business model. Ironically, it is one they are already very familiar with: an advertising-based business model.

Here, however, content providers have struggled to realize that free means not only providing free advertising-supported viewing but also providing a delivery mechanism that is at least as good as that used by the free competitors, including providing all South Korean content rather than only content produced by one network. Since illegal competitors like mysoju.in do not need to be bothered with the content licensing process, they are able to provide viewers full and diversified content, regardless of its producer.

South Korean content providers are striving for an unbiased third party to distribute content online that will share advertising profits. In response, OnDemandKorea has entered the market to fill this role. OnDemandKorea works just like Hulu, Amazon, or Roku, streaming original, high-quality dramas and providing revenue back to the content producers. However, it remains to be seen whether consumers of online content will be willing to watch advertisements or subscribe to the streaming service to watch high-quality content, or if they will be more likely to continue consuming content from pirate websites.

Case Discussion Questions

1. What might make consumers willing to pay for content (by watching ads or buying subscriptions) when free options are available?
2. If OnDemandKorea is going to be successful in competing with content pirates, what kind of relationships does it need to foster with South Korean content producers?
3. What is the biggest threat to OnDemandKorea?

Endnotes

[1] Farhad Manjoo, "Even Uber Couldn't Bridge the China Divide," *New York Times*, August 1, 2016. https://www.nytimes.com/2016/08/02/technology/uber-china-internet.html?_r=0

[2] Digital Egypt for Universities. A leaning and teaching resource for higher education. Stephen Quirke. University College London. 2000. www.ucl.ac.uk/museums-static/digitalegypt/administration/law.html (accessed February 17, 2016).

[3] Robert C. Ellickson and Charles Dia Thorland, "Ancient Land Law: Mesopotamia, Egypt, Israel," *Chicago-Kent Law Review* 71 (1995): 321.

[4] "North Korea Defense Chief Hyon Yong-chol 'executed'," BBC News, May 13, 2015. http://www.bbc.com/news/world-asia-32716749

[5] Jenna Fisher, "Kim Jong-un's 6 Super-duper Titles," July 18, 2012. www.csmonitor.com/World/Asia-Pacific/2012/0718/Kim-Jong-un-s-6-super-duper-titles/Marshal-of-the-Democratic-People-s-Republic-of-Korea.

[6] Graham Bowley and Jon Hurdle, "Bill Cosby's Challenge to Criminal Case Fails," *New York Times*, July 7, 2016. www.nytimes.com/2016/07/08/arts/television/bill-cosbys-challenge-to-criminal-case-fails.html.

[7] Aaron Smith, "Chipotle Exec Charged in Sweeping Cocaine Bust," CNN Money, July 6, 2016. http://money.cnn.com/2016/07/06/news/companies/chipotle-executive-cocaine-bust/

[8] The Reliable Source. The Washington Post. June 28, 2011. https://www.washingtonpost.com/blogs/reliable-source/post/whats-the-matter-with-illinois-with-blagojevich-conviction-state-has-most-imprisoned-governors/2011/06/28/AGZVjnpH_blog.html?utm_term=.ea51e2e96da4

[9] Robert J. Barro, "*Rule of Law, Democracy, and Economic Performance*," in G. O'Driscoll, K. Homes, & M. Kirkpatrick (Eds.), *2000 Index of Economic Freedom*. Washington D.C.: Heritage Foundation. (2000), 31–51.

[10] "Full Text: G20 Leaders' Communque, Hangzhou Summit," China.org.cn, September 6, 2016. www.china.org.cn/world/2016-09/06/content_39245577.htm.

[11] World Bank, *World Development Report 1997: The State in a Changing World* (New York: Oxford University Press), 1997.

[12] David Segal, "Petrobras Oil Scandal Leaves Brazilians Lamenting a Lost Dream," *New York Times*, August 7, 2015. www.nytimes.com/2015/08/09/business/international/effects-of-petrobras-scandal-leave-brazilians-lamenting-a-lost-dream.html?_r=0/.

[13] Tsvetana Paraskova, "Brazil Seizes $655M Odebrecht, OAS Assets in Petrobras Damage Compensation," Oilprice.com, August 19, 2016. http://oilprice.com/Latest-Energy-News/World-News/Brazil-Seizes-655M-Odebrecht-OAS-Assets-in-Petrobras-Damage-Compensation4372.html.

[14] Stephan Haggard and Lydia Tiede, "The Rule of Law and Economic Growth: Where Are We?" *World Development* 39 no. 5 (2011): 673–85.

[15] Louisa Lombard, "Elder Counsel," *Legal Affairs*, September/October 2005. https://www.legalaffairs.org/issues/September-October-2005/scene_lombard_sepoct05.msp (accessed June 26, 2009).

[16] Spencer Hearth MacCallum, "A Peaceful Ferment in Somalia," *The Freeman* 48, no. 6 (June 1998). http://rkba.org/libertarian/maccallum/MacCallum-Somalia98.html.

[17] Michael Van Notten, *The Law of the Somalis: A Stable Foundation for Economic and Social Development in the Horn of Africa* (Trenton, NJ: Red Sea Press, 2005).

[18] "Fintech Set to Become Game Changer for Islamic Finance," *Pakistan Observer*, February 19, 2016. http://pakobserver.net/fintech-set-to-become-game-changer-for-islamic-finance/.

[19] *Brulotte v. Thys Co.*, 379 U.S. 29 (1964).

[20] Adam Liptak, "In Spider-Man Toy Patent Case, Supreme Court Stands by Past Decision," *New York Times*, June 22, 2015. www.nytimes.com/2015/06/23/business/in-spider-man-toy-patent-case-supreme-court-stands-by-past-decision.html?_r=0.

[21] "Key Features of Common Law or Civil Law Systems," Public-Private-Partnership in Infrastructure Resource Center, World Bank Group. http://ppp.worldbank.org/public-private-partnership/legislation-regulation/framework-assessment/legal-systems/common-vs-civil-law (accessed February 19, 2016).

[22] "Geneva Conventions and Commentaries," International Committee of the Red Cross. www.icrc.org/en/war-and-law/treaties-customary-law/geneva-conventions (accessed October 2016).

[23] James Kraska and Brian Wilson, "Fighting Piracy," *Armed Forces Journal*, February 1, 2009. http://armedforcesjournal.com/fighting-piracy/.

[24] "Q&A: What Do You Do With a Captured Pirate?" BBC News, January 25, 2011. www.bbc.com/news/world-africa-11813168.

[25] "Convention of 1 July 1985 on the Law Applicable to Trusts and on their Recognition," HCCH. www.hcch.net/en/instruments/conventions/full-text/?cid=59 (accessed May 22, 2017).

[26] "United Nations Convention on Contracts for the International Sale of Goods (Vienna, 1980) (CISG)," United Nations Commission on International Trade Law. www.uncitral.org/uncitral/en/uncitral_texts/sale_goods/1980CISG.html (accessed March 2, 2016).

[27] Bernard E. Le Sage, "The Choice of an International Arbitration Forum: Contracting Parties can Avoid the Uncertainty of Foreign Courts," *Los Angeles Lawyer*, September 1998.

[28] Ya-Wei Li, "Dispute Resolution Clauses in International Contracts: An Empirical Study," *Cornell International Law Journal* 39, no. 3 (2006): Article 15. scholarship.law.cornell.edu/cilj/vol39/iss3/15. Shahla F. Ali, "Approaching the Global Arbitration Table: Comparing the Advantages of Arbitration as Seen by Practitioners in East Asia and the West," *Review of Litigation* 28, no. 4 (2009). http://ssrn.com/abstract=1542609.

[29] Dennis Campbell and Christian Campbell, *International Liability of Corporate Directors*, 2nd Edition. 2011. (Huntington, NY: Juris Publishing, Dec. 1, 2011) ISBN 1578232856.

[30] Campbell and Campbell, *International Liability of Corporate Directors*.

[31] *Daimler AG v. Bauman*, Certiorari to the United States Court of Appeals for the Ninth Circuit, January 14, 2014.

[32] Menno T. Kamminga, "Corporate Obligations under International Law," paper presented at the 71st Conference of the International Law Association, plenary session on Corporate Social Responsibility and International Law, Berlin, August 17, 2004; Catherine Putz, "Forced Labor Persists in Uzbek Cotton Harvest: Tashkent continues to coerce citizens into picking cotton, and harass human rights activists making not of it," *Diplomat*, September 25, 2015. http://thediplomat.com/2015/09/forced-labor-persists-in-uzbek-cotton-harvest/.

[33] See the Charter of Fundamental Rights of the European Union" *Consolidated Versions of the Treaty on European Union and the Treaty on the Functioning of the European Union* (Luxembourg: Office for Official Publications of the European Communities, , 2010).

[34] "EU Law." http://europa.eu/eu-law/index_en.htm (accessed February 26, 2016).

[35] David Gilbert, "Safe Harbor 2.0: Confusion Reigns as US, EU Send Mixed Messages Over 'Privacy Shield' Data-Sharing Rules," *International Business Times*, February 5, 2016. www.ibtimes.com/safe-harbor-20-confusion-reigns-us-eu-send-mixed-messages-over-privacy-shield-data-2294215#_blank.

[36] "International Law." Global Issues. United Nations, 2016. Web. 4 June 2016. http://www.un.org/en/sections/issues-depth/international-law-and-justice/index.html Accessed May 31, 2017.

[37] Courtney Hillebrecht and Scott Straus, "Last Week, the International Criminal Court Convicted a War Criminal. And That Revealed One of the ICC's Weaknesses," *Washington Post*, March 28, 2016. www.washingtonpost.com/news/monkey-cage/wp/2016/03/28/last-week-the-international-criminal-court-convicted-a-war-criminal-and-that-revealed-one-of-the-iccs-weaknesses/.

[38] Leila Abboud and Jeremy Wagstaff, "Legal Troubles, Market Realities Threaten Uber's Global Push," Reuters, October 5, 2015. www.reuters.com/article/us-uber-global-insight-idUSKCN0RZ0A220151005.

[39] Sam Levin, "Uber Lawsuits Timeline: Company Ordered to Pay out $161.9m Since 2009," *Guardian*, April 13, 2016. www.theguardian.com/technology/2016/apr/13/uber-lawsuits-619-million-ride-hailing-app.

[40] "2015 Investment Climate Statement – China," U.S. Department of State, Bureau of Economic and Business Affairs, May 2015. www.state.gov/e/eb/rls/othr/ics/2015/241518.htm.

[41] "2015 Investment Climate Statement – China."

[42] "Foreign Direct Investment," Make in India. http://www.makeinindia.com/policy/foreign-direct-investment (accessed August 29, 2016).

[43] World Bank Group, "Doing Business: Measuring Business Regulations," Ease of doing business in India, 2016 rankings. www.doingbusiness.org/data/exploreeconomies/india?topic=enforcing-contracts#dealing-with-construction-permits.

[44] "2015 Investment Climate Statement – India," U.S. Department of State, Bureau of Economic and Business Affairs, May 2015. www.state.gov/e/eb/rls/othr/ics/2015/241595.htm.

[45] World Bank Group. 2016. "Doing Business 2016: Measuring Regulatory Quality and Efficiency." Washington, DC: World Bank. © World Bank. https://openknowledge.worldbank.org/handle/10986/22771 License: CC BY 3.0 IGO. Accessed May 31, 2017.

[46] "Doing Business 2016," 14.

[47] Edmond Blair, "Eritrea Looks to Build Mining Sector to Kick-start Economy," Reuters, February 26, 2016. www.reuters.com/article/us-eritrea-mining-idUSKCN0VZ13S/.

[48] Lorraine Chow, "It's Official: 19 European Countries Say 'No' to GMOs," EcoWatch, October 5, 2015. http://ecowatch.com/2015/10/05/european-union-ban-gmos/.

[49] "Factbox: Asia, Africa Tiptoe into GMOs; Europe Reluctant," Reuters, February 16, 2016. http://in.reuters.com/article/gmo-crops-factbox-idINKCN0VO2GX/.

[50] Adario Strange, "U.S. Government Declares Hoverboards Unsafe," Mashable, February 19, 2016. http://mashable.com/2016/02/19/hoverboards-unsafe/#Iyu2zFTkWGq4/.

Seung Lee, "The US Government Says Hoverboards Are 'Unsafe,'" *Newsweek*, February 19, 2016. www.newsweek.com/us-government-says-hoverboards-are-unsafe-428635/.

[51] Roar Rude Trangbaek, "The Lego Group Expands Factories to Reach Even More Children with Great Play Experiences," Lego Group Newsroom, October 20, 2015. www.lego.com/en-us/aboutus/newsroom/2015/october/factory-expansion/.

[52] 2012 Minerals Yearbook: Botswana. US Geological Survey. December 2013. Accessed May 31, 2017. https://minerals.usgs.gov/minerals/pubs/country/2012/myb3-2012-bc.pdf

[53] Norimitsu Onishi, "'No One Is Safe': Zimbabwe Threatens to Seize Farms of Party Defectors," *New York Times*, August 24, 2016. www.nytimes.com/; "Title to Come: Property Rights Are Still Wretchedly Insecure in Africa," *The Economist*, July 16, 2016. www.economist.com/news/middle-east-and-africa/21702175-property-rights-are-still-wretchedly-insecure-africa-title-come/; Jack Newsham, "Zimbabwe May Owe $310M in 'Land Reform' Case, ICSID Says," Law360. www.law360.com/articles/758171/zimbabwe-may-owe-310m-in-land-reform-case-icsid-says (accessed March 16, 2016).

[54] Kirk Semple, "Evictions by Armed Men Rattle a Mexican Tourist Paradise," *New York Times*, August 16, 2016. www.nytimes.com/.

[55] "What Is Intellectual Property?," WIPO World Intellectual Property Report. www.wipo.int/edocs/pubdocs/en/intproperty/450/wipo_pub_450.pdf (accessed March 10, 2016).

[56] Neil Gough, "China Moves to Crack Down on Counterfeit Disney Products," *New York Times*, November 5, 2015. www.nytimes.com/2015/11/06/business/media/disney-china-trademark.html/.

[57] "China Says Disney to Get Special Trademark Protection," Reuters. November 5, 2015. www.reuters.com/article/us-walt-disney-china-idUSKCN0SU1ED20151105/.

[58] The Deadline Team, "Iger: Behind the Scenes of Disney in China," Deadline, June 7, 2013. http://deadline.com/2013/06/bob-iger-behind-the-scenes-of-disney-in-china-515526/.

[59] Valarie Tan, "Shanghai Disneyland Casts Spell on Surrounding Property Prices," Channel NewsAsia, January 29, 2016. www.channelnewsasia.com/news/asiapacific/shanghai-disneyland-casts-spell-on-surrounding-property-prices-8211754/.

[60] Jason Burke, "Ethiopian Olympic Medallist Seeks Asylum After Marathon Protest," *Guardian*, August 22, 2016. www.theguardian.com/world/2016/aug/22/ethiopian-olympic-medallist-feyisa-lilesa-seeks-asylum-after-marathon-protest-oromo-rio/.

[61] Michelle Perrett, "Patagonia Launches UK Environment Campaign in London's Shoreditch," *Event Magazine*, November 2, 2016. www.eventmagazine.co.uk/patagonia-launches-uk-environment-campaign-londons-shoreditch/brands/article/1414216/.

[62] Serina Sandhu, "Ikea Sells Toys Designed by Kids to Raise Money for Save the Children and Unicef," *The Independent*, October 19, 2015. www.independent.co.uk/news/uk/home-news/ikea-sells-toys-designed-by-kids-to-raise-money-for-save-the-children-and-unicef-a6713181.html/.

[63] Jennifer Alsever, "Equity for Coffee Farmers," *Fortune*, December 29, 2015. http://fortune.com/2015/12/29/coffee-farmers-equity-fair-trade/.

[64] Jeffrey Ballinger, "The New Free-Trade Heel: Nike's Profits Jump on the Backs of Asian Workers," *Harper's Magazine*, August 1992; Bob Herbert, "Brutality in Vietnam," *New York Times*, March 28, 1997. www.nytimes.com/1997/03/28/opinion/brutality-in-vietnam.html/.

[65] John H. Cushman Jr., "Nike Pledges to End Child Labor and Apply U.S. Rules Abroad," *New York Times*, May 13, 1998. www.nytimes.com/1998/05/13/business/international-business-nike-pledges-to-end-child-labor-and-apply-us-rules-abroad.html/.

[66] "World's Most Admired Companies Report," *Fortune*, 2017. http://beta.fortune.com/worlds-most-admired-companies/list. Accessed May 30, 2017.

[67] Claudine Beaumont, "Google Hires Goats to Cut Grass," *The Telegraph*, May 8, 2009. www.telegraph.co.uk/technology/google/5297097/Google-hires-goats-to-cut-grass.html; "How We Care for Googlers,"

Google Careers. www.google.com/about/careers/how-we-care-for-googlers/ (accessed May 22, 2017).

[68] Tom Lavell, "Volkswagen's Europe Market Share Falls for First Time Since 2007," Bloomberg Business, January 15, 2016. www.bloomberg.com/news/articles/2016-01-15/volkswagen-s-europe-market-share-falls-for-first-time-since-2007/.

[69] "Universal Declaration of Human Rights," General Assembly resolution 217 A, United Nations General Assembly, December 10, 1948. www.un.org/en/universal-declaration-human-rights/.

[70] "Cuba Visit: Obama and Castro Spar Over Human Rights," BBC News, March 22, 2016. www.bbc.com/news/world-latin-america-35867590/.

[71] Ian Urbina, "'Sea Slaves': The Human Misery That Feeds Pets and Livestock," *New York Times*, July 17, 2015. www.nytimes.com/2015/07/27/world/outlaw-ocean-thailand-fishing-sea-slaves-pets.html?_r=0/.

[72] "Sourcing Standards & Resources: Standards for Suppliers," Walmart. http://corporate.walmart.com/sourcing-standards-resources (accessed August 30, 2016).

[73] M. Schudson, "Notes on Scandal and the Watergate Legacy," *American Behavioral Scientist* 47, no. 9 (2004): 1231–38.

[74] Matthew Vree et al., "Corruption in the Crosshairs: A Brief History of International Anti-Bribery Legislation," Frontline World, April 7, 2009. http://www.pbs.org/frontlineworld/stories/bribe/2009/04/timeline.html/.

[75] "SCANDALS: Lockheed's Defiance: A Right to Bribe?" *Time Magazine*, August 18, 1975. http://content.time.com/time/magazine/article/0,9171,917751-1,00.html; "Japan: Bribery Shokku at the Top," *Time Magazine*, August 9, 1976. http://content.time.com/time/magazine/article/0,9171,914484,00.html.

[76] Elliot L. Richardson, "Memorandum for the President: Questionable Corporate Payments Abroad," The White House, June 8, 1976. www.tc.pbs.org/frontlineworld/stories/bribe/images/pdf/richardson_memo_1.pdf.

[77] "Foreign Corrupt Practices Act: An Overview," U.S. Department of Justice. www.justice.gov/criminal-fraud/foreign-corrupt-practices-act/ (accessed March 30, 2016).

[78] Eric Lichtblau and Carter Dougherty, "Siemens to Pay $1.34 Billion in Fines," *New York Times*, December 15, 2008. www.nytimes.com/2008/12/16/business/worldbusiness/16siemens.html

[79] The Bribery Act 2010, Ministry of Justice www.gov.uk/government/uploads/system/uploads/attachment_data/file/181762/bribery-act-2010-guidance.pdf (accessed March 30, 2016).

[80] Sadhana Chathurvedula, "FTC Tells InMobi to Pay $950,000 Penalty," Livemint, June 23, 2016. www.livemint.com/Consumer/C1tNu9hGCF1wEdJj9dHwoM/FTC-tells-InMobi-to-pay-950000-penalty.html/.

[81] Richard Adhikari, "Consumer Advocates Bemoan Senate Vote to Lift ISP Privacy Restrictions," *E-Commerce Times*, March 25, 2017. www.ecommercetimes.com/story/84407.html/.

[82] Celine Ge, "China's Cross-Border e-Commerce Trade Facing Uncertainties Amid Government Regulation," *Southern China Morning Post*, September 8, 2016. www.scmp.com/business/companies/article/2017646/chinas-cross-border-e-commerce-trade-facing-uncertainties-amid/.

[83] Reuters, "EU Data Protection Watchdogs Warn WhatsApp, Yahoo on Privacy," *Fortune*, October 29, 2016. http://fortune.com/2016/10/29/eu-data-protection-yahoo-whatsapp/.

[84] "Sending Personal Data Outside the European Economic Area (Principle 8)," Information Commissioners Office. https://ico.org.uk/for-organisations/guide-to-data-protection/principle-8-international/ (accessed May 22, 2017).

[85] "Lost in the Splinternet," *The Economist*, November 6, 2016. www.economist.com/news/international/21709531-left-unchecked-growing-maze-barriers-internet-will-damage-economies-and/.

[86] "CJ E&M to Open 'Hallyu' Channels in Malaysia, Vietnam, Hong Kong," *Yonhap News*, April 3, 2017. http://english.yonhapnews.co.kr/culture sports/2017/04/03/0701000000AEN20170403003900315.html/.

[87] Jung-a Song, "China Awash with Korean Wave Fever 'Hallyu' Extends Reach Beyond Films and K-pop into Fashion, Food and Beauty Products," *Financial Times*, April 12, 2016. www.ft.com/content/167338ec-fa0b-11e5-8e04-8600cef2ca75/.

[88] Choi Mun-hee, "China Circulates Pirated Version of Hallyu Contents while Retailing S. Korea," Business Korea, March 23, 2017. www.businesskorea.co.kr/english/news/national/17615-two-faced-china-china-circulates-pirated-version-hallyu-contents-while-retailing/.

CHAPTER **5**

Economic Systems

AFP Footage/Getty Image

Introduction

The health and growth of a country's economy play a significant role in creating the business opportunities available there. For instance, China's recent rapid growth has created millions of new middle-class consumers who command rising levels of *discretionary income*, or money available to spend on nonessential items. In contrast, Japan's slow growth over the past two decades has resulted in limited spending power and consumption. It follows that international opportunities often depend on the economic conditions in a given country, but how do you assess the health of an economy? How do you know whether business opportunities are increasing or decreasing there? And, if an economy is already healthy and growing, what can that country's leaders do to manage it and maintain that growth?

Since World War II, governments have been using two major tools to speed up or rein in economic growth: fiscal policy and monetary policy. To use these policies, of course, a government must constantly measure the economy's output and monitor changes in its growth rate. We'll discuss all these topics and more in this chapter.

LEARNING OBJECTIVES

After you explore this chapter you will be able to:

1. **Describe** how economic systems differ
2. **Compare** ways to measure countries' economic activities or output
3. **Describe** the tools governments use to slow down or speed up their economies
4. **Explain** how inflation, deflation, and the concentration of wealth affect international business opportunities

5.1 Understanding Economic Systems

LEARNING OBJECTIVE

Describe how economic systems differ.

An important consideration for international businesses is the type of economic system a country has. **Market-based economies**, for instance, encourage individuals and businesses to determine how much they privately consume and invest in the economy. **Capitalism** is an economic system in which factors of trade and production are controlled by private owners rather than by the state. **Capital** generally refers to a resource that can serve to generate wealth, such as factories, equipment, investment accounts, software, land, and education. In a capitalist economic system, individuals have property rights, meaning they can own capital, make decisions about how to use it, and reap the returns or losses of their business activities.

A significant by-product of property rights and capital ownership is that individuals can generate personal wealth from their capital. During the 1800s, many industries **industrialized**, or began building businesses and manufacturing on a large scale. As a result of industrialization, individuals who owned and had control over valuable capital resources became extremely wealthy. One of the most famous capitalists in history is John D. Rockefeller, who founded Standard Oil in 1870. As a partner in Standard Oil Company, Rockefeller owned land, rights to petroleum, and the equipment needed to refine oil into its profitable by-products. By the late 1800s Rockefeller controlled 91 percent of all oil production in the United States, and, as a result, he became the first billionaire in history. Adjusted for inflation, Rockefeller's personal fortune is estimated to have been somewhere between $300 billion and $600 billion in today's dollars.[1] Microsoft founder Bill Gates is the richest person in the United States today, with assets of about $75 billion, and his wealth, like Rockefeller's, is the result of his ownership of personal capital, in this case Microsoft stock.[2] Not only has Gates's ownership of Microsoft generated billions for him and other shareholders, but his company's inventions have also changed many of the ways in which business is done.

Proponents of capitalism argue that the opportunity to earn personal wealth is what drives people to experiment with new ideas, create new inventions, and work hard to bring those inventions to market, thereby increasing their ownership of personal capital—which is thus the incentive that drives the economy. Scottish philosopher Adam Smith (1723–1790) claimed that people who own capital and use it to generate personal wealth and deliver goods and services desired by society guide the economy toward a state of balance, called *equilibrium*, as if by an "invisible hand." This invisible hand removes inferior contenders from the market and encourages innovation and advancement, creating long-term market efficiency as consumers and investors allocate resources to the best performers in the market.[3] Because the system is regulated by the market forces of supply and demand, capitalism is also known as a **market-based economy**. Customer demand in the market for a good or service determines how much of that good or service should be produced; if demand increases, businesses step in to increase the supply or invent new products that create demand.

The success or failure of international businesses operating in countries with market-based economies is determined by their ability to respond to market forces. However, not all economies are market based. While capitalism operates under an "invisible hand," authoritarian states often operate under an "obvious hand," where the regime plans and controls all economic activity. In other words, the government determines where investments should be made, sets production targets, and allocates production tasks to workers.

The most common command-based system evolved out of the inequality inherent in capitalist systems. Specifically, many argue that although capitalist systems allow individuals to own and control capital, they have significant flaws. For instance, Karl Marx, an author, philosopher, and the founder of communism, argued that capitalism would lead to dramatic inequality between the relatively few rich capitalists who owned the means of production and the thousands of poor workers they employed. In turn, this inequality would open the door to a widespread worker revolution. The outcome of the revolution, Marx argued, would be a political system called communism, in which the workers collectively owned the factors of production, and the production outputs—goods and services—were allocated to workers based on their needs.

Capitalism operates under market forces, whereas communism calls for the workers themselves to organize the economy, but this means no single person is in charge—a characteristic of communism often perceived as a weakness. In reality, most "communist" states actually lean more toward socialism. Under socialism, the central government plans the economy, owns the factors of production, and distributes the goods and services made.

Because of the governmental or collective control over what is produced and how it is allocated in society under socialism and communism, they are often referred to as command-based

market-based economies an economic system in which prices of goods and services determine decisions regarding investment, production, and distribution

capitalism an economic system in which factors of trade and production are controlled by private owners rather than by the state

capital a resource that can serve to generate wealth, such as factories, equipment, investment accounts, software, land, and education

industrialized the process of building businesses and manufacturing on a large scale

market-based economy an economic system in which factors of trade and production are controlled by private owners rather than by the state; also known as *capitalism*

systems. These systems differ from market-based systems in that they value the collective above the individual; eliminate or reduce private ownership; and allocate investment, production, and consumption based on a central plan. For instance, in 1928, Joseph Stalin, General Secretary of the Central Committee of the Communist Party of the Soviet Union, announced the country's first "five-year plan" for the Russian economy. It was designed to increase industrial production by 350 percent by switching workers from farms to industry. The plan was successful in meeting its target and was followed by twelve more such plans, ending only with the fall of the Soviet Union in 1991.[4] Log in to WileyPLUS to watch a video that will help you understand how to measure a country's economic health.

WileyPLUS

See Whiteboard Video:
Measuring Economic Health

While the various economic systems control production in different ways, they produce the same thing: output (see the video on determining economic health). International business managers need to understand not only how to work in different economic systems but also how to identify underlying economic trends. For example, according to *Forbes* magazine, China had 66 billionaires in 2009. Just four years later, that number had increased to 168, and by 2015 it had reached 213.[5] Similarly, China's total output of goods and services was worth just $1.02 trillion in 1998, but it has since risen dramatically, reaching $10.36 trillion in 2015.[6] Where did China's more than tenfold increase in output come from? And how did so many people become wealthy so quickly?

A country increases output in any of three ways: (1) by increasing the supply and efficiency of *labor*, (2) by increasing the amount of investment or *capital* in the economy, or (3) by increasing *total factor productivity*, or the efficiency with which labor and capital work together.

How do market-based and command economies increase the supply and efficiency of labor? They can encourage people to work more hours or to work harder and acquire more experience. They can also add more advanced skills to the existing labor force. Formal and informal education, training, apprenticeships, and similar activities are all aimed at increasing the skill of workers, enabling them to produce at a higher rate of output.

Another option is for governments to increase the supply of workers. For instance, if a government increases the retirement age, the supply of labor increases because older people who might otherwise have retired now stay on the job longer. Allowing immigrants to enter and work in a country also increases the supply of labor. An estimated 250,000 Malaysians cross into Singapore each day to work and then return home each night,[7] significantly increasing Singapore's labor supply.

Many impoverished countries are tempted to use child labor to increase their labor supply. Children are generally given low-skill, manual jobs like textile manufacturing, as shown in **Figure 5.1**, tending livestock, weaving rugs, and even engaging in grueling factory work. Yet,

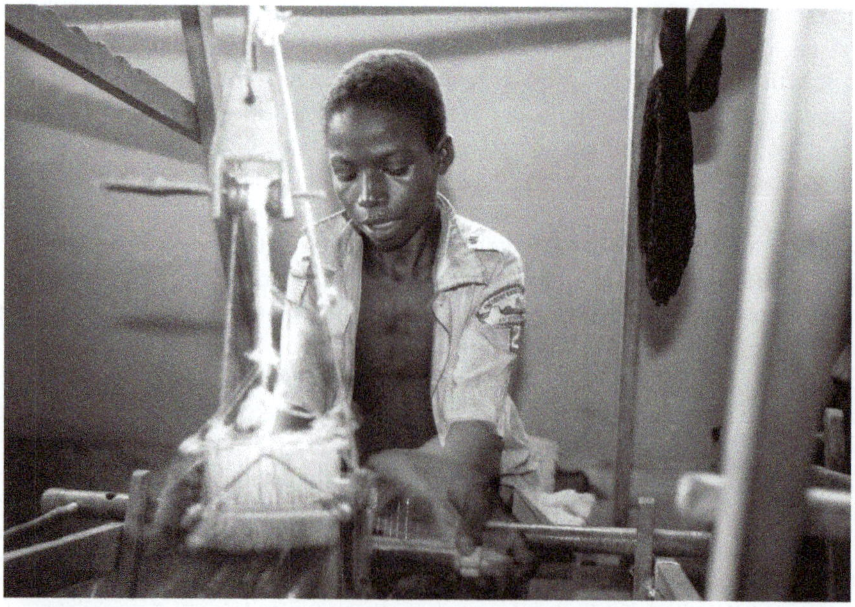

H. Christoph/ullstein bild/Getty Images

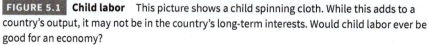

FIGURE 5.1 Child labor This picture shows a child spinning cloth. While this adds to a country's output, it may not be in the country's long-term interests. Would child labor ever be good for an economy?

Pulsar Images/Alamy Stock Photo

Scott Wallace/Getty Images

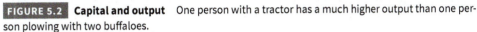

FIGURE 5.2 **Capital and output** One person with a tractor has a much higher output than one person plowing with two buffaloes.

although using child labor to produce goods and services increases the short-term output of an economy, it isn't in a country's long-term interests because it usually denies children the opportunity for education, limiting the skills they can develop. Moreover, the types of labor in which children are commonly employed can injure and permanently damage their bodies, limiting their future output.

In addition to increasing the supply of labor and the skill level of workers in a country, a larger supply of capital can also increase output per person. Capital includes monetary investments in factories, equipment, and technology. For instance, a construction worker using a hammer can drive only a certain number of nails per hour. With a pneumatic nail gun, however, the same worker can drive many more nails in the same hour. Similarly, a tractor allows one person to produce much more output than someone using two buffaloes to plow, as shown in **Figure 5.2**.

Finally, in addition to more labor and capital, increased **total factor productivity (TFP)** can raise output. TFP measures the efficiency with which labor and capital come together. For example, in 1913 Henry Ford increased the output of his Michigan factory by adopting the assembly line for auto production. In doing so he created a model for modern factories that aimed to minimize the time and effort between production steps. Instead of workers walking from car to car, the cars moved from worker to worker, enabling workers to keep necessary tools and parts at their workstations instead of dragging them around a factory floor. The change cut assembly time from twelve hours to two and a half.[8]

total factor productivity (TFP) a measure of the efficiency with which labor and capital are utilized together

5.2 Measuring Output

LEARNING OBJECTIVE

Compare ways to measure countries' economic activities or output.

How do international business leaders measure a country's economic performance? Several measures help determine how well a country is performing.

The growth of a population's wealth and spending often creates new markets and business opportunities. For example, as China's economy has grown, its market for automobiles has become the world's largest, with over 20 million vehicles sold in 2015[9]; the smartphone market in China grew to over 100 million units sold per quarter in 2015.[10] Companies seeking to expand internationally thus typically monitor the economic growth of target countries—both how wealthy individuals are and how fast their wealth increases. As income increases, people's discretionary spending increases, and they demand both more goods and services, and higher quality. Because economic growth typically translates into a rough measure of opportunity in a country, it is a key proxy for the health of a country's economy.

WileyPLUS

See Video: Measuring a Country's Economic Performance

Output per person is a common measure of the strength of an economy, and when looked at over time, it is a good way to observe growth and potential growth, indicating where multinational companies should invest and grow and where they should leave. For instance, many luxury brands such as Gucci, Hermes, and Rolex observed the increase of output in China and rushed into the market. On the other hand, Clorox, a U.S. company, observed the contraction in the economy of Venezuela and decided to exit the market in 2014.[11] We commonly measure output in different ways, but with the PEST framework, the ultimate goal of the economic component is to understand what opportunities international businesses will have in a particular country.

Gross Domestic Product

gross domestic product (GDP) the value of finished goods and services produced within a country's borders

A key measure of output is the **gross domestic product (GDP)**, the value of finished goods and services produced within a country's borders, whether by domestic or foreign companies.[12] A country's *GDP per capita*, or the level of output per person, can be calculated by dividing the GDP by the country's population. GDP per capita is a useful measure for comparing the output of different countries, particularly those that differ in size. It allows international businesses to predict the level of discretionary income consumers are likely to have in a country and is a rough first attempt to measure the potential opportunity. **Figure 5.3** presents a map showing GDP per capita values worldwide.

One key point for measuring GDP is identifying the *final* goods and services produced in the country. For instance, the various component parts that go into a car—such as door handles, steel frames, windows, and engines—are not counted in GDP until they have been incorporated into the final product in the form of a car. Note that the value of a used car does not

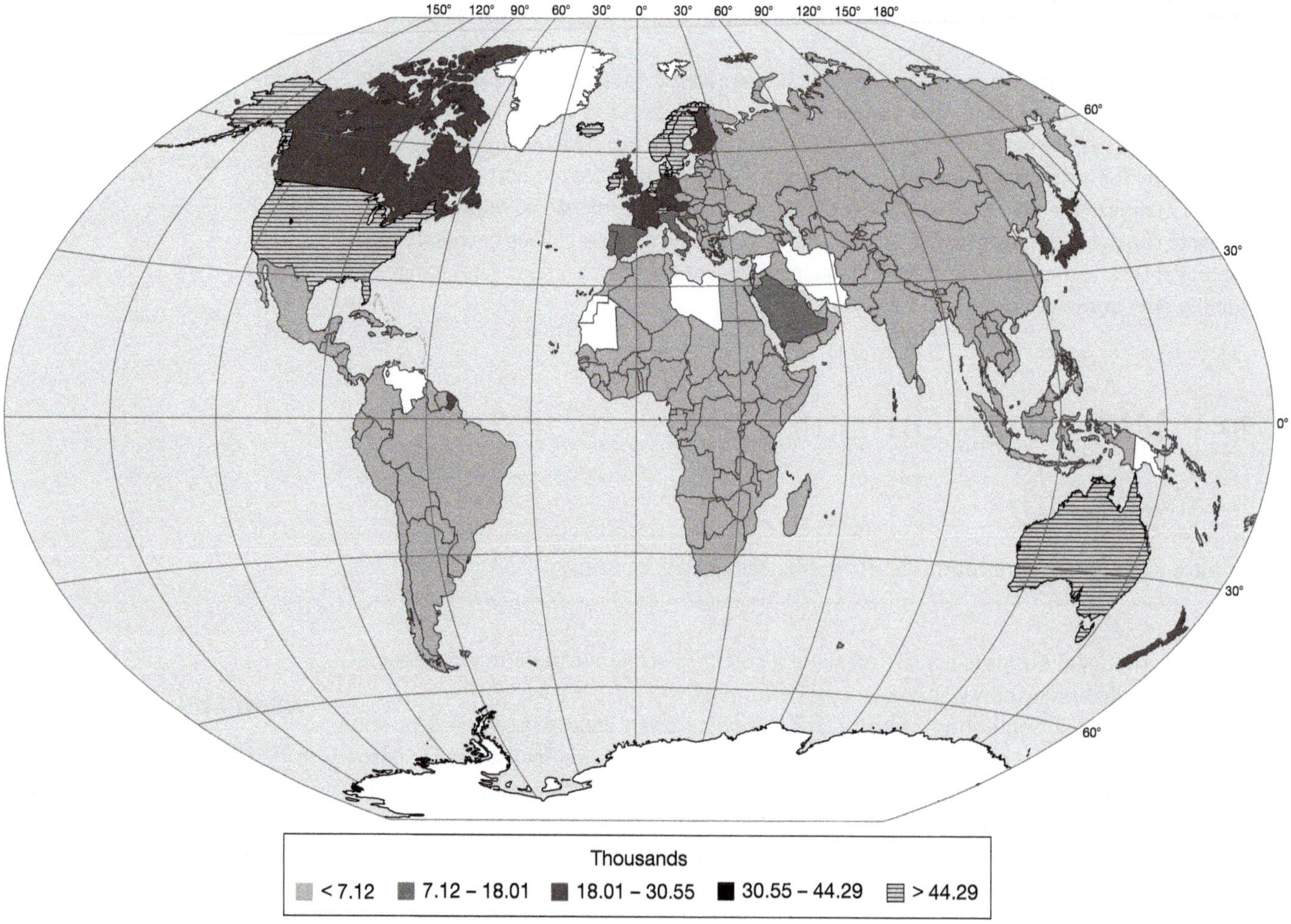

FIGURE 5.3 **GDP per capita** This map shows GDP per capita, in U.S. dollars, of countries across the globe. **Source:** World Bank, "GDP per capital (current US$)." Data from World Bank national accounts data and OECD National Accounts data files. http://data.worldbank.org/indicator/NY.GDP.PCAP.CD?end=2015&start=2015&view=map&year=2015.

count in GDP even if it is sold to a new owner, because its value was already included in GDP in the year the car was produced.

Another key point is that GDP focuses on domestic production. If Toyota—a Japanese firm—builds some of its cars in the United States, this output counts toward the United States' GDP, not Japan's, even though the goods produced are owned by a foreign firm. On the flip side, if GE—a U.S. company—builds aircraft engines in Europe, these products are not counted in the U.S. GDP; rather, they count in the country where GE's factory is located. For the purposes of calculating GDP, who owns the asset producing the output doesn't matter; what *does* matter is where the output is produced.

Gross National Product

A second way to measure the opportunities for international businesses present in a foreign country is a measure that takes into account the international income of a country. This measure is captured as the **gross national product (GNP)**; this differs from GDP in that it counts the output that domestic companies make abroad. Specifically, GNP adds net income from foreign assets owned by nationals, also called net income receipts (NRs), and subtracts net payments to foreign owners, also called net payment outflows (NPs):

gross national product (GNP) is the total value of final goods and services provided by a country; it equals the gross domestic product plus the net payment outflows of a country

$$GNP = GDP + NR - NP$$

In the United States, the difference between GDP and GNP is relatively small because the income received in from foreign assets owned by U.S. individuals and the payments made to foreigners are similar. For instance, in 2014, foreigners owned about $6 billion more ($5,539.3 million) of U.S. assets than U.S. nationals owned of foreign assets, although that gap has been growing over recent years, as shown in **Figure 5.4**.

In some countries, however, the GDP and GNP are quite different. In Ireland, for example, a large portion of the economy is owned by foreigners. Thus, while Ireland's GDP is relatively high, when the net income earned by foreigners is removed, the GNP is significantly lower. This means that Ireland may offer fewer opportunities for international businesses than would be expected by looking at GDP. As shown in **Figure 5.5**, GDP in Ireland in 2014 was about US$245 billion, whereas GNP was just $208 billion.[13] This means that roughly 15 percent of Ireland's output actually goes to foreign owners.

Other Measures of Prosperity and Opportunity

While GDP and GNP allow international businesses a rough way to begin understanding opportunity in different countries, they are far from perfect measures of a country's overall prosperity. First, they don't measure people's well-being. If a worker at General Motors takes time off to go

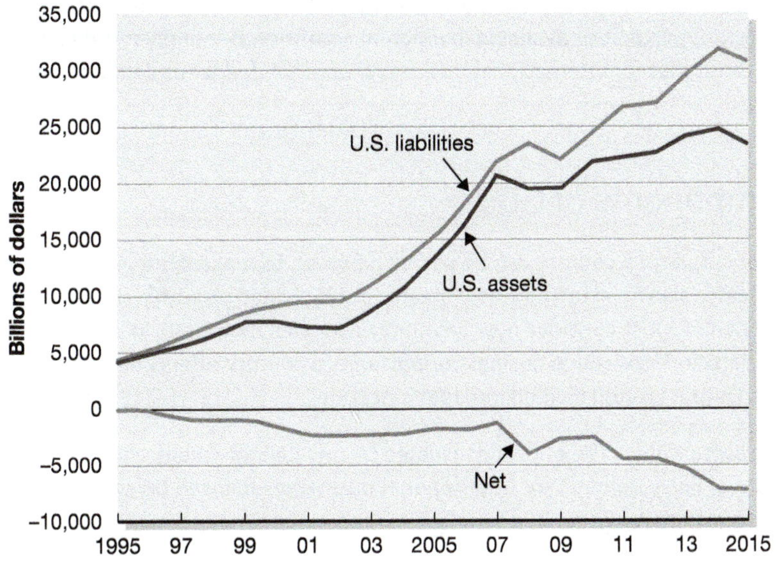

FIGURE 5.4 U.S. net international investment position This figure depicts the difference in U.S. assets and U.S. liabilities from 1995 to 2015. **Source:** "International Investment Position Graph: U.S. Net International Investment Position at the End of the Year," U.S. Department of Commerce, Bureau of Economic Analysis. www.bea.gov/newsreleases/international/intinv/iip_glance.htm. Accessed June 2, 2017.

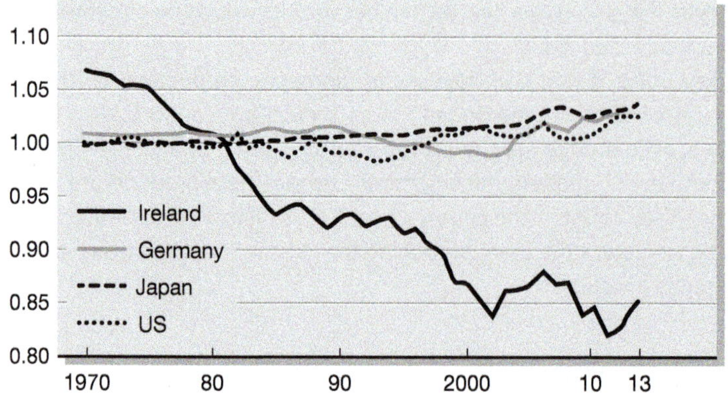

FIGURE 5.5 Ireland's ratio of GNP to GDP

Source: Valentina Romei. "Ireland is the wealthiest economy in Europe . . . or not." Financial Times Blog. May 13, 2015. http://blogs.ft.com/ftdata/2015/05/ http://blogs.ft.com/ftdata/files/2015/05/G109X-Datawatch-Wed.png

on vacation or care for a sick child, output and GDP will decrease, but the worker (and the sick child) will benefit. A person who delays entering the workforce in favor of getting additional education won't be directly boosting GDP, but he or she will be building the foundation for a better life in the future.

GDP also fails to tell us who is benefiting from a country's production. If a very few people own all the factors of output, they can claim all the benefits of increasing it. When wealth is concentrated, opportunities for international businesses also are concentrated. The rich get richer while the poor get poorer. This could limit opportunities for international businesses that focus on traditional goods but increase opportunities for international businesses that focus on luxury goods such as private aircraft, yachts, private banking, and high-end fashion. Finally, producing a particular output could require companies to destroy the environment, force child labor, or endanger the lives of workers. In cases like these, opportunities might increase in the short run, but long-term opportunities for international businesses may be restricted.

Moreover, measuring GDP can be problematic. Imagine you mow your neighbor's lawn. Does this count toward GDP? It should—you provided a finished service—but if you are paid in cash and operate outside a lawn care business, your output is difficult to track. Such informal cash transactions are generally not reported on tax forms or anywhere else where their value can be tallied. This kind of "shadow" economic activity is estimated to account for about 7 percent of the U.S. economy and about 25 percent of Greece's economy (see **Figure 5.6**)—and even those values are small compared with the estimated 68 percent of the Bolivian economy that operates "underground."[14]

Because of the disconnect between GDP and actual well-being, several alternative measures of prosperity are also useful to international businesses. One of these, developed by the United Nations, is the **Human Development Index (HDI)**, a broad measure of well-being focused on health, education, and economics (see **Figure 5.7**). The goal of this measure is to look beyond simple economics and output by focusing on the presence or absence of opportunity.

Human Development Index (HDI) a measure used to rank countries into tiers of human development, composed of factors including life expectancy, education, and per capita income

All of these measures—GDP, GNP, HDI—provide different ways for international businesses to assess likely opportunities available in different countries. But understanding the effects on specific opportunities for international business requires a deeper understanding of how they are calculated.

The Components of GDP

Knowing the output of a country can be useful; however, to make strategic decisions, international businesses also need to know how that output is divided up within the economy. In other words, companies must consider how a country allocates its output to different activities in order to understand how much business opportunity a country offers and where those opportunities are. Output is often divided into four categories:

1. *Private consumption:* the output consumed by private individuals and businesses; a good measure of likely demand for international businesses focused on selling goods and services to consumers

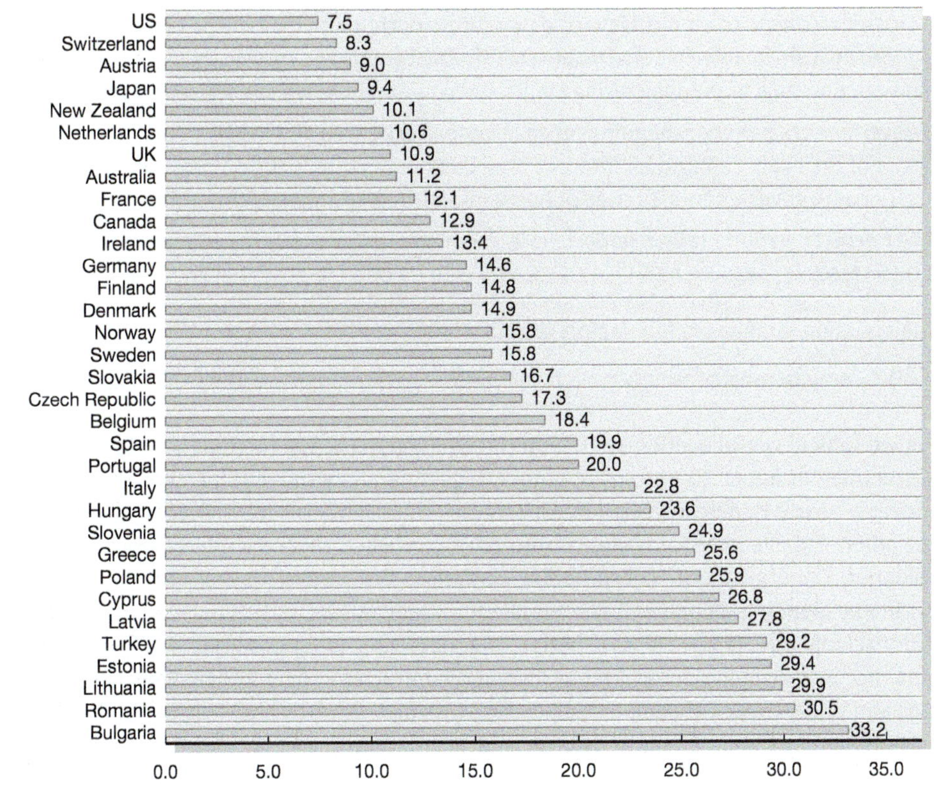

FIGURE 5.6 "Shadow" economic activity as a percentage of GDP The percentage of the GDP that is underground, or "shadow" economic activity, is difficult to measure but may be an important part of a country's output. **Source:** Dominik H. Enste, "The Shadow Economy in Industrial Countries," IZA World of Labor, February 2015. http://wol.iza.org/articles/shadow-economy-in-industrial-countries-1.pdf

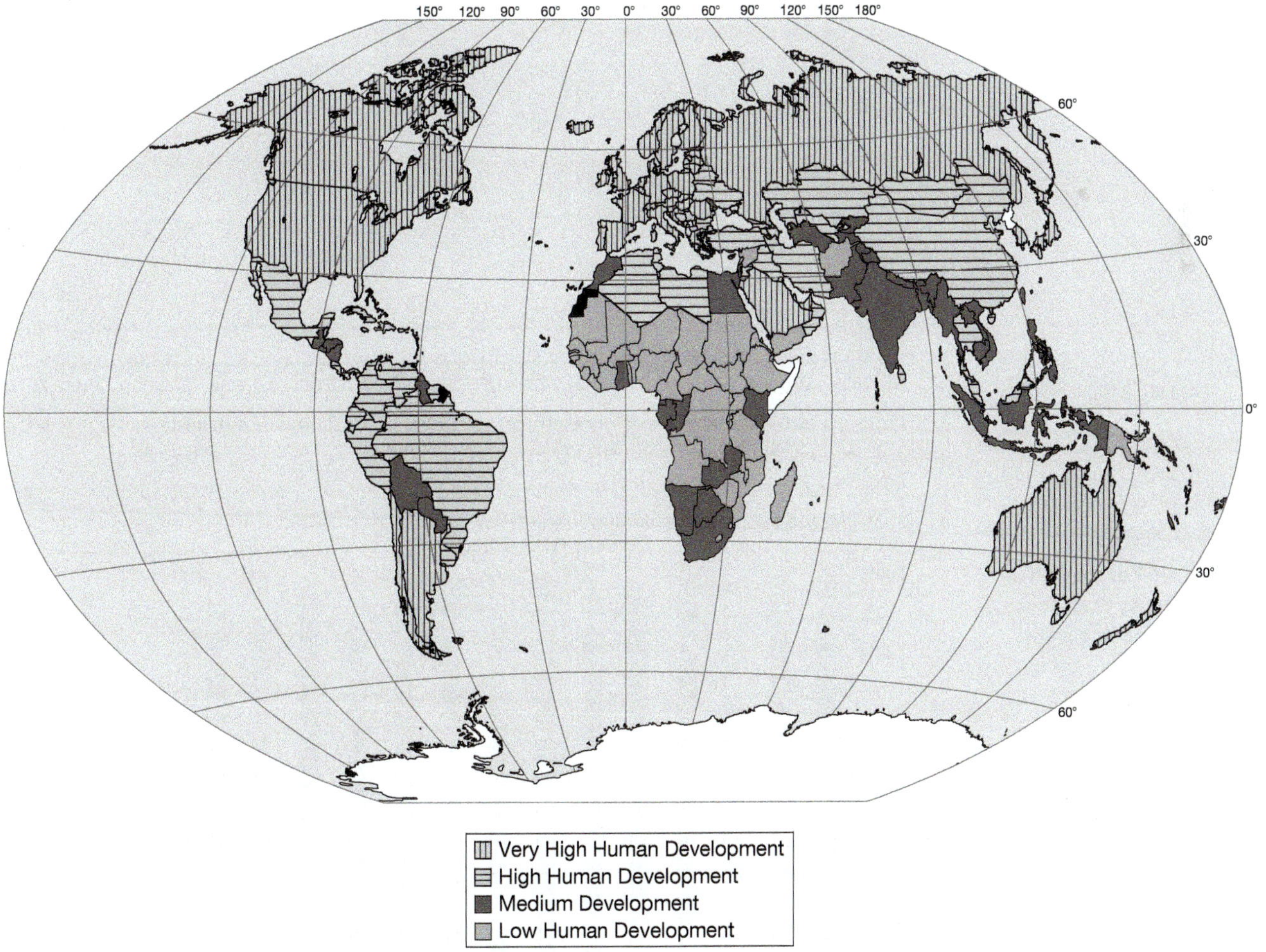

FIGURE 5.7 HDI World Index The Human Development Index. **Source:** International Human Development Indicators. The United Nations Development Programme. http://hdr.undp.org/en/countries accessed June 2, 2017.

2. *Gross investment*: the output invested into future output and that will be consumed later; a good measure for international businesses that sell goods and services focused on factors of production such as manufacturing plants and equipment as well as education and training,
3. *Government spending*: spending on government expenses and investments; a good measure of the likely demand for international businesses that focus on providing goods and services to governments, such as building infrastructure and sourcing military equipment
4. *Net exports*: exports minus imports in a given country; a proxy that allows international businesses to measure how likely a country is to be open to potential imports.

In equation form, these four factors look like this:

GDP = private consumption + gross investment + government spending + net exports.

If we look at the allocation of U.S. output in **Figure 5.8**, we see that private consumption accounts for about 70 percent of output, investment is around 15 percent, government spending is nearly 20 percent, and net exports are −5 percent—actually reducing overall GDP. These amounts have been fairly stable from 2012 through 2014 as the chart below indicates. Considering China's output, consumption comprises 35 percent; investment, 48 percent; government spending, 13 percent; and net exports, 4 percent.

Unpacking GDP leads us to a better understanding of opportunity for international companies. For instance, international defense contractors such as the French company Thales and pharmaceutical companies like the Swiss firm Novartis are likely to monitor levels of government spending because defense and health care are large government expenses.

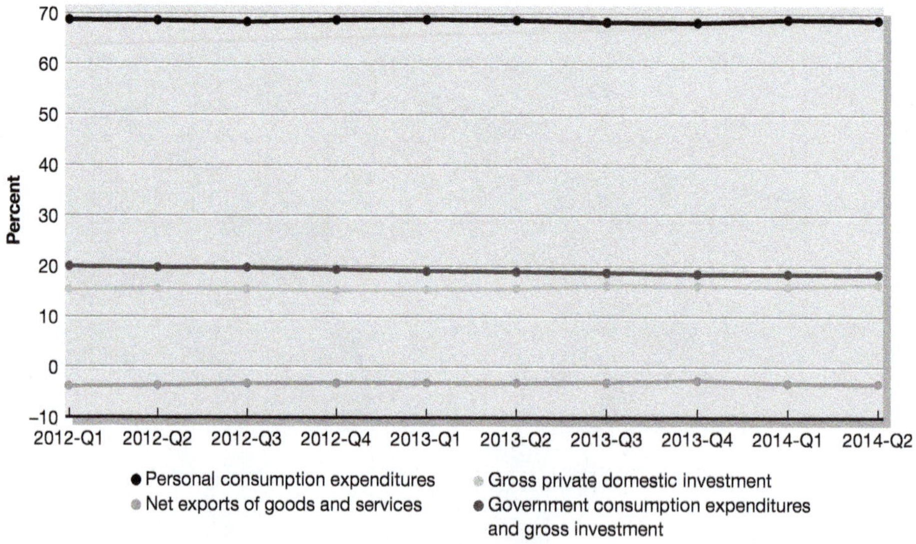

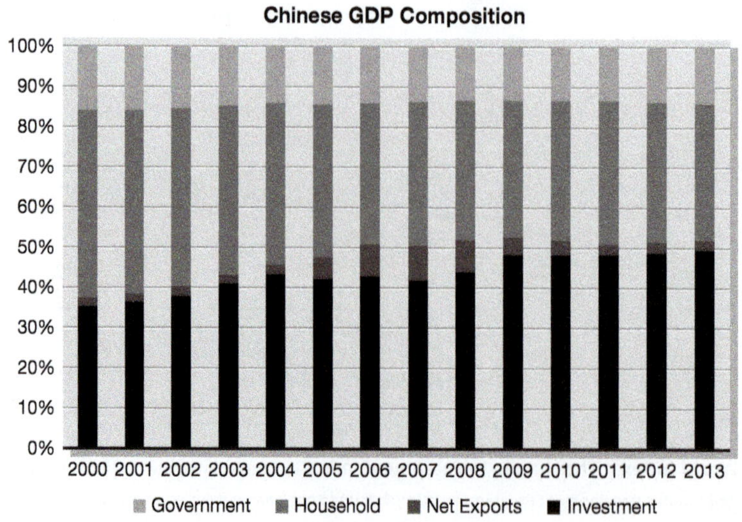

FIGURE 5.8 **GDP of the United States and China, by type: consumption, investment, government, and net exports** Using what you know about the economic systems in the United States and China, estimate the levels of consumption, investment, government, and net exports for each country. **Source:** Data from "GDP & Personal Income: National Data," U.S. Department of Commerce, Bureau of Economic Analysis. Accessed June 2, 2017. www.bea.gov/iTable/iTable.cfm?ReqID=9&step=1#reqid=9&step=3&isuri=1&903=14.

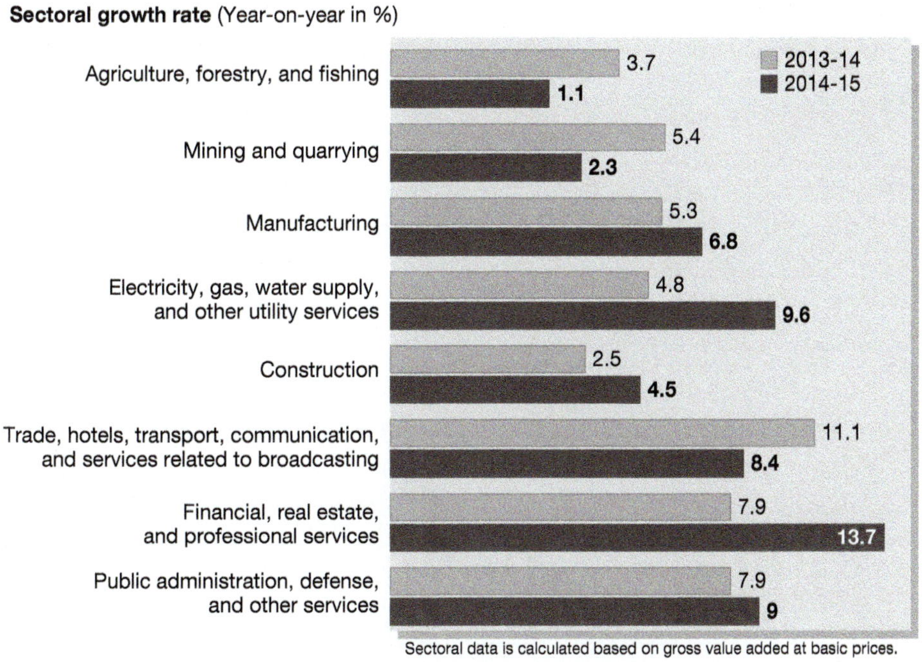

FIGURE 5.9 **Breakdown of GDP in India by sector in 2014 and 2015** **Source:** Asit Ranjan Mishra, "New GDP Measure Puts India's Economy at $2.1 Trillion," *Live Mint*, February 10, 2015. www.livemint.com/Politics/xziKtmtOxBJntZb41p2hDL/India-GDP-seen-surging-74-in-data-that-has-puzzled-economi.html.

On the other hand, international oil service providers like the United States' Halliburton and construction firms like Samsung Heavy Industries are likely to focus on levels of investment in other countries. Finally, international retail firms for both clothing, like PriMark of Ireland, and food, such as McDonald's, are keenly interested in levels of personal consumption.

Moreover, GDP is often broken down into other categories such as agriculture, services, manufacturing, and construction. This breakdown helps international businesses identify trends in their particular market sectors. **Figure 5.9** shows how India's mining sector grew more slowly in 2015 than in 2014, whereas its utility services increased nearly twice as fast in 2015 compared with 2014. An international business looking to sell electrical infrastructure equipment needs to recognize the accelerated growth in India and capitalize on that opportunity.

5.3 Governmental Economic Controls

WileyPLUS

See Whiteboard Video: Fiscal and Monetary Policy

LEARNING OBJECTIVE

Describe the tools governments use to slow down or speed up their economies.

Throughout most of modern history, world output per person has been growing, as shown by the positive percentages for the past 700 years displayed in **Figure 5.10**.

During periods of growth, well-being is likely to increase. However, when output shrinks rather than expands, general well-being also declines. If such a period of world GDP contraction lasts for at least two consecutive quarters within a year, it is called a **recession**. If the contraction is particularly long-lived or very severe, it is called a **depression**. In the past 30 years, only three periods—1990, 1998, and 2008–2009—qualified as recessions, during which the world GDP per person was contracting. Though it is useful to consider the measures of overall global growth and contraction, expansion and contraction of an economy are often localized within countries. For instance, the International Monetary Fund suggests that the world economy will increase at about 3.5 percent annually, but Venezuela, Brazil, Greece, Russia, and Ecuador all experienced recessions in 2015.[15]

recession a period of GDP contraction that lasts for at least two consecutive quarters within one year

depression a severe, sustained period of economic contraction in one or more economies

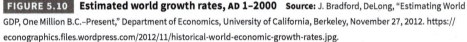

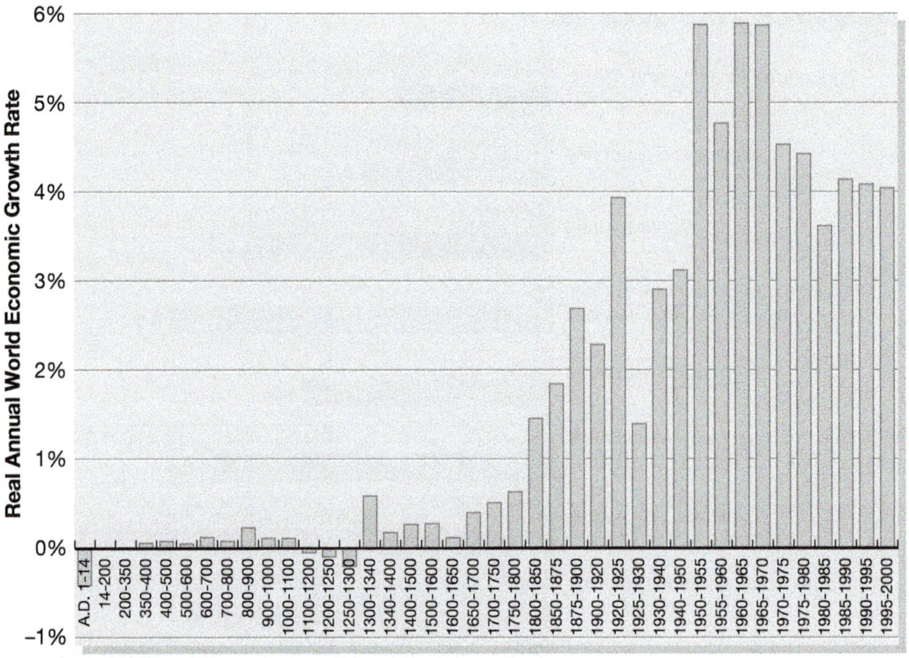

FIGURE 5.10 **Estimated world growth rates, AD 1–2000** **Source:** J. Bradford, DeLong, "Estimating World GDP, One Million B.C.–Present," Department of Economics, University of California, Berkeley, November 27, 2012. https://econographics.files.wordpress.com/2012/11/historical-world-economic-growth-rates.jpg.

To keep economies out of recession, or at least reduce the amount of time they are in recession, policymakers can use both fiscal policy and monetary policy to encourage growth. Think of an economy as a car traveling down the road; these policy tools are like the gas pedal, spurring economic growth.

Remember, GDP can be calculated using a particular formula:

$$\text{GDP} = \text{Private consumption} + \text{Investment} + \text{Government spending} + \text{Net exports}$$

or

$$\text{GDP} = \text{C} + \text{I} + \text{G} + \text{NE}$$

When the growth of GDP slows, it most often does so because private consumption and investment decline. People may be concerned about the future, and so decide to delay large discretionary purchases such as a home or car and the financial burdens such purchases impose. Similarly, companies are unlikely to make investments if they see a slump in demand. With that in mind, the goal of governments using fiscal policy is to jump-start spending and investment.

Fiscal Policy

fiscal policy government actions intended to spark or diminish consumption

Fiscal policy consists of government actions intended to spark or diminish consumption. In most cases governments struggle to stimulate growth, but in rare cases governments must try to slow an economy that is growing too rapidly. These policies include taxation and spending actions, such as increasing government spending—paid for by either raising taxes or running budget deficits—or encouraging private spending by lowering taxes to increase individuals' discretionary income. In the United States, such fiscal policy actions must be initiated by the president or by Congress. For instance, a decision by the United States to increase its government spending can benefit certain industries. For example, when military spending increases in the United States, the three largest defense companies in the world—Lockheed Martin, Northrop Grumman, and Boeing—benefit substantially. As a result, these companies will hire more talent and invest more in new technology. Similarly, increased government spending in general helps construction firms and information technology systems consultants who develop computer systems for public sector organizations.[16] Despite these obvious benefits, the overall effect of government spending, and whether it actually helps a country's economy and private sector, is a hotly debated topic.

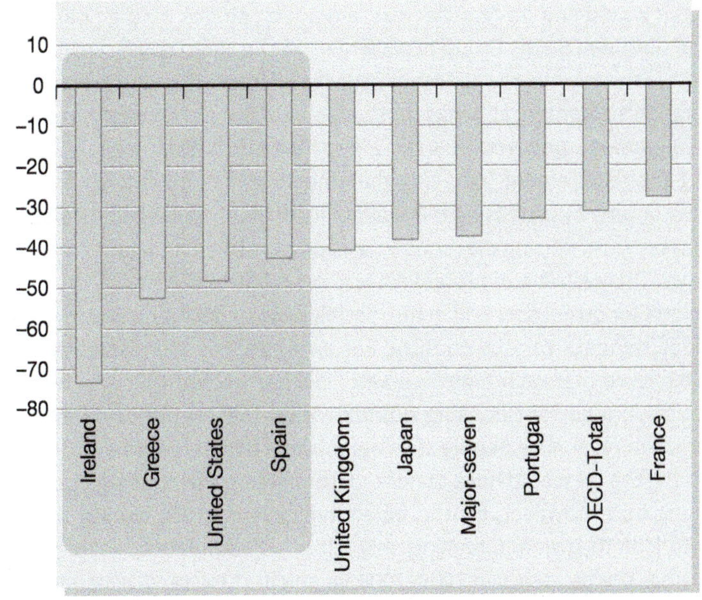

FIGURE 5.11 Cumulative annual government deficit as a percentage of GDP, 2008–2012 During the recession of 2009, many countries borrowed and spent heavily in an attempt to stimulate consumption. **Source:** Tyler Durden, "Presenting the Fund-tastic Four: Ireland, Greece, Spain and . . . the U.S.," ZeroHedge, December 10, 2012. www.zerohedge.com/news/2012-12-10/presenting-fund-tastic-four-ireland-greece-spain-and-us/.

Many nations responded to the global recession of 2008–2009 with significant new government spending programs. For instance, as **Figure 5.11** shows, Ireland, Greece, Spain, and the United States all incurred deficit spending of 40 percent or more of their GDPs during the period 2008–2012. Unlike more moderate government spending, which is paid for with increased taxes, deficit spending does not just replace flagging private consumption with government spending; rather, it attempts to spark consumption by borrowing from investors with a promise of future repayment. These investors are typically foreign institutions—like the European banks and governments that own Greece's debt, or like China and Japan, which own around $3 trillion and $1 trillion of U.S. debt, respectively.

Monetary Policy

Monetary policy has the same general goal as fiscal policy. However, **monetary policy** consists of manipulations in the interest rates, banking rules, and the volume of currency in a country. In the United States, these policies are tools of the Federal Reserve Bank, or the Fed, which operates independently of Congress and the administration. Three primary levers operate monetary policy: (1) the discount rate, (2) the reserve requirement, and (3) open market operations.

monetary policy manipulations in the interest rates, the banking rules, and the volume of currency in a country, with a goal to spark or diminish consumption

Central banks such as the European Central Bank (ECB) in the European Union, the Bank of Japan, and the Fed decide how much to charge commercial banks for borrowing money. That interest rate is called the **discount rate**. In reality, banks rarely borrow directly from central banking authorities; more often, they borrow from one another to meet their short-term cash needs. However, because a nation's banks have the option to borrow directly from the central bank, the central bank's discount rate sets the interest rate for interbank loans as well. Thus, when the central bank lowers the discount rate, the cost of borrowing becomes cheaper throughout the economy—typically increasing consumption and investment but at the expense of savings (people spend rather than save).

discount rate the interest rate a central bank charges commercial banks to borrow money

If the economy slows, central banks can lower interest rates to encourage spending. For example, if the discount rate goes down from 2% to 1%, then Bank of America will be able to get loans from other banks and the central bank at 1%. This means a loan for a car that would have cost you 5% would most likely now go down to 4%. This is great news for people who need loans for consumption and investments. But it also means that people who want to save their money with Bank of America will likely receive a lower interest rate on their savings account. On the other hand, when the Fed raises the discount rate, the banking industry profits as a result of stemming the decline in banks' net interest margins. Simply put, because some of the interest rates that banks charge on loans are directly tied to the Fed's target rate, banks immediately earn more interest on those loans. For example, on December 16, 2015, when the Fed announced that it would end its zero interest rate policy, shares of large banks like JPMorgan Chase & Co. and Goldman Sachs Group both surged on the same day.[17]

reserve requirement the minimum amount of cash reserves a commercial bank must hold

Adjustments in the **reserve requirement** have the effect of enlarging or shrinking the amount of money the nation's commercial banks must keep on hand as a safety measure. By raising or lowering the requirement, policymakers can affect how much money banks have available for loans. Lowering the requirement (reducing the amount banks must keep in reserve) releases money into the economy by increasing the availability of funds banks can lend businesses to fuel spending and investment. Raising the requirement, on the other hand, forces banks to keep more money in reserve. This restricts the total value of loans banks can make, thereby reducing the availability of credit for businesses and in turn shrinking their spending and investment.

Reserve requirements vary by country. For example, the Chinese government typically requires their banks to maintain high reserves. This has helped China to reduce what many people feel could be a current housing bubble within the country. However, knowing that banks have sufficient reserves if people start defaulting on their loans helps to keep the market stable—something the US would have benefited from before the housing bubble burst in 2008.

For the most part, however, central banks typically operate behind the scenes, letting the economy work on its own and making only minor adjustments to keep growth under control. However, since the recession in 2008–2009, in an effort to stabilize economies around the world, central banks have increased their direct involvement in money markets, using tools called open market operations.

open market operations operations by a central bank to buy or sell government bonds, corporate bonds, or equities

Open market operations are operations by a central bank to buy or sell government bonds, corporate bonds, or equities. These actions include policies such as *quantitative easing*, whereby a central bank prints money and uses it to buy government bonds, corporate bonds, or equities (stock shares). This action increases the amount of money in the economy, with the expectation that it will flow to banks that will lend it to consumers and investors, increasing consumption and investment and thus economic growth. Since the recession of 2008–2009, the Fed has engaged in unprecedented levels of open market operations in the United States. As a result, the Fed owns nearly $2 trillion worth of the U.S. government's debt and nearly $1.2 trillion of U.S. mortgage debt. The Fed's goal is eventually to sell these securities back into the market and return the money supply to its original level, but it must be careful of the speed at which it sells them because it doesn't want to drive down the price of the securities. Like policymakers in the United States, Japan's Prime Minister Shinzō Abe has encouraged the Bank of Japan to increase the money supply to try to fuel economic growth. This action is a direct attempt to reverse a nearly 20-year trend of declining output.[18]

Similarly, in 2014 the ECB set out to stimulate growth in the Euro zone (the 19 EU member countries that have adopted the euro as their common currency). The bank introduced negative interest rates and cheap long-term funding for banks in order to encourage them to increase credit availability to businesses. Then, in January 2015, the ECB began a $1.1 trillion program of quantitative easing to further increase the money supply. Under the program, the ECB purchases €60 billion per month of mostly government bonds from EU member countries. While the full results have yet to be seen, growth is still slow across Europe.[19]

5.4 Currency Fluctuation and Concentration Effects

LEARNING OBJECTIVE

Explain how inflation, deflation, and the concentration of wealth affect international business opportunities.

Our discussion in this chapter so far has assumed that an increase in GDP means an increase in output for a country. However, it is possible for GDP to increase *without* an increase in the value of output. In this case, the *price* of goods and services has increased, rather than the quantity produced.[20]

For instance, suppose a country sells exactly one hundred cars every year and nothing else. Since the cars represent the total output of the country, we can measure GDP as the dollar value of the cars produced. Now assume that over a ten-year period, the average price of a car (a measure of its value for GDP purposes) increases from $20,000 to $25,000—a 25 percent jump. Under these conditions, GDP will also seem to increase by 25 percent, because the value of the output has increased. However, if *all* prices rise by 25 percent during that same ten-year period, the actual value of GDP relative to the general price level will remain the same.

Let's define a few terms you may already be familiar with. The general rise in prices in an economy is called **inflation**. A general decline in prices is called **deflation**. **Real GDP** is GPD that has been adjusted to account for the effect of inflation. On the other hand, GDP that has *not* been adjusted to take inflation into account is called **nominal GDP**. Because policymakers are most interested in measuring and stimulating actual growth, they typically use real GDP in their calculations. We'll discuss inflation again later in the chapter.

inflation the general rise in prices in an economy

deflation the general decline in prices in an economy

real (inflation-adjusted) GDP GDP that has been adjusted to account for the effect of inflation on its value

nominal GDP GDP that has not been adjusted to account for inflation

Purchasing Power Parity and the Law of One Price

Inflation isn't the only factor for which international businesses have to adjust GDP. They also need to account for the fact that similar goods and services cost different amounts from one country to the next. For instance, a car that costs $20,000 in the United States may cost $100,000 in Singapore, where significant regulations apply to car ownership and increase its cost. Homes, fuel, clothing, food, and services like haircuts, dry cleaning, medical care, and education are also priced differently across countries. In theory, however, if goods and services could move freely across national borders without the friction of, say, trade barriers, transportation costs, or perishability, any given good would carry the same price everywhere. This principle is the **law of one price**, and you can see it in action in the prices of goods and services that *do* move easily across borders. For instance, gold, which flows relatively freely around the globe, is priced equivalently in the United Kingdom, the United States, and Brazil,[21] whereas haircuts—which do not flow freely across boundaries—are not.

law of one price assumption that any given good or service would carry the same price everywhere if allowed free movement across national borders

The reality, in fact, is that the law of one price applies to few of the ordinary goods and services most people rely on, and therefore the *cost of living* differs across countries. To account for this difference and to enable true comparisons of this important yardstick across countries, we standardize the cost of living in each country using a measure called **purchasing power parity (PPP)**. PPP compares the costs of common products and services in terms of one local currency. For instance, if a similar type of rice is cheaper in China than in Indonesia when measured in the same currency (whether China's or Indonesia's), then China's PPP will be higher than Indonesia's because Chinese consumers can get more rice for the same amount of money than consumers in Indonesia can.

purchasing power parity (PPP) a measure that compares the costs of common products and services in terms of one currency

How do differences in PPP affect GDP figures? In China in 2015, GDP per capita was just $10,500, but the PPP-adjusted GDP figure is nearly half as much again, at $15,095. This means the average person in China is able to live as if he or she were earning $15,095, not $10,500, because his or her money buys more than a U.S. consumer's dollars buy. In contrast, Japan's GDP was $44,646 per person in 2015, but its PPP-adjusted GDP was only $35,804. This drop in purchasing power highlights the high cost of living in Japan. For the purposes of comparison, GDP figures make it seem as though the Japanese earn four times more per person than the Chinese, but PPP shows that the Japanese standard of living is only about two times higher.

What this means is that today I bought a Subway sandwich, chips, and a drink (**Figure 5.12**) for ₹220 (Indian rupees). This cost just US$3.29 at current exchange rates. On average, this meal in the United States would cost over twice as much, at $7.20. If you looked across all purchases in India, you would find that while India's GDP is just $1,805

Michael Neelon(misc)/Alamy Stock Photo

FIGURE 5.12 **A subway sandwich, bag of chips, and a drink cost ₹220 (Indian Rupees)**

Country	Per Capita GDP (Nominal)	Per Capita GDP (PPP)
United States	51,486	52,549
Finland	45,288	38,642
Germany	45,269	44,053
United Kingdom	40,933	38,657
Japan	44,646	35,804
Mexico	9,517	16,501
Brazil	11,159	14,454
China	10,500	15,095
India	1,805	5,730

FIGURE 5.13 **GDP and PP: Adjusted GDP** This chart compares the nominal GDP of several countries with their PPP-adjusted amounts. **Source:** Data from "GDP per Capital, PPP (Current International $)," *World Bank.* http://data.worldbank.org/indicator/NY.GDP.PCAP.PP.CD/. *Accessed June 2, 2017.*

per person, when adjusted for purchasing power, the average GDP per person increases to $5,730. **Figure 5.13** compares the nominal GDP of several countries with their PPP-adjusted amounts.

The Gini Coefficient

Another challenge for international businesses in using GDP, even when adjusted based on PPP, is that an increase in GDP may not be equally beneficial to everyone in the economy. When ownership of the means of creating output is concentrated in the hands of a few people, the benefits of increased output go only to those few because they likely own the factors of production. The **Gini coefficient**—named for the Italian statistician Corrado Gini (1884–1965)—is a measure of the distribution of wealth within a country.[22] A country in which one person owns all the wealth will have a Gini coefficient of one; on the other hand, if everyone in the country has an equal share of the country's wealth, its coefficient will be zero. Thus, the closer to zero the Gini coefficient, the more equal the distribution of wealth in a country. As shown in **Figure 5.14**, Brazil has a significant concentration of wealth, whereas Norway, Canada, and Italy have more equal distributions.

Gini coefficient a measure of the distribution of wealth within a country

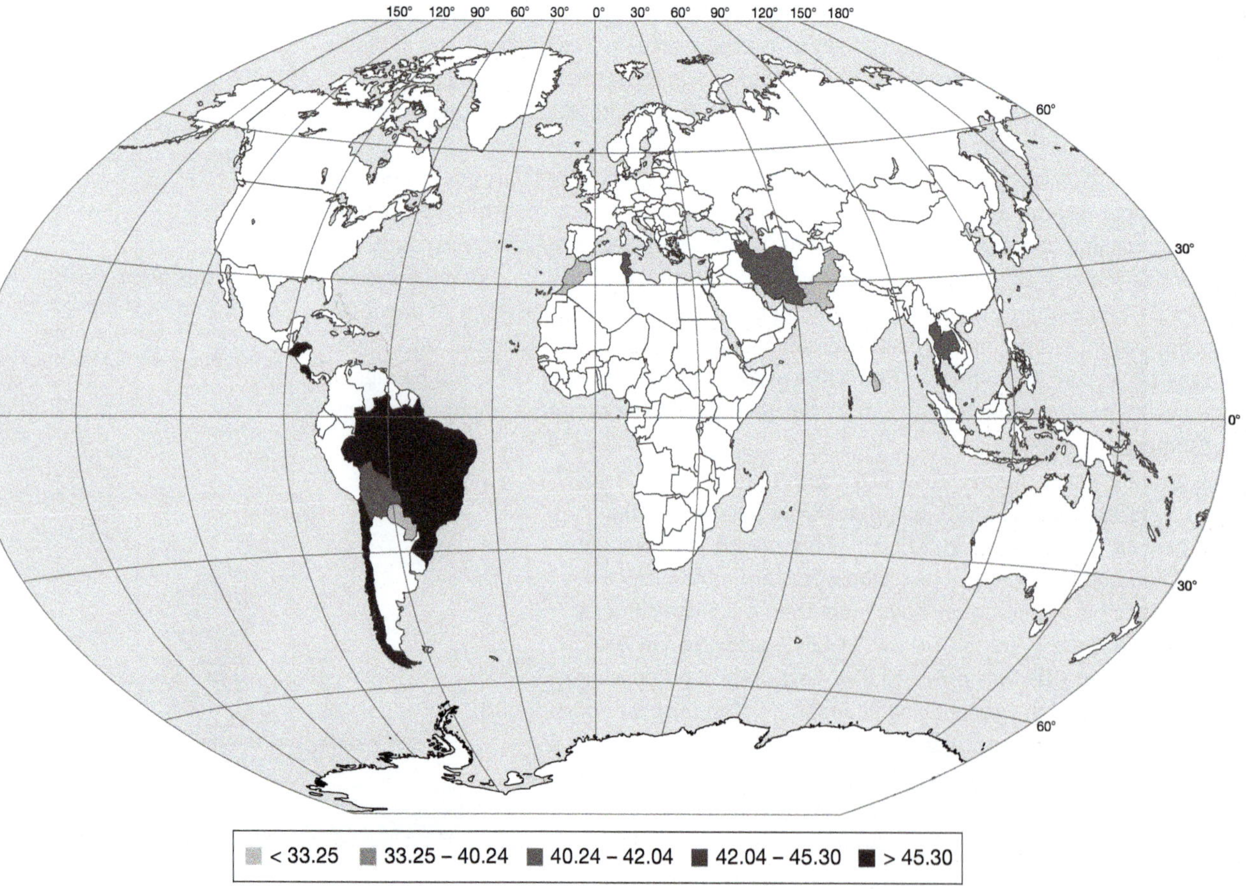

FIGURE 5.14 **Global map of the Gini Index, 1981–2013** This chart plots the Gini coefficient of countries globally. **Source:** "GINI Index (World Bank Estimate)," World Bank. http://data.worldbank.org/indicator/SI.POV.GINI?view=map. Accessed June 2, 2017.

The Gini coefficient is an important indicator of well-being and equality, in that if it is high, the buying power of everyone in the general population will not increase to the same degree when output increases. This handicap limits the opportunities for international companies who sell goods and services to average consumers. On the other hand, even small increases in GDP in countries with highly concentrated income distributions (high Gini coefficients) mean that the owners of the factors of production in those countries are likely to have significantly more spending power, and makers of luxury goods should take note.

Some observers worry that changes in fiscal and monetary policies will fuel inflation. However, most economists actually believe a little inflation is a good thing, and many countries aim to manage inflation in their economies so it is around 2 to 3 percent a year. In practice, inflation is measured by looking at the **Consumer Price Index (CPI)**. This index tracks the price of a specific set of consumer goods across time, watching for general price increases or decreases. A look at the CPI index for the U.S. economy from 2006 to 2016, illustrated graphically in **Figure 5.15**, shows that in 2009, for example, the United States was in a period of deflation compared with the preceding year.

Consumer Price Index (CPI) an index that tracks the price of a specific set of consumer goods across time to identify general price increases or decreases

A problem with inflation is that it leads to a loss of the value of assets. For instance, in 2016 Apple had nearly $90 billion in cash or equivalents. If this money is evenly spread across the globe and the average inflation rate in 2016 was 3.2 percent, then Apple will lose roughly $2.8 billion in the value of its cash every year. Inflation eats into the value of savings. The higher the inflation rate, the faster it causes those savings to lose value. In addition to the loss of value, international companies face "menu costs": companies have to spend a lot of money constantly changing and reprinting their prices on menus, e-commerce sites, and the like.

On the other hand, in Japan, deflation has been a long-term problem. As Figure 5.16 demonstrates, in most years since 2001 prices in Japan have fallen rather than risen—meaning the same products cost less each year than the year before. In 2012, Shinzō Abe was elected prime minister of Japan on his promise to break the deflationary cycle in the economy. Deflation is problematic because it often causes people, companies, and banks to hoard their money. In deflationary cycles, things will cost less next year than they do this year. Hence, customers, businesses and even governments are technically better off by putting off purchases and investment because they will be cheaper next year.

For instance, restaurants and supermarkets can be hit hard when deflation occurs. In 2016 Kroger, a grocery store, posted its slowest comparable-store sales growth in six years.[23] While low prices may be good for consumers, they force supermarkets to stay competitive by further lowering their prices and engaging in expensive promotions. However, when people hoard money, reduced spending leads to reduced demand and, eventually, reduced supply. But until supply falls to meet demand, prices will also fall, causing further deflation. This cycle can continue reinforcing itself and, without effective intervention, may spiral out of control. International businesses observing deflation are unlikely to invest in a country experiencing this trend because next year the investment may be less expensive and because demand is likely waning within the country.

How do countries break a deflationary cycle? Japan has sought to do so by increasing the money supply, which would make more money available to purchase the same amount of goods, driving up prices. The country also worked to increase the rate at which money in the country changed hands, which would also result in more money being spent on the same number of goods. If more money purchases the same number of goods, the prices of those goods increase. Prime Minister Abe sought to build a program focused on encouraging Japan's central bank, the Bank of Japan, to dramatically increase the money supply.

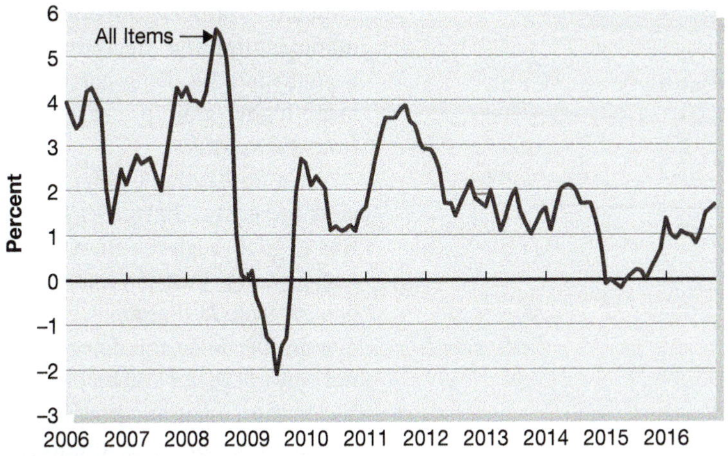

FIGURE 5.15 **U.S. consumer price index, 2006–2016** **Source:** Malik Crawford, Jonathan Church, and Bradley Akin, eds., "CPI Detailed Report: Data for December 2016," U.S. Department of Labor, Bureau of Labor Statistics, 4. www.bls.gov/cpi/cpid1612.pdf/.

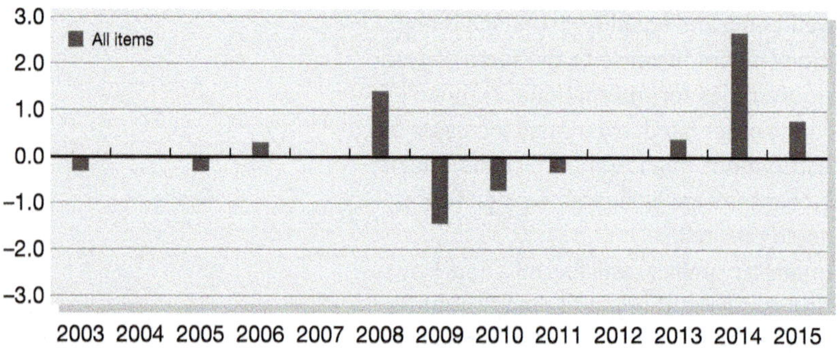

FIGURE 5.16 **Japan's consumer prices, 2003–2015** This graph shows the percentage change in the price of goods across more than a decade. **Source:** "Consumer Price Index: Japan 2016," Statistics Bureau, Ministry of Internal Affairs and Communications. www.stat.go.jp/english/data/cpi/158c.htm (accessed January 29, 2016).

He also encouraged increased government spending to drive the speed at which money changes hands. At the same time he sought to engage in economic reforms such as reducing trade tariffs.[24] All these actions were intended to increase the price of goods and services and have had some effect on Japan's CPI, as shown in **Figure 5.16**.

The dangers of deflation are the reason most countries try to ensure a low level of inflation. However, inflation can also be a problem if it gets too high. As we discussed above, high inflation erodes the value of money, discouraging savings and increasing transaction costs—all of which harm the economy. If inflation exceeds 50 percent in a month, it is termed *hyperinflation*. If the prices of necessary goods climb out of reach of consumers, disastrous consequences—including riots, food and other shortages, and widespread panic—can result.

Hyperinflation is most often caused when governments attempt to fund budget shortfalls by simply printing money. This increases the money supply without corresponding increases in output quantity, causing prices to rise as more money chases the same number of goods and services. The more money the government prints, the more quickly prices will rise. Many nations have had periods of hyperinflation in the past, leading to the devastation of their output and well-being. **Figure 5.17** documents the highest monthly inflation rate on record for different countries.

The record for hyperinflation was set by Hungary after World War II, with a monthly inflation rate of 12,950 trillion percent. Before long, the government was forced to print National Bank notes denominated in 100 quintillion—or 100 million million million—pengős, the currency at the time.[25] Even with rapid pay raises, this hyperinflation eroded the real wages of workers by over 80 percent and significantly hurt the economy. It was stopped by drastic reform in Hungary's financial system and efforts by the government to control the money supply and back its currency with gold.

Inflation can have significant impacts on international business. A country with high levels of inflation can be a less attractive investment opportunity because it is difficult to preserve the value of earnings and to engage in most aspects of business. During periods of high inflation, for instance, worker's salaries must increase frequently (sometimes daily), the cost of supplies increases rapidly, and the pricing of goods and services produced is difficult. Inflation in the United States in 2011 forced Whirlpool, an American multinational manufacturer and marketer of home appliances, to cut jobs and close plants in order to account for the rising costs of steel. Similarly, the multinational food retailer Kellogg's faced higher grain prices and as a result announced intentions to raise its cereal prices from 3% to 4%.[26]

In a more extreme example, Brazil has experienced such runaway inflation that one grocery store owner said that during Brazil's periods of high inflation he had to hire someone whose job was to go through the store and constantly relabel the prices. Similarly, in 1983–1985 Bolivia had such high inflation that the price of a movie ticket would have increased as you stood in line to buy it. At that point, companies did not list prices because they were changing too frequently. Of course, this damages international businesses, as they must constantly try to adjust not only prices but also employee pay.

In sum, inflation, growth, distribution of wealth, and measures of well-being are important considerations for international businesses. Opportunities can increase or decrease as the economies of different countries change, and global firms that recognize these trends earlier than their peers can position themselves to capture these opportunities or avoid significant threats.

No	Country	Year(s)	Highest Inflation per month (%)
1	Argentina	1989–90	196.60
2	Armenia	1993–94	438.04
3	Austria	1921–22	124.27
4	Azerbaijan	1991–94	118.09
5	Belarus	1994	53.40
6	Bolivia	1984–86	120.39
7	Brazil	1989–93	84.32
8	Bulgaria	1997	242.70
9	China	1947–49	4,208.73
10	Congo(Zaire)	1991–94	225.00
11	France	1789–96	143.26
12	Georgia	1993–94	196.72
13	Germany	1920–23	29,525.71
14	Greece	1942–45	11,288.00
15	Hungary	1923–24	82.18
16	Hungary	1945–46	1.295×10^{16}
17	Kazakhstan	1994	57.00
18	Kyrgyzstan	1992	157.00
19	Nicaragua	1986–89	126.62
20	Peru	1988–90	114.12
21	Poland	1921–24	187.54
22	Poland	1989–90	77.33
23	Soviet Union	1922–24	278.72
24	Taiwan	1945–49	398.73
25	Tajikistan	1995	78.10
26	Turkmenistan	1993–96	62.50
27	Ukraine	1992–94	249.00
28	Yugoslavia	1990	58.82
29	Yugoslavia	1992–94	313,000,000.00

Note 1.295 × 1016 equals 12,950,000,000,000,000

FIGURE 5.17 Hyperinflation in the 20th century **Sources:** Peter Bemholz, *Monetary Regimes and Inflation*, Cheltenham, UK: Edward Elgar Publishing, 2003; and Steve H. Hanke

Summary and Case

Summary

LEARNING OBJECTIVE 5.1 Describe how economic systems differ.

International businesses must understand how economic systems differ. Countries around the globe typically adopt one of two economic systems: a market-based system or a command-based system. In market-based systems, supply is determined by the demand, whereas in a command-based system, supply is planned. International businesses need to understand the opportunities in foreign countries. To do so they need to look to output as a metric of economic health. Output can be increased in three main ways: by increasing labor, by increasing the skill of laborers, and by increasing invested capital. Total factor productivity (TFP) measures the efficiency with which labor and capital come together.

LEARNING OBJECTIVE 5.2 Compare ways to measure countries' economic activities or output.

To assess whether to do business in a country, international businesses need to gauge the level of opportunity in that country. Two measures, gross domestic product (GDP) and gross national product (GNP), help businesses determine these opportunities. The Human Development Index (HDI) aims to capture a broader view of national well-being. However, when only a few individuals in a country control the means of production and thus profit more from increased output than everyone else, opportunities may be concentrated.

LEARNING OBJECTIVE 5.3 Describe the tools governments use to slow down or speed up their economies.

Governments closely monitor the growth and contraction of their economies in order to manage the well-being of their citizens. When economies grow, well-being generally increases. When economies contract, the resulting reduced consumption usually causes hardship. To avoid contraction (also called recession), governments use fiscal and monetary policies to stimulate the economy. Fiscal policy operates based on government budgets, spending, and tax rates. Monetary policy is a tool of central banks and consists of changes to monetary supply and interbank lending rates.

LEARNING OBJECTIVE 5.4 Explain how inflation, deflation, and the concentration of wealth affect international business opportunities.

Other important measures of the economy, such as inflation, deflation, and the concentration of wealth, affect international business opportunities. Inflation is a condition of generally rising prices. Real GDP is adjusted for inflation. Purchasing power parity (PPP) reflects what people in one country must spend to buy the same goods as people in another country. The Gini coefficient measures the distribution of income in GDP and PPP, and it helps businesses understand the economic situation in a country and identify business opportunities.

Case Study

Comparing GDP Growth in China and India

In 1990, India had a GDP of $326 billion, whereas China had a GDP of $358 billion.[27] Over the next 25 years, however, China's GDP grew to $10.8 trillion in 2015, while India's GDP grew to $2.07 trillion[28] (see **Figure 5.18**). While both are impressive rates of growth, China's growth is over 33 percent whereas India's is just above 6 percent.

The rapid growth of GDP in China has resulted in the rise of a wealthy class where there previously was none. For instance, *Fortune* compiles a yearly report of the world's billionaires. In 1990, it reported that China had no billionaires. In 1995 it still had none. Even in 2000 it had none. But just 15 years later, in 2015, it had over 300, as shown in **Figure 5.19.**[29]

But, not only has the vast increase in wealth affected the lives of the billionaires; the World Bank suggests that 800 million people have also moved out of poverty in China. The poverty rate fell from 88 percent of the population in 1981 to just above 4 percent of the population in 2014.[30]

India, on the other hand, cut its poverty level from 60 percent to 30 percent of its population between 1981 and 2012.[31] However, the population also increased, so the number of Indians in poverty had declined only from 429 million to 400 million.[32]

The effects of the rapid growth in China's GDP are seen everywhere in its economy. The rise of a middle class has turned China into the world's largest market for many goods, such as automobiles. India is also growing, but at a slower rate.

Case Discussion Questions

1. What are some reasons that China's GDP growth could outpace India's growth?
2. How could India match China's growth?
3. What are the effects of the rapid growth in both these countries for international businesses?

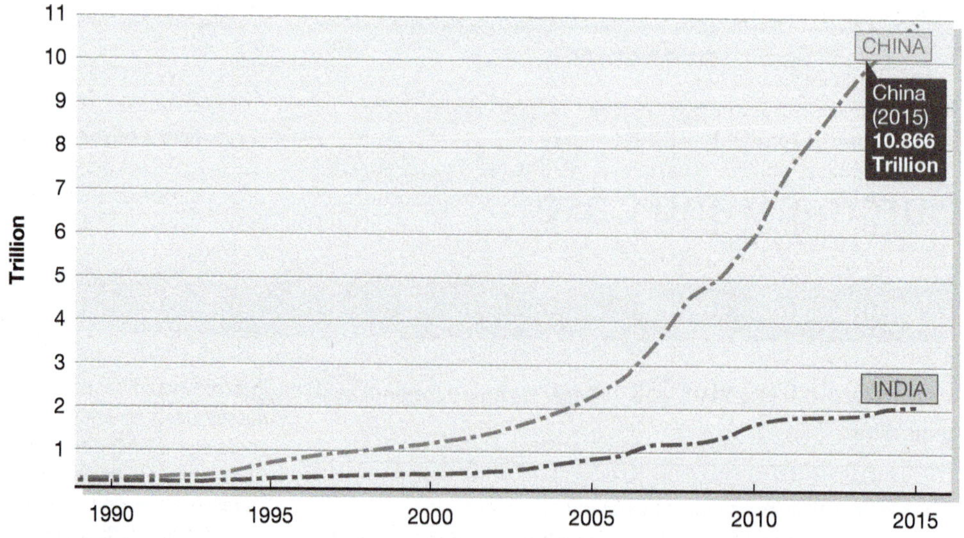

FIGURE 5.18 **Comparison of China's and India's GDP from 1990 to 2015** **Source:** "GDP (current US$)," World Bank. http://data.worldbank.org/indicator/NY.GDP.MKTP.CD?end=2015&locations=CN-IN&start=1990/. Accessed June 2, 2017.

Number of Billionaires, by Year							
	1990	1995	2000	2005	2010	2015	2016
United States	99	129	49	341	403	526	525
China	0	0	0	15	89	152	335
India	2	2	9	27	49	84	84
Worldwide		423	322	691	1011	1826	1810

FIGURE 5.19 Number of Billionaires in the United States, China, and India, 1990–2016
Source: www.forbes.com/billionaires/.

Endnotes

[1]Kat Huang, "When the Rockefellers Ruled the World: American Dynasty: The Rockefellers Create a Remarkable Cultural Legacy," *Avenue*, December 2013, 61–64.

[2]Chase Patterson-Withorn, "The Full List of Every American Billionaire 2016," *Forbes*, March 1, 2016. https://www.forbes.com/sites/chasewithorn/2016/03/01/the-full-list-of-every-american-billionaire-2016/#37acb47e37ac

[3]Smith, Adam. *An Inquiry into the Nature and Causes of the Wealth of Nations* (ed. RH Campbell, AS Skinner, and WB Todd) (1976); Karl Marx and Friedrich Engels, *Manifesto of the Communist Party* (Trier: Friedrich-Ebert-Stiftung, Musum Karl-Marx-Haus, 1848).

[4]Martin Sixsmith, *Russia: A 1,000-Year Chronicle of the Wild East* (New York: Overlook Press, 2014).

[5]"The World's Billionaires: China," *Forbes*. www.forbes.com/billionaires/list/#version:static_country:China (accessed June 2, 2017).

[6]World Development Indicators for China, data form the World Bank, 2015. http://data.worldbank.org/country/china/. (accessed September 28, 2016).

[7]CK Tan, "Malaysia-Singapore Commute a Daily Grind," *Nikkei Daily Review*, March 12, 2015. http://asia.nikkei.com/magazine/20150312-ASEAN-Linked-lands-meshed-markets/On-the-Cover/Malaysia-Singapore-commute-a-daily-grind?page=1/.

[8]"This Day in History: December 1, 1913: Ford's Assembly Line Starts Rolling," History.com. www.history.com/this-day-in-history/fords-assembly-line-starts-rolling/.

[9]Tycho De Feijter, "5 Stunning Facts About the Chinese Car Market You Need to Know," *Fortune*, May 16, 2016.

[10]Kavit Majithia, "Chinese Smartphone Market Returns to Growth" MobileWorldLive, July 29, 2016. www.mobileworldlive.com/asia/chinese-smartphone-market-returns-to-growth/.

[11]"Multinationals in Venezuela: Stay or Go," *The Economist*, September 17, 2016. http://www.economist.com/news/business/21707257-companies-age-chavismo-stay-or-go/.

[12]"*GDP* per Capita (current US$)," World Development Indicators, World Bank, 2015. http://data.worldbank.org/indicator/NY.GDP.PCAP.CD/countries/1W?display=default/ (accessed).

[13]Valentina Romei. "Ireland is the wealthiest economy of Europe . . . or not." FT.com. May 13, 2015. http://blogs.ft.com/ftdata/2015/05/13/ireland-is-the-wealthiest-economy-in-europe-or-not/.

[14]Dominik H. Enste, "The Shadow Economy in Industrial Countries," IZA World of Labor, February 2015, 127. http://wol.iza.org/articles/shadow-economy-in-industrial-countries-1.pdf/; Kathleen G. Beegle et al., "Informal Economy and the World Bank," Policy Research working paper; no. WPS 6888 (Washington, DC: World Bank Group, May 1, 2014). http://documents.worldbank.org/curated/en/416741468332060156/Informal-economy-and-the-World-Bank/.

[15]Andre Tartar, Catarina Saraiva, and Cynthia Li, "Meet 2016's Worst Economic Performers," Bloomberg, January 10, 2016. www.bloomberg.com/news/articles/2016-01-11/meet-2016-s-worst-economic-performers-flirting-with-disaster./

[16]"External Environment: Government Spending" Tutor2u, Accessed October 6th, 2016. http://www.tutor2u.net/business/reference/external-environment-government-spending

[17]James Garrett Baldwin, "The Impact of a Fed Interest Rate Hike," Investopedia, January 6, 2016. www.investopedia.com/articles/investing/010616/impact-fed-interest-rate-hike.asp/.

[18]Andy Sharp, "Abenomics: Japan's Economic Shock Therapy," Bloomberg, August 3, 2016 (updated February 10, 2017). www.bloomberg.com/quicktake/abenomics/.

[19]P. W., "Mario's Hint: The European Central Bank Prepares to Extend Its Quantitative-Easing Programme in December," *The Economist*, October 22, 2015. www.economist.com/blogs/freeexchange/2015/10/marios-hint.

[20]W. E. Diewert, "Index Numbers," in J. Eatwell, M. Milgate, and P. Neuman (eds.), *The New Palgrave Dictionary of Economics*, 2nd ed. ([1987] 2008, pp. 767–780). London: Macmillan Press.

[21]www.gold.org/investment/interactive-gold-price-chart (accessed September 23, 2016).

[22]"Who, What, Why: What Is the Gini Coefficient?" BBCNews, March 12, 2015. www.bbc.com/news/blogs-magazine-monitor-31847943/; "An Overview of Growing Income Inequality in OECD Countries: Main Findings," Organisation for Economic Co-operation and Development, 2011. www.oecd.org/els/soc/49499779.pdf (accessed June 2, 2017).

[23]Jeremy Bowman, "Food Deflation is Bad News for Restaurants and Supermarkets," Motley Fool, September 13, 2016. www.fool.com/investing/2016/09/13/food-deflation-is-bad-news-for-restaurants-and-sup.aspx/.

[24]Charles Riley, "Japan's 'Abenomics' Experiment Is on the Rocks," CNN Money, October 5, 2015. http://money.cnn.com/2015/10/05/news/economy/japan-economy-abenomics-experiment/.

[25]William Bomberger and Gail Makinen, "The Hungarian Hyperinflation and Stabilization of 1945–1946," *Journal of Political Economy* 91, no. 5 (October 1983): 801–24.

[26]"The Ten Industries Most Damaged By Inflation," 24/7 Wall St, February 23, 2011. http://247wallst.com/investing/2011/02/23/the-ten-industries-most-damaged-by-inflation/.

[27]"GDP by Country," World Bank (accessed September 14, 2016).

[28]"GDP by Country," World Bank (accessed September 14, 2016).

[29]"The World's Billionaires," *Forbes*. www.forbes.com/billionaires/ (accessed June 2, 2017).

[30]"China: Overview—Results," World Bank. www.worldbank.org/en/country/china/overview#3/ (accessed September 14, 2016).

[31]"India Has Highest Number of People Living Below Poverty Line: World Bank," Business Today India, October 3, 2016. www.businesstoday.in/current/economy-politics/india-has-highest-number-of-people-living-below-poverty-line-world-bank/story/238085.html/.

[32]Prachi Salve, "India's Unchanging Statistic: 400 Million Poor Over 30 Years," India Spend, May 15, 2013. www.indiaspend.com/investigations/indias-unchanging-statistic-400-million-poor-over-30-years/.

CHAPTER 6

Currency and Foreign Exchange

TUNTI/Creatas Video/Getty Images

Introduction

Money makes it easier to buy and sell goods around the world. In fact, thanks to electronic banking, paper money and coins no longer need to change hands.

However, despite electronic advances in the ways we can transfer currency, the value of money fluctuates across countries, adding a layer of complexity to international business. One country's currency may be undervalued, which makes buying products from another country more expensive. Or a country may have an overvalued currency, which makes buying products and services from other countries disproportionately cheaper, but makes the home country's own exports more expensive. Currency exchange is the process by which countries and companies swap one nation's currency for that of another.

The values of different currencies depend on a number of factors, such as the supply of and demand for a particular currency, the level of political stability in the country that issues it, and the economic policies imposed by its government. The disparity between currencies can create arbitrage opportunities (opportunities of taking advantage of price differences in multiple markets) for firms engaging in currency exchange, but it can also expose them to financial loss. Companies planning on doing business internationally need to first understand the opportunities and risks associated with currency exchange and then learn how to effectively respond to these threats and opportunities through various risk-management techniques.

LEARNING OBJECTIVES

After you explore this chapter you will be able to:

1. **Identify** the three functions of money
2. **Explain** why foreign exchange rates fluctuate
3. **Discuss** the causes and consequences of under- or overvaluation of currency
4. **Describe** how companies settle international monetary transactions and manage exchange rate risk

6.1 What Is Money?

LEARNING OBJECTIVE

Identify the three functions of money.

For thousands of years, people have used physical money in various forms to facilitate exchange. The ancient Romans minted coins with a set value across the Roman empire; Pacific Islanders used rare shells to buy and sell goods; soldiers and prisoners of war in World War II used cigarettes as currency. In every case, currency provides two major functions. First, money acts as a *medium of exchange*; this function allows us to conduct transactions without having to wait for what economists call a "double coincidence of wants" in which, say, I want your car and you want my airplane, so we simply trade. But what if I want your car and you *don't* want my airplane? With money we can still trade because we don't first have to look for someone who not only has something you want but also will trade it for my airplane. Instead we just exchange your car for my money.

Second, money is a *unit of account*. As a means to keep track of value, money makes it easier for people to agree on the value of goods and trade with each other. Third, money is a *store of value*. Because it keeps its value over time, it allows people to save it and delay consumption from today into the future. For instance, it is a lot easier to carry paper money around than chickens, cars, or airplanes.

Historically, currencies were made of material that had intrinsic value, such as precious metals like gold or silver (or rare shells). Later they were made of paper and coins, but these forms of money still represented the precious metals governments had stockpiled to back up their currency with something that had intrinsic value. Before 1973, for instance, the currency of the United States (and those of many other countries) was based on the **gold standard**. In other words, a dollar had intrinsic value because anyone holding it could trade it for a specified amount of gold (1/35 of an ounce) at a government-approved bank.[1] Since the 1970s, however, most of the world's currencies have been **fiat currencies**. This means they no longer represent the value of a government's store of gold or silver and cannot be traded for a precious metal. Instead they are just pieces of paper and coins that have value simply because the issuing government says they do (a fiat is a decree)—and because people put their faith in the currency as a medium of exchange, a store of value, and a unit of account. Since the United States dropped the gold standard in 1973, the U.S. dollar (USD) has retained its value only because the Federal Reserve says it has value and citizens conduct transactions with it as though it has value.

gold standard a currency where the value is determined by the ability to trade it for a specified amount of gold (i.e., $1 for 1/35 of an ounce) at a government-approved bank

fiat currencies a currency that the government has declared to be legal tender but is not backed by any physical commodity

WileyPLUS

See Whiteboard Video: The Bretton Woods System

Bitcoin (shown in **Figure 6.1**) and other digital forms of money have recently emerged. These currencies, often called *cryptocurrencies*, have no physical form and are not backed by

Chris Ratcliffe/Bloomberg/Getty Images

FIGURE 6.1 Bitcoin Even though bitcoin is not a physical currency, its symbol is represented in this picture of physical coins.

any government; rather they are electronic currencies that are monitored by distributed peer networks that simultaneously keep track of currency ownership and trades. No one institution controls the currency. Digital currencies are valuable because they store value, they facilitate trade, and they are not controlled by intermediaries. Though the price of bitcoin fluctuates as supply and demand increase or decrease, its value was just over $2,658 per coin in 2017. In April 2017, Japan formally accepted bitcoin as a new legal currency.[2]

Currencies tied to the value of an underlying standard like gold rise and fall depending on the value of that commodity. The value of fiat currencies fluctuates more readily, depending on many other factors. For instance, a fiat currency can be worth more or less in international markets depending on how trustworthy the government is that printed it, and the available supply of and level of demand for the currency. A country can undermine the value of its fiat currency, rendering it valueless. In the early 2000s, Zimbabwe experienced a period of such rapid hyperinflation that money printed there held almost no value (1 trillion Zimbabwean dollars could not even buy an apple).[3] The government was trying to print its way out of a budget deficit and eventually minted so large a supply of currency that people didn't believe Zimbabwean dollars had value anymore. Zimbabwe's currency was worth less than paper, as shown in **Figure 6.2**.

ZINYANGE AUNTONY/AFP/Getty Images

FIGURE 6.2 Worthless Zimbabwean dollars Hyper-inflation left the Zimbabwean dollar worthless. This man displays millions of Zimbabwean dollars on his hat; using the useless dollars for decoration.

6.2 Understanding Exchange Rates

LEARNING OBJECTIVE

Describe the foreign exchange market and why rates fluctuate.

The value of a fiat currency—like the U.S. dollar or the European euro—relative to the value of any other fiat currency is influenced by individuals' perceptions of the currency's value. That value depends on the supply of and demand for the currency, and the political stability and economic policies of the country that issues it. Fluctuations are termed **appreciation** when the value of a currency increases relative to other currencies, and **depreciation** when a currency's value decreases relative to other currencies. Such fluctuations are signaled by changes in a currency's **exchange rate**—the ratio that tells us how much of one currency we need in order to buy an equivalent amount of purchasing power in a different currency.

appreciation an increase in the value of one currency relative to another currency

depreciation a decrease in the value of one currency relative to another currency

exchange rate the value of one currency when being converted to another currency

For instance, imagine Apple Inc. wants to open stores in England (**Figure 6.3**). To finance the stores' rent and payroll and pay its taxes, Apple will need to sell U.S. dollars and acquire British pounds. The actual cost for a U.S. company to rent a store in the United Kingdom thus depends not only on the price of the store space in British pounds but also on the price of the British pound in U.S. dollars, because the company will first have to acquire the currency it needs to do business in England.[4] If the demand for pounds is high, then their price will go up, or appreciate, meaning it will take more U.S. dollars to buy them. On the other hand, if the demand for pounds drops, then fewer U.S. dollars will be needed to buy the same number of pounds—in which case the pound has depreciated relative to the dollar. Similarly, hundreds and even thousands of currency transactions happen every day to facilitate activities such as distributing foreign aid, making interbank transfers, purchasing and selling foreign bonds, sending remittances, and trading in goods and services.

Foreign exchange rates are in fact determined largely by the supply of and demand for currencies. For instance, if you are traveling to Japan, you will need to buy Japanese yen in order

FIGURE 6.3 **Apple in England** The actual cost for a U.S. company to rent a store in the United Kingdom depends not only on the price of the space in British pounds but also on the price of the British pound in U.S. dollars.

to buy and sell goods and services once you arrive. Thus, you will buy yen from a bank or currency trader using your local currency (dollars, if you are from the United States). You can look at this transaction as selling your local currency and taking Japanese yen as payment. Every day, thousands of companies, governments, institutions, and even individuals may also need to buy or sell yen. If on a given day the demand for yen by those who want to buy them is higher than the supply available from those selling them, the price of yen compared with other currencies will appreciate. Conversely, if more people wish to sell yen than wish to buy, the price will depreciate.

In the recession of 2008–2009, many international companies were worried about the future and sought to switch their currency holdings to U.S. dollars for safety; after all, many of their transactions and loan payments are paid in dollars. As a result, demand for the dollar was high and its cost appreciated relative to that of many other currencies. For instance, in 2007 it took about 950 South Korean won to buy US$1. A year later the value of the won had depreciated, and it cost over 1,200 KW for US$1.

In addition to demand and supply, political stability also plays an important role in determining exchange rates. In 2011, North Korea bombed a South Korean island, and the fear of a war that could damage the South Korean economy led companies doing business there to move their money out of South Korea to safer countries. Many sold their Korean won, depreciating its value from 1,200 to 1,600 KW per U.S. dollar, as they purchased U.S. dollars or other stable currencies such as the Japanese yen and the euro. A few months later, the fear of conflict subsided and the Korean won appreciated back to 1,300 KW per US$1.

While the price of a currency is a function of economic and political trends, it can also be directly affected by government intervention. Four main types of government policy affect currency valuations and foreign exchange rates, and each has a different impact.

float an exchange rate system where the price of the currency is determined by the supply and demand of the currency in the foreign exchange market

currency exchange the process by which entities swap one nation's currency for that of another

managed float an exchange rate system where the price of the currency is largely determined by the supply and demand in the foreign exchange market but where central banks attempt to influence the rate by actively buying and selling currencies

peg an exchange rate system where the price of the currency is fixed against another currency or against a basket of other currencies

1. According to the International Monetary Fund (IMF), 29 countries allowed their currencies to **float**, meaning that their governments do not explicitly or directly influence the price of their currency by directly intervening in **currency exchange** or by limiting currency flows.[5] Even without direct intervention, however, government actions such as printing more money and buying other countries' currency—or even exiting the European Union—can indirectly affect the exchange rate by increasing (or decreasing) investment in the country and thereby increasing (or decreasing) demand for the currency.
2. The IMF records that 36 countries engage in a **managed float**, or *dirty float*, meaning that they generally don't interfere in the value of the currency, but they will explicitly intervene if their currency depreciates or appreciates beyond a certain amount. Under these conditions, a government will make efforts to adjust the price of its currency—usually by directly increasing or decreasing the supply of money or by using its reserves of foreign currency to buy its own currency.
3. Some countries **peg** or fix their currency to a foreign currency or a basket of currencies—usually stronger or more stable ones. For instance, Saudi Arabia pegs its currency, the riyal, to the U.S. dollar at 3.75 riyal per dollar. This practice holds the price of the riyal steady in relationship to the U.S. dollar. Other countries that also peg their currency to the U.S. dollar are Bahrain, Egypt, Vietnam, Hong Kong, and Panama (see Figure 6.4). Some countries peg their currencies to another currency: countries such as Mali, Niger, and Congo peg their currencies to the euro, whereas South Africa, Namibia, and Botswana peg theirs to a basket, or combination, of currencies (see **Figure 6.4**).

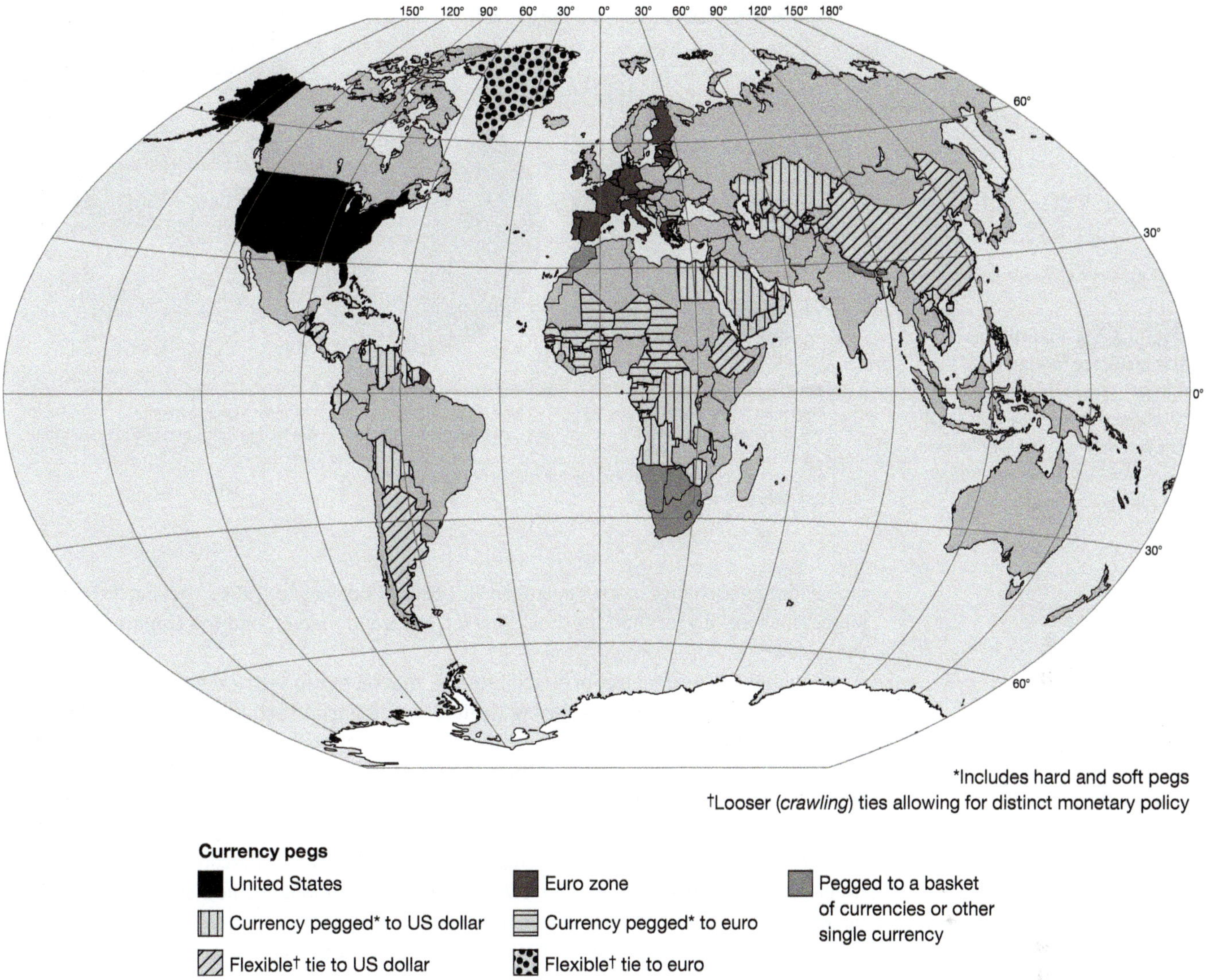

FIGURE 6.4 **Pegged currencies** This map indicates countries that peg their currencies to the U.S. dollar, the euro, or a basket of other currencies. **Source:** "Pegger Thy Neighbor," *Economist*, January 30, 2015. www.economist.com/blogs/graphicdetail/2015/01/daily-chart-17?zid=300&ah=e7b9370e170850b88ef129fa625b13c4.

4. Finally, some countries abandon their currency altogether and use U.S. dollars or another currency instead. This practice is known as **dollarization**. For instance, as mentioned earlier, Zimbabwe's currency was nearly worthless following a bout of hyperinflation from 2008 to 2009. To end the crisis, the government announced plans to switch to the U.S. dollar. Other countries including El Salvador, the Marshall Islands, the Federated States of Micronesia, Palau, and the islands of the Caribbean Netherlands also use the U.S. dollar as their official currency.[6] Similarly, Kosovo, Montenegro, and San Marino use the euro as their official currency.[7]

dollarization the process of a country abandoning their currency and using U.S. dollars or another currency instead

What Instituations Make Foreign Exchange Happen?

The Bank for International Settlements (BIS) was founded in 1930 and includes as members the central banks of 60 countries, representing 95 percent of world GDP. The BIS is headquartered in Basel, Switzerland, with a mission to help central banks achieve stability and to foster international cooperation by acting as a bank for central banks. It also studies and reports on the global foreign exchange market. A report by the BIS in September 2016 indicated that the

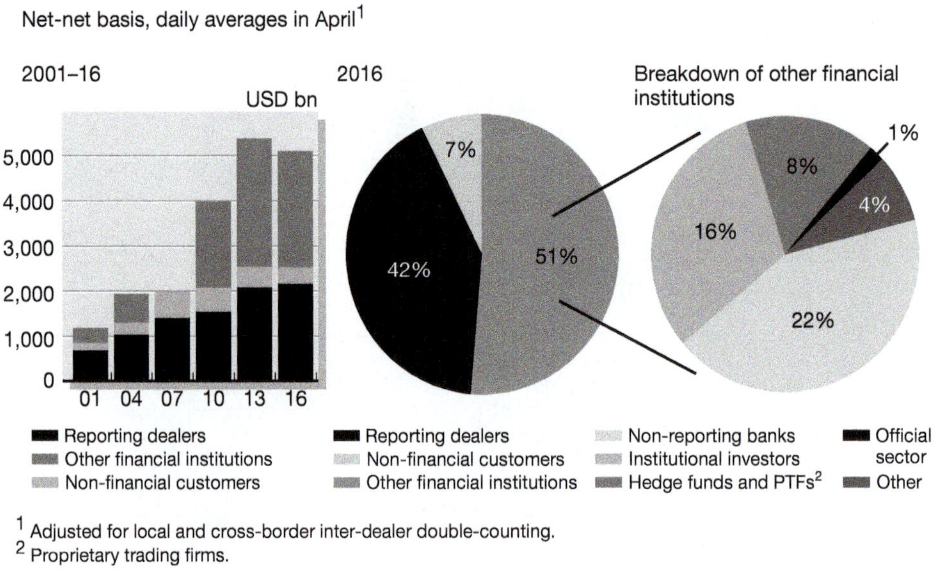

FIGURE 6.5 Institutions that facilitate foreign exchange **Source:** Bank for International Settlements, "Triennial Central Bank Survey: Foreign Exchange Turnover in April 2016," September 2016. http://www.bis.org/publ/rpfx16fx.pdf.

global foreign exchange market averaged $5.1 trillion a day in April 2016, making it the world's largest market—bigger than the stock market, the bond market, and the commodity market combined.[8]

Roughly 1,500 organizations facilitate the market for foreign exchange. These organizations are categorized into reporting dealers, nonfinancial customers, and other financial institutions. *Reporting dealers* are large banks such as JP Morgan Chase, HSBC, Royal Bank of Scotland, Goldman Sachs, Barclays, Deutsche Bank, UBS, Citi, Credit Suisse, and Morgan Stanley. These banks make markets in foreign currencies that in April 2016 accounted for 42 percent of all foreign exchange transactions (see **Figure 6.5**). *Nonfinancial customers* include individuals, governments, and businesses. This segment accounted for 7 percent of foreign exchange transactions in April 2016. Finally, *other financial institutions* include smaller commercial banks, currency funds, investment banks, hedge funds, pension funds, and money-sending companies such as Western Union. This segment accounted for 51 percent of foreign exchange in April 2016.

London is the center of the foreign exchange universe and accounts for roughly 37 percent of the global volume. New York is second, with 19 percent; other cities such as Hong Kong and Singapore also facilitate a large share of global exchange.

U.S. dollars form one side—about 88 percent—of the world's currency transactions, meaning these transactions trade U.S. dollars for a given currency. For instance, in April 2017, it took about US$1.25 to buy £1, about US$1.07 to buy €1, and about US$0.15 to buy 1 Chinese RMB.[9] The use of U.S. dollars facilitates exchange. For instance, if a company wanted to trade kip (the currency in Laos; see **Figure 6.6**) for pesos (the currency in Chile), it might have to trade kip for U.S. dollars and then the dollars for pesos, because few companies, governments, or individuals likely are seeking to trade kip for pesos in a given day. But exchanging kip for dollars first combines all trades for kip and pesos across all transactions for the currencies, including those buying the currencies to purchase commodities, to buy foreign bonds and loans, and even to engage in humanitarian aid. This in turn helps to clarify the market demand and price for these currencies.[10]

spread the difference between the buy and sell price for a currency

spot exchange rate buying foreign currency at present-day rates in anticipation of future transactions

Commercial banks make money in foreign exchange by charging a **spread** on the exchange, essentially a retail markup on the currency. For instance, if you are selling U.S. dollars and buying Korean won, the **spot exchange rate**—or the rate banks charge each other for won—may be 1,150 KW to the dollar. However, you are unlikely to get that discounted rate anywhere because you are not a bank. Instead, the bank may give you 1,130 KW for each dollar you sell. On the other hand, if you are selling Korean won to buy U.S. dollars, the bank may charge you 1,170 KW for each dollar you buy. The 20-KW difference between the spot rate and the rate you get as a trader is the spread (**Figure 6.7**). Banks compete in

Serjio74/iStock/Getty Images

FIGURE 6.6 **A 1,000 kip note (Laos) alongside a 1,000 peso note (Chile)**

The spot exchange rate: US$1 = 1,150 KW. This is the wholesale rate, or the rate at which banks exchange currency.

The exchange rate to **sell** U.S. dollars and buy Korean won, minus the 20-KW **spread** (the price you pay for the trade):

$$(1{,}150\,\text{KW/US\$1}) - 20\,\text{KW} = 1{,}130\,\text{KW}$$

The exchange rate to **buy** U.S. dollars and sell Korean won, plus the 20-KW **spread** (the price you pay for the trade):

$$(1{,}150\,\text{KW/US\$1}) + 20\,\text{KW} = 1{,}170\,\text{KW}$$

FIGURE 6.7 **How the spread operates in foreign exchange transactions**

the foreign exchange business by offering discounts on the spread in order to win customers. For simplicity, the spread is usually quoted as the average of the buy and sell rates, or as the spot rate.

In an effort to reduce the spread, or cost, of foreign exchange for retail customers, some organizations now charge a flat fee to link buyers and sellers in a virtual market. For instance, TransferWise, a peer-to-peer exchange company in the United Kingdom, charges just a 0.5 percent fee to match buyers and sellers. This peer-to-peer foreign exchange market is still small—just £250 billion a year—but it has been growing at 500 percent annually.[11]

Determining Exchange Rates

So how, exactly, do we determine an exchange rate? The formula is simple:

$$e = P^*/P$$

where e is the exchange rate, P^* represents the price of the foreign currency, and P is the price of the domestic currency.

The key is to know which currency is considered the *domestic* currency and then set it as the denominator of the equation. For the purposes of the exchange rate formula, the currency you are holding and want to trade is the domestic currency. For instance, if you want to trade U.S. dollars for euros when the exchange rate is €0.80 to US$1, the dollar is the domestic currency, and the equation will look like this:

$$0.8 = €x/US\$1$$

To solve, multiply both sides of the equation by 1, which gives us x = €0.80.

It then follows that the related exchange rate for trading euros for dollars is 1.25: if we put euros in the denominator as the domestic currency, we get

$$e = US\$1 / €0.80$$
$$e = 1.25$$

Note that we express exchange rates in terms of the domestic currency—the one in the denominator. Thus, expressing the dollar-to-euro exchange rate as 1.25 means we are considering the euro the domestic currency. To make the calculation, remember to simply multiply the amount of currency you have by the rate; this will tell you what your money is worth in terms of the other currency. Thus, if you have €0.80, multiply by 1.25 to find you have the equivalent of US$1. The exchange rate between euros and dollars has ranged between 0.83 to 1.59 dollars per euro over the past few years (**Figure 6.8**).

As they do with the stock and bond markets, many investors, speculators, businesses, and governments try to understand and predict the foreign exchange market. Doing so correctly can earn an investor a lot of money. However, it is difficult to predict how exchange rates will fluctuate.

Under- or Overvalued Currency

Because most currency values are based on the perceptions not only of inflation (as expressed in interest rates) but also of supply and demand among those who buy and sell currency, rates fluctuate constantly. As a result, a country's currency can sometimes be perceived as over- or undervalued, meaning analysts believe it is too expensive or too cheap relative to other currencies. How can that happen?

The law of one price tells us that a given good or service should sell for the same price anywhere in the world. This means, for instance, that gold sold in England should in theory cost the same as gold sold in China, Chile, or Canada. The related concept of purchasing power parity (PPP) tells us that a basket of goods sold anywhere in the world should cost the same amount. These concepts enable us to determine what the ideal exchange rate should be.

Big Mac Index a tool developed by the *Economist* magazine that demonstrates the over- or undervaluation of a currency as compared to the U.S. dollar using the price of the McDonalds' Big Mac

One popular scale for figuring out whether a currency is over- or undervalued is the **Big Mac Index** (see http://www.economist.com/content/big-mac-index). Based on PPP theory and originally developed by the *Economist* magazine as a light-hearted comparison, this tool is now standard and well-studied. This index gives the cost of a Big Mac in one country and

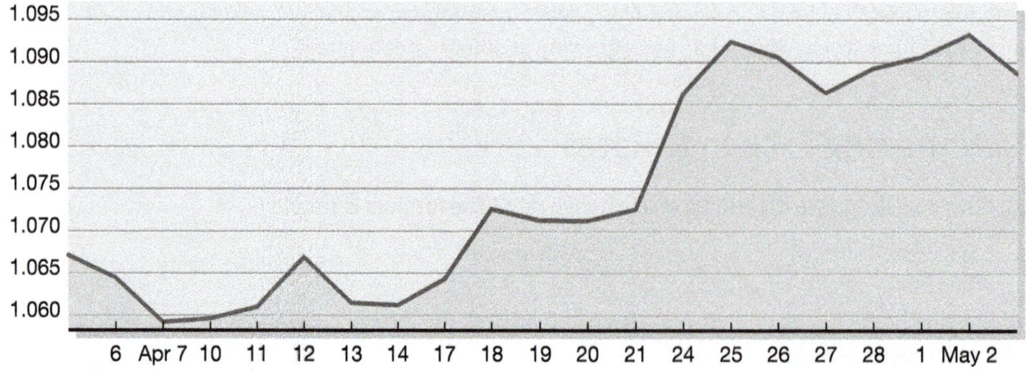

FIGURE 6.8 **Euro to U.S. Dollar Exchange Rate in 2017** **Source:** Google Finance, "Euro (€) to US Dollar ($)." www.google.com/finance?q=EURUSD&ei=Ha7iWOnmCoPDjAGV3o6gAQ.

compares it to the equivalent cost of a Big Mac in other countries, and then compares it to the actual exchange rates. If the Big Mac is relatively more expensive in the comparison currency than in the base currency, the comparison currency is probably overvalued. If the Big Mac is less expensive, the comparison currency is likely undervalued.

Let's look at a specific example. A Big Mac you purchased in Omaha, Nebraska, should cost the same relative amount in the local currency as a Big Mac purchased in Oslo, Norway. In July 2015, those Big Macs would have cost US$4.62 in Omaha and 48 kroner in Oslo. Dividing the foreign price by the domestic price gives us a predicted exchange rate of 10.01 kr per US$1. However, the actual exchange rate at the time was only 8.51 kr per US$1. This suggests that the krone is overvalued by 17.6 percent compared with the U.S. dollar. In other words, using U.S. dollars to buy kroner provides fewer kroner than we would expect.

If we think a currency is over- or undervalued, what could we do as an international business? One option is to practice Big Mac arbitrage. We could buy Big Macs for $4.62 in the United States, fly to Oslo with them in a suitcase, and sell them there for 48 kr each. Then we could go the bank and exchange the 48 kr for US$7.76, making US$3.14 in profit on each sandwich! Before you start packing, however, you should recognize two things. First, an airline ticket to Oslo would be expensive, so transportation costs would likely remove any potential profit. Second, even if we figure out transportation issues, if this exchange happened frequently enough, the value of kroner would decrease as we kept selling them in Norway to buy dollars in order to take our profit out of Norway and back to the U.S. In theory, if everyone did this with every product, not just a Big Mac, and could do it long enough to deflate the exchange rate of the kroner, the ability to engage in arbitrage would disappear—and with it the opportunity to profit.

While it's not practical to fly Big Macs around the world, imagine instead that we are doing the same thing with gold, which is just as good after a long plane flight as before. What happens? Interestingly, there is no mispricing and no room for arbitrage here. Instead, PPP and the law of one price work perfectly. For instance, the price of gold in the United Kingdom in 2012 was about £1,046 per ounce and, at the same time, $1,680 per ounce in the United States. This implies that, based on PPP, the exchange rate should be £1,046/$1,680 = £0.622 per US$1. Not surprisingly, the exchange rate really was 0.622 at that time.

So, why does PPP work perfectly with gold but not with Big Macs? One reason PPP breaks down in some instances is that some goods or services aren't easily tradeable. First, some, like Big Macs, are perishable and expensive to transport. Second, some goods and services are not perfect substitutes across borders. The law of one price requires goods and service to be identical from one country to the next, so it works reasonably well with commodities, but Norwegians might perceive a Big Mac as a luxury good rather than a fast meal, even if the product is nearly identical in both Norway and Nebraska. This would inflate the price of Big Macs in Norway and lead to a breakdown of the law of one price. After all, it works only for identical goods.

6.3 The Consequences of Under- or Overvalued Currencies for International Businesses

LEARNING OBJECTIVE

Discuss the causes and consequences of under- or overvaluation of currency

Undervalued Currency

Why would a country want to manipulate the value of its currency? The answer is simple: changes in the price of currency can have huge implications for a country's foreign trade and investment. As an example, in China, millions of people are moving from farms to cities, and these individuals need work. Historically, developing economies had implemented the strategy of employing their large, unskilled populations in manufacturing. China is no exception, and as a result, it has become a huge producer of textiles, electronics, machinery, shoes, appliances, toys, and other goods.

Until recently, very little demand existed within China for such products because incomes have traditionally been quite low, and most of what China produced was actually too expensive for the average Chinese consumer. If the goods were also comparatively expensive in the world market, they wouldn't have been competitive, demand would be weak, and few manufacturing jobs would be created. To prevent that situation, the Chinese government has made a concerted attempt to keep its currency valuation low. Because of those efforts, Chinese goods are comparatively cheap on the world market, fueling demand for them, encouraging the development of Chinese industry, and driving employment in the country.

To keep its currency cheap, China had pegged the renminbi to the U.S. dollar at what many Western observers considered an undervalued rate until 2015.[12] Even so, by some estimates (like the Big Mac index), the renminbi is more than 40 percent undervalued—meaning that you could buy as much as 40 percent more with renminbi than with the equivalent value in U.S. dollars. This also means that when goods are manufactured in China and sold in the United States, the difference in the exchange rate alone allows the goods to be priced 40 percent lower than they would be if the currency were appropriately valued, as shown in **Figure 6.9**. Yet even with low prices, the undervalued renminbi means Chinese manufacturers can still be profitable. How? The answer is that Chinese goods are also produced at a relatively low cost. So, relative to goods produced in the United States, the goods produced in China are actually even cheaper than the exchange rate makes it seem.

China's currency policy, along with investment in infrastructure and in manufacturing, has been very effective and has made it one of the fastest-growing economies in the world. Here is an example that helps illustrate why. Suppose Haier, a global appliance manufacturer headquartered in China, builds a refrigerator and sells it in the United States for $1,000. It then goes to the bank and exchanges the U.S. dollars for 6,140 Chinese RMB, which it sends back to China. However, the PPP exchange rate according to the Big Mac index is only 3.52 RMB to the dollar.

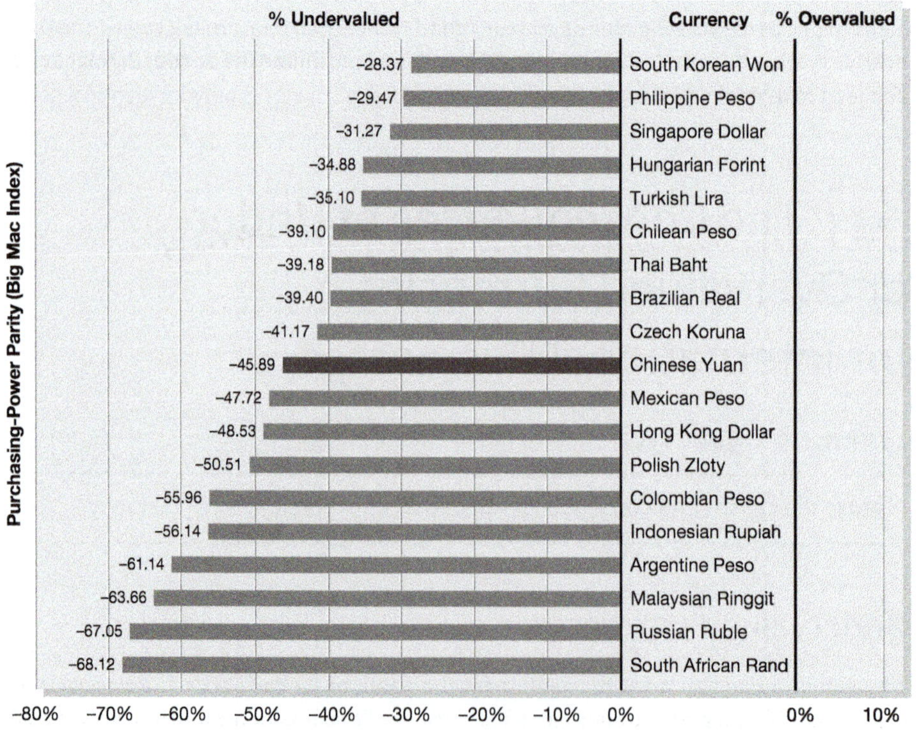

FIGURE 6.9 In 2016, the Chinese yuan was undervalued against the U.S. dollar by 45.89 percent **Source:** Roger Edgley et al., "Have Currencies Around the World Overshot Fair Value?" Advisor Perspectives, February 23, 2016. www.advisorperspectives.com/commentaries/2016/02/23/have-currencies-around-the-world-overshot-fair-value.

This means that Haier should get only 3,520 RMB (3.52 × 1,000) for the sale of that refrigerator. Since Haier actually gets 6,140 RMB (6.14 × 1,000), it is essentially doubling its earnings because of the currency valuation.

This exchange rate benefit is huge; Haier could afford to discount the appliance heavily compared with competitors' prices and still earn significant profits. In fact, given only the currency undervaluation, Haier could discount its goods by 40 percent and still achieve parity with profits of a comparable U.S.-based manufacturer. Now consider how Haier would fare against a manufacturer in Sweden. If the Swedish krone is 24.2 percent overvalued against the U.S. dollar, the advantage of the renminbi against the krone is even larger!

Overvalued Currency

Japan, by contrast, has had chronically overvalued currency for the past 20 years or more. This means that Japanese goods—like cars, computers, and TVs—are relatively more expensive than the same goods produced by foreign rivals simply because of the high price of the yen. How does this work? Consider that Toyota produces the Reiz (similar to a Camry) in Japan and sells it in China. When Toyota wishes to return the profits to Japan, it must sell the renminbi it earned in the car sale and buy Japanese yen to bring them home. At that point, the roughly 15-percent overvaluation of the yen will immediately diminish the amount the company ends up with.

This is why Shinzo Abe, the prime minister of Japan, returned to power in 2013 with the explicit goal of reducing the value of the yen on world markets. He wanted to make Japanese exports more attractive again. This strategy caused the Bank of Japan to dramatically increase the supply of yen in an effort to devalue the currency in international markets. While the outcomes for Japan are still uncertain, for the policy to work it has to make Japanese goods less expensive in world markets.

In general, manufacturing-dependent nations prefer to have their currency undervalued in an effort to help drive exports, but some countries prefer an overvalued currency. For instance, Thailand in the 1990s supported an overvalued Thai baht. Why would a country want an overvalued currency? There are two main reasons. First, it makes imports cheaper. The cost of buying foreign goods or taking a foreign vacation goes down with an overvalued domestic currency. Second, an overvalued currency can make foreign debt comparatively cheaper to pay off. This was the case for Thailand. Because the country had a large amount of debt denominated in foreign currencies such as dollars, euros, and pounds, it first had to trade baht for whatever currency its debt was denominated in before it could make payments on the debt. Having an overvalued currency meant the debt was relatively cheaper to pay off.

6.4 Understanding and Managing Exchange Rate Risk

LEARNING OBJECTIVE

Describe how companies settle international monetary transactions and manage exchange-rate risk.

The fluctuation of exchange rates is a significant risk factor for businesses that buy and sell across borders, and this risk takes several forms. For example, 2Plant is a U.S.-based importer of flower bulbs from the Netherlands. The company orders significant quantities of bulbs in the late fall and then pays for them a few months later in the spring. Buy now, pay later might sound like a good strategy on the surface, but this is actually a risky exchange because

Transaction Exposure

The extent to which the income from individual transactions is affected by fluctuations in foreign exchange values

e.g., being held to a previously agreed contract price

Translation Exposure

The impact of currency exchange rate changes on the reported financial statements of a company (**typically assets**)

e.g., value of foreign subsidiary

Economic Exposure

The extent to which a firm's future international earning power is affected by changes in exchange rates

e.g., market cap value of the firm

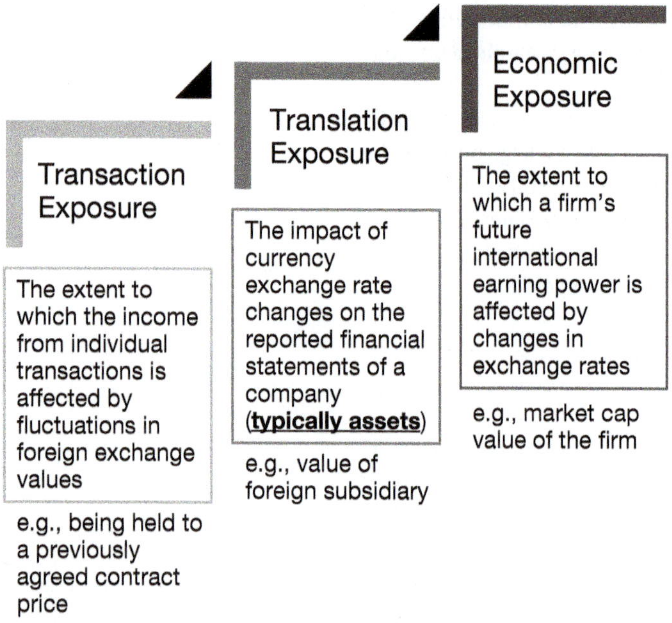

FIGURE 6.10 **Foreign exchange risk** Foreign exchange entails three types of risk: transaction exposure, translation exposure, and economic exposure.

transaction exposure the extent to which income from foreign transactions is exposed to currency fluctuations before payment is made

translation exposure the impact of currency exchange rate changes on the financial statements of a company

economic exposure a company's exposure to unexpected change in foreign exchange rates

the true cost of the bulbs can swing dramatically with currency shifts (see **Figure 6.10**).

For instance, suppose 2Plant ordered 100,000 bulbs priced at €1 each in December 2015, when the exchange rate was €0.80 per dollar. At that time, the company would owe its Dutch supplier $125,000, but it doesn't actually pay for the bulbs until spring. Fast forward to the spring of 2016, and the cost of purchasing the bulbs increased because the exchange rate increased to €0.75 per dollar. In other words, the cost to 2Plant would now be $133,333 instead of $125,000! Of course, if the exchange rate had moved in the other direction in 2016, as it did in 2017, the cost would have gone down. If it had gone from €0.80 to €0.94 to the dollar (the price in April 2017), for instance, the cost for 100,000 bulbs would have decreased from $125,000 to $106,685, leading to a nearly $9,000 profit.

This means that 2Plant not only has to negotiate the price of the bulbs it buys, but it also must manage its exchange rate risk. A 10 percent change in the exchange rate could wipe out the entire year's profits—or provide a surprise windfall of extra profit for the company. Most companies prefer to avoid this kind of **transaction exposure**, or the extent to which income from foreign transactions is exposed to currency fluctuations before payment is made, and they actively seek to control it.

For example, Toyota, which sells hundreds of thousands of cars each year in the United States, has been troubled at times because of large currency swings between the U.S. dollar and the currency of the company's home market, Japan—the yen. It's possible for the company to have growing sales but declining revenue in the United States if the yen appreciates against the dollar throughout the fiscal year. This can sometimes nearly erase profits and cripple a company as it moves forward in a globalized economy. On the other hand, the U.S. dollar appreciated nearly 20 percent against the yen during 2013. This pushed Toyota's profits up more than 50 percent.[13]

To help manage transaction exposure, some financial services firms have created options that allow them to take on this currency exchange risk for their customers, for a fee. These banks trust that their dedicated currency analysts will be able to predict the exchange rate fluctuations better than the corporate analysts employed by their corporate clients. And they typically offset some of their own risk by finding investors to buy the other side of the transaction.

Another kind of exchange rate risk international firms face is **translation exposure**, the impact of exchange rate fluctuations on the company's financial statements. For instance, suppose Samsung, the Korean electronics conglomerate, earned $1 million through sales made in the United States, but before the company could bring that money back to Korea, the exchange rate shifted such that the $1 million was only worth $800,000. In this instance, translation exposure will hurt Samsung's reported financial performance, because the value of the assets it posts in its financial reporting will drop by $200,000.

Similarly, the dollar value that Ford Motor Company lists on its balance sheet for its manufacturing plant in Koln, Germany, varies based on the value of the euro. If the euro appreciates, then the value of Ford's property, plants, and equipment as expressed in dollars will increase, thereby increasing Ford's equity. This change could in turn increase the company's ability to borrow and cause its stock price to fluctuate.

Finally, international companies also face **economic exposure**, or their exposure to unexpected change in foreign exchange rates. Economic exposure occurs, for instance, if a company earns a significant portion of its revenue in one market and that market contracts. For instance, following Britain's 2016 vote to the leave the European Union and the rapid devaluation of the British pound, the value of Burberry, a British clothing retailer, was virtually unaffected because only 10 percent of Burberry's revenues come from the United Kingdom. By contrast, the value of Barratt, a British home builder that earns a majority of its money in the United Kingdom, fell nearly 30 percent. Unlike transaction and translation exposure, economic exposure from shifting exchange rates is difficult to mitigate because it is by nature a surprise movement of currency.

For example, in 2016, McDonald's received about 70 percent of its revenues from overseas markets. Its analysts might predict a gradual depreciation of the U.S. dollar against major global currencies and factor that into its operating forecasts for the next few years. If, however, the U.S. dollar appreciates instead of depreciating as McDonald's had predicted, the company faces economic exposure. The dollar's newfound strength means that 70 percent of the revenues and cash flows the company receives will be worth less than anticipated when converted back into dollars, which will have a negative effect on its profitability and stock price.

Managing Exchange Rate Risks

Exchange rate risks can be a serious hurdle for companies wanting to do business internationally, but several strategies are available to mitigate them. First, companies can take advantage of spot exchange rates. This simply means buying foreign currency at present-day rates in anticipation of future transactions. For instance, 2Plant could buy euros on the same day it buys the bulbs, even if it doesn't use the euros to pay for the bulbs until a future date. This would help insulate the company against future fluctuations by guaranteeing that it got the euros at the current rate, eliminating the risk of the time delay.

Second, 2Plant could also engage in **forward exchange rate transactions**. In these deals, two parties, usually a company and a bank, agree to exchange currency at some future date—usually 30, 90, or 180 days out—at a specific rate they agree to at the time of the deal, which is most often based on the forward rate provided by the *Wall Street Journal* or Bloomberg. For instance, **Table 6.1** shows the spot and forward rates from the *Wall Street Journal* for exchanging British pounds for U.S. dollars in December 2016, March 2017, and June 2017. It suggests that the pound will depreciate from the current rate of 1.2964 to 1.2875 per U.S. dollar in March 2017, but then rebound slightly to 1.2927 per U.S. dollar in June 2017.

forward exchange rate transactions a transaction involving two parties that agree to exchange currency at some future date at a specific rate they agree to at the time of the deal

The forward rate is a prediction of future spot rates. In this way, the company again bypasses uncertainty in the currency market and locks in an acceptable rate.

Third, companies can engage in **FX swaps**, which are the simultaneous purchase and sale of a given amount of currency at two different rates. In other words, a spot transaction is coupled with a forward transaction, but both are completed at the same time. For example, 2Plant could engage in a swap to pay for its bulbs. To do so, the company would sell dollars at the current rate and agree to buy euros in 30 days at a fixed forward price. In this way, 2Plant locks in the price of the exchange, again eliminating the risk from currency fluctuations in the future.

FX swaps the simultaneous purchase and sale of a given amount of currency at two different rates

In addition to these direct strategies that involve the actual buying and selling of currency, companies may also hedge their exchange rate risk by buying options and or futures. An *option* is the purchase of the right to buy a certain amount of currency at a given exchange rate, but is not an obligation to buy. In this case, a bank will sell 2Plant an option to buy euros at a certain price on a certain day for a fee. 2Plant pays the fee and can exercise the option or not, depending on the actual movement of the exchange rates. A *future* is similar to a forward contract, but rather than purchasing it from a bank, it is traded on an exchange.

British Pound (CME)-£62,500; $ per £							Lifetime		
	Open	High	Low	Settle	Chg	High	(Δ ∇)	Low	Open Lnt
Dec 16	1.2964	1.2967	1.2835	1.2875	–.0122	1.5000		1.2827	242.899
Mar 17	1.2967	1.2985	1.2862	1.2899	–.0123	1.4735	∇	1.2862	1,584
Jun 17	1.2929	1.2956	1.2896	1.2927	–.0122	1.5003	∇	1.2896	416

Est vol 124,551; vol n.a. n.a.; open int. 245.000, n.a.

Sources: SIX Financial Information; WSJ Market Data Group; historical data prior to 6/15/11: Thomson Reuters; WSJ Market Data Group

TABLE 6.1 **Forward rate for British pound-to-U.S. dollar exchange, 2016–2017**

Source: "Market Data Center: Currencies," *Wall Street Journal*. wsj.com/mdc/public/page/2_3023-fut_currency-futres.html?mod=mdc_curr_pglnk. Accessed June 5, 2017.

WileyPLUS

See Whiteboard Video: Managing Foreign Exchange Rate Risk

Finally, as part of a global company's strategy to reduce exchange rate risk, it can diversify its production to the global markets in which it operates. For instance, Porsche nearly went out of business in the 1990s because it sold the vast majority of its cars in the United States and exchange rates devalued the U.S. dollar, wiping out Porsche's profits. In response, global auto manufacturers such as Volkswagen, General Motors, and Toyota have diversified production to different global markets in an attempt to hedge against the risk of currency changes. Nearly two-thirds of GM cars are produced outside the United States, often in the region where they are sold. This approach limits the amount of money GM needs to exchange and thus reduces its foreign exchange rate risk.

Predicting Exchange Rate Shifts

It is often said that the best way to make a small fortune in trading foreign currencies is to start with a large fortune. Predicting exchange rate movements is indeed a difficult endeavor, and even experts are often wrong. However, four key indicators may help predict future exchange rates: economic growth, the level of foreign direct investment (FDI) in a country, fiscal and monetary policies, and political stability.

Economic Growth. Strong economic growth is a sign that a nation's currency will appreciate in value against other currencies, because a nation's growth means its people have rising levels of disposable income and will need more places to spend it. On the other hand, countries that experience negative GDP growth usually have a depreciated currency. Currency links back to economic growth because, when GDP increases, citizens prosper and begin demanding more imports. The country will then develop a negative trade balance, which requires an infusion of foreign capital to offset the outflow of money.

Foreign Direct Investment. When foreign companies or individuals decide to invest in a country by purchasing land, constructing production facilities, or hiring and training new workers, they create demand for that currency. Mexico, for instance, has recently seen strong growth in such FDI. This FDI puts pressure on the Mexican peso to appreciate, because investments in factories, inventories, land, and salaries for Mexican employees must be paid in the home currency, which ties up pesos and increases demand for them, likely driving up the price.[14]

Monetary and Fiscal Policies. Monetary policies are the methods by which a central bank attempts to control the supply of its currency—generally with the goal of maintaining price stability and thereby improving the country's global competitiveness. Central banks can print money, increasing the supply, which may in turn stimulate borrowing and growth. However, increasing the supply of money can increase inflation and thus likely lead to depreciation of a country's currency. Central banks can also raise interest rates and use quantitative easing as tools to try to manage their currency to the advantage of their own economy. Exporting nations often deliberately weaken their currency to make their exports cheaper, and importing nations often try to strengthen their currencies to increase their purchasing power.[15]

Moreover, fiscal policies can also affect foreign exchange rates. As a government's debt grows, its currency tends to depreciate. For instance, China's debt, both public and private, quadrupled in just 10 years, to 247 percent of GDP in 2015.[16] Many investors fear that up to 25 percent of those loans are loans that are not being paid back by the borrower (also called *non-performing loans*) funded by state-controlled banks. That means if the loans are written off, it could amount to 35 percent of China's GDP being written off.[17] If they are not written off, the loans will be a drag on China's growth. This worry puts pressure on the Chinese renminbi to devalue relative to other currencies.

Political Stability. Although political stability doesn't necessarily directly affect a country's economy, global perceptions of the country's steadiness and safety do affect the strength of its currency. In general, the more politically stable a country is, the stronger its currency will be. For example, North Korea is known for its widespread poverty, authoritarian leadership, and closed economy. As a result, it is a poor candidate for a strong and widely traded currency.

Wars, riots, revolutions, terrorist attacks, and natural disasters induce chaos and affect currency markets by introducing widespread uncertainty in the minds of investors and potential investors. They begin to ask questions: "Will this civil uprising result in an overthrow of the government and the issuance of new currency?" "Will this tropical storm hurt economic growth over the long term for this country?" "Will this war change the way firms treat this country's currency moving forward?" Any of these results will affect the relative value of the currency in question.

New Zealand has high political stability. It is seen as well-run and peaceful, with very low levels of government corruption. New Zealand also benefits from a close political and economic relationship with the United Kingdom, another politically stable nation. On the other hand, Syria, Libya, Egypt, Iran, and Somalia have recently been very unstable for various reasons, including war, violent regime change, piracy, drought, and mass migration, leading to wild swings in their currency prices.[18]

Sometimes unsettling positive and negative events can occur simultaneously, and companies must decide which to weigh more heavily. For example, Canada has recently experienced strong economic growth, but the country also has increasing levels of public debt. Malaysia has experienced major tropical storms, but it has also received healthy inflows of FDI. Israel is working to cut government spending in an effort to whittle down public debt, but it also faces constant threats from neighboring nations and terrorist groups. The World Trade Center attacks of 2001 tested the United States' general political and economic stability, causing temporary fluctuations in the dollar's value. Currency analysts today struggle constantly to make accurate predictions, modifying forecasts in response to any new information. Even the most experienced and savvy foreign exchange traders make bad trades from time to time, proving that currency trading is a difficult profession.

Summary and Case

Summary

LEARNING OBJECTIVE 6.1 Identify the three functions of money.

The three functions of money are to facilitate trade, to serve as a unit of accounting, and to enable the storage of value so that people can delay consumption (save). Historically, currencies were either made of valuable materials like precious metals or were backed by such materials. Today, most governments have shifted to fiat currencies, or currencies that have value only because the government says they do.

LEARNING OBJECTIVE 6.2 Explain why foreign exchange rates fluctuate.

Today's fiat currencies are valued based largely on factors such as supply and demand, political stability, and economic policy. Exchange rates are based on purchasing power parity (PPP) and the law of one price, which imply that identical goods should have the same prices across country borders. Currencies manipulated by their governments can be either under- or overvalued, depending on whether they buy less or more foreign goods than predicted by PPP.

LEARNING OBJECTIVE 6.3 Discuss the causes and consequences of under- or overvaluation of currency.

Undervalued currencies tend to make domestic production more appealing for foreign trade, potentially boosting domestic manufacturing sectors. Overvalued currencies make it easier for a country to pay down foreign debts and for citizens to buy foreign-produced product and services. Governments sometimes interfere with natural currency values to keep foreign trade conditions more favorable for domestic industries.

LEARNING OBJECTIVE 6.4 Describe how companies settle international monetary transactions and manage exchange rate risk.

Three types of exchange rate risk—transactional, translational, and economic—can affect company profits, earnings, and balance sheets. Three major tools—spot exchanges, forward contracts, and currency swaps—help firms eliminate currency risk by locking in an exchange rate, whether payment is made now or in the future. Companies can also avoid risky situations by considering countries' current and expected rates of growth, level of foreign direct investment, fiscal and monetary policies, and political stability.

Case Study

BMW and Foreign Exchange Rate Risk

BMW, owner of the BMW, Mini, and Rolls-Royce brands, has been a major presence in Europe since 1916. The company still sells 46 percent of its cars in Europe, and growth is highest there. However, China is becoming one of BMW's most important markets. As shown in **Figure 6.11**, in 2016, the company sold over 520,000 cars in China, and BMW has turned to the Chinese market as a primary focus for future sales.[19]

Despite rising sales revenues, BMW is conscious that its profits are often wiped out by changes in exchange rates. The company has pointed out that it was hit particularly hard by China's currency devaluation in late 2015. BMW Brilliance Automotive Co. Ltd., BMW's subsidiary in China, imports about half its components from Europe and elsewhere, and it faced major declines in profit because of the negative effects of unfavorable exchange rates.[20]

However, BMW did not want to pass those exchange rate costs on to consumers through price increases. Its rival, Porsche, had done that in the United States at the end of the 1980s, and sales plunged as a result. Instead, BMW took a two-pronged approach to managing its foreign exchange exposure.

The first strategy was to use a "natural hedge" against risk, meaning the company would develop ways to earn and spend money in the same currency. To do so, BMW sought ways to keep revenues in the country and spend in the local currency. The company tried to import fewer products from Europe, and instead sourced products locally from factories in China. It also worked with local Chinese vendors to spend more of the renminbi it earned in China. By moving more of its production to China and other Asian markets, the company not only reduced its foreign exchange exposure but also benefitted from being closer to its new customers.

However, not all exposure could be offset in this way, so BMW decided it would also use formal financial hedges and currency options.[21] To achieve this second strategy, BMW set up regional treasury centers in the United States, the United Kingdom, and Singapore. These centers took on the responsibility of monitoring and reviewing exchange rate exposure in each region in which the company operated. Staff there produced weekly reports for the finance operations staff in BMW's Munich headquarters, so the company could monitor when and where to move currencies across countries, when to buy currency hedges, and what currency options it needed to mitigate foreign exchange risk.[22]

Case Discussion Questions

1. What types of exchange risk does BMW face when selling cars in China?
2. How can BMW best manage risks from currency exchange exposure in China?
3. How do the different types of hedging help BMW reduce currency risk?

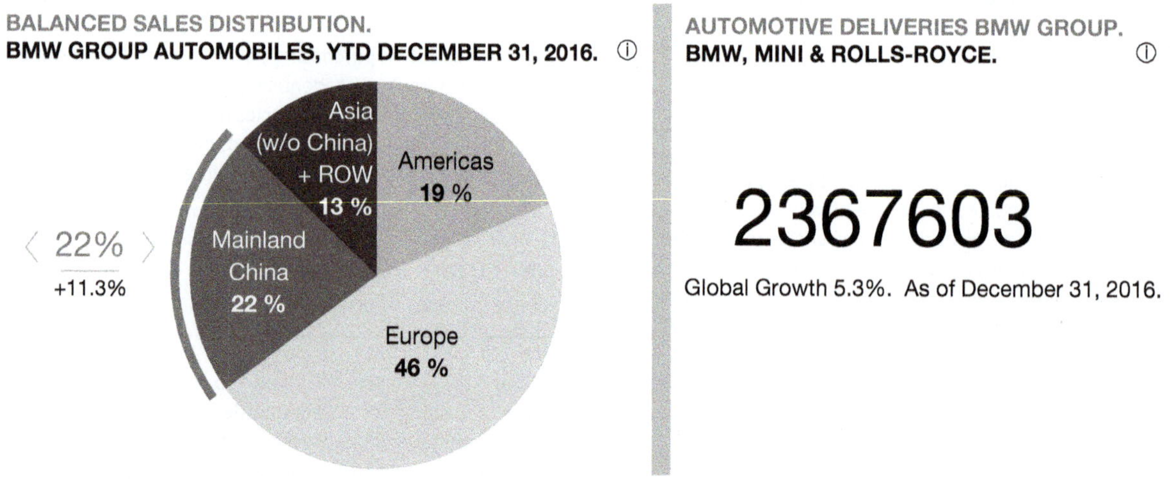

FIGURE 6.11 BMW global sales in 2016 Asia is quickly becoming a key market for the company; China's sales increased by 11.3 percent, and sales throughout the rest of Asia grew by 4 percent.

Source: "Investor Relations," BMW Group. www.bmwgroup.com/en/investor-relations.html. Accessed April 14, 2017.

Endnotes

[1]Francis X. Diebold, Steven Husted, and Mark Rush, "Real Exchange Rates under the Gold Standard," *Journal of Political Economy* 99, no. 6 (1991): 1252–71.

[2]Jonathan Garber, "Bitcoin Spikes after Japan Says It's a Legal Payment Method," *Business Insider,* April 3, 2017. www.businessinsider.com/bitcoin-price-spikes-as-japan-recognizes-it-as-a-legal-payment-method-2017-4.

[3]Dominic Frisby, "Zimbabwe's Trillion-Dollar Note: From Worthless Paper to Hot Investment," *Guardian*, May 14, 2016. www.theguardian.com/money/2016/may/14/zimbabwe-trillion-dollar-note-hyerinflation-investment.

[4]Jonathan Prynn and Mark Prigg, "Apple Changes Regent Street to Its Core," *Evening Standard*, November 20, 2009. www.standard.co.uk/news/apple-changes-regent-street-to-its-core-6760493.html.

[5]International Monetary Fund (IMF), *Annual Report on Exchange Arrangements and Exchange Restrictions*, October 2014. www.imf.org/external/pubs/nft/2014/areaers/ar2014.pdf.

[6]Matt Vasilogambros, "Zimbabwe's Own U.S. Dollar Bills," *The Atlantic*, May 6, 2016. https://www.theatlantic.com/international/archive/2016/05/zimbabwe-money/481518/

[7]IMF, *Annual Report on Exchange Arrangements and Exchange Restrictions.*

[8]Anirban Nag and Jamie McGeever, "Foreign Exchange, the World's Biggest Market, Is Shrinking," Reuters, February 11, 2016. www.reuters.com/article/us-global-fx-peaktrading-idUSKCN0VK1UD.

[9]XE Currency Converter: CNY to USD. www.xe.com/currencyconverter/convert/?From=CNY&To=USD (accessed April 2, 2017).

[10]Hendrik van den Berg, *International Economics: A Heterodox Approach* (New York: Routledge, 2014).

[11]Aliya Ram, "Peer-to-Peer Forex Platforms Come of Age: Exchanges Using Crowdsource Model Set to Eclipse Existing Currency Services in UK by 2019," *Financial Times*, April 1, 2015. www.ft.com/content/60aa6e8a-8798-11e4-bc7c-00144feabdc0.

[12]Linette Lopez, "A Perfect Example of How China Confuses Wall Street to No End," *Business Insider*, February 16, 2016. www.businessinsider.com/chinese-yuan-peg-to-dollar-and-basket-of-currencies-2016-2.

[13]Christoph Rauwald and Dorothee Tschampa, "VW to BMW Plan $25 Billion Hedge by Building Autos Abroad," Bloomberg, April 15, 2013. www.bloomberg.com/news/articles/2013-04-16/vw-to-bmw-plan-25-billion-hedge-by-building-autos-abroad

[14]Linda S. Goldberg and Michael W. Klein, "*Foreign Direct Investment, Trade and Real Exchange Rate Linkages in Developing Countries,*" *Managing Capital Flows and Exchange Rates: Perspectives from the Pacific Basin*, ed. Reuven Glick (Cambridge: University of Cambridge, 1998), 73–100.

[15]"Effect of Monetary Policy," Investopedia.com, http://www.investopedia.com/exam-guide/cfa-level-1/global-economic-analysis/monetary-policy-exchange-balance-payments.asp?lgl=myfinance-layout-no-ads. Accessed June 5, 2017.

[16]Roger Bootle, "Chinese Authorities Need to Guard Against Bad Debt Crisis," *Telegraph*, October 2, 2016. www.telegraph.co.uk/business/2016/10/02/chinese-authorities-need-to-guard-against-bad-debt-crisis/.

[17]Jing Sun, "Digging into China's Growing Mountain of Debt," Bloomberg, August 28, 2016. www.bloomberg.com/news/articles/2016-08-28/digging-into-china-s-growing-mountain-of-debt/.

[18]Jason Van Bergen, "6 Factors That Influence Exchange Rates," Investopedia.com, updated March 7, 2017. www.investopedia.com/articles/basics/04/050704.asp?ad=dirN&qo=investopediaSiteSearch&qsrc=0&o=40186.

[19]"Investor Relations," BMW Group. www.bmwgroup.com/en/investor-relations.html (accessed April 14, 2017).

[20]Xu Bin and Liu Ying, "The Case Study: How BMW Dealt with Exchange Rate Risk," *Financial Times*, October 29, 2012. www.ft.com/content/f21b3a92-f907-11e1-8d92-00144feabdc0.

[21]Sofia Horta e Costa, "Hey Auto Bulls, BMW Has Been Hedging the Euro for Years," Bloomberg, March 16, 2015. www.bloomberg.com/news/articles/2015-03-17/hey-auto-bulls-bmw-has-been-hedging-against-the-euro-for-years/.

[22]Bin and Ying, "The Case Study."

CHAPTER 7

Trade

antadi1332/Getty Images

Introduction

World trade in goods and service totals nearly $20 *trillion* a year. That's trillion with a "T." This is quite different from just a generation ago. Then, world trade was less than $2 trillion, as the graph shows. The rapid growth in trade is significant; trade now represents over a quarter of the world's GDP. For some people, the idea of world trade evokes fear. They believe jobs and opportunities are being lost to competitors in other countries because of increased trade. Several global leaders such as President Donald Trump in the United States argues for decreasing global trade and halting the loss of jobs from the United States to other markets. Others believe trade increases specialization, which increases quality and output, increasing the standard of living for everyone.

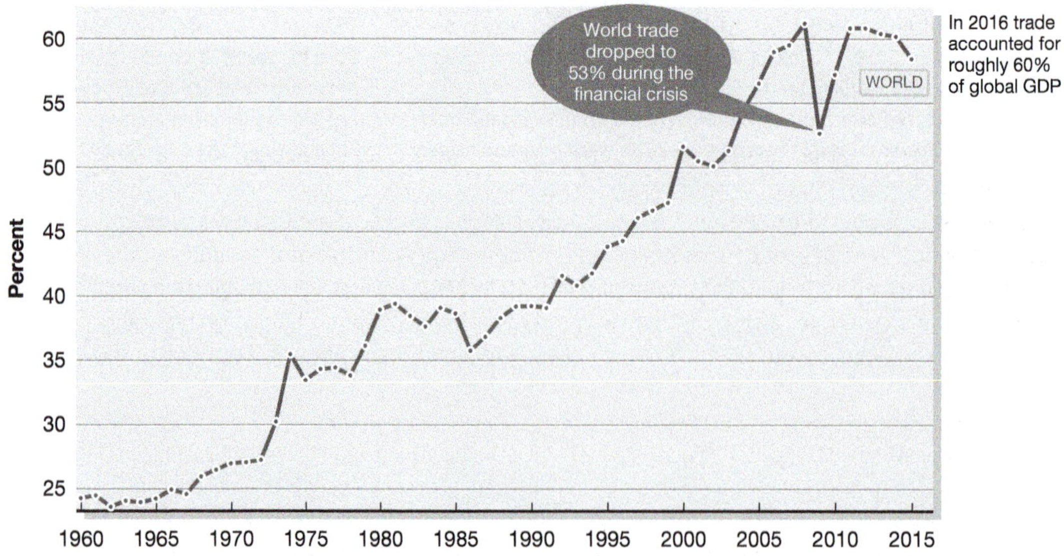

Regardless of your feelings about world trade, most countries are dependent on it, importing energy, food, and goods and services. This graph highlights each country's trade in goods and services as a percentage of its GDP. For instance, in 2015 trade was 73 percent of Saudi Arabia's GDP, a result of the country trading its abundant oil. In the same year, Hong Kong's trade as a percentage of its GDP was a world-record high of 401 percent. On the other hand, only

28 percent of the U.S. GDP comes from trade.[1] Regardless of the proportion of trade in a country, international commerce is a major part of the economic activity of most countries.

LEARNING OBJECTIVES

After you explore this chapter you will be able to:

1. **Compare** theories about why countries trade
2. **Describe** trade imbalances and their consequences
3. **Identify** patterns of trade such as regionalization
4. **Classify** government policies that affect trade patterns

7.1 Theories of Trade

LEARNING OBJECTIVE

Compare theories about why countries trade.

International trade has been an important force in the world for thousands of years. Throughout the ages, different theories have directed governments' approach to international trade. These approaches can be categorized into different theories that explain why countries trade. We will now explore these theories.

WileyPLUS

See Whiteboard Video: The Benefits of Trade

Interventionist Theories

Since antiquity, trade patterns have been shaped by the sovereign nation-states in which trading companies operated. These companies were heavily dependent on government support. In fact, they often were owned by those governments and their activities were used to promote the ruler's specific objectives, usually building up gold reserves to fill the national treasury.

Mercantilism. In 1519 the Spanish conquistador Hernán Cortés sailed from the island of Hispaniola in the West Indies to conquer the interior of Mexico for the Spanish Empire. Upon his arrival, Cortés overthrew the Aztec Empire, built colonies, and sent gold, silver, and slaves back to Spain. These acts of conquest and colonization were the result of mercantilism, the dominant theory of trade in Europe from about 1500 to 1800. **Mercantilism** suggested that trade generates wealth for a country that exported more than it imported, thus forcing trade partners to pay it in gold and silver, which enriched its coffers. The result was a positive trade balance, or **trade surplus**.

To ensure they exported more than they imported and so amassed wealth, countries created policies to restrict and tax imports, subsidize exports, and control the sale of finished goods. In addition to strictly governing trade, mercantilist regimes were active in establishing colonies overseas. Colonies provided a steady market for finished goods produced in the home country and served as a stable source of raw materials—all under the political control of the home country and contributing to a trade surplus. Often the gold and silver reserves thus accumulated were used to fund military actions and global conquest.

mercantilism a trade theory which suggests that trade generates wealth for a country with a trade surplus, with emphasis on colonization and military conquest

trade surplus the result when a country engaged in trade exports more than it imports, also called positive trade balance

neo-mercantilism a trade theory which suggests that trade generates wealth for a country with a trade surplus, with emphasis on rapid economic development

Neo-mercantilism. Like mercantilism, **neo-mercantilism** favors a positive balance of trade for the purpose of achieving a social or political objective. The word *neo-mercantilism* literally means a new or revived form of mercantilism. However, rather than focusing on

protectionist actions actions taken by a country to protect domestic industry

tariffs taxes on foreign products that discourage imports

subsidies government support for industries

monetary measures efforts related to the supply of money

free trade trade without government intervention or restrictions

absolute advantage the ability of a country to produce a specific good or service more efficiently than any rival

military development, neo-mercantilism today emphasizes running a trade surplus to fund rapid economic development. China, for instance, is often described as a neo-mercantilist country. It uses **protectionist actions**, in this case actions taken by a country intended to ensure a trade surplus, including implementing **tariffs**, which are taxes on foreign products meant to discourage imports; **subsidies**, which are price supports for industries, thereby encouraging exports; and **monetary measures**, which are government actions related to the supply of money in order to keep its currency, the renminbi, significantly undervalued[2]—all with the intention of increasing exports and rapidly developing the economy.[3] Countries like Japan, Thailand, and Singapore also engage in neo-mercantilist policies for various reasons, including maintaining political influence, protecting domestic industries, and encouraging economic independence to build self-sufficiency.

North Wind Picture Archives/Alamy Stock Photo

FIGURE 7.1 **David Hume**

Free-Trade Theories

Several negative effects resulted from mercantilistic trade policies. For instance, countries that engaged in mercantilism often distorted their economies, causing high inflation in their home markets. Some early economists began to point out that countries should not try to artificially support or suppress trade. They argued that allowing countries to trade freely allows them to gain wealth through specialization. Let's review the reasoning that led them to support **free trade**, which is trade without government intervention or restrictions.

Theory of Absolute Advantage. Even while mercantilism remained the dominant trade policy in Europe, economists began to question its logic. In 1752, the Scottish philosopher David Hume (see **Figure 7.1**), one of the first of these skeptics, stated that mercantilism was a fallacy because the inflow of currency to the home country would merely cause inflation as the larger amount of money available—a result of hoarding gold—chased the same amount of goods and services as before. Inflation would in turn affect trade by causing exports to become relatively more expensive and imports to become relatively less expensive. At the same time, the outflow of gold and silver from the trade partner's economy would cause deflation there, and foreign goods would become relatively more expensive. As a result, Hume argued, the home country would face significant pressure to import the cheaper goods produced by its trade partners, exporting less and importing more. All the while, the trade partner would have a drive to export more and import less. Thus, over time, it would be difficult to run a perpetual trade surplus, and the objective of mercantilism would fail.

Building on the work of Hume, fellow Scotsman Adam Smith (see **Figure 7.2**), a pioneer in the new field of Economics, proposed in his 1776 book *The Wealth of Nations* that different countries possessed different abilities to produce goods. Countries that were better at producing a specific good or service than any rival had an **absolute advantage** in the production of that good. For example, the English had an absolute advantage in producing textiles, whereas the French had an absolute advantage in producing wine. Hume argued that both England and France would be better off if England focused on producing cloth and France focused on producing wine, and then traded with each other.

Culture Club/Hulton Archive/Getty Images

FIGURE 7.2 **Adam Smith**

This theory shifted the view of trade from the zero-sum game (for every winner there is a loser) of mercantilism to a way of increasing productivity and wealth for both countries. For instance, as shown in **Figure 7.3**, country A is able to produce 100 pounds of rice per hour, while country B is able to produce only 25 pounds per hour. Conversely, country B is able to produce 100 pounds of wheat per hour, while country A is able to produce only 25 pounds per hour. Without trade, in two hours country A would produce 100 pounds of rice and 25 pounds of wheat, while country B would produce 25 pounds of rice and 100 pounds of wheat. But *with* trade, country A could specialize its production and produce 200 pounds of rice, while country B could specialize its production and produce 200 pounds of wheat. Then each could trade and have 100 pounds of rice and 100 pounds of wheat, dramatically increasing output and benefiting both countries.

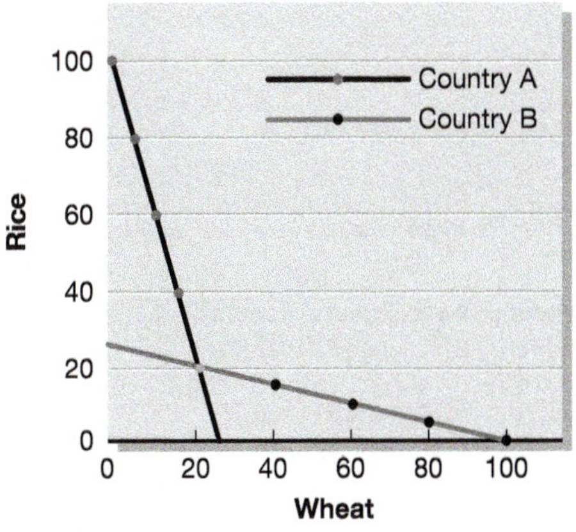

FIGURE 7.3 **Rice and wheat production by country A and country B**

Theory of Comparative Advantage.

In 1817, English economist David Ricardo took Smith's work a step further, suggesting that countries do not need juxtaposed absolute advantages in order to benefit from trade (see **Figure 7.4**). Ricardo suggested that **comparative advantage**, or the ability of a country to conduct one economic activity more efficiently than another activity, is sufficient to encourage trade.

For instance, suppose England had an absolute advantage over France at producing both rice *and* wheat (see **Figure 7.5**). Ricardo argued that England would still benefit from trading with France as long as the French had a comparative advantage in producing one product over the other. In this case, a comparative advantage could mean that it costs less for France to produce wheat than to produce rice. Even though it may not have an absolute advantage, a country can use a comparative advantage to increase its total output by specializing in what it is comparatively efficient at producing, then engaging in trade. This theory suggests that even countries without an absolute advantage can benefit from trade, and that countries with an absolute advantage can still benefit from trading with their disadvantaged neighbors.

comparative advantage the ability of a country to produce a specific good or service at a lower opportunity cost than a rival

WileyPLUS

See Whiteboard Video: Theories of Trade

Trade Pattern Theories

Free-trade theories show how economies grow through specialization and trade. However, they do not account for trade patterns that are related to a country's natural endowments or consumer preferences. As a result, several additional theories have developed that provide alternative explanations and help predict trade patterns.

Heckscher-Ohlin Theory of Factor Endowments.

In 1933, the **Heckscher-Ohlin theory of trade** introduced the idea that the basis for trade was related to differences in the availability of resources or other factors, such as labor or capital. For instance, Brazil's abundant lumber and China's abundant labor provide unique factor endowments that suggest

Heckscher-Ohlin theory of trade a theory that suggests that trade flows from countries with abundant factor endowments and to countries with scarce factor endowments

FIGURE 7.4 **David Ricardo** "You must factor in opportunity costs!"

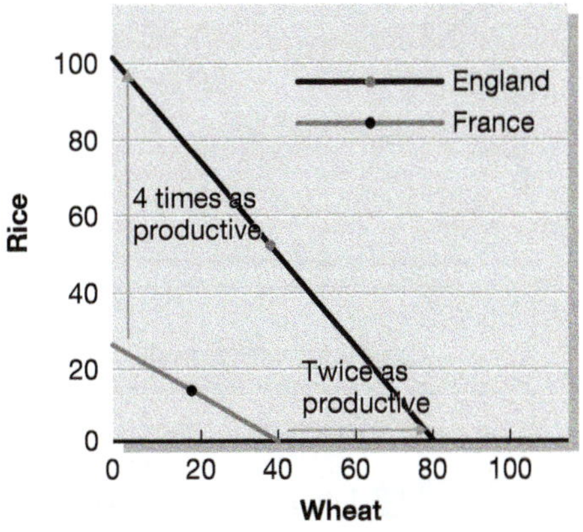

FIGURE 7.5 **Comparative advantage**
England has an absolute advantage over France in rice and wheat production, but is four times as productive in rice production and only twice as productive in wheat production.

Brazil should specialize in lumber production while China should specialize in labor-intensive industries; then both countries can trade with each other. This theory suggests that a country will trade primarily with other countries that have different factor endowments, rather than with countries that have factor endowments similar to its own. Thus, for instance, oil-rich Saudi Arabia is more likely to trade with technology-rich Germany than with oil-rich Russia.

theory of overlapping demand a theory that suggests that trade is the result of customer demand and that customers of similar wealth are likely to demand similar products and services

Theory of Overlapping Demand.

In contrast to the Heckscher-Ohlin theory, the **theory of overlapping demand** suggests that trade is the result of customer demand and that customers of similar wealth are likely to demand similar products and services. For instance, wealthy individuals in China, Brazil, and the United States are likely to have similar preferences in clothes, automobiles, and electronics. Rich countries will trade with rich countries with similar customer needs, and poorer countries will trade with poorer countries with similar customer needs. As a result, this theory suggests, because of similar levels of demand, a country is likely to engage in trade with other countries that have similar levels of GDP per person.

international product life cycle a theory that suggests that the level of trade in a product at any given time is a function of the current stage in the product's life cycle, which life cycle consists of introduction, maturity, standardization, and decline

Theory of the International Product Life Cycle.

Another theory of trade proposes the **international product life cycle**. This theory was outlined by U.S. economist and scholar Raymond Vernon in 1966. This theory suggests that the level of trade in a product at any given time is a function of the current stage in the product's life cycle, and that products go through four distinct phases during this cycle: introduction, maturity, standardization, and decline. Product life cycle theory suggests that trade patterns are a function of the patterns inherent in product life cycles, and that production will naturally shift from developed to developing countries (see **Figure 7.6**).

In the *introduction stage*, technically advanced products are produced and consumed in developed nations. At this point, the producer focuses on the domestic customer, who provides market feedback, allowing the producer to adjust the product to better respond to demand. This is easily the most expensive stage of production. Because no labor-saving developments have

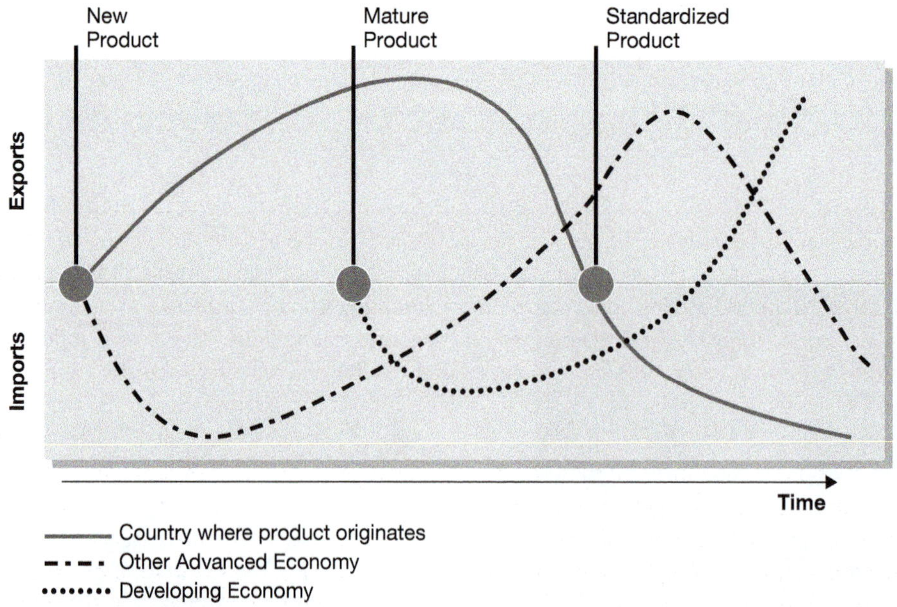

FIGURE 7.6 **International product life cycle** This theory of trade suggests that the level of trade is function of where a product is in its life cycle. **Source:** Created by the authors, based on Raymond Vernon, "International Investment and International Trade in the Product Cycle," *Quarterly Journal of Economics* 80, no. 2 (May 1966): 190–207.

occurred yet, production includes higher labor costs. To offset these higher costs, companies often engage in price skimming to initially engage eager customers who will pay the high prices, then later reduce prices to capture more of the market.

As these products *mature*, sales increase, leading to increased competition, exports, and capital intensity. As sales and awareness of the product grow, the company will begin to build brand loyalty by selling to new customers and creating repeat buyers. Mass production and the use of labor-saving processes and technologies enable the producer to produce in excess of domestic demand and export the surplus to other countries, including less developed countries.

As the products become *standardized* through widespread use, several things happen: production by the innovating company declines, global sales taper off, and prices fall. As the per-unit cost decreases, the company is forced to cut prices to deal with competitors. To continue decreasing the per-unit cost, the company will often move production to developing countries where cheap labor is available. At this point, local companies in foreign markets may begin to produce the product—often using some cheaper inputs such as labor and parts. Given their cost advantage in the production process, the foreign companies then could begin exporting the products back to the product's home country, whereby the exporter becomes the importer.

As the product enters the *decline* phase, sales spiral downward. The product will first experience a sales decline in more affluent countries, while less-developed countries become the only producers—and consumers—of the product. In time, revenue from sales of the product will drop to the point that investments are minimized. The company that invented the product will often cease producing the product, and other high-cost producers then follow suit. At the same time, the products produced in developing markets continue to enjoy price advantages, and production shifts fully to the developing market. Eventually only the firm with the lowest production costs remains in the market to produce and export the product to fewer and fewer customers around the globe.

For instance, the U.S. companies Caterpillar Inc. and John Deere invented many heavy-equipment machines, which first sold at home and then were exported globally, both to other developed countries and later to developing countries. As the products have matured, however, Chinese manufactures such as SANY, Zoomlion, and LuiGong have begun producing high-quality equipment at a fraction of the price, with the intention to export it to the United States and other markets.[4] Product life cycle theory indicates that trade flows are likely to be fluid, evolving from rich-country exports to rich-country imports—a process widely considered to be accelerating in many industries as products mature more quickly.

Regional Clusters. In addition to the theories predicting trade as a function of national resources, or product life cycles, some theories predict the level of trade as it relates to regional clusters. For instance, Harvard professor Michael Porter suggested, in his model of trade called the "Diamond Model," that competition among clusters of firms can drive innovation in a particular industry to develop best-in-the-world capabilities. The textile industry in Pakistan and the high-tech industry in Silicon Valley, California, are surrounded by a supportive network of technology, skilled labor, distribution, regulations, and other factors that foster the development of world-class businesses that produce goods and services that are exported from these clusters to customers all over the world. More specifically, Porter suggests that rivalry among firms clustered together drives innovation as a result of support from labor, capital, natural resources, and other factors (suppliers, competitors, and complementary firms) that provide the cluster a unique competitive advantage. Moreover, the world's most demanding customers come to these innovation centers with the most complex problems, further pushing innovation. Together, these factors foster an environment in which global industry dominance will occur. As a result, trade will flow from the industry center out to the rest of the world. To understand how this happens, consider the four factors of **Porter's Diamond Model** represented in **Figure 7.7**.

Porter's Diamond Model a model that assesses the competitive potential of industries

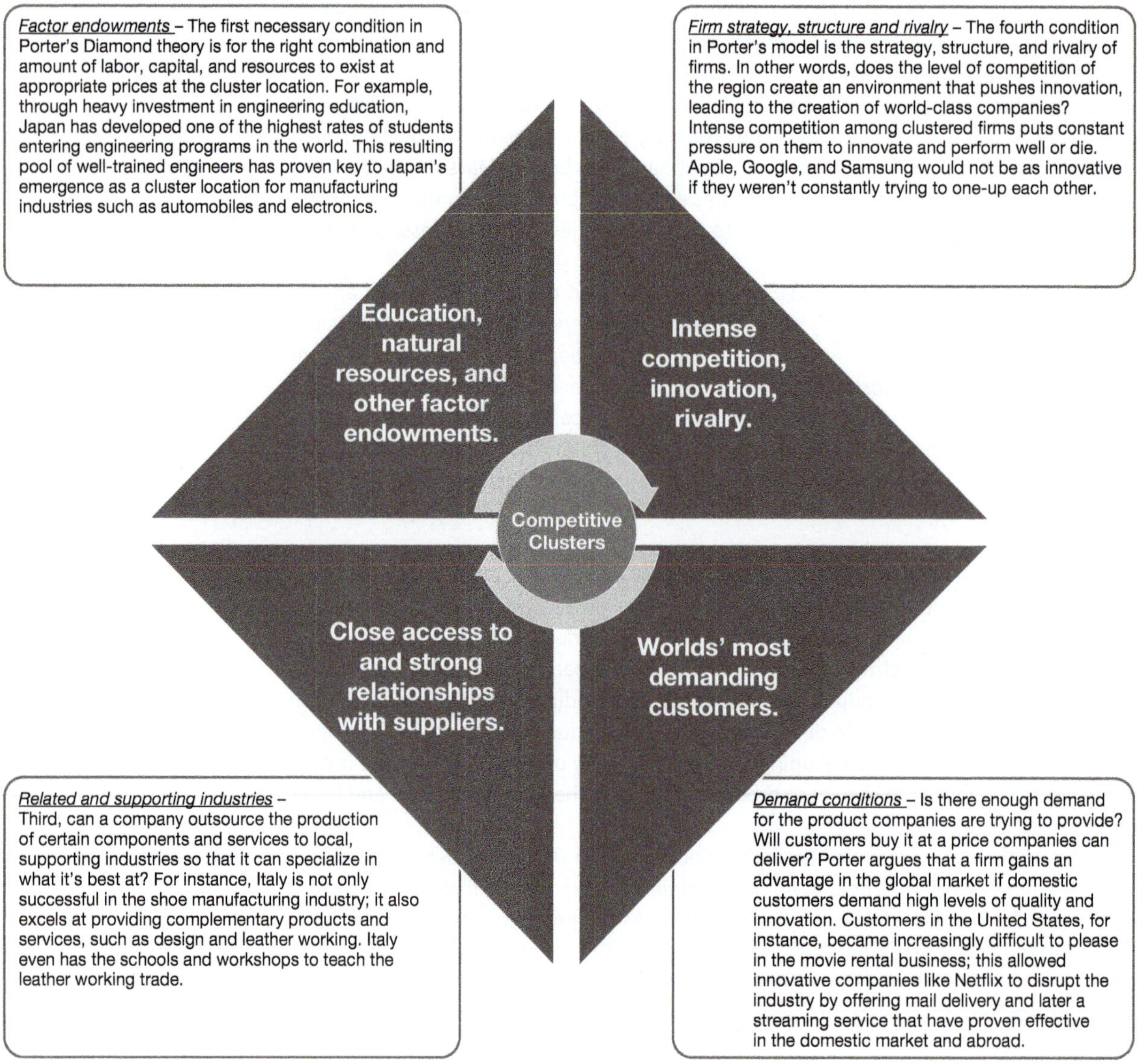

Factor endowments – The first necessary condition in Porter's Diamond theory is for the right combination and amount of labor, capital, and resources to exist at appropriate prices at the cluster location. For example, through heavy investment in engineering education, Japan has developed one of the highest rates of students entering engineering programs in the world. This resulting pool of well-trained engineers has proven key to Japan's emergence as a cluster location for manufacturing industries such as automobiles and electronics.
Firm strategy, structure and rivalry – The fourth condition in Porter's model is the strategy, structure, and rivalry of firms. In other words, does the level of competition of the region create an environment that pushes innovation, leading to the creation of world-class companies? Intense competition among clustered firms puts constant pressure on them to innovate and perform well or die. Apple, Google, and Samsung would not be as innovative if they weren't constantly trying to one-up each other.
Education, natural resources, and other factor endowments.
Intense competition, innovation, rivalry.
Competitive Clusters
Close access to and strong relationships with suppliers.
Worlds' most demanding customers.
Related and supporting industries – Third, can a company outsource the production of certain components and services to local, supporting industries so that it can specialize in what it's best at? For instance, Italy is not only successful in the shoe manufacturing industry; it also excels at providing complementary products and services, such as design and leather working. Italy even has the schools and workshops to teach the leather working trade.
Demand conditions – Is there enough demand for the product companies are trying to provide? Will customers buy it at a price companies can deliver? Porter argues that a firm gains an advantage in the global market if domestic customers demand high levels of quality and innovation. Customers in the United States, for instance, became increasingly difficult to please in the movie rental business; this allowed innovative companies like Netflix to disrupt the industry by offering mail delivery and later a streaming service that have proven effective in the domestic market and abroad.

FIGURE 7.7 Porter's Diamond Model of competitive clusters Firms embedded in competitive clusters become world-class firms and produce goods demanded all over the world. This model predicts that trade is likely to flow from these clusters to global customers.
Source: Michael E. Porter, "The Competitive Advantage of Nations," *Harvard Business Review*, March–April 1990, pp. 73–93.

Economies of scale the cost advantages companies achieve as they progress down the learning curve and spread fixed costs over more units of output

Theory of Economies of Scale. The final trade theory suggests that trade is a function of a specific company's strategic initiatives, not country-level factors, production factors, or even industry characteristics. This theory suggests that companies pursue international trade in an attempt to achieve economies of scale. **Economies of scale** are the cost advantages companies achieve as they progress down the learning curve and can spread fixed costs over more units of output. For instance, in the 1950s, Honda built a huge motorcycle manufacturing facility to gain efficiencies in production of the Super Cub motorcycle (see **Figure 7.8**). Because of this investment, Honda built capacity for more motorcycles than were demanded in all of Japan and was forced to trade internationally to sell the surplus bikes. Honda's objective was to reduce per-unit costs while improving quality—all of which it was able to do through economies of scale. Honda has since produced and sold over 90 million Super Cubs and over 300 million motorcycles worldwide.

To a point, economies of scale improve with volume, so this theory predicts that companies will be better off producing a product for multiple world markets in a single location.

For example, Intel gains a production advantage in microprocessors when it produces huge quantities in a single location and then exports the microprocessors to other countries. The economies of scale theory also suggests that the first entrant into the world market that can rapidly expand production and move along the learning curve is the most likely to be successful; thus, trade patterns are a function of firms pursuing economies of scale.

Taken together, these theories provide a variety of reasons for international trade. Despite their differences, one thing they agree on is that trade benefits consumers by increasing output and availability, driving innovation and advancement, and encouraging specialization to improve quality.

Kyodo News/Getty Images

FIGURE 7.8 **The Honda Super Cub** Honda produced this motorcycle in large quantities and exported the product to many countries in order to reduce the cost of production.

Using Trade Theory as a Global Manager

Why is it important to understand different theories of trade? Knowing the trade theory under which a country's government operates helps in three main areas of business: timing market entry, accounting for government policy, and choosing locations. By understanding what theory your company considers important, you as a manager can maximize the benefits of trade. For instance, if your company is increasing production to quickly move down the learning curve, and if international trade can provide new markets to drive demand, the theory of economies of scale suggests that your firm may wish to aggressively enter new markets. It argues that businesses that successfully enter new markets first—that are the **first movers**, in other words—are in the best position to dominate trade in their product in those markets. For instance, Coca-Cola's first-mover advantage into foreign markets has allowed the firm to dominate their industry globally. Coca-Cola expanded into foreign markets in Europe, Latin America, and Africa beginning in the 1920s and 1930s.[5] Pepsi, on the other hand, did not enter foreign markets until the 1960s, with entry into Japan and Europe.[6] Coke's early entry continues to pay off: its market share in the global cola market in 2014 was nearly 42%, compared with Pepsi's 30%.[7]

first movers businesses that successfully enter new markets first

Government Policy. Imagine having already slim profit margins and trying to enter a foreign market that places a tariff on your product. You could end up spending more to get your product to market than you could ever recoup in sales. On the other side of this equation are businesses so active in international trade that they have great influence on government trade policies, such as DeBeer's influence on diamond trade policies. In Botswana, DeBeer has a joint venture with the government that ensures Botswana trades diamonds only when DeBeers agrees.[8] Companies must understand which trade theories and policies are operating in a country or countries and how these are likely to affect its business in order to succeed there.

Location. Most theories build on the idea that countries have comparative advantages in different industries. This means that businesses can increase efficiency and reduce costs by locating production in countries that have the appropriate comparative advantage. For example, Nike sources shoe manufacturing to 14 countries, including Vietnam, which produces 43% of Nike's footwear; China, which produces 32%; and Indonesia, which makes 20%.[9] Spreading production to advantageous locations results in a connected global environment that maximizes efficiency. Ignoring this opportunity puts businesses at a serious disadvantage on an international—and even domestic—level.

7.2 Trade Imbalances and Their Consequences

LEARNING OBJECTIVE

Describe trade imbalances and their consequences.

Understanding why countries trade can help international businesses determine how much support or hostility they are likely to face when entering a foreign market. Countries that are more open to trade are likely to have more foreign investment enter their country. But trade imbalances can have significant consequences for countries and the international companies that operate in these countries. In this section we will explore how we measure trade as well as the consequences of trade for countries and companies.

WileyPLUS

See Whiteboard Video: The Consequences of Trade

The Balance of Trade

balance of trade a measure of the difference between exports from and imports into a country

The accounting for trade flows between countries shows up in the **balance of trade** measure. This measure looks at the difference between the exports from a country and the imports into the country, and then factors in the net income received by the country from investments abroad. China has consistently run a positive trade balance, or trade surplus, over the past decade[10] (see **Figure 7.9**).

balance of payments the value of exports minus the value of imports and the net amount received from investments

What does a having a positive or negative trade balance mean for a country? To understand this, we need to learn how trade balances relate to the **balance of payments**, which is simply the value of imports into the country and the net amount received from investments subtracted from the value of exports. Think of the balance of payments as a country's balance sheet for foreign transactions. It indicates whether a country is producing more than it consumes or vice versa. It consists of two parts: the current accounts and the capital accounts.

current account an account of a country's exports and imports of goods, services, and income

The **current account** calculates a country's exports and imports of goods, services, and income. In 2014, according to the Bureau of Economic Analysis, the United States had a current account deficit of 2.9% of GDP, or $505 billion, an increase over the $476.4 billion recorded in 2013.[11] In other words, the United States is buying foreign goods and services on credit (spending more than it is making).

capital account an account of a country's transfer of capital to or from other countries

The **capital account** measures the transfer of capital to or from other countries. *Capital* includes land, resources, and monetary investments such as investments in Treasury bills (or T-bills; bonds that are issued by the Federal Reserve). When a country runs a trade deficit (importing more than it exports), it loses capital. When a country runs a trade surplus (exporting

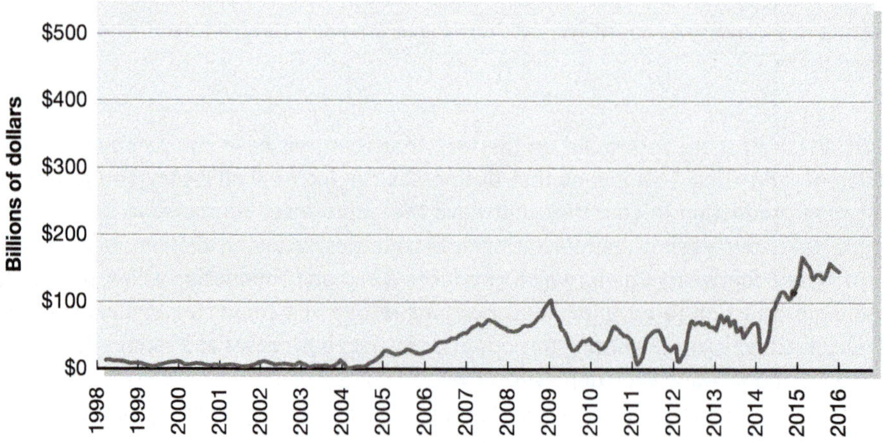

Note: This chart imputes a return to 2016 monthly averages in March.

FIGURE 7.9 China's balance of trade, 1985–2014 Beginning in 2004, China incurred a large trade surplus. **Source:** Brad W. Setser, "China's Confusing Trade and current Account Numbers," Follow the Money blog, April 4, 2017. http://blogs.cfr.org/setser/2017/04/04/chinas-confusing-trade-and-current-account-numbers/.

more than it imports), it gains capital. From a global perspective, payments are always balanced. The equation for the balance of payments is as follows:

$$\textit{Balance of Payments} = \textit{Current Accounts} + \textit{Capital Accounts}$$

If the global market is always balanced, why are countries' trade balances important? Recall that under the mercantilist theories of trade, countries sought to sustain large trade surpluses in order to build their treasuries. But what are the consequences of a trade surplus or a deficit? David Hume suggested that continually running a surplus causes inflation in the country's domestic prices, whereas a trade deficit causes deflation. As a result, over time it will become more and more difficult to sustain the trade surplus.

Today, countries running trade imbalances face even more pressures. Changes in the value of one currency relative to others not only cause inflation and deflation in the price of exports and imports, they also can directly affect exchange rates. For instance, the United States has a large trade deficit with China, meaning it imports from China about $500 billion of goods more than it exports to China each year. As a result, China's currency, the renminbi, should get more expensive relative to the U.S. dollar (meaning a dollar would buy fewer renminbi), as U.S. companies buy more and more renminbi to pay for the goods they have imported. If the renminbi were priced at about 3 to the dollar, as many currency pricing measures suggest would be appropriate, goods exported to the United States from China would be expensive for U.S. consumers and they would buy fewer of them. On the other hand, goods produced in the United States would be cheaper in China, encouraging Chinese consumers to buy more U.S.-made products. Thus, over time, the trade imbalance between the two countries should even out.

However, the Chinese government has fixed the value of the renminbi at about 6 to the dollar, so the imbalance does not even out. For this reason, and because the trade deficit between the two countries persists, the United States must figure out a way to pay for the deficit. It has two options: (1) it can borrow money or (2) it can sell assets. Which is the United States doing to fund the deficit? The answer is both. Currently, the United States has borrowed about $6 trillion from itself and other governments, such as $1 trillion from China and $1.1 trillion from Japan,[12] in part to fund the deficit in its current account. The government and U.S. companies have also sold assets such as property and stocks to foreigners. In 2013, these foreign investments into the United States equaled $236.3 billion, and the cumulative total of foreign direct investment is now $2.8 trillion,[13] or about 35% of the U.S. GDP.

Throughout the ages countries have used different strategies to try to balance their deficits. For instance, in the early 1700s the British fell in love with Chinese tea and by 1800 were buying 23 million pounds of it per year. At the same time, the Chinese were buying very few products from the British. In an effort to balance trade, the British began selling opium to the Chinese. However, China had severe restrictions on opium trade, and the imbalance persisted. In 1839, war broke out between the Chinese (who were tired of the British smuggling opium into China) and the British (who needed the smuggling to continue) (see **Figure 7.10**). The British eventually won the war, opened the opium trade to balance the deficit, and took control of Hong Kong until 1997—more than 150 years.[14]

Why Trade Imbalances Exist and Persist

Three main theories help explain why countries have trade imbalances: mercantilism, the theory of underconsumption, and the infant industry theory.

Mercantilism. As we saw earlier, mercantilism starts with a government adopting policies to actively promote a positive trade imbalance. These policies can include export subsidies and/or import restraints that artificially force capital assets to enter the economy. One purpose of this policy is to provide economic power to the country, building a treasury that in the past was often used to fund wars. We also learned that countries practicing neo-mercantilism today often do so with the intent of using foreign assets to grow their domestic industries. These countries use the inflow of capital to build new roads, ports, and industry. They also buy

Culture Club/Hulton Archive/Getty Images

FIGURE 7.10 The Opium Wars These wars led to more than 150 years of British control of Hong Kong.

foreign assets, as Haier did in purchasing GE's appliance business, or they purchase foreign currency (known as foreign currency reserves) to allow them to strengthen or weaken their own currency. The investments in output-producing assets, coupled with investments abroad and piles of cash, strengthen the domestic economy and provide abundant jobs.

theory of underconsumption a theory which states that recessions are the result of insufficient demand relative to the supply, and underconsumption is often caused by wealth inequality

The Theory of Underconsumption. The **theory of underconsumption** says trade imbalances result when local demand doesn't meet the amount produced in the economy. This lack of demand is attributed to increasing income disparity and concentration of wealth. Essentially, as rich people get richer, they buy less common, more expensive goods, rather than purchasing a larger quantity of common goods. At the same time, the poor are getting poorer and buying fewer common goods. The leftover goods are then sold internationally. Meanwhile, the wealthy typically use their increased income to make investments in foreign economies—investments that represent capital flowing out of the domestic economy.

infant industry theory a theory which states that certain emerging industries need to be protected and nurtured for a period of time or they will be unable to compete against established foreign firms

The Infant Industry Theory. The **infant industry theory** was first proposed in 1791 by Alexander Hamilton, the United States' first secretary of the Treasury. It argues that certain emerging industries need to be protected and nurtured for a period of time until they become established, or they won't be able to compete against established foreign firms. For example, from the 1960s until the early 2000s, South Korea protected its young automobile manufacturers, Hyundai, Kia, and Daewoo, against foreign competition by placing large tariffs on the import of foreign cars. This strategy preserved the domestic market for Korean manufacturers such as Kia and Hyundai, decreasing the outflow of capital assets during the market development period and allowing the domestic firms to survive until they were strong enough to face foreign competition. As Kia and Hyundai have begun to successfully compete in global markets, Korea has changed its stance and reduced tariffs on imported automobiles.

What About the US Dollar and International Trade?

Roughly 85 percent of global trade is generally processed in U.S. dollars. Some people believe this insulates the United States from trade imbalances because all other countries are forced to build up their stock of dollars (known as U.S. dollar foreign reserves) if they want to participate in international trade. In reality, the position of the U.S. dollar as a global reserve currency is much more the result of foreign policies than of the design of the U.S. government. In fact, it is not in the United States' best interest to have vast amounts of its capital pulled out of the domestic market and reserved by foreign governments and companies. China and Japan had reserves of US$3.23 trillion[15] and $1.24 trillion,[16] respectively, at the end of January 2016, giving them significant power over U.S. monetary policy. If either or both were to sell significant amounts of their dollar reserves, they could materially affect the value of the U.S. dollar in world markets. Additional research suggests that large foreign exchange reserves may not be beneficial to the country holding them because this strategy may reduce consumption in an economy.[17]

7.3 Patterns of Trade: Increased Regionalization

LEARNING OBJECTIVE

Identify patterns of trade such as regionalization.

For centuries, business leaders, scholars, and governments have argued for and against international free trade. Today, international free trade in a competitive marketplace is widely accepted as the most efficient and beneficial form of trade for any given nation's economy. Several recent studies found that free-trade policies cause long-term economic growth and that this relationship is reciprocal, meaning that growth increases freer trade which increases growth.[18] If free trade is beneficial, why have markets taken so long to adapt to and adopt free-trade policies? The answer is that they are caught in what we call a prisoner's dilemma. Consider the following scenario:

> *Two criminals are caught during a burglary. They are put in separate rooms so they cannot communicate with each other, and their respective lawyers lay out their options: Confess or stay quiet. If they both stay quiet, each will be sentenced to only 1 year in prison before going free. However, if one confesses and the other stays quiet, the confessor will walk immediately while the other will spend 20 years in prison. If they both confess, each will spend 5 years in prison before being freed (**Figure 7.11**). If you were one of the prisoners, which option would you choose?*

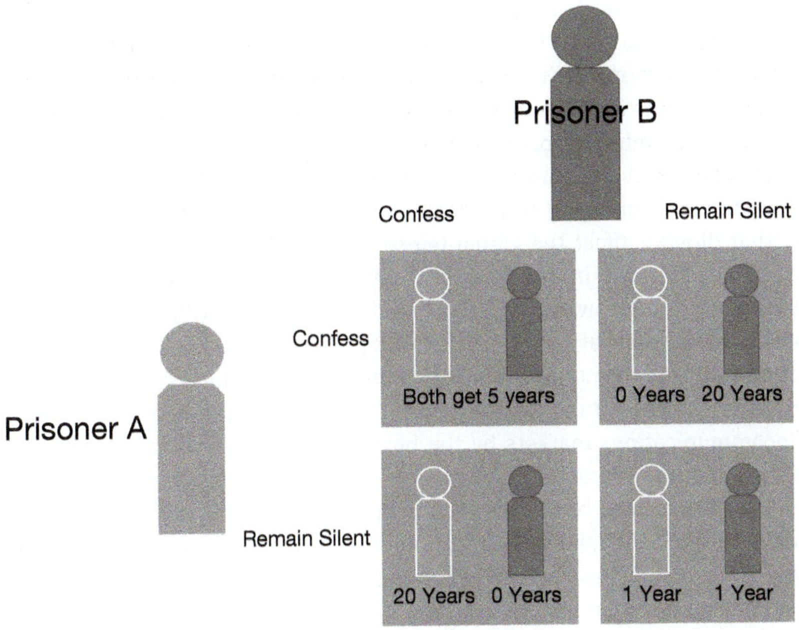

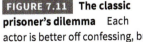

FIGURE 7.11 The classic prisoner's dilemma Each actor is better off confessing, but only if the other prisoner does not confess.

In a prisoner's dilemma, each prisoner has personal incentives to confess but only if the other person does *not* confess. It mirrors the dilemma countries face with trade decisions. They are best off if their trade partners offer open trade policies while they maintain trade barriers. However, if both erect trade barriers, both are worse off. The middle ground is where both allow free trade. The most common result is that both criminals confess—even though that eliminates the possibility of their both getting out of prison in a year. Why do they talk? Because confession eliminates the risk of being in jail for 20 years.

This situation is similar what happens between two countries that are considering opening their borders to free trade. If both do so, then both benefit. However, if only one country opens its borders, the other country can take advantage of the increased market size while protecting its domestic markets from increased competition. The country that opened its borders will be worse off. Just as in the prisoner's dilemma, many countries are tempted to choose the seemingly safe path: they keep their borders shut and hope their trade partners allow free trade.

Global Integration

To solve this dilemma and allow both countries to benefit from free trade, a third party needs to make sure the two are playing by similar rules. This mediator should be unbiased and have the power to sanction or penalize any country that breaks the rules. Such a mediator was created by representatives of 23 nations meeting in Geneva, Switzerland, in 1947; these representatives signed a treaty called the **General Agreement on Tariffs and Trade (GATT)**. GATT was intended to reduce tariffs and other trade barriers while eliminating trade preferences, or a country's buying from a preferred partner, and providing a multilateral forum in which to resolve trade disputes between member countries. Over the next 46 years, a total of 105 additional nations joined the pact, bringing the total to 128 members[19]; in 1995, GATT was reestablished as the World Trade Organization (WTO). The WTO also expanded its mandate to include the protection of intellectual property rights.

General Agreement on Tariffs and Trade (GATT) a treaty that has the purpose of reducing trade barriers and tariffs while eliminating trade preferences and providing a multilateral forum to resolve trade disputes between member countries

As of 2017, 164 member nations of the WTO have signed on to nearly "30,000 pages consisting of about 30 agreements and commitments."[20] These agreements seek to increase global integration through trade negotiations, monitoring, and dispute settlement. One of the key characteristics of the WTO is the **most favored nation clause**. As a result of this clause, any deal reached between WTO member countries extends to every other member as well, limiting favoritism and ensuring equitable standards for all members. Only a few limitations apply to the most favored nation clause, such as protections for developing countries, agreements in regional trade blocs like the European Union (EU), and allowances for trade restrictions against specific trade partners.

most favored nation clause a clause applying to members of WTO which states that any deal reached between WTO member countries extends to every other member as well

A mediator like the WTO can be effective only when it can enforce the agreements made between the parties, so the WTO enforces decisions by excluding violating members from benefits and other procedures until they become compliant. The majority of trade disputes are still handled by the disagreeing countries, but many have needed intervention. The WTO increasingly helps members resolve trade issues.

As technology and communication have advanced, the WTO has evolved too, adding agreements to cover emerging technologies such as the trade of services and intellectual property that directly affect the global telecommunications and financial services industries. The changes began in 1997, when the WTO negotiated basic telecommunications services. The key problem was that often countries did not allow foreign ownership of telecommunication or financial services. The new agreements paved the way for foreign ownership of domestic telecommunication companies and introduced competition to markets that had historically been run by monopolies. The United States, Japan, and the EU opened their telecommunications markets by the beginning of 1998, and deregulation has since become a standard for acceptance into the WTO. Similarly, the financial services industry was significantly reformed by the WTO at the beginning of 1999, affecting about 95 percent of the industry. As in the telecommunications market, these reforms released the monopolistic grip some companies had had on markets such as banking and insurance, enabling more competition and freer trade.

Policy Implications of the WTO

Many business firms regularly conduct international trade, whether by dealing with foreign markets or by competing at home with foreign firms. Because trade regulations can have a huge impact on these companies, they often lobby heavily for preferable conditions. They may either promote protectionism or support the WTO and free trade between international markets.

Governments favoring protectionism can implement different trade policies, such as tariffs, subsidies, quotas, and antidumping actions. These policies in turn can help domestic firms stay competitive with foreign firms; however, they are not without repercussions. **Quotas** and **tariffs** restrict imports, thus keeping prices higher in the importing country. This protects less efficient domestic production from foreign competition, rather than promoting efficiency. Higher prices also deter potential sales that might have taken place if the prices were lower. Like tariffs and quotas, **subsidies** support inefficiency because the government gives money to inefficient domestic firms to keep them in business. The difference is that prices stay low because the government covers the difference. **Antidumping actions** protect domestic industries from foreign firms that price products below cost in order to cut other firms out of the market. For example, in 2004, after being urged on by domestic shrimp producers, the United States imposed an antidumping duty on the large quantities of shrimp coming from China. In 2006, China requested that the WTO review the matter.[21] As a result, a panel of individuals from the EU, Honduras, Japan, Korea, Thailand, and Vietnam reviewed the case and in 2013 determined that the actions of the United States were inconsistent with the Antidumping Agreement and gave the United States eight months to change its duty.[22]

quota a direct limit on the number of goods that can be imported into or exported from a country

tariffs taxes on foreign products aimed to discourage imports

subsidies government support for industries

antidumping actions a class of protective tariffs imposed by a domestic government on foreign imports that are thought to be priced below fair market value

The biggest problem is that these different trade policies are often poorly executed and end up having ripple effects on other markets. Because of these side effects, many economists push for a free-trade environment and a stronger WTO, arguing that if true free trade becomes a reality, efficient firms will enjoy increased access to foreign markets, and the long-term benefits to both producers and consumers will immensely outweigh any short-term costs.

With the world becoming increasingly globalized, it's easy to see that both businesses and consumers benefit from trade. Countries like China and Chile have seen tremendous economic growth as they have enacted free-trade policies. However, global free-trade regulations aren't always the most practical way to encourage free trade; getting countries to agree to these regulations can be difficult. As a result, many countries are turning to bilateral trade agreements.

Bilateral Trade Agreements

Because the WTO is such a large organization comprising so many nations, it has a difficult time getting multinational agreements approved. As a result, many nations pursue **bilateral trade agreements**, that is, agreements regarding trade between just two countries. Such agreements are allowed by the WTO and are exempt from the most favored nation clause agreed to by WTO members.[23] For instance, in 2012 the United States formed trade agreements with South Korea and Colombia to increase trade, reduce tariffs, and increase intellectual property protection. The United States is a party to many such trade agreements. Let's look at just a few.

bilateral trade agreements a trade agreement between just two countries

U.S.-Israel Free-Trade Agreement. The free-trade agreement (FTA) with Israel in 1985 was the first bilateral agreement the United States entered. Its purpose was to reduce trade barriers and increase investment between the two countries. The FTA has changed over the years to decrease regulations in both countries, in particular regarding agricultural trade. By 2013, the total value of goods and services traded between the United States and Israel was $46 billion. At that time it was estimated that as many as 40,000 U.S. jobs were supported just by the goods exported to Israel.

U.S.-Australia Free-Trade Agreement. The U.S.-Australia FTA was enacted in 2005, and by 2009, the total value of goods and services traded between the United States and Australia was $26.7 billion, up 23 percent from 2004. The two nations meet on a regular basis to discuss how they are implementing the agreement and to explore ways to improve it. They recently traded views on agricultural issues and sanitation.

U.S.-Korea Free-Trade Agreement. The agreement between the United States and South Korea was enacted in 2012. This agreement made almost 80 percent of consumer and industrial exports to Korea duty free, meaning imports are not taxed. The remaining 20 percent will become duty free within the next five to ten years. This agreement was the most commercially significant FTA for the United States in almost two decades and added an estimated $10–12 billion to its annual GDP.

U.S.-Colombia Free-Trade Agreement. Around the same time the FTA was enacted between the United States and South Korea, the United States was also drafting an FTA with Colombia. The U.S.-Colombia agreement focuses on removing barriers to trade in services, including financial services. Over the ten years after implementation, the agreement is projected to increase U.S. GDP by $2.5 billion. This is particularly important as the U.S. economy continues to shift toward services and away from manufacturing.

U.S.-Chile Free-Trade Agreement. The FTA between Chile and the United States was enacted in 2004. Like many other FTAs, it eliminates tariffs and reduces barriers to trade in services. The FTA also expands protection to include many facets of intellectual property. An important component of this FTA is that all goods traded between the two countries receive **national treatment**, which means foreign and local goods are treated equally.

national treatment the equal treatment of foreign and local goods

Regional Trade Agreements

A third form of trade agreement happens at the regional level and focuses on regions consisting of many nations. In general, regional trade deals are easier to reach because the countries in the agreement often share interests, cultures, and backgrounds—and sometimes a border. The EU is the largest regional trade bloc, or union, consisting of 28 countries. It accounts for just 7% of the world's population but nearly 20% of the global volume of trade.[24]

Other regional agreements include the North American Free Trade Agreement (NAFTA), the Southern Common Market (MERCOSUR), the ASEAN Free Trade Area, the Pan Arab Free Trade Area (PAFTA), and the Common Market of Eastern and Southern Africa (COMESA) (see **Figure 7.12**). All these regional agreements and blocs aim to increase the free flow of goods, services, capital, and labor among member states in an effort to grow each one's economy by increasing specialization and reducing barriers.[25]

European Union (EU) a politico-economic union made up of 28 countries in Europe

The **European Union (EU)** is a politico-economic union made up of 28 countries in Europe. It is the realization of an idea that greater cooperation would aid countries in the process of recovery after World War II. Several regional organizations emerged during that time, including the European Coal and Steel Community. In 1957 the Treaty of Rome created the European Economic Community (EEC), or "common market," among the countries of Belgium, France, Germany, Italy, Luxembourg, and the Netherlands. The EEC eventually became the European Community and later the EU.[26]

The purpose of the EU is to grant free movement among member countries of goods, services, persons, and capital. Many member countries have adopted a single currency, the euro (€). The EU organization includes administrative bodies such as the European Commission, the European Council, the European Parliament, the European Court of Justice, and the European Central Bank. Understanding the EU and the way it functions is especially vital for companies seeking to access the European market. For instance, in 2015 Google was accused by the EU of having abused its dominant position among search engines.[27] If these allegations are proven true, Google could face a multibillion-euro fine—similar to the €497 million fine the EU levied on Microsoft in 2004 for abusing its dominant position in operating systems.

North American Free Trade Agreement (NAFTA) a trade agreement between the United States, Mexico, and Canada

The **North American Free Trade Agreement (NAFTA)** went into effect between the United States, Canada, and Mexico on January 1, 1994. Like the EU, NAFTA is an FTA. It removes all tariffs between the United States, Mexico, and Canada, and grants each most favored nation

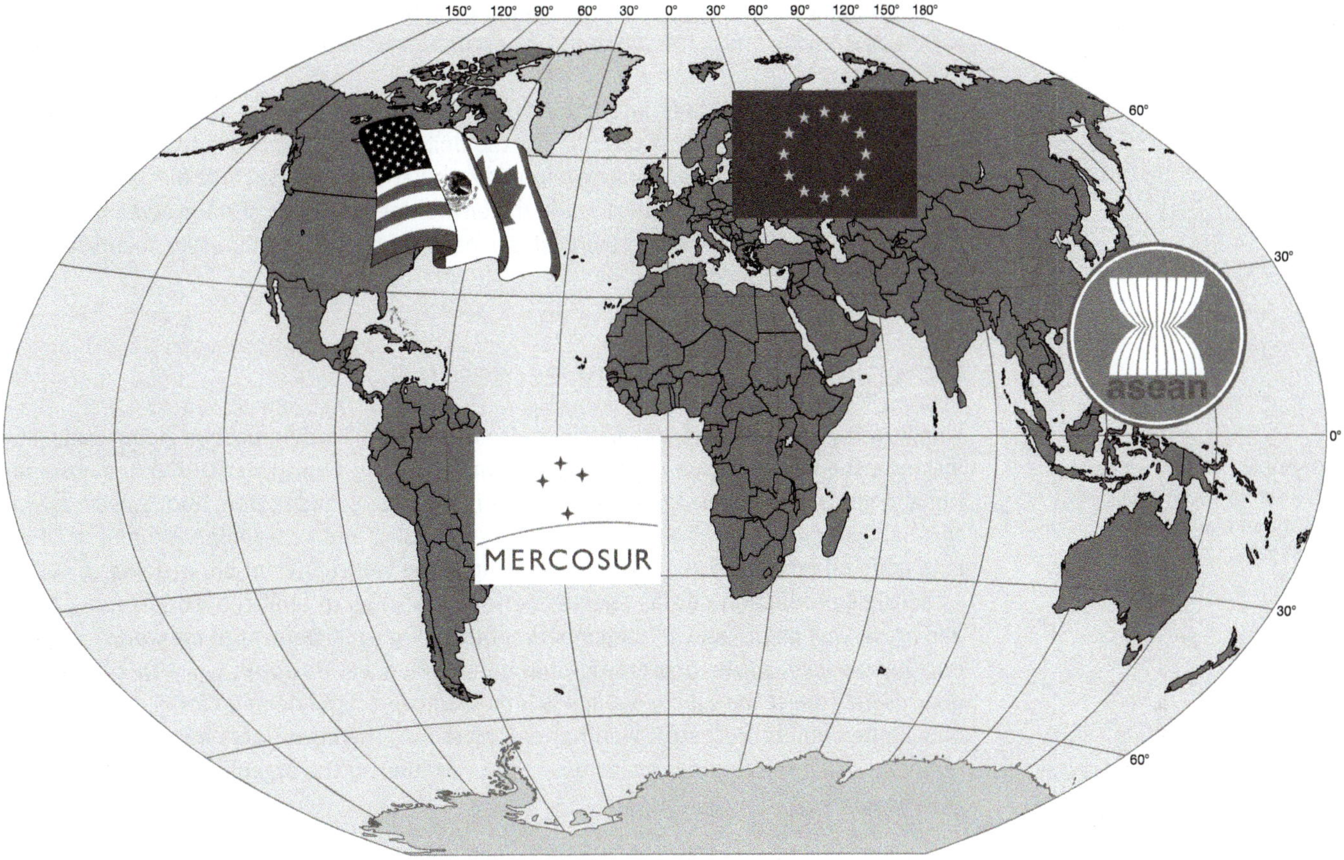

FIGURE 7.12 **Significant regional trade agreements.** Agreements have created regional trade unions including NAFTA, MERCOSUR, the European Union, and ASEAN. **Source:** http://explainedwithmaps.com/world-trade-organization/#iLightbox[56be198deccff]/0

status with the others. In essence this enables the countries to bypass the normal costs related to exports and imports.

The result? NAFTA has led to an increase in competitiveness for all three countries because each has been able to specialize in what it does best. The trade agreement has also increased trade and investment within each of the three countries. The United States has benefited from the agreement in the form of increased high-tech and service jobs. Mexican workers have benefited from an increase in manufacturing jobs.[28] The agreement has also made it significantly easier for U.S. consumers to purchase Canadian and Mexican goods. However, although effective to some degree, NAFTA has been controversial because of job losses (agricultural jobs in Mexico and manufacturing jobs in the United States), increased immigration from Mexico to the United States, and the persistence of some trade regulations.[29] President Trump has made repeated threats to repeal the agreement, citing that the United States is getting the short end of the bargain.

The **Mercado Comum do Sul** (**MERCOSUL**; Portuguese) or **Mercado Común del Sur** (**MERCOSUR**; Spanish) is a trade agreement among five countries in South America: Argentina, Brazil, Paraguay, Uruguay, and Venezuela. Like NAFTA and the EU, MERCOSUR was created to promote free trade. In addition to its five full members, MERCOSUR also has five associate members: Bolivia, Chile, Colombia, Ecuador, and Peru. Today MERCOSUR is a full-customs union and trading bloc that accounts for 75 percent of South America's GDP, making it the third largest trading bloc in the world.

Mercado Comum do Sul (MERCOSUL)/Mercado Común del Sur (MERCOSUR) a trade agreement between Argentina, Brazil, Paraguay, Uruguay and Venezuela

The **Association of Southeast Asian Nations (ASEAN)** was organized in August 1967 by Indonesia, Malaysia, Singapore, Thailand, and the Philippines to accelerate economic growth by reducing tariffs among member countries. Several other countries, including Brunei Darussalam (on the island of Borneo), Cambodia, Laos, Myanmar, and Vietnam, were later added to the trade bloc. ASEAN has been particularly successful in attracting foreign

Association of Southeast Asian Nations (ASEAN) a trade agreement between Indonesia, Singapore, Thailand, and the Philippines

direct investment, reducing tariffs, and enabling the rise of a major manufacturing hub in the region. Textiles are one of the successful export products from ASEAN, yielding almost US$10 billion a year.[30]

Transatlantic Trade and Investment Partnership (TTIP) a proposed trade and investment agreement between the European Union and the United States

The **Transatlantic Trade and Investment Partnership (TTIP)** is a proposed trade and investment agreement between the EU and the United States intended to increase economic growth in both regions by focusing on reforming regulations and standards that govern public health, agriculture, pharmaceuticals, and the environment. Like most trade agreements, the TTIP faces criticism because a partnership can make it more difficult for governments to regulate their domestic markets.[31]

Other Forms of Trade Agreements

Organization of the Petroleum Exporting Countries (OPEC) a multinational organization with the goal to unify oil producers

Finally, other international organizations also have a significant impact on global trade. For instance, the **Organization of the Petroleum Exporting Countries (OPEC)** is a multinational organization whose members are Algeria, Angola, Ecuador, Iran, Iraq, Kuwait, Libya, Nigeria, Qatar, Saudi Arabia, the United Arab Republic, and Venezuela. The goal of OPEC is to unify oil producers in an attempt to control the world price of oil. In doing so, OPEC establishes production quotas for member nations so as to limit the world supply of oil and preserve high prices. OPEC members control roughly 30 percent of the world's oil production capacity, so the organization has some influence. However, while OPEC's overall policies may affect the supply of oil, it is unable to control the demand for oil and thus has only limited ability to control world prices. Moreover, member states individually benefit from exceeding their quotas to increase their revenue, so the organization's control is far from absolute.

WileyPLUS

See Whiteboard Video: Trade Restrictions

7.4 Government Policies Directed at Trade

LEARNING OBJECTIVE

Identify government policies that affect trade patterns.

WileyPLUS

See Whiteboard Video: Trade Agreements

Governments have many different reasons to pursue free trade, but they also have reasons to deliberately restrict trade. For instance, a government may forbid a politically sensitive industry (like defense contracting) to export certain products or technologies, or it may erect barriers to competition around a particularly important domestic industry threatened by global competition. These barriers can reduce the importation of foreign goods and services or eliminate the exportation of domestic goods and services.

Another reason a government may seek to limit trade is to protect its "infant industries," as we saw above. A third reason countries may erect trade barriers is to adjust the balance of trade. For example, if a country has a significant trade deficit with a trade partner, it may enact a trade tariff on goods or services imported from that country in an effort to reduce the deficit.

Fourth, a country or multinational organization may aim to restrict trade as a bargaining tool. The United Nations frequently uses trade sanctions or limitations on trade against countries in an effort to change those countries' behaviors. For instance, in 2006 it placed sanctions on Iran to stop its nuclear weapon development programs. Those sanctions were lifted in 2016 when Iran agreed to put limits on its nuclear program.[32] In addition to stopping nuclear proliferation, sanctions are often aimed at fixing human rights abuses or stopping the import of endangered animal products, such as elephant ivory or rhinoceros horns.

Fifth, a country may introduce trade protections if it feels a trade partner is engaging in "dumping," or selling goods below the cost of production. For instance, in 2015 the United States won a WTO case in which it accused Chinese manufacturers of selling tires below their

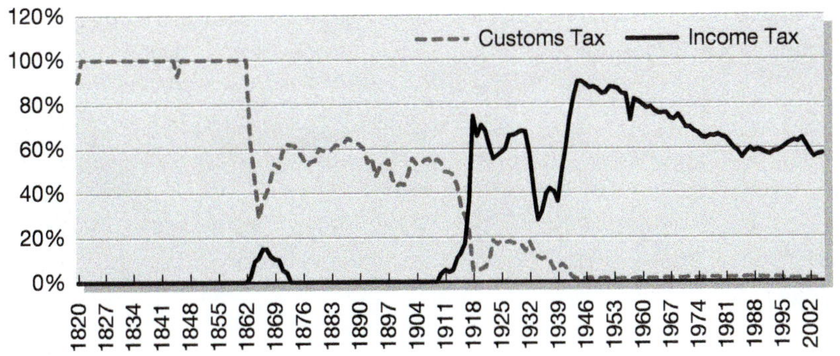

FIGURE 7.13 The U.S. federal government was primarily funded by tariffs until the early 1900s **Source:** Data from Thomas L. Hungerford, "U.S. Federal Government Revenues: 1790 to the Present," CRS Report for Congress, September 25, 2006. http://congressionalresearch.com/RL33665/document.php?study=U.S.+Federal+Government+Revenues+1790+to+the+Present (accessed April 12, 2017).

manufacturing cost. As a result, the United States has levied tariffs ranging from 19 to 88 percent on tires imported from China.[33]

Governments can use a number of specific actions to enforce the limits they wish to place on trade. Let's look at some specifics.

Tariffs. As we mentioned above, a tariff is a tax levied on goods as they cross the border of a country, whether coming in or going out. For instance, China imposes a 105.4 percent tariff on U.S. poultry, and the United States imposes a 163.8 percent tariff on peanuts from Brazil, Argentina, Malawi, or other markets and a 350 percent tariff on imported tobacco.[34]

Historically, tariffs were the primary source of revenue for the U.S. government until the government implemented the income tax in the early 1900s. **Figure 7.13** highlights this shift from tariffs to income tax by considering the percentage of the federal budget that was funded by tariffs and income tax.

Import and export tariffs can be separated into two categories, specific tariffs and ad valorem tariffs. Specific tariffs are levied as a specific amount per unit, like $0.20 per kilogram or $5 per laptop. Ad valorem tariffs are levied as a fixed percentage of the value of the imported good. For instance, South Korea has automobile tariffs on cars from the EU pegged at 3.2 percent and on cars from the United States pegged at 4 percent. In general, import tariffs are meant to protect domestic production by raising the price of imported goods in order to ease competition with domestic industries. Tariffs produce revenue for the domestic government.

Generally, import tariffs lead to increased prices for consumers and easier conditions for domestic manufacturers. In other words, tariffs harm consumers and benefit producers by creating artificial economic inefficiencies.

Import tariffs are usually more common than export tariffs. A government might impose export tariffs to raise revenue and reduce exports for political reasons. Governments typically impose export tariffs to ensure a certain amount of a product remains in the country. China, for example, levied tariffs on major grain products to discourage farmers from selling abroad at high prices while people in China weren't getting enough to eat. Tariffs offer countries a level of protection, but excessive tariffs come under scrutiny by the WTO. In 2014, the WTO ruled that tariffs imposed by the United States on Chinese solar panels were a violation of international trade rules.[35]

Subsidies. Subsidies are a form of direct assistance to domestic producers in the form of tax breaks, grants, cash payments, low-interest loans, and government-owned equity in domestic companies, which may bring favorable political treatment. The U.S. government has distributed billions of dollars in state subsidies, federal grants, tax credits, federal loans, and bailout assistance to the automobile, finance, airline, alternative energy, and agricultural industries, among others. Good Jobs First is a watchdog group in the United States that tracks subsidies and their recipients. The group found that five of the top fifty recipients of federal subsidies were also among the top fifty recipients of state and local subsidies: Boeing, Ford Motor Company, General Electric, General Motors, and JPMorgan Chase (**Figure 7.14**).[36] Governments give subsidies to firms for many reasons, but the general goal is to increase the competitiveness of domestic industries relative to their foreign rivals.

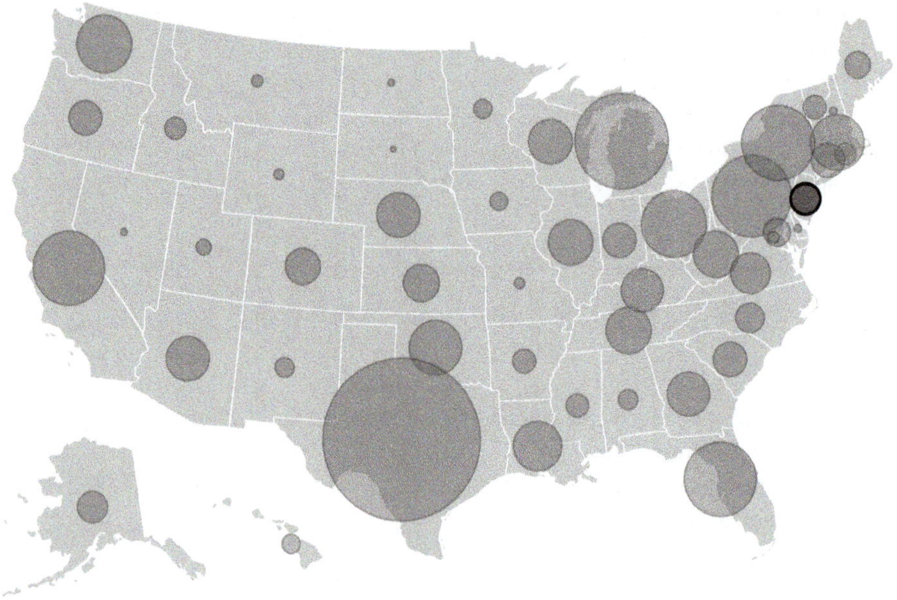

FIGURE 7.14 Subsidies in the United States Different states try to support business by offering subsidies. This map shows where the majority of subsidies are provided. **Source:** http://www.nytimes.com/interactive/2012/12/01/us/government-incentives.html?_r=0#MI

Loans. Governments provide domestic firms with subsidized loans at low interest rates in order to support industry development. Ideally, these cheap loans enable young industries to grow and have the funds to increase production capacity until they can compete on a global scale, at which time they repay the money. For instance, South Korea provided inexpensive government loans to companies developing high-technology products such as silicon chips, flash memory, and cell phones. Similarly, the EU provided Airbus, the aerospace company headquartered in France, with numerous government loans.

Quotas. Quotas are a direct limit on the number of goods that can be imported into or exported from a country. For instance, OPEC restricts the amount of oil its member countries can export in an effort to limit world supply and keep the price high. Sugar imports to the United States are limited to about 1.2 million tons a year. Beyond that quantity, heavy tariffs come into play to protect U.S.-based sugar producers.[37]

content requirements a minimum level of materials, parts, or inputs that must originate in the local country rather than be imported

Local Content Requirements. **Content requirements** set a minimum level on the materials, parts, or inputs that must originate in the local country rather than be imported. For example, Ghana gives preference to oil and gas companies that have at least 5 percent indigenous ownership, and foreign companies can enter the country only through a joint venture that has at least 10 percent local ownership.[38]

Standards. Standards such as labeling and safety requirements are designed to protect consumers from products perceived as dangerous while also limiting the inflow of foreign goods. For instance, the EU has strict requirements governing the sale of most foods containing or made from genetically modified organisms.[39] These requirements keep most U.S. soybean and corn products out of European markets.

Administrative Delay. Governments typically have customs offices to monitor and inspect imports. By delaying a product in customs, a government can restrict an industry in a nonmonetary way. Sometimes this is done for safety reasons, as in 2012 when South Korea hand-checked all incoming shipments of U.S. beef following a case of mad cow disease. The action significantly delayed and limited the importation of U.S. beef.

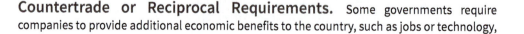

Countertrade or Reciprocal Requirements. Some governments require companies to provide additional economic benefits to the country, such as jobs or technology, when making trade agreements. A government may require certain parts to be produced in or purchased from the country in order for a foreign business to operate there. For example, as part of the deal for some commercial aircraft that U.S. manufacturer Boeing sold to China, the firm also had to agree to build component parts in China. Boeing has been able to access the multibillion-dollar Chinese market by exchanging technology, promising to establish a headquarters in Beijing, and building a spare-parts service center in the country. Last, Boeing also agreed to provide training to Chengdu Aircraft Maintenance & Engineering Company.[40]

Embargoes. **Embargoes** are a particular type of quota that limit all forms of trade on entire categories of goods and services. For instance, the United States enacted an embargo against the Castro-led Cuban government, which started in 1960 with an embargo on all products except food and medicine. The intent was to weaken the country and overthrow communism in the island state. In 1962, the embargo was strengthened to include almost everything.[41]

embargo a quota that limits all forms of trade on entire categories of goods or services

Summary and Case

Summary

LEARNING OBJECTIVE 7.1 Compare theories about why countries trade.

Trade theories argue that governments directly affect trade through intervention, such as in mercantilism and neo-mercantilism, and by free-trade policies enacted when a country has an absolute or comparative advantage. Some theories suggest that trade is a function of factor availability or overlapping demand, or that it is due to a product's life cycle or to industry clusters. Still another theory argues that trade reflects a company's desire to achieve economies of scale.

LEARNING OBJECTIVE 7.2 Describe trade imbalances and their consequences.

Trade is accounted for in the balance of payments, that is, in the current account (which measures the balance of trade for goods and services) and the capital account (which measures the transfer of capital to and from other countries). Globally, trade deficits and surpluses must balance. At the country level, countries with a surplus invest that surplus into countries with deficits, either by lending money to the country with the deficit or by purchasing assets from it.

LEARNING OBJECTIVE 7.3 Identify patterns of trade such as regionalization.

International trade is akin to a prisoner's dilemma in which each country is better off maintaining trade restrictions while trading with partners that have no restrictions. Because of these dynamics, multilateral trade organizations, bilateral trade deals, and regional trade blocs have formed to encourage freer trade, enforce existing trade deals, and resolve trade disputes.

LEARNING OBJECTIVE 7.4 Identify government policies that affect trade patterns.

While many people argue for free trade, governments may have specific reasons to affect trade patterns and the tools to do it. These tools include import tariffs, export tariffs, subsidies, loans, quotas, local content requirements, standards, administrative delay, countertrade requirements, and embargoes. All these tactics seek to alter the efficacy of trade, often to protect or promote domestic companies.

Case Study

Globalization and the Fight to Keep 1,000 Carrier Jobs in Indiana

Willis Carrier invented the air conditioner in 1902; in 1915 he started Carrier Corporation to sell his invention. The company is now part of United Technologies Corporation (UTC) based in Farmington, Connecticut. It designs and manufactures heating, ventilation, and air conditioning (HVAC) systems. During the 2016 presidential election, the company announced a plan to move 1,200 jobs to a new factory in Mexico. The move would reportedly save the company $65 million a year. In the hypercompetitive HVAC industry, keeping costs low is key to success, because there is little product differentiation. One heater does the job just about as well as the next. Carrier's rivals—including Lennox, Ingersoll Rand, and Rheem Manufacturing—had already closed their U.S. plants and moved production to Mexico.[42]

While the Indiana plant was profitable, UTC realized that its costs are higher than those of its competitors and are higher than those of its other operations already in Mexico. According to Wayne Dale, a United Steelworkers subdistrict director in Indiana, "the company has repeatedly told the union that the Indianapolis plant is 'highly profitable.'" A representative from Carrier said that the Indy factory is making money, "but it [is] one of our least profitable in terms of the actual cost of production vs. what we were seeing at other facilities, particularly in Mexico."[43] The key difference in costs between the United States and Mexico are due to differences in wages. In the United States the average wage is about $25 an hour, whereas in Mexico it is $25 a day. In addition, turnover and absenteeism are lower in Mexico.

The company's plan drew fire from President Trump. In fact, it was a key part of the Trump-Pence presidential campaign, with Trump arguing that free trade in general, and NAFTA in particular, was to blame for Carrier's proposed move to Mexico. He proposed protectionist policies to "Keep it Made in America." President Trump and Vice President Pence upped the pressure on the company to keep the jobs in Indiana. After several months and $7 million in concessions from the state of Indiana, as well as about $20 million in concessions from the union, the company agreed to keep the manufacturing plant in Indiana.

Yet, while the company kept its plant in Indiana, the CEO of UTC continued to argue, "If you have a low-skilled job, they're not safe no matter where you are," he says. "The forces of globalization are not going to slow down."[44] Bloomberg reports that the forces of globalization continue on. It noted, "Not far from Carrier, Rexnord LLC closed a bearings plant and shipped production to Mexico. Trump tweeted about it: 'This is happening all over our country. No more!' Rexnord's 350 workers are expected to be out of their jobs by summer. Elsewhere in the state, the auto parts supplier CTS Corporation in Elkhart sent production to Asia and Mexico, cutting 230 jobs. Welbilt Inc. closed its Sellersburg beverage systems factory in January and sent production to Mexico, eliminating more than 70 jobs. Harman Professional Solutions shifted some operations in Elkhart to Mexico, killing 125 jobs." Moreover, others argue that the costs of keeping jobs in the United States is too high. According to a Good Jobs First report, in the past 35 years, 240 deals similar to the Carrier deal have been made, costing companies an average of $465,000 per job saved.[45] Moreover, Gary C. Hufbauer and Kimberly A. Elliott, in a paper titled "Measuring the Costs of Protection in the United States," examined the effects of trade protections in the U.S. luggage industry. They argued that U.S. consumers paid $1,285,000 a year for each job "saved" as a result of barriers to imports. This is a huge sum, particularly when you consider that more than one job was "saved." Other industries had similar large costs, such as $199,000 annually for each textile worker's job that was saved, $1,044,000 for each softwood lumber job saved, and $1,376,000 for every job saved in the benzenoid chemical industry.[46]

Case Discussion Questions

Some people see free trade as a good thing, leading inevitably to increased output, more jobs, and cheaper products and services. Other people see it as a bad thing, leading to unemployment, loss of production capabilities, and reliance on foreign firms.

1. On which side of this argument do you fall?
2. What are the disadvantages of free trade?
3. What are the advantages of free trade?

Endnotes

[1]"Merchandise Trade (% of GDP)," World Bank.http://data.worldbank.org/indicator/TG.VAL.TOTL.GD.ZS/countries?display=map (accessed January 11, 2017).

[2]Lingling Wei, "China Moves to Devalue the Yuan," *Wall Street Journal*, August 11, 2015. www.wsj.com/articles/china-moves-to-devalue-the-yuan-1439258401.

[3]Robert D. Atkinson, "Why China Needs to End Its Economic Mercantilism," Huffington Post, January 30, 2008, updated May 25, 2011. www.huffingtonpost.com/robert-d-atkinson-phd/why-china-needs-to-end-it_b_84028.html.

[4]"Digging for Victory" *Economist*, December 21, 2013. www.economist.com/news/business/21591864-chinas-best-makers-construction-gear-are-now-world-class-digging-victory.

[5]"History of Bottling," Coca-Cola Company. www.coca-colacompany.com/our-company/history-of-bottling/ (accessed January 11, 2017).

[6]"Our History," PepsiCo. www.pepsico.com/Company/Our-History (accessed January 11, 2017).

[7]StreetAuthority, "Coke Vs. Pepsi: By the Numbers," Nasdaq, March 24, 2014. www.nasdaq.com/article/coke-vs-pepsi-by-the-numbers-cm337909.

[8]Supply Chain. Globally it is broadly accepted that the creation of a Sustainable future for Africa lies in its ability to develop and maximise the continent's abundant natural resources. Debswana.com. www.debswana.com/About-Us/Pages/Supply-Chain.aspx (accessed January 11, 2017).

[9]Nike Inc., 2015 Annual Report and Notice of Annual Meeting, 67. https://s1.q4cdn.com/806093406/files/doc_financials/2015/ar/docs/nike-2015-form-10K.pdf (accessed January 11, 2017).

[10]"China Balance of Trade 1983–2017" *Trading Economics*. www.tradingeconomics.com/china/balance-of-trade (accessed June 3rd, 2015).

[11]"U.S. International Trade in Goods and Services" December 2014. U.S. Census Bureau. U.S. Bureau of Economic Analysis." February 5, 2015. https://www.bea.gov/newsreleases/international/trade/2015/trad1214.htm

[12]"Major Foreign Holders of Treasury," *Treasury*. http://ticdata.treasury.gov/Publish/mfh.txt (accessed June 13, 2017).

[13]"Foreign Direct Investment in the United States: 2014 Report," Organization for International Investment. www.ofii.org/sites/default/files/FDIUS2014.pdf (accessed June 3, 2015).

[14]Peter C. Purdue, "The First Opium War: The Anglo-Chinese War of 1839–1842," MIT Visualizing Cultures. http://ocw.mit.edu/ans7870/21f/21f.027/opium_wars_01/ow1_essay01.html (accessed June 3, 2015).

[15]"China Foreign Exchange Reserves: 1980–2017," *Trading Economics*. January 2016. www.tradingeconomics.com/china/foreign-exchange-reserves (accessed April 3, 2015).

[16]"Japan Foreign Exchange Reserves: 1957–2017," *Trading Economics*. January2016.www.tradingeconomics.com/japan/foreign-exchange-reserves (accessed April 3, 2015).

[17]Fukuda, S., and Y. Kon. 2010. Macroeconomic Impacts of Foreign Exchange Reserve Accumulation: Theory and International Evidence. ADBI Working Paper 197. Tokyo: Asian Development Bank Institute. Available: http://www.adbi.org/workingpaper/2010/02/19/3515.macroeconomic.impact.forex.reserve.accumulation

[18]Thomas Gries and Margarete Redlin, "*Trade Openness and Economic Growth: A Panel Causality Analysis*," International Conferences of RCIE, KIET, and APEA, March 2012; Fatma Zeren and Ayse Ari, "Trade Openness and Economic Growth: A Panel Causality Test," *International Journal of Business and Social Science* 4, no. 9 (2013): 317–24; Jamel Jouini, "Linkage between International Trade and Economic Growth in GCC Countries: Empirical Evidence from PMG Estimation Approach," *The Journal of International Trade & Economic Development* 24, no. 3 (2015): 341–72.

[19]"The 128 Countries That Had Signed GATT by 1994," World Trade Organization. www.wto.org/english/thewto_e/gattmem_e.htm (accessed April 13, 2017).

[20]"The WTO Agreements," World Trade Organization. www.wto.org/english/thewto_e/whatis_e/inbrief_e/inbr03_e.htm (accessed April 13, 2017).

[21]"Shrimp Cocktail," *The Economist*, August 3, 2006. www.economist.com/node/7258544.

[22]."DS422: United States — Anti-Dumping Measures on Shrimp and Diamond Sawblades from China," Dispute Settlement, World Trade Organization, March 26, 2013. www.wto.org/english/tratop_e/dispu_e/cases_e/ds422_e.htm.

[23]Liz Brownsell, "Bilateral and Regional Trade Agreements," Advocates for International Development. Lawyers Eradicating Poverty. 2012. http://newsite.diplomaticlawguide.com/bilateral-and-regional-trade-agreements

[24]"The Economy," European Union, last updated June 8, 2016. https://europa.eu/about-eu/facts-figures/economy/index_en.htm (accessed June 3, 2015).

[25]How Does the World Trade Organization Work? Explained with Maps. explainedwithmaps.com. http://explainedwithmaps.com/world-trade-organization/#iLightbox[56be198deccff]/0 (accessed June 13, 2017).

[26]"The History of the European Union," European Union, last updated June 8, 2016. https://europa.eu/european-union/about-eu/history_en (accessed April 12, 2017).

[27]Alyssa Newcomb, "Why the European Union Is Taking on the Company," ABC News, April 15, 2015. http://abcnews.go.com/Technology/google-european-union-taking-company/story?id=30332730.

[28]"NAFTA at 20: Deeper, Better, NAFTA," *The Economist*, January 4, 2014. www.economist.com/news/leaders/21592612-north-americas-trade-deal-has-delivered-real-benefits-job-not-done-deeper-better.

[29]Lee Hudson Teslik and Mohammed Aly Sergie, "NAFTA's Economic Impact," Council on Foreign Relations, March 21, 2008. www.cfr.org/treaties-and-agreements/naftas-economic-impact/p15790 (accessed June 13, 2017).

[30]"Textile and Apparels: Where to Invest?" Invest in ASEAN. http://investasean.asean.org/index.php/page/view/textiles-and-apparels (accessed June 30, 2015).

[31]"Trading Places," *Nature* 521, no. 7553 (May 26, 2015). www.nature.com/news/trading-places-1.17616.

[32]Lesley Wroughton and Yeganeh Torbati, "Nuclear Sanctions Lifted as Iran, U.S. Agree on Prisoner Swap," Reuters, January 17, 2016. www.state.gov/e/eb/tfs/spi/iran/index.htm.

[33]Elizabeth Williamson and Tom Barkley, "U.S. Beats China in Tire Fight," *Wall Street Journal*, December 13, 2000.https://www.wsj.com/articles/SB10001424052748703727804576017473322868118

[34]Gus Lubin, "25 American Products That Rely on Huge Protective Tariffs to Survive," *Business Insider*, September 27, 2010. www.businessinsider.com/americas-biggest-tariffs-2010-9.

[35]Ian Clover, "US Solar Duty Violated Trade Rules, WTO Finds" *PV Magazine*, July 15, 2014. www.pv-magazine.com/news/details/beitrag/us-solar-duty-violated-trade-rules--wto-finds_100015741/#axzz3eV1v3h00.

[36]Niraj Chokshi, "The United States of Subsidies: The Biggest Corporate Winners in Each State," *Washington Post*, March 18, 2015. https://www.washingtonpost.com/blogs/govbeat/wp/2015/03/17/the-united-states-of-subsidies-the-biggest-corporate-winners-in-each-state/?utm_term=.5496f440b761.

[37]Leslie Josephs, "U.S. Increases Sugar Quota for Second time" *Wall Street Journal*, June 23, 2011. www.wsj.com/articles/SB1000142405270230333990457640353026010O672.

[38]Jessica Cull and Alex Msimang, "Regulations, Local Content Requirements on the Rise in West Africa," *Offshore*, February 5, 2014. www.offshore-mag.com/articles/print/volume-74/issue-2/departments/regulatory-perspectives/regulations-local-content-requirements-on-the-rise-in-west-africa.html.

[39]Timothy Josling, "A Review of WTO Rules and GMO Trade," *Biores* 9, no. 3 (April 13, 2015): 4–7; Grant E. Isaac and William A. Kerr, "GMOs at the WTO—A Harvest of Trouble," *Journal of World Trade* 37, no. 6 (2003): 1083–95.

[40]Ashley Moretz, "China's Booming Economy," BarterNews (accessed July 2, 2015). http://barternews.com/countertrade_republic_of_china.htm. More examples of countertrade can be found at www.barternews.com/countertrade_republic_of_china.htm. http://barternews.com/countertrade_republic_of_china.htm

[41]Gary Clyde Hufbauer et al., "Case Studies in Economic Sanctions and Terrorism. Case 60-3. US v. Cuba (1960–: Castro)," Peterson Institute for International Economics, updated October 2011. https://piie.com/publications/papers/sanctions-cuba-60-3.pdf (accessed December 29, 2013); Merrill Fabry, "The US Trade Embargo on Cuba Just Hit 55 Years." *Time*, October 19, 2015. http://time.com/4076438/us-cuba-embargo-1960/

[42]Bryan Gruley and Rich Clough, "Remember When Trump Said He Saved 1,100 Jobs at a Carrier Plant? Well, Globalization Doesn't Give a Damn," Bloomberg Business week, March 29, 2017. www.bloomberg.com/news/features/2017-03-29/remember-when-trump-said-he-saved-1-100-jobs-at-a-carrier-plant.

[43]Gruley and Clough, "Remember When Trump Said He Saved 1,100 Jobs at a Carrier Plant?"

[44]Gruley and Clough, "Remember When Trump Said He Saved 1,100 Jobs at a Carrier Plant?"

[45]Henry Grabar, "Trump Saved Jobs at Carrier by Making the Same Deal American Politicians Always Make," *Slate*, November 30, 2016. www.slate.com/blogs/moneybox/2016/11/30/trump_saved_jobs_at_carrier_by_making_a_bad_deal_for_america.html.

[46]Gary C. Hufbauer, and Kimberly A. Elliott, *Measuring the Costs of Protection in the United States* (Washington, D.C.: Institute for International Economics, 1994).

CHAPTER **8**

Culture

ImagesBazaar/Getty Images

Introduction

The social side of international business is about communication between two or more people seeking to maximize gains in the presence of scarce resources. Working across cultures can sometimes increase the difficulty of getting what we want. For example, an uncomfortable initial greeting can color the whole interaction and reduce the chances of achieving a mutually beneficial agreement.

The reality is that we don't always know whether to shake hands, kiss, or bow. We hope our attempts to be understanding and sensitive will bring success, but in fact most international business deals don't work out perfectly. This chapter provides you with the tools you need to start overcoming cross-cultural barriers and make effective international business deals.

LEARNING OBJECTIVES

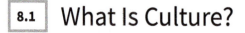

After you explore this chapter you will be able to:

1. **Define** *culture* and describe its characteristics
2. **Describe** the business implications of culture
3. **Identify** ways to manage cultural differences in the workplace
4. **Discuss** how to adapt to different cultures

8.1 What Is Culture?

LEARNING OBJECTIVE

Define *culture* and describe its characteristics.

Culture has important implications for international business. Understanding and responding to cultural differences can make or break business deals, keep employees happy, and be the difference between satisfied or frustrated customers.

What Is Culture?

Culture is a society's unique set of values and norms that govern how people live and interact. Culture manifests itself at many levels—the nation-state level, the professional level (norms for educators, lawyers, businesspeople, students), the functional level (how norms differ between professors and administrators, or between managers and employees), and even at the level of gender, where different norms exist for men and women. Any type of unifying attribute can form the basis for a level of culture. Typically, culture's influence works on a deep level, and as a result we often take it for granted, so its deepest effects on us are usually difficult for us to identify and address from within our own culture.

Think of culture as an iceberg. Just as an iceberg has a part you see and a part hidden under the water, culture has aspects that are readily observable and others that are difficult to discern. For instance, in Thailand you might easily observe people politely putting their hands together in front of them and bowing to each other as a greeting (called a *wai*)—even Ronald McDonald does it, as shown in **Figure 8.1**. But less well understood is that the greeting reflects the strictly hierarchical society of the Thai, which corresponds to the shape of the human body. The crown of the head is the highest and most important point on the body—never touch a Thai adult's or even a child's head; it is gravely offensive—while the soles of the feet are the lowest point. In the act of greeting, the height of your hands is indicative of the degree of respect you are showing the other person. Hands in front of the upper chest and neck with a slight bow is an informal greeting reserved for friends. However, a more formal greeting requires a deeper bow and hands in front of the face. When you are greeting a Buddhist monk or royalty, your hands must be in front of your forehead while you make a deep bow or kneel on the ground with your head bowed.

The principle of the head being the most important part of the body and the feet the least important leads us to understand why it is considered improper to step on coins stamped with the king's image (the king would be under your feet) and why it is important not to have your head be higher than the king's. A Bangkok taxi driver, having been cut off by another driver, was observed to weave through traffic and pull up next to the offending driver. He then took his foot off the gas pedal and stuck it out the window with the bottom toward the other driver, giving him an ultimate insult.[1]

Most of a culture's influence is hidden beneath the surface, like an iceberg (see **Figure 8.2**). When international business leaders ignore the underlying parts of an unfamiliar culture, they are more likely to crash and sink in its intricacies. Therefore, while a first step in examining any culture is to observe the visible aspects of language, institutions, and actions, an important second step is to look for the underlying norms, values, beliefs. These core elements of culture inform a guiding set of principles that establish what is socially acceptable and what isn't.

Robert Holmes/Alamy Stock Photo

Thaiways/Alamy Stock Photo

FIGURE 8.1 Greetings Thailand's main form of greeting is putting the hands together and bowing. Even the Ronald McDonald statues in Thailand perform this common greeting.

culture a society's unique set of values and norms that govern how people live and interact with each other

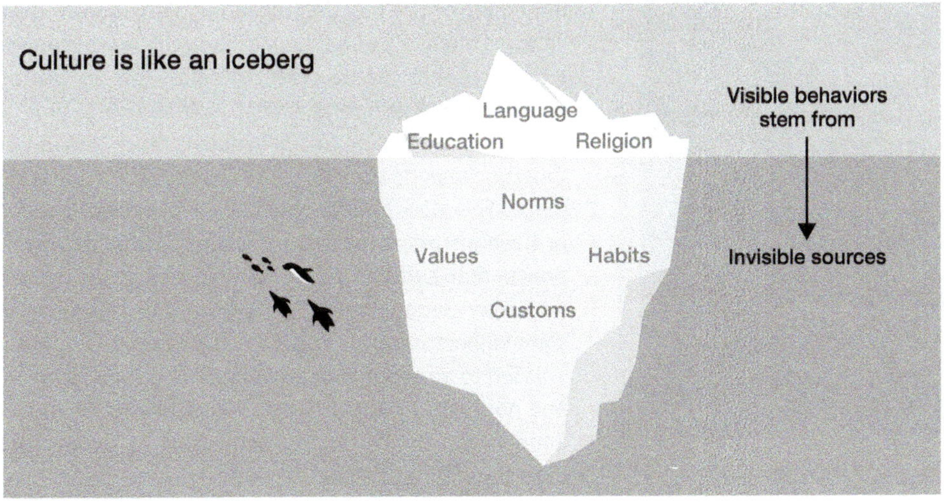

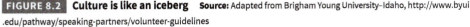

FIGURE 8.2 Culture is like an iceberg **Source:** Adapted from Brigham Young University-Idaho, http://www.byui.edu/pathway/speaking-partners/volunteer-guidelines

Values. A society's values are its backbone, the shared assumptions that identify what its members believe is good, right, and desirable. Consider the hypothetical example of a U.S. manager explaining to a Cambodian colleague that it is illegal under U.S. law, as well as distasteful, to offer bribes to government officials in exchange for their attention and quick action. The Cambodian colleague replies that many government workers are not paid enough to survive and must rely on bribes to help them make ends meet. "Your view is fair," says the Cambodian, "but we believe in taking care of those in need of help."

Values determine, in part, the culture's attitudes toward core social ideals like honesty, freedom, and equality, and toward various kinds of interactions: personal interactions like friendship and love, societial interactions like religion and education, political interactions like government and sufferage, and family interactions like child-rearing and the role of marriage. Values shape and are shaped by the organizations in which they are embedded. For instance, societies that value freedom are more likely to organize around democracies, individual choice, and strongly protected property rights. Expansive personal freedoms in turn encourage people to internalize freedom as a value. In some cases, however, societal values are not reflected in governmental systems, and a society may revolt to bring the system in line with people's values.

The Arab Spring uprising (see **Figure 8.3**) that took place primarily in 2011–2012 was a historic event in which a critical mass of people in Tunisia, Egypt, Libya, and Yemen demonstrated against their governments in an attempt to change their political and economic systems. In some of these countries, change came about and new values were recognized by political leaders. In others, the protests were less effective at instituting change. Nonetheless, this movement was not just a one-time event for the Arab world. Rather, it represents a long-term revolutionary process for liberation that, while not always visible, is still alive and well in the hearts of many people,[2] like the underwater part of an iceberg.

norms the social rules that govern people's interactions

customs socially approved standards of behavior that are not morally significant

Norms. If values are the backbone of a culture, **norms** are the social rules that govern people's interactions within that culture. Norms can be either customs or social mores. In general, **customs** are socially approved standards of behavior that are not morally significant, such as how to greet one another (see **Figure 8.4**), how to dress, what to eat, and how to behave toward neighbors. People follow customs out of tradition or convenience. Breaking a custom does not usually have serious consequences, but it can sour a relationship and make it more difficult to develop trust.

An example of a cultural custom relevant to business is people's attitude toward time. In countries like the United States, Japan, Germany, and Britain, businesspeople are very conscious of schedules. They can be quickly irritated when time is "wasted" because a partner or client is late for a meeting or the meeting runs long. People from these cultures often talk about time as though it were money—a resource that can be saved, invested, lost, or wasted. Many Arabic, Latin, and African cultures view time as more elastic; keeping to a schedule is much less important than making sure the proper interactions have taken place. This view of time may have evolved by necessity or have historical roots. For instance, flexibility toward time in Arab cultures has been influenced by the region's nomadic, Bedouin heritage; saying you would arrive somewhere tomorrow might end up meaning next week. This led to an attitude of accepting people as they come and not focusing too much on *when* they come. In fact, Saudis tend to see time as something to share rather than something to steal.[3]

MOHAMMED ABED/AFP/Getty Images

FIGURE 8.3 Antigovernment crowds throng Cairo's Tahrir Square During the Arab Spring, tens of thousands of protestors rallied in central Cairo for a new government.

Most customs are rooted in some historical or deeper value in the society. For example, during the

Stephen Pond - EMPICS/PA Images/ Getty Images

Jason Dorday/Stringer/Getty Images

FIGURE 8.4 **Different greeting customs** Tennis greats Serena and Venus Williams shake hands with opponents after a tennis match, as is the Western custom (left). German Chancellor Angela Merkel greeting a dancer in New Zealand. The traditional custom for greeting in the Maori culture, called *hongi*, consists of pressing noses together with eyes closed (right).

initial greeting between businesspeople in Japan, the Japanese executive will hold his or her business card in both hands by the corners and bow while presenting the card to the foreigner.[4] This custom carries deep cultural symbolism: The card symbolizes the manager's rank, which is important in a hierarchical society like Japan's. The bow is a sign of respect; the more deeply you bow, the more respect you show. Thus, foreigners doing business in Japan should realize that if someone is older or of higher status, they should bow low to that individual, always receive the business card with two hands, offer their own card with two hands, and examine the card of the person with the higher status right after receiving it. In fact, if you sit down for the meeting after the introduction, you should leave the other person's card on the table in front of you to continue to show respect for that person; in Japan's culture, the card symbolizes to some extent the person who gave it to you—putting it in your back pocket and sitting on it is not a good idea.

Social mores are strict norms that control moral and ethical behavior in a culture. They form the basis for what people believe is right and wrong, and thus, unlike customs, are deeply, morally significant; violating them could result in ruined business deals or worse. Social mores include feelings about such things as murder, theft, adultery, incest, and cannibalism. In many societies they are even codified into law. However, social mores differ widely from culture to culture. For example, U.S. adults generally accept the consumption of alcohol, whereas in many parts of India it is viewed as a violation of important social mores and is punishable by law.

social mores strict norms that control moral and ethical behavior in a culture

Sometimes cultures will enact similar laws based on different cultural mores. For example, based on Islamic codes of morality and fidelity, the sexually conservative country of Saudi Arabia bans strip clubs and online pornography.[5] Iceland, culturally very different from Saudi Arabia, is more sexually liberal yet has also proposed banning strip clubs and online pornography—but this proposal is not based on religion. Most Icelanders believe pornography and strip clubs have serious negative effects on young people, objectify women, and lead to an increase in violent crimes.[6]

Determinants of Culture

The values and norms of a culture do not just happen. Political and economic conditions contribute to them, as do the language, religion, history, and education of a society. Of course, the chain of causation runs both ways: norms and values also influence language, religion, education, and politics. In a sense, all these factors evolve together, but language, religion, and education are easy to recognize, and their effects are easier to observe than those of other factors. Let's take a look at each.

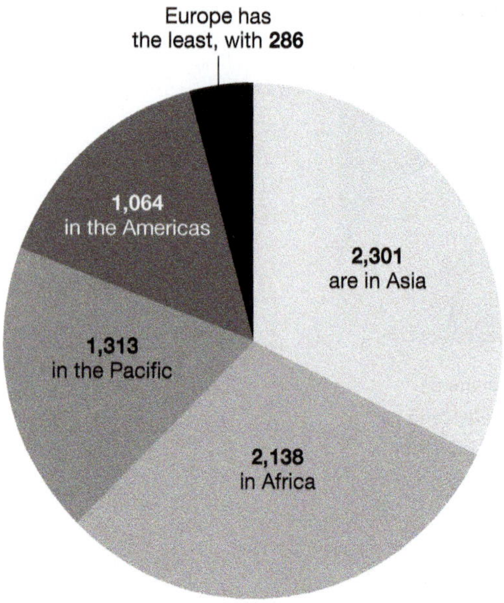

FIGURE 8.5 Languages and their locations At least 7,102 living languages are spoken throughout the world. **Sources:** Rick Noack and Lazaro Gamio, "The World's Languages in 7 Maps and Charts," *Washington Post*, April 23, 2015, https://www.washingtonpost.com/news/worldviews/wp/2015/04/23/the-worlds-languages-in-7-maps-and-charts/?utm_term=.173438a9d96e; M. P. Lewis, G. F. Simons, and C. D. Fennig, *Ethnologue: Languages of the World*, 18th ed. (Dallas: SIL International, 2015). Online version.

Language. One observable difference between countries and cultures is language, both spoken and unspoken. Research shows that we are more likely to see a certain image when we are given verbal cues, even if the image does not exist.[7] In other words, language helps us define and comprehend our reality. For instance, the language of Sanskrit, which traces its origin to India and Iran, has 96 words for love; ancient Persian has 80, Greek has 3, and English only 1.[8] This makes it difficult for many English speakers to express and define how we love one another. Do you love me like a friend, like a brother, like an admirer, or like a lover? Just as in personal relationships, business relationships may be influenced by this limitation on expressions of different types of love.

Because language shapes the way people see the world, it also helps to define culture, so countries with more than one language often have more than one culture. For example, Canada has two official languages, English and French. The French-speaking part of Canada considers itself unique, with a distinct culture. Consultants working with General Mills found that people are very familiar with the company in the English-speaking part of Canada, but it is almost unknown in the French-speaking part. French-speaking Canadians feel a stronger cultural connection to their distant French relations than they do to their English-speaking neighbors. As a result, they are more interested in French than U.S. brands.[9]

At least 7,102 living languages are spoken throughout the world, as shown in **Figure 8.5**. A living language is one spoken by a native population somewhere, whereas a dead language (such as Latin) is no longer native anywhere. Asia, despite being dominated by large countries like Russia, India, and China, has the most spoken languages of any continental area, whereas Europe, despite comprising many nation-states, is at the bottom of the pack with just 286.[10]

Chinese is the native language of the largest number of people, followed by Hindi and then English (also spoken in India). The statistics on languages are interesting because they show that two-thirds of the world's population share just 12 native languages—of the 7,102 available. In fact, a mere 3 percent of the world's people account for 96 percent of all languages spoken. As many as 2,000 languages have fewer than 1,000 native speakers alive today. According to some estimates, half the world's spoken languages could disappear by the end of the century.[11]

Despite being only third in the number of native speakers, thanks to language study courses the most widely spoken language is English, followed by Arabic, French, Chinese, and then Spanish. English is spoken in 101 countries. Next in line is Arabic, spoken in 60 countries, then French in 51, Chinese in 33, and Spanish in 31. English, French, and Spanish are so widely dispersed because of the imperialistic histories of the nations where they originate.[12]

English is the unofficial language of business and of the Internet. Overall, more people learn English than French, Spanish, Italian, Japanese, German, and Chinese combined. That said, some languages have only recently gained attention. The number of U.S. colleges teaching Mandarin Chinese has risen by 110 percent over the past 20 years. During that same time, the number of college courses offering Russian *decreased* by 30 percent. These trends reflect the shifting U.S. interest in countries that speak these languages. In fact, studying certain languages can increase graduates' earning potential.[13] For instance, learning German can mean earning an extra $128,000 over the course of a career (enough to buy a German car or two). Studying Chinese is also becoming a lucrative proposition. In addition to increasing earning potential, speaking more than one language has been shown to lead to increased creativity, negotiation skills, and problem-solving ability.[14]

religion a system of shared beliefs and rituals expressing the way adherents interpret their place in the universe

ethical system sets of moral principles or values that guide and shape behavior

Religion. A **religion** is a system of shared beliefs and rituals expressing the way adherents interpret their place in the universe. **Ethical systems** are sets of moral principles or values that guide and shape behavior, ensuring people can interact and live together effectively. Most—but not all—of the world's ethical systems are a product of religions, making the relationship between religion, ethics, and society complex. Thousands of religions are practiced worldwide today (see **Figures 8.6** and **8.7**), but four in particular stand out for their influence on society and global economic systems. Christianity is currently the world's largest religion, with roughly 2.2 billion adherents. The vast majority of Christians live in Europe and the Americas, although their numbers in Africa are growing rapidly. Christianity grew out of Judaism and is similarly monotheistic (declaring belief in one God, whose son is Christ). Max Weber, a famous sociologist, claimed that Christianity—in particular Protestant Christianity—led to a culture of rugged individualism and self-sufficiency in the United States, often called the *Protestant work ethic*.[15] In general, Christian teaching holds that it's fine to make money from business, but the purpose of making money should not be to buy material possessions; rather, money is for bettering the lives of those around you.[16]

Islam is the second-largest global religion, with 1.6 billion adherents. It is monotheistic and has connections to both Judaism and Christianity (viewing Jesus Christ as one of God's prophets). The Qur'an, the Islamic book of scripture, establishes some economic principles, many of which encourage free enterprise. The Prophet Muhammad was once a trader, and the Qur'an speaks approvingly of free trade and the protection of the right to private property.[17] As in Christianity, property and all other material goods are believed to originate from God (Allah). As a result, profiting from property is acceptable, but money should be used in a righteous, socially beneficial, prudent manner. One economic principle of Islam that differs from Christianity is its prohibition on paying or receiving interest. When you borrow money from an Islamic bank, it will therefore not charge you interest, but under the terms of a contract called a *mudarabah*, it will ask for a percentage of the profits you earn from the loan. Likewise, when you deposit money you will get a share of the profits the bank makes from using your money for investments. Islam currently represents the fastest-growing major religion, and by 2050, its adherents are expected to be as numerous as Christians.[18]

The third-largest worldwide religion is Hinduism, with just over 1 billion adherents. Major traditions within Hinduism include worship of the gods Vishnu and Shiva. Hinduism is the most geographically concentrated of the major religious groups, with more than 99 percent of adherents in the Asia-Pacific region (94 percent live in India, 2 percent in Nepal, 1 percent in Bangladesh).[19] Hindus believe that a moral existence in society requires the acceptance of certain responsibilities, called *dharma*. Hindus also believe in *karma*, the spiritual progression of each person's soul. By following *dharma* to perfect the soul, an individual can eventually achieve *nirvana*, a state of complete spiritual perfection. From a business perspective, dharma roughly translates into your moral obligation to be productive and contribute to the greater good of society.[20] This ideal is similar to the Protestant work ethic, in which work almost becomes an end in itself. At the same time, many Hindus will argue that the pursuit of material wealth can interfere with karma and stifle the path to nirvana, further reinforcing the idea that work should be undertaken for work's sake alone—not for monetary benefit.

Finally, Buddhism claims nearly half a billion adherents, mostly in Central and Southeast Asia. Buddhism was founded in the sixth century B.C.E. by Siddhartha Gautama, in what is now Nepal. Siddhartha was not completely happy with Hinduism, and in his process to achieve nirvana he became the Buddha (which means "the awakened one"). Based on the insight that spiritual liberation is attained by avoiding extremes, some people claim that Buddhism represents the *middle way* between the competing models of capitalism and socialism. It supports the conventional forces of a free market and competition so long as they don't destroy either nature or human society, and it promotes interconnectedness among all living things.[21]

Percentage of the global population

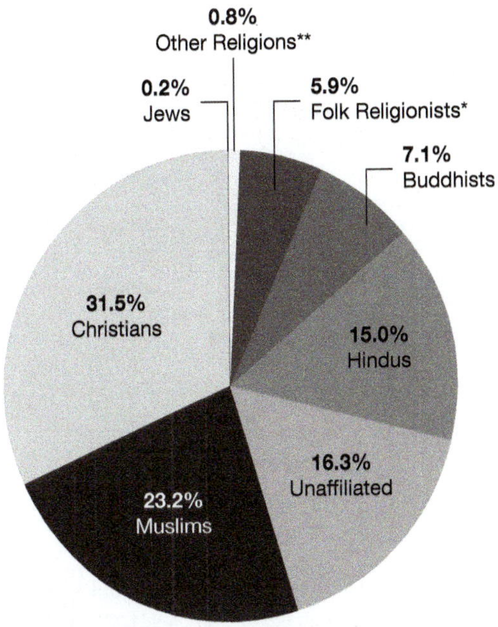

* Includes followers of African traditional religions, Chinese folk religions, Native American religions, and Australian aboriginal religions.

** Includes Bahai's, Jains, Sikhs, Shintoists, Taoists, followers of Tenrikyo, Wiccans, Zoroastrians, and many other faiths.

Percentages may not add to 100 due to rounding.

FIGURE 8.6 Sizes of major religious groups

Source: "The Global Religious Landscape," Pew Research Center, Religion & Public Life, December 18, 2012. http://www.pewforum.org/2012/12/18/global-religious-landscape-exec/.

Education. Education plays a key role in shaping a society's culture. It helps children learn the language of a society and the conceptual and mathematical skills needed to function and progress within it. It helps instill cultural norms and values in individuals, maintaining and sustaining a society's culture. Education also helps individuals think critically about their own

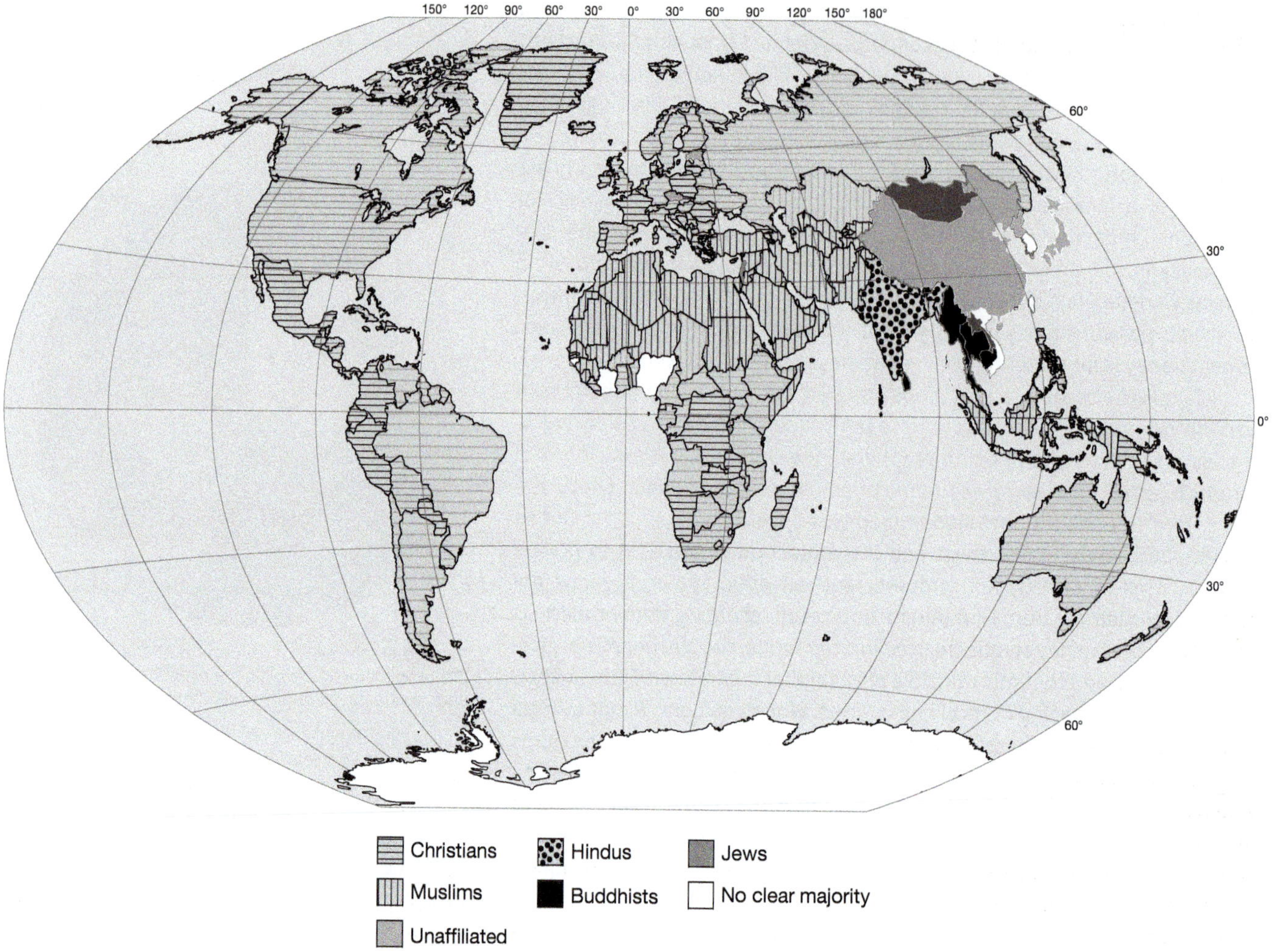

Note: Countries are colored according to the majority religion. Darker shading represents a greater prevalence of the majority religion.

FIGURE 8.7 Majority religion by country **Source:** "The Global Religious Landscape," Pew Research Center, Religion & Public Life, December 18, 2012. http://www.pewforum.org/2012/12/18/global-religious-landscape-exec/.

cultural biases, enabling them to work to change the prevailing culture for the better. For example, cultural research has shown that many people see women as undervalued in their respective cultures, and the majority who have received formal education say they do not feel this is right and that it should change.[22]

From an international business perspective, education can shape a country's ability to compete. Universities and colleges have boomed in the past decade as the world has moved to a knowledge-based economy. For example, in the past 20 years the number of universities in China has increased 600 percent and that in India, 1,600 percent. In 2014, an estimated 8 million vacant job positions were available in Europe and the United States, and at the same time, 8 million people were unemployed in Europe alone. This indicates that the current educational infrastructure in some countries does not prepare people to bridge the skills gap.[23] The United States is consistently ranked near the top globally for the quality of its universities, for example, but students still often struggle to match their educations to the job market. Many feel the squeeze of increasing tuition and fees but can't find a job after college.

Overall, education offers opportunities to both reinforce and shape a culture, but it must also ensure students are receiving the appropriate skills and knowledge to compete in the new global environment. Today's employment landscape requires a sound understanding of political, economic, sociocultural, and technological factors. With such an education, students are able to see the necessary culture changes that allow them, their businesses, and their countries to compete in the global market.

8.2 What Does Culture Mean for Business?

LEARNING OBJECTIVE

Describe the business implications of culture.

The implications of culture on international business are profound. Because global business cuts across cultural boundaries, its leaders must be ready to cope with cultural differences and all the complications they entail. Here we cover the more common areas of difference, which have been extensively studied—social stratification, work motivation, relationship preferences, tolerance for risk, and the handling of information.

Social Stratification

Social stratification is the hierarchy created by society to cluster people into groups according to characteristics such as status, power, and wealth. Every society develops a form of social stratification, but the sorting criteria can be very different because each society emphasizes different features. They can be characteristics **ascribed** at birth—such as gender, age, ethnicity, or family—or they can be **acquired** through activities and choices, such as religion, education, political affiliation, and profession. For example, U.S. culture values accomplishment and achievement regardless of age, whereas Japanese culture values the wisdom and experience of age.[24] An interaction between people from each culture could be a failure if a manager from the United States, intending to motivate his or her employee, praises a young employee's accomplishments, while the person from Japan may interpret the praise as pride or narcissism and would have likely praised the boss of the individual or the organization as a whole.

ascribed characteristics an individual is born with

acquired characteristics an individual takes on through experience

South Korea's culture has foundations in Confucian ideology. In Confucian thought, society stratifies individuals into four categories: scholars, farmers, artisans, and merchants and traders, known in Korean as *sa*, *nong*, *gong*, and *sang* (사농공상). Because of this stratification, "scholars," including university professors, are given great respect. For instance, students will not show their backs to a professor because it is a sign of disrespect. Instead they will walk backward out of the professor's office. Students also use formal titles when speaking to professors, such as "professor" or "doctor professor."[25] In the United States, by contrast, professorship doesn't carry the same social standing. Students may think of professors as "just" teachers and may even refer to them by first name.

A lack of understanding regarding the social stratification in a country can derail a company's success in that market. Ignorance or disregard can cause significant confusion and conflict. On the other hand, understanding how much respect to give and how to communicate in other cultures can boost a company's reputation and help it succeed in a foreign market.

Work Motivation

All people work for a reason, but that reason may differ systematically across different cultures. Understanding what motivates people to work will help businesses manage employees from different cultures and countries. For instance, workers in some countries are motivated by *materialism*, or the ability to buy and own property and merchandise. Harder, smarter work is encouraged because it earns greater rewards, enabling individuals to acquire more goods. This materialistic drive in a culture is likely to lead to more development and to foster economic growth, but it also is likely to lead to greater concentration of wealth and higher income disparity.

By contrast, increasing the opportunity for leisure is a motivator for work in countries that highly value spare time. People in these cultures are likely to prefer to work fewer hours, take more time off, and spend more of their hard-earned money on leisure activities rather than acquiring things.[26] A classic example is the culture of France. The French have 30 days of mandated vacation time, compared with the 0 days mandated in the United States. Full-time work in France consists of 35 hours a week, compared with 40 hours in the United States.

Other forms of motivation include fame or honor, stability and security, avoiding disdain or saving face, providing for family, and meeting other personal needs and goals. For instance, saving face and preserving the family name are critical in Korea. A South Korean woman sold her expensive home in Seoul and moved into a cheap apartment so that she could give the money to her brother, who had made some bad investments and needed money to avoid bankruptcy. She noted, "it was needed to save the reputation of the family."[27] Hence, culture also shapes the factors that motivate people.

Relationship Preferences

Different cultures often have different perceptions about how interpersonal relationships should function and how power is distributed within the work place. This cultural characteristic affects both management styles and interpersonal relationships between the employee and the company. Several measures of culture have been created to classify country cultures, including Hofstede's dimensions of national culture (https://geert-hofstede.com/national-culture.html) and the GLOBE's model of national culture (see http://globeproject.com/). We highlight a few of the key measures here.

power distance the degree to which subordinates in an organization accept that power is distributed unequally

Power distance is the degree to which subordinates in an organization accept that power is distributed unequally. Higher power distance means little consultation is likely to occur between managers and subordinates. Either the managers will act with unlimited authority (exercising autocratic, top-down leadership), or they will manage by anticipating and supplying the needs of those under them, as a parent does for a child (using paternalistic leadership). For example, a professor got a job in a country with high power distance and strong paternalistic leadership. When asked what her annual salary would be, she replied, "I don't know. They said they would take care of me." In other words, with high power distance, it is inappropriate to ask questions that might seem fundamental in the United States, like that of salary, but the paternalistic nature of the culture allowed her to trust that what the managers say, goes. She took the job.[28]

On the other hand, low power distance results in a more collaborative environment. Managers are open to and may solicit the ideas and opinions of their subordinates, who usually feel they are on a more equal footing with their manager. Yet, while low power distance may increase collaboration, it may also increase inefficiency. Most militaries around the world instill a high degree of power distance to speed decision making. Imagine an army with low power distance calling a "time out" so that they could work out a mutually agreed approach to their battle.

How does power distance affect international businesses? Sweden has a comparatively low power distance, for instance. How do you think the Swedish multinational company IKEA had to adapt when entering the Philippine market, characterized by high power distance?

individualism the belief that the needs of the individual are more important than the needs of society

collectivism the belief that the needs of society are more important than the needs of the individual

Another way relationship preferences vary across cultures is in whether the individual or the collective is more important. This distinction is known as "**individualism** *versus* **collectivism**." *High collectivism* means that individuals defer to the collective rather than looking for individual outcomes. For instance, during the Asian financial crisis of the 1990s, South Korea was in need of foreign currency or gold equivalent to prop up the economy and avoid defaulting on its loans. The government asked citizens to donate any gold they might have, and thousands took off wedding rings and other gold jewelry and gave it to the government.[29] All told, the government collected over 227 tons of gold, valued at more than $3 billion, which it used to pay down government loans. In collectivist cultures, employees are more likely to rely on the organization for benefits, training, and socialization. They usually prefer working in groups to complete projects, and job security is a principal motivator.

On the other hand, in a culture of *high individualism* people are more focused on individual activities and outcomes. They are likely to prefer working independently, and they will look outside the organization to satisfy personal needs such as friendship and to find leisure activities and even training. They want money rather than benefits as compensation, and they take more responsibility for their life independent of the organization. The opportunity to overcome challenges and grow is often a main motivator for employees.

Risk-Taking Behavior

Risk taking is another important business-related aspect of culture. Risk-taking behavior reflects people's belief in their ability to control the outcomes of their lives. It depends on factors such as uncertainty avoidance, level of trust, future orientation, and assertiveness.

Uncertainty avoidance measures how we deal with an unknown future. High uncertainty avoidance suggests that employees are more risk averse. They prefer to avoid the unknown by following established rules and regulations—even when those rules are perceived to be ineffective. Managers in cultures with high uncertainty avoidance are often more successful when they provide detailed instructions and clear guidelines. On the other hand, employees in cultures with low uncertainty avoidance typically are less loyal to their current employers because they are willing to face the uncertainty of unemployment in an attempt to find more favorable work conditions. Consumers also display their degree of uncertainty avoidance in their willingness to adopt new products early. Those with high uncertainty avoidance are less likely to try products that have not been proven safe, effective, or desirable by the majority of the market.[30]

uncertainty avoidance a business-related aspect of culture that measures how persons deal with an unknown future

As the name suggests, **future orientation** is the degree to which a culture chooses future rather than immediate results. A culture with a strong future orientation, such as the Netherlands, is more willing to postpone rewards now for greater benefit in the future. People with a strong future orientation are more willing to save resources and place more emphasis on long-term success. Cultures with weak future orientation are more likely to spend now and to emphasize short-term goals and objectives.[31]

future orientation the degree to which a culture chooses future rather than immediate results

Assertiveness measures how competitive and aggressive a culture is. Cultures that are highly assertive tend to have more competitive work environments. Communication is more direct and unambiguous. People like to have control over their environments and are more willing to take responsibility for events. Low-assertion cultures place greater value on teamwork and relationships than on results. Their communication tends to be more indirect and vague in order to avoid placing blame and causing confrontation.[32]

assertiveness a measure of how competitive and aggressive a culture is

Information

A final dimension of culture relevant to international business is the way different cultures acquire and process information. This characteristic often influences cultures' perceptions of products, people, and ideas. For instance, communication varies across cultures. Some cultures are **low-context cultures** and rely on direct means of conveying messages with little background information (or context). The most important factor in understanding the message is the words themselves, and they are often straightforward and concise. For instance, the message "Your performance was poor due to your frequent absences" is a low-context phrase.

low-context cultures cultures that rely on the direct means of conveying messages with little background information

On the other hand, **high-context cultures** use more implicit messaging and contextual elements to convey information, including body language and tone of voice. Speakers of Korean don't say "my house" or even "my spouse"; rather, they say "our house" or "our wife/husband." Whether they are referring to their own house or their friend's house is implied by the context surrounding the conversation. Low-context cultures include those in much of North America and Western Europe, whereas high-context cultures include those throughout much of Asia, Africa, and South America.[33] Some differences are highlighted in **Figure 8.8**.

high-context cultures cultures that rely on implicit messages and contextual elements to convey information

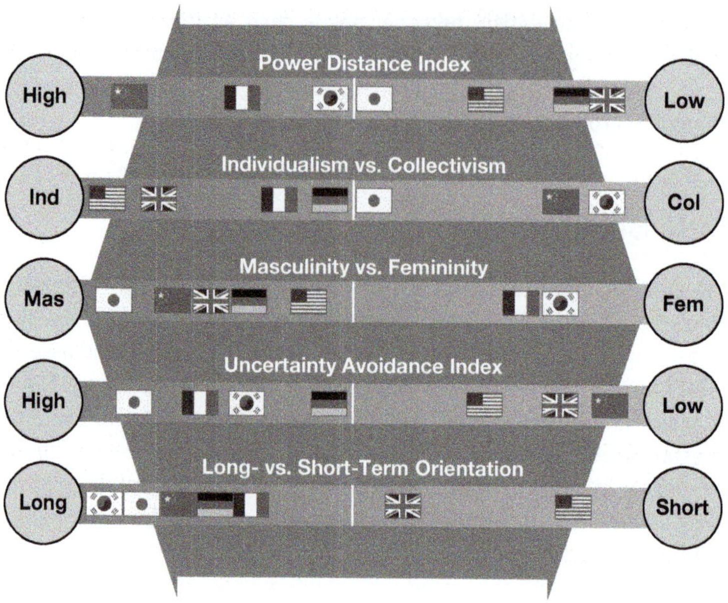

FIGURE 8.8 Cultural dimensions. This chart shows where particular countries fall with regard to various cultural dimensions. **Source:** G. Hofstede, "Dimensionalizing Cultures: The Hofstede Model in Context," *Online Readings in Psychology and Culture* 2, no. 1 (2011), 8; Edward T. Hall, *Beyond Culture* (New York: Anchor Books, 1989).

8.3 Managing Cultural Differences

LEARNING OBJECTIVE

Identify ways to manage cultural differences in the workplace.

Open interaction can help to bridge cultural differences. Each party often has a different perspective, but they are also each likely to realize something important about the other through their conversation. Building a platform of common understanding improves the quality of future communication and helps bring about a positive resolution to the situation.

Three key steps can help you achieve this kind of mutual understanding and so manage business across cultures. These steps—the three Rs of recognition, respect, and reconciliation (shown in **Figure 8.9**)—offer a framework to help you not only tolerate differences but also embrace and capitalize on them. In this way you can create greater value than if you hadn't acknowledged the differences. Let's consider each step in turn and learn how to implement them.

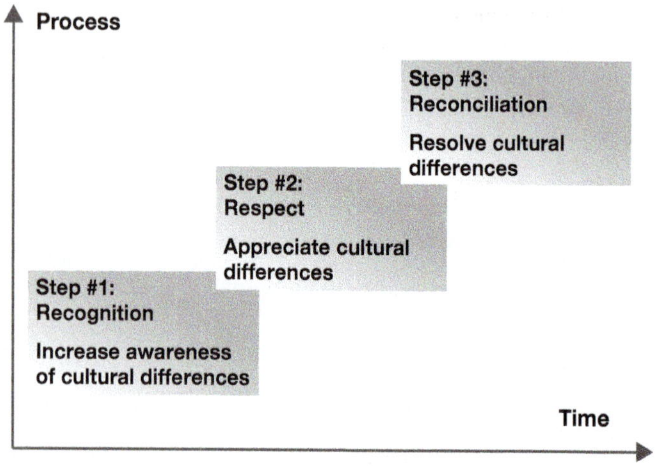

FIGURE 8.9 The 3 Rs of managing cultural differences.

Recognize Differences

Before doing business with someone from another culture, ask yourself, "What do I know about this person's culture?" Recognizing cultural differences begins with assessing your factual knowledge about the other culture. In Section 8.2, we covered several different cultural dimensions and the ways they influence business. Recognizing what to expect when working with people from different cultures can be the first step in helping you to respond and react correctly. It can help you avoid offending your business partners and understand why a deal you've been trying to structure may be taking so long.

Recognizing differences consists of first selecting which cultural dimension(s) to examine and then assessing their impact on the specific business you are attempting. This may sound easy, but many managers underestimate the challenges that come with bridging cultures. Management styles develop from habits we learn not only from experience as a manager but throughout our lifetime.

For example, Heineken, the Dutch brewing company, bought a large brewery based in Monterrey, Mexico. In connection with the merger, some Mexican employees began working at Heineken's headquarters in Amsterdam. One of these was Carlos, director of marketing for the Dos Equis brand. Carlos relates how he struggled during his first year after the merger, having developed a specific management style throughout his whole life in Mexico that no longer applied. "It is incredible to manage Dutch people, and nothing like my experience leading Mexican teams. I'll schedule a meeting to roll out a new process, and during it, my team starts challenging the process, taking us in various unexpected directions, ignoring my process altogether, and paying no attention to the fact that they work for me. Sometimes I just watch them, astounded. Where is the respect?" says Carlos. "I know this treating-everyone-as-pure-equals thing is the Dutch way, so I keep quiet and try to be patient. But often I just feel like getting down on my knees and pleading, 'Dear colleagues, in case you haven't forgotten, I. AM. THE. BOSS.'"[34]

WileyPLUS

See Whiteboard Video: Managing Cultural Differences

Respect Differences

Once you have recognized cultural differences, the next step is to respect them. *Respect* is defined as esteem for the worth of a culture. Demonstrating such respect might mean changing and adapting your own views of the world to better appreciate the elements of that culture. To shift your perspective in this way, you need to do two things—decenter then recenter.[35]

To **decenter** means that you take what you have learned about another's culture and use that knowledge to adapt your own behavior and thinking. Stand back from someone's culture and try to understand why people in the culture do what they do, to identify the underlying assumptions behind the behaviors you observe. Once you understand the underlying context, you will be able to see the value in the norms and customs of that culture.

decenter to take what you have learned about another's culture and use that knowledge to adapt one's own behavior and thinking

After decentering, the next step is to **recenter**. Recentering is finding or creating shared ground, or areas of overlap between old and new behaviors and understanding. To recenter, you first need to identify the situation and then adjust your thinking or behavior to it, rather than defaulting to your cultural conditioning. This adaptation doesn't necessarily mean you agree with the differences, but it does mean you can relate to the situation. For example, during team meetings in the United States, employees analyze information and make decisions. In Korea, however, team meetings are often held to publicly confirm decisions that smaller groups of team members have already made. The intensive discussion before the meeting explores everything just as thoroughly as the U.S. model does, but it saves face for the participants by ensuring that any conflict is aired in private rather than in public.

recenter to find or create shared ground between old and new behavior and understanding

This example shows how much we take for granted by thinking everyone has the same assumptions about the purpose of meetings. In Mexico, a meeting is a time to build relationships and learn trust. Once you trust someone, decisions can be made quickly and easily at any time. In the Netherlands, a meeting may be a time to identify the weaknesses of a particular plan.[36]

Reconcile Differences

Although respecting differences helps you find common ground with others, it doesn't necessarily mean you can simply blend everything together and make good decisions. For good decisions, you need to apply knowledge and cultural empathy to the task of reconciling differences. That means bringing different cultures into agreement or harmony in a way that allows all concerned to work toward a common goal or objective. You will need to solicit uncommon information, leverage ideas, and make a plan.

Uncommon information is information not available to all the decision makers. It can be special skills or relationships, intelligence, or experience, or even restricted data or access. Social psychologists have found that the component pieces of information for a "best option" are most often spread among group members.[37] Consider this real-life exchange among a culturally diverse team of managers from a national bank. The team was reviewing its decision-making process, and one of the managers said, "Actually, I think we've been very good. We listen to everyone. We always make sure we ask whether anyone disagrees with where we're going."

Another manager concurred. "I think you're right . . . . We get all the right ideas out from everyone, right, gang?" After a few more minutes of this self-congratulation, one woman, originally from Korea, cleared her throat and tentatively raised her hand. She took a deep breath and said, "Not one of you understands how hard it is for me to talk in meetings with you. I have to rehearse everything I'm going to say fifteen times in my mind. . . . Half the time, by the time I say my piece, you think you've gone beyond the point, and my information doesn't get considered. What frustrates me most is that the team really isn't getting my best ideas, the ones that could make a difference!" In the silence that followed, one of the men quietly said that, as an Indonesian, he also struggled to be heard by the rest of the group.

By adjusting the way meetings were run so that members took turns expressing ideas and everyone took time to consider each person's thoughts, the team was able to reconcile some of those differences. Soon they were generating a broader pool of ideas to draw from. For example, members assigned one person the role of "process leader." This person was given responsibility to curb the dominance of any individual and invite more participation from members who tended to be quieter.

Another approach to soliciting uncommon information is to change the way meetings are run in order to incorporate different cultural styles. This gives everyone a chance to contribute in a comfortable way.[38] For example, the team began asking for feedback on discussion items and concerns to be exchanged via email before meetings took place, allowing critical or dissenting voices a safe forum in which to voice their concerns and suggestions. Members also began allowing time at the beginning of the meeting to discuss personal items not necessarily related to the agenda that day—creating a time for people to build personal relationships and trust.

Soliciting uncommon information is necessary to effectively reconcile differences, but it's not enough. The shared knowledge has to be applied by the group or company, and this can be the hardest part. People from one culture might be more reluctant to implement practices from another culture because of the *not-invented-here (NIH) syndrome*.[39] The NIH syndrome is a process in which a person or group resists accepting new ideas from culturally different persons or groups inside or outside the organization. It causes an unwillingness to apply knowledge, and it may spring from a person's lack of appreciation for new knowledge. Because its origin is culturally distinct, it can be overcome by developing a shared vision and a common understanding that bridge the cultural divide so that people can focus on the results, not on the process.[40]

8.4 Building Cultural Intelligence

LEARNING OBJECTIVE

Discuss how to adapt to different cultures.

cultural intelligence the knowledge to function effectively across cultural contexts

Managing cultural differences in the workplace is key to a company's survival, but it is also key to an individual's ability to contribute to society. To operate effectively in a global world requires the use of **cultural intelligence**, or the knowledge to function effectively across cultural contexts. Cultural intelligence is measured by a person's *cultural intelligence quotient (CQ)*.[41] A person with high CQ can differentiate features of a behavior that relate to culture, features that are universal, and features that are specific to an individual. For example, if you attended a meeting in Finland and your Finnish colleague didn't do a lot of talking but then summarized what you said, would that be a common cultural communication pattern found among Finns or is it unique to that individual? If it is not unique to the individual but is a behavior common in Finnish culture, then it can give you a clue about how you might want to structure your own conversations with other Finnish colleagues.

Take, for example, a U.S. manager who was serving on a design team that included two German engineers. As other team members offered ideas, the two Germans shot the ideas down—even describing them as not applicable or too immature. After a fair amount of interaction with these engineers, the U.S. manager concluded that Germans, in general, were rude and aggressive people. Had she possessed a higher level of cultural intelligence, however, the U.S. manager might have realized that she was conflating the merit of ideas and the merit of the people offering them—two factors the Germans were able to make a sharp distinction between.[42]

Many managers would probably empathize with the team members whose ideas were being criticized and propose a new style of discussion for the team that would protect people's feelings while allowing for candor. However, without being able to distinguish how much of the engineers' behavior was culturally determined and how much was unique to them as individuals, the manager couldn't know how to influence their actions or how easy or difficult it might be to do so.

Assessing Cultural Intelligence

Cultural intelligence is rooted in research across many different countries and profoundly affects the way businesses work and the success of cross-border leadership.[43] Three factors determine a person's level of CQ. It's not enough to be good at just one or two—all three are necessary to effectively and appropriately adjust behaviors in a foreign culture.[44] These three factors, which we discuss next, are cognitive CQ, behavioral CQ, and motivational CQ.[45]

Cognitive CQ. *Cognitive CQ* is our level of understanding about how cultures are similar and different. Most corporate training programs focus on developing cognitive CQ, or understanding the beliefs, customs, and taboos of foreign cultures. Unfortunately, understanding everything about every possible culture is impossible. For that reason, the point of cognitive CQ is not to be an expert on every culture; rather, it's to understand key cultural differences and how they affect everyday business interactions. For example, communication styles, predominant religious beliefs, and role expectations for men and women often differ across cultures. Culture can also influence managers' effectiveness in specific business functions.[46]

Behavioral CQ. Knowing about someone else's culture doesn't help much unless you can adapt your personal behavior accordingly. Your actions need to demonstrate to the people in the other culture that you have entered and understood their world. *Behavioral CQ* measures your ability to do this. For example, do you know how you pass your business card to someone from the other culture? Do you know how to hail a taxi? Your ability to mimic and mirror the customs and habits of the people around you proves that you value and respect those cultural norms enough to follow them.[47] In fact, studies show that job candidates who adopt some of the mannerisms of recruiters with cultural backgrounds different from their own are more likely to receive a job offer.[48]

While adapting your behavior to local norms is important, behavioral CQ also covers knowing when *not* to adapt. For example, U.S. managers who do not to speak up at all in a meeting with Chinese colleagues might violate those colleagues' expectations make them worry that they'd caused offense. Overcompensating or taking a cultural norm to an extreme is easy; the challenge is to adapt in the right way. In addition, you shouldn't adapt to cultural practices that are unethical or potentially harmful to you or your company, such as giving or receiving bribes and discriminating against or objectifying ethnic or gender groups.

Motivational CQ. Sometimes people have the knowledge and ability to make cultural adaptations but don't care to do so. *Motivational CQ* assesses your level of interest, drive, and energy to adapt cross-culturally; this can come from both an innate (intrinsic) desire as well as external (extrinsic) forces. Intrinsic forces are internal motivations, like the enjoyment you get from having culturally diverse experiences. People with high levels of intrinsic motivation are often more extraverted and open to new experiences.[49] Extrinsic motivation, on the other hand, comes from external motivators, like taking a job in a foreign country or realizing that distinct professional or personal benefits can be gained from an experience. For example, an individual could be motivated to understand different cultures because research shows that people who increase their cross-cultural experiences are more innovative and are better able to share and work with others from different cultures.[50] Ultimately, motivational CQ measures your sense of desire to learn about and function effectively in different cultural settings.

Improving Cultural Intelligence

Our level of cultural intelligence is not locked in at birth and can be developed with effort. So, if you're not happy with where you are after assessing your current CQ, you can follow three steps to improve your cultural intelligence. Identify your strengths and weaknesses, undertake some training, and make time every day to reinforce that training.[51] Let's consider some specific ways to implement these steps.

Step 1: Identify CQ Strengths and Weaknesses. Identify your target areas of CQ by looking at your results from the CQ assessment above. For example, perhaps your cognitive and motivational CQs are high, but your behavioral CQ is low. Knowing this, you can focus on some of the specific questions with low scores and brainstorm ways you can build skill in those areas.

You can also ask for feedback from peers or your boss, based on cross-cultural interactions they've witnessed. Request specific comments about what you could have done differently to improve your cultural adaptation and how motivated and informed you seemed. Ask how well you adapted your behaviors to interact in the multicultural environment. This type of feedback is most effective if you can ask your colleague or boss *before* an upcoming encounter so he or she can prepare to analyze what you do well and what you can do better. In this way, the other person can be better prepared to observe the specifics of your behavior and offer detailed and helpful feedback.

Step 2: Select and Apply Training to Focus on Weaknesses. Once you've received feedback on your strengths and weaknesses, develop specific training to correct those weaknesses. Don't forget to practice your strengths, too, because CQ can deteriorate over time if not used. For example, to improve your cognitive CQ, you could read books that help you understand how different cultures interact and communicate. You could also visit a museum and focus on the art of a specific country or culture.

If you lag in behavioral CQ, you could enroll in an acting class or role-play specific behaviors that differ from your typical style. Reading about and playing a role as someone from a culture different from your own can be enlightening and help you act in ways that might otherwise feel uncomfortable at first. Finally, if you're struggling with motivational CQ, interview someone who has worked or traveled extensively and ask him or her about cross-cultural interactions.

Step 3: Organize Daily Tasks to Align with Training. The last step in improving your cultural intelligence is to integrate your training into your daily tasks as much as possible. Most people are too busy to worry about how they interact cross-culturally. This is a major reason so many people aren't better at it. The key is to find ways to improve your CQ while on the job. Many of the ideas suggested above can be incorporated into your daily work.

Find coworkers who can help you improve your skills by acting as a translator and ensuring that your interpretation is correct. They may be from a different culture or simply have lived or worked in one. People who grew up in a bicultural family (with parents from two different countries) have personal experience with understanding multiple cultural perspectives and are especially good at identifying ways to bridge them.[52]

Another tip is to find out what resources your company has access to or is willing to provide. Some companies (usually multinationals) have access to training materials and will sometimes offer reimbursement for cultural training. Managers often look favorably upon people who want to improve their CQ. That desire shows not only that you are interested in improving a skill set but also that you are a potential candidate for a foreign assignment. When selecting people for these assignments, managers look especially for willingness and ability to live and work in a foreign environment.

Summary and Case

Summary

LEARNING OBJECTIVE 8.1 Define *culture* and describe its characteristics.

Culture is a society's unique set of values and norms, which governs how people live and interact with each other. Values are a society's guiding principles about what is good, right, and desirable. Norms are the social rules that govern people's interactions; these can be customs or social mores. Language, religion, and education are three measurable factors that influence culture, with other factors operating behind the scenes.

LEARNING OBJECTIVE 8.2 Describe the business implications of culture.

Because international businesses span geographic and cultural boundaries, culture plays a critical role in determining the appropriate approach for business leaders in foreign markets. Cultural factors such as social stratification, work motivation, relationship preferences, risk-taking behavior, and information and task processing have huge implications for the ways employees and consumers interact with their environments. Ignorance or disregard of these factors can easily lead to business failure.

LEARNING OBJECTIVE 8.3 Identify ways to manage cultural differences in the workplace.

To conduct business across cultural boundaries, managers need to build common ground. They can do so by recognizing that differences exist, respecting and even embracing those differences, and then reconciling differences to build a framework that both sides understand and can operate within.

LEARNING OBJECTIVE 8.4 Discuss how to adapt to different cultures.

Cultural intelligence (CQ) is a measure of an individual's cultural awareness. It represents the ability to distinguish cultural traits from those that are universal and those that are specific to a given individual. CQ has three aspects: cognitive, behavioral, and motivational. Managers can cultivate CQ by taking assessments or getting other feedback, undertaking training to remedy weaknesses, and then organizing daily activities to reinforce that training.

Case Study

A Cultural Challenge in Managing Ace Adams

Ace Adams had been working as a consultant for a company called Management Systems International (MSI) in Washington, D.C., for three years, but he wanted more cross-cultural experience. When he was younger, just after college, he had worked for two years in Bulgaria with the Peace Corps. It was there that he learned Bulgarian and fell in love with the country's culture and people. Being fluent in Bulgarian and ready to move abroad, Ace asked his boss whether he could be transferred for a year to their Bulgarian office.

MSI had a small office in Bulgaria because one of its clients had moved there to manufacture skis. However, once the company realized the potential to consult with a growing set of foreign and domestic information technology (IT) companies that were capitalizing on the high levels of education and IT specialization within the country, it decided to set up a permanent office. As a U.S.-based consulting company, MSI was good at managing its consultants in the United States and allowing its foreign offices quite a bit of autonomy. The situation was no different for its Bulgarian office. The team in Bulgaria consisted of the country manager, a Bulgarian named Stoyan, and a group of ten other Bulgarian consultants. Stoyan had received his MBA from Temple University in the United States and gone back to help MSI start up a consulting branch in his home country.

Once Ace arrived in Bulgaria, reporting to Stoyan, he started a large-scale project with a cluster of IT companies based in Sofia. These companies had collectively hired MSI to provide benchmarking data about the local IT market. The project first required Ace to collect survey information about the different companies. He spent a couple of weeks interviewing managers from the different companies and then quickly developed and sent out a survey.

Stoyan soon received an email from one of the companies asking whether it was a legitimate survey and, if so, why there were so many spelling and grammatical errors in it. Moreover, why did it come from someone named Ace, and not from Stoyan himself? Stoyan couldn't understand why Ace had sent the survey without checking with him first. He felt he understood how to manage Americans, but this incident came as a bit of a shock to both him and the other Bulgarian colleagues. He wondered why Ace had done what he did.

Stoyan began to reflect on his understanding of the cultural differences between Bulgaria and the United States. After all, Bulgaria does seem to differ from the United States in terms of cultural dimensions. For one, Bulgaria ranks 70 on power distance, whereas the United States ranks 40. This means employees in Bulgaria tend to accept a hierarchical order in which everybody has a place. Subordinates usually expect to be told what to do, and the ideal boss is one who is kind but makes most of the major decisions. U.S. employees tend to bristle at hierarchy and prefer to be treated as equals. This means they don't like to be told what to do by their boss. Rather, they like to be "supported" and "empowered" by their bosses and be allowed to make some major decisions on their own.

Moreover, in the United States, employees are highly individualistic, ranking 91 on the individualism index. This high score in individualism combined with a low score in power distance (40) means U.S. employees and their managers tend to share information openly with one another. It also means employees are likely to look after themselves and take the initiative. Their managers often expect them to be self-reliant.

Stoyan wasn't sure whether he had to handle a cultural misunderstanding or whether Ace simply didn't realize the significance of his actions. He needed to talk to Ace about this, but he wasn't sure what to say.

Case Discussion Questions

1. How could Stoyan conduct his meeting with Ace?
2. How should Stoyan separate Ace's culture from his character as an individual?
3. What should Stoyan do to correct the situation? What should Ace do?

Endnotes

[1] James Oldroyd's personal experience.

[2] K. B. Anderson, "Lessons from the Arab Spring," Jacobin, September 12, 2016. https://www.jacobinmag.com/2016/09/arab-spring-syria-egypt-war-imperialism-revolution/

[3] R. Banham, The Risks and Opportunities of Doing Business in the Middle East," *Risk Management* 63, no. 2 (2016), 20; K. Al-Seghayer, "The Problems of Punctuality and Productivity in Saudi Arabia," Al Arabiya News, February 26, 2013 http://www.alarabiya.net/views/2013/02/26/268452.html; P. W. Moore, *Doing Business in the Middle East: Politics and Economic Crisis in Jordan and Kuwait*, vol. 20 (Cambridge: Cambridge University Press, 2004).

[4] Gary P. Ferraro and Elizabeth K. Brody, *The Cultural Dimension of Global Business*, 8th ed. (New York: Routledge, 2015).

[5] Saudi Arabia: How to stay safe & out of (big) trouble. World Nomads. www.worldnomads.com/travel-safety/Saudi-Arabia/A-Guide-to-Saudi-Law-and-Customs (accessed October 2016).

[6] "A User's Manual: Hardcore, Abundant and Free: What Is Online Pornography Doing to Sexual Tastes—and Youngsters' Minds?" *The Economist*, September 26, 2015 http://www.economist.com/news/international/21666113-hardcore-abundant-and-free-what-online-pornography-doing-sexual-tastesand. See also www.worldbulletin.net/world/139477/iceland-wants-to-ban-internet-porn.

[7] Gary Lupyan and Emily J. Ward, "Language Can Boost Otherwise Unseen Objects into Visual Awareness," *Proceedings of the National Academy of Sciences* 110, no. 35 (2013): 14196–201.

[8] S. Paul, "96 Words for Love," *Huffington Post*, July 4, 2012. http://www.huffingtonpost.com/sheryl-paul/96-words-for-love_b_1644658.html

[9] Authors' personal experience.

[10] Rick Noack and Lazaro Gamino, "The World's Languages, in 7 Maps and Charts," *Washington Post*, April 23, 2015. https://www.washingtonpost.com/news/worldviews/wp/2015/04/23/the-worlds-languages-in-7-maps-and-charts/?utm_term=.ba5bd10c60cf

[11] Noack and Gamino, "The World's Languages."

[12] Noack and Gamino, "The World's Languages."

[13] Boaz Keysar, Sayuri L. Hayakawa, and Sun Gyu An "The Foreign-Language Effect: Thinking in a Foreign Tongue Reduces Decision Biases," *Psychological Science* 23, no. 6 (2012): 661–68.

[14] Paula Caligiuri, *Cultural Agility: Building a Pipeline of Successful Global Professionals* (San Francisco: Josey-Bass, 2012); S. S. Morris and S. A. Snell, Intellectual Capital Configurations and Organizational Capability: An Empirical Examination of Human Resource Subunits in the Multinational Enterprise," *Journal of International Business Studies* 42, no. 6 (2011): 805–27.

[15] Max Weber, *The Protestant Ethic and the Spirit of Capitalism: And Other Writings* (New York: Penguin, 2002).

[16] 1 Timothy 6:17–19; 1 John 3:17; Matthew 19:23.

[17] T. Kuran, "The Economic System in Contemporary Islamic Thought: Interpretation and Assessment," *International Journal of Middle East Studies* 18, no. 2 (1986): 135–64.

[18] Daniel Burke, "The Worlds' Fastest-Growing Religion Is . . .," CNN, April 3, 2015. www.cnn.com/2015/04/02/living/pew-study-religion/.

[19] "The Global Religious Landscape," Pew Research Center, Religion & Public Life, December 18, 2012. www.pewforum.org/2012/12/18/global-religious-landscape-exec/ (accessed October 2016).

[20] Rajesh Kumar and Anand Kumar, *Doing Business in India* (New York: Palgrave Macmillan, 2006).

[21] Shinichi Inoue, *Putting Buddhism to Work: A New Approach to Management and Business*, trans. Duncan Williams (Japan: Kodansha International, 1997).

[22] Jagdeep S. Chhokar, Felix C. Brodbeck, and Robert J. House, eds, *Culture and Leadership Across the World: The GLOBE Book of In-Depth Studies of 25 Societies* (New York: Routledge, 2013).

[23] Global Talent Competitive Index. Insead knowledge. 2015/2016 Report http://global-indices.insead.edu/gtci/ (accessed October 2016).

[24] Paula Caligiuri, *Cultural Agility*.

[25] Authors' personal experience.

[26] Paula Caligiuri, *Cultural Agility*.

[27] Authors' personal experience.

[28] Authors' personal experience.

[29] "Koreans Give up Their Gold to Help Their Country," BBC News, January 14, 1998. http://news.bbc.co.uk/2/hi/world/analysis/47496.stm

[30] Geert Hofstede, Gert Jan Hofstede, Michael Minkov, *Cultures and Organizations: Software of the Mind—Intercultural Cooperation and Its Importance for Survival*, 3rd ed. (New York: McGraw-Hill USA, 2010).

[31] Cornelius N. Grove, " Introduction to the GLOBE Research Project on Leadership Worldwide," 2005. www.grovewell.com/pub-GLOBE-intro.html http://www.tlu.ee/~sirvir/IKM/Leadership%20Dimensions/future_orientation.html

[32] Grove, "Introduction to the GLOBE Research Project on Leadership Worldwide."; More details on the Globe Study can be found here: www.tlu.ee/~sirvir/IKM/Leadership%20Dimensions/assertiveness.html.

[33] Hofstede, Hofstede, and Minkov, *Cultures and Organizations*.

[34] Erin Meyer, "Why a Mexican Manager Had a Very Hard Time Running a Dutch Team," *Business Insider*, February 4, 2015. http://www.businessinsider.com/why-a-mexican-manager-had-a-very-hard-time-running-a-dutch-team-2015-2.

[35] Joseph J. Distefano and Martha L. Maznevski, "Creating Value with Diverse Teams in Global Management," *Organizational Dynamics* 29, no. 1 (2000): 45–63.

[36] Distefano and Maznevski, "Creating Value with Diverse Teams in Global Management."

[37] D. Gigone and R. Hastie, "The Common Knowledge Effect: Information Sharing and Group Judgment," *Journal of Personality and Social Psychology* 65, no. 5 (1993): 959.

[38] Distefano and Maznevski, "Creating Value with Diverse Teams in Global Management," 45–63.

[39] R. Katz and T. J. Allen, "Investigating the Not Invented Here (NIH) Syndrome: A Look at the Performance, Tenure, and Communication Patterns of 50 R & D Project Groups," *R&D Management* 12, no. 1 (1982): 7–20.

[40] Morris and Snell, "Intellectual Capital Configurations and Organizational Capability," 805–27.

[41] P. Christopher Earley and Soon Ang, *Cultural Intelligence: Individual Interactions Across Cultures* (Stanford, CA: Stanford University Press, 2003).

[42] Authors' personal experience.

[43] Thomas Rockstuhl et al., "Beyond General Intelligence (IQ) and Emotional Intelligence (EQ): The Role of Cultural Intelligence (CQ) on Cross-Border Leadership Effectiveness in a Globalized World," *Journal of Social Issues* 67, no. 4 (2011): 825–40.

[44] P. C. Earley and R. S. Peterson, "The Elusive Cultural Chameleon: Cultural Intelligence as a New Approach to Intercultural Training for the Global Manager," *Academy of Management Learning & Education* 3, no. 1 (2004): 100–115.

[45] Ilan Alon et al., "The Development and Validation of the Business Cultural Intelligence Quotient," *Cross Cultural & Strategic Management* 23, no. 1 (2016): 78–100; K.A. Crowne, "What Leads to Cultural Intelligence?" *Business Horizons* 51, no. 5 (2008): 391–99.

[46] K.Y. Ng, L. Van Dyne, and S. Ang, "From Experience to Experiential Learning: Cultural Intelligence as a Learning Capability for Global Leader Development," *Academy of Management Learning and Education* 8, no. 4 (2009): 511–26.

[47] Earley and Ang, *Cultural Intelligence*.

[48] Flannery G. Stevens, Victoria C. Plaut, and Jeffrey Sanchez-Burks, "Unlocking the Benefits of Diversity: All-Inclusive Multiculturalism And Positive Organizational Change," *The Journal of Applied Behavioral Science* 44, no. 1 (2008): 116–33.

[49] S. Ang, L. Van Dyne, and C. Koh, "Personality Correlates of the Four-Factor Model of Cultural Intelligence," *Group & Organization Management* 31, no. 1 (2006): 100–23.

[50] Morris and Snell, "Intellectual Capital Configurations and Organizational Capability," 805–27.

[51] Earley and Ang, *Cultural Intelligence*.

[52] A. Mok and M. W. Morris, "Asian-Americans' Creative Styles in Asian and American Situations: Assimilative and Contrastive Responses as a Function of Bicultural Identity Integration," *Management and Organization Review* 6, no. 3 (2010): 371–90.

CHAPTER 9

Sustainability

Eyal Bartov/Getty Images

Introduction

Globalization has not only made the world richer; it has also contributed to climate change and population growth. These shifts in the ecological environment have implications for businesses and their role in creating a more sustainable world—a world that will enable our children and our children's children to enjoy fresh air, clean water, and an eco-friendly environment.

International businesses have reasons besides the fate of future generations to make their operations more sustainable. Sustainability efforts affect long-term growth, but they can also have immediate, profitable effects on a business. In fact, many companies have found that it can be quite profitable to be environmentally sustainable. This chapter shows that sustainability initiatives are more than a global guilt trip; they can, in fact, be an opportunity to improve the financial status of the company.

LEARNING OBJECTIVES

After you explore this chapter you will be able to:

1. **Analyze** the risks and opportunities associated with globalization and sustainability
2. **Explain** how to fight short-termism
3. **Identify** ways to collaborate globally for sustainability
4. **Discuss** how sustainability can drive innovation

9.1 What Is Sustainability?

LEARNING OBJECTIVE

Analyze the risks and opportunities associated with globalization and sustainability.

A common message of this book is that globalization tends to lead to increased economic well-being for a majority of the world's population. As businesses specialize and trade their specialized products across borders, more people have access to these products and the ability

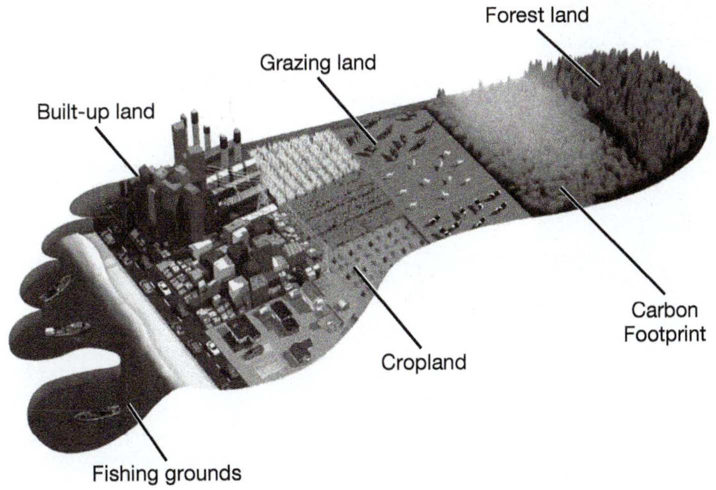

FIGURE 9.1 Globalization puts pressure on the ecological environment We sometimes refer to this impact on the environment as an "ecological footprint." **Source:** Adapted from Earth Overshoot Day, "What Is an Ecological Footprint?" http://www.overshootday.org/kids-and-teachers-corner/what-is-an-ecological-footprint-2/.

to help in their production. However, one potentially negative effect of globalization falls on the ecological environment. The **ecological environment** consists of the air, water, land, minerals, resources, and organisms that underpin our ability to survive on this planet (see **Figure 9.1**).

ecological environment the air, water, land, minerals, resources, and organisms on this planet

Globalization often puts extreme pressure on the ecological environment. As we try to figure out how to support what will likely be 9.7 billion people living on Earth by 2050 (with a good chance at 11.2 billion by 2100), we also need to consider that globalization helps a growing world population to become richer, healthier, better educated, and freer.[1] In many respects, this is a good thing. With over a billion people poised to enter the global middle class in the next few decades, demand will increase for more meat for meals, more oil to fuel mobility, more copper for electronics, more wood for homes, more water for lawns, and more electricity for lights and cell phones.

From a short-term perspective, there is much money to be made from producing these commodities and goods for the rising middle class. From a long-term perspective, however, producing meat uses up incredible amounts of land and resources, oil and copper are finite resources, harvesting too much wood without replenishing it can be destructive to natural habitats, and using water for watering lawns has become a major problem in many drought-ridden parts of the world. Sustainable business tries to figure out a way to support current growth while ensuring we have these resources to draw on and a healthy planet on which to live in the future. **Sustainability** describes a way of doing business that supports the long-term ecological balance of the environment. For example, Tesla, the car company based in California, has a specific mission "to accelerate the advent of sustainable transport by bringing compelling mass market electric cars to market as soon as possible."[2] Being able to plug your car into the wall for power means that you are no longer dependent on nonrenewable fossil fuels to move. Rather, electricity can come from multiple sources, including renewable energy sources.

sustainability a way of doing business that supports the long-term ecological balance of the environment

Right now the world is facing two significant challenges that heighten the need for sustainability: (1) climate change and (2) a limited supply of resources. These challenges to business as usual—and even to life as usual—are introducing new risks and opportunities in the ways companies operate and customers consume. While agreement has been elusive regarding how to face climate change and resource constraints, global companies that understand the arguments behind these challenges can reduce the potential business risks associated with unsustainable business practices while simultaneously creating new opportunities. Business leaders have a responsibility to figure out how to navigate them.

For instance, concerns about climate change are driving the growth of entire industry sectors, such as energy, retail, and tourism, with the goal of creating a **clean economy**, or one that produces goods and services with environmental benefit.[3] These industries often receive substantial money from both governments and private investors trying to boost clean technologies.[4] Resource constraints are also increasingly problematic because the rising global middle class is demanding a higher standard of living, more products, and improved services.

clean economy an economy that produces goods and services with environmental benefit

Everett Collection Historical/Alamy Stock Photo

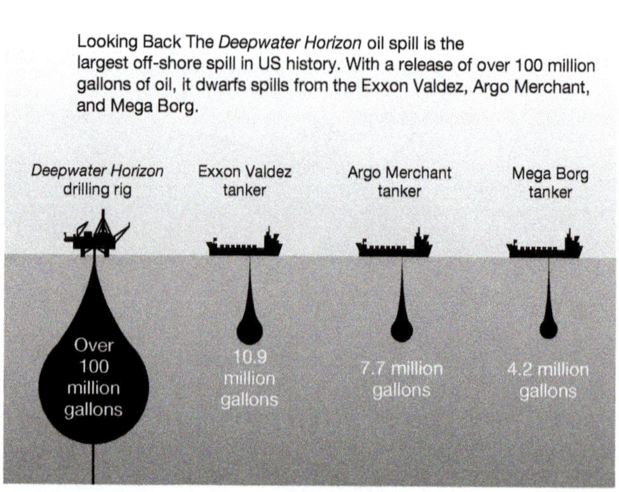
Looking Back The Deepwater Horizon oil spill is the largest off-shore spill in US history. With a release of over 100 million gallons of oil, it dwarfs spills from the Exxon Valdez, Argo Merchant, and Mega Borg.
Deepwater Horizon drilling rig
Exxon Valdez tanker
Argo Merchant tanker
Mega Borg tanker
Over 100 million gallons
10.9 million gallons
7.7 million gallons
4.2 million gallons

FIGURE 9.2 **The Deepwater Horizon** The spill was so monumental in terms of the amount of oil spilled into the ocean that it was made into a movie staring the ever-popular Mark Wahlberg. **Source:** "2010—Deepwater Horizon Oil Spill," Homeland Security Digital Library. https://www.hsdl.org/c/event/2010-deepwater-horizon-oil-spill/.

The push for more and better products means that companies have to think differently about how to produce by using new and innovative fuels, raw materials, and manufacturing and transportation processes, as well as new ways to use water and find energy sources that are sustainable and therefore plentiful and often low cost.

Sustaining Sustainability. As the world has become more and more outspoken about the challenges of sustainability, companies have followed suit by putting their money where their mouths are, creating whole units to sustain their sustainability efforts. In many cases these efforts are being led by a chief sustainability officer (CSO). The United States' first CSO was hired at DuPont in 2004. Since then, more than 36 public U.S. companies have followed suit by enlisting CSOs.[5]

What exactly does a CSO do? Does the job make a difference? Doubts about whether having a sustainability officer matters have been raised in the wake of disasters caused by companies that have appointed them. For example, in 2010 an company that drills offshore oil and operated the Deepwater Horizon rig was responsible for the largest accidental marine oil spill in the history of the industry[6] (see **Figure 9.2**).

The company that owned the rig had a sustainability officer who had not sufficiently addressed the issues that led to the disaster. Sometimes disasters occur regardless of what we do to stop them, but it later became apparent that this case could have been prevented.[7]

In other cases, a CSO has brought measurable change. Kathrin Winkler, the CSO of EMC, a global information technology company, institutes sustainability requirements for every software and hardware product, including an energy-efficiency review before launch. To date, these changes have led to more energy-efficient products and increased savings for the company. But Winkler points out that what she does also affects the company's employees, making them more engaged: "People care about their legacy and want to know that their work makes a positive impact. They want to work for companies whose values align with their own."[8]

Climate Change

Significant scientific evidence argues that climate change is happening. The earth's average temperature has risen by 1.4° Fahrenheit over the past century, and it is expected to continue to rise over the next hundred years.[9] This is a growing global concern because small changes in average global temperatures can translate to large and potentially dangerous changes in climate and weather (see **Figure 9.3**).

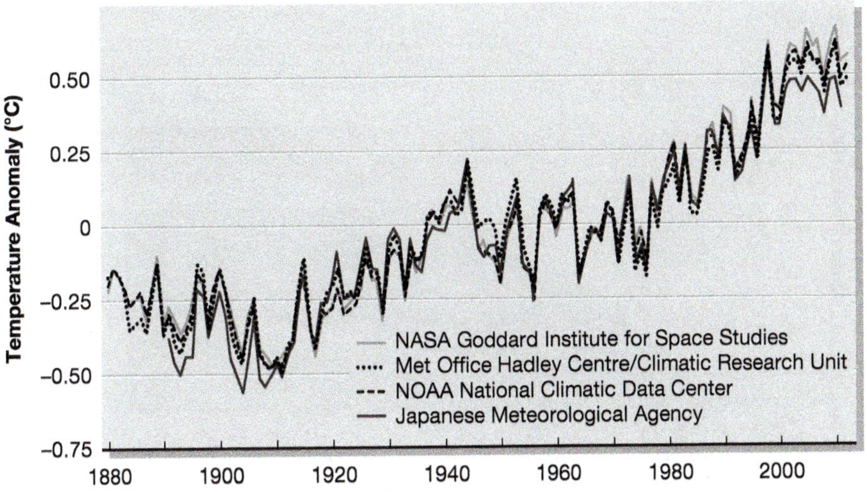

FIGURE 9.3 **Temperature change over time** Multiple independent research institutes have found evidence pointing to higher average global temperatures over the past century. **Source:** U.S. Environmental Protection Agency, "Climate Change: Basic Information." http://www.epa.gov/climatechange/basics/ (accessed October 5, 2016).

This warming is due in part to carbon dioxide (CO_2) and other greenhouse gases that have been released into Earth's atmosphere,[10] mostly by the burning of fossil fuels (oil, coal, and natural gas) to produce energy (see **Figure 9.4**). Greenhouse gases act like a blanket around the Earth, trapping heat in the atmosphere and causing it to warm. If the trend continues, by the latter decades of this century the weather in Illinois could feel more like Texas does today.[11] On a small scale, if things get too hot in Texas, a family can simply move; a business can also sometimes move, but an entire city or agriculture zone can't just pick up and go elsewhere to escape a changing climate.

Increases in global temperature are not the only result of climate change. Global sea levels are also on the rise. On average, they have risen about 6.7 inches in the past century, and the process seems to be speeding up. The rate of rise during the past decade alone was nearly double that of the entire past century.[12] Ocean temperatures are also growing warmer, and the mass of the ice sheets in Greenland and Antarctica have decreased. Glaciers are retreating almost everywhere around the world—including in the Alps, the Himalayas, the Andes, the Rockies, Alaska, and Africa.[13] Record-high atmospheric temperatures have been increasing in frequency since 1950, and average snowfall is decreasing[14] (see Figure 9.4). This all means that it is becoming more difficult for people, plants, and animals to stay alive on planet Earth.

Changing Climate Change. As a country's GDP grows, so do the amounts of CO_2 and other greenhouse gases it releases.[15] The connection has been so clearly identified that McKinsey Consulting's Global Institute actually calculated how much carbon the world needs to release in order to drive the global economy. They predict that the world realizes $740 of GDP for every ton of CO_2 produced.[16] In other words, globalization encourages (or at least contributes to) climate change (see **Figure 9.5**).

One reason for this effect is that many of the largest companies in the world are energy companies, with huge reserves of fossil fuels from which they expect trillions of dollars in profits over the coming decades. If we don't burn the fuel, then companies stand the chance of losing this money.

By comparison, recent research has shown that energy consumption in emerging markets, such as Nigeria and Mexico, has led to decreases in GDP growth. In fact, these studies point out that a primary reason developed countries, like the United States and France, continue to see

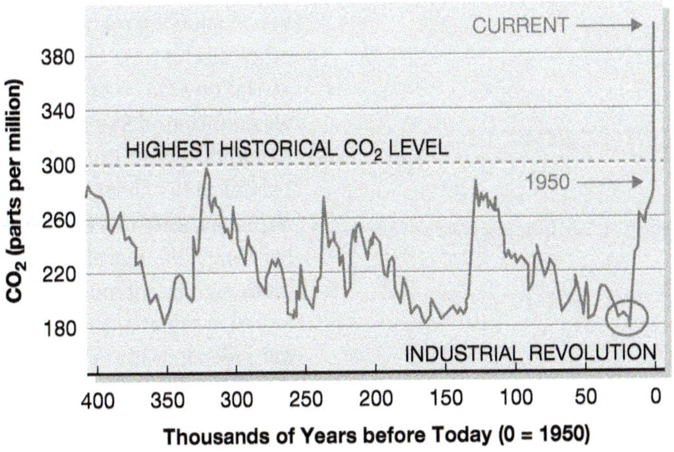

FIGURE 9.4 **Historical carbon dioxide levels** This graph, based on comparisons of atmospheric samples contained in ice cores and more recent direct measurements, provides evidence that atmospheric carbon dioxide (CO_2) has increased since the Industrial Revolution. **Credit:** Vostok ice core data/J.R. Petit et al.; NOAA Mauna Loa CO2 record. **Source:** NASA, "Global Climate Change: Vital Signs of the Planet." http://climate.nasa.gov/evidence/ (accessed October 5, 2016).

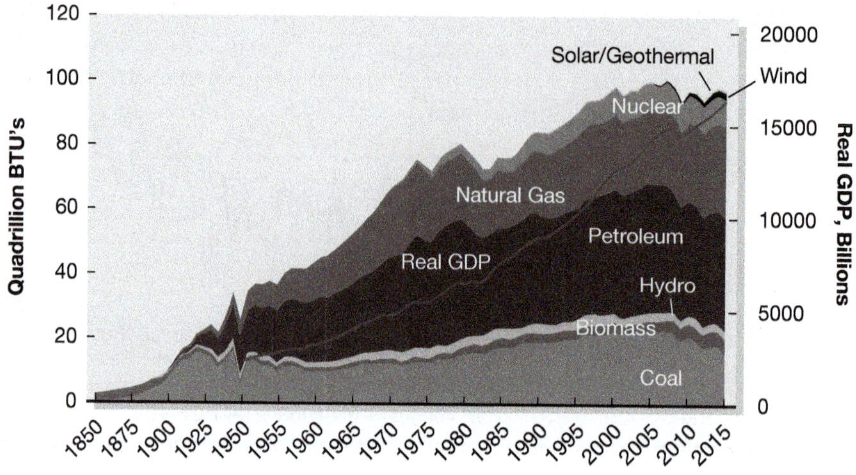

FIGURE 9.5 GDP vs. energy consumption As a country's GDP grows, so does its energy consumption. However, notice the slight trend occurring in the past few years in which energy consumption has gone down while GDP growth has continued to increase. **Source:** Institute for Energy Research, "Energy Overview." http://instituteforenergyresearch.org/topics/encyclopedia/energy-overview/ (accessed October 10, 2016).

growth with energy consumption is that they are focused more on clean energy technologies and sources.[17] In fact, more than 20 developed countries, including Austria, Finland, France, Germany, Ukraine, Uzbekistan, the United Kingdom, and the United States, have recently experienced a decline in CO_2 emissions but positive GDP growth.[18]

Though this is a good start, the Intergovernmental Panel on Climate Change says we must cut 80 percent of the world's CO_2 emissions by the year 2050 to have a chance of holding global warming to an increase of just 2° Celsius (about 3.6° Fahrenheit). Being able to reduce global warming by even this much increases our chances of preserving life as we know it. With that in mind, how do we convince companies to help reduce consumer demand for energy that requires the burning of oil, gas, and coal?

The Business of Climate Change. Getting more global companies to make their businesses ecologically sustainable requires helping them recognize two things. First, science-based targets for reducing emissions can be quite profitable. One study indicates that reducing CO_2 emissions to reach the 2° mark would actually produce a value of $780 billion for U.S. companies alone[19]—and that's just within the next decade. In another study, 79 percent of companies reported receiving higher returns on investment for emission-reduction investments than on other business investments.[20] For example, the insurance provider Nationwide recently began allowing many of its employees to work from home.[21] Not requiring people to be in the office all the time can provide significant savings in real estate and energy costs. Steve Ebert at Nationwide manages a large group of private and public company investors within the western United States, where he spends much of his time. After traveling out of the company's headquarters in Columbus, Ohio, for a few years, he finally decided to move to a location central to his clients. Ebert says he has saved countless hours once spent in airports and on airplanes, and now can drive to many of his clients' locations. This has been great not only for his family life, but also for the environment.[22] The German technology company Siemens has made significant money by selling eco-friendly energy solutions. "Come to find out," said Bryce Morris, a regional sales manager at Siemens, "the real money in this business is coming from our green initiatives. For us, green equals gold!"[23]

The second thing business leaders need to realize is that their efforts can affect entire industries. As competitors come together and collaborate on climate issues, they generate goodwill with the public and push innovation, ensuring that they stay on the cutting edge of new technologies. In 2014, Adobe became the first Fortune 500 company to install and manage an energy-intelligence system that automatically responds to spikes in its buildings' electricity use.

The system draws on power stored during off-peak hours to level energy demands without affecting operations. The company has also invested heavily in alternative and renewable energy sources, such as wind turbines, to generate power for its buildings.[24] In fact, three-quarters of the world's biggest companies now say they address climate change in their business strategies (up from one-tenth in 2010). Eight in 10 have identified actual risks to their business stemming from climate change, and more than a third see these risks as "immediate."[25]

These changes are not just happening in large western multinationals. Waste Ventures India, an Indian company focused on composting food waste, collects food waste from Indian cities, turns it into nutrient-rich soil, and sells the soil to farmers.[26]

Similarly, the Recycling and Economic Development Initiative of South Africa takes worn-out tires and recycles them, rather than allowing improper collectors to burn them in order to recover the metal inside. In just two years the initiative has collected 70 percent of discarded tires and recycle them through high-value material recovery processes. The efforts have not only reduced waste and pollution but also provided many employment opportunities.[27]

Climate change is a critically relevant issue for large global international businesses and local emerging-market opportunities. Companies are quickly figuring out that a shift of this magnitude in the business environment creates large-scale opportunities, and they want in. Taking advantage of these new opportunities, however, creates resource constraints.

Resource Constraints

Everything we use to keep warm and to clothe, move, or feed ourselves comes from resources found on Earth. **Resource constraints** are limits on the availability of such factors as materials, equipment, food, and fuel that reduce a company's ability to produce goods and services. For example, producing enough food in Nicaragua may seem fairly easy at the outset. The soil is rich, the land is plentiful, and farming has a long heritage. However, overfarming and deforestation have left much of the land vulnerable to landslides that sweep away the nutrients needed to grow food. Landslides and heavy rains destroy crucial transportation infrastructure such as roads and bridges and cause tremendous destruction to crops. As a result, despite what might seem on paper like ideal conditions, Nicaragua experiences resource constraints around food that make it the second-poorest country in the Western Hemisphere (Haiti is the first). The constraints are so severe that Nicaragua struggles to feed its population.[28]

resource constraints limits on the availability of factors of production that reduce a company's ability to produce goods and services

China is another example. With 1.4 billion citizens, China consumes more than 25 percent of the world's soybeans and more than 40 percent of its global steel and aluminum production.[29] Aware of its own resource constraints, the Chinese government has been purchasing natural resource companies all over the world. It has learned that the growing global population means increased need for nonrenewable natural resources (like minerals). In other words, the more we grow and consume, the more we will need natural resources such as copper, zinc, oil, and gas. The more of these resources we extract, the more we have to shift to less concentrated sources. This shift translates to lower quality and higher cost (see **Figure 9.6**).

Limits of Renewable Energy.

Even turning to renewable energy sources will not solve all our resource -constraint problems. In fact, sometimes the change can increase resource consumption. The new wave of electric cars made by companies like Tesla, Nissan, and BMW can run on electricity generated by renewable energy sources, making them seem like the best alternative for the future. However, the vehicles themselves require two to three times more copper than standard vehicles that burn fossil fuels, and the batteries to power them contain lithium and other rare metals. Or consider a standard wind turbine as a source of alternative energy (see **Figure 9.7**). The electrical components needed for just one turbine include 9.9 tons of copper, for which approximately 1,980 tons of rock must be mined—and that's just for one input. Many more natural resources are needed to make one wind turbine, and often these must be imported from different countries.[30]

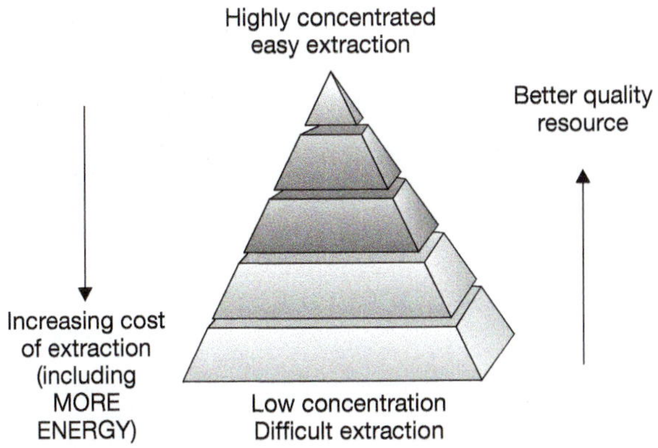

FIGURE 9.6 **Resource pyramid** As we use more of Earth's natural resources, the quality of the remaining resources decreases and the cost of extracting them increases.

Source: Kurt Cobb, "Energy: The Achilles Heel of the Resource Pyramid." Scitizen.com http://scitizen.com/future-energies/energy-the-achilles-heel-of-the-resource-pyramid_a-14-2760.html, accessed June 14, 2017.

FIGURE 9.7 **Wind energy** Wind energy fields are being built all over the world.

The Business of Resource Constraints. When working with limited resources, the realities are that companies must learn how to reduce their material use and must operate at a much more efficient level. Why? Resources won't last forever and aren't always readily available, and consumers and governments are taking an ever-increasing interest in their use. For example, Coca-Cola was once asked to leave India because the company used too much of the local water, and in India, water is life. The problem arose when a government official was visiting a small rural village and was told that it was not safe to drink the water, only the Coke. Angered by this statement, the official said, "Thirty years of freedom and planning, and we have Coke that has reached the villages, but we do not have drinking water that the villagers can consume." After that, he introduced a Foreign Exchange Regulation Act that limited Coca-Cola (and all foreign companies) to 40 percent equity in domestic enterprises. He summoned the managers of Coca-Cola and said, "Listen, you have two options. One is to fold up and go, and the other is to have an Indian partner and tell them what your technology is." Coca-Cola refused to share its secret formula and was forced out of the country. It wasn't until the Indian government eased the rules and Coca-Cola showed it was willing to increase the supply of clean water, rather than just use it up, that the company was allowed back in the country.[31]

Global consumers and governments are demanding that companies use the resources they consume more efficiently. Those that are able to help consumers use less and reduce their own ecological impact will be the winners of globalization.

9.2 Fighting Short-Termism

LEARNING OBJECTIVE

Explain how to fight short-termism.

It's almost an article of faith: We believe the world would be better off if businesses stopped thinking of only short-term results and focused more on the long term. Peter Drucker, one of the world's top business thinkers, once said, "You have to produce results in the short term, but you also have to produce results in the long term, and the long term is not simply an adding up of short terms."[32] **Short-termism** describes an excessive focus on short-term results, even at the expense of long-term interests and objectives. Short-termism is largely a creation of stock markets and the modern capitalistic system. As companies sell off parts or shares of their company in a publicly traded forum (stock exchanges), they must focus on what the new owners want—profitability.

short-termism an excessive focus on short-term results, even at the expense of long-term interests and objectives

Between 1975 and 2010, the average period of time an investor would hold stock shares on the New York Stock Exchange declined from six years to about six months.[33] Now, imagine you have recently graduated from college and are working as an analyst for Dell Computers. Your boss gives you a proposal for a new project, and your analysis shows the project will make money after a few quarters—but it will reduce your earnings this quarter. Do you invest in it? When that scenario was posed to 400 real CEOs, a majority said that they wouldn't invest in the project—they wanted to but felt they couldn't. Their argument was that they are stuck between a rock and a hard place.[34] They want to invest in projects that will make long-term profits, but they don't feel they can do so at the cost of short-term earnings.

The reason CEOs are so reluctant to make these longer-term investments goes back to what the shareholders want. If the majority of investors buy shares of a company for short-term gains, then CEOs will be conditioned to provide short-term returns—eliminating the likelihood that they will make long-term investments without immediate pay-offs.

Sources of Short-Termism

John Bogle, founder of the investment company Vanguard, points out the following about investors: "If market participants demand short-term results and predictable earnings in an inevitably unpredictable world, corporations respond accordingly. When they do, there is heavy pressure to reduce the workforce, to cut corners, to rethink expenditures on research and development . . . to make the numbers."[35] The primary reason for this short-term thinking by CEOs and companies is the relationship between these companies and their investors. Investors can be either individuals trying to figure out what stocks to buy and sell or companies that buy and sell stocks for themselves or other companies. Most company investors belong to one of two groups: (1) analysts on Wall Street or (2) institutional investors, which are made up of big funds like Blackrock and Fidelity, and asset owners that pool individual investments in pensions, retirement funds, and endowments.

Analysts on Wall Street are entirely focused on quarterly earnings, whereas institutional investors are more concerned with the long term. *Long-term* means looking at investments in terms of years, not quarters. Institutional investors care how a company will hold up in a volatile world over years.[36]

Fighting Short-Termism

Companies don't have to choose between the long term and the short term. Several strategies enable them to maintain a short-term view and blend it with a long-term outlook.

Strategy 1: Focus on Stakeholders, Not Just Shareholders. One of the striking differences between Eastern and Western cultures is the time frame leaders consider when making decisions. Eastern leaders tend to consider a longer horizon in their decisions and often have a 10-year plan to guide their companies' efforts. For instance, Samsung considers investments from a long-term perspective and even considers what will allow the company to survive for multiple generations.[37]

Theoretically, long-term logic is also foundational to Western notions of capitalism. For example, Adam Smith, the father of capitalism, wrote that "The wise and virtuous man is at all times willing that his own private interest should be sacrificed to the public interest."[38] Smith believed there is a deep interdependence between business and society. He also argued that a long-term perspective is vital for sustainability. However, Western companies especially have gravitated toward short-termism.

To create value for the long term, you must take into account the needs of employees, shareholders, the ecological environment, customers, and communities connected to the company. These different parties represent *stakeholders* because they are all affected by the company's actions. Overwhelmingly, executives and investors agree that focusing on all the stakeholders—rather than just shareholders—can create value in the long term.[39] This is especially true in a global business environment. As an example, Unilever, the maker of both Tide and Axe Body Spray, has decided to shift focus more to its stakeholders and away from its shareholders. Unilever CEO Paul Polman broke with Wall Street norms by canceling his quarterly meetings with analysts. He said, "Unilever has been around for 100-plus years. We want to be around for several hundred more . . . If you buy into this long-term value creation model, which is equitable, which is shared, which is sustainable, then come and invest with us . . . If you don't buy into this, I respect you as a human being, but don't put your money in our company."[40]

Polman still cares about the shareholder too, though. He points out that by focusing on other stakeholders and solving long-term problems for them, Unilever helps to create a sustainable world and drives shareholder value. To include what all stakeholders want means to play by stakeholder rules by focusing more on long-term cash flow instead of short-term earnings.[41]

Strategy 2: Convince Wall Street to Change the Rules. Not all managers are (or can be) as bold as Polman. In fact, only a few so far have followed his lead. In our work with companies, we frequently hear CEOs tell their employees they need to be more innovative, make long-term investments, and see a greater horizon down the road. Ironically, in the same breath those CEOs often ask their employees why they aren't hitting quarterly quotas or other short-term goals. It's true that workers today need to do both, but you can see why this message often creates tension within a company.

The value of a publicly traded company's stock is determined in large part by what Wall Street analysts are saying to shareholders about it. Some companies take advantage of that relationship and, rather than walking away from analysts and shareholders, try to engage with them to promote understanding about how long-term and sustainable activities might actually be good for profits, too. Financial analysts all over the world are beginning to see why sustainability matters. In fact, most banks now have analysts responsible for incorporating environmental and sustainability issues into their company analyses.[42] This is actually an emerging area for jobs in the financial sector.

The key role of a company's managers is to make analysts' jobs easier by communicating sustainability information in all company reports. For example, Kevin Anton, an executive at aluminum giant Alcoa, says, "We weave a sustainability thread into shareholder and analyst communications because it is embedded into our core business strategy. It's impactful to have our business leaders talk about how we create value for customers by improving energy efficiency in airplanes, cars, and buildings."[43]

The Dutch health care and lighting company Philips similarly talks to analysts about how it is trying to make its products use fewer natural resources and be less toxic to the environment—even though doing so may increase costs. The company talks about these changes to show it's developing efficiencies that will lead to profits in the long term *and* will help the environment. Its explanation helps investors understand that the company is still trying to maximize profits. These successes show that even companies that can't break out and play by different rules (like Unilever) can still change the existing rules by getting financial markets and analysts to see the value of long-term approaches to business.[44]

Even government organizations like the Sovereign Wealth Fund of Norway are taking note and taking steps toward sustainability. Sovereign wealth funds are state-owned institutional investments used to invest a country's wealth in things like stocks and bonds. Norway's Sovereign Wealth Fund is the world's largest, valued at $900 billion. It was initially created to responsibly manage and reinvest the massive profits from Norway's oil sales. Nearly 60 percent of that $900 billion is invested in shares of various companies around the world. Over the years, those investments have resulted in the organization owning 1.3% of all publicly traded companies globally.[45] In 2015 through 2017, Norway's sovereign wealth fund cut its backing of the global coal industry. Specifically, the organization sold its shares in firms that made more than 30 percent of their revenue from coal-related activities.[46] Coal is the largest source of greenhouse gas emissions in the world, and Norway and many other governments and organizations are intent on seeing coal—once known as the king of fossil fuels—become the fuel of yesterday.

Strategy 3: Get the Board of Directors to Think Long Term. The final strategy to help a company take a long-term approach to business is to get the board of directors to catch the vision. The way boards are currently structured often doesn't help them serve as a sufficient proxy for stakeholders. For example, the board of Merrill Lynch, a company crushed by the 2008 financial crisis, wasn't even aware of the company's soaring exposure to subprime mortgage instruments until it was too late. In fact, many scholars argue that it wasn't a failure of risk management that caused the financial crisis; it was actually a failure of corporate governance. Board members were not asking the right questions of the financial services companies that were providing subprime mortgage instruments; rather, they were looking at the short-term earnings these companies were bringing in while ignoring the long-term perspective.

One way to make boards orient more around a long-term perspective is to bring in board members who are already committed long-term owners. This strategy is known as **ownership-based governance**, and it requires that board members have both relevant industry experience *and* a stake in the company. In turn, boards should ensure that the CEO's pay is tied to achieving long-term objectives—like innovation and efficiency—and not just to increasing the short-term share price. This treats the CEO more like an owner. Taking this a step further, some experts suggest that new executives should invest a year's salary in the company and that performance evaluations attached to bonuses should be extended to three- or even five-year terms instead of the traditional annual review. In essence, to create a long-term focus, companies must change the way their boards operate, the way investors and analysts value the company, and the way managers and CEOs are incentivized. Such changes aren't necessarily easy, but they bring significant benefits to future generations.

ownership-based governance a strategy that requires board members to have both relevant industry experience and a stake in the company

WileyPLUS

See Whiteboard Video: Long-termism vs. Short-termism

9.3 Collaborating for Sustainability

LEARNING OBJECTIVE

Identify ways to collaborate globally for sustainability.

Increased threats to the global climate and resources require governments, businesses, and the community to come together and make appropriate changes. Companies today need to build relationships with an increasingly diverse set of actors, such as other companies, governments, nonprofit organizations, universities, and mobile, global, vocal customer bases.

For example, the Sustainability Consortium (SC) is a collaboration of the world's largest retailers, consumer products companies, nongovernment organizations (NGOs) and universities. Some of the key companies include Kroger, Best Buy, Tyson's, Disney, Dow, Unilever, Samsung, and 3M. The key universities include Arizona State University, the University of Arkansas, Wageningen University in the Netherlands, and Nanjing University in China. Established with funding from Walmart, the SC aims to reduce the impact of global consumption by gathering data on the life cycle of consumer products and then putting that information into the hands of relevant companies.[47] This helps the companies begin to reduce the detrimental impacts of their products on the environment and society. As John Johnson, the head of the SC, says, "It's easier to change a few hundred big brands than it is to change a few hundred million consumers."[48]

Why Companies Want to Collaborate

Some companies may ask whether what they do to stop climate change or to address resource scarcity really matters. To be fair, even a company as large as Walmart, with revenues nearing 2 percent of U.S. GDP, cannot unilaterally change things, like decreasing the price of solar power for its operations or making food available to the masses. However, while individual actions, in isolation, may not have much of an impact on global sustainability, they begin to add up at the collective level, so each action really *does* matter.

The challenge of achieving global sustainability is not the responsibility of companies alone; it is also required of governments, NGOs, universities, and individual members of society. Sustainability is a challenge everyone faces, so it requires solutions developed in common. The secondary challenge for businesses is that working for society's collective good is not always enticing when an organization is primarily responsible for making money for its shareholders. Companies need other reasons to engage in global sustainability collaborations. In a survey of company executives, 78 percent said that a strong reason for such collaboration is to build brand or company reputation.[49]

Benefits of Collaboration. While it may seem discouraging that companies are collaborating only to look good to the public, consider that around 81 percent of a company's stock market value is determined by its "intangible assets,"[50] such as brand and reputation. So, having a reputation as a sustainable company has a beneficial effect on a company's bottom line—even in the short term—and to be sustainable requires that companies collaborate with each other. For example, companies like Walmart need a network of sustainable suppliers willing to make products that are better for the environment and to use resources more efficiently. They also need sustainable customers who are conscious of their purchases and the effects of those purchases on the environment. Finally, companies need a world that supports sustainable business by offering renewable energy sources and safe ecological conditions. To achieve these goals, companies must become collaborators in a global effort toward sustainability.

Goals of Collaboration. Collaborating for sustainability can take multiple forms, depending on a company's goals. Primary goals include the following:

- Developing product standards and common practices
- Sharing information to help spark innovation and new ideas
- Creating a consolidated base of power to influence policymakers, suppliers, and buyers
- Sharing investments to spread cost and risk

Achieving some of these goals requires that traditional tensions between for-profit companies and not-for-profit NGOs be set aside. For example, the highly active and controversial NGO Greenpeace criticized Asia Pulp & Paper for its supply chain practices, causing many of Asia Pulp & Paper's customers to withdraw orders. As a result, the company was pressured to change the way it acquired its wood products. To do so, the company executives invited Greenpeace into the boardroom to give input on how the company could stay profitable but also help end deforestation in Asia (**Figure 9.8**).

One manager from Asia Paper & Pulp commented, "Never in our history would our shareholders sit in the same room with a 'radical' NGO like Greenpeace. So it's quite groundbreaking that we sit together in our boardroom and discuss strategy and incorporate their input."[51] By collaborating with Greenpeace, Asia Pulp & Paper was able to spark new ideas on how to more effectively reduce deforestation.

Another example of collaboration with the goal of sharing both investment costs and ideas comes from the Israel-based company Netafim. Founded in the 1950s on a small kibbutz in Israel, Netafim has become the largest drip irrigation company in the world. The system it makes was originally designed for farmers in areas where water is a scarce resource, but it has proven to be a cheap and efficient watering system regardless of climate. After achieving success in Israel and developed markets, Netafim turned its attention to developing markets—where water often is scarce.

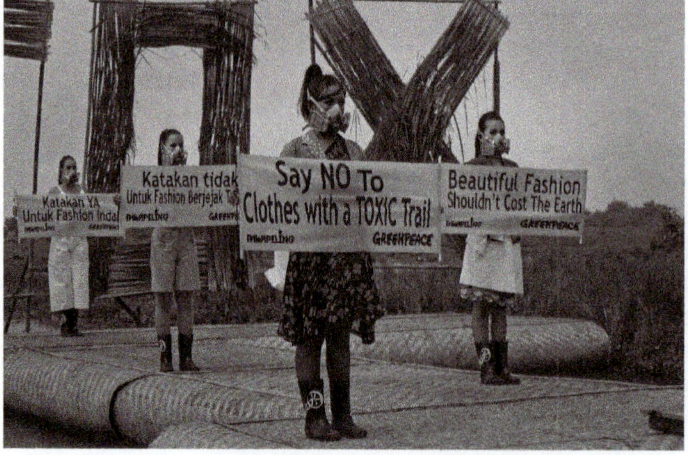

ROMEO GACAD/AFP/Getty Images

FIGURE 9.8 Greenpeace in Indonesia. Asia Pulp & Paper responds to Greenpeace's efforts in Indonesia, and Greenpeace rallies Indonesian citizens to protect their forests.

Because potential customers in developing markets are generally small farmers in remote rural areas, Netafim needed partners who knew the farmers and the culture—partners that could help sell to and train the farmers. By partnering with governments, NGOs, and financing organizations such as the International Finance Corporation (IFC) of the World Bank, the company has turned emerging markets into its largest market and has been able to help millions of farmers survive droughts and farm more efficiently.

How to Collaborate Successfully

To successfully engage in collaborative initiatives for sustainability, managers need to practice five key behaviors: conduct due diligence, develop a shared language, create entrance strategies, create exit strategies, and engage the board. These steps are based on a special collaborative report from the United Nations, the Boston Consulting Group, and the Massachusetts Institute of Technology;[52] it can help companies ensure that collaborations are valuable to themselves, their partners, and the environment. Let's look at each step.

Conduct Due Diligence. When deciding whom to involve in a sustainability initiative—for example, sourcing cacao for chocolate from organic farms—companies need to be sure the objectives of any potential partners (other companies, NGOs, governments, universities) are consistent with their own. This often requires that internal, top-level managers adopt a transformative new agenda to make a truly positive impact on sustainability, rather than just improving the organization's public image. It means all partners should be thinking as broadly as possible to address any environmental challenges for their industry. For example, the founders of the Zotter chocolate company, based in Austria, revealed that they travel to Nicaragua and other locations where they get their cacao in order to be sure the farmers are using organic and sustainable farming techniques. This ensures not only that the chocolate is of high quality but also that the environment in which the cacao is grown is sustained.[53]

Companies, then, should start with a detailed discussion of the deal. Is it a good opportunity? What is the best solution from each partner's perspective? What, if any, are the overlapping objectives of each organization? Once these foundational questions have been settled, managers can address more controversial questions, like the partners' willingness and ability to monitor certain standards. For example, Zotter executives not only spend time with cooperative cacao farming leaders, they also talk with the farmers at their farms to understand exactly how they are carrying out their organic farming practices (**Figure 9.9**).

This is also the point at which the partners identify risks to their respective reputations. For example, if Zotter works with a local farming cooperative and the news media later finds out that the farmers were secretly using pesticides, what are the implications for Zotter's reputation? Will people still trust the quality of its chocolate? It is also important to identify the implications for the cooperative. Does supplying Zotter make them look good? Will this help bring more buyers from other chocolate makers?

The final part of this first step is to map out who will be affected by the initiative. Does it consist of a small change, or will it have effects outside the industry? In the case of Zotter and the Nicaraguan farmers, Zotter might identify that fair-trade organic cacao beans would not only affect its customers and the farmers, but that it would affect other chocolate producers and other farmers who might see increased opportunities. They could create a larger consortium of small chocolatiers interested in improving the quality of their chocolates and the sustainability of how cacao is harvested.

Thierry Tronnel/Corbis News/ Getty Images

FIGURE 9.9 **Zotter chocolate.** Zotter's owner, Josef Zotter, meets with farmers on a regular basis to ensure the cacao beans meet organic standards.

For example, in developing the SC, Walmart realized that the problem it was trying to solve would affect all retailers and everyone who supplied goods to those retailers. As a result, it decided to expand the consortium to include both retailers and companies providing consumer packaged goods. By similarly mapping out everyone affected by the objectives, companies can expand the collaboration to even more interested parties.

Develop Shared Language. After assembling the collaborative group, the next step is to acknowledge that governments, NGOs, and businesses will often speak from different contexts and have different terms for environmental issues. These differences in vocabulary can be potential sources of misunderstanding and might delay collaborative success unless they are resolved first. To help create a shared terminology, some groups even hire a professional facilitator to serve as a neutral actor and help bring the parties together through shared terms.

Before inviting Greenpeace into Asia Pulp & Paper's boardroom, for example, the company hired a "translator" to help executives understand the jargon Greenpeace was using and bridge the way the two organizations talked about sustainability. Eventually the terminology barrier fell, and the partners developed a common language.

Create Entrance and Exit Strategies. Successful collaborations need clear entrance and exit strategies. An entrance strategy provides specific ways a new partner can enter a collaboration. It helps set a framework for what organizations are required to do within that collaboration so they can evaluate their own performance and that of their peers.

Entrance strategies can also specify when certain organizations are needed in the collaborative effort. For example, in the case of the irrigation system company Netafim, engaging the IFC to help finance small farmers was necessary only once the specific farmers had been identified. Local governments were first asked to find rural farmers, then IFC would be responsible for funding loans for irrigation equipment, and finally Netafim would come in to sell the product and train the customers. Partners could engage and disengage at different stages, avoiding wasted time and bloated bureaucracy.

Exit strategies help partners know when they've reached an appropriate time to disengage. The exit strategy can apply on an individual basis, as in the case of Netafim and the IFC, or it can apply to the entire collaborative effort. For example, an exit strategy might help the group know when a project is complete, or when a strategy should be abandoned because it has drifted too far from its mission or the environmental factors have changed so much that the intended goal is no longer reasonable. A collaborative group set up to ensure that all governments comply with certain environmental standards, for instance, could disband once a specific set of objectives has been met.

Get the Board on Board. Getting the board of directors to buy into the collaboration is also a key behavior for success. For example, BASF, a German chemicals company, wanted to turn all its products into sustainability all-stars. To do this, company executives carefully engaged the board of directors and asked them to form a sustainability board, chaired by one of the board members. The sustainability board was then asked to make an initial proposal to the board of directors to review all the products, after first going to the business units to secure buy-in from the leaders and have them draft implementation strategies. Because the board was asked to get involved, members engaged with the initiative and drew in the management team as a result.

Because short-termism is so deeply entrenched in capital markets, fighting it in the boardroom is no small matter. Part of the key to changing this mind-set and getting boards to embrace collaborative sustainability is to get them to see a meaningful story in which stakeholders and material risks are most important to the company's long-term goals, and then to communicate that story to the market.[54]

9.4 Sustainability and Innovation

LEARNING OBJECTIVE

Discuss how sustainability can drive innovation.

Shifts in thinking about international business and in behaviors related to sustainability are changing the competitive landscape. To keep up, companies need to change the way they think about products, technologies, processes, and business models. In fact, innovative thinking is what brought companies out of the 2008 financial crisis and is what will bring them out of future crises. By innovating for sustainability, early movers will develop organizational capabilities that competitors will struggle to match. This process starts with companies learning to recognize opportunities rather than focusing solely on reducing risk.

Companies that already possess this competitive advantage have typically gone through four distinct stages.[55] Each stage is increasingly more difficult to navigate and requires firms to develop new capabilities, but being able to move through all the stages can help them be the winners in the global game of goods and services. What are the four stages?

Stage 1: View Compliance as Opportunity

The first step companies usually take is complying with existing laws aimed at protecting the environment. This is sometimes difficult because laws differ by country and by region. In 2015, Hawaii became the first U.S. state to ban plastic bags at store checkouts. While many plastic bag companies maintained their existing strategies in spite of this decision, others saw Hawaii's law as a trend that could extend to other states and countries. In anticipation of this, they used it as a rationale to shift their strategies and begin making other types of reusable bags, both plastic and cloth.

Companies often feel compelled to abide by voluntary codes or certifications, such as the Greenhouse Gas Protocol or the Forest Stewardship Council code. Many of these codes and certifications are developed by NGOs or industry groups interested in improving the environment. They are often stricter than existing laws and are frequently used to persuade companies to follow a set of environmental best practices—especially in countries where environmental laws may not be very strict. For example, the Greenhouse Gas Protocol was started by the World Resources Institute (an NGO) and the World Business Council on Sustainable Development (an industry association) to encourage companies to adopt standards and tools in order to manage their emissions and become more efficient, especially in countries like China and India.

Another related opportunity is to turn antagonistic regulators into allies by going above and beyond current laws. This strategy often makes companies first movers in innovative sustainability techniques. For example, when the European Union created laws that required all electronics manufacturers to bear the cost of recycling the products they sold, Hewlett Packard teamed with three other electronics makers—Sony, Braun, and Electrolux—to create the European Recycling Platform. This organization works with more than 2,500 companies to help recycle the equipment its member companies sell.[56]

Stage 2: Make Value Chains Sustainable

Once companies learn to turn compliance into opportunity and antagonists into allies, the next step is to focus on resource constraints. Typically, firms can achieve this goal by using fewer natural resources or more renewable sources of energy. *Eco-efficiency* is very profitable today, and there are countless examples of companies using less energy, water, or other materials.

Take the example of dyeing clothing, a surprisingly water-intensive activity. When Adidas, the sporting-goods manufacturer, decided to reduce the amount of water it used in the dyeing process, it first tried to figure out a way to use no water. Working with the Thai fabric and clothing maker Yeh Group, it came up with the "DryDye" process. This new process uses heat and pressure to force pigment into the fibers, consumes only half as much energy and chemicals as traditional dyeing, and requires zero water.[57]

Likewise, during the 2012 Olympics, Nike introduced a new shoe upper (the top of the shoe, without the sole) that was knit from one strand of fabric rather than being assembled from different pieces. Compared with most other shoes, the new Nike "single-strand" shoe reduced material waste by as much as 80 percent.[58] By analyzing each link in the value chain, companies like Nike can increase the sustainability of their supply chains and operations—improving their own bottom lines while minimizing environmental effects. In another example, Nike has spent significant amounts of money to ensure its suppliers' shop floors are ecologically and structurally safe. Much of this effort occurred in response to revelations by environmental and human rights groups about Nike's overseas labor practices that tarnished its name in the 1990s. After making changes in several locations, Nike found that the factories were actually more productive and used fewer resources, reducing the cost of production.

Stage 3: Design Sustainable Products and Services

As companies make their value chains more sustainable, they realize that more sustainable products and services are often more profitable too. For example, Kimberly-Clark, the $21 billion company that makes tissues and toilet paper, questioned the simple assumption that toilet paper roles need to have cardboard tubes to hold their shape. As a result, the company developed Scott Naturals, a toilet paper roll without the cardboard tube[59] (see **Figure 9.10**). The product is cheaper to make—creating savings that can be passed on to the consumer—and avoids all the waste generated when the tubes are thrown out. While this innovation may not seem significant, it still required developing an innovative new rolling technology that remains an industry secret.

Did you know that 100,000 pairs of conventional shoes create about 31 garbage trucks' worth of waste and garbage throughout the production process and product life cycle? The shoe company Puma realized how much waste it was creating and introduced a new collection of products that are either recyclable or biodegradable. The Puma InCycle Collection uses biodegradable polymers, recycled polyester, and organic cotton to eliminate the need for pesticides, chemical fertilizers, or other hazardous chemicals in the creation of its raw materials. Puma even installed recycling bins in its stores and outlets to help in the collection of the recyclable material, giving consumers a handy place to recycle and the company a free source of recyclable materials.[60]

To invent sustainable products and services, companies must understand consumer concerns and carefully examine product life cycles or product origins before production and where they go afterward. This helps companies know how to reduce, reuse, and recycle. Next, companies often need to partner with NGOs, governments, universities, and even other companies to get a fresh view of how different ideas and technologies can solve those customer problems. Reaching out in this way helps connect

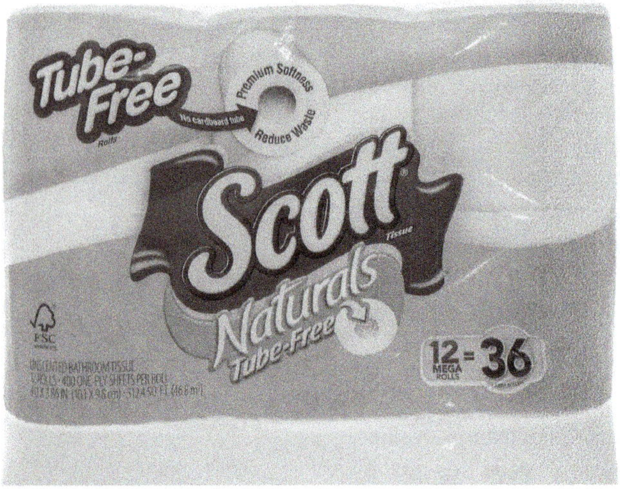

Keith Homan/Shutterstock

FIGURE 9.10 **Scott Naturals** A natural toilet paper without the cardboard tube created savings for Scott and for consumers.

existing knowledge with real-world problems, bringing about new insights like tubeless toilet paper and biodegradable shoes.[61]

Stage 4: Develop New Business Models

The final stage in sustainable innovation provides the highest returns but also requires taking the biggest risks. To develop new business models, managers must think differently about a traditional industry and the way they operate within it. For example, Elon Musk, the founder of Tesla, started making electric cars by questioning assumptions about the entire auto industry—from the way cars are initially sold through the way they depend on an infrastructure powered by burning fossil fuels. Today Tesla does not use a go-between dealership. Instead, the company sells cars directly to customers online. It has also built more than 4,000 charging stations throughout the world, where motorists can rapidly recharge their electric cars (see **Figure 9.11**). Where possible, these charging stations are solar-powered.[62]

Mark Reinstein/Corbis/Getty Images

FIGURE 9.11 **A Tesla charging station**

Tesla has upended an established industry, but the company is still waging an uphill battle against some norms. For instance, some U.S. automobile retailer consortiums have felt threatened by Tesla's direct-to-consumer model and have convinced state governments in New Jersey, Arizona, Michigan, and Texas to block direct car sales.[63] Fighting against institutional pressures as strong as those from the auto industry can be a potential roadblock for innovative companies trying to make their business more sustainable.

In spite of these setbacks, many companies—including Tesla—have found tremendous public favor and success by questioning traditional business models. Part of this progress has come as consumers become more educated and informed about the need to fight climate change and manage resource constraints. To keep up with public opinion, most global companies have embraced some level of sustainability. The winners of the changing business landscape will not be just those able to comply with laws, adapt their supply chains, or even modify their products; the winners will change their business model to one that is also sustainable.

In summary, environmental changes and resource constraints have added new challenges for companies. Those that respond well understand that these challenges are not simply risks to be avoided; they are opportunities to differentiate the firm from its competition and to safeguard the environment. Companies can best respond to the risks and opportunities that come from globalization by taking a long-term perspective; collaborating with other companies, governments, and civil society; and innovating around sustainability (see **Figure 9.12**).

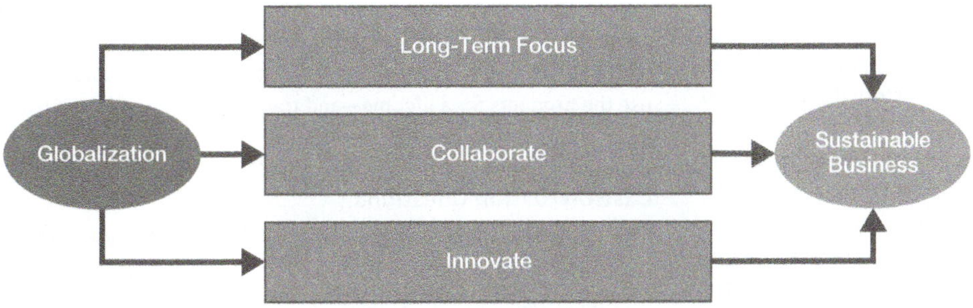

FIGURE 9.12 **Responding to risks and opportunities that come from globalization**

Summary and Case

Summary

LEARNING OBJECTIVE 9.1 Analyze the risks and opportunities associated with globalization and sustainability.

Sustainability efforts face two significant issues: climate change and resource constraints. Climate change is influenced by human activities, compelling companies to reduce CO_2 emissions through improved efficiency and other creative means. Similarly, the finite supply of minerals and raw materials on Earth requires that businesses develop more efficient methods to use resources. Companies that dedicate themselves to sustainability can find ways to save money and even profit from such practices.

LEARNING OBJECTIVE 9.2 Explain how to fight short-termism.

Businesses exist to make money for investors and employees. Thus they default to short-termism—the excessive focus on short-term results at the expense of long-term objectives. Three strategies to fight short-termism are to focus on stakeholder interests as opposed to shareholder interests; to engage Wall Street investors and analysts in discussions about the profitability and importance of pursuing sustainable practices; and to align the interests of board members with those of stakeholders by applying ownership-based governance.

LEARNING OBJECTIVE 9.3 Identify ways to collaborate globally for sustainability.

The best practice is for governments, businesses, and communities to collaborate to find solutions. Sustainable business models save money and directly affect a company's reputation—and subsequently its stock market value. To collaborate successfully with other organizations, businesses can conduct due diligence, develop a shared language, create entrance and exit strategies, and convince the board of directors of the need for collaboration.

LEARNING OBJECTIVE 9.4 Discuss how sustainability can drive innovation.

Businesses can thrive by learning to recast challenges as opportunities in four phases. First, laws related to sustainability can show companies which sustainability measures to target for the maximum effect on public opinion. Second, companies can improve supply chains by enforcing ecologically friendly standards to increase efficiency and profitability. Third, they can completely reimagine products, using fewer resources or discontinuing certain materials altogether. Finally, they can develop new business models designed to challenge traditional, inefficient industry practices.

Case Study

Patagonia Invests in Repair and Recycle

It was a bright spring day—perfect for a walk in the park—and the words "Patagonia Worn Wear" came into view. They were painted on a refurbished food truck bouncing down the overused road. As the truck came to a halt and the doors opened, however, there was no food to be had. Instead, the truck was full of repair equipment. A team of people started to unload it, handing out flyers to the curious crowd that began to gather. To everyone's amazement, the truck belonged to an outdoor athletic clothing company and was there to fix worn gear and clothing.[64]

Patagonia, the outdoor athletic clothing company, had decided to address the vast amounts of resources required by the apparel industry—and the even larger volume of waste the industry produced. It had found its inspiration in a *New York Times* story discussing how consumers needed better-quality clothing that wouldn't create so much waste. In launching an anticonsumerism movement, Patagonia hoped people would reuse and recycle purchased items because of the clothing's great quality. To help consumers catch on to this idea, Patagonia started creating repair kits and traveling around to help people repair their worn or damaged clothes. If their existing clothing lasted longer, people wouldn't have to buy so much.[65]

Patagonia is one of the world's foremost suppliers of outdoor apparel and equipment. Like all retailers, the company makes its money by selling new products. The more it sells, the more money it makes. However, Patagonia isn't interested only in profits. It hopes its high-quality outdoor gear will give people the tools to fall in love with the out-of-doors, and it also wants to be known as a company that truly believes in what it sells.[66] After all, if you love the outdoors, then you're going to do everything you can to keep the environment clean and safe. In keeping with that philosophy, Patagonia's initiative is to get people to use their Patagonia gear forever. "Buy a jacket from us," a company ad says, "and you should never have to buy another jacket from us again."

The refurbished food truck was just one more step in Patagonia's pursuit of its mission. The company has developed repair and recycle shops all over the world to ensure that its customers are getting a lifetime of use from its products. Its hope is that all its customers will use the products for a lifetime—and then maybe the outdoors will be around for many more lifetimes.

Case Discussion Questions

1. What are some disadvantages of Patagonia's model of sustainability?
2. What are some advantages?
3. Do the advantages outweigh the disadvantages for Patagonia?
4. Is this model of sustainability viable for the long run?

Endnotes

[1]"World Population Prospects: The 2015 Revision," UN Department of Economic and Social Affairs, July 28, 2015. https://esa.un.org/unpd/wpp/.

[2]Tesla Mission Statement, Tesla website. www.teslamotors.com/blog/mission-tesla (accessed July 8, 2015).

[3]Geoff Williams, "3 Industries Most Likely to be Affected by Climate Change," American Express Open Forum, May 20, 2014. https://www.americanexpress.com/us/small-business/openforum/articles/3-industries-most-likely-to-be-affected-by-climate-change/.

[4]Andrew S. Winston, *The Big Pivot: Radically Practical Strategies for a Hotter, Scarcer, and More Open World* (Boston: Harvard Business Review Press, 2014).

[5]Christine Bader, "What Do Chief Sustainability Officers Actually Do?" *The Atlantic*, May 6, 2015. www.theatlantic.com/business/archive/2015/05/what-do-chief-sustainability-officers-actually-do/392315/.

[6]Richard Pallardy, "Deepwater Horizon Oil Spill of 2010," *Encyclopedia Britannica*, last updated March 31, 2017. www.britannica.com/event/Deepwater-Horizon-oil-spill-of-2010 (accessed June 14, 2017).

[7]Bryan Alexander, "Deepwater Horizon Shows Human Side of Oil Spill," *USA Today*, September 29, 2016. https://www.usatoday.com/story/life/movies/2016/09/29/deepwater-horizon-shows-human-side-infamous-bp-oil-spill/91208486/.

[8]Jacob Morgan, "Creating an Engaged Organization by Focusing on Sustainability in the Workplace," *Forbes*, July 5, 2016. https://www.forbes.com/sites/jacobmorgan/2016/07/05/creating-an-engaged-organization-by-focusing-on-sustainability-in-the-workplace/#689897cc734f.

[9]"Climate Change: Basic Information," U.S. Environmental Protection Agency website. http://www.epa.gov/climatechange/basics/ (accessed July 8, 2015).

[10]Ninety-seven percent of climate scientists agree that climate-warming trends over the past century are very likely the result of human activities, and most of the leading scientific organizations worldwide have issued public statements endorsing this position; see "Scientific Consensus: Earth's Climate Is Warming," NASA Global Climate Change, http://climate.nasa.gov/scientific-consensus/ (accessed October 5, 2016).

[11]"Confronting Climate Change in the U.S. Midwest.". Union of Concerned Scientists. July 2009: 5. http://www.ucsusa.org/sites/default/files/legacy/assets/documents/global_warming/climate-change-ohio.pdf (accessed June 14, 2017).

[12]R.E. Kopp et al., "Temperature-Driven Global Sea-Level Variability in the Common Era," *Proceedings of the National Academy of Sciences* 113, no. 11 (2016): E1434–41; Church, John A., and Neil J. White. "A 20th century acceleration in global sea-level rise." *Geophysical Research Letters* 33.1 (2006).

[13]WGMS, and National Snow and Ice Data Center (comps.). 1999, updated 2012. *World Glacier Inventory, Version 1*. [Indicate subset used]. Boulder, Colorado USA. NSIDC: National Snow and Ice Data Center.doi:http://dx.doi.org/10.7265/N5/NSIDC-WGI-2012-02(accessed July 8, 2015).

[14]Derksen, Chris, and Ross Brown. "Spring Snow Cover Extent Reductions in the 2008–2012 Period Exceeding Climate Model Projections." *Geophysical Research Letters* 39.19 (2012).

[15]K. Saidi and S. Hammami, "The Impact of CO2 Emissions and Economic Growth on Energy Consumption in 58 Countries," *Energy Reports* 1 (2015): 62–70; U. Soytas and R. Sari, "Energy Consumption and GDP: Causality Relationship in G-7 Countries and Emerging Markets," *Energy Economics* 25 no. 1 (2003): 33–37.

[16]Eric Beinhocker et al., "The Carbon Productivity Challenge: Curbing Climate Change and Sustaining Economic Growth," McKinsey Global Institute, July 2008. http://www.mckinsey.com/business-functions/sustainability-and-resource-productivity/our-insights/the-carbon-productivity-challenge.

[17]S. K. Mathur et al., "Does Domestic Energy Consumption Affect GDP of a Country? A Panel Data Study," *Global Economy Journal* 16, no. 2 (2016): 229–73.

[18]Nate Aden, "The Roads to Decoupling: 21 Countries Are Reducing Carbon Emissions While Growing GDP," World Resources Institute, April 5, 2016. www.wri.org/blog/2016/04/roads-decoupling-21-countries-are-reducing-carbon-emissions-while-growing-gdp.

[19]"The 3% Solution," World Wildlife Organization, 2017. www.worldwildlife.org/projects/the-3-solution.

[20]"Global 500 Climate Change Report," CDP, 12 September 2013. http://www.sustainablebrands.com/digital_learning/white-paper/cdp-global-500-climate-change-report-2013 Most of the world's largest companies now respond to the CDP survey.

[21]Laura Shin, "Work from Home: The Top 100 Companies Offering Telecommuting Jobs in 2015," *Forbes*, January 21, 2015. https://www.forbes.com/sites/laurashin/2015/01/21/work-from-home-the-top-100-companies-offering-telecommuting-jobs-in-2015/#20d0336d263c.

[22]Steve Ebert, personal interview with the authors, Salt Lake City, Utah. October 2016.

[23]Bryce Morris, personal interview with the authors, South Jordan, Utah. October 2016.

[24]Energy Conservation. Adobe Corporate Responsibilty. www.adobe.com/corporate-responsibility/sustainability/energy-conservation.html (accessed July 9, 2015).

[25]"Extreme Weather Events Drive Climate Change up Boardroom Agenda in 2012," Carbon Disclosure Project, November, 2012. http://www.duurzaam-ondernemen.nl/extreme-weather-events-drive-climate-change-up-boardroom-agenda-in-2012/

[26]Hauke Engel, Martin Stuchtey, and Helga Vanthournout, "Managing Waste in Emerging Markets," McKinsey & Company, February 2016 www.mckinsey.com/business-functions/sustainability-and-resource-productivity/our-insights/managing-waste-in-emerging-markets.

[27]Engel, Stuchtey, and Vanthournout, "Managing Waste in Emerging Markets."

[28]Vanya Walker-Leigh, "Country Profile—Nicaragua," New Agriculturalist, August 2011. www.new-ag.info/en/country/profile.php?a=2143 (accessed July 13, 2015).

[29]Jeremy Grantham, "Time to Wake up: Days of Abundant Resources and Falling Prices Are Over Forever," The Oil Drum, April 29, 2011. http://www.theoildrum.com/node/7853

[30]Vince Matthews, "Who Is Going to Get the Global Goodies?" Presentation, Arizona State University. Global Institute of Sustainability. 2014. https://sustainability.asu.edu/media/video/global-goodies/ (accessed June 14, 2017).

[31]"Backwash: Coke Returns from India Exile." *Multinational Monitor*, 16 (July/August 1995): 7–8.

[32]Rich Wartzman. "Why 'Pay for Performance' Is a Sham." *Forbes*. March 26, 2013. https://www.forbes.com/sites/drucker/2013/03/26/pay-for-performance-is-a-sham/#2c3e451061b1

[33]Dominic Barton and Mark Wiseman, "Focusing Capital on the Long Term," CPP Investment Board/McKinsey & Company, May 22, 2013. http://www.mckinsey.com/global-themes/leadership/focusing-capital-on-the-long-term.

[34]John Graham, Campbell Harvey, and Shiva Rajgopol, "The Economic Implications of Corporate Financial Reporting," *Journal of Accounting and Economics* 40 (2005): 3–73.

[35]John C. Bogle, *The Clash of the Cultures: Investment vs. Speculation* (Hoboken, NJ: Wiley, 2012).

[36]Claire Miller and Nick Bilton, "Google's Lab of Wildest Dreams," *New York Times*, February 14, 2011. http://www.nytimes.com/2011/11/14/technology/at-google-x-a-top-secret-lab-dreaming-up-the-future.html; Adam Lashinsky, "Inside Apple," *Fortune*, May 23, 2011. http://fortune.com/2011/05/09/inside-apple/.

[37]Paige Tanner, "What Is Samsung's Growth Strategy in the Semiconductor Space?" Market Realist, March 11, 2016. http://marketrealist.com/2016/03/samsungs-growth-strategy-semiconductor-space/.

[38]Smith, Adam. *The Theory of Moral Sentiments*. Penguin, 2010.

[39]Sheila Bonini and Stephan Görner, "The Business of Sustainability: McKinsey Global Survey Results," McKinsey & Company, October 2011. www.mckinsey.com/insights/energy_resources_materials/the_business_of_sustainability_mckinsey_global_survey_results (accessed July 13, 2015).

[40]Josie Ensor, "Unilever's Polman Hits out at City's Short Term Culture," *Telegraph*, July 5, 2011. http://www.telegraph.co.uk/finance/newsbysector/retailandconsumer/8617022/Unilevers-Polman-hits-out-at-Citys-short-term-culture.html.

[41]Dominic Barton, "Capitalism for the Long Term," *Harvard Business Review*, March 2011. https://hbr.org/2011/03/capitalism-for-the-long-term.

[42]Winston, *The Big Pivot.*

[43]Winston, *The Big Pivot.*

[44]Winston, *The Big Pivot.*

[45]Norges Bank Investment Management website. http://www.nbim.no/en/ (accessed August 18, 2015).

[46]"Norway's $900bn Sovereign Wealth Fund Told to Reduce Coal Assets" *Guardian*, May 27, 2015. www.theguardian.com/world/2015/may/27/norway-sovereign-fund-reduce-coal-assets.

[47]"TSC's John Johnson: Retailers, Governments and NGOs Need to Drive Sustainable Change," Sustainability Consortium, May 23, 2011. www.sustainabilityconsortium.org/consortium-news/tscs-jon-johnson-retailers-governments-and-ngos-need-to-drive-sustainable-change/.

[48]"TSC's John Johnson."

[49]Andrew S. Winston, *The Big Pivot: Radically Practical Strategies for a Hotter, Scarcer, and More Open World* (Boston: Harvard Business Review Press, 2014).

[50]Winston, *The Big Pivot.*

[51]David Kiron et al., "Collaboration and Leadership for Sustainability: The Growing Importance of Corporate Collaboration and Boards of Directors to Sustainable Business," *MIT Sloan Management Review*, January 2015. http://sloanreview.mit.edu/projects/joining-forces/.

[52]David Kiron, Nina Kruschwitz, Knut Haanaes, Martin Reeves, Sonja-Katrin Fuisz-Kehrbach, Georg Kell. Joining Forces: Collaboration and Leadership for Sustainability. *MIT Sloan Management Review*. January 12, 2015. http://sloanreview.mit.edu/projects/joining-forces/

[53]Personal interview with the author, Julia Zotter. Shanghai, China. November 2016.

[54]Robert G. Eccles and Michael P. Krzus, *The Integrated Reporting Movement: Meaning, Momentum, Motives, and Materiality* (New York: John Wiley & Sons, 2014).

[55]Ram Nidumolu, C. K. Prahalad, & M. R. Rangaswami, "Why Sustainability Is Now the Key Driver of Innovation," *Harvard Business Review*, September 2009. https://hbr.org/2009/09/why-sustainability-is-now-the-key-driver-of-innovation

[56]European Recycling Platform website. http://erp-recycling.org (accessed October 2016).

[57]Leon Kaye, "Adidas Rolls out Waterless 'DryDye' T-Shirt," TriplePundit, August 9, 2012. http://www.triplepundit.com/2012/08/adidas-waterless-drydye-shirt/.

[58]Winston, *The Big Pivot.*

[59]Scott Tube-Free Toilet Paper. Scottbrand.com. https://www.scottbrand.com/products/toilet-paper/tubefree (accessed October 2016).

[60]Sondja Brugmann and Thomas Kolster, "Dare to Stand Out: Develop Follow-Worthy Brands," New Hope Network, March 27, 2015. http://www.newhope.com/managing-your-business/dare-stand-out-develop-follow-worthy-brands.

[61]Morris, Shad S., Bijuan Zhong, and Mona Makhija. "Going the Distance: The Pros and Cons of Expanding Employees' Global Knowledge Reach." *Journal of International Business Studies* 46.5 (2015): 552–573.

[62]Tesla website. www.teslamotors.com (accessed October 2016).

[63]Brent Snavely, "Auto Dealers Chief Warns of Tesla Direct Sales Model," *USA Today*, October 7, 2016. https://www.usatoday.com/story/money/cars/2016/10/06/auto-dealers-chief-warns-teslas-direct-sales-model/91649750/.

[64]Bob Smith, "Get Your Outdoor Clothing Fixed at Patagonia's Worn Wear Tour Workshops," *Grough Magazine*, April 6, 2016. https://www.grough.co.uk/magazine/2016/04/07/get-your-outdoor-clothing-fixed-at-patagonias-worn-wear-tour-workshops

[65]J. B. Mackinnon, "Patagonia's Anti-Growth Strategy," *New Yorker*, May 21, 2015. http://www.newyorker.com/business/currency/patagonias-anti-growth-strategy; "Patagonia Worn Wear," *Alabama Chanin Journal*, September 2, 2015. http://journal.alabamachanin.com/2015/09/patagonia-worn-wear/.

[66]Avi Shankar and Robin Canniford, "If Patagonia's Business Model Is a Paragon of Virtue, Should More Companies Follow Suit?" The Conversation, September 29, 2016. https://theconversation.com/if-patagonias-business-model-is-a-paragon-of-virtue-should-more-companies-follow-suit-66188

Poverty

sidefx/Getty Images

Introduction

This heat map represents the world's population. Darker areas of red represent large amounts of people. As you can see from the map, countries like China, India and Indonesia have some of the most densely populated areas. At the same time, most of the world's economic activity still resides in North America, Europe and the Far East. Yet, little economic activity exists and poverty may be widespread in significant population centers of the world.

Although living standards differ around the world, in essence people are poor when they lack the ability to purchase products and services. Low-income societies represent more than

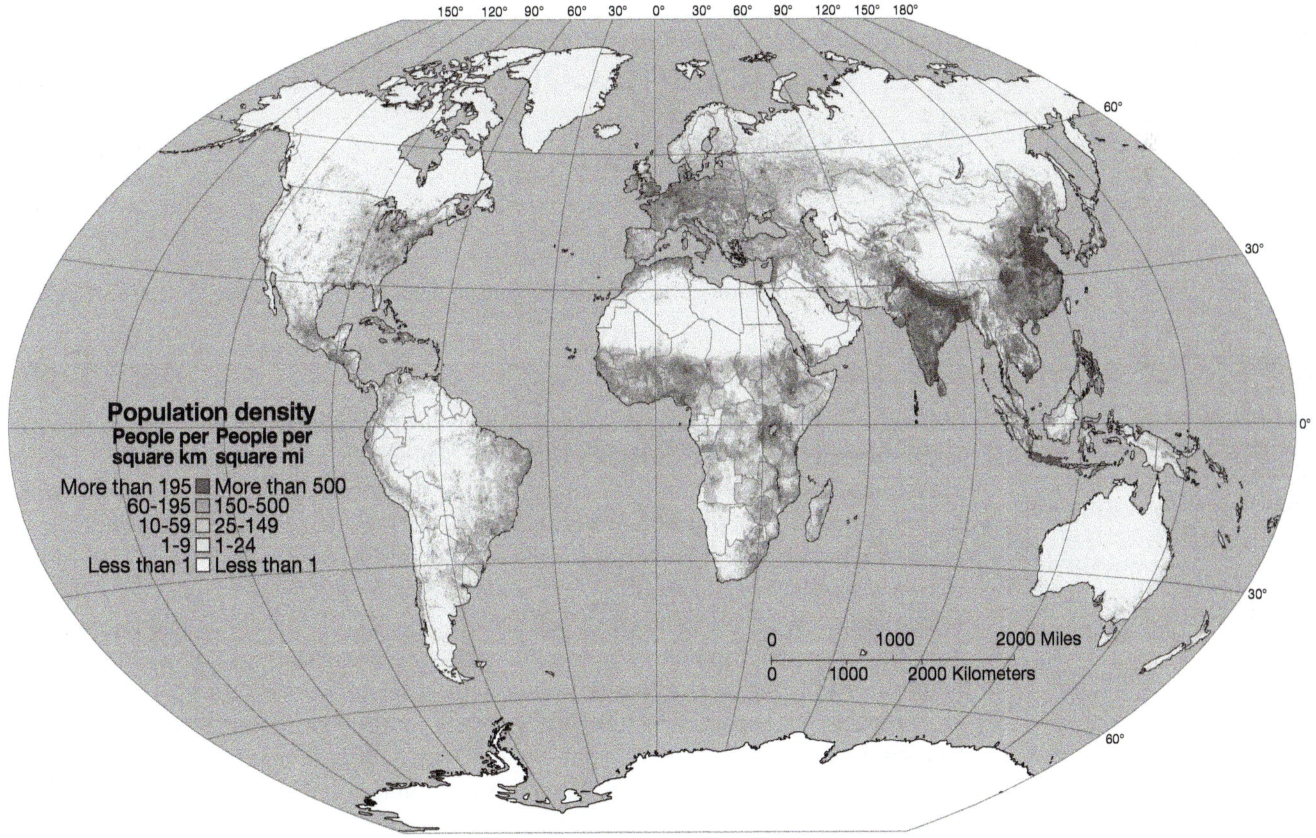

Source: http://ww.theatlantic.com/past/docs/images/issues/200510/world-is-spiky.pdf

4 billion potential consumers who are largely unreached by international companies. For example, although Vietnam has a population of 80 million people, Ford may struggle there because few can afford to buy a car.

For this reason, most multinational companies target their products and services to the wealthier segments of society. But consider an analogy: would you rather pick up a thousand $100 bills ($100,000) or a billion pennies ($10,000,000) in the same time frame? Most Western companies are organized to pick up the $100 bills, but companies willing and able to pick up the pennies may have huge opportunities.

Countries with a low average income and untapped human capital also present opportunities for companies to cut labor costs. For example, hiring a machine shop worker in Switzerland will cost over $38 per hour, whereas hiring a similarly qualified laborer in the Philippines costs under $2 per hour.[1] And not least, the opportunity to alleviate poverty by hiring and training low-income workers and improving conditions in their communities provides a secondary benefit to companies that have made a commitment to demonstrate corporate social responsibility in their business practices.

LEARNING OBJECTIVES

After exploring this chapter you will be able to:

1. **Identify** the causes and consequences of global poverty as they apply to international business
2. **Discuss** traditional approaches to alleviating global poverty
3. **Compare** traditional approaches and business solutions to poverty
4. **Describe** ways that businesses can make money while also doing good

10.1 Causes and Consequences of Global Poverty

LEARNING OBJECTIVE

Identify the causes and consequences of global poverty as they apply to international business.

poverty a general scarcity or lack of material possessions or money for consumption; a persistent lack of income that deprives an individual of the ability to obtain appropriate levels of food, water, clothing, shelter, health care, and/or education

Defined as a social factor, **poverty** is a general scarcity or lack of material possessions or money for consumption, a persistent lack of income that deprives an individual of the ability to obtain appropriate levels of food, water, clothing, shelter, health care, and/or education.[2] However, poverty is not just a lack of money. It is also the inability to effectively participate in society. It means not having enough resources to feed and clothe a family, not having access to schools or clinics, not having land on which to grow food or a job through which to earn a living. It means insecurity, powerlessness, and exclusion for individuals, households, and communities. It means susceptibility to violence, and it often forces people to live in marginal or fragile environments, frequently without access to clean water or sanitation (see **Figure 10.1**).[3]

Because of its impact on millions of lives, playwright George Bernard Shaw called poverty "the greatest of evils and the worst of crimes."[4] The tragedy of poverty is that it wastes so much potential. Lives are battered, happiness is stunted, creativity is wasted, and freedoms are eroded by the misfortunes of poverty.

Why does poverty exist? Countless books have been written about the causes of poverty, but no clear consensus has been reached. What we do know is that poverty is usually the convergence of multiple social factors beyond the reach of individuals, and of multiple individual

FIGURE 10.1 Poverty The poor in South Africa struggle to find clean water.

factors beyond the reach of governments. In the developing world, many social factors can contribute to poverty, including limited access to credit and capital markets, extreme environmental degradation, lack of public health care, poor infrastructure, and war.[5]

The Poverty Trap

What is most notable, however, is that the poor generally also have a much lower level of individual capability—for health, education, nutrition, and hope. Increased personal ability can be a way out of poverty; without it, the poor are often considered to be "trapped" in poverty or in a **poverty trap**. As Nobel Prize–winning economist Amartya Sen points out, poverty deprives individuals of key capabilities, limiting their ability to achieve and earn, thus keeping them poor and limiting their opportunities to increase their capability. For the very poor, the rate of return from investing in food, education, or a business is so low that, given their resources, they cannot improve their circumstances. As a result, they get poorer and poorer and remain trapped in poverty. Poverty often leaves people without the opportunity, education, or resources necessary to progress out of poverty. Raised beyond a certain threshold, however, their investments can become productive enough so that their income can increase over time.[6] This poverty trap is explained in the whiteboard video "The Poverty Trap."

poverty trap an economic condition in which it is difficult for an individual to obtain enough capital and/or credit to escape poverty; it causes poverty to persist and is also called the "cycle of poverty"

WileyPLUS

See Whiteboard Video: The Poverty Trap

From a business perspective, poverty is about a person's lack of ability to purchase the things they need. Businesses may be interested in alleviating poverty because doing so may increase the base of potential consumers, employees, and citizens. The goal is to improve the capabilities necessary to participate effectively in society, consume more products and services, and become steady and reliable employees. In addition, international businesses are increasingly aware of the opportunities to provide goods and services to the poor, understanding that collectively they make up a significant market.

Risks of Poverty

Before they can consider taking advantage of the economic and social responsibility opportunities found in poor markets, companies first need to consider the risks in targeting the poor as consumers or employees. These risks are three-fold.

1. Low to No Consumption The poor have many unmet needs. If a business could satisfy those needs and make a profit in the bargain, it would have a painless, profitable way to solve the problem of poverty. Unfortunately, profitably meeting the needs of the poor is no easy task. The consulting firm Monitor Group concluded, after an extensive survey, that few examples exist of profitable businesses marketing truly beneficial goods in low-income markets and operating on a large scale. The problem is that the market for selling to the poor is very small, and the poor have very little individual purchasing power, which means the market isn't often attractive for companies.[7]

In fact, the truly impoverished do not really represent an actual market at all. To have a consumer market, businesses need to build a lifestyle around a product or service. For instance, in the 1970s bottled water was a foreign idea in the United States, where paying for water was not part of the consumer lifestyle. It took decades of marketing before large numbers of consumers changed their lives to accept paying for water. Now, bottled water is a large and profitable U.S. business. Likewise, many poor consumers balk at the idea of paying for clean water or sanitation. Many international companies make the mistake of assuming that a base of customers willing to pay for a product already exists.

Consider the Tata Nano, the "world's cheapest car." After examining the local environment in India, Ratan Tata of the Tata Group had the idea to develop a family car at a price of about $2,500—less than half what it cost to buy the next-cheapest car at that time. He followed this vision, and after five years of hard work, his group of engineers developed the Nano to meet the needs of the poor, who had always wanted a car they could afford.

But were they really successful? While the car was the world's cheapest by a large margin, the Nano (shown in **Figure 10.2**) was not an instant success and even suffered from early problems with quality. Even today it is only slowly building a market. One reason is that for the poor in India a car is a status symbol, not just a convenience. To get from place to place, they already use public transportation or other cheaper means, such as motorcycles. Their lifestyle does not require a car, and if they were going to buy a car as a status symbol, they might not be interested in owning the "world's cheapest status symbol."

2. Low to No Cost Savings Offshoring jobs to poor countries is often seen as an opportunity to reduce production costs in a globally integrated world. However, as more companies take advantage of these pockets of low-cost labor, the price of that labor goes

travelib environment/Alamy Stock Photo

FIGURE 10.2 **Tata Nano** This vehicle was developed to be the "world's cheapest car."

up. This causes companies to move to the next poor market in order to reduce labor costs once again. The cycle can be good for the countries in which such companies are competing, because attracting firms requires building infrastructure and developing labor skills; however, this "country hopping" also presents certain risks for the companies themselves.

For instance, offshoring jobs to poor countries ends up being much more expensive than most companies predict. In fact, nearly 50 percent of all outsourced projects fail.[8] The problem is that companies often fail to assess the operational and structural risks of offshoring jobs. **Operational risk** comes from a firm's inability to document the work remote employees do, to describe the different situations they might face, and to direct what their responses should be in each scenario. For example, companies like Deloitte and IBM have had to spend millions of dollars managing and interacting with remote vendors in poor countries to ensure that the quality of their work can be effectively measured and tracked. **Structural risk** is the risk that arises as firms realize that their vendors may have different incentives than the client. Often these relationships do not work as expected. For example, a vendor may promise to hire workers with a certain skill set but fail to do so, or they may alter the terms of a contract as they operate.[9] Apple has had to work more closely with its vendors in China to ensure they are treating employees appropriately and not using exploitive management practices.

operational risk a firm's inability to document the work remote employees do, describe the different situations they might face, and direct their responses in each scenario

structural risk a firm's difficulty when relationships with vendors do not work as expected

Moreover, because the poor have limited access to health care, education, and any kind of insurance, they are subject to higher turnover and absenteeism, and they often need more training than their wealthier counterparts. Setting up a call center in a poor, rural village in India may seem attractive from a cost perspective—wages are just a fraction of those paid in wealthier markets—but international businesses will often end up paying for employees' training, retraining, health care, and recovery from natural disasters.

3. Low to No Respect Most multinationals operating in developing markets might at some point mutter the phrase, "I get no respect." That is, when they mess up, they are exposed in their home markets for exploiting the poor abroad. Typically, company reputations suffer and firms find themselves targeted by consumer boycotts, social media campaigns, and liability lawsuits. While they can be damaging to the company, these responses are actually necessary to ensure proper accountability.[10]

For example, the collapse of the Rana Plaza textile factory in Bangladesh in 2013 killed 1,129 garment workers, and an explosion at the packaging factory of Tampaco Foils in Bangladesh in 2016 killed 34 people and critically injured many more (see **Figure 10.3**).

Mamunur Rashid/Alamy Stock Photo

FIGURE 10.3 The Rana Plaza collapse This collapse of a clothing factory was Bangladesh's largest industrial accident. Owners of the Rana Plaza building urged employees to return to work even after an engineer had inspected the building the day before the collapse and deemed it unsafe.

It also created a backlash from media and advocacy groups in the industrialized world, such as the Clean Clothes Campaign and Labour Behind the Label.[11] These groups placed the blame on companies such as Primark, Walmart, and Benetton that used the Bangladeshi vendor to manufacture their clothes. The groups pointed out that workers in developing countries lack the rights, legal protections, and union representation enjoyed by their counterparts in developed countries. Because they lack bargaining power, those workers do not benefit from an increase in the demand for labor and their wages do not go up. They may have no choice but to work in sweatshops, suffering unhealthy or dangerous conditions, excessive hours, and physical abuse. All these negative attributes are then linked back to the firms that use the labor for profit.[12]

10.2 Traditional Responses to Poverty

LEARNING OBJECTIVE

Discuss traditional approaches to alleviating global poverty.

Many organizations have as their express mission ending or alleviating poverty. For instance, the first United Nations Millennium Development Goal is to "eradicate extreme poverty and hunger."[13] Using different approaches, various organizations, governments. and businesses provide direct assistance to and develop resources within impoverished areas. Meanwhile researchers have begun seeking ways to scientifically measure the effects of these interventions and better design future efforts. While poverty is still a huge world problem, there are some bright spots in efforts to reduce it.

Poverty Programs

foreign aid money and programs provided by governments, NGOs, or corporations to help alleviate poverty

Two major schools of thought drive the discussion about how to alleviate poverty. The first says the world's poor are poor simply because they are unable to break out of the "poverty trap." Economist Jeffrey Sachs says the solution is simple. Like a car with a dead battery, poor countries require a "jump start"—an infusion of foreign aid to lift poverty-stricken countries out of the poverty trap and onto the path to growth. **Foreign aid** consists of money and programs, such as education and healthcare, directly provided by governments, nongovernmental organizations, or even corporations to help alleviate poverty. According to Sachs, $195 billion a year, invested by rich countries over the course of 20 years, would be enough to jump-start all the poor countries of the world.[14]

However, others, such as economist Dambisa Moyo, make up a second school of thought and call foreign aid a waste of resources. In her book *Dead Aid*, Moyo notes that transfers of food, money, and other resources do little to help poor countries and may actually be detrimental to their progress. Her reasoning is that aid suffers from three problems. First, it may undermine innovation in those countries that receive it. Second, it frequently goes to corrupt leaders who build personal wealth rather than the infrastructure their countries need. Third, aid creates an unnatural reliance on foreign donors. Some countries even use it to enhance their efforts to get more aid rather than to make economic or social progress.[15]

These schools of thought represent different views of foreign aid. The first is based on the idea that markets by themselves may generate more general wealth but often unfairly neglect the poor. The second is based on the idea that providing aid undermines the incentives built into market economies. If people are given aid, then a false incentive system develops, thereby motivating them to search for handouts from others rather than create the benefits themselves. Below we discuss how the different types of foreign aid organizations are interacting with markets so you can better understand what these "poverty programs" look like.

While the debate is still unfolding, most developed countries have set up governmental aid agencies: the Australian Agency for International Development, the Kuwait Fund for Arab Economic Development, Irish Aid, and the Agencia Brasileira de Cooperacao (Brazilian

Cooperation Agency). These agencies have been created by their respective governments to help end poverty, cultivate economic resilience, and advance global security and prosperity. Governments fund them because they believe their own countries are safer and stronger when fewer people around the world face destitution, their trading partners are doing well, and basic human rights are protected—including by other sovereign nations.

The US Agency for International Development (USAID) reported that in 2015 the United States provided foreign countries with $18 billion in total economic assistance (www.usaid.gov). The biggest recipient was Afghanistan, followed by Israel, Egypt, and the West Bank/Gaza. **Figure 10.4** presents a historical chart of the aid the U.S. government has provided, in the form of both economic and military assistance, from 1946 to 2015. Worldwide, the United States contributed much more than the United Kingdom, the next-highest donor. However, as much as the United States gives, the amount of U.S. foreign aid is still less than 0.2 percent of the gross national income each year, as depicted in **Figure 10.5**.

Believing that poverty is a primary cause of war and financial crises, many nations decided to team up and provide foreign aid collectively. Collectively owned aid agencies are known

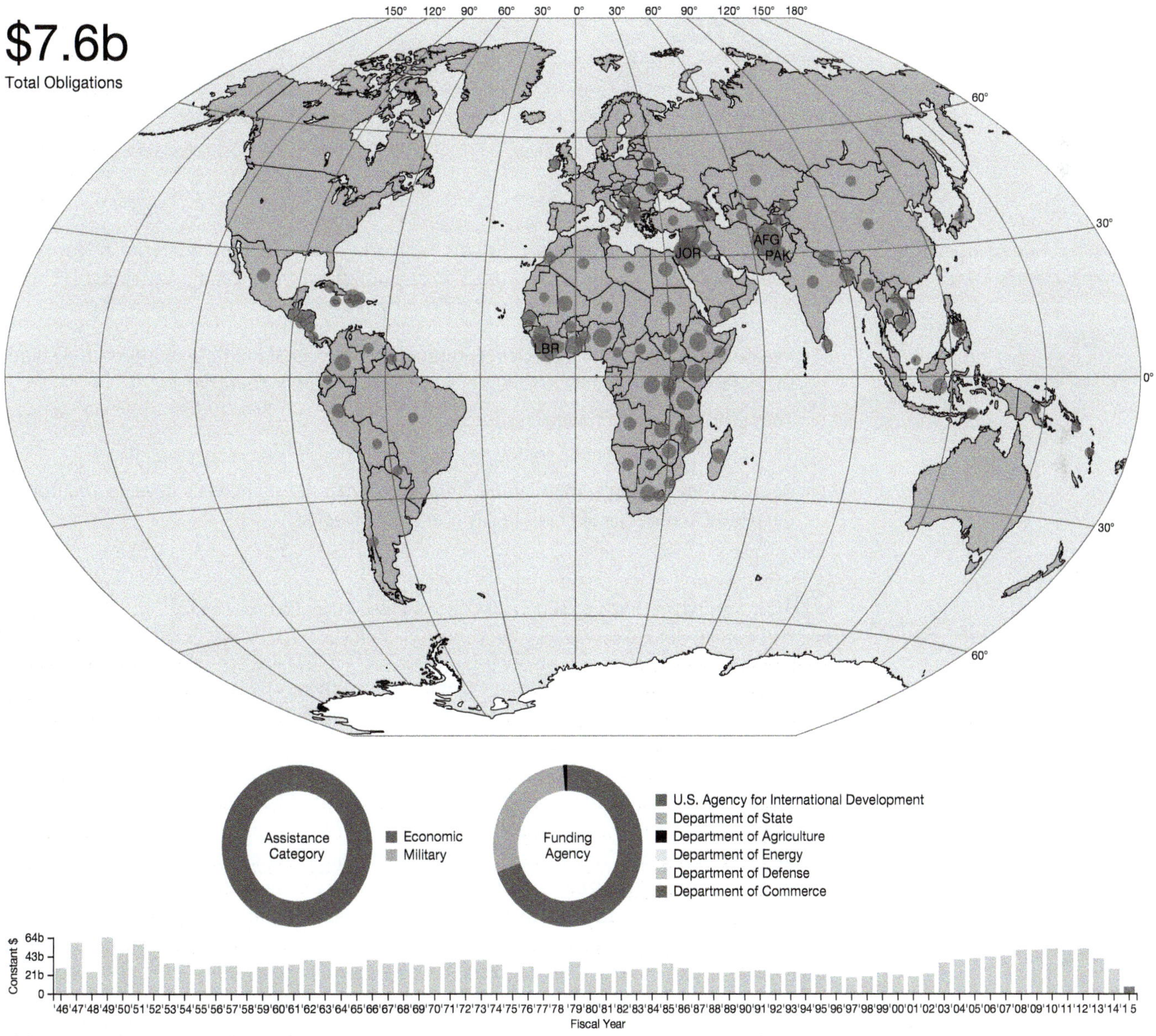

FIGURE 10.4 **U.S. foreign aid worldwide, 1946–2015** **Source:** USAID Foreign aid explorer, fiscal year 2015. https://explorer.usaid.gov/aid-trends.html. Accessed June 12, 2017.

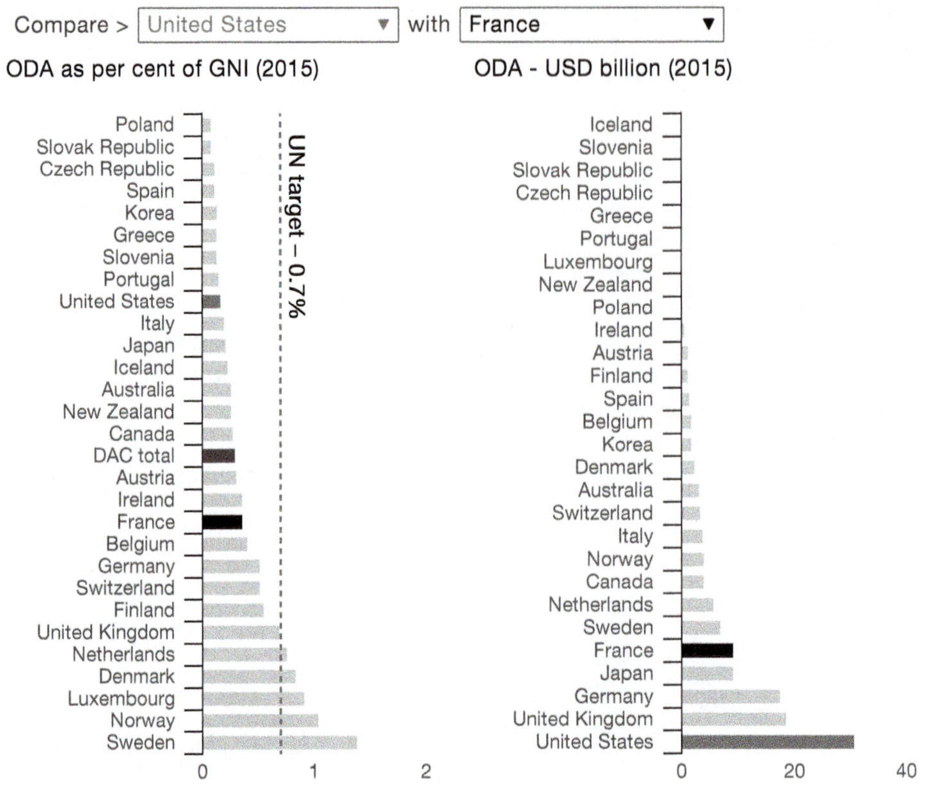

FIGURE 10.5 U.S. foreign aid given as development assistance, by country, 2015 **Source:** Organisation for Economic Co-operation and Development. Development Co-operation Report 2015: Mobilizing Resources for Sustainable Development. OECD (2015), *Development Co-operation Report 2015: Making Partnerships Effective Coalitions for Action*, OECD Publishing, Paris. Accessed June 12, 2017. DOI: https://dx.doi.org/10.1787/dcr-2015-en

multilateral aid agencies collectively owned aid agencies

as **multilateral aid agencies**; they include the World Bank and the International Monetary Fund, which were introduced in the discussion of multilateral organizations in Chapter 1. These entities differ from government aid agencies in various ways:

- Because multilateral aid agencies represent the interests of multiple countries, they tend to be less tied to the political self-interests of specific donor countries.
- They efficiently pool financial resources.
- They foster a sense of cooperation among nations that further reduces conflict.
- Because they are large, multilateral aid agencies can simultaneously develop and utilize deep local knowledge of needs in any given global region.

Other Types of Organizations That Fight Poverty

In addition to governments and multilateral aid agencies, many individuals are directly trying to eliminate poverty, often through special types of private organizations known as nonprofit organizations. Nonprofits, such as the Human Rights Watch and the Red Cross, usually have a social mission that is not about making money but rather about offering a service the for-profit sector does not provide. In a nonprofit organization, all profits made (if any) must be put back into the organization to further its charitable goals. By contrast, for-profit organizations may tie the sales of a product to actions to alleviate poverty. For instance, a small pizza franchise in Utah called Malawi's Pizza donates a "nutritious meal to a child in Malawi, Africa" for each meal purchased.

Another type of organization often focused on poverty elimination is a foundation. Foundations are nonprofit organizations that channel a wealthy donor's resources toward his or her aims. For instance, one of the primary aims of the Bill and Melinda Gates Foundation is to reduce extreme poverty. This organization pays salaries to its employees and has other operating costs, but the bulk of its funds are used to help reduce poverty. It has an endowment of over $38 billion from contributions by Microsoft cofounder Bill Gates (about $28 billion) and mega-investor Warren Buffett (about $10 billion). The Gates Foundation contributes to fighting diseases that primarily afflict the poor, such as polio, malaria, tuberculosis, and HIV/AIDS. In addition, it has funded multiple microfinance institutions such as the Grameen Foundation and

Pro Mujer, with the aim of giving would-be entrepreneurs in poor countries the capital they need to start or grow their businesses.

Other organizations try to alleviate poverty by supporting the payment of a fair wage to laborers abroad. For instance, Fair Trade USA helps to certify products such as tea, coffee, and sugar that come from developing countries as **Fair Trade** products. This certification indicates that the farmers or workers producing the goods have been paid a fair wage, often above the global market price. The guaranteed minimum sale price ensures that the farmer receives enough money to invest in high-quality production or other infrastructure. For instance, certified Fair Trade coffee growers receive a minimum of $1.40 per pound for their coffee beans, regardless of the price in the world market.

Fair Trade a trade movement which pays a guaranteed price to farmers in exchange for commodities

With the additional money they receive, the farmers collectively invest in improving farming techniques, improving distribution and product quality, and building schools and health care clinics in their communities. Companies like Starbucks that purchase this coffee are able to formally brand it as "Fair Trade." Fair Trade products usually sell for higher prices, but consumers are willing to pay a premium for the perceived higher quality and the realization that they are doing some good.

Poverty Science

In addition to governments, nonprofits, foundations, and Fair Trade organizations, many educational institutions have become engaged in the study of poverty. One approach in research relies on randomized experiments to explore the effects of interventions on reducing poverty. This research has generated a new field of **poverty science**, a movement by economists, policy researchers, and even business researchers, in cooperation with aid agencies, to use randomized controlled experiments in order to understand what types of activities and interventions might more effectively alleviate poverty. These researchers aim to bring increased rigor to poverty alleviation so businesses, governments, and nonprofits can make the most effective use of the resources they have dedicated to this cause.

poverty science a movement by economists, policy researchers, and business researchers to understand what types of activities and interventions might more effectively alleviate poverty

For instance, Abhijit Banerjee and Ester Duflo have summarized a host of experiments in their book, *Poor Economics: A Radical Rethinking of the Way to Fight Global Poverty*. They explore topics such as, "How much more food will a person living on 99 cents a day buy when given more money?" The answer is that an individual will spend on food about 67 percent of the money above the 99 cents he or she earns, but much of it will go to upgrading the person's existing diet to include more meat and more expensive grains rather than simply increasing the number of calories. As a result of this research, we can steer organizations to not just fight hunger. Making sure people have enough money to get sufficient calories on which to live is important, but making sure they have enough money for the right kinds of calories is even more important. When people increase the protein and the quality of grains in their diets, it increases their vitality and, in children, promotes proper growth and brain development. These factors make a big difference in helping people in the workforce improve their skills and abilities.

With knowledge such as this, poverty science is changing the way organizations are addressing poverty by providing scientific evidence for and against different poverty-reduction initiatives. Though the field is still young, its discoveries seem likely to help us more efficiently design and fund efforts aimed at reducing poverty.

10.3 A Business Response to Poverty

LEARNING OBJECTIVE

Compare traditional approaches and business solutions to poverty.

Operating in both poor and rich countries presents opportunities and constraints for multinational companies. In many developing countries, governments are skeptical of foreign companies' intentions. Foreign companies often have (and sometimes deserve) a reputation for entering a new market simply to extract resources and profits, then sending the money back to their home-country headquarters.

The Poor as a Social Responsibility

corporate social responsibility (CSR) a form of corporate self-regulation used to further some social good beyond the requirements of law

To alleviate some of this concern and to proactively do good in the world, many companies have developed a **corporate social responsibility (CSR)** approach to doing business. CSR is a form of corporate self-regulation used to further some social good beyond the requirements of law. Such policies are created for many reasons, but if used strategically, they can have beneficial effects on both poverty alleviation and the firm's performance.

While trade-offs may exist between social goals and short-term profitability, long-term gains generally occur when companies are socially responsible. In fact, research has shown that managers can choose the right level of CSR to maximize long-term profitability; to do so they need to conduct a cost-benefit analysis in the same way they would for any other investment.[16] For example, avoidable tragedies like the Rana Plaza textile building collapse in Bangladesh have caused companies to think more about improving the lives and working conditions of their suppliers' employees. This is responsible, and it also makes sense strategically. Gone are the days when companies could be concerned only about their shareholders and employees.

Drug companies, for instance, are increasingly pricing life-saving drugs lower in developing countries. Traditionally, these firms developed drugs in a few research locations and then sold them throughout the world at the same price. They want to be paid for their time and investment, which can run to $1 billion and 15 years of research and development effort. However, many developing-country governments have pushed back against the high prices charged for drugs and vaccines—often the very ones most needed in their markets. As a result, companies like GlaxoSmithKline are offering to poorer countries tiered pricing for vaccines. *Tiered pricing* sets the price in proportion to the income levels in the countries where the drug is sold. For example, a typical consumer in the United States might pay $200 for a polio vaccine, whereas that same vaccine is priced at $20 or even $2 in a developing country.

The Poor as Profitable Clients

If you ask around, you will find few people in the United States who will pick up a penny from the street. Increase the amount to a nickel, and a few more will say yes. At a quarter, nearly half will bend down. When you get to a $5 bill, most people will gladly pick it up, even from a dirty snowbank. The same is true for most U.S. companies: They are unwilling and sometimes unable to cost-effectively pick up "small change" and instead cover the globe looking for figurative $5 bills (or higher).

Still, some companies are realizing they could make huge profits by picking up pennies. For instance, Bharti Airtel, which primarily does business in India, is one of the world's largest telecommunications companies, but it was nearly bankrupt in 2001. Airtel's business model from 1999 to 2001, like that of most of its competitors, had been focused on increasing the average revenue per user. This means the company looked for clients who were likely to spend more than the average of $50 per month on telecom services, and then it recruited them as customers. However, because all of Airtel's competitors were also focused on these same customers, competition was intense, and the costs of providing service were also high.

In 2001, nearly bankrupt because of high costs and low revenue, Airtel realized it was fighting too hard for too small a market and developed a new strategy focused on its total revenue. In this way the company could add any customer it could profitably serve—and it wanted to serve them all—which meant it had to significantly lower costs. To do that, Airtel outsourced most of its support functions, including technology, sales, and service, and switched focus to acquiring any customer it could. The results have been dramatic.

The company now has an average revenue per user of just $6 per month (far shy of the $50 it used to target), but it has been making large profits and expanding to other markets, particularly in Africa, that companies have historically avoided—"walking past pennies," so to speak.

Airtel provides just one example of how companies can effectively work with poor clients and do so profitably. The transition required reorganization, a shift in strategic focus, and the development of new employees' skills, but the results speak for themselves. Some of the world's fastest-growing companies have figured this out. The key requirement is to recognize the pennies that others are walking past and figure out how to gather them profitably.

Base of the Pyramid Strategies

We can conceptually divide the world population into segments based on the amount of income received each day. As you can see in **Figure 10.6**, roughly 1 billion people—the very poor—live on less than $2 a day. Businesses have difficulty operating at this level because most activity in this segment is humanitarian. The next segment, which lives on $2–10 a day, accounts for about 3 billion people, who collectively make up a $5 trillion market. These two groups are often called "the base of the pyramid." Two other segments, those who make between $10 and 60 a day and those who make more, constitute a $12.5 trillion market that is well served by many companies' products and services. However, little competition occurs at the base of the pyramid; these markets are difficult to access, difficult to serve, and difficult to develop profitable products and services for.

Picking up pennies efficiently and profitably requires innovations and efficiencies that enable a company to deliberately target the **base of the pyramid (BOP)** (Figure 10.6). The BOP (represented in yellow in the figure) is the largest but poorest socioeconomic group in the global economy and consists of 4 billion people who survive on less than $10 a day.[17] They often live in rural areas largely unserved by companies. This means there is little competition for these potential clients. By focusing on the poor as clients—rather than as victims in need of handouts—profit-seeking companies can play a larger role in alleviating poverty and can make significant profits in the process. However, serving the BOP market often requires a major shift in the way a company thinks about business. For example, it needs to focus on overall revenues (pennies) rather than on revenues per unit sold (dollars).

base of the pyramid (BOP) the largest but poorest socio-economic group in the global economy

Another and very obvious shift is to acquire a much deeper understanding of the poor and their living and working conditions: How do they make purchases? What are their preferences? To understand the poor and meet their needs as clients, companies must view them as partners with capabilities and insight that can be capitalized on. This means ensuring personal contact

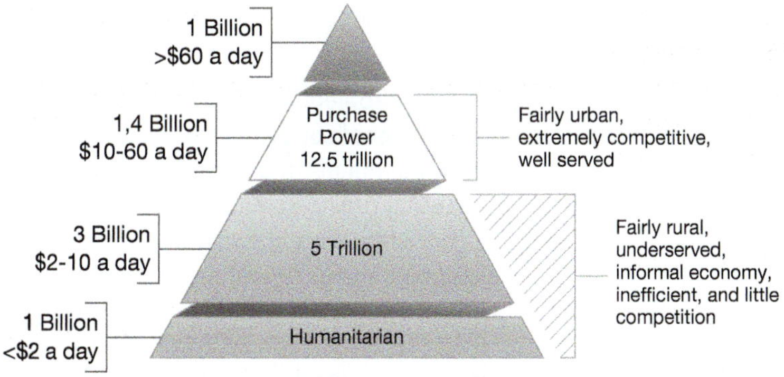

FIGURE 10.6 **Market opportunities based on the income pyramid** Most products and services are targeted to the blue section at the very top of the income pyramid. Companies have also started focusing on white section as well. However, the majority of the world's population represents over $5 trillion of consumption potential. **Source:** Adapted from World Economic Forum 2014 Sketches. https://www.flickr.com/photos/worldeconomicforum/2892099522/in/set-72157607529973530/

between the community and company representatives, which in turn calls for highly decentralized decision making and incentives for employees who collaborate with local community, government, and social enterprises.

For example, when Unilever sought to build successful operations in BOP markets in rural India, the company took a team of top leaders and dropped them into a rural Indian village for over a month. Their goal was to learn what the environment is like, to understand what it means to live in an environment without infrastructure and what it is to have little money and even fewer products to buy. The team learned a great deal and built—from the ground up—a new distribution approach that centered on the women of the village. The results have been exceptional.[18]

In addition to a deep, personal understanding of how the poor live and work, companies often need to increase their ability to quickly access and combine ideas already in place elsewhere within their organizations. Ironically, providing valuable services to the poor requires combining local knowledge of the problem with knowledge from technologies, designs, and systems outside the local context. Consulting others within the organization but outside the local context helps local representatives understand valuable principles behind company products, services, or systems that may produce an innovative solution to a problem the local market has not been able to solve. As a result, when company representatives expand their reach to include others in geographically distant locations, they increase their chances of finding relevant and valid information that can improve their own solutions.

For example, while working on a project in Serbia with the International Finance Corporation of the World Bank, one of the authors of this text turned to some colleagues in China and Ukraine to help develop a better product for the client. Research has found that subsidiary operations in a particular country are better able to meet the needs of the poor, particularly in emerging markets, when they turn to other teams outside that country for advice. While the local contexts differ across countries, many elements of the problems the poor face are consistent across borders.[19]

Global knowledge often provides novel and better solutions to local problems than can be implemented within a local context. For example, we interviewed a project leader from a company focused on emerging markets. Her team has effectively accessed knowledge from foreign units in different countries: "Here in India we took lessons from Chad and from Azerbaijan. We directly turned to people who were involved in earlier projects to be involved in this new project. So from India we pulled in [particular project members] from the [given] project so they could help us in our talks to the client and help brainstorm on what is a good approach in this environment based on their experience."

However, as attractive as it sounds to lift the poor out of poverty while making money, few companies have been successful in doing so. Part of the problem is developing a decentralized organization with strong local expertise, and then pairing that organization with a highly efficient way to come up with innovative solutions that can be marketed to populations large enough to generate overall profit.

For instance, DuPont ran into profitability problems with a venture it piloted from 2006 to 2008. DuPont's subsidiary Solae, a manufacturer of soy protein, operated in Andhra Pradesh, India. The goal of the project was to alleviate malnutrition and open a new market for the company by getting mothers in rural areas and urban slums to cook with soy protein as part of their daily routine. The product set consisted of small packets of protein isolate (which provided about half a woman's average daily protein needs) and a range of packaged, soy-fortified snack foods—all priced below 30 U.S. cents. The isolate's profit margins were on a level with those of Solae's core business-to-business products (which were good), but sales proved inconsistent. Sales were stronger for the snack foods but the margins were significantly lower—so low, in fact, that the company couldn't reach effective economies of scale in the limited available markets. Unable to see a path to profitability, Solae ultimately closed the pilot.[20] Such experiences prove the need to take specific precautions and ensure that your business model avoids traps related to BOP markets; **Figure 10.7** provides a list of these traps. For example, to sell to the poor requires different distribution channels than those used for top-of-the-pyramid markets.

Designing a Business Model to Profitably Sell to the Poor

To Cost of Capital Trap

To be sustainable in the long term, a business has to earn more profits than the opportunity cost of capital employed in the business. It is not enough to just cover operating costs.

The Unmet Needs Trap

The size of a market is determined by the number of people willing to pay a price for the product that is higher than the cost of producing the product, not by the number of people who need the product.

Affordability Trap

The poor can afford only low-priced products because they have very little purchasing power and many competing demands on their meager income.

Adaptability trap

It is usually necessary to reduce quality in order to significantly reduce costs; the challenge is to make the cost-quality trade-off acceptable to the poor. Starting with the product sold to affluent markets and adapting it to the poor often does not work.

Distribution Trap

Successful business models often piggyback on existing distribution networks and try to achieve economies of scope. Distribution networks to serve the poor often do not exist or are very inefficient.

Multiple Objective Trap

Successful ventures have a narrow focus on profitably selling beneficial products to the poor. Trying to serve multiple social objectives usually leads to failure.

FIGURE 10.7 **A business model to sell to the poor** When designing a business model for base-of-the-pyramid markets, businesses must take into account certain considerations (traps) that do not necessarily apply to the top of the pyramid. **Source:** Aneel Karnani, "Selling to the Poor," World Financial Review, December 28, 2010. http://www.worldfinancialreview.com/?p=2787.

Reverse Innovation

Product life-cycle theory suggests that international trade across countries follows a product's life cycle. New products are invented and exported to developed markets; then, as the product matures, production shifts overseas, and the export nation eventually becomes the import nation. Developed when innovation came almost entirely from developed markets, product life-cycle theory sees emerging markets as imitators, full of poor people who understandably want the rich person's product. But why would a rich person want a poor person's product?

When companies take innovations developed in emerging markets and repackage them for developed markets, the process is known as **reverse innovation**. Reverse innovation begins when a company focuses on the need to develop low-cost products and services for low-income populations in emerging markets. Once the goods have been developed, they are sold elsewhere—even to developed markets—often at significantly lower prices than in the countries where they were originally developed. Selling at low prices helps create new markets and capture market share, which can help fund additional innovations.[21]

reverse innovation the process of taking innovations developed in emerging markets and repackaging them for developed markets

Normal innovation for emerging markets typically starts as companies try to adapt their established products and services by removing more expensive, premium features in order to reduce the product's price. However, this approach is not a source of sustainable advantage for the company. In fact, "defeaturing" products usually makes them less valuable without sufficiently reducing the price to bring them within reach of the poor. In other words, this approach targets only the most affluent segments within an emerging market, if anyone. Reverse innovation, on the other hand, creates new products from the ground up to meet the specific needs of the poor. These products are unique because they have been developed, tested, and marketed in emerging markets first and then upgraded for sale and delivery in the developed world.[22]

Jeffrey Immelt, CEO of General Electric (GE), noted that in countries like India, only 10 percent of the population could afford medical devices that had been developed in the United States and sold elsewhere. That led GE to increase its understanding of the local context—with transformational results. The company soon developed a portable, battery-operated electrocardiograph that sold for $500—that's $19,500 less than the bulky machine made for the U.S. market. Given the dramatically different price but similar functionality, it made little sense for GE to continue selling its $20,000 machine. So the company made some adaptations, added some premium features, and started selling the new portable, battery-operated machine in the U.S. and other developed markets.

"Local companies in these markets are really smart," said innovation expert Vijay Govindarajan. "If you don't do it, they will do it. And if they do it, not only do you lose the market in China or India, but they can bring those products here."[23] To avoid being one-upped by emerging-market challengers, many multinationals have established research and development centers in BOP markets like India and China, with the aim of producing innovative products and services not only for these markets but for the whole world.

The Poor as Entrepreneurial Producers

In addition to lifting people out of poverty by making them better consumers, some businesses see opportunities to make money and move people out of poverty by making them better producers. Resource-constrained environments often make the poor entrepreneurial. Visiting Mumbai, India, you may be surprised to see children gathering sand from the beach and taking it to the road to be dried by the heat from the wheels of passing cars. The children then return to the slums to package the dry sand into packets made from discarded newspapers. They sell these sand packs to local women, who use them to scrub their dishes. This form of ingenuity comes from the necessity to create something out of almost nothing.

However, turning such entrepreneurial spirit into a country-changing force requires business training and financing for the would-be entrepreneurs. **Microfinance** is a source of financial services for entrepreneurs and small businesses lacking access to banking and entrepreneurial training. Global organizations such as Grameen Bank and Kiva Microfinance are taking banking to the poor. Traditionally, the poor have been considered "unbankable" because they have little to no collateral that a bank could take in the event of a loan default. However, leaders such as Nobel Prize winner Muhammad Yunus have worked to develop innovative business models that provide loans to the poor in a way that is both profitable and helpful, with minimal risk to the lender. One such model consists of giving loans to lending groups, rather than to individuals. This makes the entire group responsible, so members must help each other pay the loan back if someone cannot make a payment. Because people lack physical resources such as homes and cars, microfinanciers use social resources such as lending groups and peer pressure to ensure the loans are repaid.

microfinance a source of financial services for entrepreneurs and small businesses lacking access to banking and entrepreneurial training

Connecting financial capital with entrepreneurship leads to increased business opportunities for the poor. Research indicates that by taking a chance on an entrepreneur, microfinanciers give hope and ambition to those who before saw no way to improve their circumstances.[24] Moreover, lending groups act both as collateral for the microfinance company and as social networks for the entrepreneurs, giving them people to talk to for business advice, marketing, and partnering.[25]

Still, microfinance is not without its problems. Just giving a loan to someone does not always help that person get out of poverty. Because most businesses run by the truly poor barely make a profit, more working capital does not necessarily improve the results. Nor does it turn a mediocre business model into a great one. This explains why giving loans to poor entrepreneurs generally does not lead to a radical transformation in their lives. While still beneficial, microfinance does not provide a foolproof solution to poverty. Rather, it is one more piece in the puzzle of the potential solutions to poverty.

10.4 Doing Well and Doing Good

LEARNING OBJECTIVE

Describe ways that businesses can make money while also doing good.

While microfinance has led to a host of new businesses in emerging markets, an equally impressive—and possibly more powerful—change has been happening in developed markets. This change is in the core value proposition of many companies. Since the end of World War II, most companies have focused on maximizing shareholder value—earning profits and then delivering those profits back to shareholders of the company through stock dividends or stock price increases. This goal has been reinforced by laws that see leaders of public companies as "agents" responsible for increasing shareholders' wealth. One result is an organizational hyper-focus on taking actions that are most likely to increase shareholder value most quickly.

However, new legislation in many countries permits companies to have a dual focus of doing well—by making money and increasing shareholder value—and doing good, by engaging in activities that promote a positive social outcome such as alleviating poverty or reducing energy consumption and waste. One critical step in bringing about this change was the passage of laws in 32 countries (including the United States) that enable public companies to create a new type of legal entity called a **benefit corporation (B-Corp)**. More than 950 B-Corps in 60 industries are "working together toward one unifying goal: to redefine success in business."[26] B-corps differ from normal corporations in that they are explicitly organized with an additional focus beyond making money. B-Corps are required to report both their profits and their social goals. Log in to WileyPLUS to view a video that introduces the concept of B-Corps.

benefit corporation (B-Corp) a legal entity explicitly organized with an additional focus beyond making money

For instance, JustNeem is a body-care products company that uses the neem tree in all its products. JustNeem is "committed to sharing the benefits of Neem with West Africa. They purchase all of their Neem raw material from Mauritania, West Africa, using existing Neem trees and paying a fair market price for labor and goods. This helps create jobs and generates income for families living with few resources. Their goal is to keep your skin healthy while at the same time improve the lives of people in West Africa."[27] Log in to WileyPLUS to access a video about JustNeem, an example of a B-Corp that has a social and profit mission.

Patagonia is another B-corp, with a dual focus of making money and preserving wild and beautiful places. The company donates time, services, and at least 1 percent of sales to hundreds of grassroots environmental groups all over the world that are working to help make the planet healthier. The company's specific focus is to "build the best product, cause no unnecessary harm, [and] use business to inspire and implement solutions to the environmental crisis." At least 75 percent of materials used in Patagonia's products are "environmentally preferred (organic, recycled, etc) and 30 percent of suppliers meet bluesign® standards for environmentally advanced apparel manufacturing."[28]

Finally, ¡Échale! a Tu Casa is a Mexico-based B-Corp focused on social housing production. Its goal is to "deliver affordable homes to communities through the implementation of innovations in construction, technology and finance." Échale's model focuses on helping individuals build their own homes. The company estimates a total housing deficit worldwide of more than 400 million homes. Many of the world's poor build their own homes, but the process is difficult because of high costs and limited financing. Échale's objective is to stop the "vicious cycle by correcting the flaws inherent to the self-build process, thus allowing it to deliver returns on economic, social, and environmental levels."[29] To do so the company helps families build their own homes and in the process seeks to strengthen communities and enable families to create wealth.

In addition to the B-Corp, other new institutional forms are emerging that highlight and even reward the good that companies are doing, encouraging more to follow suit. For instance, Standard and Poor's and the International Finance Corporation of the World Bank provide a **green index** of businesses in emerging markets that allows investors to track the companies' carbon use. The goal is to increase the transparency of corporate environmental policies and drive more than $1 billion in investments to those that are more carbon-efficient. Other "green" indexes enable investors to find and invest in companies that are more efficient or produce

green index an index that allows investors to track a company's carbon use

cleaner energy, build more efficient transportation, reduce water use, utilize greener building technologies, or engage in sustainable farming and forestry.

Individual companies are also creating indexes of their own. For instance, Timberland, the outdoor shoe and apparel maker, has created a green index to measure all its products on a scale of 0 to 10 (with 10 being the most resource-greedy). The scale is based on the product's impact on the climate, the chemicals used during manufacturing, and the resources used in production. Timberland's objective is not only to make the impact of its apparel manufacture transparent but also to encourage others to join in.

This trend among global companies is increasing as they seek to reduce poverty and win customers. Individuals can have a significant impact on global companies by rewarding those who are actively engaged in efforts that seek to eliminate poverty. As companies, governments, and individuals come together, innovate, and create new opportunities, many people can move out of poverty, giving some hope that poverty can be eliminated. The United Nations reports that more than 1 billion people have moved out of extreme poverty, and the portion of undernourished people in developing countries has been cut in half since 1990.[30]

Summary and Case

Summary

LEARNING OBJECTIVE 10.1 Identify the causes and consequences of global poverty as they apply to international business.

Poverty is the general scarcity or lack of material possessions or money for consumption. If the poor are boosted beyond a certain threshold, they are able to become more productive and gain wealth. Focusing on poor markets can provide unique opportunities for companies to increase profitability and competitiveness, but there are risks.

LEARNING OBJECTIVE 10.2 Discuss traditional approaches to alleviating global poverty.

The traditional response to poverty is the distribution of foreign aid by government aid agencies, multilateral aid agencies, and nonprofit organizations. Educational institutions have recently begun studying aid distribution and effectiveness. Foreign aid can alleviate poverty, but, if not carefully implemented, it can also stifle innovation, encourage corruption at the government level, and cause dependence.

LEARNING OBJECTIVE 10.3 Compare traditional approaches and business solutions to poverty.

Businesses have traditionally played a role in alleviating poverty through corporate social responsibly (CSR) initiatives. But some companies have gone further and see the poor as clients or employees rather than victims. This strategy represents a base-of-the-pyramid (BOP) approach to doing business, which relies on scaling up low-cost strategies and learning new ways to tackle old problems. This knowledge can not only help in poor markets but also bring improved products back to developed markets in a process known as reverse innovation.

LEARNING OBJECTIVE 10.4 Describe ways that businesses can make money while also doing good.

B-Corporations present an alternative business model that promotes a dual focus on profitability and social good. Investors want not only to earn a return on investment but also to make a difference in the world. Because the B-Corp standards provide a framework for being both profitable and socially conscious, such companies are able to better serve their communities and be a force for change.

Case Study

Grameen Bank Considers Lending to the Non-Poor

Grameen Bank was founded in 1976 by economics professor Muhammad Yunus in Bangladesh. This private bank makes small loans, known as microcredit, to the poorest of the poor without requiring collateral. It was founded on the principle that loans interrupt poverty better than charity because loans offer people the opportunity to take the initiative in business or agriculture, generating earnings and enabling them to pay off debt. The bank and its founder were jointly awarded the Nobel Peace Prize in 2006.

After decades of operation, Grameen Bank faced a serious dilemma. Many of its borrowers had done well enough to become small businesses with employees and real physical assets, and at that point they needed more than a "micro" loan. The average loan offered by Grameen Bank was under $400. These businesses needed more like $4,000. As a profitable microcredit bank, Grameen could extend its existing products to include larger loans for small and medium-sized enterprises. This would not only enable the bank to grow with its existing clients; it would also help it move some of its clients to the next level of wealth creation.

Dr. Yunus pondered the issue. On the one hand, expanding the organization's objectives to include lending to small and medium-sized enterprises would fill a need and continue to help clients secure a better economic livelihood. It would also fill a gap underserved by traditional banks in the markets where Grameen operated. Moreover, including small and medium-sized enterprise loans in the bank's portfolio would likely increase profits.

On the other hand, to offer small- and medium-sized loans, Grameen Bank would have to switch to a business model completely different from its origins in microlending. This would mean adopting practices related to traditional banking and no longer focusing on lending only to the truly poor. Dr. Yunus realized that this decision required some additional insight.

Case Discussion Questions

1. Should Dr. Yunus expand the scope of Grameen Bank to provide small and medium-sized loans? Defend your answer.
2. How would lending to small- and medium-sized companies affect the way Grameen Bank is organized? Would the bank have to change its lending strategy? Would it have to change the expertise of its loan officers? How would the lending risks change?
3. What can other companies learn from Grameen about dealing with poverty?

Endnotes

[1]"International Comparisons of Hourly Compensation Costs in Manufacturing, 2012," Bureau of Labor Statistics, August 9, 2013. www.bls.gov/fls/ichcc.pdf.

[2]Paul Godfrey, *More Than Money: Five Forms of Capital to Create Wealth and* Eliminate *Poverty* (Stanford, CA: Stanford University Press, 2013).

[3]David Gordan, "Indicators of Poverty for Youth," University of Bristol, December 14, 2005. www.un.org/esa/socdev/unyin/documents/ydiDavidGordon_poverty.pdf (accessed May 27, 2011).

[4]Shaw, George Bernard. *Major Barbara* (London: Penguin, 2000, p. 87). http://public-library.uk/pdfs/7/738.pdf

[5]Matthew H. Bonds, Donald C. Keenan, Pejman Rohani, and Jeffrey D. Sachs, "Poverty Trap Formed By the Ecology of Infectious Diseases," *Proceedings of the Royal Society of London Series B* 277 (2010): 1185–92.

[6]Dipak Mazumdar, "The Marginal Productivity Theory of Wages and Disguised Unemployment," *Review of Economic Studies* 26, no. 3 (1959): 190–97; Debraj Ray, "Aspirations, Poverty, and Economic Change," in *Understanding Poverty*, ed. Abhijit Vinayak Banerjee, Roland Bénabou, and Dilip Mookherjee (Oxford: Oxford University Press, 2006), 409–21; Abhijit Banerjee and Esther Duflo, *Poor Economics: A Radical Rethinking of the Way to Fight Global Poverty* (New York: Public Affairs, 2012).

[7]Aneel Karnani, "Selling to the Poor," *World Financial Review*, December 28, 2010. http://www.worldfinancialreview.com/?p=2787.

[8]Dave Rodenbaugh, "The Outsourcing Low Cost Lie," Lessons of Failure blog, June 10, 2009. www.lessonsoffailure.com/companies/outsourcing-cost-lie/.

[9]Ravi Aron and Jitendra Singh. "Getting Offshoring Right." *Harvard Business Review*. December 2005. https://hbr.org/2005/12/getting-offshoring-right

[10]Wayne Visser, "Corporate Responsibility in a Developing Country," *Ethical Corporation*, issue 20, August 2003. www.waynevisser.com/wp-content/uploads/2012/07/article_myths_devcos_wvisser.pdf.

[11]Sarah Butler, "Benetton Agrees to Contribute to Rana Plaza Compensation Fund," *Guardian*, February 20, 2015 https://www.theguardian.com/business/2015/feb/20/benetton-agrees-contribute-rana-plaza-compensation-fund; Palash Kamruzzaman, "Industrial Accidents in Bangladesh Are Another Sign of Inequality," PhysOrg, September 22, 2016. https://phys.org/news/2016-09-industrial-accidents-bangladesh-inequality.html

[12]"The Butterfly Effect," *Economist*, October 31, 2013. www.economist.com.

[13]"We Can End Poverty: UN Millennium Development Goals and Beyond 2015," United Nations. www.un.org/millenniumgoals/poverty.shtml (accessed April 20, 2017).

[14]Jeffrey Sachs, *The End of Poverty: How We Can Make It Happen in Our Lifetime* (New York: Penguin, 2005).

[15]Dambisa Moyo, *Dead Aid: Why Aid Is Not Working and How There Is a Better Way for Africa* (New York: Farrar, Straus and Giroux, 2009).

[16]Andreas Wieland and Robert B. Handfield, "The Socially Responsible Supply Chain: An Imperative for Global Corporations," *Supply Chain Management Review* 17, no. 5 (2013): 22–29.

[17]World Bank. 2013. *The World Bank Annual Report 2013.* Washington, DC. © World Bank. https://openknowledge.worldbank.org/handle/10986/16091 License: CC BY 3.0 IGO. Accessed June 12, 2017.

[18]Alexa Roscoe, "Is Big Business Appropriating Social Enterprise?" November 17, 2013. https://alexaroscoe.com/2013/11/17/is-big-busness-appropriating-social-enterprise/

[19]Shad S. Morris, Bijuan Zhong, and Mona Makhija, "Going the Distance: The Pros and Cons of Expanding Employees' Global Knowledge Reach," *Journal of International Business Studies* 46, no. 5 (2015): 552–73.

[20]Erik Simanis, "Reality Check at the Bottom of the Pyramid," *Harvard Business Review*, June 2012, https://hbr.org.

[21]Vijay Govindarajan and Ravi Ramamurti, "Reverse Innovation, Emerging Markets, and Global Strategy," *Global Strategy Journal* 1, nos. 3–4 (2011): 191–205.

[22]Vijay Govindarajan and Chris Trimble, *Reverse Innovation: Create Far from Home, Win Everywhere* (Cambridge, MA: Harvard Business School Publishing, 2013).

[23]Natalie Zmuda, "P&G, Levi's, GE Innovate by Thinking in Reverse: Marketers Are Increasingly Creating Products in the Developing World and Importing Those Ideas Into More Mature Markets," June 13,

2011. http://adage.com/article/global-news/p-g-levi-s-ge-innovate-thinking-reverse/228146/.

[24]Abhijit Banerjee and Esther Duflo, *Poor Economics: A Radical Rethinking of the Way to Fight Global Poverty* (New York: Public Affairs, 2012).

[25]Shad S. Morris, Warner P. Woodworth, and Shon R. Hiatt, "The Value of Networks in Enterprise Development: Case Studies in Eastern Europe and Southeast Asia," *Journal of Developmental Entrepreneurship* 11, no. 4 (2006): 345–56.

[26]Kenneth Lander. "What Do Third-Party Certifications Reveal About Your Brand?" *Sustainable Brands*. March 14, 2017. http://www.sustainablebrands.com/news_and_views/collaboration/kenneth_lander/what_do_third-party_certifications_reveal_about_your_bra

[27]JustNeem Named Among "Best for the World" B Corp. April 26, 2017. https://www.justneem.com/justneem-named-among-best-for-the-world-b-corp-2/.

[28]Patagonia Environmental and Social Initiatives, 2015. Page 30. Accessed June 12, 2017. http://www.patagonia.com/on/demandware.static/Sites-patagonia-us-Site/Library-Sites-PatagoniaShared/en_US/PDF-US/patagonia-enviro-initiatives-2015.pdf

[29]Anne Field. 92 "Best for the World" B Corps. *Forbes.* March 19, 2014. https://www.forbes.com/sites/annefield/2014/03/19/new-list-reveals-92-b-corps-with-the-most-impact/#424665974073

[30]"We Can End Poverty," United Nations. http://www.un.org/millenniumgoals/ accessed June 12, 2017.

Technological Change and Infrastructure

simonkr/Getty Images

Introduction

In response to RCA's introduction of the television at the World's Fair in New York in 1939, the *New York Times* reported on the future of the television. The newspaper noted, "Television will never be a serious competitor for radio, because people must sit and keep their eyes glued on a screen; the average American family hasn't time for it."[1] People have obviously found the time for television—and for many other activities that glue eyes to screens. The *New York Times* underestimated the role of TV and screens in the future economy—a role still unfolding.

In the postwar boom of the 1950s, economists such as Moses Abramovitz and Robert Solow sought to understand which stimulus contributed more to economic growth—adding labor and capital, or advancing technology. They discovered that the addition of labor and capital could explain only about 15 percent of growth. The rest must result from the advancement of technology, which fuels massive economic growth and thereby generates abundant opportunities for international businesses.[2] We have since come to understand that technology is also a disruptive force that can both create and eliminate entire industries. In the world of television, for instance, the global market for TV sets has grown to over $110 billion.[3]

Successful global leaders understand how technology opens (or limits) opportunities in international markets. In the PEST acronym, the T, for *technology*, indicates the prominence of technology and its impact on international business. We introduce in this chapter a framework that identifies changes in technological infrastructure and in the structures and facilities that support business. These changes can occur in the physical infrastructure (the hardware), the information infrastructure (the software), and the human capital infrastructure (the "brainware") of a country. Using this framework helps global business leaders assess the level of technology in a country and understand how changes to that level are likely to affect international business opportunities. The ultimate goal is to understand how leaders can capitalize on changes in technology across industries such as agriculture, medical, textiles, manufacturing, sanitation, and energy, just to name a few.

LEARNING OBJECTIVES

After exploring this chapter you will be able to:

1. **Assess** the impact of physical infrastructure on international business opportunities
2. **Identify** the way information infrastructure creates business opportunities
3. **Describe** the effect of human capital on opportunities in a global business
4. **Discuss** how global business leaders position their firms to take advantage of technological opportunities

11.1 Technology as Physical Infrastructure

LEARNING OBJECTIVE

Assess the impact of physical infrastructure on international business opportunities

Beginning with the inventions of the wheel, irrigation, and writing, technological improvements have been responsible for countless changes to the way we live and trade. For global business leaders, knowing how to understand, evaluate, and harness technological trends at the global and country levels is an increasingly important skill. In this chapter, we introduce a framework to help you understand the impact of technology and technological changes on the global enterprise and how global leaders can capitalize on these opportunities. This framework consists of physical infrastructure, information infrastructure, and human infrastructure (see **Figure 11.1**).

International businesses must consider an important factor: the level of physical infrastructure present in a given country. Countries with low levels of physical infrastructure may be less attractive to international businesses because producing and distributing goods and services are often difficult. Countries with high levels of physical infrastructure, however, present fewer challenges for international businesses.

The physical infrastructure includes elements such as the availability of raw materials like plastics, metals, and minerals; the availability of machinery and equipment like weaving looms for textiles, precision weighing and mixing equipment for pharmaceuticals, and metal stamping and welding equipment for automobiles; transportation networks that enable goods to move between producers and customers; and the energy resources that provide power to producers and consumers alike. Key questions for assessing the physical infrastructure are shown in Figure 11.1.

For instance, when Hindustan Unilever—a global seller of soaps, shampoos, and lotions—sought to move from urban cities to rural towns in India, it quickly recognized a problem. Competition was fierce in urban India, but while the country had over a billion potential customers, getting products to the half who lived in rural villages would be exceptionally challenging because of the country's undeveloped physical infrastructure. The lack of roads made transportation burdensome, the very small number of large retail stores made distribution channels difficult to establish, and a general lack of information made monitoring the distribution process nearly impossible.[4]

In assessing the physical infrastructure of a market, global leaders need to consider a host of factors, including access to raw materials, manufacturing capabilities and techniques, transportation networks, and energy resources.

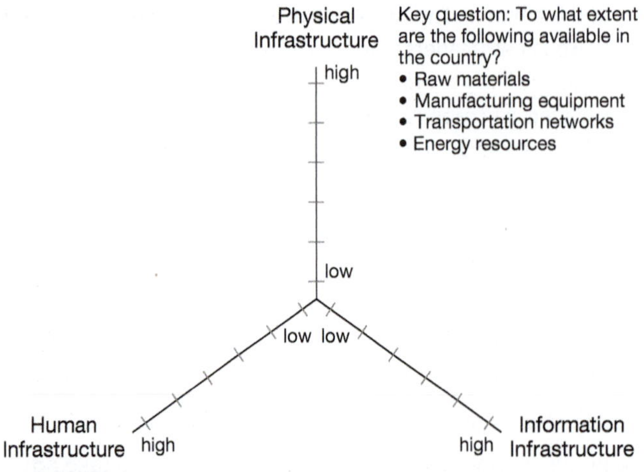

FIGURE 11.1 Assessing the level of physical infrastructure
Physical Infrastructure includes raw materials, manufacturing equipment, transportation networks, and energy resources.

Raw Materials

Raw materials are the basic materials from which goods and components of goods are made. While many raw materials are abundant around the globe—such as the elements oxygen, silicone, aluminum, and iron—others are rare enough that companies' needs for them can influence global business decisions. For instance, many of today's batteries are lithium-ion batteries. Bolivia and Chile control nearly half the world's supply of lithium.[5] This means foreign companies may struggle to gain access to an ample supply. They may not need to move to Chile or Bolivia, but managers of international companies should certainly build healthy trade relationships with Chilean and Bolivian suppliers and governmental officials.

raw materials the basic materials from which goods are made

Often, governments will use access to raw materials as a source of advantage for their domestic companies.[6] For instance, a RAND Corporation report[7] suggests that China, which controls nearly 90 percent of the world's rare earth elements, charges global electronics firms much higher prices than what domestic Chinese competitors pay for rare earth elements such as lanthanum and cerium, which are often used in electronics (see **Table 11.1**). As a result, Chinese electronics firms may have a significant cost advantage in addition to preferred access to critical elements. In addition, China's near monopoly has forced other countries to develop alternative approaches that work around the requirements for some elements. For instance, when China cut off sales of rare earth elements to Japan in 2010 during a spat over the fate of Chinese fishermen who were caught fishing in Japanese waters, Japan, among other nations, began seriously investing in finding alternative materials that could substitute for rare earth metals.[8]

Manufacturing Equipment

In the past decade, the advances of new manufacturing equipment and techniques have changed many global industries. For instance, horizontal drilling allows vertical wells to twist and turn horizontally for over a mile underground. Coupled with hydraulic fracturing (in which a high-pressure solution is pumped into a well to crack the rock and release nearby pockets of hydrocarbons), this technique has increased production of natural gas from shale gas to more than eight times the rate of any earlier technologies.[9] This capability reduces the bargaining power of OPEC producers, significantly altering the global oil and gas industry. This is just one example of how new technologies can overturn commonly held beliefs in any sector, even manufacturing.

Another manufacturing innovation with a dramatic impact on global business is the creation of global manufacturing clusters,[10] which concentrate suppliers and producers of a given industry in the same geographic location.[11] This proximity facilitates the free flow of ideas, people, and resources between firms and for well-designed hubs often results in global dominance. For instance, in Silicon Valley, tech firms cluster together, attracting talent, investors, and ideas from around the world.[12] Similarly, Italy is the world's center for leather craft[13] and high-end automobiles.[14] France is the center of the fashion industry. South Africa is the center of the

TABLE 11.1 China's Two-Tiered Pricing of Rare Earth Elements

Material	International Prices (USD/kg)	Chinese Domestic Prices (USD/kg)
Lanthanum	66.46	18.28
Cerium	59.31	20.65
Neodymium	244.23	122.76
Praseodymium	209.62	106.94
Samarium	95.31	14.48
Dysprosium	2032.31	1085.35
Europium	3800.00	2228.38
Terbium	2973.85	1767.93

Source: Richard Silberglitt et al., "Critical Materials: Present Danger to U.S. Manufacturing," RAND National Defense Research Institute, 2013, www.rand.org/content/dam/rand/pubs/research_reports/RR100/RR133/RAND_RR133.pdf.

world's mining industries. China is the center of the world's garment industry.[15] No rules exist that require new businesses to locate near the existing ones in their industry, but new entrants are still likely to benefit from proximity to them.

Transportation Networks

Transportation technologies play a vital role in the success of international businesses. Transportation, whether between production facilities or from supplier to customer, relies on a network that links shipping, air, rail, and road; in the not-too-distant future it may even include delivery drones.

Ships Perhaps the most important technological advancement in the transportation industry in the past twenty years has been the invention of the standardized shipping container. With ports, shippers, and transportation companies all agreeing to standard twenty-foot and forty-foot designs, ships, trains, and trucks can be loaded and unloaded quickly using standardized equipment.[16]

Maersk Line is the world's largest transporter of shipping containers today. It ships goods to and from 115 countries using 600 container vessels. That may not seem like much, but container ships are huge.[17] In 2014, the company introduced the Triple-E (**Figure 11.2**), the world's largest container ship, which carries 18,000 shipping containers.[18] To put that in perspective, if those containers were lined up end to end, they would stretch for sixty miles. Standardization of shipping containers has enabled this kind of specialized ship, which in turn has increased efficiency and reduced costs in the shipping industry.[19]

Sea Ports and Canals. Like ships, ports have grown dramatically to keep pace with the demands of global shipping. Shanghai, China, is the world's busiest port, handling the equivalent of more than 15 million forty-foot containers per year. China exports so many goods that it is responsible for six of the ten busiest ports in the world. What does this mean for international businesses? China's investment in transportation makes it relatively easy for global firms to manufacture in China and ship to other markets[20] and for Chinese businesses to export their products abroad.[21]

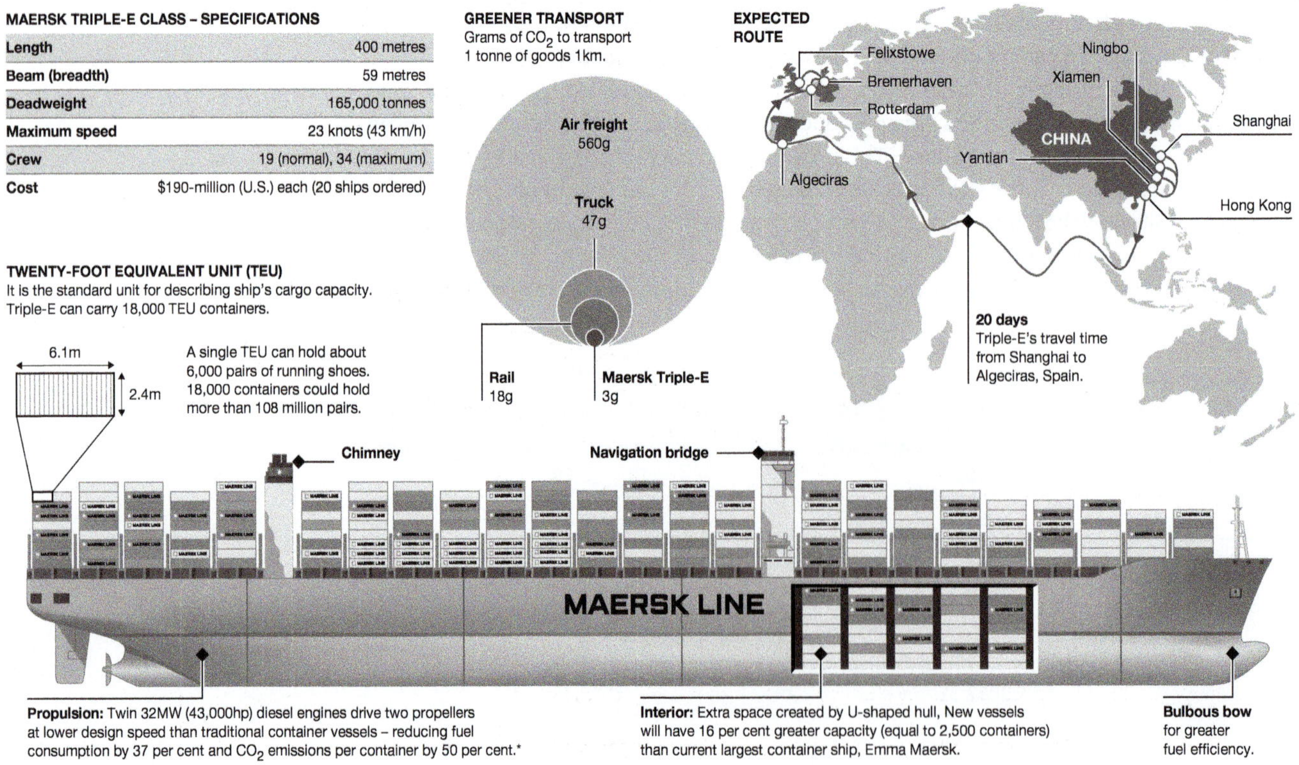

FIGURE 11.2 Maersk's Triple-E The world's largest container ship boasts improved fuel efficiency, reduced emissions, and enormous size. **Source:** Vitron Trading Ltd. 2017. www.vesseltracking.net/wp-content/uploads/2015/12/final_maersk.jpg

Air Transport Major technological changes have increased the safety and efficiency of air transportation and air travel; these changes have led to reductions in their cost.[22] The World Bank estimates that the number of air passengers worldwide has increased from around 300,000 per year in 1970 to over 3.4 billion per year in 2015,[23] equating to more than 6 billion passenger-kilometers, or the number of kilometers flown multiplied by the number of passengers on the planes. The relative ease of travel has increased foreign business travel and foreign vacations, but perhaps more important, it has also increased the ease of shipping goods as air cargo (see **Figure 11.3**).[24] With the rise of several global e-commerce sites like Alibaba.com and Amazon.com, international air cargo is set to grow quickly because nearly a third of all e-commerce is from foreign customers who buy goods abroad and have them shipped to their home market.[25]

Rail and Roads Shipping by sea is cheap but slow and limited to coastal ports. Air freight is fast but expensive and limited to regions with established airports. Ground transportation bridges the gap between the two: trucks and trains take the containers shipped over the oceans and move them inland, where much of the world's population lives. In addition, many overland routes exist between countries like Mexico and the United States or Germany and Turkey, and these are best traveled by truck and/or train.

Overall, the combination of improvements in shipping, ports, air, rail, and roads has made much of the world more easily and quickly accessible. As **Figure 11.4** shows, a few areas are still remote—like the Arctic tundra, the Amazon basin, the Sahara, the Tibetan plateau, Antarctica, and Siberia—but thanks to advanced physical infrastructure, it is fairly easy to ship goods to most of the rest of the world.

Energy Resources

During a recent visit to an electronics manufacturer in Delhi, India, a U.S. consultant observed the power go out. The lights flickered for a moment, then an alternative power generator kicked in, and the lights hummed back on. Such events are common, and no one else even seemed to notice. Unfortunately, the next building over had no backup power, and it remained dark until the power was restored.[26] Power outages are common in India and other developing markets. In India, businesses lose more than a third of their data because of power outages, and as a result most companies in emerging markets like India must maintain contingency plans for power failures, including backup generators and backup data recovery operations.[27]

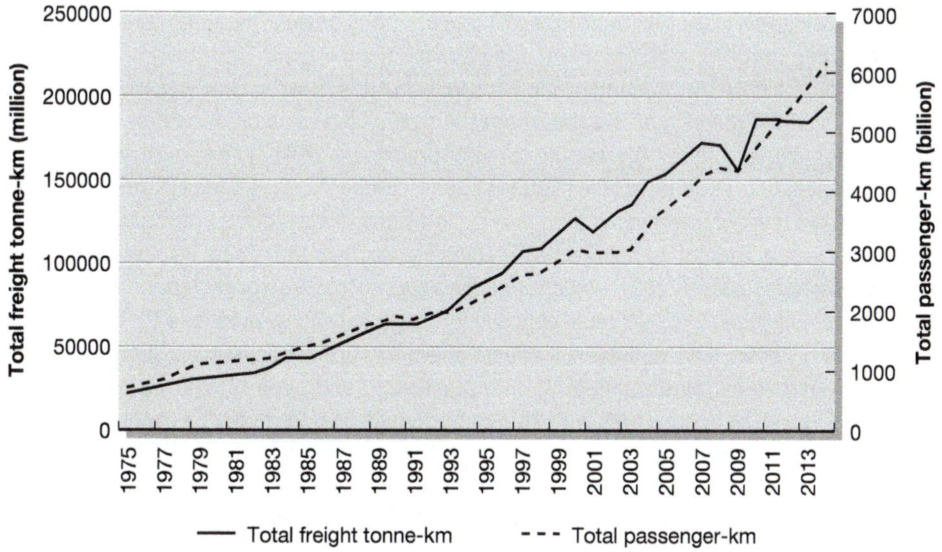

FIGURE 11.3 **The rapid growth of air travel and air cargo from 1975 to 2014**

Source: Franziska Kupfer et al., "The Underlying Drivers and Future Development of Air Cargo," Journal of Air Transport Management 61 (June 2017): 6–14, www.sciencedirect.com/science/article/pii/S0969699715301678.

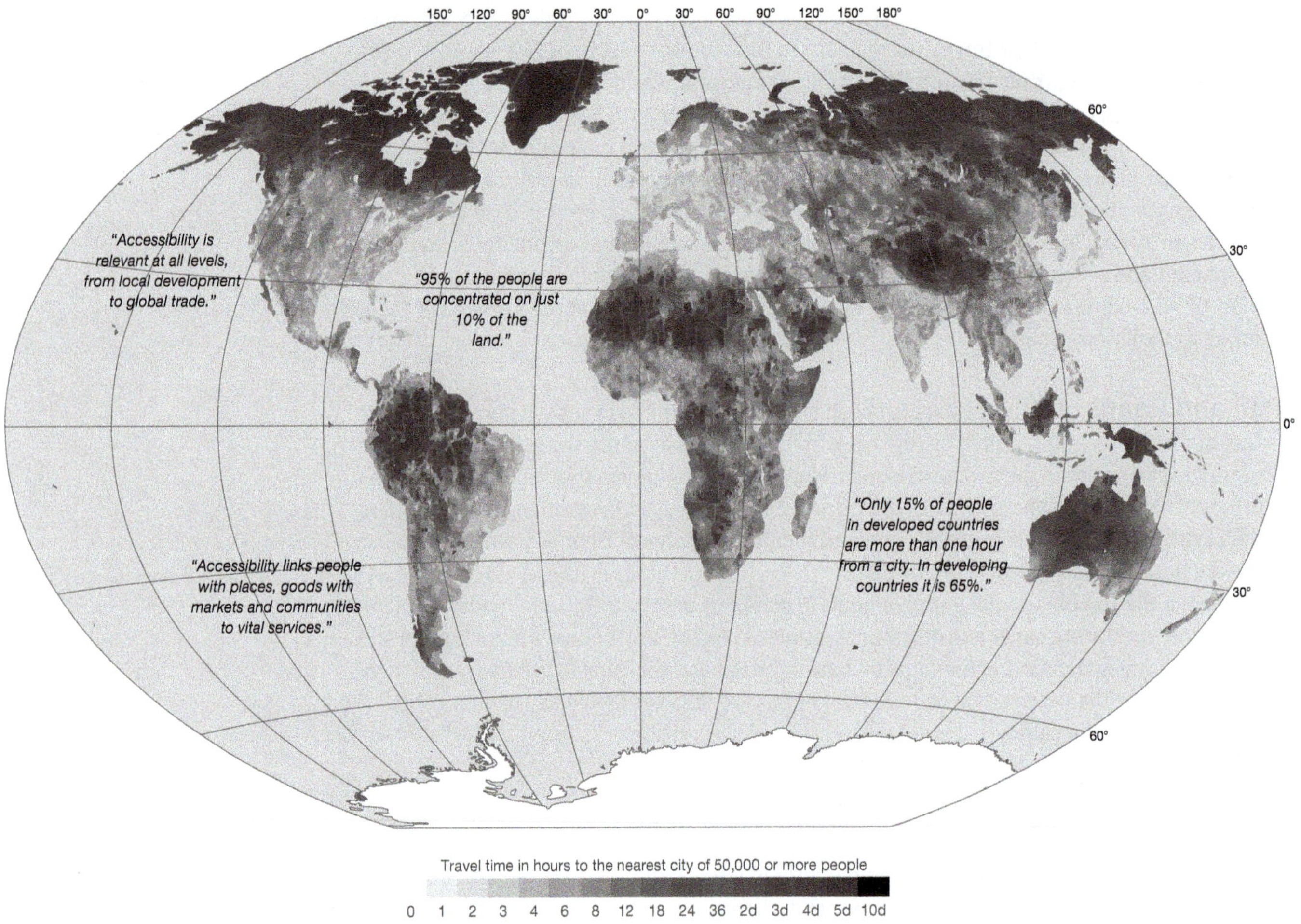

150° 120° 90° 60° 30° 0° 30° 60° 90° 120° 150° 180°
60°
30°
0°
30°
60°
"Accessibility is relevant at all levels, from local development to global trade."
"95% of the people are concentrated on just 10% of the land."
"Only 15% of people in developed countries are more than one hour from a city. In developing countries it is 65%."
"Accessibility links people with places, goods with markets and communities to vital services."
Travel time in hours to the nearest city of 50,000 or more people
0 1 2 3 4 6 8 12 18 24 36 2d 3d 4d 5d 10d

FIGURE 11.4 **Accessibility of the world's major cities** **Source:** *European Commission, Joint Research Centre.* http://forobs.jrc.ec.europa.eu/products/gam/download/accessibility.png.

Production of Power Beijing and other areas of northern China are often blanketed in thick smog from both cars and factories as well as from coal-fired power plants.[28] China's energy needs have increased from just 7 percent of the world's power consumption in 1973 to 22 percent in 2013.[29] The country produces over 45 percent of the world's coal supply and imports even more, using this fossil fuel to produce 75 percent of its power.[30] Beijing citizens are angry about the smog that frequently blankets the city (see **Figure 11.5**), and the government has tried to lessen the haze by reducing traffic and even shutting down businesses when pollution levels are high.[31] Estimates indicate that more than 100,000 people died in China in 2013 as a result of smog, making it the fifth-leading cause of premature death in the country.[32]

As a result of China's smog problem, global energy companies have seen a dramatic increase in the country's level of interest in clean energy solutions. Today, power production in China needs to be clean in addition to being reliable. GE Energy expects that China will double its use of renewable energy sources by 2021—which could be a big win for GE's world-class wind and hydroelectric power products. The shift could also help other global energy providers.[33]

High energy costs have substantial effects on international businesses. Energy-intensive industries—such as aluminum smelting, manufacturing, and even bitcoin mining—gain an advantage by locating in countries with cheaper energy costs. Germany has average electricity costs of $0.19 per kilowatt hour, much higher than the $0.10 in the United States or the $0.07 price in Sweden. In fact, a recent reduction of industrial electricity costs in the United States has led some U.S. companies to bring their manufacturing operations back home. GE recently moved its manufacturing facilities for household appliances such as washing machines, fridges, and heaters from China to Kentucky, partly because energy costs in the state are so low.[34]

Kevin Frayer/Getty Images

FIGURE 11.5 **Smog in Beijing** The view from the same location in Beijing in photos taken less than three months apart: the one on the left was taken September 27, 2015, and the one on the right was taken December 1, 2015.

The production of power is a global business. Emerging markets like Vietnam are seeking foreign investment in power production. For instance, the Japanese firm Orix recently joined Singapore's United Overseas Bank to buy a 10 percent stake in Vietnam's Bitexco power company. Vietnam plans to invest nearly $150 billion in energy projects in the next 16 years.[35] But even developed countries often rely on foreign investment to build power infrastructure. The United Kingdom just agreed to have a consortium of French and Chinese investment companies build a $24 billion nuclear power plant at Hinkley Point in southern England.[36]

Power Distribution and Storage

Electricity distribution and storage also have important implications for global companies. Many companies are looking for ways to store electricity production during off-peak times in order to provide it to customers during periods of peak demand. For instance, the city of Los Angeles, California, is planning a huge battery farm to soak up solar power produced during the daily hours of peak sunshine that is not needed until people return home in the evenings. The system involves planned use of 18,000 lithium-ion batteries, each strong enough to power a car, to provide power during periods of peak demand, enabling conventional generation methods to function at their most efficient levels rather than try to scale up or down with the fluctuation in demand.[37]

Some companies, such as AES Corporation and Tesla, are working on solutions that enable power to be produced, stored, and used on site (**Figure 11.6**). The idea is for a home to produce

petrmalinak/Shutterstock

FIGURE 11.6 **Is that battery art?** In the future, energy will likely be produced by individual homes, dramatically decreasing the need for grid energy systems.

enough power to meet the needs of the occupants, storing it during peak production and making it available during peak usage times. Power produced on site would have the added benefit of reducing the need for the massive energy infrastructure that currently transports power over the 300,000 miles of high-voltage and transmission lines within the United States.[38] For example, nearly $283 billion is spent each year on both new lines and replacements for existing grid systems.[39] Local household production of power could eliminate much of the vast system of electrical transmission lines in the United States.

11.2 Technology of Information Infrastructure

LEARNING OBJECTIVE

Identify the way information infrastructure creates business opportunities.

WileyPLUS

See Whiteboard Video: Technology Infrastructure

UPS estimates that it saves nearly 1 million gallons of gas each year across North America just by using mapping technology that minimizes left turns (drivers turning left risk being delayed by oncoming traffic). The mapping system has also eliminated millions of miles of travel by matching packages, delivery times, and truck locations in order to optimize routes and maximize delivery densities.[40] By tracking this data in real time and running complex analytics, the firm is able to improve efficiency, thereby saving time and money. Digital technologies make this possible (see **Figure 11.7**).

In a similar way, the country Estonia uses digital technology to run many government operations. Estonia began the process of digitizing its operations in 1997. The system now enables citizens to register vehicles, file health insurance claims, and even vote, all through an electronic platform called X-Road. The system is so successful that over 900 agencies—some global, including energy, telecom, and banking—offer services through the site. Because of the boost in efficiency, the platform saves an estimated five days a year per citizen by eliminating trips to government offices by both citizens and businesses, which can access information such as land deeds. The efficiency of the system adds 7 million workdays to the Estonian economy.[41] For instance, in Estonia taxes can be filed in five minutes using prefilled, auto-generated reports; by contrast, most Germans hire tax consultants to help them fill out tax forms and spend hours on the process.[42]

Digital infrastructure like the Internet can also help international businesses improve their communication networks, data storage, and information processing, as we'll see next.

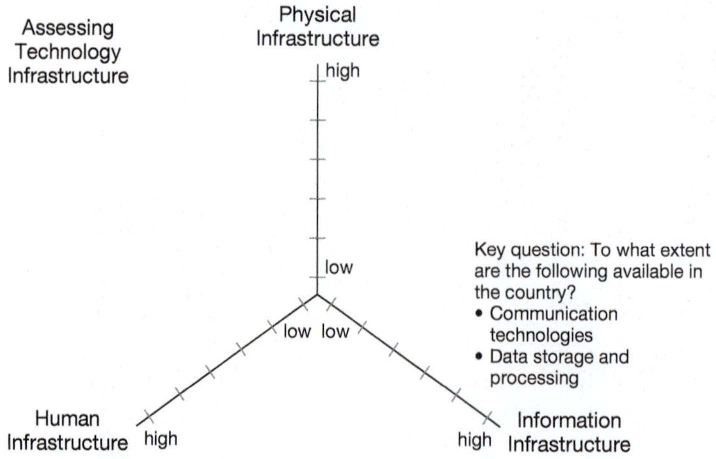

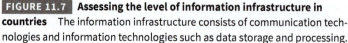

FIGURE 11.7 Assessing the level of information infrastructure in countries The information infrastructure consists of communication technologies and information technologies such as data storage and processing.

Communication Technologies

Changes in communication technologies can dramatically affect international business opportunities. For example, even in Brazil's poorest *favelas* (slums), satellite TV and even Internet access are nearly ubiquitous (**Figure 11.8**).[43] Because nearly all consumers have access to media, international companies like Samsung, LG, and Apple can market their electronics to global customers. Companies can launch products in new markets more quickly and efficiently when they can harness global media.

PABLO PORCIUNCULA/AFP/Getty Images

FIGURE 11.8 Satellite TV antennae on the houses of Brazil's poorest neighborhoods

Nearly 43 percent of people on the planet have access to the Internet. In the OECD countries, mobile broadband is used by more than 95% of the population. This is 1.27 billion people with access to the Internet. Japan has the highest level of access to the Internet of any country in the world, with close to 150 mobile broadband subscriptions per 100 people. In other words, almost half of the Japanese people have more than one broadband subscription. The numbers are almost as high in Finland as well (see **Figure 11.9**). The United States primarily relies on DSL and cable, whereas in Japan, fiber-optic networks dominate the country. There are now more than 7 billion cellular subscriptions worldwide—that is almost one for every man, woman, and child alive today—and 95 percent of the world's population is covered by a cellular network.[44]

This statistic highlights the need for international business managers to understand how such nearly universal connectivity affects them. In rural fishing villages in India, for instance, economists recorded the market price that fishermen received for their daily catch before and after the introduction of phones in three separate markets. Look at **Figure 11.10**; you can see on the left side of each chart that the price of the daily catch varied significantly up and down in each market. Once phones were introduced in these markets, fishermen were able to compare prices efficiently with other fishermen, and prices quickly converged (notice the large price discrepancies on the left side of each chart). That is, prices now varied within a much smaller

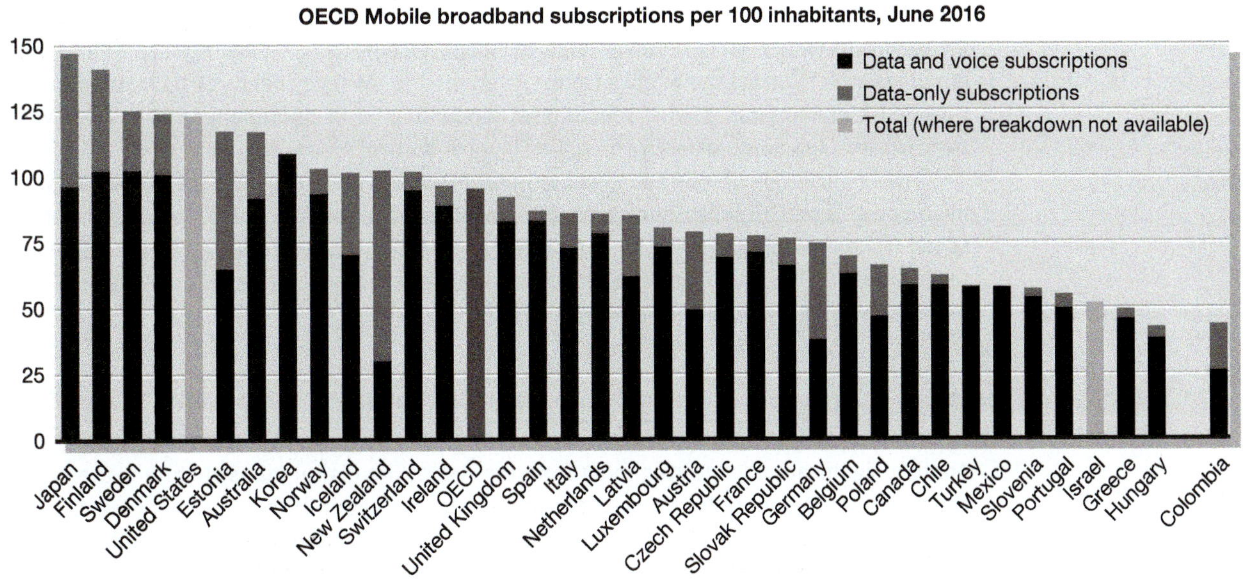

FIGURE 11.9 Mobile Broadband, by country, 2016 **Source:** Andrew Burger, February 2017, "OECD Mobile Broadband Penetration Rises to 95%, Now Reaches 1.2 Billion," Telecompetitor. http://www.telecompetitor.com/oecd-mobile-broadband-penetration-rises-to-95-percent-now-reaches-1-2-billion/

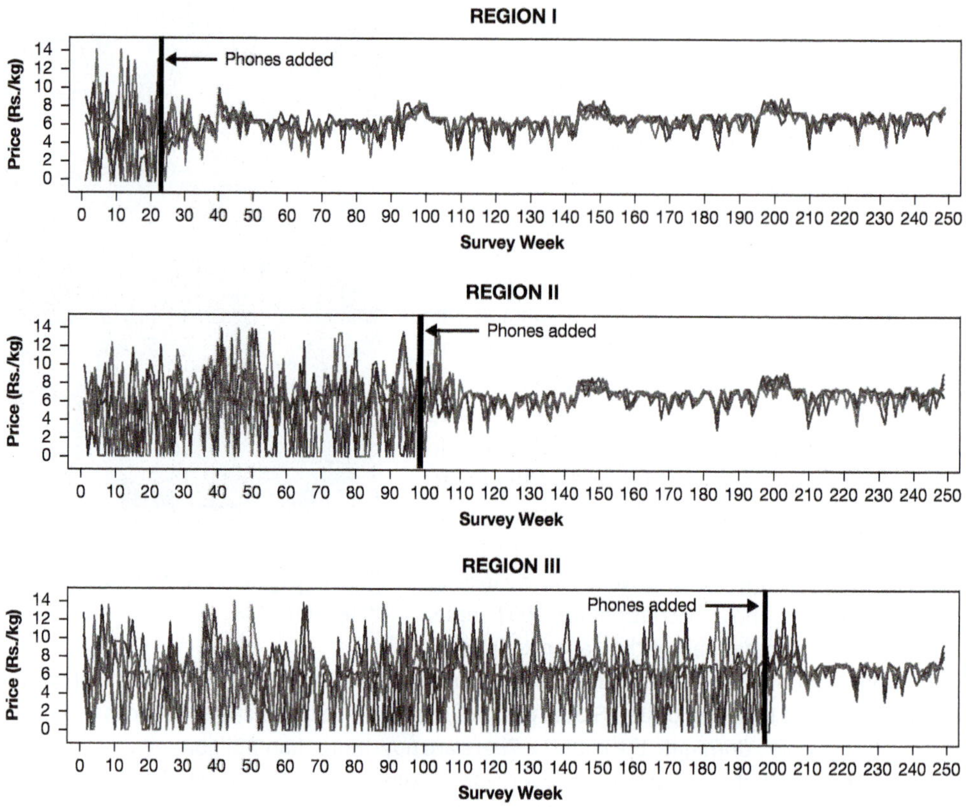

FIGURE 11.10 The price of fish in rural India before and after cell phones were introduced **Source:** Robert Jensen, "The Digital Provide: Information (Technology), Market Performance and Welfare in the South Indian Fisheries Sector," Quarterly Journal of Economics 122, no. 3 (2007): 879–924.

range than before, because fishermen were able to verify the actual market price.[45] The power of connectivity helped the fishermen better understand their markets, price their catch properly, and earn more money. This study demonstrates an effect that has been witnessed around the world: when more communication is available, information flows more freely, and producers and consumers all benefit.[46]

Speed of the Internet

Not only is global access to the Internet increasing, but the speed of the Internet itself is also increasing. As **Figure 11.11** demonstrates, the global Internet runs on average at 5.6 Mbps, but in Korea—which boasts the world's fastest Internet—the average speed is 21.1 Mbps. By contrast, much of Africa has Internet speeds less than 2 Mbps.[47] This discrepancy means that a web page will load ten times faster in Korea than in most parts of Africa.

The implications of Internet speed are more than simple inconvenience for people who have slower access. Companies operating in global markets need to consider the local Internet speed when designing content for their Internet presence. For example, embedding a video testimonial on a website might be effective in Japan, where download speeds are high, but less effective in India, where speeds are slow.

Peer-to-Peer and the Shared Economy

shared economy a system in which an owner rents something they are not using, such as a room, a car, or even a service, to a stranger using peer-to-peer services

Another significant change stemming from the rise of the digital infrastructure is the emergence of peer-to-peer (P2P) transactions in a virtual marketplace that is sometimes referred to as the "shared economy." A **shared economy**, also called collaborative consumption or the peer economy, is a system in which owners rent to strangers something they are not using, such as a room, a car, or even a service, using peer-to-peer services.[48] Constant connectivity and access saturation have enabled people, especially in industrialized nations, to rent their

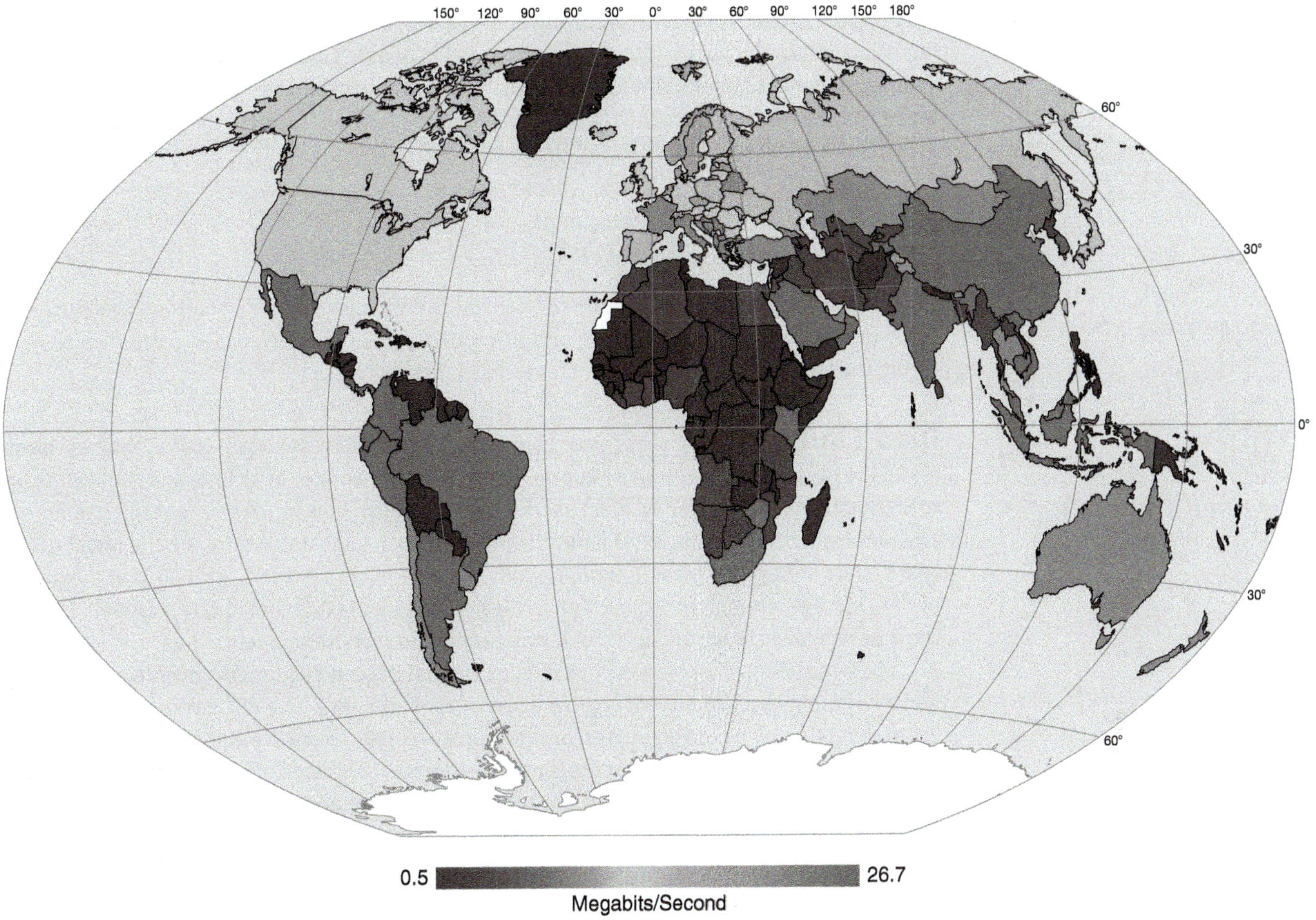

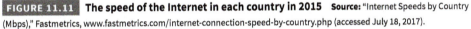

FIGURE 11.11 The speed of the Internet in each country in 2015 **Source:** "Internet Speeds by Country (Mbps)," Fastmetrics, www.fastmetrics.com/internet-connection-speed-by-country.php (accessed July 18, 2017).

goods and services directly to other people. Hotels, car rental agencies, and even banks have experienced some unexpected competition from the shared economy. For instance, the world's largest renter of rooms is not technically a hotel; it's the lodgings broker Airbnb, which matches individuals willing to rent out space in their own homes to people who want to rent that space. Airbnb's online market for lodgings in private residences boasts over 1.5 million listings around the globe. The average Airbnb host in New York City earned more than $5,000 in 2016.[49] But in some markets such as San Francisco and New York City, the company faces laws that make renting out rooms illegal unless the renters register with the city.[50]

Similarly, Turo, a car-sharing service, enables individuals in the United States and Canada to rent their cars to others. The service matches car owners with prospective renters. Turo then offers insurance to protect the car owner and detailed reviews to protect the renter.[51]

People can even "share" their money now. Those who need money go to the appropriate P2P site, enter the amount they would like to borrow, name the terms, and include details of their employment, location, and other personal information. Lenders from around the globe agree to loan the money at a certain rate. If both parties agree, the deal is completed and the P2P lender, such as Bitbond, Prosper, Upstart, or SoFi, receives a fee between 1 and 5 percent of the loan. The loans can be used to consolidate debt, buy a car, or remodel a house.[52]

The P2P phenomenon is not limited to developed markets. Taobao is a Chinese global market platform similar to eBay, bringing buyers and sellers together in both an auction and a fixed-priced model. The company's site is one of the world's most visited and has over 7 million sellers posting over a billion products. Taobao is so large that it represents over 80 percent of online commerce in China and is growing quickly abroad. Similarly, Yu'ebau is changing China's financial industry by paying interest on money left in people's Taobao Alipay accounts. Alipay is Taobao's payment system, similar to PayPal. With a simple click of a button, users can transfer money from their online account to an attached savings account, where they can earn interest. In just 3 years, the service has accumulated over $60 billion.[53]

Data Storage and Processing Technologies

In addition to the explosion of information that is dramatically affecting international business opportunities, the cost of gathering and using information has decreased dramatically. As a result, the store of global data has increased exponentially.

Data Storage Thirty years ago, computer systems like the Atari 1040ST helped bring about the personal computing revolution. The Atari was a wonder of its time and could store up to 360 kilobytes of data. Today, most users don't even know how much storage their computers have—the amount is so large it is almost irrelevant. Such large data stores are the result of the cost of data storage decreasing exponentially over the past sixty years. In 1960, one megabyte of data storage, enough to store about 870 pages of plain text,[54] costed about $4,000. In 1994 the cost had fallen to $1, and by 2010 it was a mere thousandth of a cent.

For international businesses, this means that data about customers, inventory, suppliers, and everything else can and does grow at an exponential rate. The BBC estimates that about 2.5 exabytes, or 2.5 billion gigabytes, are created every day; that's the equivalent of 960 trillion pages of plain text.[55] Experts estimate that 40 zettabytes (40 *trillion* gigabytes) of data will have been created by 2020.[56] Companies are bursting with data, and many are using it to improve operations and interactions. For instance, Shell Oil Company now integrates millions of observations obtained when its crews are looking for oil and gas to determine how much is present and how easy recovering it will likely be.[57]

However, this explosion of information has challenges of its own. As economist Herbert Simon predicted over fifty years ago, global leaders today face a hard limit on their ability to use all available data. Simon noted, "In an information-rich world, the wealth of information means a dearth of something else: a scarcity of whatever it is that information consumes. What information consumes is rather obvious: it consumes the attention of its recipients. Hence, a wealth of information creates a poverty of attention and a need to allocate that attention efficiently among the overabundance of information sources that might consume it."[58] This information explosion has global leaders feeling overloaded in a flood of information.[59] Indeed this problem affects not only leaders of organizations; a 2015 study by *Fortune* found that 65–76 percent of companies struggle with employees who feel overwhelmed.[60]

The Rise of Global Data Centers With the creation of so much data, global companies have emerged to help companies securely store their data either on-site, in remote data centers, or in "cloud-based" storage options. For instance, Interxion is a pan-European data storage company with 42 data centers in 12 countries.[61] Its nondescript London location is tucked away in the remains of an old brewery. But inside is a state-of-the-art, high-security data center conveniently close to London's financial companies. These firms could save money by using a center outside London rather than one right in the heart of the city, but the milliseconds required to send and retrieve the data from a more distant location would slow the time-sensitive trades they make. As the pace of business increases, even the smallest fraction of a second can mean the creation or loss of a fortune.

Increased Processing Power As the cost of data storage has been reduced, the importance of the ability to process data has increased. In 1965, Gordon Moore, a cofounder of Intel, suggested that processing power—measured by the number of transistors that amplify or switch signals and electrical power on a microchip—would double every 24 months. This prediction has become known as **Moore's law**, and so far it has proven to be largely true. Processing power has increased by 3,500 times over the past fifty years, even as the cost has come down.[62]

Moore's law the prediction that processing power will double every 24 months

Energy use in microchips is 90,000 times more efficient today than in 1965, and the price per transistor has decreased by a factor of 60,000 over the same period.[63] While these improvements have fueled many innovations—such as smartphones and tablets—some argue that the trend predicted by Moore's law has reached its limit.[64] Horst Simon, the deputy director of Lawrence Berkeley National Laboratory, is among those who say our need for computing power may have plateaued.[65] As a result, while Intel has led the pack in driving innovation, companies in Taiwan, Korea, and China are capturing an increasingly large share of the memory chip market by producing chips that are cheaper because they are sufficient for most purposes.

Access to Data Another major hurdle for international business today is ensuring access to critical data. In the past, companies kept their own data on site in order to maintain integrity and security. However, keeping data in-house makes it more difficult for an increasingly mobile workforce to access. For that reason, companies are moving to cloud-based solutions.

In the United States, Amazon, Google, Microsoft, and others offer cloud-based hosting for data from hundreds of global companies via remote data centers with more than a million servers to handle the flow of the data.[66] Spotify, the Swedish music streaming company, uses Google to host its music streaming services.[67] Netflix uses Amazon's twelve regions to stream films to global markets.[68] One important advantage for global business is that cloud-based solutions enable companies to quickly take their electronic content global. For instance, Amazon has existing infrastructure in the United States, Canada, Brazil, the European Union, India, Singapore, Australia, China, Korea, and Japan.[69] The company's services span thirty-five of the world's thirty-eight time zones. Thanks to cloud-based applications, Amazon's data centers in India can host the same business processes as those in the United States.

Despite the availability of data, a persistent challenge faced by global firms is sharing knowledge across country boundaries. Global companies frequently need to transfer data across borders in order to complete credit card transactions, make reservations, or transfer employees, yet such actions can actually be illegal. Different nations often have different rules for how data must be handled, and passing data across borders can cause companies to accidentally run afoul of those laws. For example, Adobe and Unilever have each been fined by the EU for transferring data to the United States in ways that did not meet the EU's data privacy standards.[70]

Another key global challenge is the security of devices and data. In February 2017, hundreds of thousands of cash register printers in the United Kingdom began printing out a picture of robot along with the phrase, "the hacker god has returned from the dead. → YOUR PRINTER HAS BEEN OWNED ←" (**Figure 11.12**.)[71] The culprit was purportedly a high school student who was upset that companies were so vulnerable and didn't seem to care.

With the proliferation of the "IOT," or the "Internet of things," everything from mundane devices such as refrigerators and headphones to critical health care products such as pacemakers and cars are connected and susceptible to hackers. Part of the problem is the volume of source code that runs major global companies. Google maintains over 2 billion lines of code.[72] Growth in global cyber security is expected to grow quickly in the coming decades.

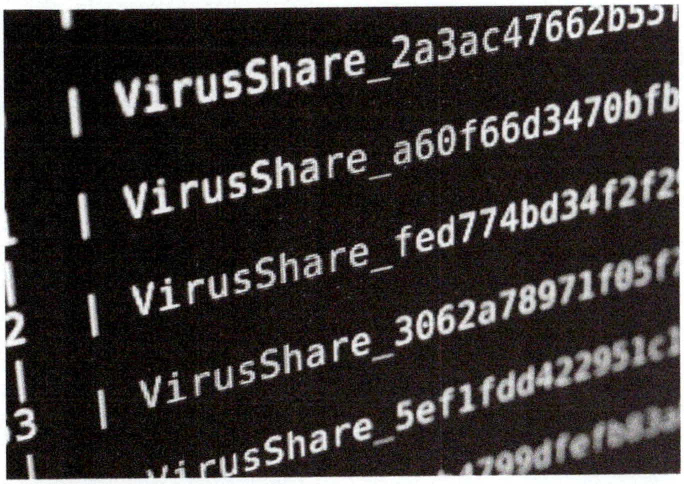

DAMIEN MEYER/AFP/Getty Images

FIGURE 11.12 **Security of devices and data**

11.3 Technology of Human Infrastructure

LEARNING OBJECTIVE

Describe the effect of human capital on opportunities in a global business.

Global companies not only face physical and information infrastructure challenges but also are often constrained by the level of human capital that is available in a market. Several factors are indicators of the availability of human capital. As **Figure 11.13** suggests, these include education, corporate training, and alignment of educational, company, and government intiative to build human capital. We now discuss each of these in turn.

Education

human capital the abilities, skills, experience, and knowledge possessed by individuals

Human capital is the abilities, skills, experience, and knowledge possessed by individuals. The quality of human capital can have important implications for the growth and development of opportunities for international business. Economic output, for instance, is a function of labor and technology. If labor (human capital) is skilled, it will produce higher output per person per hour, leading to growth. Education is thus positively associated with positive economic outcomes. According to the National Center for Education Statistics, the United States spends about $12,000 per child per year for elementary and secondary education and more than $26,000 per student per year for postsecondary education—the highest amount in the OECD (see **Figure 11.14**).[73] Note the positive slope of the line in Figure 11.14; this suggests that higher spending on education is correlated with higher GDP per person in a country. In other words, the more a country invests in education, the more wealthy it is likely to be.

skills shortage a difficulty finding people with the right skills to fill vacant positions

ManpowerGroup conducts surveys of global business leaders each year to ask them questions about hiring global talent. According to the 2016 survey, 40 percent of the 42,000 participating employers indicated they were facing a **skills shortage**, or having difficulty finding people with the right skills to fill vacant positions. The survey reaches companies in forty-three countries, so this is not a localized effect. Basic skills like reading, writing, and math are not the problem; rather, specific skills like mobile app design, nursing, and sales are in short supply.[74] This skill shortage is particularly acute in Japan, where 83 percent of employers report having trouble.[75] Some economists argue that a skills shortage should not exist because the unemployed would just move to fill the jobs, but others are quick to point out that those currently unemployed simply do not have the skill sets needed for the available jobs,[76] and in many countries laws prohibit those who do have the skills from immigrating to the country. For instance, given the United Kingdom's 2016 decision to leave the EU ("Brexit"), many are fearful that the skills shortage in the United Kingdom will increase.[77]

Students at a university in Seoul, South Korea, come from across the world—Brazil, Kenya, Pakistan, India, Nigeria, Turkey, Romania, Vietnam, and other countries—because their own countries faced severe skills shortages. Samsung recognized the skills shortages in these countries when it tried to find people who could run its global electronics operations. To combat the shortage, the company recruited the brightest undergraduate students from their home countries and gave them scholarships to study for an MBA in Korea. Upon graduation, the students would work for Samsung in Korea for a couple of years to further refine their skills. After that time, they would return to their home countries with all the skills to lead Samsung's

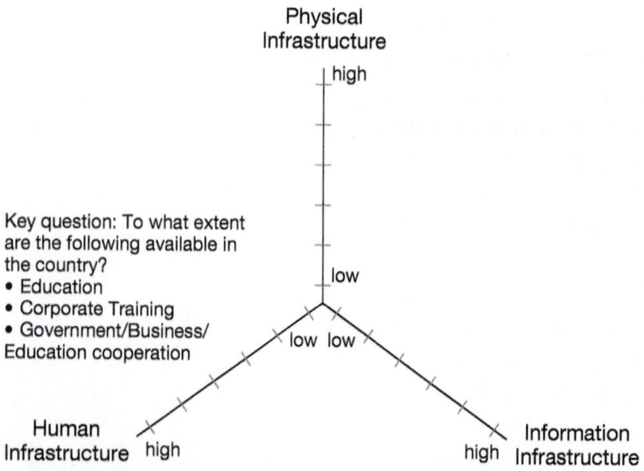

FIGURE 11.13 A Framework for assessing the level of technological infrastructure in countries Human capital infrastructure includes education, corporate training, and cooperation between companies, educational institutions, and governments.

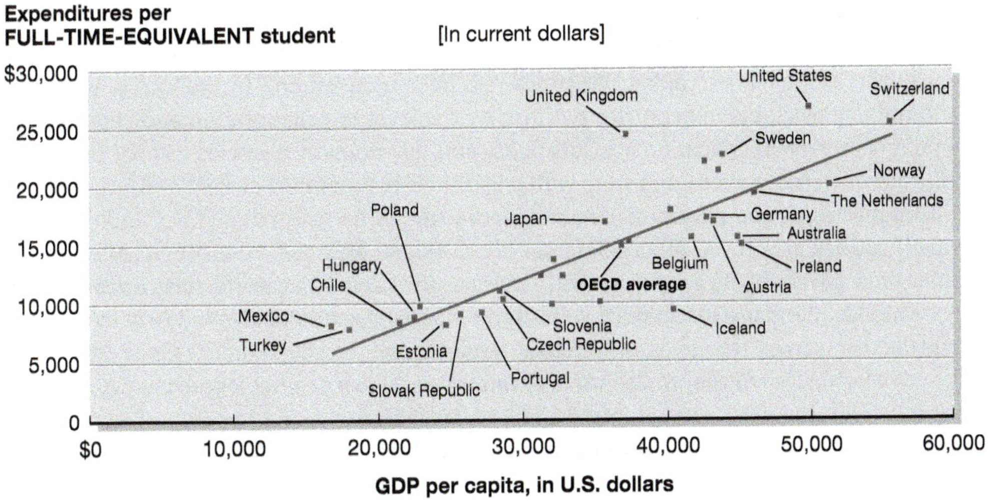

FIGURE 11.14 Postsecondary Spending In 2012, among OECD countries, the United States spent the most per student on postsecondary education. **Source:** "Education Expenditures by Country," National Center for Education Statistics, Institute of Education Sciences, May 2017, http://nces.ed.gov/programs/coe/indicator_cmd.asp.

businesses in these markets. This solution was effective for a time, but it was expensive for Samsung. Worse still, the newly trained employees were often hired away by other global companies in the local markets—after all, they were often some of the most skilled employees in their country.[78]

While most countries provide primary education for the majority of their populations, the quality of this education varies greatly.[79] India operates the largest education system in the world, and that alone brings many challenges.[80] Often, schools lack basic resources such as desks, books, and even teachers. In response, despite the availability of public education, roughly 40 percent of families choose to send their children to private schools—even though private education represents a significant cost to the family.[81] This trend is common throughout Asia. In Japan, Singapore, and Korea, families commonly invest heavily in private education, sending their children to after-school classes for math, English, and the sciences. After-school classes are so aggressive and competitive in Korea that the government instituted laws requiring schools to close at 10 p.m. and not start again before 6 a.m.[82]

Corporate Training and Development

In addition to the level of education within a country, corporate training has important effects on human capital. Global companies spend over $130 billion a year on corporate training—nearly double the estimated $70 billion spent on public education in the U.S. alone.[83] This training is designed to develop a range of skills such as leadership, negotiation, and sales. Many global companies have formal leadership development programs that recruit employees into two- to four-year rotational programs with opportunities to learn different facets of the company.[84] MetLife, GE, IBM, and many others offer such programs across a host of functional areas, including global human resources, global supply chain, global leadership, and global marketing.

In addition to these longer formal programs, most global companies offer skill-based training, much of which takes advantage of new technologies by moving online.[85] New companies such as edX, Coursera, and Udemy offer classes for people around the globe. The use of virtual technologies has shifted corporate training closer to employees and has made it more hands-on.[86]

In addition to providing internal corporate training, some companies partner with employers and employees to identify the skills lacking in the labor market and then develop those skills, working directly with individuals to build them. For instance, LabourNet is a service in India with a mission to provide training and skill development to workers who are not in formal jobs, with a goal of providing vocational training to 1 million workers.[87]

Industry, Education, and Government

The quality of the human capital infrastructure is influenced not only by the level of education and training available in countries but also by the level of collaboration and coordination among companies, educational institutions, and government agencies. Global industries struggle when companies don't work with universities to determine current and future needs, when universities and governments don't work together on research and development, and when industry and government fail to set priorities and agendas. When companies, universities, and governments work together, however, they can build world-class opportunities. For instance, Germany successfully cultivated a booming synthetic dye industry by bringing together companies' resources, universities' research, and the government's money.[88]

Similarly, Silicon Valley in California became a world-class center for technology by bringing together academics from Stanford and Berkley, including tech firms from the Valley, and gaining government support from nearby municipalities.[89] The city of Tel Aviv, Israel, sought to replicate the Silicon Valley model by combining government support, educational resources, and business forces to create a tech hub.[90] The government requires all men and women to join the Israeli army and puts the brightest in high-tech intelligence units such as its famous Unit 8200, where it trains them on cutting-edge technologies and encourages them to pursue tech opportunities after their two-year military service.[91] The businesses of the country also spend the most per capita on research and development. Finally, universities in Israel provide world-class programs, particularly in engineering and information technology. The combination of these forces has resulted in an abundance of tech start-ups that have created significant economic growth.[92]

On the other hand, where governments, industries, or educational institutions are not supportive and do not work together, businesses are forced to develop or find resources on their own, narrowing the margins for success.

business incubator a company that helps found and grow new businesses

One of the key organizations that can bring firms, universities, and governments together is a "business incubator." A **business incubator** is a company that helps found and grow new businesses. It provides new companies with space, tools, and leadership skills to help accelerate their early growth. For instance, MIT has created an organization called the Global Startup Lab (GSL), which provides resources to undergraduate students from emerging markets. In addition to providing resources directly to students, the GSL partners with institutions such as governments, businesses, and universities in emerging markets, with the goal of helping students develop commercial opportunities.[93]

11.4 Technology Trends in International Business

LEARNING OBJECTIVE

Discuss how global business leaders position their firms to take advantage of technological opportunities.

The creation of new technologies can have a profound impact on global business opportunities. For instance, Safaricom (one of the largest mobile operators in Kenya) and Vodacom (the African arm of Vodafone of the United Kingdom, which owns a 40 percent stake in Safaricom) teamed up ten years ago to provide a new product called M-Pesa. This simple but effective phone-based money transfer system enables individuals to deposit, withdraw, transfer, buy mobile minutes and data, and even pay for goods and services with a simple text message. Most Kenyans don't have access to a bank and don't have enough funds to open a bank account anyway. M-Pesa provides an alternative to the traditional banking system but provides similar benefits for individuals: they are able to securely store and use their money.

The product has been very successful in Kenya. In that country of 44 million people, M-Pesa has nearly 20 million registered users, including 90 percent of adults. The system is supported by more than 90,000 M-Pesa agents who act as points of contact for customers, enabling them to deposit and withdraw money from their M-Pesa accounts.[94] M-Pesa payments now represent over 40 percent of the country's GDP.[95] Nearly everyone in the country is using the service to buy and sell goods and services and to send money. Because it provides benefits like those of banking—with perhaps even more convenience—it has improved the lives of millions.

Not only is the technology of M-Pesa providing individuals with value, it has provided many opportunities for business. For instance, because it offers a secure payment process, employers use it to pay salaries. When M-Pesa entered Afghanistan, the government there also began using M-Pesa to pay salaries. Immediately, police officers saw a roughly 30 percent increase in their paychecks because the process cut out corrupt officials who had been skimming the officers' salaries.[96] M-Pesa also reduces crime because individuals are not walking around with cash, so there is less incentive for robberies. The service not only benefits the companies and customers that use it, but according to Bob Collymore, the CEO of Safaricom, the company makes a $250-million-a-year profit.[97]

In addition to making money for the company and providing a valuable service to millions, this new technology has paved the way for a flood of entrepreneurial ventures. For instance, M-KOPA Solar offers customers in Kenya, Tanzania, and Uganda a "4-watt rooftop solar panel, a control box that attaches to the wall of a home or business, three lamps, and mobile-phone chargers."[98] To purchase the $200 unit, the company requires a roughly $35 down payment and then a daily payment of 40 Kenyan shillings, or about 40 cents, for 365 days, until the unit is paid off. The customer uses M-Pesa to make the daily payment, and if the payment is not made, the lights will not turn on until payments resume. The $200 cost may seem high, but it is actually cheaper than the kerosene lamp alternative most Kenyans currently use. Moreover, once the unit is paid for, the customer gets free power. The opportunity to invest in their personal energy needs has improved the lives of over 400,000 customers.[99]

Similarly, the village of Njogu-ini installed a clean-water well that uses mobile payments through the M-Pesa platform. Residents simply walk to the well and use their phone to pay the small fee to activate the pump, providing them access to clean water. Water obtained this way costs about $6 a month per person. The critical feature is that the technology allows micropayments that are reasonable in the context of Kenyan life, while still enabling villagers to get clean water.[100]

Now that the technology has been established, Safaricom is using the M-Pesa platform to expand to provide other services, such as mobile health care initiatives. The mHealth Kenya service enables doctors to remotely diagnose patients using cell phones, and patients can pay providers using their M-Pesa accounts. In addition, the government of Kenya is using M-Pesa to distribute e-vouchers for prenatal care in an effort to increase the health of mothers and babies.[101]

M-Pesa has changed the economic landscape in Kenya and is expanding to Tanzania, Afghanistan, South Africa, India, Eastern Europe, and more. The simple but effective technology is also starting to be copied by other companies in more advanced markets. Tencent—a large computer technology company in China—has announced WeChat mobile payments, and even Apple is working on a text-based payment system that would enable users to text money to one another.[102]

All these opportunities—and countless more—came about because a new technology enabled millions of Kenyans, traditionally overlooked by international businesses, to safely store money and make mobile payments.

The Globalization of Research and Development

Historically, international companies conducted their research and development (R&D) at their corporate headquarters and pushed the products they invented there to the rest of the world. Over the past decade, this strategy has changed in two ways. First, international companies are spending more money on R&D.[103] Second, they have moved R&D to locations around the world, particularly China and India.[104]

When looking at R&D trends, most analyses focus on the level of gross expenses on research and development (GERD). For instance, total worldwide GERD in 2001 was just $753 billion. Five years later, in 2006, it had ticked up to $1.05 trillion, and in 2011, the amount passed $1.43 trillion—nearly double the 2001 figure. The trend has accelerated, with GERD topping $1.88 trillion in 2015. At that level, roughly 1.75 percent of world GPD is being spent on R&D. Of that, over $1.80 trillion is being spent by the top forty countries ranked by GDP. The United States represents more than 26 percent of global spending, China accounts for over 20 percent, and Japan comes in third with nearly 9 percent of worldwide R&D spending.[105]

While the amount of R&D spending is increasing everywhere, it is growing most rapidly in Asia, as global companies rush to fill the needs of the world's largest markets—China and India.[106] A recent National Science Foundation report highlights this increase, noting that, while R&D spending is increasing in the United States and the European Union, the increase is proportional to increases in the countries' GDP.[107] In Asia, on the other hand, R&D is increasing at a rate faster than the growth of GDP. These trends are highlighted in **Figure 11.15**.

Private businesses, governments, higher education institutions, and private nonprofit donors typically invest in R&D. In the United States, nearly 70 percent of R&D is funded by businesses; that's less than the 83 percent in Israel but much more than the 36 percent funded by businesses in India. Perhaps more interesting is the nearly universal increase in business-sponsored funding (see **Figure 11.16**), indicating that global businesses are recognizing the competitive advantages that come from being at the forefront of technology.

The shift toward business-sponsored R&D is driven by the rise within emerging markets of local companies that develop advanced products for local and global customers. In response,

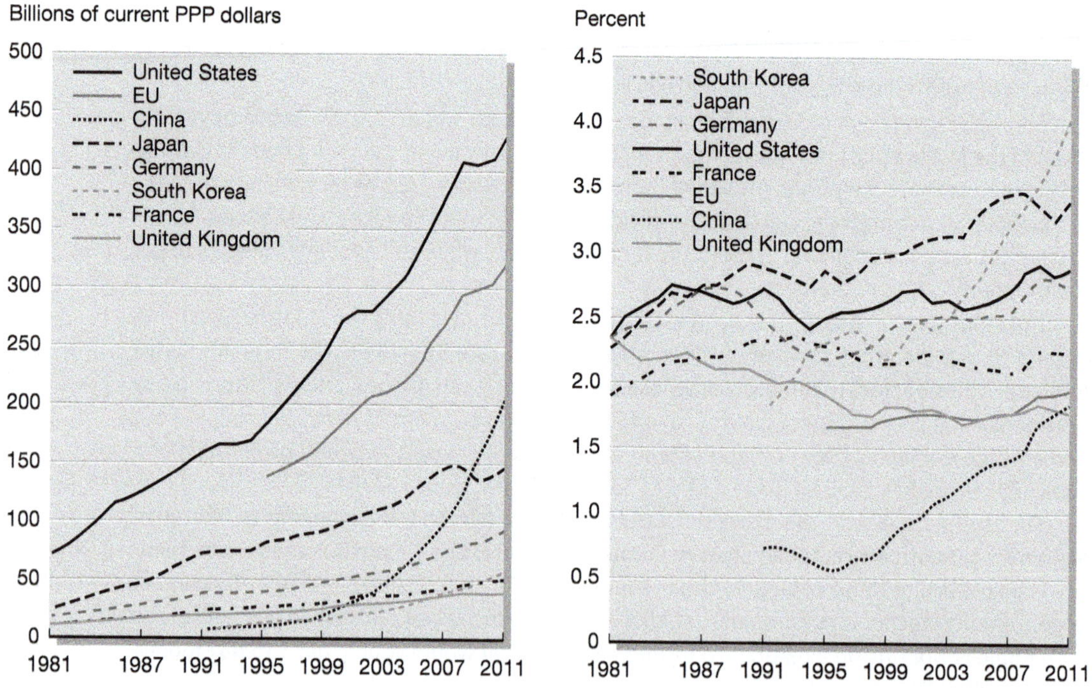

EU = European Union; PPP = purchasing power parity.

NOTES: Data are not available for all countries in all years. Data for the United States in this figure reflect international standards for calculating gross expenditures on R&D, which vary slightly from the National Science Foundation's approach to tallying U.S. total R&D. Data for Japan for 1996 onward may not be consistent with earlier data because of changes in methodology. EU data for all years are based on the current 27 EU member countries.

EU = European Union; GDP = gross domestic product.

NOTES: Data are not available for all countries in all years. The table includes the top seven R&D-performing countries. Figures for the United States reflect international standards for calculating gross expenditures on R&D, which differ slightly from the National Science Foundation's protocol for tallying U.S. total R&D. Data for Japan for 1996 onward may not be consistent with earlier data because of changes in methodology.

FIGURE 11.15 **Total R&D spending and R&D spending as a percentage of GDP for select countries, 1981–2011** **Source:** "Chapter 4. Research and Development: National Trends and International Comparisons," in "Science and Engineering Indicators 2014," National Science Foundation, February 2014, www.nsf.gov/statistics/seind14/index.cfm/chapter-4/c4s2.htm.

Country	GERD PPP ($billions)	Share of total (%) Business	Government	Institutions of higher education	Private nonprofit
		R&D funding sources			
United States (2011)	$429.1	58.6%	31.2%	6.4%	3.8%
China (2011)	$208.2	73.9%	21.7%	NA	1.3%
Japan (2011)	$146.5	76.5%	16.4%	6.6%	0.5%
Germany (2010)	$93.1	65.6%	30.3%	0.2%	3.9%
South Korea (2011)	$59.9	73.7%	24.9%	1.2%	0.2%
France (2010)	$51.9	53.5%	37.0%	1.8%	7.6%
United Kingdom (2011)	$39.6	44.6%	32.2%	6.2%	17.0%

** = included in data for other performing sectors; NA = not available.
GERD = gross expenditures on R&D; PPP = purchasing power parity.

FIGURE 11.16 **Percentage of GERD by funding source, 2005–2011** Gross expenditures on R&D for selected countries, by performing sector and funding sources: 2011 or most recent year **Source:** Adapted by the authors from "Chapter 4. Research and Development: National Trends and International Comparisons," in "Science and Engineering Indicators 2014," National Science Foundation, February 2014, www.nsf.gov/statistics/seind14/index.cfm/chapter-4/c4s2.htm.

many multinational companies are shifting R&D into those same markets to reclaim an edge.[108] For instance, GE built R&D centers in China and India in 2000,[109] expanded to Israel and Brazil in 2011,[110] and entered Saudi Arabia in 2015.[111] As a result, GE has introduced to its global customer base new products that were designed for a local market such as India. As a result, the company is now meeting customer needs different from those it traditionally focused on.

Summary and Case

Summary

LEARNING OBJECTIVE 11.1 Assess the impact of physical infrastructure on international business opportunities.

Physical infrastructure takes the form of raw materials, manufacturing, transportation, and energy. Changes in the availability of raw materials, the emergence of new manufacturing equipment and techniques, larger transportation networks, and more plentiful energy resources are changing the global competitive landscape. Ignoring any component of the physical infrastructure can expose a company to problems that will make it unable to complete its objectives.

LEARNING OBJECTIVE 11.2 Identify the way information infrastructure creates business opportunities.

Access to abundant information has opened markets for new services such as cloud-based storage and the shared economy, and has made many transactions more efficient in industries from agriculture to e-commerce. Improvements in data storage and processing technologies can shape business opportunities by changing how and where companies host their data. This in turn enables new ranges of products, such as car sharing and peer-to-peer loans, and the rise of online brokers like Taobao.

LEARNING OBJECTIVE 11.3 Describe the effect of human capital on opportunities in a global business.

The abilities, skills, experience, and knowledge possessed by individuals is called human capital. Level of education has a strong, positive correlation with economic prosperity, meaning that companies that enrich human capital are enriched by it in return. Managers assess the value of human capital in a country by considering the country's educational infrastructure, the company's global corporate training and development, and the level of collaboration between companies, educational institutions, and governments.

LEARNING OBJECTIVE 11.4 Discuss how global business leaders position their firms to take advantage of technological opportunities.

Technology trends can change opportunities in international markets. Increased spending on R&D in both developed and emerging markets is changing international business. Many organizations are expanding their R&D centers to emerging markets, many in Asia, because of the need to be close to the world's largest and fastest growing markets.

Case Study

LinkedIn in Brazil

In 2015, LinkedIn had over 400 million users, 120 million of whom were from Brazil. Brazil is Linkedin's third largest market, behind the United States and India.[112] The company is looking to grow its operations in Brazil by opening what would be its first regional office in Latin America. The market entry strategy team has been tasked with determining whether expansion into Brazil is a good idea, given its physical, information, and human capital infrastructures.

Consistent economic growth policies have affected every level of Brazil's infrastructure by lifting more than 29 million Brazilians to the middle class between 2003 and May 2014.[113] This explosion in economic growth and improvement in human infrastructure, along with a commitment to improve the country's physical infrastructure, have led to a quickly developing information and technology sector.

Despite recent improvements in Brazil, however, the country is still plagued by serious infrastructure problems. In 2017, the World Economic Forum ranked Brazil as 123rd in the world for ease of doing business.[114] Furthermore, Brazil is notorious for its poor physical infrastructure. Roads in rural areas are generally underdeveloped, and railways and airports are in need of better funding and further expansion.[115]

On the other hand, Brazil's rapid growth has led to the development of tech hubs and business centers that are attracting companies from around the world. If LinkedIn decides to invest in a regional office in a large city such as Rio de Janeiro, it will join the research facilities and offices owned by the likes of General Electric, Halliburton, Baker Hughes, and Schlumberger. As a tech company that offers online services, LinkedIn should not be hampered by the poor physical infrastructure that might seriously affect an e-commerce business such as Amazon.com.

One of the most significant challenges that LinkedIn will likely face is the limited human capital that Brazil produces. Opening a tech company in Brazil presents a difficult challenge for recruiters, who will be hard-pressed to find technically capable workers. Brazil's education system is largely to blame. Over the past 20 years, Brazil has done an excellent job of including more students in the education system. More than inclusion rate, however, is the problem of the quality of education in Brazil, which has led to a professional shortage. According to research by the Instituto Paulo Montenegro, 38 percent of Brazilian undergraduates are functionally illiterate.[116] This has in turn resulted difficulties retaining talent as foreign and local businesses compete for qualified workers.[117] If LinkedIn opens offices in Brazil, will a talent shortage and competition in recruiting undermine the firm's success?

For the past two decades, Brazil's mobile subscription and Internet penetration have steadily increased, making business such as e-commerce and cloud systems increasingly more attractive in the country. For example, in 2012, several high-profile companies—Microsoft, Cisco Systems, and Foxconn—announced multimillion-dollar investments to build research centers in Rio de Janeiro. Despite the political and economic crises that occurred in 2015 and 2016—which resulted in significant economic decline and the impeachment of President Dilma Rousseff, as well as the ousting of many politicians and business leaders who were caught taking money from Petrobras, the national oil company[118]—the tech industry, along with the country's technological and information infrastructures, is growing in size in the double digits.[119]

Case Discussion Questions

As part of the market entry team, you have been asked to analyze whether LinkedIn should establish headquarters in Brazil.

1. Use the tool referenced throughout the chapter to assess the level of physical, information, and human infrastructure in Brazil.
2. Are the positive aspects of Brazil's infrastructure enough to outweigh the negatives?
3. Would you recommend that LinkedIn open an office in Brazil? Give three reasons to support your answer.

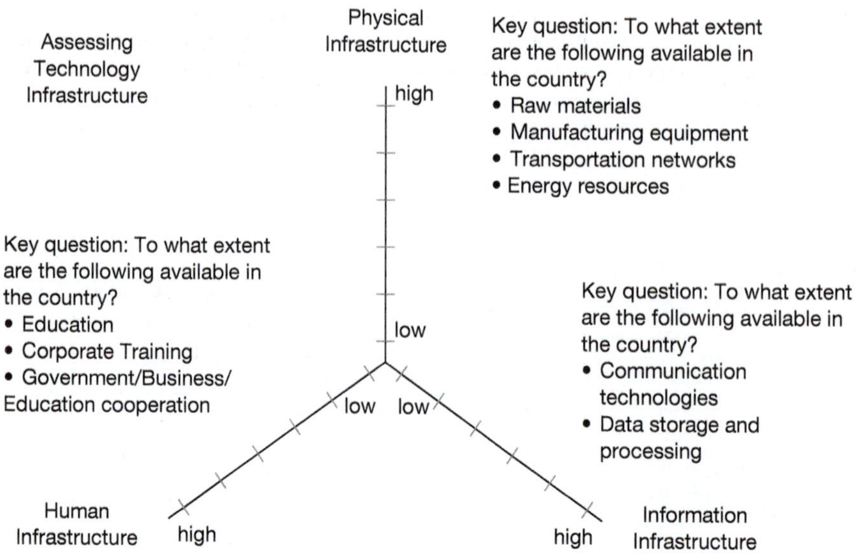

Endnotes

[1]A *New York Times* editorial from March 19, 1939, as quoted in Jeffrey A. Harris, *Transformative Entrepreneurs: How Walt Disney, Steve Jobs, Muhammad Yunus, and Other Innovators Succeeded* (New York: Palgrave Macmillan, 2012).

[2]Moses Abramovitz, "Catching up, Forging Ahead, and Falling Behind," *Journal of Economic History* 46, no. 2 (1986): 385–406; Robert M. Solow, "Technical Change and the Aggregate Production Function," *Review of Economics and Statistics* 39 (1957): 312–20.

[3]GfK, "TV Sales Revenue Worldwide from 2013 to 2016 (in Billion Euros)," *Statista - The Statistics Portal*, www.statista.com/statistics/461324/global-tv-market-sales/ (accessed November 17, 2016).

[4]"Marketing to Rural India: Making the Ends Meet," Knowledge@Wharton, March 8, 2007, http://knowledge.wharton.upenn.edu/article/marketing-to-rural-india-making-the-ends-meet/.

[5]"An Increasingly Precious Metal: Amid a Surge in Demand for Rechargeable Batteries, Companies Are Scrambling for Supplies of Lithium," *Economist*, January 16, 2016, www.economist.com/news/business/21688386-amid-surge-demand-rechargeable-batteries-companies-are-scrambling-supplies.

[6]Daniel J. Packey, "Interesting Developments in the Rare Earth Market," *Economic Papers* 32, no. 4 (2013): 454–61, http://onlinelibrary.wiley.com/doi/10.1111/1759-3441.12047/pdf.

[7]Richard Silberglitt, James T. Bartis, Brian G. Chow, David L. An, and Kyle Brady, "Critical Materials: Present Danger to U.S. Manufacturing," Santa Monica, CA: RAND Corporation, 2013, http://www.rand.org/pubs/research_reports/RR133.html.

[8]Jonathan Soble, "Japan Warns on Island Dispute with China," *Financial Times*, August 17, 2012, www.ft.com/content/efd92786-e853-11e1-8ffc-00144feab49a.

[9]Seamus McGraw, "Is Fracking Safe? The 10 Most Controversial Claims About Natural Gas Drilling," *Popular Mechanics*, May 1, 2016, www.popularmechanics.com/science/energy/g161/top-10-myths-about-natural-gas-drilling-6386593/.

[10]Neil M. Coe and Henry Wai-Chung Yeung, *Global Production Networks: Theorizing Economic Development in an Interconnected World* (Oxford: Oxford University Press, 2015).

[11]Liang Wang, Anoop Madhok, and Stan Xiao Li, "Agglomeration and Clustering over the Industry Life Cycle: Toward a Dynamic Model of Geographic Concentration," *Strategic Management Journal* 35, no. 7 (2014): 995–1012.

[12]Cristobal Cheyre, Jon Kowalski, and Francisco M. Veloso, "Spinoffs and the Ascension of Silicon Valley," *Industrial and Corporate Change* 24, no. 4 (2015): 837–58.

[13]Tiberio Daddi et al., "Enhancing the Adoption of Life Cycle Assessment by Small and Medium Enterprises Grouped in an Industrial Cluster: A Case Study of the Tanning Cluster in Tuscany (Italy)," *Journal of Industrial Ecology* 20, No. 5 (2015): 1199-1211.

[14]Frank Pyke and Peter Lund-Thomsen, "Social Upgrading in Developing Country Industrial Clusters: A Reflection on the Literature," *Competition & Change* 20, No. 1 (2015): 53-68 1024529415611265.

[15]Global Textile Report, Euler Hermes, February 2016, www.eulerhermes.com/economic-research/sector-risks/Global-Textile-Report/Pages/default.aspx.

[16]Marc Levinson, *The Box: How the Shipping Container Made the World Smaller and the World Economy Bigger* (Princeton, NJ: Princeton University Press, 2016).

[17]William Kremer, "How Much Bigger Can Container Ships Get?" *BBC News*, February 19, 2013, www.bbc.com/news/magazine-21432226.

[18]Liz Stinson, "A Gorgeous Tour of the Largest Ship in the World," *Wired*, October 16, 2014, www.wired.com/2014/10/matz-maersk-triple-e/.

[19]Jane Lister, "Green Shipping: Governing Sustainable Maritime Transport," *Global Policy* 6, no. 2 (2015): 118–29.

[20]M. S. S. El Namaki, "Dynamic Synergy Analysis in International Business: The Concept and Application to Two Players China and Russia," *Scholedge International Journal of Management & Development* 3, no. 7 (2016): 129–36.

[21]Nadège Rolland, "China's New Silk Road," National Bureau of Asian Research, February 12, 2015, http://www.nbr.org/research/activity.aspx?id=531.

[22]Derek Thompson, "How Airline Ticket Prices Fell 50% in 30 Years (and Why Nobody Noticed)," *The Atlantic*, February 28, 2013, www.theatlantic.com/business/archive/2013/02/how-airline-ticket-prices-fell-50-in-30-years-and-why-nobody-noticed/273506/.

[23]The World Bank, 2016, http://data.worldbank.org/indicator/IS.AIR.PSGR. (Accessed July 18, 2017).

[24]Franziska Kupfer et al., "The Underlying Drivers and Future Development of Air Cargo," *Journal of Air Transport Management* 61,(2016): 6-14.

[25]"Air-Freight Industry Challenged by Cross-Border e-Commerce Growth," Global E-commerce Facts, April 21, 2016, http://e-commercefacts.com/17-general/6029-air-freight-industry-challenged-by-cross-border-e-commerce-growth.

[26]Personal experience of the James Oldroyd, November, 2016.

[27]Prijanka Sangani, "Indian Enterprises Lose Almost a Third of Their Data During Disruptions: Zerto," *India Times*, November 5, 2016, http://tech.economictimes.indiatimes.com/news/corporate/indian-enterprises-lose-almost-a-third-of-their-data-during-disruptions-zerto/55257801.

[28]Edward Wong, "Coal Burning Causes the Most Air Pollution Deaths in China, Study Finds," *New York Times*, August 17, 2016, www.nytimes.com/2016/08/18/world/asia/china-coal-health-smog-pollution.html?_r=0.

[29]"Key World Energy Statistics 2016," International Energy Agency, October 19, 2016, www.iea.org/publications/freepublications/publication/KeyWorld_Statistics_2015.pdf

[30]"Key World Energy Statistics 2016," 14.

[31]Li Jing, "Why Does China's Choking Smog Persist Despite Beijing's Clean-up Efforts?" *South China Morning Post*, November 9, 2016, www.scmp.com/news/china/policies-politics/article/2044383/why-does-chinas-choking-smog-persist-despite-beijings.

[32]Wong, "Coal Burning Causes the Most Air Pollution Deaths in China."

[33]Scott Cendrowski, "This Is What GE's $8 Billion China Business Is Facing," *Fortune*, March 1, 2016, http://fortune.com/2016/03/01/ge-china-public-procurement-hospitals/.

[34]"Coming Home: A Growing Number of American Companies Are Moving Their Manufacturing Back to the United States," *The Economist*, January 19, 2013, www.economist.com/news/special-report/21569570-growing-number-american-companies-are-moving-their-manufacturing-back-united.

[35]"Vietnam Trying to Juice up Power Sector with Foreign Investment," *Nikkei Asian Review*, September 6, 2016, http://asia.nikkei.com/Politics-Economy/International-Relations/Vietnam-trying-to-juice-up-power-sector-with-foreign-investment.

[36]"Hinkley Point: UK Approves Nuclear Plant Deal," BBC News, September 15, 2016, www.bbc.com/news/business-37369786; Laurence Arnold and Will Kennedy, "Quick Take Q&A: Britain and France's $24 Billion Nuclear Gamble," Bloomberg, September 15, 2016, www.bloomberg.com/news/articles/2016-09-15/quicktake-q-a-britain-and-france-s-24-billion-nuclear-gamble.

[37]John Fialka, "World's Largest Storage Battery Will Power Los Angeles," *Scientific American*, July 7, 2016, www.scientificamerican.com/article/world-s-largest-storage-battery-will-power-los-angeles/.

[38]"Electricity Explained: How Electricity is Delivered to Consumers," U.S. Energy Information Administration, December 22. 2015, www.eia.gov/energy_in_brief/article/power_grid.cfm.

[39]William Pentland, "Perverse Economics of the Electric Grid: As Generation Gets Cheaper, Transmission Costs Soar," *Forbes*, January 2, 2013, www.forbes.com/sites/williampentland/2013/01/02/the-perverse-economics-of-the-electric-grid/#305b4daf7739.

[40]David Zax, "Brown Down: UPS Drivers vs. the UPS Algorithm," *Fast Company*, January 3, 2013, www.fastcompany.com/3004319/brown-down-ups-drivers-vs-ups-algorithm.

[41]"How the Internet Promotes Development," in "World Development Report 2016: Digital Dividends," World Bank, May 27, 2016, www.worldbank.org/en/publication/wdr2016; Leonid Bershidsky, "Envying Estonia's Digital Government," Bloomberg, March 4, 2015, www.bloomberg.com/view/articles/2015-03-04/envying-estonia-s-digital-government.

[42]Bershidsky, "Envying Estonia's Digital Government."

[43]"Rio Favela Facts," CatComm.org, http://catcomm.org/favela-facts/; Fabio Brisolla, "Morador de favela está 'superligado' à internet, diz pesquisa," Folha de São Paulo, February 17, 2013, www1.folha.uol.com.br/cotidiano/2013/02/1231878-morador-de-favela-esta-super-ligado-a-internet-diz-pesquisa.shtml.

[44]"ICT Facts and Figures," ICT Data and Statistics Division, Telecommunication Development Bureau, International Telecommunication Union, May 2015, www.itu.int/en/ITU-D/Statistics/Documents/facts/ICTFactsFigures2015.pdf.

[45]Robert Jensen, "The Digital Provide: Information (Technology), Market Performance and Welfare in the South Indian Fisheries Sector," *Quarterly Journal of Economics* 122, no. 3 (2007): 879–924.

[46]Funda Sahin, and E. Powell Robinson, "Flow Coordination and Information Sharing in Supply Chains: Review, Implications, and Directions for Future Research," *Decision Sciences* 33, no. 4 (2002): 505–36.

[47]"Internet Speeds by Country," Fastmetrics, https://www.fastmetrics.com/internet-connection-speed-by-country.php (accessed January 13, 2017).

[48]"Airbnb, Snapgoods and 12 More Pioneers of the 'Share Economy'," Forbes, www.forbes.com/pictures/eeji45emgkh/airbnb-snapgoods-and-12-more-pioneers-of-the-share-economy/#2fc727607226 (accessed July 18, 2017).

[49]Madeline Farber, "Here's How Much New York City Airbnb Hosts Earn in a Year," *Fortune*, July 8, 2016, http://fortune.com/2016/07/08/how-much-money-airbnb-hosts-make-new-york-city/?iid=leftrail.

[50]Katie Benner, "Airbnb in Disputes with New York and San Francisco," *New York Times*, June 28, 2016, www.nytimes.com/2016/06/29/technology/airbnb-sues-san-francisco-over-a-law-it-had-helped-pass.html?_r=0.

[51]Rick Broida, "Rent Private Cars for Cheap with Turo," CNET, February 22, 2016, www.cnet.com/how-to/rent-private-cars-for-cheap-with-turo/.

[52]Anya Martin, "How Online Lenders Can Finance Home Improvements," *Wall Street Journal*, June 29, 2016, www.wsj.com/articles/how-online-lenders-can-finance-home-improvements-1467212248.

[53]"Can Alibaba's Ant Financial Become as Successful as Taobao?" *Fortune*, May 30, 2016, www.forbes.com/sites/ckgsb/2016/05/30/can-alibabas-ant-financial-become-as-successful-as-taobao/#2d2bcfc3204a.

[54]"How Much Is 1 Byte, Kilobyte, Megabyte, Gigabyte, etc.?" Computer Hope, www.computerhope.com/issues/chspace.htm. (Accessed July 18, 2017).

[55]Matthew Wall, "Big Data; Are You Ready for Blast-Off?" BBC News, March 4, 2014, www.bbc.com/news/business-26383058.

[56]Daniel Price, "Surprising Facts and Stats about the Big Data Industry," Cloud Tweaks, March 17, 2015, http://cloudtweaks.com/2015/03/surprising-facts-and-stats-about-the-big-data-industry/.

[57]Rick Delgado, "Commercial Use Cases: 5 Companies Using Big Data to Make Money," CTOvison.com, July 28, 2015, https://ctovision.com/2015/07/commercial-use-cases-5-companies-using-big-data-make-money/.

[58]H. A. Simon, "Designing Organizations for an Information-Rich World," in *Computers, Communication, and the Public Interest*, ed. Martin Greenberger (Baltimore: Johns Hopkins University Press, 1971), 40–41.

[59]Daniel J. Levitin, *The Organized Mind: Thinking Straight in the Age of Information Overload* (New York: Penguin, 2014).

[60]Vanessa Loder, "75% of Companies Struggle with Overwhelmed Employees - Here Are Three Tips to Cope," *Forbes*, April 24, 2015, www.forbes.com/sites/vanessaloder/2015/04/24/75-of-companies-struggle-with-overwhelmed-employees-here-are-three-tips-to-cope/#49b4a8404f0e.

[61]"An Interactive Guide to Our Global Coverage," Interxion.com, www.interxion.com/Locations/ (accessed January 13, 2017).

[62]"After Moore's Law," *The Economist*, March 12, 2016, www.economist.com/technology-quarterly/2016-03-12/after-moores-law.

[63]"50 Years of Moore's Law: Fueling Innovation We Love and Depend on," Intel, www.intel.com/content/www/us/en/silicon-innovations/moores-law-technology.html (accessed December 16, 2016).

[64]"After Moore's Law."

[65]Tom Simonite, "Moore's Law Is Dead. Now What?" *MIT Technology Review*, May 13, 2016, www.technologyreview.com/s/601441/moores-law-is-dead-now-what/.

[66]Jack Clark, "5 Numbers That Illustrate the Mind-Bending Size of Amazon's Cloud," Bloomberg, November 11, 2014, www.bloomberg.com/news/2014-11-14/5-numbers-that-illustrate-the-mind-bending-size-of-amazon-s-cloud.html.

[67]Sooraj Shah, "Spotify Wants Google to Improve Cloud Platform after Going All-in on GCP," Tech Week Europe, October 25, 2016, www.techweekeurope.co.uk/cloud/spotify-google-cloud-aws-gcp-199408#Sw45rpyJYqc8ROoX.99.

[68]Jon Brodkin, "Netflix Finishes Its Massive Migration to the Amazon Cloud," ARS Technica, February 2, 2016, http://arstechnica.com/information-technology/2016/02/netflix-finishes-its-massive-migration-to-the-amazon-cloud/.

[69]"AWS Global Infrastructure," Amazon Web Services, https://aws.amazon.com/about-aws/global-infrastructure/ (accessed January 13, 2017).

[70]Julia Fioretti, "German Privacy Regulator Fines Three Firms over U.S. Data Transfers," Reuters, June 6, 2016, www.reuters.com/article/us-germany-dataprotection-usa-idUSKCN0YS23H.

[71]"Why Everything Is Hackable," *The Economist*, April 8, 2017, www.economist.com/news/science-and-technology/21720268-consequences-pile-up-things-are-starting-improve-computer-security.

[72]"Why Everything Is Hackable."

[73]"Education Expenditures by Country," National Center for Education Statistics. May 2017, http://nces.ed.gov/programs/coe/indicator_cmd.asp.

[74]Roy Maurer, "Employers Are Facing the Worst Talent Shortage Since 2007," Society for Human Resource Management, November 7, 2016 www.shrm.org/resourcesandtools/hr-topics/talent-acquisition/pages/employers-facing-worst-talent-shortage-2007.aspx; James Bessen, "Employers Aren't Just Whining – the 'Skills Gap' Is Real," *Harvard Business Review*, August 25, 2014, https://hbr.org/2014/08/employers-arent-just-whining-the-skills-gap-is-real/.

[75]Enda Curran and Connor Cislo, "Japan Opens up to Foreign Workers (Just Don't Call It Immigration," Bloomberg, October 25, 2016, www.bloomberg.com/news/articles/2016-10-25/a-wary-japan-quietly-opens-its-back-door-for-foreign-workers.

[76]Patrick Gillespie, "America's Persistent Problem: Unskilled Workers, CNN Money, August 7, 2015, http://money.cnn.com/2015/08/07/news/economy/us-economy-job-skills-gap/.

[77]Fergal O'Brien, "U.K. Companies Worry Brexit Will Worsen Skills Shortage: Chart," Bloomberg, November 10, 2016, www.bloomberg.com/news/articles/2016-11-10/u-k-companies-worry-brexit-will-worsen-skills-shortage-chart.

[78]James Oldroyd's personal experience 2007–2013.

[79]Agnès Van Zanten, Stephen J. Ball, and Brigitte Darchy-Koechlin, eds, *World Yearbook of Education 2015: Elites, Privilege and Excellence: the National and Global Redefinition of Educational Advantage* (New York: Routledge, 2015).

[80]Rebecca Winthrop and Xanthe Ackerman, "Meet the Man Fixing India's Broken Education System," *Newsweek*, November 15, 2016, www.newsweek.com/india-broken-education-system-solution-521294.

[81]"Indian Students Increasingly Prefer Private Education," *Times of India*, May 16, 2016, http://timesofindia.indiatimes.com/home/education/Indian-students-increasingly-prefer-private-education/articleshow/52292067.cms.

[82]Elise Hu, "The All-Work, No-Play Culture of South Korean Education," NPR Parallels, April 15, 2015, www.npr.org/sections/parallels/2015/04/15/393939759/the-all-work-no-play-culture-of-south-korean-education.

[83]Josh Bersin, "Spending on Corporate Training Soars: Employee Capabilities Now a Priority," *Forbes*, February 4, 2014, www.forbes.com/sites/joshbersin/2014/02/04/the-recovery-arrives-corporate-training-spend-skyrockets/#49a6df354ab7.

[84]Richard McGill Murphy, "How Do Great Companies Groom Talent?" *Fortune*, November 3, 2011, http://fortune.com/2011/11/03/how-do-great-companies-groom-talent/.

[85]Bersin, "Spending on Corporate Training Soars."

[86]David Wentworth and Mollie Lombardi, "5 Trends for the Future of Learning and Development," Training, August 28, 2014, https://trainingmag.com/5-trends-future-learning-and-development.

[87]Chitra Unnaithanl, "LabourNet to Provide Vocational Training to 1 Million Workers in 6 Years," *Times of India*, March 9, 2014, http://timesofindia.indiatimes.com/city/ahmedabad/LabourNet-to-provide-vocational-training-to-1-million-workers-in-6-years/articleshow/31735932.cms.

[88]Johann Peter Murmann, "The Co-development of Industrial Sectors and Academic Disciplines," UNSW Australian School of Business Research Paper No. 2012 STRE 02, *Science and Public Policy* 40, No. 2 (August 29, 2012): 229-246; Johann Peter Murmann, *Knowledge and Competitive Advantage: The Coevolution of Firms, Technology, and National Institutions* (Cambridge: Cambridge University Press, 2003).

[89]Michael H. Best, "Silicon Valley and the Resurgence of Route 128: Systems Integration and Regional Innovation," in *Regions, Globalization, and the Knowledge-Based Economy*, ed. John H. Dunning (Oxford: Oxford University Press, 2000), 459–506; Christophe Lécuyer, *Making Silicon Valley: Innovation and the Growth of High Tech, 1930–1970* (Cambridge, MA: MIT Press, 2006).

[90]Ben Rooney, "How Tel Aviv Became a Tech Hub," *Wall Street Journal*, January 27, 2012, http://blogs.wsj.com/tech-europe/2012/01/27/how-tel-aviv-became-a-tech-hub/; Gil Avnimelech and Morris Teubal, "Venture Capital Start-up Co-evolution and the Emergence & Development of Israel's New High Tech Cluster: Part 1: Macro-Background and Industry Analysis," *Economics of Innovation and New Technology* 13, no. 1 (2004): 33–60; Jarunee Wonglimpiyarat, "Government Policies Towards Israel's High-Tech Powerhouse," *Technovation* 52-53 (2016): 18-27.

[91]Jonathan Kandell, "Israel's Silicon Wadi Is Bringing in Billions from Investors," Institutional Investor, October 26, 2016, www.institutionalinvestor.com/article/3596157/banking-and-capital-markets-trading-and-technology/israels-silicon-wadi-is-bringing-in-billions-from-investors.html#.WHpGoFUrKpo.

[92]"Tales from Silicon Wadi," *The Economist*, June 4, 2016, www.economist.com/news/finance-and-economics/21699920-military-insecurity-can-boost-economy-up-point-tales-silicon-wadi.

[93]Zafar Anjum, *Startup Capitals: Discovering the Global Hotspots of Innovation* (Haryana, India: Random House India, 2014).

[94]Ian Allison, "Bitcoin versus M-Pesa: Digital Payments Rumble in the Jungle," *International Business Times*, December 1, 2015, http://www.ibtimes.co.uk/bitcoin-versus-m-pesa-digital-payments-rumble-jungle-1531208.

[95]Eric Wainaina, "42% of Kenya GDP Transacted on M-pesa and 9 Takeaways from Safaricom Results," Techweez, May 7, 2015, www.techweez.com/2015/05/07/ten-takeaways-safaricom-2015-results/.

[96]"Mobile Money in Afghanistan," USAID Afghanistan, August 24, 2011, www.youtube.com/watch?v=VJtjEhFYorU.

[97]Leslie Stahl, "The Future of Money," *60 Minutes*, aired on November 22, 2015 (Shachar Bar-On and Alexandra Poolos, producers), www.cbsnews.com/news/future-of-money-kenya-m-pesa-60-minutes-2/.

[98]Sarah McGregor, "Kenya's M-KOPA Gives Phone-Loans to Put Solar Power in Reach," Bloomberg Business, October 5, 2012.

[99]"Small-Scale Solar Power Is Surging Ahead," *The Economist*, November 1, 2016, https://www.economist.com/news/middle-east-and-africa/21709297-small-scale-solar-power-surging-ahead-africa-unplugged.

[100]Stahl, "The Future of Money."

[101]"Safaricom: Avoid the Little Fragments by Finding Partners," Mobile World Live, November 13, 2012, www.mobileworldlive.com/safaricom-avoid-the-little-fragments-by-finding-partners/.

[102]Tom Griffiths, "China's Mobile Payments War Is Going Global," Advertising Age, November 30, 2015, http://adage.com/article/opinion/china-s-mobile-payments-war-global/301488/; Katie Collins, "Apple Reportedly Considering Person-to-Person Payments," CNET, November, 12, 2015, www.cnet.com/news/apple-reportedly-investigating-person-to-person-payments/.

[103]Barry Jaruzelski, Kevin Schwartz, and Volker Staack, "The 2015 Global Innovation 1000: Innovation's New World Order," *Strategy + Business*, October 27, 2015. http://www.strategyand.pwc.com/reports/2015-global-innovation-1000-media-report

[104]"2016 Global R&D Funding Forecast," *R&D Magazine*, Winter 2016, www.iriweb.org/sites/default/files/2016GlobalR%26DFundingForecast_2.pdf.

[105]"2016 Global R&D Funding Forecast."

[106]"2016 Global R&D Funding Forecast."

[107]National Science Foundation, National Center for Science and Engineering Statistics, "Business Research and Development and

Innovation: 2013," Detailed Statistical Tables NSF 16-313, August 2, 2016. www.nsf.gov/statistics/2016/nsf16313/.

[108]Feng-Shang Wu and Robert Haak, "Innovation Mechanisms and Knowledge Communities for Corporate Central R&D," *Creativity and Innovation Management* 22, no. 1 (2013): 37–52.

[109]Jeffrey R. Immelt, Vijay Govindarajan, and Chris Trimble, "How GE Is Disrupting Itself," *Harvard Business Review* 87, no. 10 (2009): 56–65.

[110]Farok J. Contractor, "'Punching above Their Weight': The Sources of Competitive Advantage for Emerging Market Multinationals," *International Journal of Emerging Markets* 8, no. 4 (2013): 304–28.

[111]"GE's US$1 Billion Investment in Saudi Arabia Creates a Path for New Initiatives in Localization, Technology Innovation and Manufacturing to Drive Country's Digital Transformation by 2020," GE Global Research, November 3, 2015, www.geglobalresearch.com/news/press-releases/ges-global-research-center-in-saudi-arabia-to-drive-cutting-edge-innovation-and-digital-transformation.

[112]Angelica Mari, "LinkedIn Surpasses 20 Million Users in Brazil," *ZD Net*, February 9, 2015, www.zdnet.com/article/linkedin-surpasses-20-million-users-in-brazil/; Harrison Weber, "LinkedIn Now Has 400M Users, but Only 25% of Them Use It Monthly," Venture Beat, October 29, 2015, https://venturebeat.com/2015/10/29/linkedin-now-has-400m-users-but-only-25-of-them-use-it-monthly/.

[113]Hellen Berger, "Finding Opportunities in Brazil," Process Development Forum, Feb. 06, 2015. http://www.processdevelopmentforum.com/articles/finding-opportunities-in-brazil/ (accessed April 22, 2017).

[114]"Doing Business 2011: Making a Difference for Entrepreneurs," World Bank, November 4, 2010, www.doingbusiness.org/reports/global-reports/doing-business-2011.

[115]"Top Challenges of Doing Business in Brazil," TMF Group, www.tmf-group.com/en/media-centre/resources/top-challenges/the-americas/brazil (accessed December 16, 2016).

[116]Cynthia Fujikawa Nes, "The Brazilian Educational System," *Brazilian Business*, August 12, 2015, http://thebrazilbusiness.com/article/the-brazilian-educational-system.

[117]"Brazil's Growth Is Dependent on Human Capital Infrastructure Development," Cision (PR Newswire), October 3, 2012, www.prnewswire.com/news-releases/brazils-growth-is-dependent-on-human-capital-and-infrastructure-development-172479701.html.

[118]Hellen Berger, "Finding Opportunities in Brazil," Process Development Forum, Feb. 06. http://www.processdevelopmentforum.com/articles/finding-opportunities-in-brazil/2015 (accessed April 22, 2017).

[119]Julie Ruvolo, "As Brazilian Economy Descends into Crisis, Tech Is Growing Double Digits," *Tech Crunch, September* 27, 2015, https://techcrunch.com/2015/09/27/as-brazilian-economy-descends-into-crisis-tech-is-growing-double-digits/.

CHAPTER **12**

Global Innovation and Intellectual Property

Hamster3d/Getty Images

Introduction

Many of the assumptions we take for granted about the future are likely to change. For instance, while owning a car may be a basic fact of life for many people throughout the world, actually driving one may soon be unnecessary. Artificial intelligence and the "Internet of things" is changing the nature of many daily tasks and jobs on a global scale. Developments in neuroscience and genetic engineering are altering the ways we treat and prevent diseases. Virtual reality may transform health care, travel, and recreation.[1]

On one hand, these innovations have the potential to increase global income levels and improve the quality of life for entire populations around the world. Improving learning and making better decisions are possible when billions of people are connected through mobile devices and have unlimited access to knowledge. On the other hand, these innovations could also yield greater global inequality, particularly given their potential to disrupt labor markets.[2] As automation and artificial intelligence continue to substitute for labor in all its forms, more jobs are likely to be done by machines—displacing the workforce.

What does this mean for you as a future (or current) global business leader? It means that to compete in such an environment you must connect seemingly different ideas in new and unique ways. It means you need to get your companies to invest in global research and development (R&D) and help members of your team become more innovative. It means that you need to develop and protect intellectual capital.

LEARNING OBJECTIVES

After exploring this chapter you will be able to:

1. **Identify** three types of innovation that can fuel global growth
2. **Outline** ways to invest in global R&D operations
3. **Describe** ways that companies drive innovation
4. **Discuss** how firms can protect their intellectual property

12.1 Innovation as a Tool for Global Growth

LEARNING OBJECTIVE

Identify three types of innovation that can fuel global growth.

Over 93 percent of global executives rate innovation as a key driver of organic global growth.[3] More importantly, research shows that around 85 percent of a company's productivity gains are related to R&D and other innovation-related investments.[4]

Innovation is the commercialization of new invention. However, many innovations do not necessarily build on new inventions. An **invention** is a new concept or product that derives from ideas or from scientific research. **Innovation**, on the other hand, is the combination of new or existing ideas to create something desired by customers, viable in the marketplace, and possible with technology (see **Figure 12.1**).[5]

invention a new concept or product that derives from ideas or from scientific research

innovation combination of new or existing ideas to create marketable value

The inputs used to innovate could be new inventions or they could be old ideas. For example, Henry Ford didn't invent the automobile. Karl Benz from Germany did. However, Ford combined scientific management concepts with the automobile production process to build automobiles more efficiently (**Figure 12.2**). This innovation built on existing inventions to usher in a new industry with the scale to meet demand.[6]

Most global managers struggle to get people in their companies to innovate. So far, no one has created a formula or model that reliably leads companies to increased innovation. Some management approaches are helpful, but none is perfect. As Dr. Brian Junling Li, vice president of Alibaba Group, puts it, "Innovation doesn't come from organized plans. It comes from our preparedness to deal with the uncertainty of the future."[7] To understand how global companies can effectively deal with the uncertainties of the future, we first need to examine the different types of innovation in which companies can invest.

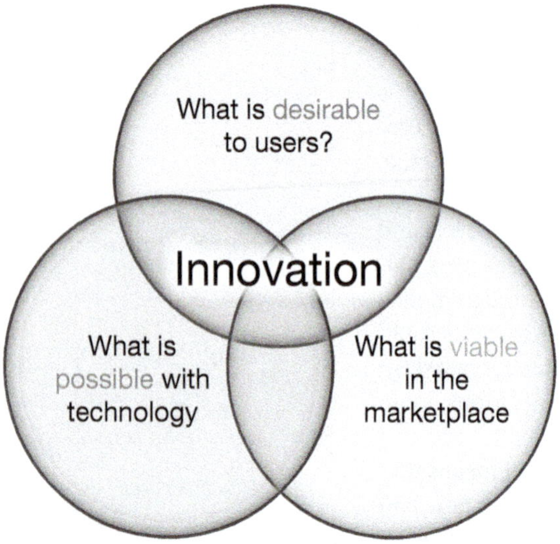

FIGURE 12.1 **Primary components of innovation**

Three Kinds of Innovation

Different types of innovation have different implications for company growth. Based on those implications, we can organize innovations into three types: those that improve performance, those that enhance efficiency, and those that create a market.[8]

artpartner-images.com/Alamy Stock Photo

Chronicle/Alamy Stock Photo

FIGURE 12.2 **Innovation in the auto industry** Carl Benz of Mercedes Benz invented the automobile (left). Henry Ford of Ford Motor Company innovated by combining ideas on assembly lines with car production (right).

Performance-improving innovations replace old products with upgraded models. Often, the improvements in these models are consistent worldwide. Performance-improving innovations keep a company growing because they provide updated products and services that customers find refreshing. Automotive and tech companies often focus on this kind of innovation.

One downside for a company updating its products is that sales of the new product typically replace sales of the old one. For instance, when Apple introduced the iPhone 8, people mostly stopped buying the iPhone 7 because they were upgrading to the new version instead. Future iPhones will likely get thinner or move away from a handheld device altogether (**Figure 12.3**).

However, most companies don't actually see this as a problem because they know their competitors will also introduce new products that will have the same effect on their sales. Apple continues to bring new phones to market each year because it knows Samsung, Huawei, and LG will also be introducing new phones that could attract current iPhone users, and Apple would rather take market share from its own existing product line than cede it to a competitor. Thus Apple needs to keep updating its phones to stay competitive.

The more serious downside of performance-improving innovations, however, is that they usually don't create a lot of new growth for a company. Incremental innovations tend to attract repeat customers rather than first-time buyers. In addition, because the company stops producing and selling the old product, all the resources used in production—such as people, technology, and equipment—merely shift to the production line for the new product. As a result, this type of innovation is often necessary to maintain sales, but it has only limited potential to create new jobs or capture additional market share.[9]

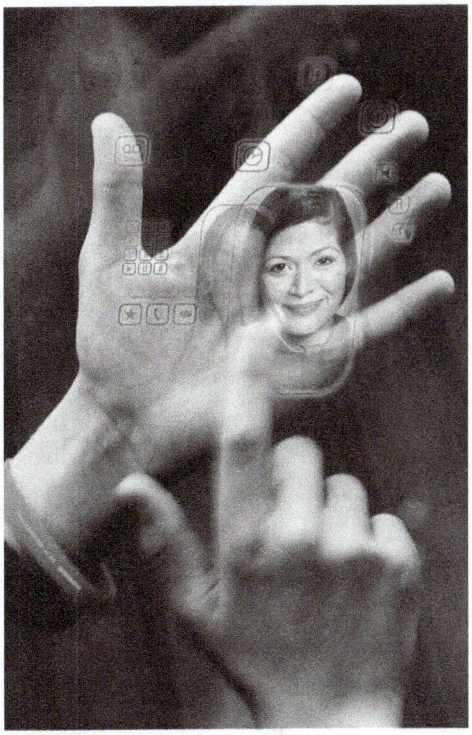

Coneyl Jay/Getty Images

FIGURE 12.3 The future of the iPhone.

Efficiency-enhancing innovations help companies make and sell existing products and services at lower price points. This type of innovation often improves process and efficiency for workers, and makes resources cheaper.[10] For example, the grocery store Aldi (**Figure 12.4**), headquartered in Germany, was founded to meet consumers' daily market needs at a much lower cost than that of its competitors.[11] Over time Aldi has taken a number of innovative steps to reduce costs and prices. These include limiting the number of products in the store, accepting only debit cards and cash, reducing store staff by stacking most products in their shipping

performance-improving innovations improvements to existing products or ideas that meet more of a customers' needs

efficiency-enhancing innovations changes to existing products or ideas that make them lower cost

B Christopher/Alamy Stock Photo

FIGURE 12.4 Aldi offers a low-cost food option The firm has been growing internationally and has stores opening across the United States.

boxes or crates, sourcing from global low-cost suppliers, stocking mostly Aldi-branded products, and having customers bag their own groceries. The company doesn't even provide shopping bags. All these innovations are focused on reducing the cost of operations, enabling the firm to make money while offering low ultra-prices.

From a growth perspective, efficiency-enhancing innovations enable companies to increase profit margins by raising productivity. They also allow companies to reach a lower-income segment of the market. This is particularly important in developing economies, where many people are "priced out" of markets for products whose prices they can't afford.

Not everything about these efficiency innovations is good for the global economy, however. Efficiency innovations often eliminate jobs. For example, Aldi was able to reduce the number of employees needed to run a store to fewer than half that required by a traditional competitor.[12] While this saves consumers money, it also means Aldi has fewer jobs to offer in a community.

market-creating innovations products or ideas that meet the needs of a group of potential consumers whose needs have not been met before

Finally, **market-creating innovations** introduce products so radically different from anything else available that they create a new class of consumers—or a new market.[13] Take the smartphone as an example. Smartphones integrated features from a whole range of electronics—phones, computers, cameras, and music and video players—and packaged them all into a device that could be carried around in a pocket almost anywhere. The smartphone took functions that had been accessible only by the rich and made them available to billions of people all over the world.

Market-creating innovations can unlock other such opportunities. The telecom systems provided in China by Western telecommunication companies like Ericson were so large and expensive that they often took up the roof of an entire building. Smaller, less affluent companies couldn't afford or house such large and complex equipment for their offices.[14] The Chinese telecom company Huawei developed and marketed a system that was a fraction of the price and size, opening a market that had been previously ignored (see **Figure 12.5**).[15]

From a growth perspective, market-creating innovations enable companies to both increase revenue and grow in size.[16] As companies reach more prospective customers, they need more employees to build and distribute products, and to sell to and support customers. That growth also works its way up the company's supply chains as its partners work to increase their supply. This potential makes market-creating innovation the form of innovation most effective for company growth; however, it's also the riskiest, as we'll see next.

WileyPLUS

See Whiteboard Video: Market-Creating Innovation

Risks of Market-Creating Innovation

While global companies often claim to invest in all three types of innovation, in fact most investment focuses on performance-improving or efficiency-improving innovation. This might seem odd, since most real economic growth comes from market-creating innovations.[17] One possible explanation comes from the work of early economists such as Adam Smith and David Ricardo.[18] According to their economic models, companies generate profits because they differentiate the performance of their product—and/or the efficiency of their product—in a way that generates higher profits than competitors earn. As a result, companies focus so much on performance- and efficiency-based innovation because traditional business models are effective at determining the value of these investments and interpreting those values for investors. For example, how much money did Disney make in China from the release of the film *Finding Dory*? Disney has advanced metrics that enable it to predict the value of this and similar performance-improving investments.

LLUIS GENE/AFP/Getty Images

FIGURE 12.5 **Huawei's innovative design significantly reduces the required space**

By contrast, market-creating innovations are much more difficult to evaluate because their potential for generating profits is ultimately uncertain. By definition, this kind of innovation results in products and services that cannot be tested in the market before release and for which demand is not obvious. For example, after incurring considerable costs and investing heavily in R&D, IBM developed the first smartphone in 1992. However, the company was so concerned that consumers wouldn't like the phone that it took two years to introduce it to the market. The phone was not successful. Many argued that there were too many problems with the phone and that its sheer size turned people away.

Rob Stothard/Getty Images

FIGURE 12.6 Evolution of smartphones IBM's Simon Smart Phone from 1992 compared with the Apple iPhone in 2007.

Some years passed before the Japanese firm NTT DoCoMo introduced the next smartphone, with the infrastructure necessary for it to gain significant customer adoption. However, the phone was successful in Japan but never made it in global markets. Many believe the phone was so customized to the Japanese market and system (for example, it didn't adopt 3G technology) that it couldn't make it as a global product.[19] It was at about this time, in 2007, that Apple's iPhone was introduced in the United States—a full 15 years after IBM's pioneering phone (**Figure 12.6**).[20] Not only was the iPhone an instant success in the United States; it was also a success worldwide because Apple had built it using hardware and software that could operate effectively anywhere in the world.

Market-creating innovations like these are rare for several reasons. First, they are costly and time-consuming to develop. Second, investment decisions are often based on short-term metrics. Specifically, managers often try to satisfy financial markets (increasing the value of the company's stock) in the short term. As a result, their approach to investing resources is focused on immediate results, not the long-term horizon of market-creating innovation. Often, the prompt results promised by performance enhancements or job-eliminating investments are more immediately attractive to shareholders than investments that create new value and jobs down the road. To put that in perspective, imagine a global leader at IBM saying, "We should invest in the smartphone starting now, even though it will be 15 years before customers are willing to buy it."

Finally, there is always a danger that the new market segment will never appear, turning the company's investment in innovation into a loss. This risk is another reason some companies avoid market-creating innovations in favor of performance or efficiency innovations of proven products and processes.

12.2 Investing in Innovation

LEARNING OBJECTIVE

Outline ways to invest in global R&D operations.

While innovation is often associated with high-tech companies, in reality, all companies must innovate if they hope to stay competitive and continue to grow in a global environment. To compete in this environment, companies have begun to spread their innovation efforts across multiple markets, including many emerging markets.[21] The benefits include developing products to meet local needs, decreasing costs of innovation by moving some R&D to countries where resources are cheaper, and bringing in new ideas from different cultures and perspectives to help solve old problems.

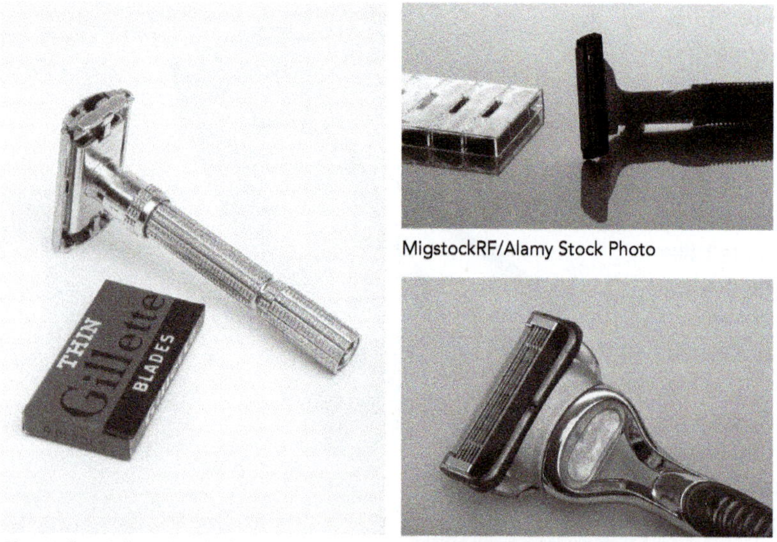

Chris Willson/Alamy Stock Photo

MigstockRF/Alamy Stock Photo

marek kasula/Alamy Stock Photo

FIGURE 12.7 **Evolution of the razor** *Clockwise from left:* A double-edge razor, a Schick Hydro, and a Gillette Guard.

For example, after developing its Fusion ProGlide razor in North America and then for years selling it in India, Gillette realized it was overlooking a 400-million-person market of low-income men who were using double-edge razors. So Gillette developed a strategy to innovate for the low-income Indian customers who could not afford its premium-priced Fusion ProGlide. It began by creating a local R&D unit in India, whose members were able to observe potential customers in their homes and on the streets in order to understand the role of grooming in their lives. The R&D team realized their potential customers weren't just interested in affordability; they were also interested in safety and ease of use—something double-edge razors did not offer. Next, Gillette's Indian R&D team collaborated with other R&D groups within the company to design a customized new product—the Gillette Guard (**Figure 12.7**).

The Guard was priced at a fraction of the cost of the premium razor and promised a high-quality shave, featuring an easy-rinse cartridge to limit water consumption and a lightweight ribbed handle for ease of use and safety (see **Figure 12.8**).[22]

Because of the benefits of distributing innovation efforts across local markets, global companies have taken to building multiple R&D centers in order to learn about local markets and take advantage of talent and ideas across the world. Estimates indicate that more than half of all U.S. and European firms have done so.[23] While building globally distributed R&D centers is

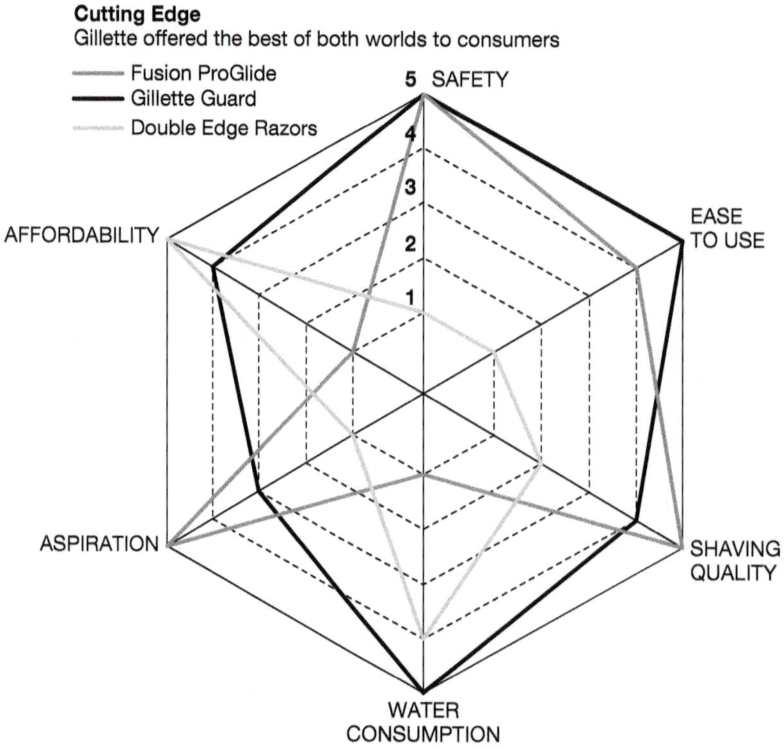

FIGURE 12.8 **Gillette Guard compared with the Fusion ProGlide and double-edge razors.** **Source:** Leonardo Scamazzo, "Sharp Focus," *Business Today*, April 13, 2014, www.businesstoday.in/magazine/lbs-case-study/gillette-innovated-improved-its-market-share-in-india/story/204517.html.

a good start for encouraging innovation, the way those centers are organized and staffed also influences the degree to which a company will generate successful innovation.

From Local to Global Innovation

R&D units often form the springboard for innovation. That said, we need to distinguish between R&D units that focus primarily on developing new or repurposing old technologies, and units that focus on incrementally updating products. One company that makes this distinction is Shell, the oil giant. Shell has three central technical centers focused on new innovation and technology invention—two in Holland and one in Houston, Texas. Shell's ten other technical centers focus on developing products, supporting marketing, or providing specific technical assistance for regional operations. These centers are scattered throughout the world, from the United Kingdom, France, and Canada to India, Qatar, and Singapore.[24] The company realizes that both types of R&D are vital for continued innovation.

How do multinationals know where they should locate their R&D or product development centers? A common philosophy says they should put them where the need for information collection and processing is the greatest.[25] For example, if a company is in an industry where consumer tastes change frequently or are difficult to assess, the center of innovation should be set up locally, close to the customers. In some cases this requires massive investments in R&D centers in local markets. For instance, LG has R&D offices in nearly 90 countries to drive local innovation (see **Figure 12.9**).

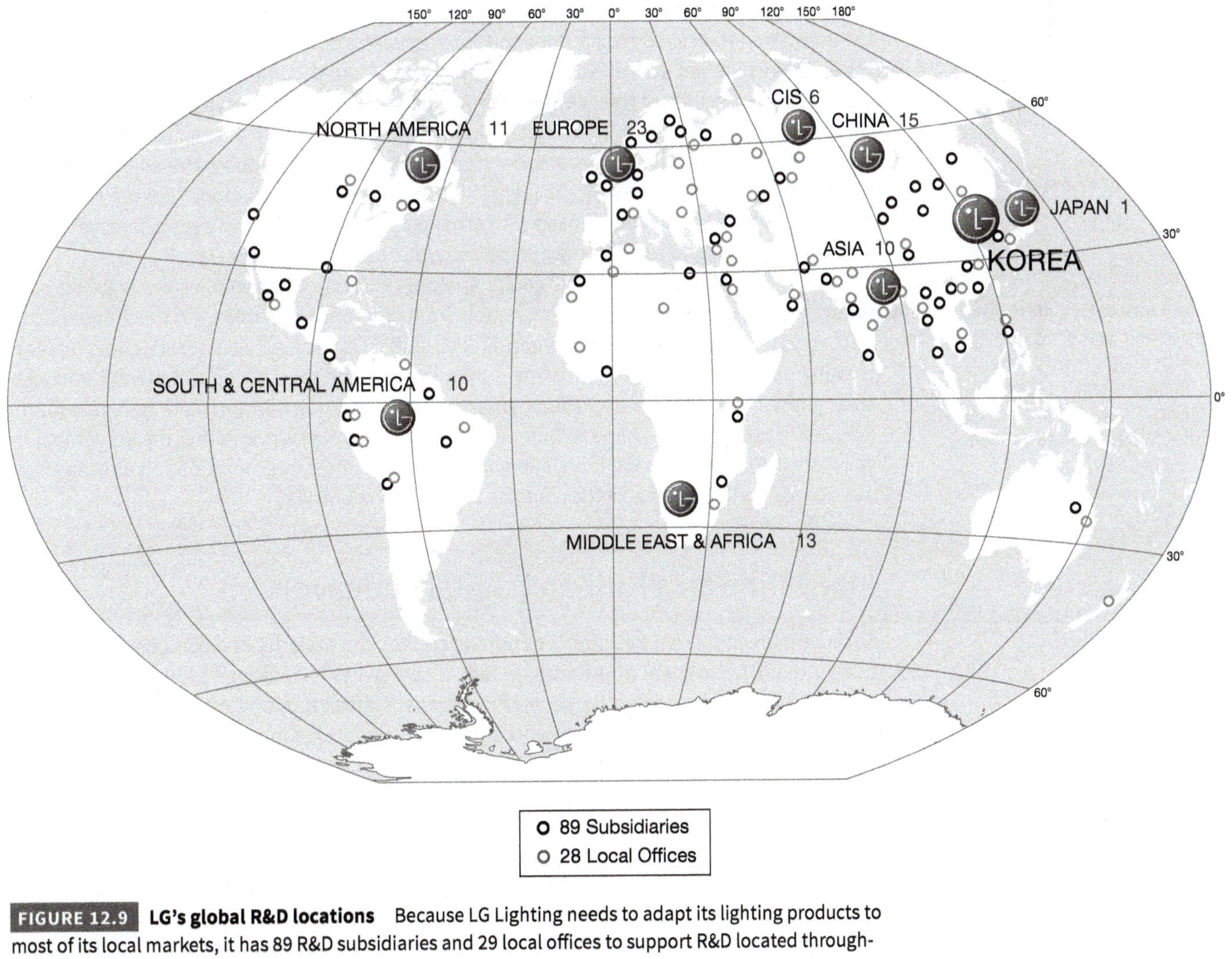

FIGURE 12.9 **LG's global R&D locations** Because LG Lighting needs to adapt its lighting products to most of its local markets, it has 89 R&D subsidiaries and 29 local offices to support R&D located throughout the world. The largest R&D operation is in Korea, but Europe, Russia, China, North America, the Middle East and Africa, and South and Central Europe all have their own R&D Centers. **Source:** "About Reliability and Sustainability," LG Lighting, http://www.lglightingus.com/reliability-and-sustainability.aspx (accessed July 18, 2017).

If the firm is in an industry dominated by technological changes driven by a centralized geographic location—like Silicon Valley for the technology industry—at least some portion of the R&D function should be located there. The idea is to establish linkages to potential sources of innovation. For instance, Zhang Ruimin, CEO of the Chinese appliance manufacturer Haier, brought the company to the U.S. market because U.S. consumers are some of the most demanding in the world. Ruimin wanted to "create zero distance with the customer," and the innovation required to succeed in the United States would in most cases be more than that required for success in other markets.[26] In other words, if Haier could meet the needs of the world's most demanding customers, it could take some of that local knowledge and apply it to other demanding markets.

Separate, regional centers of innovation have a downside: they can lead to duplication of effort. If the various centers don't communicate, innovators in different places can end up working on similar problems without sharing their results. Email, messaging, videoconferencing, computerized databases, and electronic forums such as Slack and Yammer, have eliminated much of the effective distance that hindered collaboration and interaction in the past, but many global companies continue to struggle with these issues.

Part of the problem is that distance is a critical obstacle to information transfer. Modern technologies can't eliminate it entirely. This is why Microsoft locates key employees primarily in its sprawling campus at Redmond, outside Seattle, Washington. It's why Cisco still locates some 15,000 people on its campus in crowded and expensive San José in the heart of Silicon Valley.[27] Putting employees together increases interaction, and interaction increases innovation.[28]

The fact is, while the Internet may have reduced the extent to which distance is an obstacle to information transfer, it hasn't done much to assist the effective blending of creative knowledge across different countries. Microsoft, Cisco, and other companies still rely on creative knowledge as a source of their competitive strength, so effective knowledge transfer is a critical part of their businesses.[29] Effectively sharing complex knowledge requires personal interaction; thus, innovation remains a social process, and distance reduces the ability to interact socially, making distance one of the biggest barriers to global innovation.[30] Research indicates that inventors are more tightly linked with other parts of the world than ever before, yet people who work closely tend to cluster geographically, just as they did in the past.[31]

open innovation platforms electronic platforms through which people from different companies and independent contractors work collaboratively with internal R&D staff to innovate

For example, many consumer goods and pharmaceutical companies are creating **open innovation platforms** through which people from different companies and independent contractors work collaboratively with internal R&D staff to innovate.[32] As a result, companies are creating open work environments where people can come together to collaborate and meet face-to-face. These spaces are also opening up to try to bring consumers in to help with the innovation process.[33] The need to bring employees and customers together means companies go where the technology and innovation are. As a result, most large multinationals today carry out extensive innovation activities outside their home countries.

Innovation as a Human Capital Endeavor

Because innovation requires intensive human capital, the majority of a company's innovation budget tends to be spent on salaries. In fact, a survey by *R&D Magazine* found that the most important factor considered by general managers is attracting and retaining staff, followed closely by the need to build a company culture that encourages innovation.[34]

For this reason, after selecting an overseas R&D location, the first step is to select the right site leader. Should a company hire a local who is unlikely to understand the company's culture but understands the country's culture? Or should it hire someone from the home country who understands the company's culture but not the local culture? Ideally, an innovation leader would understand both cultures, but if a company is forced to choose between the two, it is more important to start with someone who understands the company's culture. That understanding will help the manager make sure the company's values are effectively translated to local members of the R&D team and will ensure that the local team draws on resources from both headquarters and other R&D locations. The manager must then accept that he or she needs to hire local managers who understand the country-specific context, and then listen to those people.

The next step is to ensure strong coordination between the local R&D center and other R&D centers within the company. Consider Panasonic's R&D management strategy. When the company globalized its R&D operations to places like the United States and Europe, many of its R&D managers at the headquarters in Japan feared their jobs would become obsolete or redundant. Instead, much of their work shifted to coordinating Panasonic's network of globally scattered R&D centers and ensuring innovations were conducted at a globally collaborated level. In addition to their normal R&D activities, their responsibility includes setting research agendas, monitoring results, and creating direct ties between sites.[35]

12.3 Driving a Culture of Innovation

LEARNING OBJECTIVE

Describe ways that companies drive innovation.

To truly become global innovators, successful companies have created a company culture in which experimentation and entrepreneurship are encouraged across all local units, and where taking a calculated risk is not frowned upon. A **company culture** is the unique combination of a company's vision, values, norms, systems, symbols, language, assumptions, beliefs, and habits. Several companies have become famous for their cultures of innovation. For instance, at Google, the "70-20-10 rule" governs the ratio of investment between the company's core business, related side projects, and new ideas. This principle even extends to the way employees are expected to divide their time: 70 percent on the main tasks, 20 percent on related projects, and 10 percent on exploratory projects. It sends a strong message to employees everywhere that they are expected to think outside the box and come up with solutions to problems that may not even have been recognized yet.[36]

company culture the unique combination of a company's vision, values, norms, systems, symbols, language, assumptions, beliefs, and habits

But a culture of innovation does not just happen. Building one requires specific investments on the part of the global company, leaders who back innovation, and strategic goals focused on innovation. And even then, innovation isn't just a corporate, high-level management effort. The company needs to foster specific behaviors that ensure employees across its diverse workforce are also engaged in the innovative efforts.

Foundations of Culture

Corporate role models are a foundational element in building a culture of innovation. Leaders who demonstrate the ideals of innovation—such as Jack Ma (founder of Alibaba, shown in **Figure 12.10**), Reed Hastings (founder of Netflix), and Elon Musk (founder of Tesla, SolarCity, and SpaceX)—help employees across the globe embody them as well. For example, at 3M—a firm known for its culture of innovation—virtually all senior line managers have pioneered successful innovations. Their experiences serve as a powerful example for other workers.[37] However, success isn't the only important model. These 3M managers have also each experienced dead ends along the way, and those too serve as an important example for the company culture. These failures demonstrate that innovation comes at a cost the company is willing to bear, and that people are expected to question existing assumptions within the company, take

dpa picture alliance/Alamy Stock Photo

FIGURE 12.10 **Jack Ma** Ma is China's richest man and a strong advocate for continual innovation.

time to experiment with unproven ideas, and search for and combine knowledge from the most unlikely of places.

stretch goals goals that represent company-level objectives that require employees of a company to do something beyond what one might reasonably expect

Another foundational element needed to drive a culture of innovation is to set stretch goals. **Stretch goals** are company-level objectives that require the company to do something beyond what others might reasonably expect, pushing efforts in new directions or to new levels. Often, the goals are difficult enough that they require new ways of looking at problems rather than simply maintaining the status quo. As it turns out, strong belief in a company's current activities and products can actually work against innovation. Too much confidence can produce a culture of complacency and limit a company to focusing solely on how to best exploit its current capabilities.[38]

For example, about a decade ago the Chinese telecom company Huawei was just a small player in the telecommunications industry. The company was searching for something to differentiate itself from other telecom companies, to gain power in the market, and to attract carriers to its business. One day, while in the Netherlands, a team of Huawei engineers met with a small Dutch company that needed help with a problem: the company needed to find a base station for its telecom networks that could fit in a very small space—about a fifth the size the existing technology required. However, major telecom companies, including Ericsson and Nokia, had refused this challenge.[39]

Even in the face of this opportunity to create something new for the Dutch company, the Huawei team was reluctant to risk moving forward. They were confident in their existing product and technology, but those options wouldn't work in this new situation. Their thinking was limited. "Because people had always been [following the leader] as the status quo," a Huawei team member noted, "we always thought we could do what the competitor did, but we never imagined that we could go beyond it." Fortunately, Huawei's innovative leader, Chairman Yu, set stretch goals to go beyond the existing product base, inspiring the development of new space-saving equipment that would meet the needs of the Dutch company. That same equipment then went on to disrupt the market and become the new standard, putting Huawei at the forefront of the industry.[40] This shift to build a more innovative culture at Huawei required a corporate role model and a stretch goal that many weren't sure could be accomplished.

The Innovator's Imperative

Role models and stretch goals provide a foundation for multinationals trying to develop a culture of innovation, but such a foundation can only get you so far. As companies take a global approach to management, they discover that innovative ideas can come from anywhere in the company, not just at headquarters or within R&D operations. Rather, innovation is likely to have its roots in the local problems of a company's globally dispersed customers.[41] Therefore, companies must effectively search for knowledge at the local level and combine that new knowledge with other knowledge found throughout the company.

innovator's imperative the need for individuals to understand local market problems, to reach out to others globally to search for unique solutions to the problem, and to uncover the causal relationships found within that foreign knowledge to ensure it is correctly applied to the local problems

Research suggests that building a culture of innovation at the global level requires three key behaviors across the multinational's globally dispersed operations. These behaviors represent the **innovator's imperative** and consist of going local, reaching out, and uncovering principles (see **Figure 12.11**).

Most established multinational companies have templates for products and processes that have been developed by headquarters and have already proven successful elsewhere.[42] As one unit manager at Shell Oil put it, "many unit leaders see these templates as the correct way to do something and barely veer from the [templates] sent from on high . . . . [M]any of the [HQ] managers tend to think this way as well."[43] But to drive innovation, we must acknowledge that no two local markets are identical. Corporate knowledge can wilt and die once it reaches the local level if it doesn't find root in the local soil.

Go Local Going local, the first of the three steps, helps units adapt standardized products and processes in ways that enable these offerings to flourish in the new context. It means

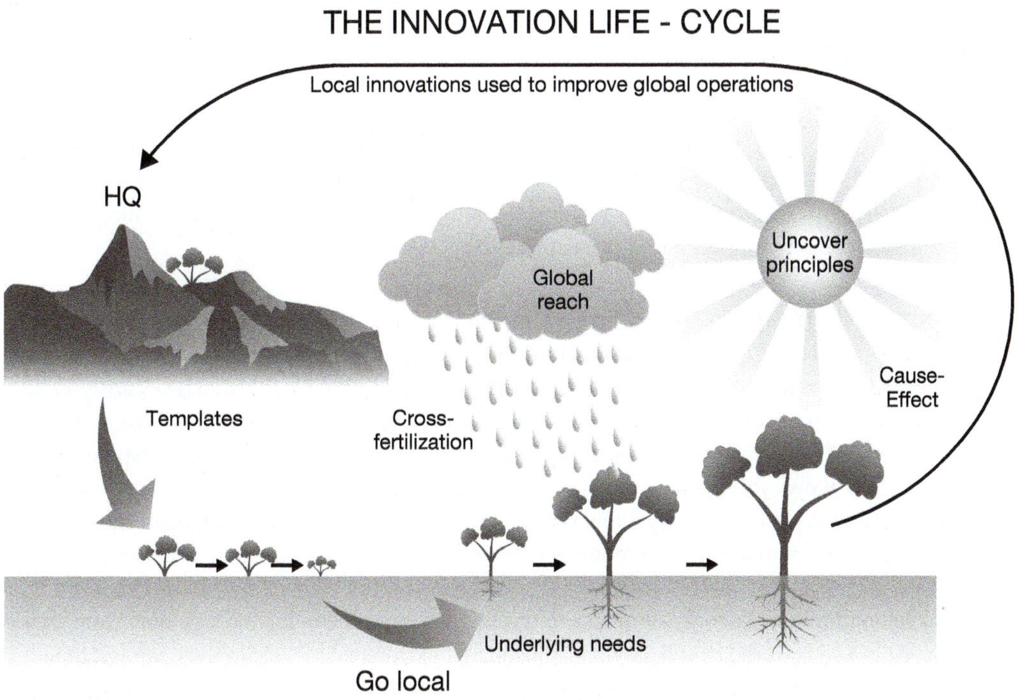

FIGURE 12.11 **The innovator's imperative** Building a culture of innovation within foreign units starts with global products and processes developed at the corporate level. Local units first modify and develop these processes and products to make them their own. Then each unit reaches outside its local context and finally tries to uncover underlying principles in knowledge from abroad.

observing the local market and the context in which potential clients live and work in order to find ways to create solutions for their local needs. This behavior includes (1) gaining a deep understanding of customers by observing how they use the product in the local environment; and (2) questioning preexisting assumptions about the customer or the way the company has done things in the past. These two actions enable employees to identify novel problems that have not been addressed before.

Let's revisit our Huawei example to show how a group of employees "went local" to understand the context of the Dutch customer. Because Huawei has a strong reputation for being customer-oriented, requiring all engineers and managers to visit customers on-site, its team was able to identify the novel problem the Dutch company was facing. As one engineer from the Huawei team working on the Dutch project pointed out, "We headed to the customer's engine rooms right after we got off the plane before we got to the hotel."[44] During one of these visits, the engineers gained a key insight: for the new base station to work, the main part of the system had to be separated into several parts, and some parts had to be located outside. To this point, no one had even wondered whether the system could be separated into different parts. Huawei's people never would have been able to identify this problem had they not spent time observing the space the Dutch company was working with, and then questioning their own assumptions and existing ways of doing things.

Reach Out Going local is a critical first step in identifying gaps in the market, but it is not enough. Understanding the client only helps identify the actual problem. The next step is for employees at the local unit or subsidiary to reach out to people at headquarters and in peer units for help examining the problem from new angles, enabling them to formulate effective, unique, and low-cost solutions. As a behavior, reaching out involves (1) collaborating with individuals, inside or outside the firm, with whom employees have developed strong relationships, in order to access diverse stores of complex knowledge; and (2) integrating the new knowledge with the local knowledge base. In essence, it helps to fertilize local ideas by improving the root structure.

After the Huawei team identified the unique problem and opportunity by going local with the Dutch company, they reached out by turning to another Huawei office in Shenzhen, where the main R&D efforts were located. Working with the head R&D group, they brainstormed many different ways to solve the problem of separating the main portion of the system into several different parts. They also attended various exhibitions on different telecommunication systems to integrate ideas from outside their local context in the Netherlands. One engineer on the Dutch team commented, "after looking and understanding, we combined learning from the industrial leading products with the existing products in Huawei."[45]

Uncover Principles Often, at the same time as they are reaching out, globally dispersed employees must also uncover why something works in another geographic location to ensure the knowledge is applicable to the local setting. Principles highlight *why* certain tasks are effective. The behavior of uncovering principles includes (1) exploring why a product, service, or process works, and (2) identifying the universal principles behind it. For example, understanding that A leads to B allows you to make the proper connection between those two variables. However, knowing *why* A leads to B may allow you to know when A or B can be replaced by C. Hence, building a culture of innovation requires that units explore the cause-and-effect relationships of their products, processes, and services. For instance, the Huawei employees realized that they needed to more deeply understand the science behind the technology they were trying to deliver. This ensured that they were transferring to others with whom they worked only the knowledge needed to solve the Dutch problem.

Going local by questioning company norms through deep customer observation, along with reaching out to different R&D groups and uncovering principles about the science behind the technology, helped Huawei to generate insight that led to the development of a new standard product called a distributed base station.[46] Today, this base station is the industry norm and has helped transform Huawei from a small, obscure Chinese telecom company to a global industry leader and the largest telecom company in the world.[47]

Following the innovator's imperative can also help companies in emerging markets to develop solutions for poor clients. Using this approach to develop unique and low-cost solutions to problems faced by the poor means that companies must first drop their assumption that the poor want what they've already been selling.

12.4 Protecting Intellectual Property

LEARNING OBJECTIVE

Discuss how firms can protect their intellectual property.

In addition to globalizing their R&D operations and building cultures of innovation, multinational companies are investing more of their financial and other resources outside their home countries. As a result, they are faced with the increasing need to protect these investments abroad, especially against the theft of intellectual property occurring worldwide. The IP Commission, an independent initiative to understand and protect intellectual property (IP), comprising leading U.S. experts from the private sector, national security, academia, and politics, recently estimated that the United States loses over $300 billion a year to such crimes.[48] In addition, the European Union estimates that counterfeiting and piracy of products cost the EU between $250 and $650 billion a year.[49] Protections such as patents and trademarks are an obvious benefit for the companies that own the IP, but they also stimulate global economic growth, according to a recent report by the United Nations Industrial Development Organization.[50] Accordingly, many companies and governments push to create and enforce IP protections in order to encourage growth.

At the Consumer Electronics Show in Las Vegas in January 2016, U.S. marshals raided the stand set up by Changzhou First International Trade and confiscated all its products and marketing materials.[51] Future Motion, a U.S. firm, argued that Changzhou had "infringed on its patents." The one-wheeled motion-board design from Future Motion retails for $1,499; Changzhou's knockoff sold online for a mere $550. Future Motion had filed a complaint with the U.S. District Court and obtained a restraining order, a seizure order, and a temporary injunction against Changzhou.

Such disputes are becoming more and more common as firms fight ever harder to protect their IP. But IP rights are often difficult to enforce globally—particularly in emerging markets with limited regulation or governmental oversight. And some losses occur not through patent violations but through theft of unpatented trade secrets. In 2014 Jun Xie, a Chinese engineer at General Electric in the United States, pleaded guilty to copying more than 2 million files regarding GE's magnetic resonance imaging technologies without authorization and sending them to relatives in China. The estimated value of GE's lost trade secrets was between $100 and $200 million.[52]

dpa picture alliance/Alamy Stock Photo

FIGURE 12.12 Louis Vuitton's checkerboard pattern Turns out that even Louis Vuitton can't patent a checkerboard pattern.

Even with IP protection, not all global companies win their complaints. Louis Vuitton lost a trademark suit and appeal in 2016 for its famous checkerboard pattern found in handbags and clothing. A court based in Luxembourg ruled that "the checkerboard pattern, as represented in the contested trademark, was a basic and banal feature composed of very simple elements."[53] It was not able to be trademarked because it lacked a monogram or other distinguishing feature (**Figure 12.12**).

Because protecting IP is so critical for companies today, next we highlight a few of the different modes businesses use in an effort to keep their intellectual property safe.

Patents

The most common protection with which global firms guard their IP is a patent. A **patent** is issued by a governmental authority to exclude anyone other than the patent holder from making, using, or selling the patented invention for a set period of time.[54] Laws of nature, physical phenomena, and abstract ideas cannot be patented. Data from the U.S. Patent Office show that the number of patents granted has dramatically increased over the past 20 years (see **Figure 12.13**).

patent a form of legal protection provided by a government that excludes anyone other than the patent holder from making, using, or selling the invention for a set period of time

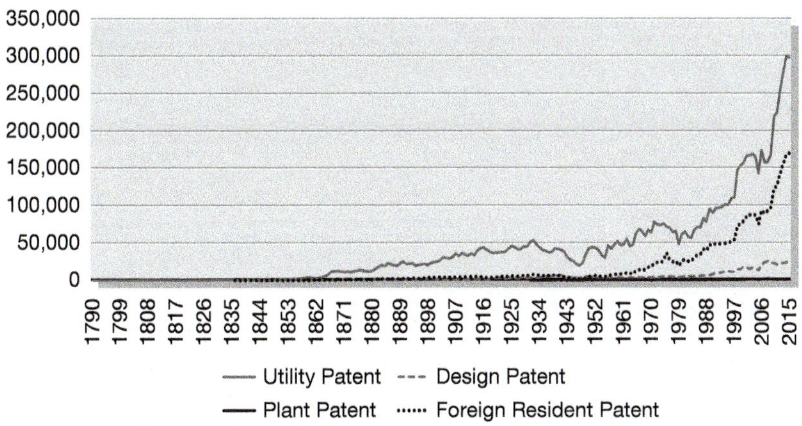

FIGURE 12.13 Number of U.S. patents granted, 1790–2015 Similar trends are evident in across the globe, particularly in China. **Source:** U.S. Patent Activity, Calendar Years 1790 to the Present, www.uspto.gov/web/offices/ac/ido/oeip/taf/h_counts.htm.

Advantages of Patents

Patents have a long history, and more than 150 countries recognize and use them. The agreement most of them have adopted enables patent applicants to seek protection in 148 countries simultaneously across the globe (see **Figure 12.14**). The biggest advantage of this system is that a company can call upon a government to back its claim and to help protect its property rights in all these countries, including asking for sanctions against patent infringers.

Disadvantages of Patents While global companies achieve many advantages by seeking patent protections, patents do have a few disadvantages. First, the patenting process is very specific and requires the inventor to disclose in full to the issuing authority the technical details of the product. Because patent applications are public records, this requirement in essence gives competitors a blueprint of exactly how to copy the invention. Second, the patent application process can be time-consuming and costly. The average cost to file a patent in the United States is about $20,000. This cost covers just filing and search fees—to ensure the inventor's idea is novel and then to file the protection status. The heaviest cost of a patent is incurred in defending it. In 2015, the typical cost to bring a patent-infringement suit in the United States ranged from $400,000 for cases with less than $1 million at risk to $3,000,000 for suits with more than $25 million at risk.[55]

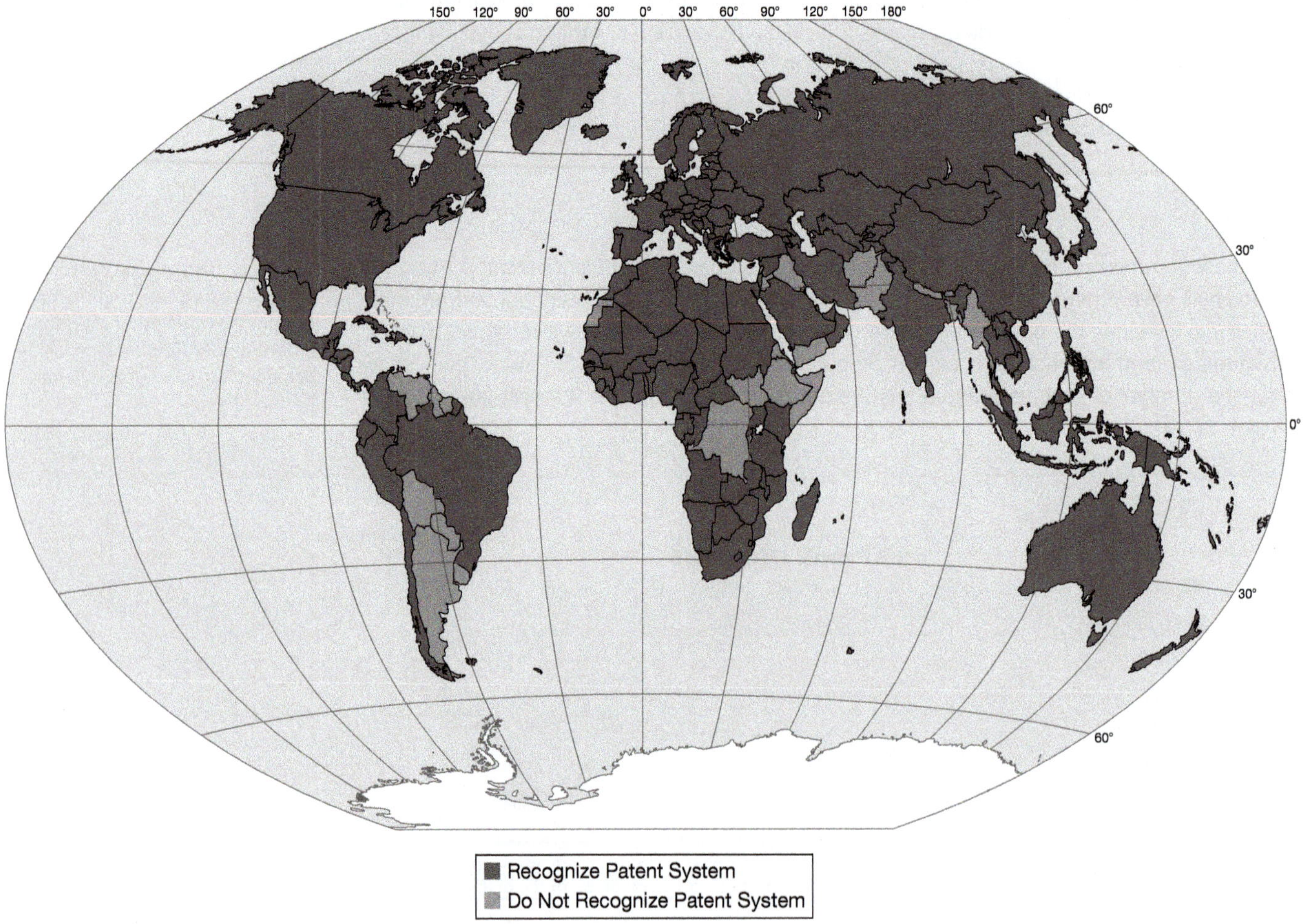

FIGURE 12.14 **Patents are recognized worldwide** Countries that recognize the international patent system as of September 2016. **Source:** "The PCT Now Has 152 Contracting States," World Intellectual Property Organization, www.wipo.int/pct/en/pct_contracting_states.html.

Copyrights

Erik Voake/Getty Images

FIGURE 12.15 **Adidas works hard to protect its iconic three strip design.**

A **copyright** is a form of IP protection granted to authors of a literary, dramatic, musical, or artistic work. The author of the work becomes the owner of the copyright unless the work was made for hire, in which case the employer is considered the author. A work is automatically protected from the moment of its creation throughout the author's life, plus 70 years after the author's death. Even though registration of copyright is not required, doing so has some advantages; for example, making a public record by registering with the appropriate copyright office allows authors to sue for copyright infringement and damages if their work is copied without authorization.[56] Not protected under a copyright is work that has not been written or recorded, such as improvised speeches or performances, titles, slogans, or lists of ingredients, and ideas, procedures, methods, or systems. While copyrights are granted by national governments, several treaties have extended the rights of copyright owners internationally. For instance, the Berne Convention of 1886 provides means for authors to control how, by whom, and under what terms their work is used.[57]

copyright a form of protection available to authors of literary, dramatic, musical, or artistic intellectual property

The German footwear maker Adidas vigorously defends its copyrights. In 2008, the company won a $305 million judgement against Payless Shoe Company after Payless copied Adidas's three-stripe design (shown in **Figure 12.15**).[58] It also filed suit against Ecco over Ecco's 2016 shoe design and filed two suits against Sketchers.[59]

Advantages of Copyrights Copyrights allow global companies, artists, and authors to invest significant resources in creating unique and highly valued work. For instance, JK Rowling, the author of the world-famous *Harry Potter* series, is worth over a billion dollars. Holding the copyright to her books allows her to profit from all the spinoffs that use her copyrighted characters as well as the book sales. Without copyright protection she would not likely have capitalized on her creative works.[60]

Disadvantages of Copyrights The disadvantages of copyrights are the costs and challenge of enforcement. Many authors of creative works simply do not have the means to pursue copyright infringement litigation. For instance, a recent case in China in which a famous novelist was accused of copying the work of over 200 other authors has moved slowly because "the cost of litigation was a barrier."[61] It is also often difficult for copyright owners to control the use of their content. For instance, during the 2016 U.S. presidential campaign, Donald Trump Jr. violated a copyright in tweeting an unlicensed image of a bowl of Skittles. The author registered his image and then filed suit. However, by the time Trump removed the image from his Twitter feed, it had been retweeted thousands of times. Each time constituted a copyright violation the author could do little to fix.[62] In response, a Vietnam-based company created a block-chain technology that would mark the work with data that would send information back to the original author, showing each time the work was transferred or downloaded.[63]

Trademarks

A **trademark** is a recognizable brand name, design, or logo, like the Nike swoosh, that calls a specific product to a consumer's mind. Service marks are like trademarks but are representations of services, such as the FedEx logo for the FedEx corporation. Trademarks and service

trademark legal protection of a recognizable brand name, design, or logo that calls a specific product to a consumer's mind

marks enable companies to brand products in an obvious way, helping customers quickly recognize the maker and thus infer the inherent quality at a glance.

Once a trademark has been registered, the holder of the mark can attach the "registered trademark" label ® to a logo or other symbol that forms the trademark. In addition to company-specific trademarks, some trademarks are issued based on geography, for goods produced in the appropriate location. For instance, Champagne, Darjeeling tea, Idaho potatoes, and Colombian coffee are products whose names include trademarked geographic indicators. These labels are based on the geographic origin of the product, not the specific company producing it.

Advantages of Trademarks Trademark laws allow companies to stop unauthorized use of their trademark by other producers of the good. Trademarks also enable customers to identify quickly and easily products produced by certain companies, thereby acting as a proxy for quality. Without such protections, consumers might mistakenly buy goods they do not want. For instance, 22 fake Apple stores were shut down in Kunming, China. These stores had copied the design of Apple stores in an effort to trick customers into shopping there.[64]

Disadvantages of Trademarks The major disadvantage of trademarks is they are costly to enforce. Like patent litigation, trademark litigation can cost from $300,000 to over $3 million. For instance, in September 2012, a federal court in California sided with the Swiss company Rolex when it claimed that Melrose.com had used Rolex trademarks illegally. Melrose had been using a tactic called "cybersquatting" in which it operated "rolexwatchforum.com" and featured the Rolex logo. In consequence of the litigation, the company was forced to give up the Melrose.com domain and pay Rolex $8.5 million in damages.[65]

Trade Secrets

trade secret any information that provides a business with a competitive advantage but isn't shared openly

A **trade secret** is any information that provides a business with a competitive advantage but isn't shared openly. Trade secrets can include designs, patterns, formulas, ideas, and processes. One of the most famous trade secrets is the recipe for Coke, the world's most popular soda. The recipe sits in a vault in the company's museum, as shown in **Figure 12.16**.

The value to the U.S. economy of goods and services protected by trade secrets is estimated to be around $5 trillion. Losses and misappropriations of trade secrets by firms that copy products are estimated to cost companies between $160 billion and $480 billion annually.[66] Companies obviously take the protection of their trade secrets seriously. In 2007, two Coca-Cola employees were arrested for trying to sell samples of the "new Coke" to PepsiCo for $1.5 million before the product was launched. PepsiCo alerted Coca-Cola to the breach, and the two employees were arrested; one was sentenced to 7 years in prison and the other to 5 years.[67]

Advantages of Trade Secrets The primary advantage of having a trade secret is that disclosure is not required, as with, for instance, a patent application. A second advantage is that there are no filing costs; the company merely needs to keep the information secure. Finally, unlike patents, trade secrets have no time limit. They last as long as the information remains secure.

Disadvantages of Trade Secrets The primary disadvantage of trade secrets is that they often don't stay secret for very long if the company has a tangible product. Competitors can simply purchase and reverse engineer the product to discover how it is made. For instance, tobacco companies have reverse-engineered competitor's changes in design and ingredients in at least 100 cases.[68] Moreover, competitors can patent the trade secret once they discover it, locking the original company out of its own invention. Finally, because trade secrets are not officially recognized, legal remedies are difficult to find once secrets have been breached.

ZUMA Press, Inc./Alamy Stock Photo

FIGURE 12.16 **The Coca-Cola Vault** Inside this vault is the recipe for Coke.

International Bodies and Laws Governing IP

In today's global market, most laws protecting IP are country-specific, but some key international organizations are actively engaged in creating IP protections. These include the World Trade Organization (WTO) and the World Intellectual Property Organization (WIPO). In 1995 the WTO sponsored the Agreement on Trade-Related Aspects of Intellectual-Property Rights (TRIPS). This agreement created a standard of IP-law enforcement across all WTO members, which include 164 countries. TRIPS focuses on only minimal levels of protection but does include the way copyrights, trademarks, and patents should be created and enforced within countries, and how IP disputes should be handled.

Established in 1967, WIPO is a UN agency with 189 invited member states including Germany, Israel, and South Africa. Its mission is to create a balanced IP system that enables innovation and creativity for the benefit of all. WIPO provides a forum to bring nations together discuss IP law, provide global services to resolve disputes, create cooperation programs to help countries develop IP rules, and act as a world reference source for IP information. For instance, WIPO reports that, in 2015, Huawei of China filed 3,898 patent applications—the most for any company in that year.[69] US companies have submitted more than 57,000 applications. The agency also has standing bodies that deal with copyrights, patents, trademarks, IP standards, enforcement, and negotiations.

Other institutions that deal with international IP issues include the U.S. Patent and Trademark Office's Strategy Targeting Organized Piracy program. This initiative provides hotlines and helps businesses to report and combat counterfeit and pirated goods. Moreover, the bilateral institution US-China Joint Commission on Commerce and Trade provides a forum for the United States and China to meet annually each year since 1983 in order to discuss trade-related matters, including technology transfer and IP.[70]

The Difficulty of Enforcement

While many organizations exist to help protect global IP, protection is only the first step. The real challenge is enforcement. Enforcement puts the teeth in IP law, and without solid enforcement, much of the law would be disregarded.

Summary and Case

Summary

LEARNING OBJECTIVE 12.1 Identify three types of innovation that can fuel global growth.

Three types of innovation are performance-improving, efficiency-enhancing, and market-creating innovations. Performance-improvement innovations introduce new features to existing products but typically take sales from the old product, effectively recycling current customers rather than attracting new ones. Efficiency-enhancing innovations update and improve internal processes and procedures, including those of suppliers, to reduce the costs of production. Market-creating innovations create entirely new products to reach untapped markets. It is the most effective form of innovation for growth over the long term.

LEARNING OBJECTIVE 12.2 Outline ways to invest in global R&D operations.

To make the most of R&D investments, companies must be strategic in where they locate R&D centers and how those centers are organized. If companies use technologies with an existing geographic focal research point, a best practice is to establish an R&D center in that location. For product development centers, regional locations keep R&D centers near the local markets they serve. Finally, R&D is a human capital–intensive endeavor, and companies need to select leaders who understand the company culture.

LEARNING OBJECTIVE 12.3 Describe ways that companies drive innovation.

To create a culture of innovation, a company first needs to build a foundation of innovative leaders and create stretch goals for employees. Next, the company must apply the innovator's imperative: they must go local by talking to and understanding the needs of their customers in each local context. Then the local units should reach out and access information and ideas from other localities and even headquarters. Finally, local units must uncover the principles behind the knowledge used from geographically distant locations in order to adapt and apply it to their local context. Doing so allows companies to build innovative cultures among their globally dispersed organization.

LEARNING OBJECTIVE 12.4 Discuss how firms can protect their intellectual property.

Forms of IP protection include patents, copyrights, trademarks, and trade secrets. Each has pros and cons. International groups like the World Trade Organization (WTO) and World Intellectual Property Organization (WIPO) work to improve IP standards, laws, and enforcement throughout their member nations.

Case

Mettler-Toledo: Measuring the Weight of Innovation

Mettler-Toledo International, Inc. (MT), is a company that researches, develops, and manufactures precision scales and other analytical equipment. Its product portfolio includes weigh modules, pipettes and tips, analytical instruments, load cells, floor scales, dynamic check-weighers, precision balances, moisture analyzers, and gas analyzers, among others.

Mettler-Toledo has always encouraged employees to get to know the needs of local customers within each country and then meet those needs. To facilitate the localization of knowledge and products, the Switzerland-based company has manufacturing centers around the world, including in the United States, Germany, the United Kingdom, Switzerland, and the People's Republic of China. By locating manufacturing in the areas served by the production facilities, MT has significantly shortened the distance for communication between R&D/fabrication and customers. This enables the company to remain agile and to quickly respond to customer needs and requests, integrating feedback to adapt products to local needs. To an extent, this process has worked well for MT, enabling the company to create templated products and services, and then to customize those to meet individual client needs.[71]

Increasingly, however, local Chinese companies have been building up and flooding the market with cheaper, inferior products. At present, the competition couldn't touch the level of sophistication in MT's product line, but the price difference was eating away at MT's hold on the region all the same. While the shift in market wasn't critical or crippling yet, one could envision a future when it might be. MT could see how other companies had come in at the low-end of an industry and built up a brand name before taking on the much larger incumbents. It had happened time and time again in industry after industry around the world, and now it was happening with precision instruments in China.

There was the very real chance that maintaining the status quo would only mean turning a blind eye to a very real threat. History dictated that sleeping giants could only maintain dominance in industry for so long without waking up. Eventually, every arrogant industry leader fell from the top and had to undergo painful—and often insufficient—changes. Many such companies never fully recovered.

By dropping down and competing with the low-cost manufacturers in their arena, MT could ensure that the competition stayed there. It could put pressure on the low-cost competition and make it harder for those companies to try to innovate and move up in the market, keeping them where they were. Even better, MT could put itself into a position to be the first to unlock the innovation that would have otherwise proven to be MT's Achilles heel. Doing so would not only preserve the company; it would also put MT on the leading edge and leave even the discount competitors behind.[72]

Case Discussion Questions

1. What should Mettler-Toledo do to make sure it develops products that meet the needs of its Chinese customers?
2. How can the company get employees to build on existing templates?
3. How can the company get employees to uncover principles?

Endnotes

[1]R. May Lee, "How Can We Teach Innovation? A View from China," World Economic Forum, June 22, 2016. www.weforum.org/agenda/2016/06/the-role-of-education-in-fostering-innovation-a-view-from-china/.

[2]E. Brynjolfsson and A. McAfee, *The Second Machine Age: Work, Progress, and Prosperity in a Time of Brilliant Technologies* (New York: W. W. Norton, 2014).

[3]Saul J. Berman et al., "How Successful Firms Guide Innovation: Insights and Strategies of Leading CEOs," *Strategy & Leadership* 44, no. 5L 21–8; David Percival, Robert Shelton, and Huw Andrews, "Unleashing the Power of Innovation," PWC, 2013, https://www.pwc.com/im/en/assets/document/unleashing_the_power_of_innovation.pdf.

[4]N. Rosenberg, "Innovation and Economic Growth," OECD report, https://www.oecd.org/cfe/tourism/34267902.pdf; R. M. Solow, "Neoclassical Growth Theory," in *Handbook of Macroeconomics*, vol. 1 (1999), 637–67; M. M. Appleyard and H. W. Chesbrough, "The Dynamics of Open Strategy: From Adoption to Reversion," *Long Range Planning* 50, No. 3 (2016): 310–321.

[5]V. W. Ruttan, "Usher and Schumpeter on Invention, Innovation, and Technological Change," *The Quarterly Journal of Economics* 75, no. 1 (1961): 596–606; "Something New under the Sun," *Economist*, October 11, 2007; W. A. Lewis, *Theory of Economic Growth*, vol. 7 (New York: Routledge, 2013).

[6]T. H. Davenport, *Process Innovation: Reengineering Work Through Information Technology* (Cambridge, MA: Harvard Business Press, 2013).

[7]Maria Pinelli, "Innovating for Growth: A Spiral Approach to Business Model Innovation," EY Online (2012), http://www.ey.com/Publication/vwLUAssets/EY_-_Innovating_for_growth/$FILE/EY_innovating-for-growth-1.pdf.

[8]Clayton Christensen and Derek van Bever, "The Capitalist's Dilemma," *Harvard Business Review*, June 2014.

[9]Maggie Qiuzhu Mei, Keld Laursen, and Kwaku Atuahene-Gima, "How Does Ambidexterity Matter for Radical and Incremental Innovation Capabilities?" *Academy of Management Proceedings* 2014, no. 1 (2014): 16696.

[10]V. Govindarajan and C. Trimble, *Reverse Innovation: Create Far from Home, Win Everywhere* (Cambridge, MA: Harvard Business Press, 2013); M. Zedtwitz, S. Corsi, P. Søberg, and R. Frega, "A Typology of Reverse Innovation," *Journal of Product Innovation Management* 32, no. 1 (2015): 12–28.

[11]Saabira Chaudhuri, "Aldi Details U.S. Expansion Plan," *Wall Street Journal*, June 11, 2015, www.wsj.com/articles/aldi-details-u-s-expansion-plan-1434033903.

[12]Lauren Greutman, "7 Reasons You Shouldn't Shop at ALDI!" *Huffington Post*, February 24, 2016, http://www.huffingtonpost.com/lauren-greutman/7-reasons-you-shouldnt-sh_b_9299162.html.

[13]Govindarajan and Trimble, *Reverse Innovation*; Zedtwitz et al., "A Typology of Reverse Innovation."

[14]Personal interview by Shad Morris with Hauwei R&D managers in China, December 2015.

[15]"Huawei Super Vector Enables Operators to Build UBB Networks Economically & Efficiently," *Light Reading*, November 1, 2016, http://www.lightreading.com/ubiquitous-ultra-broadband/huawei-super vector-enables-operators-to-build-ubb-networks-economically-and-efficiently/d/d-id/727447.

[16]B. Forés, and C. Camisón, "Does Incremental and Radical Innovation Performance Depend on Different Types of Knowledge Accumulation Capabilities and Organizational Size?" *Journal of Business Research* 69, no. 2 (2016): 831–48; M. G. Colombo, C. Franzoni, and R. Veugelers, "Going Radical: Producing and Transferring Disruptive Innovation," *The Journal of Technology Transfer* 40, no. 4 (2015): 663–69.

[17]M. Mazzucato, "From Market Fixing to Market-Creating: A New Framework for Innovation Policy," *Industry and Innovation* 23, no. 2 (2016): 140–56; Bryan C. Mezue, Clayton M. Christensen, and Derek van Bever, "The Power of Market Creation: How Innovation Can Spur Development," *Foreign Affairs* 94 (2015): 69; D. J. Teece, *Intangibles, Market Failure and Innovation Performance* (New York: Springer, 2015).

[18]Paul Walker, "The Past and Present of the Theory of the Firm: A Historical Survey of the Mainstream Approaches to the Firm in Economics," June 25, 2015, available at papers.ssrn.com; Kathleen R. Conner, "A Historical Comparison of Resource-Based Theory and Five Schools of Thought Within Industrial Organization Economics: Do We Have a New Theory of the Firm?" *Journal of Management* 17, no. 1 (1991): 121–54.

[19]Patrick Budmar, "Why Japanese Smartphones Never Went Global," *PC World*, July 11, 2012, https://www.pcworld.idg.com.au/article/430254/why_japanese_smartphones_never_went_global/.

[20]Steven Tweedie, "The World's First Smartphone, Simon, Was Created 15 Years before the iPhone," *Business Insider*, June 14, 2015, http://www.businessinsider.com/worlds-first-smartphone-simon-launched-before-iphone-2015-6.

[21]G. J. Costello and B. Donnellan, "IT-Enabled R&D for Business Value in a Global Framework," *Journal of the Knowledge Economy* 7, No. 3 (2015): 782–796.

[22]F. Zhu, S. Zou, and H. Xu, "Launching Reverse-Innovated Product from Emerging Markets to MNC's Home Market: A Theoretical Framework for MNC's Decisions," *International Business Review* 26, No. 1 (2016): 156–163; Leonardo Scamazzo, "Sharp Focus," *Business Today*, April 13, 2014, http://www.businesstoday.in/magazine/lbs-case-study/gillette-innovated-improved-its-market-share-in-india/story/204517.html.

[23]G. J. Tellis, A. B. Eisingerich, R. K. Chandy, and J. C. Prabhu, "Competing for the Future: Patterns in the Global Location of R&D Centers by the World's Largest Firms," *ISBM Report*, 06-2008, 2013, http://citeseerx.ist.psu.edu/viewdoc/download?doi=10.1.1.799.7667&rep=rep1&type=pdf.

[24]Vlado Pucik, Paul Evans, Ingmar Bjorkman, and Shad Morris. *The Global Challenge: International Human Resource Management*, 3rd ed. (Chicago: Chicago Business Press, 2017).

[25]D. Jolly and F. Masetti-Placci, "The Winding Path for Foreign Companies: Building R&D Centers in China," *Journal of Business Strategy* 37, no. 2 (2016): 3–11; S. Athreye, G. Batsakis, and S. Singh, "Local, Global, and Internal Knowledge Sourcing: The Trilemma of Foreign-Based R&D Subsidiaries," *Journal of Business Research* 69, No. 12 (2016): 5694–5702.

[26]Bill Fischer, Umberto Lago, and Fang Liu, "The Haier Road to Growth," *Strategy + Business*, April 27, 2015, www.strategy-business.com/article/00323?gko=c8c2a.

[27]Steve Johnson, "Cisco Systems to Cut 6,000 Jobs," *San Jose Mercury News* August 13, 2014 www.mercurynews.com/business/ci_26330332/ciscos-sales-and-profit-slightly-down-quarter.

[28]J. V. Gray, E. Siemsen, and G. Vasudeva, "Colocation Still Matters: Conformance Quality and the Interdependence of R&D and Manufacturing in the Pharmaceutical Industry," *Management Science* 61, no. 11 (2015): 2760–81.

[29]Thanks to Joe Santos for this observation on Microsoft and Cisco.

[30]S. S. Morris, B. Zhong, and M. Makhija, "Going the Distance: The Pros and Cons of Expanding Employees' Global Knowledge Reach," *Journal of International Business Studies* 46, no. 5 (2015): 552–73.

[31]S. Morris, S. Snell, and I. Björkman, "An Architectural Framework for Global Talent Management," *Journal of International Business Studies* 47, no. 6 (2016): 723–47.

[32]Appleyard and Chesbrough, "The Dynamics of Open Strategy."

[33]"Workplace Forecast: Liberated from Old Constraints, Prepared to Go Where the Talents Are Best Supported, an Urban Workforce Will Reshape Work and Its Settings," 2016 Gensler Design Forecast, www.gensler.com/2016-design-forecast-workplace (accessed June 23, 2017).

[34]"2016 Global R&D Funding Forecast," *R&D Magazine*, winter 2016, https://www.rdmag.com/article/2016/02/2016-global-rd-funding-forecast-0.

[35]"Panasonic Announced Its R&D Concept and Launched the R&D 10-Year Vision Website," Panasonic, April, 11, 2016, http://news.panasonic.com/global/topics/2016/45049.html.

[36]Peter Crush, "70:20:10 Training Model Is 'Most Effective for Learners', Research Finds," *People Management*, February 3, 2016, http://www2.cipd.co.uk/pm/peoplemanagement/b/weblog/archive/2016/02/03/training-model-70-20-10-is-39-most-effective-for-learners-39-research-finds.aspx.

[37]Dan Schiff, "How 3M Drives Innovation Through Empathy and Collaboration," *Forbes*, March 31, 2016, https://www.forbes.com/sites/ashoka/2016/03/31/how-3m-drives-innovation-through-empathy-and-collaboration/#315b37a571dd; Regina Koh, "Inspiring Disruptive Innovation: 3M's Story," *Human Resource Magazine*, October 2, 2015, http://www.humanresourcesonline.net/inspiring-disruptive-innovation-3ms-story/.

[38]S. S. Morris, J. B. Oldroyd, and S. Ramaswami, "Scaling Up Your Story: An Experiment in Global Knowledge Sharing at the World Bank," *Long Range Planning* 49, no. 1 (2016): 1–14.

[39]W. Shepard, "China's Huawei 'Growing Up' to Become the World's No. 1 Smartphone Brand," *Forbes*, May 25, 2016, https://www.forbes.com/sites/wadeshepard/2016/05/25/chinas-huawei-growing-up-to-become-the-worlds-number-one-smartphone-brand/#4d25bf113adf; D. De Cremer and T. Tao, "Huawei's Culture Is the Key to Its Success," *Harvard Business Review*, June 11, 2015.

[40]Personal interview by Shad Morris with Huawei managers in Shanghai, China, July, 2015.

[41]Morris, Snell, and Björkman, "An Architectural Framework for Global Talent Management," 723–47.

[42]Morris, Zhong, and Makhija, "Going the Distance," 552–73.

[43]Quote taken during research conducted by Shad Morris with a group of multinational corporations.

[44]S. Morris, D. Chng, J. Han, and J. Oldroyd, "The Role of Employees in Creating Firm Value: A Process Approach to Exploration and Exploitation," working paper (Provo, UT: Brigham Young University, 2016).

[45]Personal interview by Shad Morris with Huawei manager in Shanghai, China, July 2015.

[46]R. Heath, S. Peters, Y. Wang, and J. Zhang, "A Current Perspective on Distributed Antenna Systems for the Downlink of Cellular Systems," *IEEE Communications Magazine* 51, no. 4 (2013): 161–67.

[47]Shepard, "China's Huawei 'Growing Up.'"

[48]"The IP Commission Report: The Report of the Commission on the Theft of American Intellectual Property," National Bureau of Asian Research, 2013, www.ipcommission.org/report/ip_commission_report_052213.pdf.

[49]"Trade Enforcement," European Commission, April 28, 2016, http://ec.europa.eu/trade/policy/accessing-markets/intellectual-property/enforcement/.

[50]Kristina Lybecker, "The Economic Case for Strong Protection for Intellectual Property," *IPWatchdog*, May 2, 2014, www.ipwatchdog.com/2014/05/02/the-economic-case-for-strong-protection-for-intellectual-property/id=49376/.

[51]Joshua Brustein, "U.S. Marshals Raid Hoverboard Booth at CES," Bloomberg, January 7, 2016, www.bloomberg.com/news/articles/2016-01-07/u-s-marshals-raid-hoverboard-booth-at-ces.

[52]Victoria Slind-Flor, "P&G Suit, Apple, U.K. Museums, GE: Intellectual Property," Bloomberg, November 4, 1014, www.bloomberg.com/news/articles/2014-11-04/p-g-suit-apple-u-k-museums-ge-intellectual-property.

[53]Véronique Hyland, "Louis Vuitton Lost Its Checkerboard Trademark Case," NYMag.com, May 1, 2015, http://nymag.com/thecut/2015/05/vuitton-lost-its-checkerboard-trademark-case.html.

[54]"Patent FAQs," United States Patent and Trademark Office, https://www.uspto.gov/help/patent-help#1902 accessed December 14, 2016.

[55]"Report of the Economic Survey 2015," American Intellectual Property Law Association, June 2015, http://files.ctctcdn.com/e79ee274201/b6ced6c3-d1ee-4ee7-9873-352dbe08d8fd.pdf.

[56]"Copyright Basics," U.S. Copyright Office, May 2012, www.copyright.gov/circs/circ01.pdf.

[57]"Berne Convention for the Protection of Literary and Artistic Works," World Intellectual Property Organization, www.wipo.int/treaties/en/ip/berne/ (accessed January 11, 2017).

[58]"Adidas Wins $305 Million in Copyright Suit," NYMag.com, May 7, 2008, http://nymag.com/thecut/2008/05/adidas_wins_305_million_in_cop_1.html.

[59]Jennie Bell, "Adidas Sues Ecco Over Trademark Infringement," Footwear News, April 22, 2016, http://footwearnews.com/2016/

focus/athletic-outdoor/adidas-ecco-lawsuit-three-stripe-copyright-infringement-214443/.

60"Forbes Profile: J.K. Rowling," *Forbes*, www.forbes.com/profile/jk-rowling/.

61Yijun Yi, "Novelist Behind Hit Chinese TV Show Accused of Plagiarizing 200 Works," *China Film Insider*, November 23, 2016, http://chinafilminsider.com/novelist-behind-hit-chinese-tv-show-accused-plagiarizing-200-works/.

62Robert Channick, "Photographer, a Former Refugee, Sues Trump in Chicago over Skittles Tweet," *Chicago Tribune*, October 20, 2016, www.chicagotribune.com/business/ct-trump-skittles-lawsuit-1021-biz-20161020-story.html.

63Steve Brachman, "Vietnam-Based Copyrobo Unveils Blockchain-Based Copyright Management Service," *IPWatchdog*, November 17, 2016, www.ipwatchdog.com/2016/11/17/copyrobo-unveils-blockchain-based-copyright-management-service/id=74559/.

64Erica Swallow, "China Cracks Down on Fake Apple Stores," *Mashable*, August 12, 2011, http://mashable.com/2011/08/12/fake-apple-stores/#X0O4NdHSHiqX.

65Rob Bates, "Melrose.com Shuts Down Following Rolex Challenge," JCK, December 2, 2013, http://www.jckonline.com/editorial-article/melrosecom-shuts-down-following-rolex-challenge/.

66Orrin Hatch and Chris Coons, "A Better Way to Protect Trade Secrets," The Agenda, *Politico*, April 4, 2016, www.politico.com/agenda/story/2016/04/a-better-way-to-protect-trade-secrets-000081.

67Rusty Dornin, "2 Sentenced in Coke Trade Secret Case. Ex-Coke Workers Sentenced to Federal Prison for Plot to Offer Rival Pepsi Sample of New Product," CNN Money, May 23, 2007, http://money.cnn.com/2007/05/23/news/newsmakers/coke/.

68Clayton Velicer, Lauren K. Lempert, and Stanton Glantz, "Cigarette Company Trade Secrets Are Not Secret: An Analysis of Reverse Engineering Reports in Internal Tobacco Industry Documents Released as a Result of Litigation," *Tobacco Control, Vol. 24, Issue 5* (2015).

69"Global Patent Applications Rose to 2.9 Million in 2015 on Strong Growth From China; Demand Also Increased for Other Intellectual Property Rights," WIPO, November 23, 2016, www.wipo.int/pressroom/en/articles/2016/article_0017.html.

70"Global Economy Week Ahead: U.S.-China Meetings, Europe PMI, Fed Minutes," *Wall Street Journal*, November 20, 2016, www.wsj.com/articles/global-economy-week-ahead-u-s-china-meetings-europe-pmi-fed-minutes-1479672001.

71"Mettler-Toledo International Inc. Reports, Third Quarter 2016 Results"; "History of Mettler-Toledo International Inc.," *International Directory of Company Histories*, vol. 30 (St. James Press, Ohio 2000).

72L. Wohlfart, M. Bünger, C. Lang-Koetz, and F. Wagner, "The Two Faces of Frugal Innovation—Bridging Gaps to Foster Successful Innovation Strategies," In *ISPIM Innovation Symposium* (December 2015): 1; M. Zeschky, B. Widenmayer, and O. Gassmann, "Frugal Innovation in Emerging Markets," *Research-Technology Management* 54, no. 4 (2011): 38–45; M. B. Zeschky, S. Winterhalter, and O. Gassmann, "From Cost to Frugal and Reverse Innovation: Mapping the Field and Implications for Global Competitiveness," *Research-Technology Management* 57, no. 4 (2014): 20–27.

CHAPTER **13**

Country Selection and Entry Modes

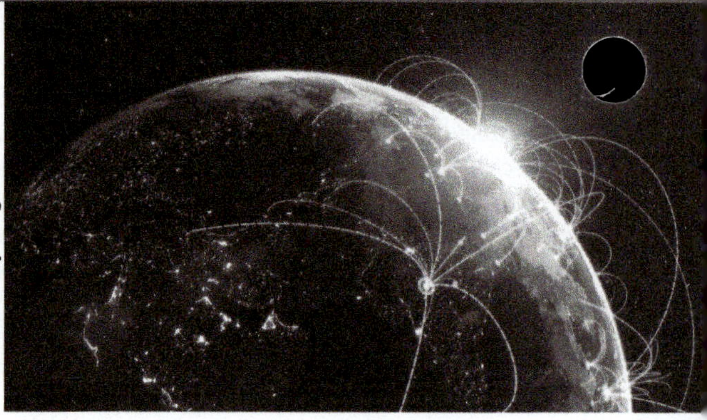
antadi1332/Getty Images

Introduction

Companies decide to move abroad for many reasons, including to pursue new markets, acquire new resources, and reduce risk. For instance, SolarWorld is a solar panel company founded in 1988 and headquartered in Bonn, Germany. The company grew within Germany and spread across Europe by acquiring the domestic solar divisions of Bayer in 2000 and Bosch in 2014. In 2006 the company moved beyond Europe with the acquisition of Shell Oil Company's solar division, including a manufacturing plant in Hillsboro, Oregon. In its international expansion, the company opened sales offices in Europe, the United States, South Africa, Singapore, and Japan, and now produces solar panels in Europe and the United States. In 2015 it earned more money in the United States than in all its other markets combined.

The decision to internationalize SolarWorld introduced a host of important questions for the company. For example, when should the company move internationally? Which market should it enter first? How should it enter that market? This chapter discusses these questions and introduces a framework to evaluate the options.

LEARNING OBJECTIVES

After exploring this chapter, you will be able to

1. **Describe** factors that determine which markets companies are likely to enter
2. **Explain** the advantages and disadvantages of different entry modes
3. **Compare** making, allying, and buying as entry tactics

13.1 Deciding Which Foreign Markets to Enter

LEARNING OBJECTIVE

Describe factors that determine which markets companies are likely to enter.

Once a company decides it wants to begin international operations, it must choose the foreign markets it will enter and how it will do so. An external analysis is an important first step in determining the attractiveness of foreign markets, and any such analysis likely includes a full PEST (political, economic, sociocultural, and technological) analysis. However, not all decisions are based solely on an opportunity. Sometimes other forces and resources at the company level may keep firms out of or pull firms into specific countries. These forces include the liability of foreignness, first-mover advantages, and the need to follow customers into specific markets.

WileyPLUS

See Whiteboard Video: Emerging Market Entry

The Liability of Foreignness

The **liability of foreignness** describes the challenges multinational companies face when entering and competing in foreign markets. This liability increases as the geographic, economic, cultural, or administrative differences between the foreign market and the domestic market increase.[1] Companies doing business in countries that are geographically proximate, are economically similar, share a common cultural base, and have few administrative differences—such as Thailand and Laos, or the United States and Canada—face a small liability of foreignness. Those doing business in the presence of large differences—such as Brazil and Saudi Arabia, or Mexico and Turkey—are likely to face a large liability of foreignness.

liability of foreignness a liability foreign firms face as the geographic, economic, cultural, or administrative differences between the foreign market and the domestic market increase

As these differences grow, and particularly when working across very different languages and cultures, global companies are more likely to face novel challenges in the foreign market, may make poorer decisions, and face increased costs to coordinate activities with the foreign division.[2] Some common ways to measure different kinds of distance are found in **Table 13.1**.

The liability of foreignness is not just a challenge a company faces as it learns how to act and react to the market. Customers, the media, and government officials in the new environment are also more likely to be biased against firms perceived as foreign. For instance, recent research founds that when firms such as BP engage in activities like reducing emissions in foreign markets, locals are more likely to focus on the harm the foreign firm causes rather than on actions the firm takes to reduce that harm.[3] Moreover, customers often exhibit an **ethnocentrism bias**, meaning they prefer and are willing to pay more for local brands even when the quality is inferior,[4] particularly when buying high-priced, infrequently purchased items like cars and electronics.[5]

ethnocentrism bias a bias indicating that customers prefer local brands over foreign brands and are willing to pay more for local brands even when the quality is inferior

In addition to customer bias, foreign firms often face a bias in the media. Local media outlets often are more negative in their coverage of foreign firms. A recent study in Germany demonstrated that foreign firms receive twice the press of domestic firms when downsizing staff, and the press coverage of foreign firms has a more negative tone than the coverage of local firms.[6] This media slant against foreign firms is another part of the liability of foreignness.

Finally, government officials are also likely to discriminate against foreign firms. A study of corporate mergers in the European Union found that governments prefer that companies remain domestically owned rather than foreign-owned, and officials can take actions that deter foreign firms from attempting to acquire local firms, such as increasing regulations and proactively looking for suitable domestic acquirers.[7]

TABLE 13.1 Common Measures of Cultural, Administrative, Geographic, and Economic Distance

Cultural Distance	Administrative Distance	Geographic Distance	Economic Distance
Different languages	Different colonial ties	Physical difference	High GINI coefficient
Different ethnicities	Different trading blocs	No shared land borders	Different natural resources
Different religions	Different currency	Different environment	Different financial resources
Different values	Different politics	Different climates	Different human resources
Different norms		Different agriculture	Different information resources
Different dispositions			

Source: Pankaj Ghemawat and Steven A. Altman, "Depth Index of Globalization 2013," IESE Business School Report. http://www.iese.edu/en/about-iese/news-media/news/2013/november/launch-of-2013-depth-index-of-globalization/

Research suggests that minimizing the geographic, economic, cultural, or administrative distances between a firm and a foreign market can help foreign firms succeed in new markets. In other words, companies that pick foreign markets similar to their home markets are more likely to succeed.[8] Hence companies may enter countries that aren't ideal according to a traditional PEST analysis but are similar to their own domestic environment, reducing the number of adaptations they must make.

As an example, AJE Group is a multinational company based in Peru that sells alcoholic and nonalcoholic beverages. Its flagship product is Kola Real, a cola beverage. The company was founded in the late 1980s, when military and terrorist conflicts in Peru made it impossible for established beverage companies like Coca-Cola and PepsiCo to distribute their products. For instance, their delivery trucks and drivers were often seized and held for ransom. In the absence of other cola products, the Añaños family began producing cola in their kitchen and distributing it with an old pickup truck. The terrorists ignored them because of their small size and lack of resources, which enabled them to maintain low costs and low prices. Their company quickly grew and expanded into nearby countries such as Venezuela and Ecuador, where similar distribution challenges and similarly price-sensitive customers existed. AJE then expanded to distant markets but continued to seek those with similar infrastructure and customer challenges, like Thailand, Nigeria, Indonesia, and Vietnam[9] (see **Figure 13.1**).

First-Mover Advantage

A second force driving companies toward specific international markets is the desire to be the first company to move into those markets. In many cases, the first entrant into a market captures a leadership position, enabling it to control critical resources such as distribution

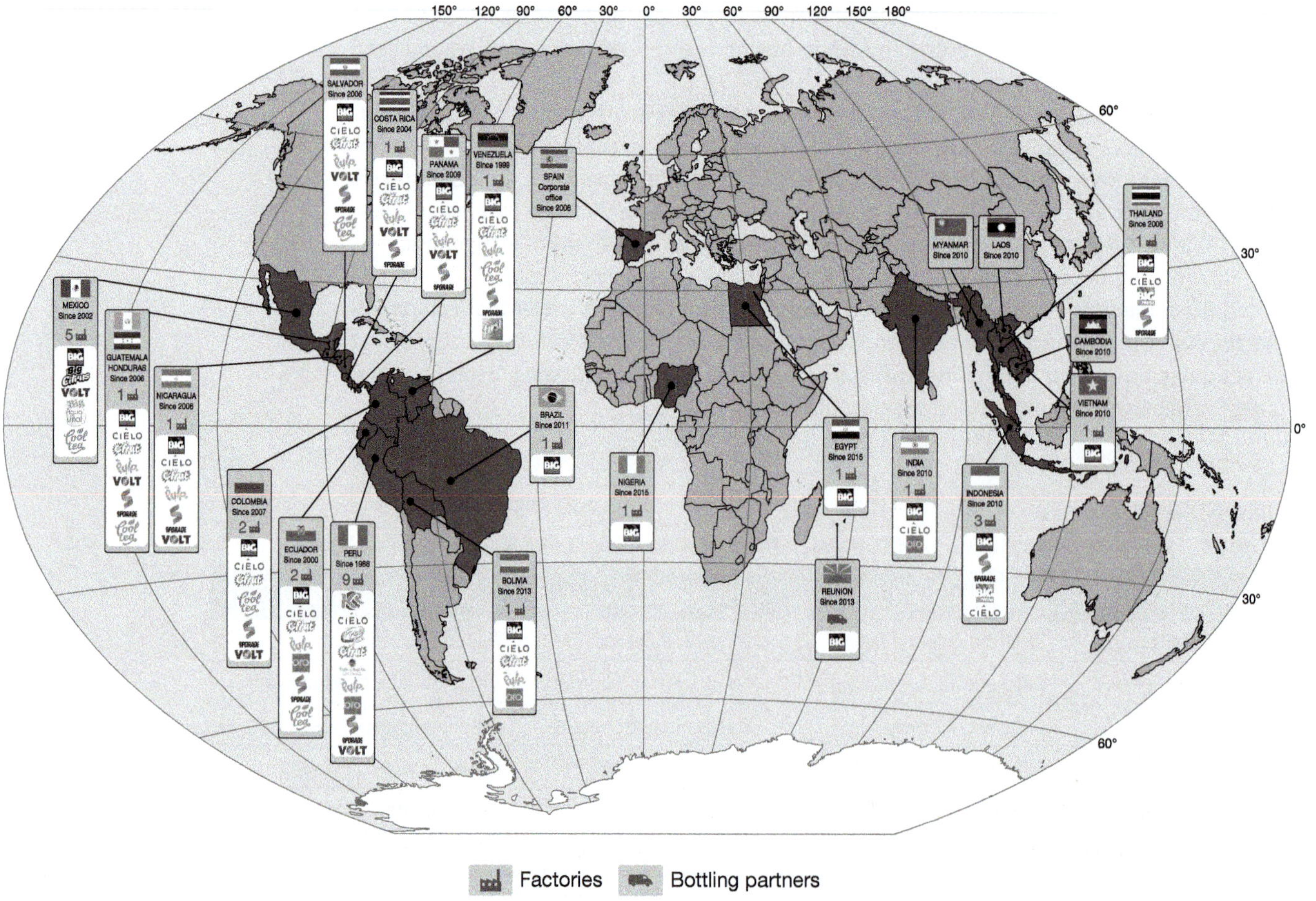

FIGURE 13.1 The global presence of AJE's brands, from the company's start in Peru in 1988 to its entry into Nigeria and Egypt in 2015 **Source:** AJE Worldwide brands. www.ajegroup.com/about-aje/a-worldwide-company/

channels and to build up buyer-switching costs, particularly where network effects or branding are important. The drive to capture this advantage sometimes pulls firms into markets they would otherwise wait to enter.

For example, Nestlé's Nescafé brand of coffee is the world leader among instant coffees, with nearly 25 percent of the market.[10] However, U.S.-based competitor Mondelēz International, maker of global coffee brands, entered South Korea in 1968, shortly after the Korean War, through a joint venture with Dongsuh Foods Corporation. As a result, Mondelēz built a strong brand and distribution presence in the country and still commands 80 percent of the market, whereas Nestlé, based in Switzerland, has just under 5 percent, even after many years in the country and heavy investments.[11] Mondelēz's first-mover advantage has given it an enduring dominant presence in South Korea.

Similarly, German car maker Volkswagen (VW) established in 1984 a joint venture in China, with a 25-year commitment to produce vehicles in Shanghai. Since then, the company has sold over 20 million cars in China. In fact, despite spending most of 2016 battling a huge scandal over cheating on emissions tests for their diesel-engine cars, VW was the largest car maker in China, providing enough sales to push Volkswagen past Toyota to become the top car seller in the world (see **Table 13.2**).[12] Six of the top ten vehicles driven in China are made by VW. VW's early entry into China earned it a strong distribution network, loyal customers, and familiarity with working with the Chinese government.[13] The company continues to invest in China and has since formed two additional joint ventures with FAW Group and SAIC Motor Corporation, both Chinese car manufacturers.

Following Clients Globally

Last, companies may expand not because they necessarily want to, but because their customers pressure them. For instance, in the mid-1990s, commercial real estate began to be driven by corporate customers, such as Microsoft and Bank of America, that were quickly expanding

TABLE 13.2 **VW's sales performance in China, 2016**

China new-auto sales for major Western, South Korean, Japanese, Chinese automakers

Number of vehicles sold *(year-on-year changes in parentheses)*

Automaker	December	2016
WESTERN		
Volkswagen Group	390,600 *(18.6)*	3,982,200 *(12.2)*
General Motors	434,799 *(-2.3)*	3,870,587 *(7.1)*
Ford Motor	149,856 *(21.3)*	1,272,708 *(13.6)*
SOUTH KOREA		
Hyundai Motor	222,815 *(3.7)*	1,792,022 *(4.6)*
JAPAN		
Nissan Motor	162,500 *(2.1)*	1,354,600 *(8.4)*
Honda Motor	132.891 *(-3.4)*	1,247,713 *(24.0)*
Toyota Motor	113,800 *(-6.7)*	1,214,200 *(8.2)*
CHINA		
Great Wall Motor	150,548 *(57.3)*	1,074,471 *(26.0)*
Zhejiang Geely Holding Group	108,230 *(101.8)*	765,851 *(50.2)*
Ford 2016 sales include Lincoln brand; Hyundai sales exclude imports		*Based on company reports, industry group surveys*

Because VW came early to the Chinese market, it has a competitive advantage there.
Source: Yu Nakamura and Shunsuke Tabeta, "China Widens Its Lead as the World's No. 1 Car Market," *Nikkei Asian Review*, January 19, 2017. http://asia.nikkei.com/magazine/20170119/Business/China-widens-its-lead-as-the-world-s-No.-1-car-market

into international markets. In response, LaSalle Partners, a U.S. real estate services company, merged with Jones Lang Wooton of London in 1999. The combined firm, named Jones Lang LaSalle, or JLL, combined LaSalle's dominance in the United States with Wooton's presence in Europe and Asia. JLL's global presence thus came about because its clients demanded that the firm provide a global solution, not because of the draw of the markets themselves.[14]

Similarly, QuintilesIMS, a U.S. company that helps pharmaceutical companies advance their new prescription medications through clinical trials, was founded in North Carolina. The company has helped over 130 drugs come to market by assisting with data collection and analysis, and by facilitating clinical trials at all stages of drug development. In 1987, 5 years after its founding, QuintilesIMS followed the growth of pharmaceutical companies into Europe and opened an operation in the United Kingdom. In 1993, the company again followed customers and expanded into Asia.[15] Currently, it helps its customers gain access to markets and provides insights into the drug development process around the globe using a network of nearly 1,000 medical doctors and an additional 900 research PhDs. The company has helped develop or commercialize all of the top 100 drugs on the market today.

13.2 Entry Modes

LEARNING OBJECTIVE

Explain the advantages and disadvantages of different entry modes

Once a firm decides it will enter a foreign market, it needs to choose the method it will use to do so. These methods can be divided into nonequity and equity modes. Nonequity modes typically carry less risk but also bring fewer rewards. They include the entry modes of exporting, turnkey operations, licensing, and franchising.[16] Equity modes require a larger investment and engage the foreign firm in local operations. This increases the risk of the activity but also allows the firm to get close to customers and thus build better products. Equity modes include joint ventures and wholly owned subsidiaries, either greenfield projects or acquisitions[17] (see **Figure 13.2**). Each has advantages and disadvantages, and some are better suited to certain industries than others, but nearly all international expansion falls into one of these six entry modes. Next we discuss the pros and cons of each.

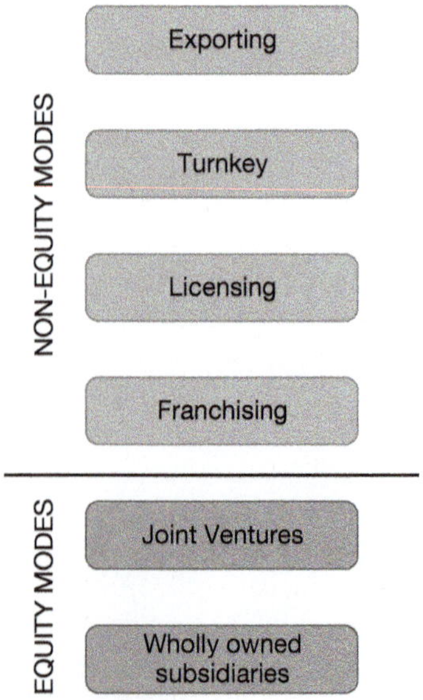

FIGURE 13.2 Foreign Market Entry Modes

Exporting

Exporting is the process of producing a good or service in one country and selling it in another country. Some large companies such as GM, LG, and Apple manufacture products in one central location and then export them to markets around the globe, but many small and medium-sized firms also rely heavily on exporting. For instance, Igus—a German producer of more than 100,000 high-end plastic products such as energy chain cables, plastic bushings, and piston rings—exports products to more than thirty-six countries. The company was started in Cologne, Germany, in 1964, with products to help preserve the cables that supply power and control to robotic manufacturing machines.[18] While the company is limited to one production facility in Cologne, Germany, by exporting, Igus is able to sell its products around the world.

Advantages A key advantage of exporting is the associated low-cost of entering a foreign market. Exporting requires little infrastructure investment, and the company needs to keep little to no inventory in different locations around the world. For instance, when Samsung sells appliances such as refrigerators, washers, and dryers in the United States, it exports the products directly from manufacturing plants in Korea and China to major U.S. retailers such as Home Depot, Lowes, and Best Buy. By monitoring these retailers' inventory levels, Samsung can export enough product to maintain stock with low surplus while tying up few of its assets in foreign markets.

Reaching other markets via exporting is also getting easier, with e-marketers such as Alibaba.com in China and Amazon.com in the United States making it possible for smaller producers to sell directly to consumers around the globe. For instance, few U.S. customers have heard of Shenzhen Kinlan Technology Limited of China, but a search for scooters on Alibaba.com quickly highlights the company's self-balancing electric scooter for sale at $140, shipped directly to any address in the United States.[19] Without Alibaba, Shenzhen Kinlan Technology Limited would have difficulty attracting global customers.

Another advantage of exporting is its flexibility. If sales decline, an export company like Samsung merely ships fewer products; if sales increase, it ships more. Exporters are thus able to respond relatively quickly to changes in global demand. This flexibility also allows firms to enter and exit markets quickly.

Finally, exporting enables firms to move quickly down the learning curve and capture economies of scale. By producing to meet worldwide demand at one facility and then exporting worldwide, companies can aggregate global demand in one production facility and accelerate the pace of learning by having the same facility produce many units. For instance, when Samsung builds a production plant in Suwon, South Korea, for dynamic random-access memory chips, engineers and laborers on the production line produce many more units of the same chip than if production were scattered around the globe. As the workers repeat the tasks, they learn how to produce the memory chips with the highest efficiency. In addition, Samsung is able to reduce the cost of production not only by gaining production efficiency but also by spreading fixed costs, such as those for research and development, across more units produced, increasing profits.

Disadvantages While exporting is a method for international operations that requires relatively low investment, it does pose a number of disadvantages. First, exports of goods and services are often subject to import tariffs. For instance, according to the World Trade Organization (WTO), Argentina imposes tariffs of 34.2 percent on imported coffee and tea, 21.4 percent on chemicals, and 35 percent on clothing; the country has an average tariff of 13.6 percent on all goods and services imported.[20] The Bahamas has the highest average tariff of WTO members, at 35.1 percent. The average tariffs for each country are shown in **Figure 13.3**. As tariffs increase in a country, the profitability of exporting to that country decreases.

Sometimes tariffs are prohibitively high. South Korea imposes a 513 percent tariff on rice imports. As **Table 13.3** indicates, this makes rice imported from China, the United States, and Thailand much more expensive in Korea than domestically produced rice, a result intended to help protect Korean rice farmers from foreign competition.

While rice farmers have few alternatives to exporting, tariffs or not, businesses in other industries can sometimes shift production into a target country in order to avoid its tariffs. For instance, Japanese automobile manufacturers have shifted the production of 3.6 million vehicles a year from Japan to the United States to avoid the 25.0 percent tariff for trucks and 2.5 percent tariff for passenger cars added to the price of vehicles imported to the United States.[21] This tariff amounts to roughly $625 per vehicle for passenger cars and 10 times that for trucks, but foreign companies can avoid it by building their manufacturing plants in the United States.

Another disadvantage of exporting is that the country where production occurs may have high relative costs, which can cause the product to be comparatively expensive—perhaps prohibitively expensive—in other markets.[22] For example, BMW manufactures cars at home in Germany and then exports them around the world. Unfortunately, because Germany's average cost of labor of $44.25 an hour is built into the price of the car, exporting affordable cars from Germany to the Philippines, where the average labor cost is $2.12 an hour, is difficult.[23] As a result, German cars are often too expensive for customers in the Philippines and other countries where low wages are common.

On the other hand, Nike turns this export reality into an advantage. Nike doesn't use shoes suppliers from the United States, because labor costs there are relatively high. Instead, Nike uses suppliers who manufacture in Indonesia, where labor is very inexpensive. This strategy allows the company to embed low labor costs into the footwear it buys from global suppliers.

A final disadvantage of exporting is the time and money required to transport goods, especially if items are heavy or bulky, or if their sale is time-sensitive. To put this in perspective,

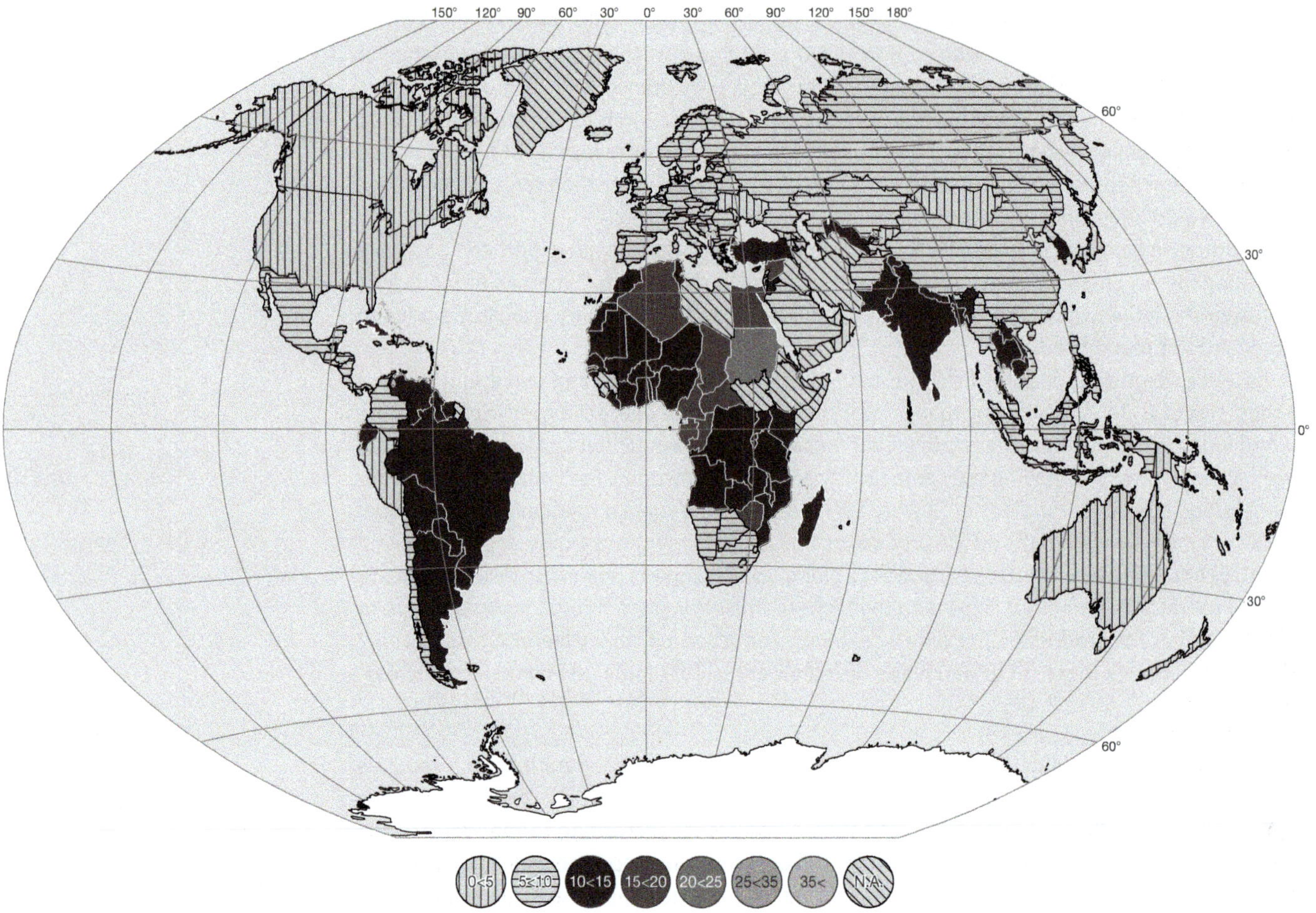

FIGURE 13.3 **Average tariff rates for WTO members** **Source:** "International Trade and Market Access Data: Tariffs," World Trade Organization, www.wto.org/english/res_e/statis_e/statis_bis_e.htm?solution=WTO&path=/Dashboards/MAPS&file=Tariff.wcdf&bookmarkState={%22impl%22:%22client%22,%22params%22:{%22langParam%22:%22en%22}} (accessed July 19, 2017).

TABLE 13.3 **South Korean Rice Tariffs**

Estimated price of rice with 513% tariff

(Unit: won per 80 kilograms)

Country	International price	Tariff	Retail price in Korea
China	85,177	436,957	522,134
United States	63,303	324,746	388,049
Thailand	45,230	232,029	277,259
Korea			175,000

Source: "Nations Complain to WTO over Korea's Rice Tariff," *Korea JoongAng Daily*, January 7, 2015, http://koreajoongangdaily.joins.com/news/article/Article.aspx?aid=2999328. Original data from South Korea's Ministry of Agriculture, Food and Rural Affairs.

consider that the cost of shipping a forty-foot container from Shanghai to Northern Europe is $950,[24] regardless of whether the container is full of iPhones or mattresses. However, because thousands of iPhones fit into the same amount of space required for a hundred or so mattresses, the cost per unit shipped is much lower for iPhones than for mattresses. As the costs of transportation continue to fall, exporting is likely to continue to increase. For instance, shipping a MacBook Pro from China to the United States costs just $1.50.[25]

Turnkey Operations

FIGURE 13.4 **The Taishan Nuclear Power Plant in China**
The French firm Areva is building this plant for the Chinese government as a turnkey project.

In a turnkey project, a company builds a facility in a foreign market for a client, makes it operational, and then hands over the "keys" to the client, which will own and operate the facility. Such projects are a way for firms to internationalize their process technologies, such as refining oil or building nuclear power stations, when opportunities for equity entry are restricted. For instance, Areva is a French company that focuses on developing and commercializing nuclear power production. In 2008, the firm started building two reactors in Guangdong, China, for the province. Once the reactors are completed in 2018 and the staff are trained to operate and maintain the facility, Areva will hand over the keys to the government, which will operate it[26] (**Figure 13.4**).

Turnkey operations are typically billion-dollar projects undertaken by governments collaborating with large multinational companies and use sophisticated technologies in industries into which governments are unwilling to let foreign companies enter directly. For instance, countries are unwilling to let foreign entities own their nuclear power or oil refineries, as these are critical industries. But they often need help to build and operate such facilities. This is the typical domain of turnkey operations.

Advantages The advantage of using turnkey projects as an entry mode is that they enable foreign firms to enter technologically complex markets and politically sensitive environments. For instance, many countries want their own operations to produce chemicals or refine oil but do not have the technology to build these facilities. The countries are also unwilling to allow foreign companies to own the facilities, but they are willing to have foreign companies build the facilities for them.

Disadvantages The major disadvantage of turnkey operations is that once the firm hands over operations to the customer, it has no further financial interest in the business. As a result, even though turnkey operations are often massive, multiyear projects, the cash flow they create does not recur. A second disadvantage is that turnkey operations can actually create potential competitors. Because the projects are fully functional upon delivery, customers can sometimes begin competing with the original firm using the design and knowledge they gained from the turnkey company. For instance, China General Nuclear Corporation (CGN) moved from being a passive investor by partnering with Areva and the EDF Group to build a nuclear power station in the United Kingdom. CGN's goal in the project is to "gain experience in the UK" that "will support their long-term objective of becoming established nuclear developers." The firm plans to have its Chinese staff work alongside members of EDF Group's project team.[27] Over time, CGN hopes to become a trusted nuclear power provider and compete with their European partners.

Licensing

A **license** is a contractual agreement between two parties, the licensor and the licensee, that grants the licensee certain rights, such as the right to produce or sell the licensor's patented goods, display the licensor's brand name or trademark, or use the licensor's intellectual property. Typically, licensing agreements cover a specific time and place. For example, when Disney expanded its theme parks internationally, it went first to Japan. The Tokyo Disney theme park opened in 1983 and is nearly an exact replica of Disneyland in California. It operates under a licensing agreement between Disney (the licensor) and the Oriental Land Company of Japan

license a contractual agreement between two parties, known as the licensor and the licensee, that grants the licensee certain rights, such as the right to produce or sell the licensor's patented goods, display the licensor's brand name or trademark, or use the licensor's intellectual property

(the licensee). In the agreement, Disney receives a 10 percent royalty on ticket sales and a 5 percent royalty on food and beverage sales in exchange for providing Oriental Land Company with the license to use Disney's brands.[28]

Advantages Internationalizing through licensing has some advantages. First, the licensing firm typically takes on very little risk in entering foreign markets. If Tokyo Disney had been unsuccessful, Disney would have had little financial liability, because the licensee typically covers the costs of developing the operation. Walt Disney is the world's largest licensor, with $23.9 billion in licensed goods sold in 2015. Meredith Corporation, the owner of the Better Homes and Garden brand, is second with $20 billion in licensed sales. The top 10 global licensors had over $137 billion in global sales in 2015, and the top 150 accounted for over $262 billion in sales.[29]

Second, licensing allows a company to grow quickly by leveraging its brand or technology into new industries and new locations. Pharmaceutical companies like Regeneron of New York often license their drugs to foreign companies such as Sanofi, a French pharmaceutical firm, to quickly penetrate additional markets.[30] Similarly, Google developed a smart contact lens that monitors blood sugar levels via miniature sensors and licensed the technology to the Swiss pharmaceutical company Novartis.[31] This arrangement enables Google to leverage the knowledge and abilities of Novartis for the purpose of commercializing its own technology.

Third, licensing allows companies to enter geographic or product markets that are outside their own strategic goals. For instance, Disney has no interest in getting into the daycare business, but it could still profit in this market by licensing its intellectual property, such as its popular characters, to firms operating in that industry.

Finally, licensing can help solve the problems of pricing a good across markets. For instance, pharmaceutical companies often face uncertain demand as they develop and sell drugs in different markets. By licensing their products rather than selling them directly, licensors can transfer the risk of potential loss to the licensees while maximizing gain by collecting up-front fees, annual fees, royalty fees, and milestone fees, or fees paid when key events occur.[32] Cellectis, a U.S.-based biotech firm, and Servier, a French biotech firm, entered a license agreement to codevelop a leukemia drug. Under the deal, "Cellectis will receive from Servier a payment of $38.2 million upon signature. In addition, Cellectis is eligible for over $300 million of milestone payments, R&D financing, and royalties on sales from Servier, based on annual net sales of commercialized products."[33] Servier gets access to a potential blockbuster drug that could be worth billions of dollars.

Disadvantages The disadvantages of licensing deals are threefold. First, in licensing technology, brands, or other intellectual property to firms, a licensor becomes one step removed from customers and loses the opportunity to get feedback directly from them. The licensor can also end up trapped by the agreement. At one point, Starbucks licensed the distribution of its coffee to Mondelēz International, a food and beverage company based in Illinois. Mondelēz then sold Starbucks-branded coffee in grocery stores and other retailers around the world and grew sales to over $500 million a year. Seeing that growth and finding itself removed from all the new customers who were buying through grocery stores, Starbucks violated its license agreement in 2010 and took over distribution of its coffee. Mondelēz sued Starbucks for breach of contract and won a settlement of roughly $2.7 billion.[34]

After the settlement, Howard Schultz, the CEO of Starbucks, noted, "We now have the flexibility and the freedom to control our own destiny." With full control of distribution, rather than distribution through license agreements, Starbucks can develop from a coffee company into a consumer products company. Nick Setyan, an analyst at Wedbush Securities in Los Angeles, said he views "Starbucks as 'a global consumer-products company rather than simply a coffee retailer now. That would be impossible if [Mondelēz] still controlled coffee distribution.'"[35] This increased scope is possible because Starbucks now has direct access to grocery stores and can expand more readily into different products.

Second, licensing agreements provide only limited control over the way in which the licensed brand, technology, or intellectual property is used. Calvin Klein sued Warnaco Group, a licensee, for selling CK jeans in low-price outlets such as Sam's Club, BJ's, and Costco, and for altering designs and using poor-quality materials. Calvin Klein viewed the licensee's actions as diminishing its brand value.[36] The companies ultimately reached a private agreement to solve the problem.

As their number of licensees increases, companies find it increasingly difficult to ensure that those licensees do not misuse the brand. In 2002, the iconic British firm Burberry had lost control of its high-end fashion brand because it had licensed its iconic tartan pattern (see **Figure 13.5**) to firms that put it on everything from hats to dog collars. As the brand began to appear on more and more products, it became associated with "people who did bad stuff," such as football hooligans. "Quite a lot of people thought that Burberry would be worn by the person who mugged them," noted one U.K. newspaper. Then, in 2009, Angela Ahrendts, the CEO of Burberry, sought to reestablish the company brand. In the process, she bought back twenty-three licenses and implemented stringent brand guidelines revitalizing the brand[37] in order to make it "Britain's premier luxury label."[38]

FIGURE 13.5 The Burberry tartan print Actress Danniella Westbrook's daughter sports Burberry's check.

A final challenge in global licensing is that the licensor may risk a loss of core capabilities. Licenses between media companies and Netflix have hurt content producers. Netflix "has become a fast-expanding, high-margin source of revenue for the biggest content owners, including Walt Disney, Time Warner, 21st Century Fox, CBS, Viacom, Discovery Communications and AMC Networks. But it is clear the presence of their shows on these platforms is hurting traditional TV ratings, which drive ad revenue, and making it easier for pay-TV subscribers to quit. While pulling content from Netflix may be the right response for media companies, the situation poses a classic prisoner's dilemma: Who will be first to forgo short-term profits for the good of the industry?"[39] Compounding the difficulty for media companies is the fact that Netflix and other streaming services such as Amazon Prime and Hulu have taken what they've learned and begun developing original content. In 2016, Netflix invested over $5 billion to produce thirty-one original series, ten feature films, and comedy and kids' shows.[40] The shows have been a huge success, snapping up critics' awards, including nine Emmys in 2016,[41] and drawing in nearly 100 million subscribers worldwide.[42]

Franchising

Franchising is a unique form of licensing in which a partner, called the franchisee, is given the right to use the franchisor's brand and other intellectual property, while the franchisor takes an active role in the ongoing operations of the firm, such as advertising, training staff, and managing inventory. As **Figure 13.6** shows, Subway is one of the world's largest fast-food companies, yet the U.S. firm does not own a single restaurant. Instead the 44,852 Subway restaurants around the world are owned by more than 21,000 franchisees in over 112 countries.[43] In choosing a franchise entry mode, Subway is able to leverage its brand while limiting its risk across the globe. In return, Subway franchisees are able to harness the operational abilities of Subway to manage their restaurants.

Some franchisors provide a master franchise arrangement rather than contracting with franchisees on a store-by-store basis. This deal provides the master franchisee the ability to create subfranchises in a specific geographic area. For instance, Burger King has master franchise agreements in Mexico, Central America, and South America.[44] Similarly, Papa John's created an agreement with Hassan Bouanaka, a master franchisee, to open thirty-eight stores across Northeast France.[45]

Advantages The advantages of the franchise entry mode are twofold. First, the franchisor can seek global growth with limited financial risk yet maintain direct involvement with the franchisees. Thus it can learn directly from local markets and transfer that knowledge to other markets. Second, the franchisor can benefit from flexibility in a licensing arrangement that enables a franchisee to respond to local customers' needs. For instance, Hilton Hotels franchises Hampton Inns. This allows Hilton to expand to global markets with local franchisees. VHM Management owns one Hampton Inn in Lodz, Poland (**Figure 13.7**) and will open a second in 2018. The VHM director said the company could "further develop the concept of internationally branded focused service hotels with an infusion of famous Polish

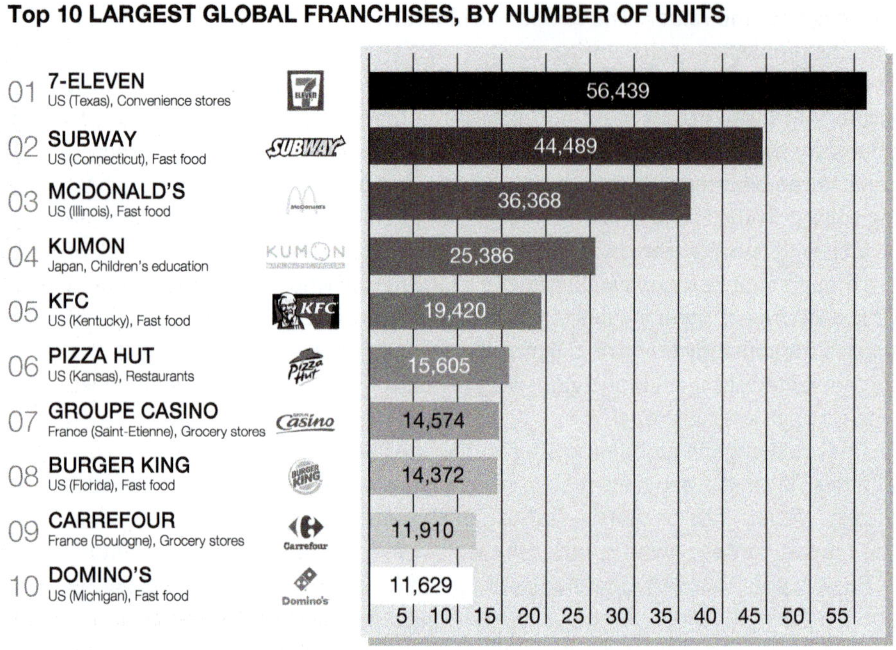

FIGURE 13.6 Top ten largest global franchises by the number of units includes U.S., Japanese, and French brands **Source:** "Top 10 Largest Franchises in the World," Raconteur, June 21, 2016, http://raconteur.net/business/top-10-largest-franchises-in-the-world (accessed April 25, 2017).

hospitality."[46] The combination of Hilton's know-how and VHM's local knowledge provides a recipe for success.

Disadvantages One of the key challenges of franchising is finding suitable franchisees. For instance, Wendy's International has had difficulty finding well-qualified franchisees, particularly in emerging markets. As a result, its strategy has been to focus on global expansion with master

Jan Kucharzyk/Getty Images

FIGURE 13.7 The Hampton in Lodz, Poland

franchisees who have previous food experience in the local market and significant financial resources to deliver the brand to international markets.[47]

A second challenge of franchising is that, to build franchisee interest in foreign markets, businesses may find they need to be the first mover. For instance, Yum Brands chose direct ownership when entering the Chinese market in order to build interest in the brand. Once it had established a presence in the country, the company switched to its preferred method of franchise agreements.[48] For an example, see **Figure 13.8**.

Lou-Foto/Alamy Stock Photo

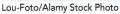

FIGURE 13.8 **KFC is the largest restaurant chain in China** Yum China had more than 7,600 restaurants in over 1,100 cities, mostly under the KFC and Pizza Hut brands.

Joint Ventures

An **international joint venture** is a new legal entity created and owned by two or more existing companies from different countries. The parent companies can have very different degrees of ownership in the joint venture, ranging from a 50/50 split to a 99/1 ownership structure or anything in between, depending on their goals, their investments in the venture, and their resources and capabilities. The more partners, the more complex the contract, although many joint ventures are simple 50/50 arrangements between two parent companies.

international joint venture a new legal entity created and owned by two or more existing companies from different countries

Joint ventures can be an attractive entry mode when a company is concerned about physically entering a new market. A local partner can provide expertise in complying with government entry requirements, ideal distribution strategies, other local market–related skills, and deep customer understanding. In some countries, foreign firms are required by law to set up joint ventures if they want to enter. For instance, both India and China have historically had provisions in place requiring most foreign firms to enter via a joint venture with a local partner.[49] The objective in requiring joint ventures is to encourage knowledge transfer from the foreign firm to the domestic firm.[50]

Advantages The advantages of a joint venture for the entering firm include reduced political risk, the opportunity to leverage local knowledge, and shared costs. In many countries, foreign companies face political risks such as unfair regulation, corruption, and even expropriation.[51] However, a joint venture with a local company can significantly reduce these risks by providing the foreign firm a local partner.

Disadvantages One of the disadvantages of entering a new market through a joint venture structure is that the partners sometimes have different goals. For instance, many multinationals invest in joint ventures in China with a focus on profitability, while their Chinese counterparts focus on growth. The lack of strategic alignment can lead to serious problems in how these firms allocate resources, market to customers, and price goods and services.[52]

In addition, joint ventures can lead to the loss of intellectual property if the less technologically advanced partner takes advantage of the relationship.[53] For instance, Fellowes, a U.S. company that manufactures paper shredders, had three joint ventures with partners in China for the manufacture of its products. The first was made in 1982, the second in 1988, and the third in 2006. In 2009, Shinri, a Chinese partner, demanded a $10 million investment from Fellowes. The company refused and a dispute erupted. According to Fellowes, its partner took several of the manufacturing machines, worth millions of dollars, and began producing its own shredders. Fellowes sought help from Chinese officials and asked several U.S. politicians to put pressure on its partner,[54] but it has recovered nothing. With few options, Fellowes built a new manufacturing facility in the United States.[55]

Wholly Owned Subsidiary

wholly owned subsidiary a new legal entity set up for operation in a foreign market that is legally a separate company but is fully owned by the parent firm

In a **wholly owned subsidiary**, the parent company sets up a new legal entity that is legally a separate company but that it fully owns. Firms can either create the subsidiary company from scratch—a process sometimes called a "greenfield" operation—or buy an existing company. In 2016 Berkshire Hathaway entered the motor vehicle insurance business in India through a greenfield operation by setting up a new company.[56] It invested about $11 million to build a call center and train sales agents in order to gain access to the market while also retaining control of the new company.[57]

Advantages One of the biggest advantages of wholly owned subsidiaries is that by retaining ownership control of the subsidiary, the parent company protects its intellectual property. Valuable knowledge can flow across country borders but still stay within the company, reducing the risk that it could leak to competitors or enable a business partner to become a future competitor. Companies whose advantage relies on their intellectual property often enter new markets through a wholly owned subsidiary.

Wholly owned subsidiaries also enable parent firms to maintain tight control over their foreign operations, opening the opportunity for a high degree of coordination. For instance, if a company needs to use profits made in one market to develop another market, a wholly owned subsidiary enables it to do so without the need to split revenues or negotiate with partners. This entry mode also enables firms to gain firsthand experience with customers and learn directly from the local market. For instance, Porsche Cars North America, Inc. is a wholly owned subsidiary of Porsche AG of Stuttgart, Germany. The subsidiary is responsible for all customer interaction—such as marketing, sales, and service of the Porsche brands—in North America and provides Porsche AG with direct access to U.S. and Canadian customers.[58]

Disadvantages The disadvantages of entering new markets via a wholly owned subsidiary are twofold. First, it is an expensive undertaking. Companies must bear initial costs such as purchasing retail or manufacturing space, hiring staff, and establishing distribution entirely by themselves, and that means putting a large investment on the line. Second, the company entering via a wholly owned subsidiary bears the entire risk of ongoing operations. If things don't go well in the market, there is no easy exit strategy other than giving up the entire investment.

Figure 13.9 compares the advantages and disadvantages of different foreign market entry modes.

		Advantages	Disadvantages
NON-EQUITY MODES	Exporting	Low cost, quick access, flexibility, economies of scale	Tariffs, embedded production costs, transportation costs
	Turnkey	Entry into restricted highly technical markets	Customers can become competitors
	Licensing	Low risk, quick growth, growth outside strategic focus of the firm, differential pricing	Distance from the customer, limited control of product and brand, loss of core capabilities
	Franchising	Limited financial risk, high degree of response to local needs	Difficult to find suitable franchisees, need to build brand in country prior to franchising
EQUITY MODES	Joint Ventures	Reduced political risk, increased local knowledge, shared development costs	Different partner goals and objectives, loss of intellectual property
	Wholly owned subsidiaries	Retain knowledge, full control of foreign operations, direct exposure to local customers	Expensive, high risk

FIGURE 13.9 Degrees of risk and control firms accept when entering foreign markets

13.3 Make, Ally, or Buy

LEARNING OBJECTIVE

Compare making, allying, and buying as entry tactics.

WileyPLUS

See Whiteboard Video: Special Considerations

In addition to considering which entry mode is best for its needs, a company must consider its objectives, its capabilities, and its resources—these will determine which entry tactic the company should take to best achieve the desired entry mode. For example, a firm may wish to internationalize through the exporting mode but lack the capabilities or skills to export on its own. In that case, it may need to find an export partner or buy a company that has expertise in exporting.

For instance, Haier—the Chinese appliance manufacturer—wanted to enter the U.S. market with a wholly owned subsidiary but recognized it had limited experience in the United States. Facing the market realities of strong competitors and no brand recognition, the company instead began by exporting compact office and dorm refrigerators to Welbilt, a U.S.-based firm, which sold the Haier appliances under the Welbilt brand. In 1999, Haier and Welbilt formed a joint venture called Haier America to begin selling products in the United States under the Haier brand using Welbilt's experience with the market. Later, in 2001, Haier invested further in a wholly owned subsidiary and built a $40 million production facility in South Carolina to produce high-end refrigerators.[59] As Haier's experience and capabilities in the U.S. market grew over time, its entry mode also evolved from exporting to joint venture to wholly owned subsidiary, and its tactics changed from partnering to making products on its own. Many firms' mode of and tactics for foreign expansion are similarly shaped by their changing capabilities.

We can categorize entry tactics as *make, ally, or buy*, meaning the firm can make or develop its own operations in the country, partner with existing firms or firms that are adept in the local market, or acquire a firm already operating in the local market. These tactics can be executed within the firm's preferred entry mode (**Figure 13.10**). For instance, a firm wanting to expand internationally via franchising can develop its own franchise operations, ally with a master franchisor, or buy the franchise operations of an existing firm. Not all tactics are available for all entry modes. For instance, a company cannot license or create a joint venture with itself. Next we discuss each entry tactic—make, ally or buy—in detail.

	Internationalization Entry Tactics		
Internationalization Entry Modes	Make (Do it yourself)	Ally (Do it with a partner)	Buy (Acquire it)
Exporting	Export support functions (Trade, lobbying, shipping, sales etc)	Export partner/ be an OEM	Purchase distributors or marketing or sales channels
Turnkey	Build and deliver	Partner on development (Consortium)	
Licensing		Contracts with licensees	
Franchise	Develop franchise operations	Master licensor agreement	Buy franchise operations
Joint venture		JV partner(s)	Buy into an existing JV
Wholly owned	Green Field		M&A / Turnkey

FIGURE 13.10 Entry modes and entry tactics This image compares the entry tactics available for different entry modes. JV, joint venture; M&A, merger and acquisition; OEM, original equipment manufacturer.

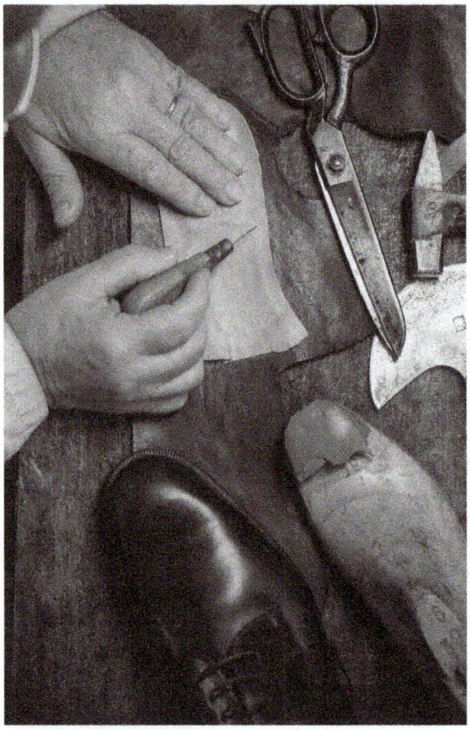

Terry Vine/Blend Images/Getty Images

FIGURE 13.11 **Scarosso** The company sells high-end Italian fashion directly to consumers in many markets via the Internet.

Make

Companies desiring to go global through an entry mode of exporting, a turnkey project, franchise, or wholly owned subsidiary can "make" or develop its own operations in a new market. Firms that choose to export can establish their own supporting functions, such as sales, distribution, lobbying, and trade. In this case the firm can directly own the exporting process. For instance, Boeing exports its commercial aircraft around the world and handles all aspects of the export process.[60] Firms are increasingly using the Internet to export directly to international customers. SCAROSSO, an Italian firm (**Figure 13.11**), exports handmade Italian shoes directly to the United States and other global markets, bypassing intermediaries and offering premium shoes at lower prices.[61]

Firms engaging in international business through turnkey projects are, by definition, developing infrastructure in foreign markets. Hence, the most common entry mode for these types of firms is "make." Turnkey providers develop facilities such as oil refineries, energy infrastructures, and production facilities; make them operational; train employees to maintain operations; and then turn those operations over to the local owners. For instance, Samsung Engineering Company, based in South Korea, is building two petrochemical plants in Malaysia for Petronas, the Malaysian national oil company. The project scope of Samsung's mission includes designing, engineering, procuring, constructing, and commissioning; the plants are to be completed in 2019.[62]

In addition, a firm can "make" by developing its own international franchise operations. For instance, RE/MAX is a global network of more than 97,000 real estate agents in over 95 countries and includes nearly 2,500 international franchisees. It was founded in 1973 and began franchising in 1975. Each franchisee is in charge of his or her own business, shares office expenses, and operates under a high commission plan.[63]

Finally, a company may choose to enter a market by creating a wholly owned subsidiary and develop the subsidiary itself through a greenfield venture. Mexico has experienced rapid growth in greenfield manufacturing investments over the past decade: annual investment in these operations has grown from $3 billion in 2005 to $16 billion in 2014.[64] Much of this investment has been poured into automobile production facilities by Nissan, Honda, Mazda, Kia, and BMW. These foreign firms not only produce for the Mexican market but also supply regional demand to more than 100 countries, especially the United States and Canada.[65]

Ally

alliance a contractual relationship between two or more companies

Allying with international partners requires an **alliance**, which is a contractual relationship between two or more companies. Firms often use allying as an important tactic in their globalization efforts. For instance, some companies wishing to export do not have the skills to do so, in which case they can ally or partner with other firms to help them. The export partners may handle one or more of the sales, distribution, and lobbying activities that are common for exporting firms. For example, many thousands of companies in countries around the world have allied with Alibaba, the giant Chinese e-commerce firm, which helps them export their products to foreign customers in China and other markets. In allying with Alibaba, a company shifts the job of developing technology to link buyers and sellers and to run the payment and delivery systems that ensure product delivery and payment. Alibaba provides an export service in industries such as textiles from India and Pakistan, seafood from Vietnam and Japan, and wine from Portugal and Argentina.[66] The British-Dutch firm Unilever formed an alliance with Alibaba (**Figure 13.12**) in 2015 to sell its products through the Alibaba platform.

As another alternative, exporting firms can offer their unbranded products to partners in the local market. These products are called "white-label goods" because they can easily be

Imagine China/Newscom

FIGURE 13.12 **Alibaba-Unilever alliance** The Chinese firm Alibaba and European firm Unilever formed an alliance in 2015 to sell Unilever's products on the Alibaba platform.

branded and sold under the partner's label. For instance, when Haier entered the European market, it exported refrigerators to the Swiss appliance company Liebherr without a label. In Switzerland, Liebherr branded and sold these refrigerators under its "Blue Line" label.[67]

In some cases, firms will enter a *consortium*, an alliance of companies pooling their resources, to deliver a turnkey project. For instance, Effiage, a French construction company; Schneider Electric, a French energy company; and Krinner, a German solar support company, have teamed up to build the largest photovoltaic plant in France for Neoen, a French renewable energy company.[68] Each company will contribute its unique strengths to offer a complete turnkey project.

In addition to exporting and turnkey modes, firms ally by forming license agreements with licensees. In fact, allying is the only entry tactic available with a licensing entry mode. For instance, 7-Eleven had 17,799 licensed stores in Japan as of August 2015. The company began licensing to Japan's Ito-Yokado Company in 1972, retaining control of its brand but limiting its exposure to the Japanese market.[69]

In many cases, firms choose the franchise entry mode and elect to form an alliance with a master franchisee. Chem-Dry, a U.S.-based carpet-cleaning franchise, recently expanded to India. Upon entering the country in 2014, the company formed a master franchise relationship in one key market and began looking for partners in other major markets.[70] The master franchise agreement enables the firm expanding internationally to form partnerships with investors who will further enlarge operations in the country. Some franchisors explicitly state in the contract a particular number of stores that the master franchisee must open within a given amount of time.

Joint ventures for foreign entry are formed when two companies from the same or different countries come together. For instance, GE Aircraft and Pratt & Whitney, two U.S. companies, have a 50/50 joint venture to develop and sell the GP7200 aircraft engine globally. The engine has become one of the most successful on the market because the two firms have shared lessons learned during their combined 25 million flight hours.[71]

In addition, joint ventures can also be formed to enter the home market of one of the parent companies, as in the General Motors/SAIC Motor Corp. venture. GM partnered with Chinese car manufacturer SAIC to enter the Chinese market. The 50/50 venture has been so successful in China, selling over 100,000 cars annually, that GM recently announced it will begin to export the Buick Envision SUV from its factory in Shandong, China, back to the United States.[72]

Last, a joint venture can be formed with the goal of helping two or more foreign firms enter an unrelated global market. For instance, Samsung Heavy Industries, a South Korean company, and Amec Foster Wheeler, a British firm, formed a joint venture, AMEC Samsung Oil & Gas, LLC, to pursue offshore oil service opportunities in the Gulf of Mexico. The venture combines the construction and service talents of Samsung with the engineering talents of Amec.[73]

The ally strategy deserves special attention because it can offer firms a hybrid mode of entry into foreign markets that combines a global company's international efforts with contracts. For instance, many airlines have joined either the Star Alliance, the Sky Team, or the Oneworld Alliance. These agreements use contracts to combine the resources of the individual airlines in a way that helps them access global flights. While each airline operates its own individual flights, all seats are sold by all the partners. This kind of alliance allows firms to enter new markets by pooling their resources.

Buy

Companies seeking to expand internationally by buying or acquiring access can engage in several entry modes. A firm can buy existing franchisee operations to enter a new international market. For instance, in 2016 Marriott International purchased Starwood Hotels and Resorts for $13.6 billion. Starwood's properties, which are largely franchised, offer Marriott a combined 5,700 hotels in more than 110 countries. The purchase gave Marriott access to 30 new countries.[74]

As another way to form a joint venture, firms can buy into an existing company, becoming a partner without purchasing the company outright. Acerta Pharma is a U.S.-Dutch biotech company working on the development of blood cancer drugs. AstraZeneca, a U.K.-based pharmaceutical company, bought 55 percent of the Acerta venture in a $2.5 billion deal, making AstraZeneca the controlling partner without its having to purchase the entire company. AstraZeneca gains access to the drugs Acerta has created and can market them around the world.[75]

Many firms enter foreign markets by purchasing the existing operations of a foreign company. For instance, Yelp entered the European market by purchasing Qype, a European local review site, and expanded into the German and French markets by acquiring Restaurant-Kritik and CityVox, respectively. These acquisitions allowed Yelp to quickly enter and expand in the European market without the lead time required or the risk entailed when developing operations from scratch.[76]

Companies' internationalization efforts are driven by several desires, such as the need to grow, to acquire resources, and to reduce risk. In choosing which markets to enter, firms not only use a PEST analysis but also factor in the liability of foreignness, the desire to be first into markets, and the need to follow clients globally. Once a company has chosen which market to enter, it must determine the preferred entry mode and decide which entry tactic to take—whether to make, ally, or buy its way into the market. These efforts are often difficult, but doing them well allows firms to succeed in the global market.

Summary and Case

Summary

LEARNING OBJECTIVE 13.1 Describe factors that determine which markets companies are likely to enter.

Once firms decide to go abroad, they can determine where to go by using a PEST analysis to identify the opportunities and risks of entering a country based on its political, economic, social, and technological factors. However, firms may choose to enter a country because of other pressures, such as the liability of foreignness, the desire for first-mover advantages, or the need to follow customers into specific markets.

LEARNING OBJECTIVE 13.2 Explain the advantages and disadvantages of different entry modes.

After firms identify a foreign market to enter, they must choose the market entry mode best tailored to their abilities and strategic objectives. While all market entry modes have downsides and risks, nonequity modes such as exporting, turnkey operations, franchising, and licensing tend to have the lowest risk for the parent company; however, they also offer the least amount of control over the venture. By contrast, equity modes such as joint ventures and wholly owned subsidiaries offer the parent company more control but at the cost of higher risk.

LEARNING OBJECTIVE 13.3 Compare making, allying, and buying as entry tactics.

Once a firm chooses a market entry mode, it must then consider the objectives of its foreign expansion as well as its own capabilities and resources in order to select the best tactic for market entry. A firm that chooses the "make" tactic develops its own operations in the country. Through the "ally" tactic, a company partners with existing firms in the local market. The "buy" tactic means the firm will acquire another firm already operating in the local market.

Case Study

Blendtec Goes Global . . . Again

Harvey Scott, vice president of international development, was in charge of Blendtec's global expansion effort. He and his team had been gathering data and meeting with international partners and contacts for months to help determine which global markets to enter, when to enter them, and how. Scott had to decide how to leverage Blendtec's existing network of international partners and distribution channels, or whether to scrap them and start over. He understood that in many international markets, if Blendtec didn't get things right, it wouldn't get a second chance.

Blendtec began in 1975 when founder Tom Dickson created a revolutionary wheat mill. Dickson next turned his attention to commercial kitchen appliances, and his blenders were an unqualified success, reducing average blending times from around fifty seconds to just thirteen.

Product performance made Blendtec the primary appliance supplier to big-name companies like Starbucks and Jamba Juice. The company also partnered with Costco to sell Blendtec blenders directly to consumers. These relationships initially stayed domestic, and Blendtec was positioned to service a predominantly U.S. market. Starbucks and Costco, however, had plans for global expansion.

Going Global

When Starbucks and Costco moved international in the early 1990s, Blendtec wasn't an international company, so it had no network in place to provide service and support to its big customers. It promised to build a global supply and support network, but it faced new and different problems in each market, which required additional innovation. For example, in Australia, the power grid could fluctuate widely in terms of voltage. Most U.S. appliances would burn up under that kind of power variation. Blendtec had to find a partner to explain how to build a power regulation system that would protect appliances from those fluctuations.

Mixing Things Up

After a few years abroad, the company wanted to enter other foreign markets using a more strategic focus, not just in reaction to customers' demands. To ensure its future, Harvey Scott needed to determine Blendtec's strategy. Future growth depended on his decision, and he wouldn't get a second chance to make a first impression on new markets and consumers.

Case Discussion Questions

1. Which markets are most likely to be most receptive to a greater presence from Blendtec? Why? What differentiates those markets from other markets?
2. Should Blendtec sell to local retail stores or rely on global retailers such as Costco?
3. Should Blendtec set up production facilities in foreign countries? For example, would it be better to manufacture units in Brazil for that market or better to ship product there and pay applicable import tariffs? Does that determination vary from market to market?

Endnotes

[1]Gongming Qian, Lee Li, and Alan M. Rugman, "Liability of Country Foreignness and Liability of Regional Foreignness: Their Effects on Geographic Diversification and Firm Performance," *Journal of International Business Studies* 44, no. 6 (2013): 635–47; Pankaj Ghemawat, *Redefining Global Strategy: Crossing Borders in a World Where Differences Still Matter*, (Cambridge, MA: Harvard Business Press, 2013).

[2]Srilata Zaheer, "Overcoming the Liability of Foreignness," *Academy of Management Journal* 38, no. 2 (1995): 341–63; and Srilata Zaheer and Elaine Mosakowski, "The Dynamics of the Liability of Foreignness: A Global Study of Survival in Financial Services," *Strategic Management Journal* 18, no. 6 (1997): 439–63.

[3]Donal Crilly, Na Ni, and Yuwei Jiang, "Do-No-Harm versus Do-Good Social Responsibility: Attributional Thinking and the Liability of Foreignness," *Strategic Management Journal* 37, No. 7 (2015): 1316–1329.

[4]Nikoletta-Theofania Siamagka and George Balabanis, "Revisiting Consumer Ethnocentrism: Review, Reconceptualization, and Empirical Testing," *Journal of International Marketing* 23, no. 3 (2015): 66–86.

[5]George Balabanis and Nikoletta-Theofania Siamagka, "The Behavioral Effects of Consumer Ethnocentrism: The Role of Brand, Product Category and Country of Origin," *2014 Global Marketing Conference at Singapore*, 2014.

[6]Guido Friebel and Matthias Heinz, "Media Slant Against Foreign Owners: Downsizing," *Journal of Public Economics* 120 (2014): 97–106.

[7]I. Serdar Dinc and Isil Erel, "Economic Nationalism in Mergers and Acquisitions," *Journal of Finance* 68, no. 6 (2013): 2471–514.

[8]Srilata Zaheer, "Overcoming the Liability of Foreignness," 341–63; Zaheer and Mosakowski, "The Dynamics of the Liability of Foreignness," 439–63; Zheying Wu and Robert Salomon, "Does Imitation Reduce the Liability of Foreignness? Linking Distance, Isomorphism, and Performance," *Strategic Management Journal* 37, No. 12 (2016): 2441–2462.

[9]"Peruvian Upstart AJE Takes on Coke and Pepsi in Asia," *Financial Times*, July 21, 2014, www.ft.com/cms/s/0/dd0e0c00-0cf2-11e4-bf1e-00144feabdc0.html#axzz3tlSFG8gv.

[10]Luc Cohen, "Factbox: With Dealmaking, JAB Holding Expands Its Coffee Empire," ed. Lisa Shumaker and Lisa Von Ahn, Reuters, December 7, 2015. www.reuters.com/article/us-keurig-green-m-a-jab-factbox-idUSKBN0TQ1ZI20151208#fFYcym4I2o49KXAH.97.

[11]"Instant Coffee Mix Not So Hot as Sales Dive," *Korea Times*, December 8, 2015, www.koreatimes.co.kr/www/news/nation/2015/12/116_192664.html.

[12]"What Emissions Scandal? VW May Have Just Become the World's Top-Selling Automaker," Associated Press, January 10, 2017, http://www.latimes.com/business/autos/la-fi-hy-vw-sales-20170110-story.html; "Volkswagen Expects to Sell Three Million VW Vehicles in China This Year," Reuters, November 17, 2016, http://www.reuters.com/article/us-volkswagen-china-idUSKBN13D085.

[13]Benjamin Zhang, "One Country Has Kept Volkswagen's Global Sales from Cratering After Its Emissions Scandal," *Business Insider*, October 17, 2016, www.businessinsider.com/volkswagen-sales-increased-after-emissions-cheating-scandal-china-2016-10.

[14]Ranjay Gulati, *Reorganize for Resilience: Putting Customers at the Center of Your Business* (Cambridge, MA: Harvard Business Press, 2013).

[15]"Our History," QuintilesIMS, 2016, www.quintiles.com/en/about%20us/our%20history.

[16]Sanjeev Agarwal and Sridhar N. Ramaswami, "Choice of Foreign Market Entry Mode: Impact of Ownership, Location and Internalization Factors," *Journal of International Business Studies* 23, no. 1 (1992): 1–27; Anne Canabal and George O. White, "Entry Mode Research: Past and Future," *International Business Review* 17, no. 3 (2008): 267–84.

[17]Jean-François Hennart and Arjen H. L. Slangen, "Yes, We Really Do Need More Entry Mode Studies! A Commentary on Shaver," *Journal of International Business Studies* 46, no. 1 (2015): 114–22.

[18]About igus® www.igus.com/AboutIgus (accessed July 19, 2017).

[19]Alibaba search for hooverboards. http://www.alibaba.com/trade/search?fsb=y&IndexArea=product_en&CatId=&SearchText=2+Two+Wheels+Electric+Balance+Hooverboard (accessed July 19, 2017).

[20]http://stat.wto.org/TariffProfiles/AR_e.htm (accessed January 27, 2017).

[21]Gabe Nelson, "Tariff Talks Lead to Auto Trade Fight," *Automotive News*, October 21, 2015, www.autonews.com/article/20131021/GLOBAL/310219851/tariff-talks-lead-to-auto-trade-fight; "The Japanese and American Auto Markets at a Glance," http://democrats.waysandmeans.house.gov/sites/democrats.waysandmeans.house.gov/files/TPP%20Japan%20U.S.%20Side-by-side_0.pdf (accessed January 27, 2017).

[22]Nina Adam, "Rising Costs Strike at German Competitiveness,", *Wall Street Journal*, July 27, 2015, www.wsj.com/articles/rising-costs-strike-at-german-competitiveness-1438039512.

[23]"International Comparisons of Hourly Compensation Costs in Manufacturing, 2011, news release, Bureau of Labor Statistics, December 19, 2012, www.bls.gov/news.release/pdf/ichcc.pdf; "International Comparisons of Hourly Compensation Costs in Manufacturing, 2013," The Conference Board, December 17, 2014, www.conference-board.org/ilcprogram/index.cfm?id=28269.

[24]Jillian Ambrose, "That Sinking Feeling for Hanjin as Falling Freight Rates Fuel a Global Shipping Crisis," *The Telegraph*, September 17, 2016, www.telegraph.co.uk/business/2016/09/17/that-sinking-feeling-for-hanjin-as-falling-freight-rates-fuel-a/.

[25]Karl West, "British Steel Industry Buckles under the Weight of Cheap Chinese Product," *The Guardian*, September 28, 2015, www.theguardian.com/business/2015/sep/28/british-steel-industry-buckles-under-weight-cheap-chinese-product-ssi-redcar.

[26]"Issues at Taishan Nuclear Plant in China's Guangdong Spark Safety Fears," Radio Free Asia, June 23, 2016, www.rfa.org/english/news/china/china-nuclear-06232016125814.html.

[27]"Structure of the Partnership for Hinkley Point C Project," press release, Areva, October 21, 2013, www.areva.com/EN/news-9986/structure-of-the-partnership-for-hinkley-point-c-project.html.

[28]Trefis Team, "Tokyo Disneyland Goes Down and Could Hurt Disney," *Forbes*, March 17, 2011, www.forbes.com/sites/greatspeculations/2011/03/17/tokyo-disneyland-goes-down-and-could-hurt-disney/#fd6dd33208bb.

[29]"The Top 150 Global Licensors," Global License!, May 1, 2015, www.licensemag.com/license-global/top-150-global-licensors-1.

[30]Michael Flanagan, "2015 in Review: Pharma's Largest in-Licensing Deals—Cancer Continues to Carry the Day," FirstWord Pharma, December 23, 2015, www.firstwordpharma.com/node/1339317?tsid=17.

[31]Mark Scott, "Novartis Joins with Google to Develop Contact Lens That Monitors Blood Sugar," *New York Times*, July 15, 2014, www.nytimes.com/2014/07/16/business/international/novartis-joins-with-google-to-develop-contact-lens-to-monitor-blood-sugar.html?_r=0.

[32]Richard Mason, Nicos Savva, and Stefan Scholtes, "The Economics of Licensing Contracts," *Nature Biotechnology*, July 11, 2008, www.nature.com/bioent/2008/080701/full/bioe.2008.7.html; Flanagan, "2015 in Review: Pharma's Largest in-Licensing Deals."

[33]"Servier Exercises Exclusive Worldwide Licensing Option with Cellectis for UCART19, an Allogeneic CAR-T Cell Therapy for Hematological Malignancies," Business Wire, November 19, 2015, www.businesswire.com/news/home/20151118006806/en/Servier-Exercises-Exclusive-Worldwide-Licensing-Option-Cellectis.

[34]Amrutha Gayathri, "Starbucks to Pay $2.76B to Mondelez International to Settle Packaged Coffee Dispute," *International Business Times*. November, 13, 2013.

[35]Chris Burritt, "Starbucks to Pay $2.79 Billion to Settle Coffee Dispute," Bloomberg Business, November 13, 2013, www.bloomberg.com/news/articles/2013-11-12/starbucks-to-pay-2-76-billion-to-settle-grocery-dispute.

[36]"Licensing Is One Fashion Trend That Isn't Going Away," The Fashion Law, April 2015, www.thefashionlaw.com/home/licensing-is-one-fashion-trend-that-isnt-going-away.

[37]Rupert Neate, "How an American Woman Rescued Burberry, a Classic British Label," *The Guardian*, June 15, 2013, www.theguardian.com/business/2013/jun/16/angela-ahrendts-burberry-chav-image.

[38]Catherine Ostler, "As Romeo Beckham Stars in Their New Ad, How Burberry Went from Chic to Chav to Chic Again," DailyMail.com, November 5, 2014, www.dailymail.co.uk/femail/article-2822546/As-Romeo-Beckham-stars-new-ad-Burberry-went-chic-chav-chic-again.html#ixzz4RcmvWTqM.

[39]Miriam Gottfried, "The Netflix Problem: Which Media Company Will Solve It?" *Wall Street Journal*, November 15, 2015, https://www.wsj.com/articles/the-netflix-problem-which-media-company-will-solve-it-1447609351.

[40]"Pay-TV Notes: Netflix and the Dish Network's Sling TV in Focus," *Forbes*, December 14, 2015, www.forbes.com/sites/greatspeculations/2015/12/14/pay-tv-notes-netflix-and-dish-networks-sling-tv-in-focus/.

[41]Tom Huddleston, "How FX Broke HBO's Grip on the Emmy Awards," *Fortune*, September 19, 2016, http://fortune.com/2016/09/19/emmy-awards-2016-hbo-fx/.

[42]Andrew Meola, "Nielsen Shines a Light on Netflix Viewership," *Business Insider*, July 1, 2016, www.businessinsider.com/nielsen-shines-a-light-on-netflix-viewership-2016-7.

[43]Chloe Lewis, "Top 5 Food Franchises," Business Review USA, November 14, 2016, www.businessreviewusa.com/top10/5638/Top-5-food-franchises.

[44]Matthew Luke, "McDonald's and Burger King Battle for Latin America," The Motley Fool, November 12, 2013, www.fool.com/investing/general/2013/11/12/mcdonalds-and-burger-king-battle-for-latin-america.aspx.

[45]"Papa John's Continues European Expansion," Pizza Marketplace, December 9, 2015, www.pizzamarketplace.com/news/papa-johns-continues-european-expansion/.

[46]"Hampton by Hilton Lodz Hotel to Open 2018 in Poland," Hotel News Resource, November 28, 2016, www.hotelnewsresource.com/article92141.html.

[47]"International Franchising," The Wendy's Company, www.wendys.com/en-us/about-wendys/international-franchising (accessed December 1, 2016).

[48]Julie Jargon, "Yum Brands to Split off China Business," *Wall Street Journal*, October 20, 2015, www.wsj.com/articles/yum-brands-to-spin-off-china-business-1445338830.

[49]Wenhui Wei, "China and India: Any Difference in Their FDI Performances?" *Journal of Asian Economics* 16, no. 4 (2005): 719–36.

[50]Weilei Stone Shi et al., "Domestic Alliance Network to Attract Foreign Partners: Evidence from International Joint Ventures in China," *Journal of International Business Studies* 45, no. 3 (2014): 338–62.

[51]Keith D. Brouthers, "Institutional, Cultural and Transaction Cost Influences on Entry Mode Choice and Performance," *Journal of International Business Studies* 44, no. 1 (2013): 1–13.

[52]Stephan Bosshart, Thomas Luedi, and Emma Wang, "Past Lessons for China's New Joint Ventures,", McKinsey & Company, December 2010, www.mckinsey.com/insights/corporate_finance/past_lessons_for_chinas_new_joint_ventures.

[53]Andrew C. Inkpen, "Learning Through Joint Ventures: A Framework of Knowledge Acquisition," *Journal of Management Studies* 37, no. 7 (2000): 1019–44.

[54]Paul Merrion, "U.S. Probes Itasca Firm's Chinese Trade Dispute," Crain's Chicago Business, January 23, 2013, www.chicagobusiness.com/article/20130123/NEWS05/130129890/u-s-probes-itasca-firms-chinese-trade-dispute.

[55]Matthew Robertson, "Fellowes, American Stationery Giant, Brought to Its Knees in China," *Epoch Times*, April 5, 2011, www.theepochtimes.com/n3/1499682-american-stationary-giant-brought-to-its-knees-in-china/full/.

[56]Shilpy Sinha, "Berkshire Can't Resist India Any More, to Return with Reinsurance Business," *Economic Times*, September 30, 2016, http://economictimes.indiatimes.com/wealth/personal-finance-news/berkshire-cant-resist-india-any-more-to-return-with-reinsurance-business/articleshow/54594516.cms.

[57]"Berkshire Hathaway Enters India Market Via Wholly-Owned Subsidiary," India Briefing, June 21, 2010, www.india-briefing.com/news/berkshire-hathaway-enters-india-market-whollyowned-subsidiary-3052.html/#sthash.aFd2gKap.dpuf/.

[58]"Porsche Cars North America Statement Regarding California Air Resources Board in Use Compliance Letter," Cision, PR Newswire, November 25, 2015, www.prnewswire.com/news-releases/porsche-cars-north-america-statement-regarding-california-air-resources-board-in-use-compliance-letter-300184719.html.

[59]Krishna Palepu, Tarun Khanna, and Ingrid Vargas, "Haier: Taking a Chinese Company Global," Harvard Business Case 9-706-401, October 17, 2005.

[60]Tim Fernholz and David Yanofsky, "Boeing Is Everything Right and Wrong about the US Export," Quartz, November 18, 2013, http://qz.com/148374/boeing-is-everything-right-and-wrong-about-the-us-export-push/.

[61]Declan Eytan, "How Two College Friends Established a Brand of Premium Italian Shoes, for a Mid-Market Price," *Forbes*, March 19, 2015, www.forbes.com/sites/declaneytan/2015/03/19/how-two-college-friends-established-a-brand-of-premium-italian-shoes-for-a-mid-market-price/#61357a6e3a18.

[62]"Samsung Wins $882m Malaysia Petchem Plants Contract," Trade Arabia, December 12, 2015, www.tradearabia.com/news/OGN_296612.html.

[63]"2016 Top Franchises from Entrepreneur's Franchise 500 List," *Entrepreneur*, 2016, www.entrepreneur.com/franchise500.

[64]Courtney Fingar, "Mexico Foreign Direct Investment Races Ahead as Brazil Sputters," *Financial Times*, August 25, 2015, www.ft.com/intl/cms/s/3/e938840a-4b13-11e5-b558-8a9722977189.html#axzz3uglk1wSX.

[65]Dudley Althus, "Mexico Sets Auto Production Record, Aims for More," *Wall Street Journal*, January 8, 2015, www.wsj.com/articles/mexico-sets-auto-production-record-aims-for-more-1420749573.

[66]www.alibaba.com/countrysearch/continent.html?spm=a2700.7224109.1998688605.11.1aP9H1 (accessed December 15, 2016).

[67]Krishna G. Palepu, Tarun Khanna, and Ingrid Vargas, "Haier: Taking a Chinese Company Global," Harvard Business School (October 2005).

[68]"Neoen Launches New Photovoltaic Farm in Cestas," Market Line, December 15, 2015, www.renewablesbiz.com/article/15/12/neoen-launches-new-photovoltaic-farm-cestas.

[69]Kazuo Usui, *Marketing and Consumption in Modern Japan* (London: Routledge, 2014).

[70]"Chem-Dry Seeks Regional Master Franchisees," FranchiseIndia.com, December 16, 2015, http://news.franchiseindia.com/Chem-Dry-seeks-regional-master-franchisees-6328/.

[71]"Emirates Selects Engine Alliance GP7200 Engines to Power Latest A380 Aircraft Order," GE Aviation, July 19, 2010, www.geaviation.com/press/gepw.

[72]John D. Stoll and Gautham Nagesh, "GM to Import Chinese-Made Buick SUV," *Wall Street Journal*, November 13, 2015, www.wsj.com/articles/gm-to-import-chinese-made-buick-suv-1447349781.

[73]"Samsung, AMEC Form Engineering Joint Venture," *Offshore Magazine*, October 25, 2012, www.offshore-mag.com/articles/2012/10/samsung-amec-form-engineering-joint-venture.html.

[74]Nancy Trejos, "After Merger, Marriott Expands into Africa," *USA Today*, October 4, 2016, www.usatoday.com/story/travel/roadwarriorvoices/2016/10/04/week-after-merging-starwood-marriott-expands-into-africa/91519616/; Aaron Smith, "Marriott and Starwood Merge: World's Biggest Hotel Company," CNN Money, November 16, 2015, http://money.cnn.com/2015/11/16/investing/marriott-starwood-hotel/; Nancy Trejos, "Marriott, Starwood Merger Is Complete, Loyalty Programs Will Reciprocate," *USA Today*, September 26, 2016, www.usatoday.com/story/travel/roadwarriorvoices/2016/09/23/marriott-starwood-merger-complete-and-loyal-customers-get-reciprocal-benefits/90885318/.

[75]Andrew Ward and Arash Massoudi, "AstraZeneca Adds 55% Acerta Pharma Stake to Swath of Deals," *Financial Times*, December 17, 2015, www.ft.com/intl/cms/s/0/6aa1c230-a48e-11e5-b73f-9545472cb784.html#axzz3uglk1wSX.

[76]Steven Leob, "Yelp Expands European Presence with Cityvox Purchase: The Deal Comes Less Than a Week after Yelp Bought German Review Site Restaurant-Kriti," Vatornews, October 28, 2014, http://vator.tv/news/2014-10-28-yelp-expands-european-presence-with-cityvox-purchase/.

CHAPTER **14**

International Strategy

Stanchev/Getty Images

Introduction

The purpose of following an international strategy is to help companies manage the differences that arise when crossing borders, whether those borders are geographic or cultural. This chapter begins by exploring what *strategy* is. Strategy consists of actions managers take to achieve their company's objectives for profitable growth. Profitable growth often comes from reducing costs and/or increasing customers' willingness to pay a premium for a product or service.

At a global level, companies can reduce costs through global integration or standardization, which consists of selling the same product or following the same operational practices within different countries. To increase customers' willingness to pay for a product, companies must respond to local needs by customizing and providing new value to products and operations at the local country level. Managers are likely to choose one of three international strategies—a multi-domestic, a meganational, or a transnational strategy—to ensure they introduce the right amount of standardization and customization in order to enable profitable growth in a global market.

LEARNING OBJECTIVES

After exploring this chapter you will be able to:

1. **Define** *strategy*
2. **Explain** why multinational companies benefit from being locally responsive
3. **Outline** the benefits of achieving global integration
4. **Identify** appropriate strategies for different company objectives and industry pressures

14.1 What Is Strategy?

LEARNING OBJECTIVE

Define *strategy*.

Choosing a market entry strategy, as described in Chapter 13, is one thing; deciding how you will manage your operations once you are in the new market is quite another. Companies determine how they will operate in a global setting largely through their international strategy.

international strategy actions by which companies manage differences across borders to create advantages over their competitors

strategy the actions managers take in pursuit of company objectives for profitable growth

growth occurs when a company is able to increase its profits relative to past profits

profitable growth when a company increases revenues in excess of expenses over time

low-cost strategy a strategy that helps companies succeed through efficiencies and by reducing costs

differentiation strategy a strategy that helps companies succeed by differentiating their product in order to persuade customers to pay more for it

value creation the process of maximizing the difference between a customer's willingness to pay and the cost of a product

value capture the process of maximizing the portion of that value the company keeps

International strategy consists of the steps by which companies manage differences across borders to create advantages over their competitors. Gaining competitive advantage is at the core of international strategy. For example, IKEA decided to enter India in 2017 by building its own storefronts and operating them as wholly owned subsidiaries.[1] This represented their market entry mode. What they did next to successfully manage the different customer demands, suppliers, and potential competitors in India depended on their international strategy. To understand their international strategy, we must first define what we mean by *strategy*.

Strategy, in its most basic form, consists of the actions managers take in pursuit of company objectives for profitable **growth**. For example, the store manager of the first IKEA that opened in Hyderabad, India, may have the objective of increasing the store's profitability by 10 percent every year. The store's strategy is the plan put in place to achieve that 10 percent growth. It will likely include tradeoffs between spending and earning, since profitability is the store's total sales minus its operating costs. For instance, the manager may decide to increase advertising and, to balance that expense, decrease the number of employees needed by adopting a more efficient inventory management system. These steps help ensure that the company is able to sell more products while reducing costs. If executed well, this strategy will lead to profitable growth for IKEA in India.

Profitable growth is exactly what it sounds like—a combination of growth and profitability—and it's harder to achieve than it might seem.[2] When talking about the need for both profitability and growth, Gary Burnison, CEO of Korn Ferry, an executive placement firm, said that profitable growth comes through two levers: reducing your costs or differentiating your product.[3] These two levers represent generic strategies companies can use to build a specific international strategy that will lead to profitable growth (see **Figure 14.1**).

A **low-cost strategy** focuses the company's efforts on seeking efficiencies and reducing costs. Through a **differentiation strategy**, firms differentiate their product in order to persuade customers to pay more for it. Chipotle, for example, tries to do both. The popular Mexican grill restaurant succeeded in differentiating itself within the overcrowded Mexican fast-food market by emphasizing the use of organic, locally sourced ingredients and meat from naturally raised animals. As a result, even though it increased its menu prices in 2014, in-store sales increased 17 percent the same year. Chipotle's dedication to quality ingredients has been such an effective marketing tool that it has also enabled the company to contain costs by having a relatively small marketing budget.[4]

Value Creation and Capture

Both low-cost and differentiation strategies help companies to create and capture value. **Value creation** is the process of maximizing the difference between a customer's willingness to pay and the cost of the product, whereas **value capture** is the process of maximizing the portion of that value the company keeps. In other words, *captured value* is the difference between the price a company charges customers and the cost of making the product.

Value creation drives profitable growth. But to persuade people to value a product and then to make a profit from selling it to them, you need to create value for both your customer and your company. **Figure 14.2** shows why capturing some of the value created is so important for profitable growth.

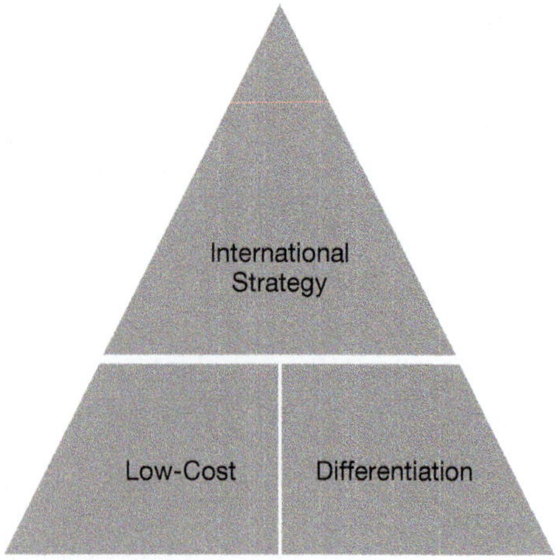

FIGURE 14.1 Generic strategy as a foundation for international strategy Firms may use a low-cost or differentiation approach underlying their international strategy.

Strategic Positioning

Any company's leaders need to be explicit about the overall strategy they are following—by leading in cost or by differentiating—and how that strategy relates to those of its industry competitors. This type of positioning helps employees know where they should focus their day-to-day efforts. If a firm emphasizes a low-cost approach, it needs to deliberately align all its internal operations—such as marketing, research and development, human resources, and so on—to support that goal. This helps the company position itself such that all managers and

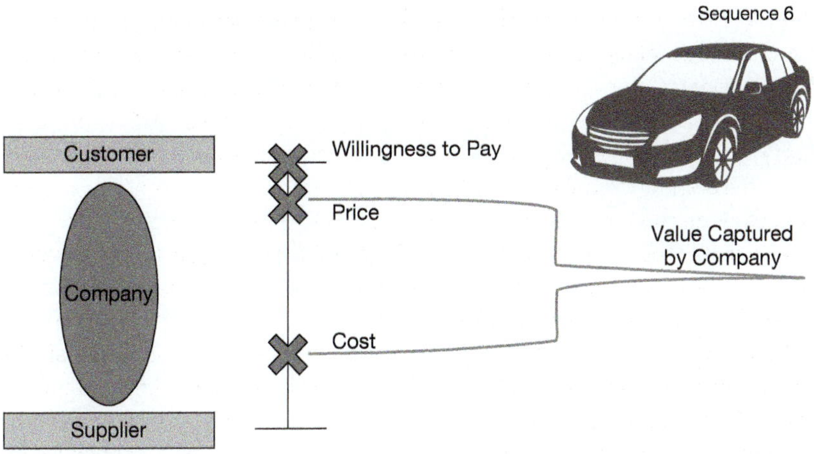

FIGURE 14.2 Value creation and capture This image illustrates how companies create and capture value to drive profitable growth.

employees can base their decisions on the same goals. If you've ever traveled to India from the United States, for example, you've probably noticed that you often arrive in Delhi at night and can't get a connecting flight to a smaller city until the next morning. As a result, many hotels cluster around Delhi's international airport, some of which compete using a low-cost approach by offering simple rooms on back streets for less than $20 a night. For instance, Hotel Delhi Airport Link costs a mere $16 a night (**Figure 14.3**).

If a firm emphasizes a differentiation approach, it needs to align its operations differently. The JW Marriott hotel chain usually offers quiet rooms with shuttle service from the local airport and a gated courtyard for about $200 a night. All the hotels are competing using different strategies, but their objectives are still the same. Each is trying to maximize the amount of value it captures, but one might try to do this by keeping costs low and competing on price, while the other might try to differentiate itself from the many alternatives by delivering high quality. Both types have their advantages. One you see in your wallet; the other you see in how well you sleep that night.

Cost Leadership Low-cost leadership describes a strategic position to create value by having the lowest cost of operation in the industry. The $20 hotels in India, many of them chains, aim to be the hotel industry's low-cost leaders for a given level of service. To keep costs down they need to ensure that they are sharing across the entire chain the cost-saving techniques learned at one location. They also need to ensure that their suppliers, such as the elevator vendor and linens supplier, are giving them the lowest possible prices.

Seeing a need for low-cost elevators in India, the Swiss-based elevator company Schindler Group decided to take a low-cost strategy and produce a standardized elevator that was safe but simple for low-end hotels.[5] The model proved successful in the Indian market, in part because competitors like Otis were catering to the higher-end hotels.

To compete in the low-cost market segment really means to improve overall efficiencies and reduce supplier costs while also reducing the features to offer a more basic product. Barti Airtel, based in India and one of the largest global telecommunications companies in the world, decided to pursue a cost-leadership strategy by reducing the costs of its product—in this case, per-minute talk time on cell phones.[6] However, it realized that it couldn't do this alone, so it outsourced most of its operations, such as building cell phone towers and providing IT solutions, to other, more efficient suppliers. This has allowed Barti Airtel to get the price of cellphone time down to 1 penny per minute—unheard of in the telecom business. Barti Airtel used this strategy to amass a large subscriber base in more than 20 different countries.[7]

PRAKASH SINGH/AFP/Getty Images

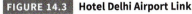

FIGURE 14.3 Hotel Delhi Airport Link

LEX VAN LIESHOUT/Stringer/AFP/Getty Images

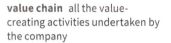

FIGURE 14.4 Starbucks adapts to a café culture This Starbucks café in Amsterdam uses locally sourced wood and avant-garde architecture to differentiate it from typical coffee shops in Europe.

Differentiation A differentiation strategy requires that companies create value by generating insights into customer behaviors, developing innovative products, and designing high-profile marketing programs. Consider, for example, the global fashion leader Zara, based in Spain. Zara differentiates itself from other youth fashion retailers like GAP and Abercrombie & Fitch by identifying the latest fashions at shows in Paris and Milan, copying them inexpensively, and bringing them to market in its stores around the world months before anyone else. Sustaining profitable growth through a differentiation approach requires that companies continuously innovate in ways that are difficult for competitors to imitate.

Starbucks has developed a unique and hard-to-replicate model for delivering coffee. However, the company knows that, at some point, its business model may be disrupted by someone else. As a result, it is continually changing the way it does things. In Europe, for instance, Starbucks is adopting that region's café culture through the use of classical architecture and chandeliers in its stores (**Figure 14.4**).[8]

Value Chain Analysis

value chain all the value-creating activities undertaken by the company

Once a firm decides whether to take a cost-leadership or differentiation strategy, managers work to align that approach with the internal operations of the company.[9] These operations, collectively called the **value chain**, represent all the value-creating activities undertaken by the company. The *primary* value chain functions are research and development, production, distribution, marketing and sales, and customer service. These contribute directly to value creation by developing and producing the product, distributing it, marketing and selling it, and assisting customers after purchase. *Support* functions, such as human resources and information systems, enable the primary functions to operate more efficiently or effectively in order to create value. Primary functions are not more important than secondary ones; both types need to be effective for a company to succeed.

Value chain analysis examines the specific operations of the company and scrutinizing each function to determine where costs can be lowered and where the company can differentiate itself from competitors. For example, with the fluctuations in the price of oil, many energy companies are evaluating parts of the value chain that can be streamlined and differentiated to help either decrease the costs of operations or to add more value for customers. Customized engineering within research and development, and production and bureaucratic management within many of the functions, are being replaced by standardized designs and leaner operations.[10]

Primary Functions Five primary functions are found in the value chain (in this order):

- **Research and development (R&D):** The process responsible for coming up with ideas for new products and production processes. For service companies, R&D focuses on developing new services. For example, banks have devised many new financial services—such as student checking accounts, alternate forms of credit, and overdraft protection—to increase customers' options. Through product innovation, a form of differentiation, R&D can increase the functionality of products, increasing customers' willingness to pay for them. R&D can also support a cost-leadership strategy by suggesting more efficient production methodologies or finding ways to reduce product costs.
- **Production:** the function that actually makes the product or provides the service. For physical products, production means manufacturing. For services such as banking and health care, production occurs when the service is delivered to the customer. At a health care facility, production occurs when a doctor or nurse diagnoses and treats a patient. At a bank, production occurs when a bank officer approves you for an auto loan or helps you open a checking account. The production function provides value by performing efficiently (cost leadership) and/or in a way that improves the quality of the product (differentiation).
- **Distribution:** the function that moves finished products from operations to wholesalers, retailers, or end consumers. This includes dealing with distribution channels, managing inventory, warehousing products, and negotiating with transportation providers. As a massive distributor, Amazon spends much time and energy on improving the way it distributes products to the end customer (cost leadership). Amazon differentiates its service by allowing customers to return items easily and by offering quality assurance for the products it sells. It pioneered "one-click" ordering and is now attempting to differentiate itself further by investing in delivery drones (**Figure 14.5**) for its planned Prime Air service, which it hopes will be able to deliver products within 30 minutes of ordering.[11]
- **Marketing and sales:** this function is responsible for finding the right market niches and promoting, advertising, and selling products in those markets. By differentiating through brand positioning and advertising, the marketing function can increase the perceived value of a product. For example, many luxury goods brands, such as Louis Vuitton and Gucci, engage in marketing campaigns to show that when you make a purchase, you are buying not only quality but also prestige. The marketing function also increases value by passing information from customers back to R&D in order to help improve product design and differentiation, as well as to lower costs.
- **Customer service:** this function provides service and support after a sale. This activity solves customer problems and supports customers in using their new products. The availability of high-quality customer service can increase a customer's willingness to pay a premium price. For example, the Seattle-based retailer Costco will take back any product at any time for full refund, no questions asked and no receipt necessary—whether you bought it at a Costco in Mexico or Australia. By adopting such an open customer service policy, Costco hopes to persuade customers to pay extra for its products (differentiation).

Amazon/ZUMA Press/Newscom

FIGURE 14.5 **Amazon proposes the use of delivery drones** Amazon's delivery drones, in the testing phase in several countries, have met some challenges in the United States from the Federal Aviation Administration (FAA) and from citizens concerned about their airspace privacy.

Support Functions The support roles of the value chain provide inputs or pathways that enable the primary roles to create value. Through their ability to help companies gain a competitive advantage, support activities can be just as important—if not more important—than primary functions.

- **Information systems:** the company's electronic networks for managing inventory, tracking sales, pricing products, selling products, and recording and monitoring customer service concerns. Information systems also help companies manage knowledge and coordinate communication across functions within the

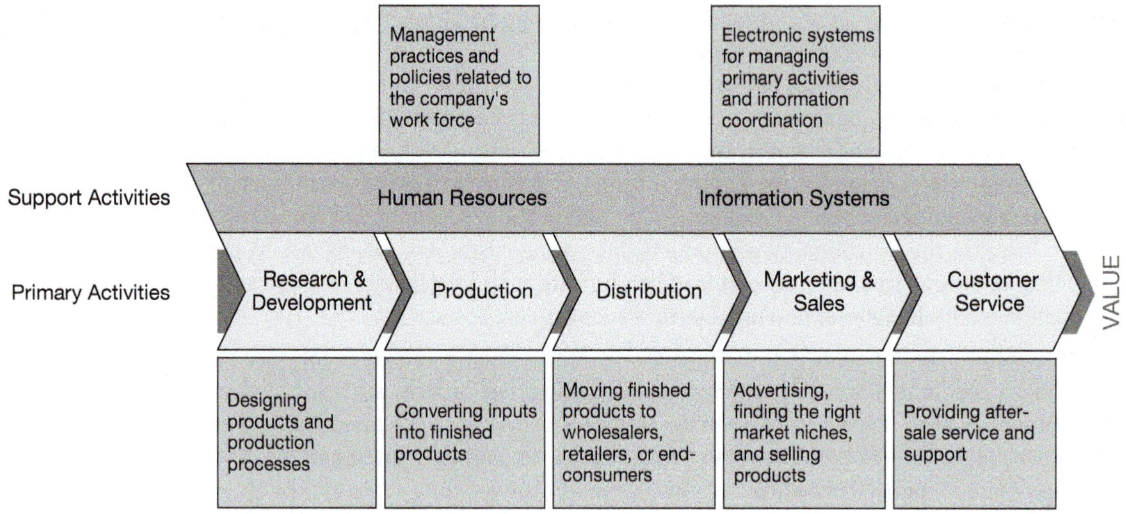

FIGURE 14.6 **Value Chain**

organization. For example, the World Bank uses its information systems to track activities in different countries, find overlaps where knowledge from one lending project might help another, and provide information about these overlaps to ensure that lending-project leaders across the globe are learning from one another.[12] This system thereby helps to eliminate redundancies in the organization's operations and make them more efficient (cost leadership). The system also coordinates new ideas between local operations that can then be customized to bring about newer and more innovative lending products that countries and companies are willing to pay more for (differentiation). These innovations are important, as the World Bank now faces more competition from other development agencies, such as the China Development Bank.

- **Human resources (HR):** this function applies management practices and policies to the company's workforce. It ensures that the company has employees with the right mix of skills to follow the organization's strategy and create value, and that they are adequately trained, motivated, and compensated to perform their value creation tasks. For example, when the World Bank implemented new information systems for knowledge management, it also had to implement the right HR policies to ensure that people were motivated, trained, and rewarded for using the systems in order to coordinate effectively worldwide.[13] HR is also instrumental in creating a culture for the organization.

Taken together, HR management and information systems can be the most powerful combination for enabling a global company to create value. While they don't directly influence products or services, they enable the primary functions to more effectively deliver products with high value at low cost. Review the value chain map in **Figure 14.6** to visualize how these factors work together to create value.

14.2 Becoming Locally Responsive

LEARNING OBJECTIVE

Explain why multinational companies benefit from being locally responsive.

When the online retail giant Amazon.com decided to enter India in 2013, its executives realized they would have to do things differently from how they had done them elsewhere. For example, Amazon couldn't simply work with a postal carrier to ship goods to households from giant fulfillment centers, as it does in the United States and Europe. Heavy traffic and imprecise addresses meant the company had to build a wide network of "micro-warehouses" that ship goods to smaller distribution centers, from which packages are whisked off by motorcycle drivers (**Figure 14.7**) and delivered in bundles at local stores, where customers can pick them up. The company has also had to build a system to allow people to pay cash upon delivery, rather than by debit or credit card when they order online, because many Indian consumers either don't have cards or prefer to use cash even when they purchase online.[14]

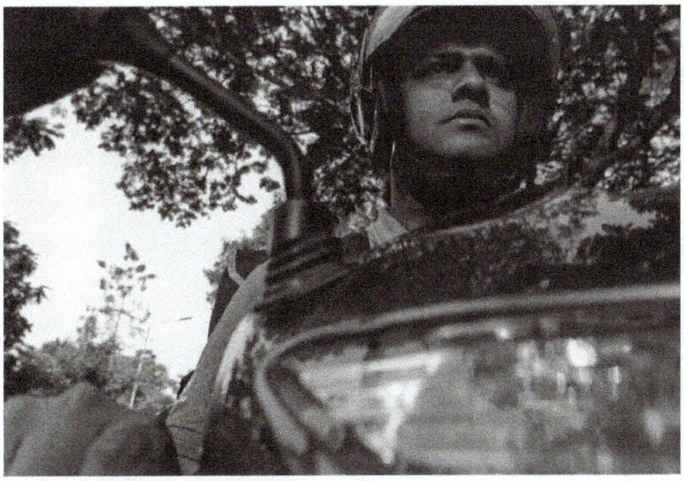

Dhiraj Singh/Bloomberg/Getty Images

FIGURE 14.7 **Amazon in India** Amazon motorcycle delivery drivers in India need to be able to navigate heavy traffic and find imprecise addresses.

To ensure that Amazon was able to respond to the local market, founder and CEO Jeff Bezos hired Amit Agarwal, a man who knew both the Indian retail market and Amazon very well. Agarwal grew up and worked in India but has also spent many years at Amazon in Seattle, shadowing Bezos. Bezos told Agarwal that he didn't need more computer scientists; instead, he needed people willing to think differently and make the adaptations Amazon needed to meet the needs of the local Indian market. These people needed to be willing to "come up with creative ideas and be unafraid of untested execution methods." They needed to be problem solvers and adapt the company's methods to the way things are done in India. So far this approach has paid off. India is Amazon's fastest-growing market and by 2025 is expected to be its second largest, after the United States.[15]

Amazon in India exemplifies the need to respond to local markets. **Local responsiveness** consists of adjusting an approach—or creating an entirely new approach—to meet the differentiated needs of local markets, of local customers, and of local stakeholders, such as government officials and employees, as well as those of suppliers and distributors. Sometimes that requires delegating decision-making authority to local managers, giving them the ability to adapt products, services, and business processes as they see fit.

local responsiveness adjusting or creating an approach to meet the differentiated needs of local markets, of local customers, of local stakeholders such as government officials and employees, and of suppliers and distributors

Being locally responsive helps companies avoid the trap of thinking customers all over the world are the same and also to overcome the liability of foreignness many face when entering new markets (see Chapter 13).[16] For example, companies in the highly regulated world of oil exploration and marketing must interact closely with local authorities, as global oil companies like Shell and Chevron recognize. One manager from Shell notes the difficulty of adhering to corporate policies when working in a 50/50 partnership with a local government. As a result, Shell must sometimes sideline corporate directives in order to respond to local partner demands and gain new business.[17]

As another example, for several years Google hosted a Chinese-language version of its search engine (www.google.com) outside China, which the Chinese government closely monitored and sometimes undermined. In 2006, Google decided to open a new version of the search engine in China (www.google.cn), agreeing, like Yahoo and Microsoft, to adhere to Chinese self-censorship laws and regulations.[18] The decision was heavily criticized in the United States, but Google executives felt it was the right strategy to try to gain some future say in those censorship laws.[19] In 2010, however, activists in China using Gmail were hacked, and Google announced it would no longer censor searches there. In response, Chinese authorities have essentially blocked access to most Google products (including Gmail and YouTube). As a result, Google online tools are essentially nonexistent in China today, but this doesn't mean the company has written off China as a future market.[20] In fact, Google has recently reentered China's market through new hardware products such as mobile phone, home speakers, and virtual reality headsets, as shown in **Figure 14.8**. Moreover, while you may not be able to check your Gmail in China or watch your favorite YouTube clips, as of 2017 you can at least use Google's Translate app.[21]

Advantages of Being Locally Responsive

A company that is locally responsive will be aware of local trends, emerging needs, and product usage patterns—and therefore less likely to miss subtle market opportunities. By presenting a local face and operating like a domestic company, the foreign company can reach a wider customer base and compete more effectively in local labor markets.

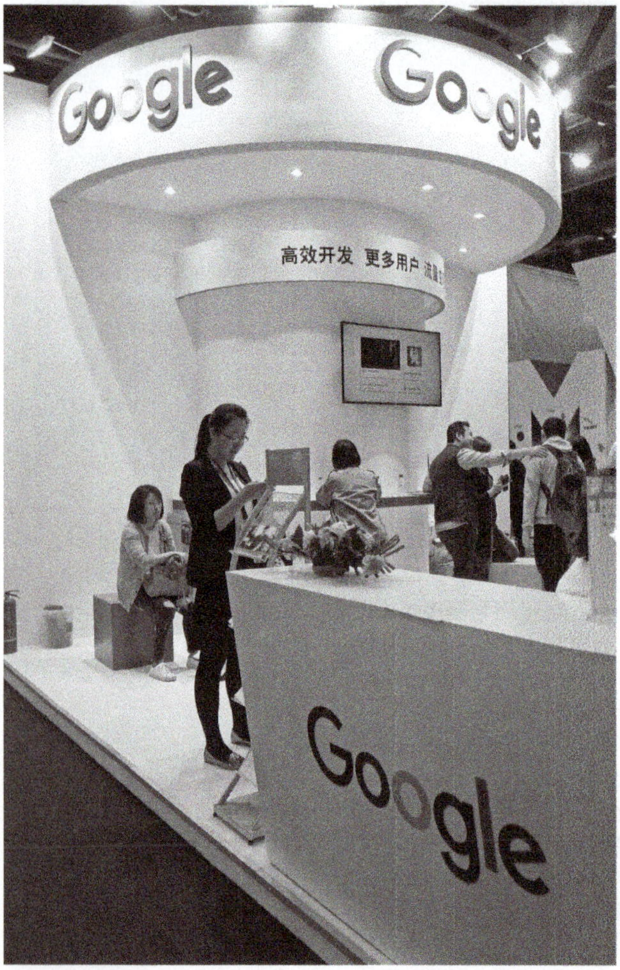

VCG/Getty Images

FIGURE 14.8 Google's Daydream View VR headset is now available in China

Conforming to local business practices and developing ties to local authorities can be especially important. If a firm becomes a local insider, it is more likely to have a say in shaping new policies and regulations. It may even be invited to play a significant role in industry or trade associations. In this way it can gain valuable information and have a better chance of participating in local partnerships. Some specific factors that can help companies take advantage of being locally responsive are described below.[22]

Acknowledging Industry Characteristics In certain business sectors, little competitive advantage can be gained by standardizing and globalizing—or even by coordinating across different subsidiaries. Local dealing works best in these industries. For example, manufacturers of nonbranded foods and of small household appliances face weak forces for global standardization because of an absence of economies of scale. Cement companies, such as Lafarge of France and CEMEX of Mexico, engage heavily in local production in every country they have entered,[23] largely because high shipping costs and tariffs outweigh any advantages of getting needed resources such as rock or lime from one central location. Similarly, many financial and legal services firms must conform to local regulations, which effectively require them to be highly localized.

Satisfying Customer Needs Historically, branded packaged-goods companies, such as France's Danone (foods) and British-Dutch Unilever (nondurable goods), have localized their foreign operations to meet different customer expectations, preferences, or requirements. Today, even businesses with global business formulas, such as McDonald's and Disney, can be forced to modify their offerings to cater to local traditions or expectations. For example, South Korean dining habits forced Subway Korean franchises to abandon long-standing no-alcohol policies that came from the United States market[24] (**Figure 14.9**).

Competing with Local Substitutes Competition from local products or services with different price or performance characteristics may force a company to either adapt or lose market share. The Swiss multinational Nestlé varies its infant cereal recipes according to the availability of local ingredients—in Europe they are made with wheat; in Latin America, with maize and sorghum; and in Asia, with soy and rice.[25]

Andrey Rudakov/Bloomberg/Getty Images

FIGURE 14.9 Subway Korea Franchises adapt to their markets.

Adapting to Markets and Distribution National differences in market structure and distribution channels can force a company to change its pricing, product design, positioning, promotion, and advertising. For example, Amazon distribution channels and packaging in India require local solutions to heavy traffic and poor roads.

Meeting Regulations of the Host Government A host government's concerns about economic development or national security may also force a business to be locally responsive. Petrochemical firms often have to build close relationships with national authorities in order to gain access to a country's natural resources. Similarly, requirements to use local sources can force a firm to develop partnerships with its suppliers. For example, when Rolls Royce won a contract to make airplane engines for a major South Korean airline, the South Korean government required the British company to partner with local steel producers to ensure that some of the jobs related to making the engines stayed in South Korea.[26]

Considering all these factors together, being locally adaptive has its advantages. Log in to WileyPLUS and watch the "Local Responsiveness" video to gain greater insight on how local responsiveness can help a company.

Disadvantages of Being Locally Responsive

Just as a company may fail by blindly applying globally standardized policies and practices to different local environments, so might it fail by focusing too closely on local markets. Often, locally responsive companies find themselves unable to leverage globally derived knowledge and lower costs through global economies of scale. The balance between harnessing global economies of scale while simultaneously trying to maintain local responsiveness is a difficult one to maintain; it often calls for managers to execute a complicated balance between decentralization and centralization.

A company doesn't always have to cater to local demands. Indeed, one of the benefits of localization is that managers who truly understand the local context have a better sense of **intracultural variation**—a tolerance for differences within a nation and the ability to identify local preferences they can safely ignore. They also tend to have a better understanding of the strength of cultural norms and the likely effects of breaking them. In addition, they know how flexible national and local institutional structures are.

intracultural variation an understanding of differences within a nation and the ability to identify local preferences that are irrelevant for global companies

To overcome the disadvantages of being too locally responsive, firms need managers who have a strong local understanding but who have also been exposed to the company's global methods and practices. Rather than simply embracing the local way, then, these managers can redefine the boundaries of what is considered "local." They can find ways to operate that don't simply mimic local firms or copy the way multinational corporations do things. Knowledge they acquire in other parts of the world may also be the seed of innovation that eventually benefits the company as a whole.

14.3 Achieving Global Integration

LEARNING OBJECTIVE

Outline the benefits of achieving global integration.

As discussed earlier, Zara is the largest apparel retailer in the world, and much of its success is attributed to its "fast fashion" business model, which consists of quickly churning out fashionable designs at affordable prices. As a result, Zara is often seen as being responsible for a major transformation in the global apparel industry and consumer purchasing patterns.[27]

The retail industry's need to respond rapidly to changes in market requirements—and for individual fashion companies to do so at lower prices than their competitors—means that Zara has to build many standardized processes to design and distribute product. The company also develops a strong corporate culture to help it deploy its processes consistently around the world and support a global brand, maintaining the same image in all countries where it does business.

While part of its success rests on its ability to define global standards that satisfy customers' fashion preferences, Zara's tight operational controls also stand out: they govern not only its cost management and operations, but all aspects of its global processes. Zara's headquarters in Spain sets the company's strategy. Each store regularly receives manuals that include information about the primary activities of the value chain and its management, including support activities of human resources practices and information systems. However, for most store processes, no exact formal template spells out how something needs to be done. Rather, each store is given guidelines based on core principles related to Zara's culture of fast communication and continual renewal.

Felipe Rodriguez/Alamy Stock Photo

FIGURE 14.10 **Zara** Zara is partly responsible for the fast fashion movement of the past decade.

This approach allows each store to respond to local expectations while maintaining a strong global brand overall. For example, corporate headquarters requires that clothes continually be turned over and refreshed in every store in different locations. How exactly this gets done depends on the country manager and individual store managers; no corporate guideline says you need to move displays and change clothing locations every so often. By focusing on principles instead of following the details of a brand template, Zara maintains an integrated global approach while still allowing for local responsiveness (**Figure 14.10**).

Zara became a leader in fashion retailing through superior pricing and speed to market, backed by standardized product design and distribution processes globally. In this kind of **global integration**, operations such as R&D, manufacturing, sales, and service are aligned across the countries in which the firm operates, so the different parts of the corporation use the same methods. Managers make decisions using a global perspective, with the goal to align operations to achieve the highest global performance.

global integration the process by which a company combines different global activities so the different parts of the corporation use the same methods

Advantages of Being Globally Integrated

Among the factors favoring integration are the emergence of global consumers who share a growing homogeneity of tastes; the diminishing impediment of country borders thanks to regional integration in Europe, Latin America, and Southeast Asia; and the increasing importance for businesses of fast decisions, rapid turnaround times, and operational speed. These are some of the reasons companies may choose to pursue tight international integration. Below are some ways companies can gain advantages by being globally integrated.[28]

Achieving Economies of Scale One of the most common ways for a company to lower its per-unit costs is to centralize production, distribution, or both. This may mean maintaining a small number of large facilities to make products for export to markets around the world. Or it could mean creating a network of specialized, focused operations worldwide that are tightly controlled by a central hub. This second method has enabled Zara to carefully manage its investments and maximize economies of scale in sourcing, production, and distribution.[29] Automobile companies, on the other hand, use a few large facilities to avoid the high fixed costs they would incur if they manufactured across many geographic locations.

Forging Links in the Value Chain Sometimes competitive advantage comes from tight links between activities in the value chain. Ensuring the process of moving a product between R&D, production, and marketing is efficient across different countries can enable a firm to stay ahead of competitive changes. For example, Mettler-Toledo, a Swiss-based maker of precision weighing scales, decided to move R&D activities for all of its low-end products to China, because that is where most of the products were manufactured and purchased anyway.[30] The move allowed the R&D group to more closely and efficiently interact with production.

Serving Global Customers When customers themselves operate on a global basis, their suppliers may be forced to adopt a similar strategy. For instance, subsidiaries that serve not only local customers but also customers all over the world may need to set global prices, quality standards, and delivery terms. International law firms are expected to deliver the same service to their global clients regardless of where they are served.[31] For example, a law firm that works for Goldman Sachs would need to ensure that the ways it bills hours and engages clients are consistent across the Goldman Sachs offices all over the world. This has caused law firms to become globally integrated, even though laws differ considerably across countries.

Using Global Branding Global branding is the process of making a product known in a consistent manner across the world. A consumer-product company like Coca-Cola promotes a unified brand image globally. Rather than adapt the product to local tastes, Coke relies on its global image as a refreshing soft drink to sell an "acquired taste" to different food cultures. Coke highly standardizes both its formula and its advertising themes (its two critical success factors), gaining efficiencies of scale through the use of marketing tools like advertising and merchandising.

Capitalizing on Capabilities Some companies expand globally by transferring capabilities developed in the home market. The international expansion of both IKEA and Walmart depends on their global supply-chain management skills, which allow these companies to pursue their traditional low-price strategies around the world.[32]

Offering World-Class Quality Assurance Companies often standardize and centrally control their key processes in order to maintain competitive advantage. Samsung designs and produces many of its memory chips centrally in Suwon, South Korea, because it finds that keeping engineering and production together quickens the design process and improves quality.[33] On the other hand, the U.S. pharmaceutical giant Merck manufactures locally in order to meet foreign government requirements, but it strictly standardizes manufacturing techniques across geographies to maintain high quality.[34]

Digital Platforms In construction, a platform is something on which to stand so you can build with greater ease. The same is true of a digital platform. With a common digital platform, people throughout the company and even outside it can easily contribute to knowledge and products. For example, online retailers like eBay, Etsy (**Figure 14.11**), and Amazon.com have each created a retail platform where members of the company and even external retailers can create spaces where different types of products are sold.[35]

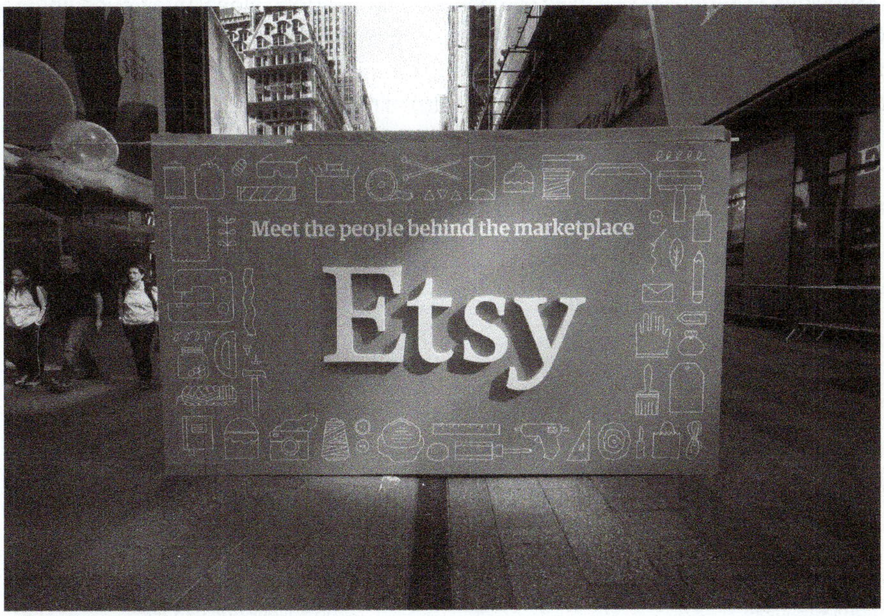

FIGURE 14.11 Etsy's digital platform Etsy allows people who create handmade products to sell their wares online.

Jane.com is another digital platform founded in the United States that sells trendy clothes from small boutique clothing shops that source fashions from Europe and other parts of the world. Providing a highly standardized platform with innovative and secure payment systems, Jane showcases products for their boutique sellers and creates an attractive audience for new, innovative products. This approach allows Jane to sell differentiated products from a standardized platform.

Jane.com provides an example of how integration does not necessarily mean selling identical products the same way all over the world. Rather, it means making decisions about how to address local customer needs and achieve market differentiation by taking an integrated, global point of view and favoring standardization. For instance, the strategies of export-driven Japanese, Korean, and Chinese manufacturing companies—relative latecomers to internationalization—typify this. Their tightly integrated product development and manufacturing functions in their domestic markets provide economies of scale in cost, quality, and product innovation, supplying the world with automobiles, cameras, copiers, consumer electronics, and other products through their sales subsidiaries abroad.

Similarly, global integration does not mean all aspects of a company's operations are centralized. Integration may be limited to a particular product, function, or value chain segment. For example, to capitalize on its ability to develop new products and quickly launch them worldwide, Nestlé strives to deliver globally branded products, such as the Kit Kat candy bar. On the other hand, advertising, ingredients, and product pricing are adapted to local needs. Zara faces the constant challenge of ensuring that global integration does not become too rigid, thereby restricting its ability to adapt quickly to shifting local consumer preferences.

A similar strategy can work in digital industries. When Google first started selling its Apps for Work in India, the products were sold online using the same approach as applied in developed markets and requiring customers to pay in U.S. dollars. After a series of complaints and the loss of many potential clients, Google customized its sales and advertising strategy for the Indian market, including an option for payment in the local currency.[36] The need for global integration, just as for local responsiveness, is always a matter of degree. **Figure 14.12** offers an opportunity to indicate where you think different advantages belong, in terms of whether they enhance local responsiveness or global integration.

Disadvantages of Being Globally Integrated

Despite many examples of successful and profitable growth through global integration, failures are equally easy to find. The Chinese messaging app WeChat and its recent attempt to go global provides a cautionary tale to all companies taking a strong global integration approach. The CEO of the company said its approach to taking WeChat global should have been "more hands-on" and "localized."[37] Strong norms about how things should be done in a company may be helpful for integration, but these norms can also blind managers when they should be making adaptations in order to succeed in a local market.

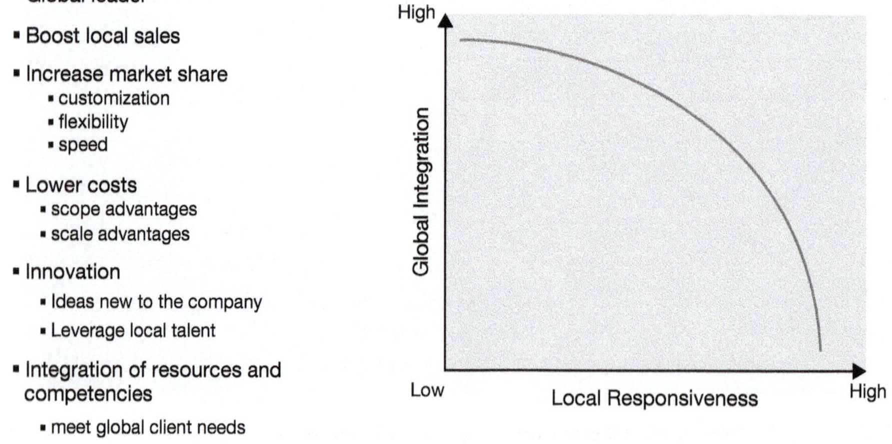

FIGURE 14.12 Advantages of local responsiveness and global integration

WeChat struggled to adapt its product offerings and marketing approach to foreign markets. In many of these markets, managers didn't realize the amount of on-the-ground work it would take to show each country how this product would meet their local needs. And because WeChat was so late to the game, it urgently needed to localize. If WeChat managers had been more open to adapting to the expectations and needs of the local markets early on, the company might have been successful in these markets.

The main weakness of global integration is probably a company's restricted ability to respond quickly to evolving local market opportunities, needs, and demands.[38] In theory, global integration does not preclude local innovation, but in practice this approach to management often leaves insufficient room for new ideas to arise or be implemented on a global scale. For instance, IKEA and Toyota may promote cross-subsidiary or cross-plant coordination, but sharing process improvement knowledge is not the same as allowing opportunities for radical new ideas to emerge directly from diverse local markets.

On the other hand, the challenge of tapping into the creative potential of employees is very much on the mind of Zara's CEO. Not only does his company need to be globally fast and efficient, it also needs to continuously improve.[39] That kind of continuous improvement requires tight control over operations—a capability at the core of Zara's competitive advantage—and building a new capability to encourage change from the bottom up.

14.4 Choosing an International Strategy

LEARNING OBJECTIVE

Identify appropriate strategies for different company objectives and industry pressures.

For global companies, the choice of international strategy depends first and foremost on a given company's generic strategic objectives. Does the firm want to be a low-cost leader or differentiate itself? These aims aren't mutually exclusive, but most companies tend to focus primarily on one over the other. The company's generic strategic objectives should be the primary factor in determining its international strategy.

Once a company has identified its generic strategic objectives, it also needs to take into account its relative needs for global integration and local responsiveness. For example, industries like pharmaceuticals run such high R&D costs that they have to defray the expense of newly invented drugs by selling them in multiple countries. Consumer goods companies like Unilever and Procter & Gamble, on the other hand, are strongly pressured to develop products that respond to specific needs of local consumers. Such customized products don't generally fare well in the broader global market.

In reality, executives often say they face both these pressures. The chair and CEO of a large Asia-Pacific industrial group asked, "How can our group of 20 diversified companies provide flexibility for each operating company to grow and innovate and at the same time leverage scarce functional knowledge, reduce administrative overheads, and employ information technology effectively across the group?"[40]

An executive of the Swiss firm Nestlé said, "We are on a course to nurture internal sources of growth rather than acquisitions. To do so, we must provide our country markets with high flexibility to operate effectively on a local basis. Yet, to compete with global brands against regional and global competitors, we must adopt common processes in our supply chains, reduce the costs on non-value-added functions, and learn to leverage IT on a global, regional, and local basis. The challenge is not if, but how to do so?"[41]

Based on their unique blend of local and global pressures, companies often adopt one of three distinct international strategies—multidomestic, meganational, or transnational (see **Figure 14.13**). Each of these three emphasizes global integration and local responsiveness in

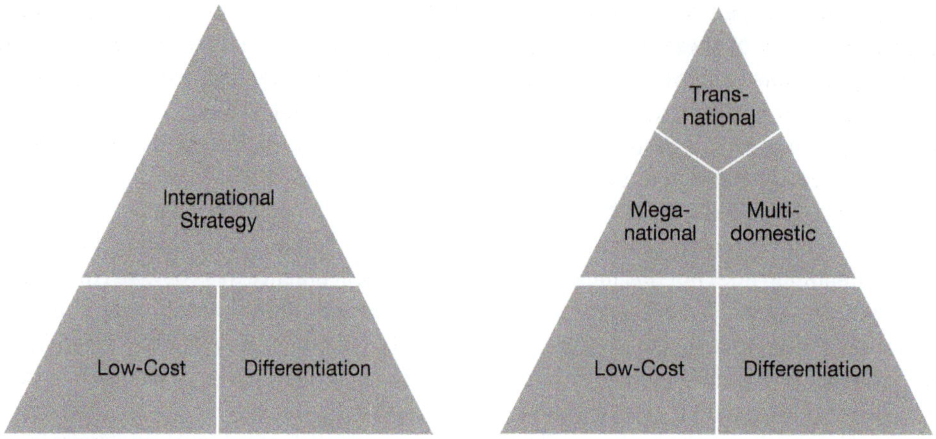

FIGURE 14.13 International Strategy Generic strategy as a foundation for multidomestic, meganational, and transnational strategies.

WileyPLUS

See Whiteboard Video: International Strategy

different proportions: multidomestic emphasizes local responsiveness over global integration; meganational emphasizes global integration over local responsiveness, and transnational tries to achieve a balance between the two.

Multidomestic Strategy

multidomestic strategy a strategy whereby global firms respond to differentiated needs and preferences in each local market in which they operate

meganational strategy a strategy whereby global firms focus on increasing profitable growth by reaping cost reductions from economies of scale and other advantages of global integration

Companies that pursue a **multidomestic strategy** focus on increasing profitability by customizing products, services, and operations so they can respond to the differentiated needs and preferences of customers and employees in each of the countries where they operate. In effect, these companies become a grouping of locally focused subsidiaries that act independently, like domestic companies, in their various local markets. In this way, the multidomestic strategy helps a company pursue a differentiation strategy at a global level. The value chain is designed by the foreign operations, not by the home office. The subsidiaries in each country make decisions on how products are designed, made, distributed, and marketed. Often the HR practices are adapted to local employment customs.

Nestlé exemplifies this strategy. One manager in China pointed out, "Why would we ever want to scale our 'sweet congee' drink to other markets? Not many other countries would ever consider consuming a congee drink." In other words, Nestlé must adapt many of its products to local tastes. In fact, Nestlé found sales of its globally branded Kit Kat candy bar were not what they expected in China. As a result, the Chinese team designed, made, and marketed a new type of chocolate wafer bar at a fraction of the cost of Kit Kat. Today it is the company's top-selling candy bar in China[42] (**Figure 14.14**).

ASSOCIATED PRESS

FIGURE 14.14 Nestlé's Crispy Shark Nestlé's main candy product in China is not the globally branded Kit Kat bar but a chocolate-covered wafer bar called Crispy Shark.

Meganational Strategy

Taking a stance opposite that of a multidomestic strategy, a **meganational strategy** focuses on increasing profitable growth by reaping cost reductions from economies of scale and other advantages of global integration.[43] In other words, this strategy helps a company pursue a cost-leadership strategy at the global level. Managers at headquarters implement design, production, and marketing standards to achieve maximum efficiency gains. The aim is to create products for a world market, manufacture them on a global scale in a few highly efficient plants, and market them through a few key distribution channels.

This strategy requires that companies exploit **location economies**, the cost advantage of performing each stage in the value chain at the lowest cost for that activity. For instance, aluminum might be produced in the United States, where electricity costs are low; manufacturing in Indonesia, where labor costs are low; and IT support in India, where service-labor costs are low. In doing this, and by making sure the product is standardized across the world, a meganational strategy is really about seeing the world as one huge national market.

location economies the cost advantage of performing each stage in the value chain at the lowest cost for that activity

The Danish shoe company ECCO has decided to sell the same shoes all over the world. It applies a common marketing strategy and has focused its manufacturing in a few key countries with competitive advantages in shoe production.[44] By choosing to avoid adaptation, the company can spend significant resources on innovations for its leather and shoe designs. In fact, it proudly promotes the fact that its products are designed and sometimes even made in Denmark, where outdoor conditions are harsh and rugged, like its shoes.

Transnational Strategy

Of course, many companies face pressure to be both locally responsive and globally integrated. The **transnational strategy** is often considered a hybrid that combines the meganational and multidomestic strategies. Rather than compromising between being global and being local, companies that follow a transnational strategy aim to be both simultaneously. However, doing so presents a paradox for any company. Locally adapting products while also ensuring they are consistent and standardized across countries is, in many ways, impossible.

transnational strategy a strategy whereby global firms take a hybrid approach that combines the meganational and multidomestic strategies, simultaneously offering the benefits of both global and local advantages

Therefore, to follow this strategy, companies must make trade-offs. For example, they must implement complex organizational structures and encourage ideas to come up from local operations, then integrate them into global standards. Companies that successfully pursue a transnational strategy tend to adopt a governance structure that is simultaneously flexible and tightly integrated. Like the multidomestic approach, the transnational strategy allows subsidiaries the discretion and autonomy to adapt and customize locally. However, that discretion is bounded by global integration and coordination from headquarters. Unlike a meganational strategy that achieves integration through decisions made mostly by headquarters, integration in a transnational organization occurs through the different subsidiaries coordinating and exchanging information to make more informed decisions.[45] **Figure 14.15** illustrates the conditions under which the transnational as well as meganational and multidomestic strategies are most appropriate.[46]

Rather than being only top-down (from headquarters to subsidiaries, as in meganational) or bottom-up (from foreign subsidiary to headquarters, as in multidomestic), coordination in a transnational strategy promotes knowledge flow throughout the organization, regardless of where the ideas originate. For example, GE is known for having globally standardized products (a meganational approach); however, it has begun to encourage foreign subsidiaries to come up with and share innovative new ideas for the rest of the global organization.[47] This has allowed multiple products originally developed for local markets—such as compact and inexpensive heart-monitoring devices—to be imported back into the global market.[48]

GE was able to do this because it allowed its local subsidiaries to decide what products to develop and sell in their local markets (a multidomestic approach). However, it also said the products should be useful for the global organization and that subsidiaries should use knowledge from other parts of the organization to help them develop their local solutions. This represented a transnational approach to strategy because it allows for the flow of information across borders, regardless of whether it originated at headquarters or in Haiti.

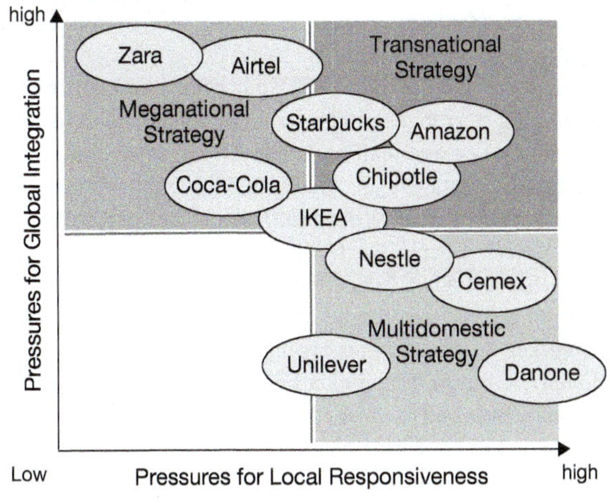

FIGURE 14.15 **International strategies**

Summary and Case

Summary

LEARNING OBJECTIVE 14.1 Define *strategy.*

Firms going abroad need to choose both their market entry mode and their broader international strategies. Those that effectively manage differences in customer preferences, political requirements, and distribution across borders will gain an advantage over competitors that cannot. The primary objective of any strategy is to create value and then capture as much value as possible by differentiating, reducing costs, or both. Once a firm decides between a cost-leadership and a differentiation strategy, it needs to align its internal operations to that strategy.

LEARNING OBJECTIVE 14.2 Explain why multinational companies benefit from being locally responsive.

Companies may have to adapt their strategy by being locally responsive to individual markets. Benefits of local responsiveness include better relationships with government authorities, improved awareness of local trends, and better connections with a wider customer base. Not everything needs to be locally adapted, however. Companies that focus too narrowly on local adaptation may struggle to reduce costs and exploit economies of scale. One factor of successful local adaptation is relying on managers who are locally knowledgeable yet experienced with the company's global practices.

LEARNING OBJECTIVE 14.3 Outline the benefits of achieving global integration.

Global integration does not necessarily mean selling identical products in the same way all over the world. It can also be achieved by standardizing a particular process, function, or way of doing business. This strategy enables companies to reap the benefits of economies of scale, maintain a unified global brand image, and offer world-class quality assurance.

LEARNING OBJECTIVE 14.4 Identify appropriate strategies for different company objectives and industry pressures.

A company's objectives and its relative needs for global integration and local responsiveness direct its choice of global strategy. Companies that focus on increasing profitability by localizing products, services, or operations often choose a multidomestic strategy. Companies that focus on increasing profitable growth through the intensive cost reductions characteristic of global integration lean toward the meganational strategy. Companies that need to be both locally responsive and globally integrated can pursue a hybrid strategy called transnational. A transnational is neither a top-down (meganational) or bottom-up (multidomestic) organization; rather, it is a lateral organization that succeeds or fails based on its ability to effectively shepherd knowledge transfer and communication between foreign subsidiaries.

Case Study

Lincoln Electric's International Strategy

The 120-year-old Ohio-based Lincoln Electric Company is the largest manufacturer of welding equipment in the world. Lincoln's culture is based on the founders' fervent belief in self-reliance, the necessity of competition for human progress, and egalitarian treatment of managers and employees. From the 1930s, Lincoln's incentive system has been based on piece rates (which pay people based on how much of something they make) and an annual bonus linked to profits that can amount to over half an employee's base income. To calculate the bonus, management appraises production employees on four criteria: output, quality, dependability, and ideas/cooperation.[49]

Abroad, Lincoln Electric had invested successfully in Canada (in 1925), Australia (1938), and France (1955), but until the late 1980s the firm still focused mostly on its domestic market, which it dominated. Led by a management team that had never worked outside the United States, the firm took a bold strategy for internationalization, spending over half its sales revenue on building plants in Japan and Latin America, and on making nineteen acquisitions across Europe and Mexico.[50] Senior executives sought to combine productivity and low costs with high-quality manufacturing operations to dominate the global market.

The expansion was challenging. Lacking managers with international experience, the firm was forced to hire local managers who were not familiar with Lincoln's culture. The only new country where the incentive system and culture took gradual hold was Mexico. In most of Europe and Japan, where piece-rate payments are viewed with deep suspicion, Lincoln's approach was rejected. In Germany, with its thirty-five-hour average work week, employees would not agree to work nearly fifty hours when asked.[51] As a consequence, the company retreated and sold off most of its international acquisitions.[52]

When Lincoln again expanded its international operations in the late 1990s, its managers had learned from its previous attempt to internationalize. They relied more on joint ventures and alliances and, when necessary, adapted to fit local conditions.[53] The company also developed managers with international experience who were transferred to the foreign units.

By 2015, the company had returned to record sales and profits, with a third of sales from foreign operations.[54] However, in spite of the significant progress it had made, Lincoln still experienced challenges in managing people in some of its overseas units. For instance, in China, the company had difficulty finding, developing, and retaining talented local professionals and managers. As a result, it was struggling to reach profitability in Asia-Pacific.[55]

Case Discussion Questions

1. Lincoln Electric's rapid expansion abroad resulted in multiple failures except in Mexico. Why do you think Lincoln succeeded in Mexico when it failed in Europe and Japan?
2. What changes did Lincoln Electric implement that led to a more successful international expansion on its second attempt?
3. What do Lincoln Electric's failures say about the importance of managers having international experience? Why does a company that is expanding abroad need leaders with international experience to be successful?

Endnotes

[1] Suneera Tandon, "After Three-Plus Years of Bureaucratic Wrangling, IKEA Has Broken Ground on Its First Store in India," Quartz India, August 11, 2016. https://qz.com/755892/ikea-india-first-store-construction/.

[2] A. Verbeke and C. G. Asmussen, "Global, Local, or Regional? The Locus of MNE Strategies," *Journal of Management Studies* 53.6 (2016): 1051–1075; R. Peshawaria, "The Three Most Important Questions for Profitable Growth," *Forbes*, January 28, 2012. https://www.forbes.com/sites/rajeevpeshawaria/2012/01/28/the-three-most-important-questions-for-profitable-growth/#397981e562bd.

[3] "Now or Never: CEOs Mobilize for the Fourth Industrial Revolution," KPMG U.S. CEO Outlook 2016, p. 4. https://advisory.kpmg.us/content/dam/kpmg-im/trends/2016-ceo-outlook.pdf.

[4] Venessa Wong, "Why Doesn't Chipotle Do Sustainability Reporting? It Hasn't Needed To," *Bloomberg*, March 6, 2014.

[5] Vishwas Tambe, "Schindler India Launches New Elevator for Premium Residential Villa Segment." PR Newswire, March 16, 2016.

[6] "Airtel's Low-Cost Strategy Unsustainable: BMI Research," *Economic Times*, March 30, 2016, http://economictimes.indiatimes.com/industry/telecom/airtels-low-cost-strategy-unsustainable-bmi-research/articleshow/51620183.cms.

[7] "Airtel's Low-Cost Strategy Unsustainable."

[8] L. Alderman, "In Europe, Starbucks Adjusts to a Café Culture," *New York Times*, March 30, 2012. http://www.nytimes.com/2012/03/31/business/starbucks-tailors-its-experience-to-fit-to-european-tastes.html.

[9] M. E. Porter, "What Is Strategy?" *Harvard Business Review* 74.6 (1996 November/December): 61–78.

[10] Ed Crooks, "How Can the Oil Industry Cut Costs?" World Economic Forum, February 29, 2016. https://www.weforum.org/agenda/2016/02/how-can-the-oil-industry-cut-costs.

[11] "Amazon Prime Air," Amazon.com, www.amazon.com/b?node=8037720011 (accessed September 7, 2016).

[12] S. Morris, J. Oldroyd, and S. Ramaswami, "Scaling up Your Story: An Experiment in Global Knowledge Sharing at the World Bank," *Long-Range Planning* 49, no. 1 (2016): 1–14.

[13] Morris, Oldroyd, and Ramaswami, "Scaling up Your Story."

[14] Sunny Sen, "How It Made Itself Indian: The Amazing Rise of Amazon in the Country," *Hindustan Times*, November 7, 2016. http://www.hindustantimes.com/business-news/how-it-made-itself-indian-the-amazing-rise-of-amazon-in-the-country/story-YfyzGUuNVTAHEHHenNmxvO.html.

[15] "Amazon Is Building an Army of 'Cowboys' and 'Jeff Bots' in India," *Economic Times*, October 5, 2015. http://m.economictimes.com/magazines/panache/amazon-is-building-an-army-of-cowboys-and-jeff-bots-in-india/articleshow/49222667.cms.

[16] S. Zaheer, "Overcoming the Liability of Foreignness," *Academy of Management Journal* 38, no. 2 (1995): 341–63; H. Gorostidi Martinez and X. Zhao, "Strategies to Avoid Liability of Foreignness When Entering a New Market," *Journal of Advances in Management Research* 14, no. 1 (2017): 46–68.

[17] Personal communication with regional manager by Shad Morris, January 2010.

[18] Google has for many years removed links to pro-Nazi websites in Germany.

[19] Google executives were called into Congressional hearings to defend their actions, and many commentators on social media were highly critical of Google. See C. Thompson, "Google's China Problems (and China's Google Problems)," *New York Times*, April 23, 2006. http://www.nytimes.com/2006/04/23/magazine/23google.html.

[20] Kevin Waddell, "Why Google Quit China—and Why It's Heading Back," *The Atlantic*, January 19, 2016. https://www.theatlantic.com/technology/archive/2016/01/why-google-quit-china-and-why-its-heading-back/424482/.

[21] Simon Denyer, "New Google Translate App Now Available in China as Company Tries to Edge Back in," *Washington Post*, March 29, 2017. https://www.washingtonpost.com/news/worldviews/wp/2017/03/29/new-google-translate-app-now-available-in-china-as-company-tries-to-edge-back-in/?utm_term=.dc9b8a81e5a9.

[22] V. Pucik, P. Evans, L. Bjorkman, and S. Morris, *The Global Challenge: International Human Resource Management*, 3rd ed. (Chicago: Chicago Business Press, 2016).

[23] T. Khanna, "A Case for Contextual Intelligence," *Management International Review* 55, no. 2 (2015): 181–90.

[24] Marcia Breen, "McDonald's Starts Selling Beer in World's Most 'Spirited' Nation," NBC News, February 17, 2016. http://www.nbcnews.com/business/business-news/mcdonald-s-starts-selling-beer-world-s-most-spirited-nation-n519681.

[25] Brian Blackstone, "CEO Dismisses Concerns That Nestle Isn't Agile, Innovative Enough," *Wall Street Journal*, June 3, 2016. https://www.wsj.com/articles/ceo-says-nestle-at-150-years-old-hasnt-lost-its-edge-1464893283?mg=prod/accounts-wsj; "Cerelac," Nestle, www.nestle-cwa.com/en/brands/babyfoods/cerelacdetails (accessed July 3, 2017).

[26] Personal correspondence with Harvey Scott at Rolls Royce by Shad Morris, June 2008.

[27] Felipe Caro, "ZARA: Staying Fresh and Fast," UCLA Case: Ref 612-006-8 (2014).

[28] Pucik et al., *The Global Challenge*.

[29] H. Marsh, "From Zara to Zambia," *London Business School Review* 26, no. 3 (2015): 8–11.

[30] S. Morris, D. Chng, J. Han, and B. Zhong, "Leveraging Local Talent: How Foreign Employees Contribute to Knowledge Creation and Sharing within MNCs," Working Paper, Brigham Young University, 2016.

[31] Rich Parkin, Reid Wilk, Evan Hirsh and Akshay Singh, "2017 Automotive Trends," Strategy&. https://www.strategyand.pwc.com/trend/2017-automotive-industry-trends. Accessed July 14, 2017.

[32] J. F. Gollnhofer and E. Turkina, "Cultural Distance and Entry Modes: Implications for Global Expansion Strategy," *Cross Cultural Management* 22, no. 1 (2015): 21–41.

[33] The authors have worked as employees of Samsung and understand its inner workings.

[34] "Our Values and Standards: The Basis of Our Success," Code of Conduct, Edition III, Merck, www.merck.com/about/code_of_conduct.pdf (accessed November 8, 2016).

[35] M. Bonchek and S. P. Choudary, "Three Elements of a Successful Platform Strategy," *Harvard Business Review*, January 31, 2013. https://hbr.org/2013/01/three-elements-of-a-successful-platform; J. Moon and S. Choi, "Impact of Mobile Platform Strategy on Platform Generativity and Competition," *Academy of Strategic Management Journal* 15, no. 2 (2016): 47.

[36] Based on personal conversations with the director of business development at Google, September 2015.

[37] Steven Millward, "WeChat's Global Expansion Has Been a Disaster," Tech in Asia, May 25, 2016. https://www.techinasia.com/wechat-global-expansion-fail.

[38] Kobrin, Stephen J. "Bricks and Mortar in a Borderless World: Globalization, the Backlash, and the Multinational Enterprise." *Global Strategy Journal* 7, no. 2 (2017): 159–171.

[39] Ton Zeynep, Elena Corsi, and Vincent Dessain, "Zara: Managing Stores for Fast Fashion," Harvard Business School, Case: 9-610-042. (2010).

[40] Personal communication with a top level executive at Sanyo by Shad Morris, June 2008.

[41] Personal communication with Nestle manager by Shad Morris, December 2015.

[42] Personal communication with Nestle talent manager by Shad Morris, December 2015.

[43] Paul Evans, Vladimir Pucik, and Ingmar Björkman, "Putting the Challenges of International Human Resource Management into Perspective," in *Readings and Cases in International Human Resource Management and Organizational Behavior*, 65th ed., eds. Günter K. Stahl, Mark E. Mendenhall, and Gary R. Oddou (New York: Routledge, 2012), 3; Shad Morris, Scott Snell, and Ingmar Björkman, "An Architectural Framework for Global Talent Management," *Journal of International Business Studies* 47, no. 6 (2016): 723–47.

[44] "ECCO's Strategy Towards 2020," World Footwear, April 6, 2015. https://www.worldfootwear.com/news.asp?id=943&ECCO%E2%80%99s_strategy_towards_2020.

[45] S. Morris, R. Hammond, and S. Snell, "A Microfoundations Approach to Transnational Capabilities: The Role of Knowledge Search in an Ever-Changing World," *Journal of International Business Studies* 45, no. 4 (2014): 405–27.

[46] S. Ghoshal and C. A. Bartlett, "The Multinational Corporation as an Interorganizational Network," *Academy of Management Review* 15, no. 4 (1990): 603–26; T. Kostova, "Transnational Transfer of Strategic Organizational Practices: A Contextual Perspective," *Academy of Management Review* 24, no. 2 (1999): 308–24.

[47] Lisa Granatstein, "How GE Is Continuing Its Legacy of Innovation in the Digital Age: From Lightbulbs to Podcasts, CMO Says Being First Matters," AdWeek, October 16, 2015. http://www.adweek.com/brand-marketing/how-ge-continuing-its-legacy-innovation-digital-age-167619/.

[48] "GE Healthcare Announces $300 Million Commitment to Support Emerging Market Health," Business Wire, September 23, 2015. http://www.businesswire.com/news/home/20150923005242/en/GE-Healthcare-Announces-300-Million-Commitment-Support.

[49] J. Siegel, "Lincoln Electric," Harvard Business Case, 2006.

[50] "Creating Cultures That Lead to Success: Lincoln Electric, Southwest Airlines, and SAS Institute," *Organizational Dynamics* 41, no. 1 (January–March 2012): 32–43.

[51] Paul J. Gollan and David Lewin, "Employee Representation in Non-Union Firms: An Overview," *Industrial Relations: A Journal of Economy and Society*, special issue "Employee Representation in Non-Union Firms," 52, no. 1 (2013): 173–93.

[52] I. Björkman, C. Galunic, and J. Lockard, "Lincoln Electric in China (B): Updates," Harvard Business Case, 2015.

[53] S. E. Jackson, R. S. Schuler, and K. Jiang, "An Aspirational Framework for Strategic Human Resource Management," *The Academy of Management Annals* 8, no. 1 (2014): 1–56.

[54] Björkman, Galunic, Lockard, "Lincoln Electric in China (B)."

[55] M. J. Yang, L. Kueng, and B. Hong, "Business Strategy and the Management of Firms," (No. w20846). National Bureau of Economic Research, 2015. http://www.nber.org/papers/w20846. ; M. J. Chen, "Presidential Address – Becoming Ambicultural: A Personal Quest – and Aspiration for Organizations," *Academy of Management Review* 39, no. 2 (2014): 119–37.

CHAPTER **15**

International Organizational Structures

ABC News VideoSource/Getty Images

Introduction

When PepsiCo initially entered China in 1981, it set up its Chinese operation with an organizational structure that maximized local autonomy, using joint ventures with local partners to produce its products in different provinces. This structure maximized local responsiveness and met the stringent investment guidelines of the government, but did not enable PepsiCo to ensure the product standardization the market preferred. As a result, PepsiCo shifted to a centralized structure with one strategic partner that gave it more direct control over marketing, sales, and production, which were needed to ensure a standardized product.[1]

A formal organizational structure establishes the firm's hierarchy, organizes its operating and functional units and their interrelationships, and specifies the processes by which the firm's members make decisions and report to managers. Adopting the correct structure, or revising an existing structure when necessary, can contribute greatly to the success or failure of an organization's strategy.

This chapter discusses how international businesses structure their operations to achieve their strategic goals of being locally responsive or globally integrated (see Chapter 14). These include the elements of formal structure, control systems, and contractual partner arrangements that allow headquarters to control subsidiaries, as well as the mechanisms to reduce the need to coordinate work with headquarters, such as virtual or modular organizational design principles. We also discuss challenges and solutions for subsidiary-to-subsidiary interactions.

LEARNING OBJECTIVES

After exploring this chapter you will be able to:

1. **Describe** how functional, divisional, matrix, and network structures help international businesses achieve their global strategies
2. **Identify** the effects of informal control systems, including bureaucratic, output, normative, personal, and incentive systems
3. **Outline** the role of virtual organizations, technology standards, and modularity in helping to coordinate work with subsidiaries
4. **Discuss** the challenges of enabling horizontal coordination and knowledge transfer among subsidiaries

15.1 Types of Organizational Structures

LEARNING OBJECTIVE

Describe how functional, divisional, matrix, and network structures help international businesses achieve their global strategies.

One of the fundamental challenges global companies face is ensuring headquarters' vertical control of and coordination with its subsidiaries. This relationship is represented in **Figure 15.1**. Some global organizations exert a high degree of control over subsidiaries, whereas others apply less pressure.

A quintessential example of this challenge is found in Philips. The company was founded in 1891 in Eindhoven, Netherlands, as a maker of light bulbs. Almost immediately it began selling internationally, and by 1915 it had invested in operations all over the world, including China, Australia, and Brazil. Over the next few decades, the company expanded its range of products to include radios, televisions, electric razors, medical equipment, and more.[2] Along the way, Philips's international arm evolved from an exporting enterprise to a full-scale operation that developed its own products for each unique market.

During World War II, Philips's operations in the United States, Brazil, and other locations were cut off from the corporate offices, which were located in German-controlled territory. As a result, each country further developed its own functional units, conducting its own research and development (R&D), finance, marketing, manufacturing, and so on. These operations were largely successful and captured significant shares of their respective markets for many years after the war's end.

Then, in the 1970s, Japanese electronics manufacturers recognized that the market for consumer electronics was more global than local—meaning that customers around the globe were demanding similar rather than unique products. Matsushita, Sony, Toshiba, and others therefore capitalized on their centralized production capabilities and began serving customers around the world from single locations.[3] As a result, they were able to drive down costs significantly while also improving design. Philips quickly recognized the inefficiency of country-based operations that had multiple redundant functions in each location, and in the 1990s the company began an arduous process of centralizing its operations, with the country leaders reporting back to product leaders at headquarters in the Netherlands.[4] In 2014, Philips announced yet another restructuring of its global product groups, stating that it was likely to split into two separate companies, one focused on health care and one on lighting.[5] The purpose of the reorganization was to further increase its global focus on these two industries.

The different paths taken by Philips and its Japanese rivals highlight the role of organizational structure in international business. Organizational structures reinforce international strategies by clarifying reporting channels, facilitating knowledge flows up and across the company, and determining where decision making happens. Some structures encourage local decision making and local market exploration, whereas others support global execution of standardized plans. Thus, aligning the organization's global structure with its global strategy is critical.

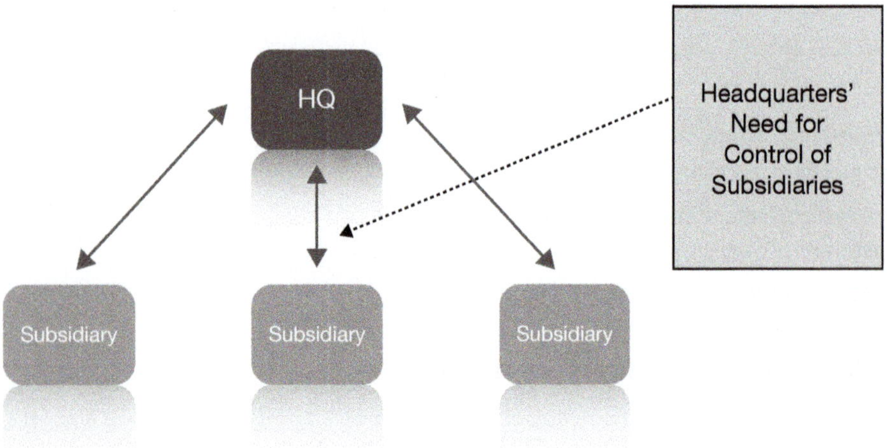

FIGURE 15.1 Global companies must determine how to control their global subsidiaries

Source: Adapted from work by Christopher Bartlett, "Kent Chemical: Organizing for International Growth," Harvard Business School Case, 2012. With permission from the author.

Organizations such as Philips can structure themselves in four different ways, each of which has advantages and disadvantages. The types of organizational structure are functional, based on what each unit *does*; divisional, based on what each unit *is*; matrix, which combines functional and divisional; and network, a temporary project-based approach with maximum flexibility.

Functional Structure

functional structure a structure that organizes a company into units identified by their functional roles, or what they do

A **functional structure** organizes a company into units that are identified by their functional roles, or what they do. For instance, a functional organization will have an R&D unit, a sales unit, a marketing unit, a manufacturing unit, a finance unit, and so on.[6] Each of these functional units serves the whole organization. **Figure 15.2** shows a typical functional structure. The company is divided into the functional groups of finance, operations, human resources, research and development, marketing, and public relations.

A president or chief executive officer (CEO) is usually at the top of a functional structure; vice presidents manage each of the functions and report to the CEO. In turn, the vice presidents have staff who report to them. Each function may be further divided into subsections. For instance, the marketing function may consist of separate groups with responsibility for design, web, trade shows and events, and customer loyalty.

The advantage of a functional structure is its efficiency in coordinating all the people who work on the same tasks. More specifically, it groups finance people to work with other finance people and operations people to work with other operations people. Thus, the people in each function are better able to coordinate their tasks, develop expertise, and mentor newcomers. International businesses with a meganational strategy (i.e., a globally integrated approach) in industries that require large capital investments and produce a limited range of products, such as semiconductors, automobiles, or aircraft, often use a functional organization structure. This structure allows the firm to maximize efficiencies in each function. For instance, Boeing uses a functional structure, which enables it to move down the experience curve in its aircraft manufacturing processes. In 2012, the functional structure of Boeing's commercial airplanes business included Ray Conner as president and CEO, with 17 functional heads reporting to him.

Yet while a functional structure excels at efficiency by streamlining the vertical flow of knowledge within each functional unit, it may also tend to limit interaction and coordination *between* functions.[7] Lacking cross-functional interaction, organizations often struggle to respond to market needs and opportunities, especially if these affect more than one functional unit simultaneously. Because the responsibility for decisions that cross-functional lines does not fall neatly on one unit head, it often escalates to the top of the organization. If this happens frequently, the CEO's time may become consumed with problems that in other organizational structures are solved at lower levels of the company. Thus, it is often not appropriate for multidomestic companies (i.e., companies that try to adapt their operations and products to local markets).

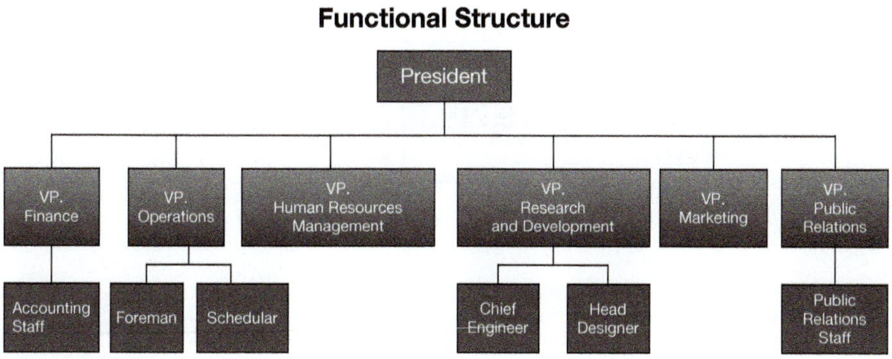

FIGURE 15.2 **Example of a functional organizational structure**

Divisional Structure

divisional structure a structure that organizes a company by units according to the products they make, the customer segments they serve, or the geographic location in which they operate

Unlike a functional structure, which organizes a company's units by their activities, a **divisional structure** organizes units by the products they make, the customer segments they serve, or the geographic location in which they operate (see **Figure 15.3**). For instance, Ford Motor Company's geographic divisional structure organizes its units into North America, South America, Europe, Middle East and Africa, and Asia Pacific.[8] Each geographic division is responsible for, and has subunits dedicated to, the developing, manufacturing, distributing, and servicing vehicles within that region. Ford's Credit Division, an exception, handles financing and leasing worldwide.[9] A divisional structure focused by region is appropriate for global businesses pursuing a multidomestic strategy, allowing them to understand and respond to the needs of local customers.

On the other hand, divisional structures organized by products or type of customer are often used to reinforce a meganational business. For instance, the United Kingdom's Virgin Group is organized by product. Virgin Atlantic is the passenger airline division, Virgin Galactic the space program, and Virgin Mobile the mobile phone service business. Virgin Vacations handles the vacation business, Virgin Money the banking operation, and Virgin Limited Edition the luxury hotels.[10] Similarly, France's LVMH—which includes luxury brands such as Louis Vuitton, Christian Dior, and Givenchy—is divided into six product groups as described in Figure 15.3: wine and spirits, fashion and leather goods, perfumes and cosmetics, watches and jewelry, selective retailing, and other activities (which includes luxury hotels, yachts, and *Les Echos*, a French media outlet).[11]

In addition, Dell Computer Corp. and Tumi Holdings Inc., both based in the United States, use a divisional structure defined by customer segments. Dell divides the company into units focused on large-enterprise, government, and consumer segments. Tumi, which makes high-end suitcases, travel bags, and accessories, focuses on premium and young adult customers. These customer segments span the globe, enabling a meganational strategy.

Some companies use both a product and geographic divisional structure. This is called a multidivisional structure. For instance, as **Figure 15.4** shows, the Swiss giant Nestlé has some global product organizations, including Nestlé Waters, Nestlé Nutrition, and other businesses, that are key to the company. By having a global division for these products, the firm ensures that they are standardized globally. In addition, the company uses geographic divisions including Zone Americas (including North and South America), Zone Asia, Oceania, and Africa; and Zone Europe (which also includes the Middle East and North Africa).[12] These geographic divisions allow the company to focus also on the unique needs of the different markets. Many global companies pursuing a transnational strategy take some form of this multidivisional structure in order to balance the need for focus on specific markets and for global standardization of products.

In general, the benefit of a divisional structure is the company's ability to develop specific and unique offerings for each target group. A divisional structure can, however, lead to

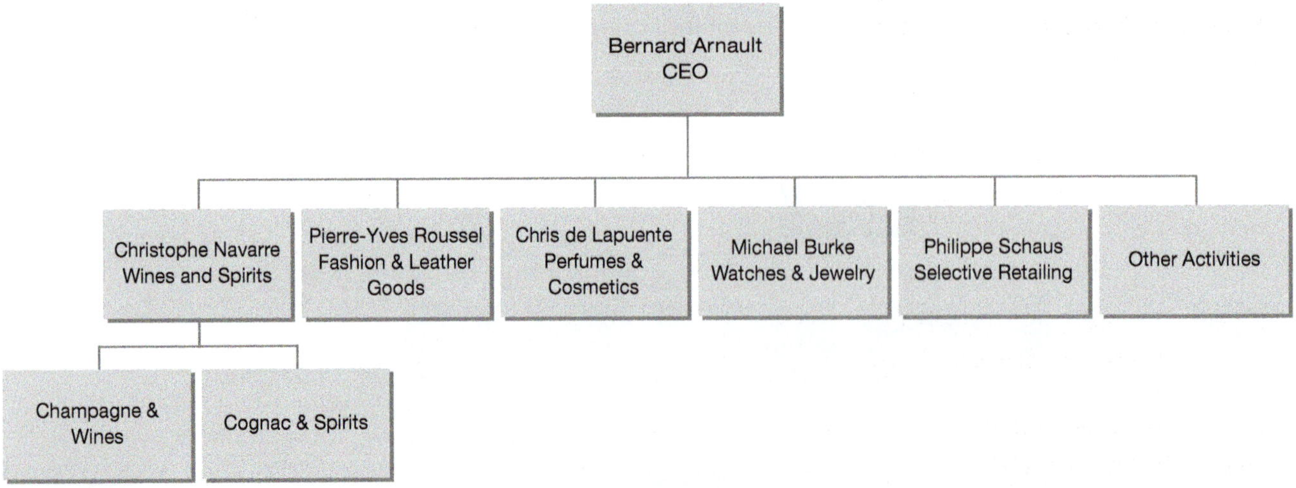

FIGURE 15.3 **Divisional organizational structure** LVMH provides an example of a divisional organizational structure, set up by product and product leaders in 2016.

Analysis of sales, trading operating profit and organic growth (OG)

By operating segment

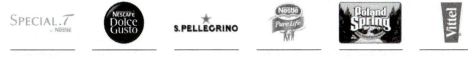

In millions of CHF	Sales	Trading operating profit	OG
Zone Europe	15 175	2 327	+1.5%
Zone Americas	27 277	5 117	+5.0%
Zone Asia, Oceania and Africa	18 272	3 408	+2.6%
Nestlé Waters	7 390	714	+5.4%
Nestlé Nutrition	9 614	1 997	+7.7%
Other businesses (a)	13 884	2 654	+7.1%
Unallocated items (b)		(2 198)	
Total Group	91 612	14 019	+4.5%

FIGURE 15.4 **Nestlé's organizational structure** Nestlé's organizational structure uses both geographic and product divisions. The data are from 2014. **Source:** "Nestlé Group 2014," www.nestle.com/asset-library/documents/library/documents/about_us/quick-facts-2014-en.pdf. Accessed July 7, 2017.

inefficient knowledge flows between units and high coordination costs. For instance, Cisco's divisional structure in the early 2000s led to the development of three separate routers that were nearly identical—one for each of its customer segments—tripling the costs of R&D and production. To remedy this coordination error, the company consolidated the structure of its R&D into functional groups based on products, which reduced redundancy of the R&D efforts.[13]

Matrix Structure

matrix structure a structure that organizes a company along multiple dimensions that may include geography, function, and division

In addition to the multidivisional form, global companies engaged in a transnational strategy also often use a matrix structure. This structure helps balance the efficiencies of a functional structure with the responsiveness of a divisional structure. A **matrix structure** is a structure in which employees have two or more reporting relationships, generally to a functional manager *and* a product manager; in global firms, employees often also report to a geographic manager. For instance, GE Healthcare, based in the United Kingdom but scheduled to move its headquarters to Chicago, Illinois, is organized based on three categories: different geographies (such as North America and Europe), different products (such as computed tomography (CT) scanners, magnetic resonance imaging machines, and ultrasound equipment), and different functions (such as equipment sales, service sales, operations, and customer advocacy).[14] These units serve the entire organization. So, as **Figure 15.5** shows, an employee who works for GE Healthcare in Japan and sells CT scanner services will have three bosses: the head of the Japanese group, the head of customer service, and the head of the CT scanner unit.

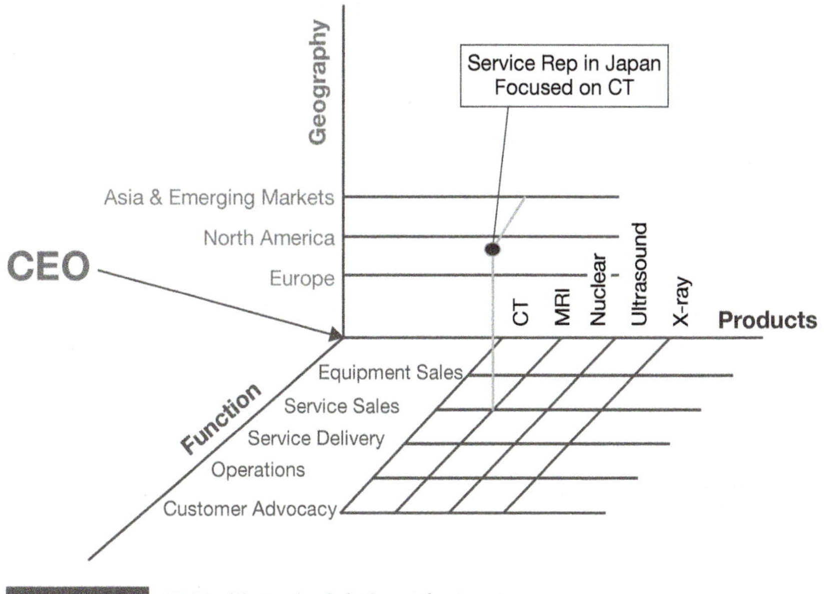

FIGURE 15.5 **GE Healthcare's global matrix structure**

The main challenge of a matrix structure is the sheer complexity of the operation. Reporting to one boss is often difficult enough, but when global employees have three bosses, often in different locations, it becomes difficult to set priorities and to manage all the expectations. To combat any confusion this situation could cause, companies often designate one boss as the "primary" boss and the other two as "secondary" bosses.

Formal organizational structures play an important part in determining how global headquarters of multinational companies control global subsidiaries. In addition to these formal organizational structures, informal organizational structures, including networks and virtual organizations, can make a critical difference in the success or failure of global ventures.

Network Structure

Some global industries are organized into fluid structures that bring people together into a group to work on a project; the group dissolves after the project is over, then re-forms, with the same or different members, when a new project becomes available.[15] For instance, the film industry brings together studios, writers, producers, actors, and technical crew for a given project. At the conclusion of the project, this group typically dissolves, and its members join other units to work on new films. Similarly, consulting companies may bring experts together to work on a project, then dissolve the team at the end of that project and form a new team for the next project. The membership of the team may be chosen based on client needs, worker expertise, availability, and other considerations. Companies like these, where people constantly move and the structure shifts, are organized through a **network structure**.

network structure a structure that organizes a company by groups that form to work on a project, and then dissolve once the project is complete

The advantage of a network organization is its ability to fluidly respond to rapid and frequent change. Because no rigid hierarchies or formal reporting lines exist, collaboration occurs in an informal and fluid manner. This adaptive nature makes the network organization ideal for rapidly changing environments.

Emerging markets are often fertile ground for large conglomerates that operate with a network organization, such as Samsung in South Korea,[16] Aditya Birla in India,[17] and Votorantim in Brazil.[18] These large organizations comprise vastly diversified companies in a loosely connected network that enables member companies to share resources and expertise while still operating essentially independently. For instance, the South Korean economy is dominated by chaebols—large conglomerates of diverse companies—such as LG, Hyundai, and Samsung.[19] Samsung's more than 90 different companies each pursues its individual, unique focus—such as cell phones and other consumer electronics, insurance, ship building, construction, or retail sales—while the corporate parent merely ties the various subsidiaries together in a loosely connected, highly flexible network, as illustrated in **Figure 15.6**.

Similarly, Nike operates in an international network that unites suppliers, manufacturers, and distributors with its design and marketing expertise. However, Samsung owns all the subsidiary companies, whereas Nike simply contracts with them on a project-by-project basis. This looser structure gives Nike operational flexibility; it can easily change suppliers, producers, and distributors as the need arises.[20]

In addition to the benefits of flexibility, network organizations constantly introduce new people with new ideas into the organization, increasing the potential for innovation. For instance, a man named James Jamison played bass for the Funk Brothers and wrote or cowrote more than 70 number-one hits—that's more than the Beatles, the Rolling Stones, the Beach Boys, and Elvis combined.[21] According to research, Jamison's success was due, in part, to his being part of a network of artists who provided insight, feedback, and critiques of his ideas.[22]

Other research has demonstrated that the ideal team structure for international consulting companies is one that gathers both international and local experts to provide global insight and local application. Network structures allow such combinations to form quickly, dissolve quickly, and then re-form as needed.[23]

However, not all organizations benefit from a network structure. Because network structures are fluid and flexible, organizations that require rigid hierarchies—such as the military, where coordination failures can cost human lives—are better served by avoiding network structures. Another potential drawback is that network structures have decentralized decision-making.

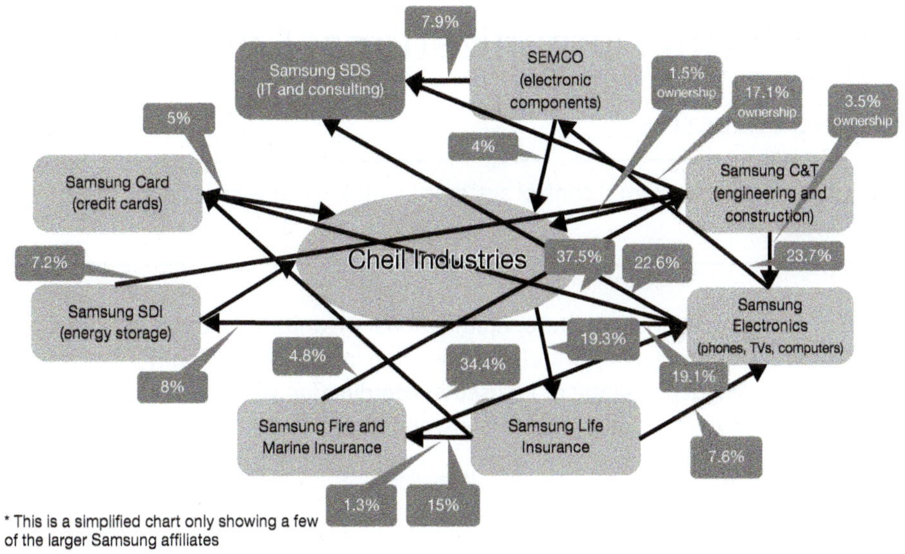

FIGURE 15.6 **Samsung's corporate network structure** **Source:** Data from "Shareholder Structure," Samsung, www.samsung.com/us/aboutsamsung/investor_relations/stock_info/ownership_structure.html; and "Why Does Samsung Have Such a Complicated Circular Corporate Structure?" Quora, www.quora.com/Why-does-Samsung-have-such-a-complicated-circular-corporate-structure.

This ambiguous structure means that international organizations that cannot tolerate incorrect decisions and mistakes should avoid network structures. For example, in 1999, a team of engineers spanning the Atlantic lost a $125 million space probe sent to explore the Mars's polar region. The problem was that one group of engineers calculated key spacecraft operations using metric units while another group used imperial units. Because of this disconnect, the probe was steered too close to Mars's atmosphere, "where it presumably burned and broke into pieces."[24] The lack of coordination in the decision-making structure meant the end of both the craft and the mission.

Figure 15.7 compares a network structure with the functional, divisional, and matrix structures we've already discussed.

The structure of global firms can facilitate or impede their ability to control subsidiaries. In general, global companies need to understand the trade-off between structures that allow subsidiaries to create localization and flexibility, and structures that enable control and globalization. On one hand, localization structures such as country-specific or regional divisions allow products and services to be fine-tuned for the local market; on the other hand, structures focused on products or functions enable firms to exert more control and establish global scale. As global companies shift their strategy, they must often also change their structure. As a result, these structures are often dynamic and change frequently.

	Functional	Divisional	Matrix	Network
Division of Labor	By inputs	By outputs	By inputs and outputs	By knowledge
Coordination	Hierarchical	Divisional	Dual reporting	Cross-functional teams
Importance of Informal Structure	Low	Modest	Considerable	High
Basic of Authority	Functional expertise	Managers	Negotiation	Network Centrality

FIGURE 15.7 **Comparison of organizational structures** Functional, divisional, matrix, and network. **Source:** Adapted from Ethan Bernstein and Nitin Nohria, "Note on Organizational Structure," Harvard Business School Background Note 491-082, February 1991 (revised May 2016), www.hbs.edu/faculty/Pages/item.aspx?num=16170.

15.2 Informal Organizational Controls

LEARNING OBJECTIVE

Identify the effects of informal control systems including company culture, incentives, and routines.

WileyPLUS

See Whiteboard Video: Formal and Informal Organizational Control

In addition to organizational structure, multinational organizations often use other tools—such as culture, incentives, and control systems—to reinforce the company's strategy. These elements can work independently or be used in coordination with the organizational structure to guide employees' actions, provide goals, and ensure that employees in different countries are doing their jobs.

Company Culture

Like countries, companies have their own cultures. Company culture is a system of shared assumptions, beliefs, and values that effect how employees behave. For instance, in some companies it is acceptable to publicly disagree with the boss and have open dissent, whereas in other companies conformity is the norm. Research suggests that a strong organizational culture can improve the success of multinational companies by encouraging employees to act in accordance with the values of the organization, increasing knowledge sharing, and providing motivation. For instance, recent research suggests that culture helps define for employees why the organization exists: what its purpose is. The research indicates that "why we work determines how well we work."[25] When employees are engaged in work and feel the company has a higher purpose, they work harder, even if it requires personal sacrifice.[26]

For instance, IKEA, the iconic company from Sweden founded in 1983 by Ingvar Kamprad, aims to bring furniture to the world "one room at a time."[27] Its employees are asked to adopt the common values of (1) working hard, (2) facing tough challenges, (3) using common sense, (4) staying true to its Swedish roots, and (5) limiting the use of resources. These embody the essence of IKEA's culture. Kamprad noted, "Maintaining a strong IKEA culture is one of the most crucial factors behind the continued success of the IKEA Concept."[28] The culture helps everyone focus on delivering consistent value through "democratic design"—in other words, through low-cost, well-designed products. A culture focused on democratic design pushes designers, employees, and even customers to think of creative solutions no matter where they are in the world.

IKEA's culture actually operates in contrast to the company's formal and rigid matrix organizational structure that organizes employees by store, country, and product. The structure is designed to deliver a consistent customer experience at any store around the world, ensuring efficiency; the culture empowers creative thinking because all employees are expected to share their innovative ideas within the company. This allows the firm to deliver low-cost and highly innovative designs globally.

Founders tend to have a profound effect on company culture.[29] Google's playfully, innovative, and egalitarian culture emerged from the desire of its founders, Larry Page and Sergey Brin, to create a company that pursues ideas they are excited about.[30] They built a company that allows employees to spend one day a week working on projects they are interested in.[31] Google's website states: "We're proud we've been able to create a company culture where employees are empowered to do cool things that matter." Similarly, Honda's focus on efficiency and quality manufacturing came from its founder Soichiro Honda, who was obsessed with the "joy of manufacturing."[32]

Culture typically takes on a life of its own and, without maintenance, can slowly change into something that no longer supports the company's objectives. Once established, organizational culture must be maintained through careful hiring, frequent employee interaction, regular company communication, and targeted incentives.[33] International businesses face the added struggle of creating a company culture that bridges national boundaries. For instance, the democratic, open context of IKEA's culture runs somewhat in opposition to the directive nature of many cultures found in Asia. Employees may struggle when company culture directly contradicts country culture.

IKEA takes many steps to preserve and strengthen its company culture when it operates in areas where the national culture runs counter to the company culture. First, it has developed a set of strict hiring criteria to focus the selection process on finding employees who can get the job done while exemplifying the company values, and on building cooperation, innovation, and diversity. Second, the company provides training, career development, and constant communication focused on the IKEA way. Finally, IKEA encourages employee interaction through activities such as *fika* (or coffee breaks) in order to bring employees together to connect, relax, and share ideas.[34]

Changing the culture can also be a daunting challenge. In 1984, when Zhang Ruimin took over a failing state-owned refrigerator factory in Qingdao, China, the company was in trouble. The organizational culture had been built around the production of low-quality, low-cost products, and the company had succeeded so far only because it supplied the only products in the market. It faced no competition, so employees faced no real pressure to perform. And, as a state-owned enterprise, the company merely turned to the government for more funds when it lost money.

Inspired by the quality of appliances he saw on a trip to Germany, Ruimin sought to change the company culture to focus on producing higher-quality goods. His first step was to convince employees that low-quality goods were no longer acceptable. To accomplish this task, he had employees take 76 refrigerators with minor flaws like scratches and dents—appliances the company would ordinarily have sold—out of the factory and smash them to bits with sledgehammers. Ruimin's point was that what was once "good enough" was no longer sufficient. This was a watershed event highlighting the company's new focus on quality. To further his efforts, Ruimin increased accountability by requiring employees to publicly explain any failures to their coworkers at the end of each day.[35] Finally, he initiated a communication strategy that focused on convincing both employees and customers that the products were high quality. These actions may seem extreme, but they worked to reset the culture and push quality to new heights. Today, Haier is the world's largest producer of refrigerators and recently purchased the appliance division of GE.[36]

Control Systems

In addition to corporate cultures, global companies use control systems to help them face the daunting challenge of maintaining control of their various subunits, which are often in different countries thousands of miles from corporate headquarters. **Control systems** are the means by which headquarters can force compliance from global subsidiaries. These systems include bureaucratic, output, normative, and personal control systems (see **Figure 15.8**).

control systems means by which headquarters can force compliance from global subsidiaries

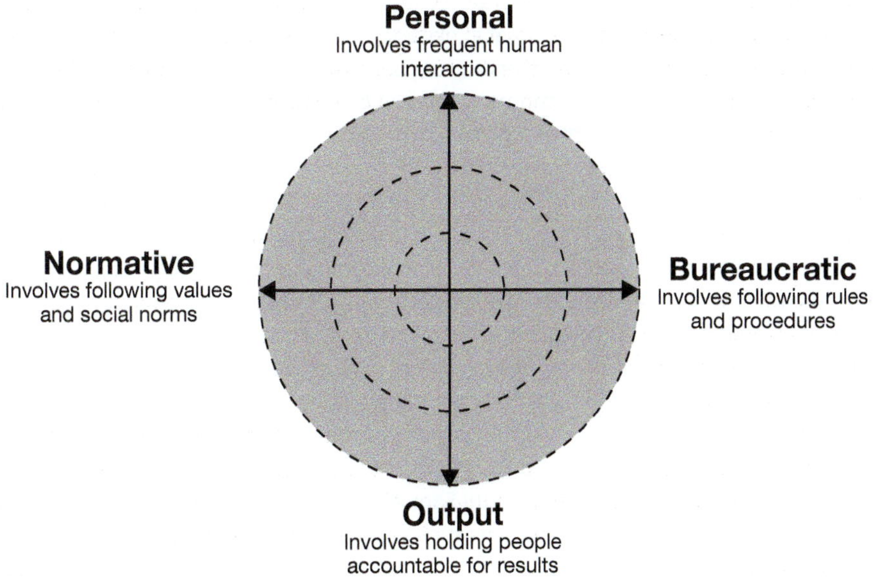

FIGURE 15.8 Control systems International businesses often use one or more control systems to help govern the efforts of their subsidiaries.

bureaucratic control control accomplished through rules and routines

Bureaucratic control is control accomplished through rules and routines. Routines are standardized methods for accomplishing recurring organizational tasks. Within international organizations, they can exert subtle yet significant control over business operations. For instance, McDonald's uses bureaucratic control in its global operations: it clearly specifies ways to complete the operational routines of taking a customer's order, preparing food, and even cleaning the store to ensure that customers in India and Indiana have similar experiences. Similarly, Uber has routines and rules that ensure that riders know what they can expect when hailing an Uber in New York or Paris.

Bureaucratic routines are advantageous because they enable a firm to control the activities of its employees by standardizing everyday customer interactions, manufacturing processes, and R&D. Such standardization can reduce errors and save time by eliminating the need for employees to search repeatedly for solutions to recurring problems. They may also help a company pursue a global strategy by allowing it to replicate practices that exist in different countries as it expands. For instance, Toyota has replicated its successful production routines in many countries, allowing the automaker to reproduce its production advantage across the globe. Another plus is that improvements made in an organizational routine in one location can easily transfer to all other locations.

On the other hand, the rigidity of routines can be problematic, particularly for companies seeking to be locally responsive. For instance, Novotel—a French hotel company with more than 400 properties in 61 countries around the world—used to provide each hotel manager with a set of operations manuals that outlined the company's routines in detail. Each manager was then held accountable for the correct and complete implementation of the company's routines. The routines that worked in France, however, didn't work as well in international markets. As one critic noted, "This system appeared to militate against more flexible practices because it left no room for empowerment of the front line worker and had no system of feedback and learning. For example, employees were given scripted greetings to give to customers and scripted methods of behavior that did not allow contextual variations."[37] As a result, Novotel has since moved away from highly rigid routines in favor of more flexible working practices that allow workers to respond to local customer needs and requirements.

output control control that focuses on profitability and/or market share

Output control focuses on profitability and/or market share. Objective standards, such as a 2 percent increase in market share, govern operations. These output measures are able to be standardized and measured consistently around the globe, allowing multinationals to hold subunits accountable based on market outcomes. Global companies that use market controls generally set difficult but achievable goals for their subsidiaries, then let the units determine how to achieve the goals. In general, day-to-day operations are at the discretion of local management. Such an arrangement is ideal when the firm's strategies are focused on localization and when the subsidiaries are highly trusted.[38]

For instance, the Swedish fashion brand H&M expanded to Puerto Rico, New Zealand, and Cyprus in 2016, opening 264 new stores globally. However, the company also simultaneously closed 53 stores. The company looks at profitability as a control mechanism. Regional managers are responsible for sales performance at existing and new stores. They thus evaluate each store and explore opportunities to achieve growth. For instance, in Germany, in the first nine months of the 2016 fiscal year, the company opened eleven stores and closed seven stores. In the United States it opened thirty-seven stores and closed seven stores, whereas in Japan it opened eight stores but closed two stores.[39]

The challenges of output control are that it can be difficult to get accurate and timely performance data, to efficiently analyze the data, and to ensure that data from one market are comparable to those from other markets. Typically, global companies rely on large-scale information systems such as Oracle or SAP to help organize these efforts, but these systems are costly, include only company information, and are limited by the accuracy of the inputs.

normative control control that gets subunits to adhere to the values of the organization

Normative control relies on strong buy-in from subunits for the values of the organization. This control reduces the need for external control factors because global employees are likely to value and seek the same thing. Walmart aims for normative control in its global operations by reiterating the values of Walmart during frequent team meetings. In these meetings, staff sing the Walmart song, discuss "What would Sam Walton do?" in different scenarios, and learn the Walmart way, which includes acronyms such as HEATKTE—High Expectations Are The Key To Everything.[40]

Normative control is particularly difficult for global companies because differences across borders make it less likely that employees will value the same thing. For instance, many new Walmart employees in the United States find the Walmart culture unique and surprising, but French or Japanese workers may find them odd.

Personal control occurs when a global company uses frequent human interaction to enforce control. This often includes the use of expatriates to staff or visit global subsidiaries. Through personal control, leaders of global companies are able to extend their focus and vision to subsidiaries. Samsung exerts personal control by sending a few trusted employees to many global subsidiaries to interact with and enforce compliance by the units. Similarly, Toyota sends consultants to their suppliers in order to teach them the Toyota production process.

personal control the use of frequent human interaction to enforce control

The downside of personal control is the high cost of individual interaction. Sending workers around the globe can be an expensive effort. These expatriate employees often require many benefits such as foreign school tuition and housing allowances. In response, some companies have tried to reduce or eliminate the cost of travel by using video technology, allowing people to join meetings remotely via technologies like Skype and GoToMeeting.

In sum, companies choose to what extent personal, bureaucratic, output, and normative controls are used by headquarters to control subsidiaries. Most companies use multiple measures. For instance, Hang Ten clothing was started by the surfer Duke Boyd, who invented board shorts, to bring California beach fashion to the world.[41] The company is now headquartered in Hong Kong and operates in twelve global markets, including the United States, Canada, Mexico, Brazil, Korea, Taiwan, Japan, China, Singapore, the Philippines, Malaysia, and South Africa (see **Figure 15.9**). It has 2000 global retail partners and over $1 billion a year in sales.[42]

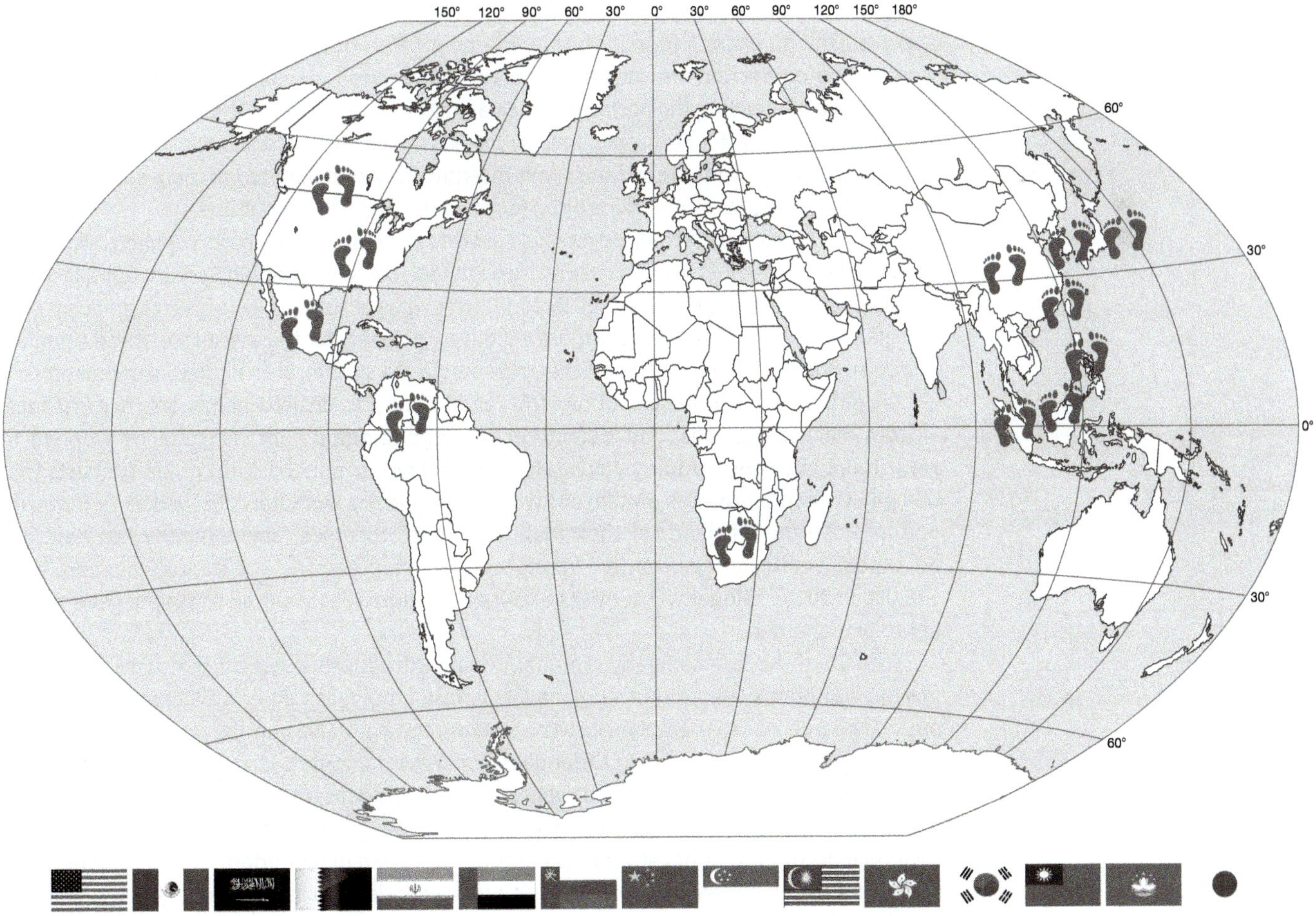

FIGURE 15.9 **Hang Ten's geographic footprint** **Source:** https://hangten.com/about.html (accessed December 12, 2016).

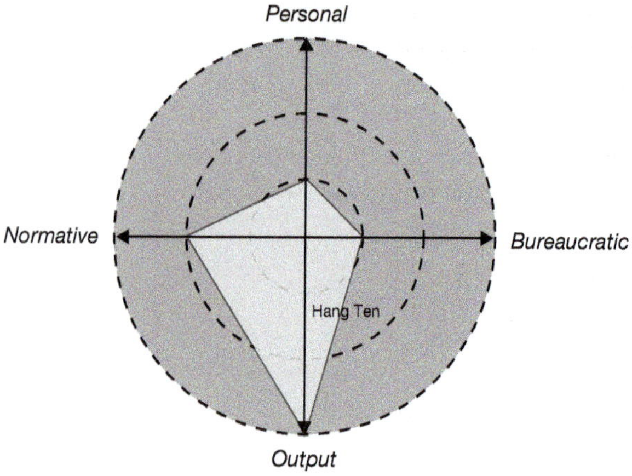

FIGURE 15.10 **Hang Ten's control mechanisms**

The company mainly uses output control to control its global operations (see **Figure 15.10**). It provides sales targets for each global market and closely monitors these targets, but each country manager determines how best to reach these targets. For instance, which designs will work, where to produce the products, and at what price are all determined by country managers. Headquarters provides some brand guidance to ensure that the units stay true to the normative values focused on the California beach culture, but the rest is determined locally. As a result, Hang Ten's control takes the shape found in Figure 15.10.

Incentives as Control

Behavioral incentives can also act as an important control mechanism by inducing subunits to act in specific ways. They add a new source of motivation to reward additional effort, whether the goal is improved individual, unit, or organizational performance. If the incentive—such as a status symbol (like a corner office), a bonus, or profit sharing—is offered to individual employees based on their personal output, then individuals are likely to increase their efforts. However, an individual incentive may also have the unintended consequence of limiting efforts to collaborate, help, and teach coworkers, because employees will be focused on earning their own individual bonuses. For this reason, managers must choose incentives carefully and accurately pair them with a desired systemic outcome.

For instance, because Toyota wants employees to share information across divisions, the company provides incentives that reward individuals and units for the performance of other divisions in addition to their own. These employees then have a stake in others' performance and are likely to share information that will help those other divisions. However, a factory worker on a production line at a Toyota plant in Indonesia may perceive that he or she has little chance of affecting the performance of a plant in Portugal, and thus incentives linked to the performance of the Portugal plant may seem unfair and decrease the Indonesian worker's motivation. For this reason, cross-unit incentives are often limited to more senior leaders, whereas incentives for line workers often focus on their own unit's output.

Taking this concept further, Toyota also provides incentives to its parts suppliers, encouraging cooperation and information sharing through the Toyota Production System. Suppliers that are members of the system open their factories to Toyota consultants, who invest significant time and effort in helping them become more effective. To qualify for the assistance, these suppliers must also open their factories to all other members in the system, even if they are competitors.[43]

Incentives enable leaders to directly reward specific desired behaviors. For instance, Lincoln Electric Co., a U.S. manufacturer of welding equipment, encourages workers to make more effort by providing pay based on each piece produced. The company insists that this pay structure provides employees with motivation to work hard, as well as to innovate and improve the efficiency of their manufacturing processes. The company has paid out an annual profit-sharing incentive for eighty-two straight years. The bonus was more than $26,000 in 2015.[44] Globally, incentives are used for more reasons than to simply get employees to work harder.

The South Korean company Hyundai Capital introduced a system that uses a negative incentive of bonus cuts to punish managers whose employees do not take enough vacation days. The issue was that employees were working too hard and burning out, so the incentive was created in an effort to create a friendlier work environment.[45]

While financial incentives can be successful, they do present some challenges for managers. If bonuses are paid regularly, for instance, employees can begin to perceive them as part of their regular compensation, at which point they may fail to induce additional effort. If bonuses are removed, employees may perceive it as a loss, with demotivating effects.[46]

Another challenge for multinational organizations is that incentives may work well in one country and not in another. For example, one U.S. technology firm gave its employees in Singapore

S$4, a nominal amount of money, to celebrate the Lunar New Year. Management thought it was making a nice overture to acknowledge the local culture. However, the number four signifies death in most Asian countries. So, instead of being grateful, employees were horrified. To fix the situation, management gave S$8 to each employee, unwittingly signifying "double death." Morale tanked, workers disengaged, and the firm eventually went out of business.[47]

Multiple Control Mechanisms Simultaneously Most global companies use more than one type of control simultaneously in order to achieve the benefits of multiple methods while minimizing the impact of the particular challenges of each. In fact, recent research suggests that Japanese subsidiaries in Europe achieve the highest performance when they have high involvement from headquarters (high personal control) and high autonomy (high outcome control).[48] The optimal combination of control mechanisms is likely to be unique for each company, based on their strategy and capabilities.

15.3 Reducing the Need for Coordination among Subsidiaries: Virtual Organizations, Standards, and Modularity

LEARNING OBJECTIVE

Outline the role of virtual organizations, technology standards, and modularity in helping to coordinate work with subsidiaries.

A primary purpose of structure and control systems is to ensure adequate levels of coordination and oversight between headquarters and subsidiaries.[49] However, international businesses also may seek to reduce the need for control and coordination.[50] To do so, they often use alternative forms of coordination, such as virtual meetings, technology standards, and modularity, to coordinate actions. We now discuss each of these alternative coordination modes in more detail.

Virtual Organizations

A **virtual organization** enables employees to coordinate and execute activities almost entirely through information technology, rather than by working in the same physical space. Their information is often remotely hosted on servers in the cloud, and workers are not required to live in a specific area, but rather telecommute to work. As a result, virtual organizations typically have either a limited or no physical structure. They often use a network structure and sometimes hire contract employees to conduct much of the work. **Contract employees** are typically outside workers who perform specific predetermined tasks for a company and are paid by the job; they are sometimes called freelancers. These workers are not employees of the organization.

Virtual organizations offer lower costs and improved flexibility. For instance, most of Jet Blue's customer service employees work from their homes using their own computers and telephones. These employees take reservations, change flights, and support customers. The company saves the money it would otherwise pay for office space, and it can hire workers who live anywhere, rather than being restricted to those within a reasonable commuting distance from a centralized office building.

One downside of virtual organizations is that it can be difficult to build a strong company culture and to socialize and train new employees or freelancers.[51] Also, because the structure limits employee interaction, it can reduce social support, limit information and knowledge

virtual organization an organization that enables employees to coordinate and execute activities almost entirely through information technology, rather than by working in the same physical space

contract employees outside workers who are hired by a firm to perform specific predetermined tasks for a company and who are paid by the job

sharing, and reduce overall morale. Finally, because contract workers and freelancers are by definition free agents, one disadvantage is that these potential contributors may not always be available for a given project when needed.

Technology Standards

Standardization of technology protocols and equipment can also act as an organizing principle because it predetermines how coordination occurs in complex products and processes. For instance, 4G wireless technology standardizes the way in which cell phones interact with towers, enabling data to be transferred across carriers and across devices. Because all equipment providers and service providers use a single industry standard, each company can develop and sell any device that complies with the standard, without further need of coordination.

Similarly, Wi-Fi Alliance is a worldwide nonprofit association of companies that has certified more than 25,000 Web-enabled products, ensuring that these devices can send and receive data using a common standard that all companies follow. Member companies include Apple, Microsoft, Sony, Samsung, Comcast, Intel, and many others. The companies collaborate to develop standards for security, spectra, and technologies that send and receive data in order to dramatically improve users' Wi-Fi experience. The association also looks for new markets for Wi-Fi, such as airlines, trains, and emerging markets.[52]

The benefit of organization through standardization is that, once the standard interface and protocols have been set, companies can create technology products that interact well, without further collaboration. This allows Apple and Samsung—fierce rivals—to develop their own equipment, but in a way that permits customers to buy products that communicate with one another, whether they are made by Apple or Samsung. In addition, companies just entering the industry don't need to develop their own technology standards; they can simply adopt those already in place.

While standards are generally helpful, they do have a few drawbacks. First, they are not always easy to establish. For one thing, companies developing standards often require licensing fees from competitors that want to use their technology; therefore competitors may prefer to set the standard rather than follow it. As a result, many competing offerings may exist, particularly early in the life of a new technology. In 2016, BMW teamed up with Intel, the U.S. tech giant, and Mobileye, an Israel-based driver assistance company, to develop a standards-based technology platform for autonomous vehicles. The system aims to allow advanced driver assistance systems to become the global standard.[53] The technology uses cameras and software to recognize and respond to activities both on and off the road. On the other hand, Tesla, Ford, and Velodyne, among others, are pushing a light detection and ranging model of autonomous driving technology that uses cameras, radars, and ultrasonic sensors.[54]

A second drawback is that the existence of multiple competing standards can undermine customer value. For instance, Apple and Android use different standards for formatting digital content. As a result, smartphone customers can't use content in one format on devices from the other company, limiting their ability to change formats. In some ways, companies like Apple and Google attempt to use this drawback to their advantage, locking customers into a specific standard, even if those customers would rather use something else.

In this way, standardization can actually backfire and restrict innovation and advancement. For example, in the late 1800s, some of the first cars were actually battery-operated electric cars. The gasoline engine, however, eventually beat out electric motors and became the standard for the next hundred years, even as the cost of batteries fell over the period. Because the standard was entrenched, it's only now—more than a century later—that companies like Tesla, Toyota, and General Motors are coming back around to question the standard of the gasoline engine and examine the electric car again.

Modularity

modular design a system in which a process, product, or service is divided into components that can be changed independently and then reintegrated into the system

Modular design is a system in which a process, product, or service is divided into components that can be changed independently and then reintegrated into the system.[55] Like standards, modularity enables companies to coordinate activities across boundaries. Car manufacturers operate based on the idea of modular design principles. Each uses a small number of base platforms on which it can build a different model for different markets with minimal modification. For instance, Volkswagen and Toyota both use platforms to build cars. VW uses the MQB platform to build the A3, Golf, Leon, and Octavia (**Figure 15.11**). Toyota uses a common platform for the Land Cruiser, the Lexus LX570, the Sequoia, and the Lexus GX460.[56] These modular platforms can then be configured to meet the needs of different countries, such as left-hand- or right-hand-drive cars,[57] and to allow the companies to achieve economies of scale.

The advantage of modularity is that companies can achieve economies of scale and simultaneously work on different aspects of a product or service. For instance, LG uses modular design to produce TVs that are nearly identical worldwide. The only real necessary modification is a change in the power module for each country, depending on the local power wattage. The modular design enables LG to achieve economies of scale while still allowing local customization of components.

The disadvantage of a modular design is that the overall design is usually not optimized. Tesla, for instance, terminated a partnership with Mobileye, a supplier of the EyeQ3 chip, which is used in autonomous driving vehicles to help recognize elements that affect driving. Tesla preferred to focus on building an integrated system that designed the hardware directly into the car. While modular systems often reduce costs, because each component is independent, they require lots of integration and may not work well with each other. For instance, Google recently terminated Ara, a fully modular phone.[58] The idea for the phone was that each of the components (battery, camera, processor, and so on) were all able to be swapped out. This had the potential to reduce production costs and allow users to upgrade only the components that they cared about. However, Google realized that separating a phone into components increased battery consumption by 20–30 percent because the different component parts required constant communication to ensure the different parts of the phone were working in sync.[59]

In sum, virtual organizations, standards, and modularity are important tools that enable companies to coordinate activities across geographies without building formal organizational structures. The flexibility of these informal organizational modes is becoming increasingly important in enabling companies to adapt to global pressures.

FIGURE 15.11 **Modular design at Volkswagen** These four cars (the Audi A3, the Leon, the Golf, and the Octavia) made by companies in the Volkswagen Group are all built off a common platform; standardizing the frame and powertrain.

15.4 Horizontal Subsidiary Coordination

LEARNING OBJECTIVE

Discuss the challenges of enabling horizontal coordination and knowledge transfer among subsidiaries.

horizontal coordination the process by which subsidiaries communicate and coordinate work among themselves

In international business, not only does headquarters need to control and coordinate interactions with subsidiaries, but subsidiaries often need to engage in **horizontal coordination**, or to communicate and coordinate work among themselves (see **Figure 15.12**). In the vertical relationship between headquarters and subsidiaries, headquarters can mandate coordination by requiring subsidiaries to share knowledge with headquarters.[60] However, because subsidiary units are peer organizations, coordination by mandating knowledge sharing often does not work; rather, units must obtain the knowledge they need through influence and persuasion. This means that the *motivation* as well as the *ability* of other subsidiaries is an important consideration in knowledge sharing. Research suggests that subsidiaries that both receive and share knowledge are likely to have higher performance.[61]

For instance, the International Finance Corporation (IFC) of the World Bank provides both money and knowledge to governments and companies around the world.[62] The regional offices report to headquarters in Washington, DC. However, many of the projects the IFC conducts are similar across different regions. The IFC is involved in many banking projects in South America and the Middle East. While these subsidiaries technically report to headquarters in Washington, they would benefit by sharing best practices among the subsidiaries. Yet, the IFC and many other global companies find it difficult to get knowledge to flow horizontally—between subsidiaries.[63]

Horizontal coordination faces challenges with motivation and ability from both the source of and the recipient of knowledge, as presented in **Figure 15.13**. A subsidiary seeking knowledge from another subsidiary may face resistance from individuals in the other subsidiary, who may be reluctant to invest the time, energy, and effort to share their knowledge. This creates a "hoarding of expertise" problem in subsidiaries. International businesses address this challenge by creating both norms and processes that encourage individuals to share, rather than hoard, knowledge.[64] For instance, at the IFC, after each project, the company sends a team to create a project completion report. This report codifies what the team learned on the project in an electronic format that is available across the organization.

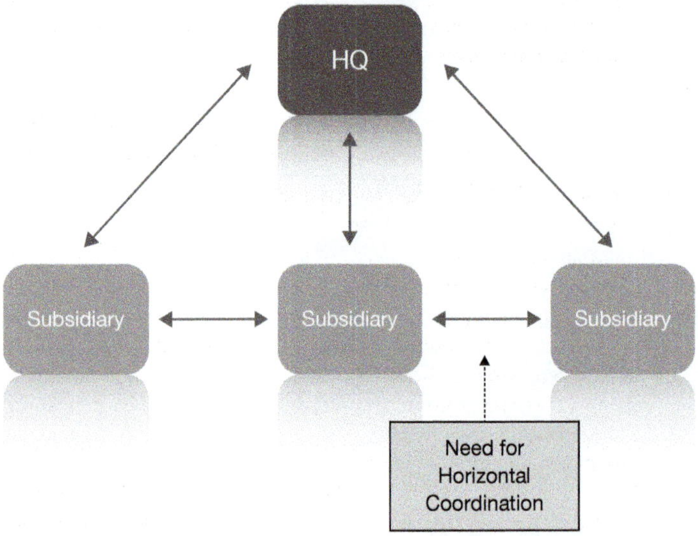

FIGURE 15.12 **Horizontal coordination between subsidiaries** Inter-subsidiary coordination is often critical in successful global organizations.

On the other hand, a subsidiary that may have discovered a best practice and tries to share this with other subsidiaries is likely to face a "not-invented-here" problem. Research repeatedly demonstrates that subsidiaries are reluctant to use knowledge that was not created in their unit, even when the knowledge is beneficial to them.[65] Organizations that successfully overcome this challenge focus on building trust among units. This trust allows subsidiaries to use the knowledge provided by other units because they trust them.[66]

In addition, even when subsidiaries may be motivated to both seek and provide knowledge, they are often limited in their ability to transfer knowledge. For instance, at the IFC, hundreds of projects are completed each year by subsidiaries across the globe. As a result, it is difficult for a project manager in Vietnam to know what prior projects are relevant for her current project. In fact, she is likely to not even be aware that similar projects have been completed within the company. This "needle-in-a-haystack" problem is particularly challenging in global

	Knowledge Seeker	Knowledge Provider
Motivation	Not-invented here problem	Hoarding of expertise problem
Ability	Needle-in-a-haystack problem	"Foreigner problem"

FIGURE 15.13 **Challenges in subsidiary to subsidiary knowledge flows** The motivation and ability of both providers and seekers of knowledge are important.

companies where personal interaction is limited. To solve this problem, global companies create extensive knowledge systems that house past projects and related questions and answers. In addition, some knowledge may be more tacit in nature and require personal interaction. Because of this, many global companies keep up-to-date contact information available so those looking for knowledge can contact those who may have relevant knowledge, and they create norms that allow quick responses to colleagues' requests. For instance, one global consulting company has a response policy that requires colleagues to respond to requests within 24 hours.

Finally, knowledge providers may face a "foreigner" problem that limits their ability to transfer knowledge across subsidiaries. This challenge relates to the ability of different subsidiaries to understand knowledge provided to them. Research suggests that when subsidiaries share a common core of knowledge, they are better able to transfer knowledge—particularly complex knowledge. As a result, global subsidiaries seeking to share knowledge may be unable to communicate in a way that is understood by other units. To address this problem, global companies must create absorptive capacity. This capacity not only increases the ability of units to understand new knowledge but also helps subsidiaries create knowledge that is useful to other units.[67]

Summary and Case

Summary

LEARNING OBJECTIVE 15.1 Describe how functional, divisional, matrix, and network structures help international businesses achieve their global strategies.

Companies typically take one of four structures: functional, divisional, matrix, or network. Functional structures are highly efficient and group employees by functional expertise. Divisional structures are highly reactive and group employees by product line, geography, or customer segment. Matrix structures attempt to compensate for the shortcomings of the functional and divisional structures by combining elements of both. Network structures are highly adaptive, forming a group of workers for a project and then disbanding, forming anew for the next project.

LEARNING OBJECTIVE 15.2 Identify the effects of informal control systems, including bureaucratic, output, normative, personal, and incentive systems.

Less direct means of controlling global organizations are company culture and control systems. *Culture* refers to the shared values of a company and has a powerful effect on employee motivation and efforts. Other control systems include bureaucratic, control by rules; output, control by business results; normative, control by common values; and personal, control through personal interaction. In addition, organizations can use incentives to shape motivation and behavior. These control systems help global companies get subunits to work toward common goals.

LEARNING OBJECTIVE 15.3 Outline the role of virtual organizations, technology standards, and modularity in helping to coordinate work with subsidiaries.

International businesses also coordinate or reduce the need to coordinate work using virtual organizations, standards, and modularity. Virtual organizations use information technology as a foundation, enabling team members across the globe to connect and collaborate on a group project. Standardization establishes a specific way of doing something or sets a specific standard. This enables competing companies to develop unique products that will still interact. Modular design is a system in which a process, product, or service is divided into components that can be changed independently and then be reintegrated into the system. Modularity enables companies to build different products from the same base parts, customizing some components to meet local needs while achieving economies of scale with other uniform components.

LEARNING OBJECTIVE 15.4 Discuss the challenges of enabling horizontal coordination and knowledge transfer among subsidiaries.

International businesses also coordinate intersubsidiary knowledge. This flow of knowledge can increase a firm's performance and allows best practices to flow between units. However, these horizontal knowledge flows are often limited by the motivation and ability of those units seeking knowledge and those providing knowledge. Interunit trust, norms, knowledge systems, and absorptive capacity can reduce these challenges.

Case Study

Control at Zara

Zara is a subsidiary of Inditex, which also owns Bershka, Pull & Bear, and Massimo Dutti fashion stores. Zara started in Spain in 1975 and now has over 7,000 stores in ninety-one countries.[68] The company uses a unique approach. For instance, Zara stores around the world receive deliveries from headquarters twice a week. All new products are centrally designed at headquarters in Spain, and most are produced close to headquarters—in Spain, Portugal, Turkey, and Morocco, instead of Asia. As a result, the products often reach stores in just three weeks. By contrast, most clothing stores have at least a six-month delay from design to store.

Zara's retail model is often called "fast fashion" because of its speed. The constant change in inventory means that customers visit the stores much more frequently, worried they will miss out on a great item. To get the inventory right requires intensive coordination between headquarters and the local stores. A couple of times a week, store managers send an order to headquarters. The order is based on the sales data for the store and anecdotal evidence from shoppers about what they like and don't like. At headquarters a "team compiles the order, adding in new products and balancing out demand with other stores, before sending it to Inditex's manufacturing hub. Within two days, the order has reached the store."[69] In addition, in-house central designers are watching the sales trends in the stores and observing emerging high-fashion trends, such as catwalk displays.

Expatriate managers also regularly rotate through the different stores to ensure consistent processes and product delivery. These expatriates ensure that Zara's common values are distributed across all stores and that all processes are carried out in exact accordance with top management's wishes. Once new items are designed, they are produced in small batches and quickly tested in stores to see what works and what doesn't. The constant change means that, rather than having Spring, Summer, Fall, and Winter seasons, Zara has 104 seasons.

Zara also centralizes distribution. "Every single item of clothing that Zara sells comes through Spain, even if it has been made in China and will ultimately be delivered back to a Chinese store. At the vast Arteixo base, home to 6,000 staff from 30 countries, a tunnel network carries a carousel that moves clothing from the on-site factories to the vast distribution center. Inside the distribution center, clothes move along the carousel until they reach their allocated box. This box, earmarked for an individual store, will be packed with different products and often reaches its destination within 36 to 48 hours."[70] This strict adherence to process controls allows the company to provide the latest fashions much faster than any other company out there, making Zara's the fast fashion company of the world.[71]

Case Discussion Questions

1. Given Zara's approach to sales and its structure, to what extent would you suggest Zara use each control mechanism—Personal, Normative, Bureaucratic, Output?
2. Why would you suggest these mechanisms and levels?
3. How would Zara compare to Hang Ten in terms of which control mechanisms are emphasized?

Endnotes

[1] "Tingyi Holding and PepsiCo Finalize Strategic Alliance in China," press release, PepsiCo, March 31, 2012, www.pepsico.com/live/pressrelease/Tingyi-Holding-and-PepsiCo-Finalize-Strategic-Alliance-in-China03312012.

[2] "Our Heritage," Philips, www.philips.com/a-w/about/company/our-heritage.html (accessed December 5, 2016).

[3] Christopher A Bartlett, "Philips versus Matsushita: The Competitive Battle Continues," Harvard Business School Case 910-410, December 2009.

[4] "The Matrix Master," *Economist*, January 19, 2006, www.economist.com/node/5380495.

[5] Olga Kharif and Elco Van Groningen, "Philips, Post Lighting Spinoff, Eyes Billion-Dollar Deals," Bloomberg Technology, June 8, 2016, www.bloomberg.com/news/articles/2016-06-08/philips-post-lighting-spinoff-eyes-billion-dollar-acquisitions.

[6] Jay R. Galbraith, *Designing Complex Organizations* (Boston, MA: Addison-Wesley, 1973).

[7] Ranjay Gulati, "Silo Busting," *Harvard Business Review* 85, no. 5 (2007): 98–108.

[8] Form 10-K, Ford Motor Company 2015 Annual Report, December 31, 2015, http://s21.q4cdn.com/450475907/files/doc_downloads/Ford-10-K-(2015).pdf

[9] Form 10-K, Ford Motor Company 2015 Annual Report.

[10] Sarah Gordon, "Virgin Goup: Brand It Like Branson," *Financial Times*, November 5, 2014, www.ft.com/content/4d4fb05e-64cd-11e4-bb43-00144feabdc0.

[11] "LVMH 2014 Annual Report," http://r.lvmh-static.com/uploads/2015/04/lvmh_ra2014_gb.pdf (accessed December 12, 2016).

[12] "Management," www.nestle.com/aboutus/management (accessed December 12, 2016).

[13] Ranjay Gulati and Phanish Puranam, "Renewal through Reorganization: The Value of Inconsistencies between Formal and Informal Organization," *Organization Science* 20, no. 2 (2009): 422–40.

[14] Ranjay Gulati, James Oldroyd, Suzanne Carpenter, and Abbas Khan, "GE Medical Systems," Kellogg School of Management Case, January 27, 2003; Kim Janseen, "GE Healthcare Moving Headquarters to Chicago from U.K.," *Chicago Tribune*, January 11, 2016, www.chicagotribune.com/business/ct-ge-healthcare-hq-0112-biz-20160111-story.html.

[15] Thomas U. Grund, "Network Structure and Team Performance: The Case of English Premier League Soccer Teams," *Social Networks* 34, no. 4 (2012): 682–90; Roger Guimera et al., "Team Assembly Mechanisms Determine Collaboration Network Structure and Team Performance," *Science* 308, no. 5722 (2005): 697–702.

[16] Amjad Hadjikhani, Joong Woo Lee, and Sohee Park, "Corporate Social Responsibility as a Marketing Strategy in Foreign Markets: The Case of Korean MNCs in the Chinese Electronics Market," *International Marketing Review* 33, no. 4 (2016): 530–554.

[17] Nabyla Daidj, *Strategy, Structure and Corporate Governance: Expressing Inter-firm Networks and Group-affiliated Companies* (Boca Raton, FL: CRC Press, 2016).

[18] Paloma Fernandez Perez and Andrea Lluch, *Evolution of Family Business: Continuity and Change in Latin America and Spain* (Cheltenham, UK: Edward Elgar Publishing, 2016).

[19] Cho Mu-hyun, "The Chaebols: The Rise of South Korea's Mighty Conglomerates," CNET, April 6, 2015, www.cnet.com/news/the-chaebols-the-rise-of-south-koreas-mighty-conglomerates/.

[20] Phalguni Soni, "An Overview of NIKE's Supply Chain and Manufacturing Strategies," Market Realist, December 2, 1014, http://marketrealist.com/2014/12/overview-nikes-supply-chain-manufacturing-strategies/.

[21] Brian Uzzi and Jarrett Spiro, "Collaboration and Creativity: The Small World Problem," *American Journal of Sociology* 111, no. 2 (2005): 447–504.

[22] Allan Slutsky, *Standing in the Shadows of Motown: The Legendary Life of Bassist Jamie Jamison* (Milwaukee: Hal Leonard, 1989).

[23] Martine R. Haas, "Acquiring and Applying Knowledge in Transnational Teams: The Roles of Cosmopolitans and Locals," *Organization Science* 17, no. 3 (2006): 367–84.

[24] "NASA's Metric Confusion Caused Mars Orbiter Loss," CNN, September 30, 1999, www.cnn.com.

[25] Lindsay McGregor and Neel Doshi, "How Company Culture Shapes Employee Motivation," *Harvard Business Review*, November 25, 2015, https://hbr.org/2015/11/how-company-culture-shapes-employee-motivation.

[26] Dana Chandler and Adam Kapelner, "Breaking Monotony with Meaning: Motivation in Crowdsourcing Markets," *Journal of Economic Behavior & Organization* 90 (2013): 123–33.

[27] "The IKEA Concept," Inter IKEA Systems B.V., http://franchisor.ikea.com/typically-swedish/ (accessed December 6, 2016).

[28] "The IKEA Concept."

[29] Diana C. Kyser and Theodore Hill, "Through the Looking Glass: Company Culture as a Reflection of Founder Personality in Entrepreneurial Organizations," (September 10, 2016), 6th International Engaged Management Scholarship Conference, Fox School of Business Research Paper No. 17-006; Aegean Leung, Maw Der Foo, and Sankalp Chaturvedi, "Imprinting Effects of Founding Core Teams on HR Values in New Ventures," *Entrepreneurship Theory and Practice* 37, no. 1 (2013): 87–106.

[30] Steven Tweedie, "Larry Page and Sergey Brin Explain Why They Just Created a New Company," *Business Insider*, August 10, 2015, www.businessinsider.com/larry-page-and-sergey-brin-explain-why-they-created-alphabet-2015-8.

[31] Charles Duhigg, "What Google Learned from Its Quest to Build the Perfect Team," *New York Times*, February 25, 2016, www.nytimes.com/2016/02/28/magazine/what-google-learned-from-its-quest-to-build-the-perfect-team.html?_r=1.

[32] "The 'Joy of Manufacturing,'" Honda History, http://world.honda.com/history/limitlessdreams/joyofmanufacturing/ (accessed December 6, 2016).

[33] Mats Alvesson, *Understanding Organizational Culture* (Thousand Oaks, CA: Sage, 2012); Edgar H. Schein, *Organizational Culture and Leadership*, vol. 2 (New York: John Wiley & Sons, 2010).

[34] "Working at the IKEA Group," IKEA, www.ikea.com/ms/en_AU/this-is-ikea/working-at-the-ikea-group/index.html (accessed December 6, 2016).

[35] Tarun Khanna, Ingrid Vargas, and Krishna G. Palepu, "Haier: Taking a Chinese Company Global in 2011," Harvard Business School Publishing Case, August 21, 2011.

[36] "Haier Sustains Pole Position in the Euromonitor Global Major," Bloomberg Business, January 9, 2015, www.bloomberg.com/article/2015-01-09/aSUb4iEQ60yA.html; Ashlee Clark Thompson, "It's Official: GE Appliances Belongs to Haier," CNET, June 6, 2016, https://www.cnet.com/news/its-official-ge-appliances-belongs-to-haier/.

[37] Conrad Lashley, *Empowerment: HR Strategies for Service Excellence* (New York: Routledge, 2012); Charles Baden-Fuller and Sidney G. Winter, "Replicating Organizational Knowledge: Principles or Templates?" Available at SSRN 1118013 (2005): 17.

[38] Björn Ambos, Kazuhiro Asakawa, and Tina C. Ambos, "A Dynamic Perspective on Subsidiary Autonomy," *Global Strategy Journal* 1, nos. 3–4 (2011): 301–16.

[39] "H&M Hennes & Mauritz AB Nine-month Report," December 1, 2015, to August 31, 2016. https://about.hm.com/en/media/news/financial-reports/2016/9/2319113.html

[40] Michael Bergdahl, "Cultural Kool-Aid Creates Cult-Like Commitment," LinkedIn Pulse, January 20, 2016, www.linkedin.com/pulse/sam-walton-way-walmart-michael-edward-bergdahl.

[41] Doris Hajewski, "Kohl's to Revive Hang Ten Brand," *Journal Sentinel*, June 12, 2008, http://archive.jsonline.com/business/29461529.html.

[42] "The Icon," Hang Ten, https://hangten.com/about.html (accessed December 10, 2016).

[43] "Toyota Company Vision," Toyota Production System, http://www.toyota-global.com/company/vision_philosophy/toyota_production_system/ (accessed July 14, 2017); Jeffrey H. Dyer and Kentaro Nobeoka, "Creating and Managing a High Performance Knowledge-Sharing Network: The Toyota Case," *Strategic Management Journal*, special issue "Strategic Networks," 21, no. 3 (2000): 345–67.

[44] Frank Koller, "Lincoln Electric, 67 Straight Years without Layoffs, 82 Straight Years of Profit-Sharing Bonuses," December 11, 2015, www.frankkoller.com/2015/12/lincoln-electric-67-straight-years-without-layoffs-82-straight-years-of-profit-sharing-bonuses/; Norman D. Fast and Norman A. Berg, *The Lincoln Electric Company*, Harvard Business School Case, 1975.

[45] "Corporate Culture in South Korea: Loosening Their Ties," *Economist*, November 28, 2015. https://www.economist.com/news/

business/21679214-punishing-work-culture-gradually-being-relaxed-loosening-their-ties.

[46] Eleni Mantzari et al., "Personal Financial Incentives for Changing Habitual Health-Related Behaviors: A Systematic Review and Meta-analysis," *Preventive Medicine* 75 (2015): 75–85; Alfie Kohn, *Punished by Rewards: The Trouble with Gold Stars, Incentive Plans, A's, Praise, and Other Bribes* (New York: Houghton Mifflin Harcourt, 1999).

[47] Rita Pyrillis, "Avoid Culture Shock When Rewarding International Employees," Workforce, August 23, 2011, www.workforce.com/articles/avoid-culture-shock-when-rewarding-international-employees.

[48] Norifumi Kawai and Roger Strange, "Subsidiary Autonomy and Performance in Japanese Multinationals in Europe," *International Business Review* 23, no. 3 (2014): 504–15.

[49] Francesco Ciabuschi, Henrik Dellestrand, and Ulf Holm, "The Role of Headquarters in the Contemporary MNC," *Journal of International Management* 18, no. 3 (2012): 213–23.

[50] Vladimir Pucik, Paul Evans, Ingmar Bjorkman, Shad Morris, "The Global Challenge: International Human Resource Management, 3rd Edition," (2017). Chicago Business Press, Chicago.

[51] Justin M. Taylor, Alecia M. Santuzzi, and Derrick L. Cogburn, "Trust and Member Satisfaction in a Developing Virtual Organization: The Roles of Leader Contact and Experience with Technology," *International Journal of Social and Organizational Dynamics in IT (IJSODIT)* 3, no. 1 (2013): 32–46.

[52] Jacob Kastrenakes, "Wi-Fi Alliance Promises Faster Wi-Fi in New Products This Year," *Verge*, June 29, 2016, www.theverge.com/2016/6/29/12053936/wi-fi-alliance-updates-80211ac-certification-faster-speeds; "Who We Are," www.wi-fi.org/who-we-are (accessed July 14, 2017).

[53] Sam Levin and Nicky Woolf, "Tesla Driver Killed while Using Autopilot Was Watching Harry Potter, Witness Says," *Guardian*, July 1, 2016, https://www.theguardian.com/technology/2016/jul/01/tesla-driver-killed-autopilot-self-driving-car-harry-potter; Yen Tran, Volker Mahnke, and Björn Ambos, "The Effect of Quantity, Quality and Timing of Headquarters-Initiated Knowledge Flows on Subsidiary Performance," *Management International Review* 50, no. 4 (2010): 493–511.

[54] Fred Lambert, "Tesla Autopilot 2.0: Next Gen Autopilot Powered by More Radar, New Triple Camera, Some Equipment Already in Production," Electrek, August 11, 2016, https://electrek.co/2016/08/11/tesla-autopilot-2-0-next-gen-radar-triple-camera-production/.

[55] Karl Ulrich, "*Fundamentals of Product Modularity*," in *Management of Design* (Amsterdam: Springer Netherlands, 1994), 219–31.

[56] Bengt Halvorson, "2014 Lexus GX 460 Review," Car Connection www.thecarconnection.com/overview/lexus_gx-460_2014 (accessed December 8, 2016).

[57] Michael A. Cusumano and Kentarō Nobeoka, *Thinking Beyond Lean: How Multi-Project Management Is Transforming Product Development at Toyota and Other Companies* (New York: Simon and Schuster, 1998).

[58] Davis Z. Morris, "Why Google Canceled Project Ara," *Fortune*, September 3, 2016, http://fortune.com/2016/09/03/why-google-canceled-project-ara/.

[59] Ina Fried, "Google Delays Test of Project Ara, Its Modular Smartphone, Until 2016," Recode, August 17, 2015, www.recode.net/2015/8/17/11617786/google-delays-project-ara-its-modular-smartphone-until-2016.

[60] Anil K. Gupta and Vijay Govindarajan, "Organizing for Knowledge Flows within MNCs," *International Business Review* 3, no. 4 (1994): 443–57.

[61] L. Felipe Monteiro, Niklas Arvidsson, and Julian Birkinshaw, "Knowledge Flows within Multinational Corporations: Explaining Subsidiary Isolation and Its Performance Implications," *Organization Science* 19, no. 1 (2008): 90–107.

[62] "Where We Work," and "Our Governance," International Finance Corporation, www.ifc.org/ (accessed May 1, 2017).

[63] Shad S. Morris, James B. Oldroyd, and Sita Ramaswami, "Scaling up Your Story: An Experiment in Global Knowledge Sharing at the World Bank," *Long-Range Planning* 49, no. 1 (2016): 1–14.

[64] Michael R. Parke, Elizabeth Margaret Campbell, and Kathryn M. Bartol, "Setting the Stage for Virtual Team Development: Designing Teams to Foster Knowledge Sharing," *Academy of Management Proceedings* January 2014, meeting abstract supplement, 17244; Yong Sauk Hau et al., "The Effects of Individual Motivations and Social Capital on Employees' Tacit and Explicit Knowledge Sharing Intentions," *International Journal of Information Management* 33, no. 2 (2013): 356–66.

[65] David Grosse Kathoefer and Jens Leker, "Knowledge Transfer in Academia: An Exploratory Study on the Not-Invented-Here Syndrome," *The Journal of Technology Transfer* 37, no. 5 (2012): 658–75.

[66] Jane F. Maley and Miriam Moeller, "Global Performance Management Systems: The Role of Trust as Perceived by Country Managers," *Journal of Business Research* 67, no. 1 (2014): 2803–10.

[67] Yi-Ying Chang, Yaping Gong, and Mike W. Peng, "Expatriate Knowledge Transfer, Subsidiary Absorptive Capacity, and Subsidiary Performance," *Academy of Management Journal* 55, no. 4 (2012): 927–48.

[68] "Who We Are," Inditex, www.inditex.com/en/our_group (accessed December 9, 2016).

[69] Graham Ruddick, "How Zara Became the World's Biggest Fashion Retailer," *Telegraph*, October 20, 2014, www.telegraph.co.uk/finance/newsbysector/retailandconsumer/11172562/How-Inditex-became-the-worlds-biggest-fashion-retailer.html.

[70] Ruddick, "How Zara Became the World's Biggest Fashion Retailer."

[71] Ruddick, "How Zara Became the World's Biggest Fashion Retailer."

CHAPTER **16**

Global Leadership

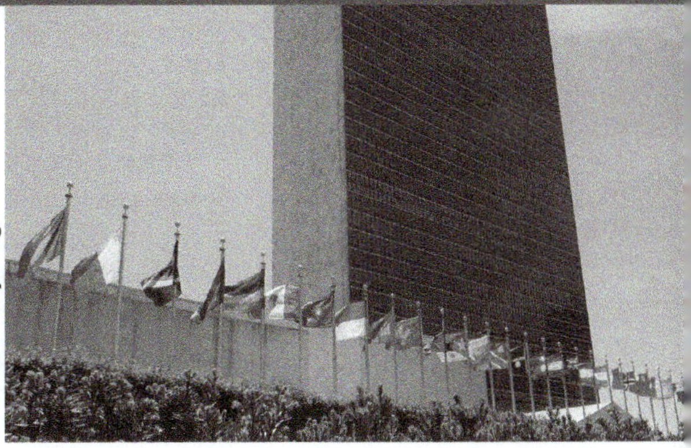
WW News/Getty Images

Introduction

Most business leaders agree that global leadership requires a different skill set than domestic leadership. Global leaders represent a rare and unique breed. These are people with cultural intelligence who are also able to manage in a globally complex world, to inspire others to collaborate across borders, and to shape the societies in which they operate.

We've identified eight key skills for global leaders, and we discuss them in this chapter. We also point out some things you can do once you become a manager in order to develop global leadership skills in others. After all, this is what global leaders do: they inspire others to pursue something greater than themselves in a global context. Finally, we show how you can develop these skills, even if you have not yet entered the workforce. The process starts with seeking opportunities in school, at home, and in work. It requires you to be flexible about your career plans and perhaps be open to visiting or living in countries and cities that might put you outside your comfort zone.

LEARNING OBJECTIVES

After exploring this chapter you will be able to:

1. **Explain** the nature and role of global leadership
2. **Identify** specific leadership competencies and their value in a global context
3. **Describe** ways to develop leadership competencies in others
4. **Develop** a plan to improve your global leadership skills

16.1 What Is Global Leadership?

LEARNING OBJECTIVE

Explain the nature and role of global leadership.

According to one survey of senior executives, 76 percent believe their companies need to develop global leadership competencies, and only 7 percent think they are doing so effectively.

In addition, roughly 30 percent of U.S. companies admit they have not fully exploited their international growth opportunities because they do not have sufficient global leaders among their ranks.[1]

global leadership the process of influencing others to adopt a positive vision in a global context

Global leadership is the process of influencing others to willingly pursue a positive vision in a global context.[2] It demands unique skills because of the context in which the leader's influence is exercised. For example, Paul Polman, CEO of Unilever, helps us understand what it means to be a leader who takes bold action and inspires others toward a positive vision in a global context. For example, Paul demonstrated courage by creating a bold plan to double his company's revenue and halve its global carbon footprint. This provided a common purpose for Unilever employees throughout the world. But he didn't stop there; he then empowered his employees to find innovative ways to achieve this goal and helped them create simple metrics to track the company's progress.

Below we discuss three contextual elements that make global leadership different from leadership in general: (1) complexity, (2) flow, and (3) presence.[3]

The Global Context of Leadership

complexity operating in multiple countries, dealing with various cultures, and, most important, recognizing that optimal solutions will vary across different countries

Global leaders need to influence others in a world that is significantly more complex than a solely domestic setting. **Complexity** arises because managers are operating in multiple countries, dealing with various cultures, and, most important, recognizing that optimal solutions will vary across different countries.[4] Global leaders must have knowledge of the different markets in which they work and must be able to deal with this complexity by adapting and adjusting to different demands. For example, a subsidiary manager based in the Philippines but in charge of customer service globally needs to know that certain customer service approaches for one country will not apply to another; he or she must be able to influence people in both settings in accordance with their own country's culture.

flow the movement of information and relations across countries and business units

presence degree to which an individual is required to move physically across geographic, cultural, and national boundaries, and not just communicate across those boundaries through the use of technology

Flow is the movement of information and relationships across countries and business units. Global leaders must be able to span boundaries by encouraging flow, that is, by getting people and business units to trust and communicate with one another and take on different perspectives.[5] For example, a manager in charge of bringing new customers to the online survey company Qualtrics must be able to share information across the different country markets in which the company operates in order to identify potential customers and learn what to do to win their business.

The final dimension that global leaders must manage is presence. **Presence** is the degree to which an individual is required to move physically across geographic, cultural, and national boundaries, and not just communicate across those through the use of technology.[6] Global leaders, such as expatriates who live and work outside their home country, require a much higher degree of presence than domestic leaders.[7] Not only must they successfully settle in a foreign country, but they must also travel back to headquarters and interact and communicate with people there.[8]

Combined, the three dimensions of complexity, flow, and presence represent the contextual demands of global leadership (see **Figure 16.1**). By influencing others within this global context, leaders understand that they play a role in transforming not only their companies but also the societies in which they operate.[9]

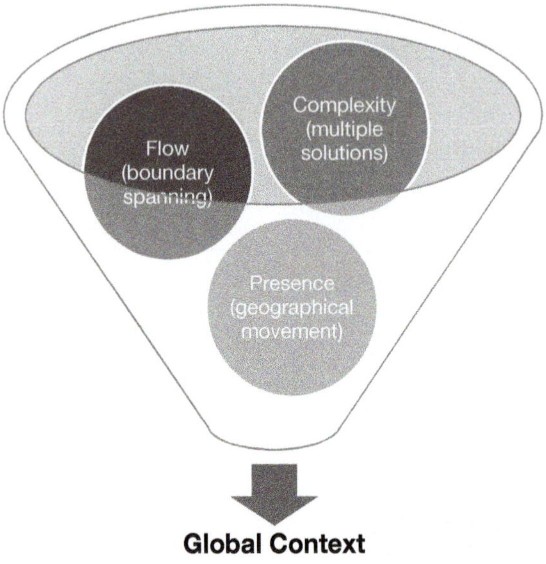

FIGURE 16.1 **The "global" in global leadership**

The Need for Global Leadership

It's sometimes said that if you can successfully lead a global company, you can successfully lead a domestic company, but the reverse is not true at all. When David Whitlam, former CEO of Whirlpool, was engaged in helping to lead the company from being a domestic U.S. player to a global company, he commented, "I've often said that there's only one thing that wakes me up in the middle of the night. It's not our financial performance or economic issues in general. It's worrying about whether or not we have the right skills and capabilities to pull the strategy off. . . . It is a simple and inescapable fact that the skills and capabilities required to manage a global company are different from those required for a domestic company."[10]

To grow successfully abroad, companies need sufficient global leadership among all ranks, but especially among those individuals who can influence decisions that are made across national borders.[11] However, many organizations struggle to develop people with global leadership skills.[12] A big part of this stems from the fact that, too often, lower-level managers don't rate developing their own global leadership as a high priority.[13] Instead, they see competencies like strategic thinking and execution, which help them with their immediate responsibilities, as most important to their performance, and they pursue those skills. As these managers rise through the organization to positions in which global leadership becomes a central priority, it becomes clear they have made little effort to develop the global competency they need. Developing global leadership is no easy task, however, and requires significant effort.

Effective global leaders become who they are by cultivating particular ways of interpreting the world. They develop competencies that enable them to interpret the world differently and to react effectively to those interpretations.[14] One defining factor is that global leaders have unique and identifiable traits.[15] For instance, global leaders are curious about the world and about people different from themselves. This interest inspires visionary initiatives that can lead organizations to span national boundaries. But while many people think leaders are born and not made, evidence indicates that leadership skills can be developed.[16]

One company that has made a lot of effort to develop global leaders is Unilever, the U.K.-based maker of Suave shampoo, Pond's beauty creams, Hellman's mayonnaise, and Lipton tea.[17] Unilever is the world's second-largest consumer goods company and operates in nearly 200 countries.[18] To develop leaders able to manage in this global context, Unilever has made tremendous efforts to put global leadership development front and center. As Unilever CEO Paul Polman points out, "The Unilever Leadership Development Program prepares our future leaders for an increasingly volatile and uncertain world where the only true differentiation between companies is the quality of leadership."[19]

The idea behind the program is to help leaders learn to think differently about their purpose as leaders and the way they manage in a global context. It consists of four days of intensive training and self-reflection, during which participants are expected to be completely open with each other about their global leadership needs. As they focus on their personal vision statement and leadership competencies, they are instructed to create a leadership development plan that identifies the training and experiences necessary to lead in a global environment. Unilever believes that for people to obtain truly global leadership skills, they need more than just international experience; they need to learn to see the world from a global perspective and be able to take context into account when making decisions. As one employee stated, "Leadership at Unilever is about being able to make quick decisions and execute amid an environment of continuous change and complexity."[20] That level of decision-making and execution ability requires a global mind-set—and much more.

Another example of a great global leader at Unilever is Anat Gabriel. Gabriel is the CEO of Unilever Israel, a relatively small operation that sells many global Unilever brands like Dove soap and Lipton tea, as well as many brands developed just for the local market, such as a breakfast cereal brand called Telma. The company expects Gabriel to be a global leader. She not only has to achieve her goals for profitable growth in Israel by selling local products that meet local tastes, but she also needs to promote the company's global brands that may not intuitively be appreciated by local consumers. Sometimes, she says, this requires trade-offs. Decisions to support global brands can take away from local brands like Telma. "I must work with my team to align our agenda locally in Israel with the broader Unilever enterprise agenda. I need to help my people see how the pieces of the puzzle fit together," she says.[21] This goal requires Gabriel to manage complexity, flow, and place—all at the same time.

Gabriel provides an example of the need for companies to develop global leaders with a strong global mind-set, an ability to work across functions, and a strong vision of what the corporation is trying to accomplish in order to serve the global company. Simultaneously, companies must also develop leaders with a deep understanding of what local customers want, the resilience to adapt to the local context, and the ability to adapt to different cultures. What this all means is that more companies are (or should be) requiring global leadership competencies of their managers.

16.2 Global Leadership Competencies

LEARNING OBJECTIVE

Identify specific leadership competencies and their value in a global context.

Every year, *Fortune* magazine creates a list of the world's fifty greatest leaders. These people are from business, government, the nonprofit sector, and sports. Some may wonder how *Fortune* determines who these leaders are. The list is compiled based on how effective people are at making life better for others. The editors of *Fortune* point out that great leaders can be found everywhere and that their sphere of influence does not necessarily have to be massive, but it must be globally impactful. For example, H. R. McMaster is the U.S. National Security Advisor under President Donald Trump. McMaster was selected as a global leader because of his innovative and unconventional practices of more humanely leading military units. McMaster was successful in stabilizing a city that had been rife with ethnic conflict.[22]

Most managers agree that global leadership competencies are different from those required to lead domestically, but that is about as far as agreement goes. The skills needed for global leadership and the best way to acquire them are often debated. Nevertheless, a substantial amount of research addresses the question of what competencies global leaders need to be effective and how these can be developed.[23] Based on the collective work of many scholars and our own experience consulting for dozens of multinational companies, we've narrowed down a core set of competencies that help to shape global leaders.

The general competencies needed to lead global organizations are collaborative synergy, contextual resilience, cultural intelligence, and personal integrity. In addition, global leaders must possess company-related competencies of corporate vision and functional excellence, as well as location-related competencies of global mind-set and market savvy (see **Figure 16.2**).[24]

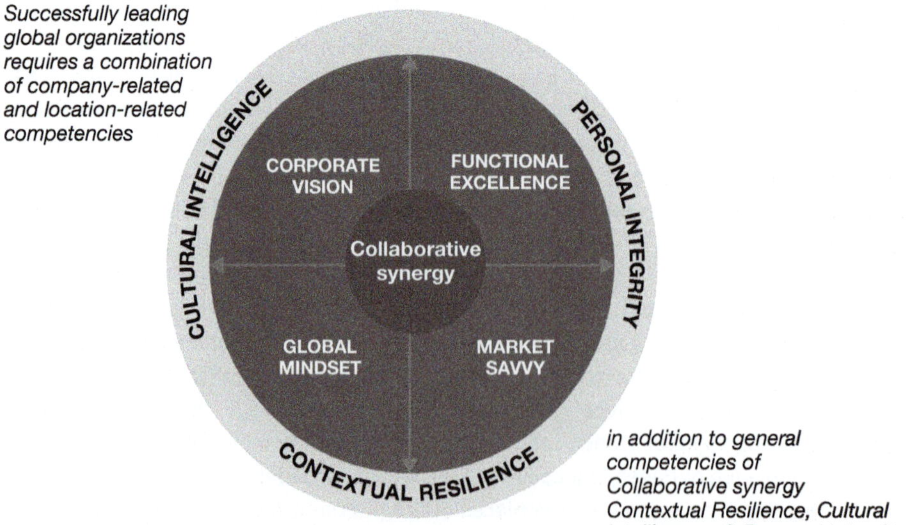
Successfully leading global organizations requires a combination of company-related and location-related competencies
CULTURAL INTELLIGENCE
PERSONAL INTEGRITY
CORPORATE VISION
FUNCTIONAL EXCELLENCE
Collaborative synergy
GLOBAL MINDSET
MARKET SAVVY
CONTEXTUAL RESILIENCE
in addition to general competencies of Collaborative synergy Contextual Resilience, Cultural Intelligence, & Personal Integrity

FIGURE 16.2 **Global leadership competencies** Central to global leaders is their ability to help people collaborate across borders. Corporate vision and functional excellence represent company related competencies. Global mindset and market savvy represent location-related competencies.

General Competencies

At the core of the global leadership competency model is collaborative synergy, which represents the foundation of leadership, regardless of whether one works in a domestic or global environment. Encircling collaborative synergy are three general competencies necessary for success in any global setting: cultural intelligence, contextual resilience, and personal integrity. These competencies represent basic leadership survival skills when operating in a foreign environment. Leaders without these skills will be unable to function in a global environment and will be on shaky ground even in a domestic posting.

ullstein bild/Getty Images

FIGURE 16.3 **Gandhi defines leadership** Gandhi helped bring people together to build synergistic collaboration. He said, "I suppose leadership at one time meant muscles, but today it means getting along with people."

Collaborative Synergy At the core of global leadership is the ability to be a collaborative leader—to create an environment where people understand that success for one member of the team means success for all members of the team. This is called **collaborative synergy**. These leaders are good at communicating with both subordinates and their leaders, helping them feel like part of a team. They foster an environment where individuals are interested in helping one another to achieve goals. They encourage others not only to reach their full potential but also to help their peers reach full potential as well.

For instance, Mahatma Gandhi, shown in **Figure 16.3**, fought against the British rule of India without a gun and won; he demonstrated a strong ability to help others see how success for one group meant success for others. One of the arguments put forth to explain why India was not ready for independence was the fighting between its different political and religious groups. Gandhi therefore communicated with Muslims, Hindus, Buddhists, and Christians to show them how gains for one group could lead to gains for the others. He helped them see the value of celebrating each other's victories. He also showed British government officials the benefits of an independent India. Gandhi thereby helped unify India in a peaceful and nonviolent manner, and the country gained independence in 1947.[25] His ability to foster collaborative synergy among all the actors in India's drive for independence is one of the core characteristics that place him among the most memorable leaders in history.[26]

collaborative synergy the ability to create an environment where people understand that success for one member of the team means success for all members of the team

cultural intelligence the ability to adapt and operate effectively across different cultural settings

Cultural Intelligence Another primary component of global leadership is **cultural intelligence**, the ability to adapt and function across different cultural settings.[27] A person with high cultural intelligence is able to differentiate features of someone else's behavior that relate to culture and alter his or her own expressions when a cultural encounter requires it. Such people are often referred to as "cultural chameleons" because they can blend into many different local environments quickly.[28] They acquire a bit of the local language and learn something about the local history and other facts before engaging in the new culture in order to show their interest in it and to learn about it more quickly while there. Higher cultural intelligence is not associated with any particular personality type. Rather, it's found in people who have the desire and understanding necessary to interact effectively with people from different cultures and to see commonalities among people[29] (see **Figure 16.4**).

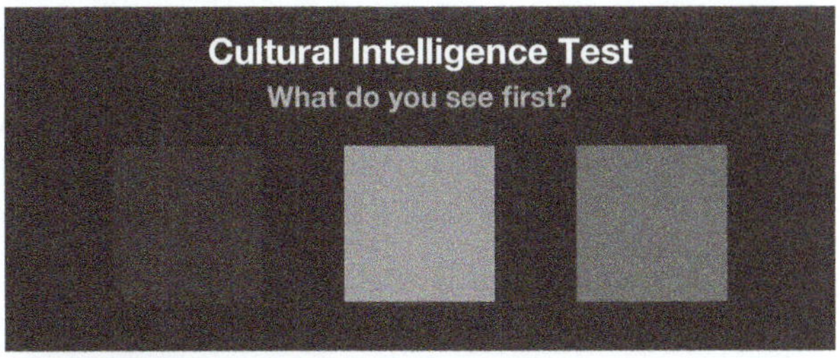
Cultural Intelligence Test
What do you see first?

FIGURE 16.4 **Cultural intelligence test** People taking this test often see different colors (what is different among the items) rather than seeing three squares (what is common to all). Seeing all three objects as squares demonstrates the ability to focus on commonalities. **Source:** Finn Majlergaard, "How Much Cultural Intelligence Do You Have?" Gugin blog, http://gugin.com/how-much-cultural-intelligence-do-you-have/.

For example, when U.S. expatriate John Larsen moved from Detroit to Shanghai to run the Smart Mobility company of Ford Motors in Asia, he recognized the need to adapt to the local culture. Ford Motors started the Smart Mobility company in 2016 in order to become part of the growing transportation services market that companies like Uber and Lyft were developing. This market represented tremendous opportunities for the company all over the world, especially in China, where the need for alternate modes of transportation was growing.[30] To engage with his employees and customers, Larsen would talk about not only business but also the local culture. He spoke Mandarin whenever he could and paused when someone behaved in a way that was inconsistent with what he expected as their boss. He would ask himself, "Is this the way of behaving consistent with cultural norms or is it an idiosyncrasy of the individual with whom I'm dealing?"[31] His strong desire and ability to adapt to the local culture provided Larsen with the cultural intelligence necessary to more effectively lead his team in China.

Another U.S. expatriate manager worked as a project leader for one of HP's subsidiaries in Israel.[32] As the manager floated ideas to the Israeli engineers on the team, they repeatedly criticized them and cited several serious flaws. Based on these interactions, the manager concluded that Israelis are rude and do not like outsiders leading them. However, a bit of market savvy would have helped him realize he was mistakenly reading open disagreement with superiors as an attack against authority. He would have understood that engineers in general are more direct than nonengineers, and that Israel is a very egalitarian country in which lower-level employees are encouraged to speak as equals with their managers. These factors produced a team whose members were very open about the way they felt, not a team that was necessarily rude or spiteful.

contextual resilience a leader's ability to anticipate roadblocks and find better ways of doing things in a complex, cross-border environment

Contextual Resilience

Contextual resilience is a leader's ability to anticipate roadblocks and find better ways of doing things in a complex, cross-border environment. It is the ability to hold fast to objectives while operating in an environment that constantly interferes with plans.[33] While most people have a certain level of ability to bounce back after encountering a difficult or unexpected situation, contextual resilience enables a leader to effectively deal with stresses and new situations—often before they become real problems for the organization.

Developing contextual resilience requires the courage to confront painful realities, the faith that a solution will be found when one isn't immediately evident, and the tenacity to hold on when it seems there is no way around a problem.[34] It also requires leaders to be self-aware. Self-awareness helps them eliminate behaviors that don't work and build on those that do.

For example, the U.S. Army is acting on research about contextual resilience to improve the resilience of soldiers deployed in harsh contexts by having them undergo a series of training exercises to help them more effectively recover from combat trauma. Soldiers are trained to minimize catastrophic thinking, for example, by identifying worst-case and best-case outcomes. Most people's natural inclination is to dwell on the worst-case scenario (catastrophe). A soldier who receives a negative performance evaluation from a commanding officer might therefore think, "I won't be recommended for promotion. I could even be kicked off my platoon." That's the worst-case scenario. The best case might be, "The negative report was a mistake." The soldiers are then taught to think about the most likely case, which is neither of these, and that means it's not as bad as the worst case.[35] By developing contextual resilience, individuals are able not only to overcome performance reviews, but to understand how more catastrophic events like the raid on a subsidiary office by government officials in Bolivia or demands for protection money from the local mafia in Bulgaria might be more effectively overcome—or at least endured.

personal integrity a demonstration of honesty and high ethical standards in work

Personal Integrity

Of all the competencies related to global leadership, integrity might be the most underappreciated. Leaders with **personal integrity** demonstrate honesty and high ethical standards in all their work. Perhaps you've heard people say, "Integrity is doing the right thing when no one is watching." However, integrity is more than this; it actually consists of two components.

The first component of integrity is adherence to a moral or ethical principle. This isn't simple compliance with rules or laws; it implies having a philosophical understanding of the reasons *behind* the rules. Thus, having integrity means knowing why a rule or social norm exists and how to apply that principle in contexts outside your home country. For example, the country manager of a German elevator company in India had to deal with informal norms of corruption that were inconsistent with his own values. He said, "I've had to fire nearly half my top-level managers due to corruption. If I were strictly following our rules, I would have fired many more."[36] He did not fire the rest because he realized that he needed to be patient in helping the employees understand the principles behind the company's philosophy on bribery.

The second component of integrity is the pursuit of continual self-improvement. Everyone makes mistakes, and doing so does not mean you are no longer a person of integrity. Instead, having integrity means you possess the strength of character to learn from mistakes and from inconsistencies in your moral principles. You act on the best information available, and if you later learn you should have acted differently, you do your best to fix any damage and then move forward again, learning from the overall experience.

The late Colonel Eric Kail, a professor at West Point, argued that integrity is a competency we develop over time, not one we are born with. This means you can begin today to develop and strengthen integrity, such as by embracing higher-level principles about how to behave, accepting that you may make mistakes in applying those principles in your life, and then learning to rise above those mistakes in the future.[37]

Company-Related Competencies

Corporate vision and functional excellence are the two company-related competencies necessary to lead global organizations. When someone has high levels of corporate vision and functional excellence, they have knowledge that is specific to the company in which they are operating. These competencies aren't transferred to other companies as easily as the more general competencies.

corporate vision understanding the company's overarching objectives and helping individuals stay focused on these objectives

Corporate Vision

Effective global leaders regularly engage with other leaders within the corporate headquarters about how to align activities to create value for the company. **Corporate vision** is about helping the organization to stay focused on its core capabilities. Such leaders need to play the difficult role of eliminating otherwise good opportunities in local countries that would distract the organization from its strategic focus.

To assess whether you have sufficient corporate vision, ask yourself, "To what extent do I build and contribute to the global company culture?" To build such a company culture you need to engage in communication with members of corporate headquarters to ensure you understand the goals of the global company and are working to meet those goals. You also need to think about your own behavior and how it relates to the corporation's vision and mission.

UPS, the worldwide leader in global shipping and logistics, has a vision of "Committed to More." This includes more sustainable solutions, more efficiency, and more ways to give back. Following this vision, the firm is pioneering the use of electric and propane-fueled trucks, as shown in **Figure 16.5**.

The company is exemplary in regularly bringing together its global subsidiary managers in order to communicate and systematically clarify the company strategy throughout the entire organization. This ensures that subsidiary managers possess a strong vision of how their local decisions need to align with and support the larger UPS organization. The subsidiary managers also engage in "strategy mapping games" so that every individual leader can translate the corporate vision into priorities and goals that matter to the company.[38]

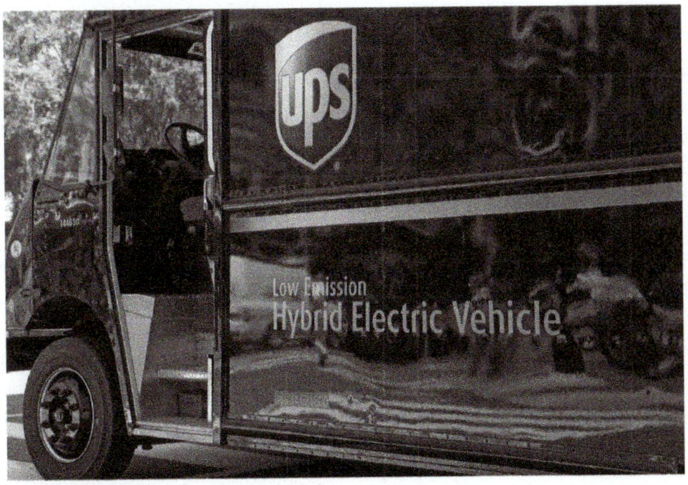

B Christopher/Alamy Stock Photo

FIGURE 16.5 UPS and innovation UPS's vision encourages its people to innovate in the development of emissions-efficient vehicles, like this hybrid electric truck.

functional excellence the ability to collaborate with different units and functions within the company

Functional Excellence Effective leaders possess functional skills that enable them to actively build and share expertise about the different functional units in their local operations. These leaders use their expertise to help employees add value to the products and services they deliver. Overall, someone who possesses **functional excellence** is effective at actively seeking ideas from different functional and operational groups within the company. He or she listens to others outside their team and function, and engages them in decision-making.

For example, one manager at Honeywell in China pointed out the need to interact across functions and divisions. As a diverse company, Honeywell makes turbo chargers for cars, engines for airplanes, and air filter systems. However, these products are developed by three separate divisions. The manager commented, "It's so easy to get into a silo mentality here. We just focus on what we're doing in our own division but often fail to recognize good ideas from other divisions that we can use." This manager then went on to explain how he made it a point to reach out to managers in other divisions on a regular basis to ensure they are coordinating their efforts and learning from one another. The most recent initiative that had come from these interactions was the introduction of turbo engine technology from one division to help improve air flow in the filter system developed in a different division. Because of his functional excellence capability, this manager was able to improve an existing product by bringing in technology from a seemingly unrelated product from a different part of the organization[39] (see **Figure 16.6**).

Location-Related Competencies

Market savvy and global mind-set are the two location-related competencies necessary to lead global organizations. Someone with a high level of market savvy and a global mind-set has knowledge specific to the contexts in which he or she is operating. Market savvy tends to be specific to one local market, whereas global mind-set is specific to multiple market contexts. Both represent a deep understanding of a local context in terms of customer needs and market gaps.

Market savvy a leader's ability to be accountable for the products and services they deliver in a local market

Market Savvy **Market savvy** is leaders' ability to hold themselves accountable for the products and services they deliver to clients and the society in which they are operating. It is more than mere knowledge of local customs, preferences, and norms; it is a skill that enables a leader to understand and observe the underlying needs of customers. To understand whether you

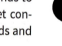

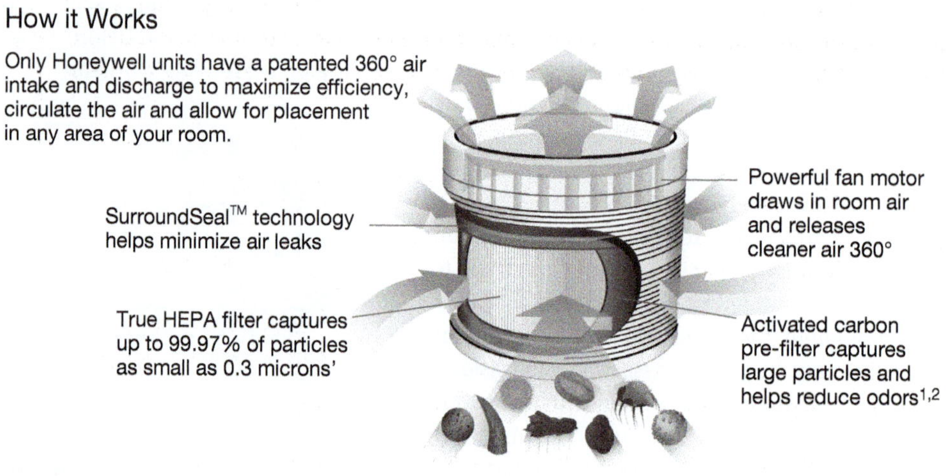

How it Works
Only Honeywell units have a patented 360° air intake and discharge to maximize efficiency, circulate the air and allow for placement in any area of your room.
SurroundSeal™ technology helps minimize air leaks
True HEPA filter captures up to 99.97% of particles as small as 0.3 microns'
Powerful fan motor draws in room air and releases cleaner air 360°
Activated carbon pre-filter captures large particles and helps reduce odors1,2

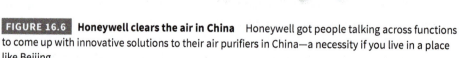

FIGURE 16.6 **Honeywell clears the air in China** Honeywell got people talking across functions to come up with innovative solutions to their air purifiers in China—a necessity if you live in a place like Beijing.

have a high level of market savvy, ask yourself, "To what extent do I work to meet or exceed the client's requests, needs, or goals to ensure successful solutions?" You can develop market savvy by observing customers in their local setting, asking probing questions, and offering unique solutions. Question your existing assumptions about what the client actually needs.

For example, one engineer at the Swiss precision-scale maker Mettler-Toledo, shown in **Figure 16.7**, took a call from a new customer who had purchased one of the company's scales and said it was broken. The marketing and sales people were not able to solve the customer's problem, so the engineer went to the site. Instead of asking what was wrong with the scale, the engineer asked the customer to show him how she used it and why. He quickly realized the client had purchased the high-end scale to measure chemicals in a different way than Mettler-Toledo had anticipated. The encounter gave the engineer an idea for developing a new scale that would meet the needs of a different client base. This example of market savvy shows the importance of understanding the client's underlying needs.[40]

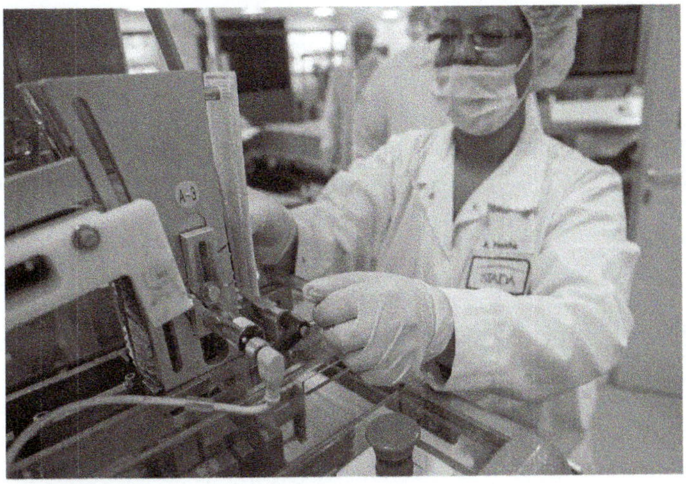

Krisztian Bocsi/Bloomberg/Getty Images

FIGURE 16.7 **Market savvy at Mettler-Toledo** Mettler-Toledo employees interact with customers to understand how they use the company's precision scales, thus increasing their market savvy.

Global Mind-set Managers with a **global mind-set** are better than their peers at bringing together ideas from diverse country contexts. They constantly scan the global environment and use this information to change their behaviors and those of people around them.[41] They monitor industry trends and assess interesting data from all over the world. The result is an improved ability to bring in best-practice ideas from different locations and combine them to drive more effective and innovative results. In contrast to what some might assume, being skilled at applying a global mind-set doesn't mean just understanding what's going on in the world; rather, it means bringing in the best ideas from different locations and being open to doing things differently.

global mind-set the ability to scan the global market and bring together ideas from diverse contexts

For example, Owens Corning has two major business units that require different leadership skills. The building materials division is based in the United States and primarily operates there. However, the composites business makes products in many different countries. Owens Corning found that in order to be competitive, managers of the composite business must possess global mind-set as a vital competency. As a result, the company focuses on building this competency in its employees. In fact, companies like Owens Corning and Honeywell include global mind-set as one of the core capabilities needed by their employees and managers, regardless of position.[42]

As a leader, it's important to assess your capabilities on these eight global skills. Section 16.4 provides some ideas on how you might develop your skills further. But before we get there, you'll learn in the next section how you can help to develop these skills in others.

16.3 Building Global Leadership Competencies in Others

LEARNING OBJECTIVE

Describe ways to develop leadership competencies in others.

Companies often consider international experience as a proxy for global leadership ability, but not all international experience is created equal. A U.S. executive who goes to Brazil could send her children to foreign schools, live and socialize in a gated compound with other expatriates, and deal only with other expatriate senior managers at work. In gaining that kind of "foreign experience," essentially bringing her native country with her, she will learn skills very different from those learned by someone who makes an effort to interact with and get to know the local employees, thereby learning something about the local culture and language.

For example, Anheuser-Busch InBev, the Belgian beer company known for producing Budweiser and Corona, says the types of challenges people experience during international assignments are more significant than the function or role in which they experience them. These employees need to have experiences that come from taking on the following roles[43]:

- Challenging people roles, in which leaders acquire experience supervising and developing large numbers of people
- Challenging functional roles, in which leaders work outside their area of functional expertise
- Challenging commercial roles, in which leaders gain the customer-facing experience essential for developing brand-related competencies
- Challenging expertise roles, in which each individual develops skills in a functional area of expertise (such as finance or marketing) to fall back on if needed

In addition to ensuring people are exposed to the right roles during their international assignments, as a manager you can also help build leaders' skills through mentoring and coaching. In fact, Millennials—people aged 18 to 35—say they want coaching 50 percent more often than older generations.[44]

Research has shown that managers who have more frequent conversations with their employees are able to get better results from them and to develop them into better leaders. The research also identifies what managers talk about during these conversations and suggests that the topics of conversation matter. The most effective conversations focus on a few key activities that make up what's called the "RAP framework."[45]

RAP stands for (1) recognizing and reviewing past behaviors, (2) aligning future behaviors for improved performance, and (3) providing purpose for those future behaviors. Let's see how these help develop global leadership competencies (see **Figure 16.8**).

R. First, managers *recognized* the strengths of potential leaders, both identifying and praising them. They made sure the individuals felt recognized for the good work they were doing and for the specific skills they possessed. Managers also provided clear developmental feedback to potential leaders. They *reviewed* past performance together, but they spent only a short time doing so. They concentrated instead on ensuring both parties understood the employee's specific skill gaps and on helping the employee create an action plan to fill in these gaps in the future.

A. Next, managers provided coaching to help the potential leader *align* his or her actions with the goals they had modified and set. The manager was careful not to provide a plan—leaving that to the individual—but rather helped the future leader ensure that his or her personal leadership development plan was in place and moving forward.

P. Finally, managers *provided purpose* and clarity to ensure the potential leader was making a difference for the company. Providing purpose is about helping the employee understand why the goals and objectives they have set are actually important for the organization and for their own personal fulfillment. For example, how does this help make a difference for the customers they are trying to serve? How does it help the employees working for the company? This served to bind the individual's vision of what they needed to do with the goals of the company and inspire the person to work hard for the organizational goals.

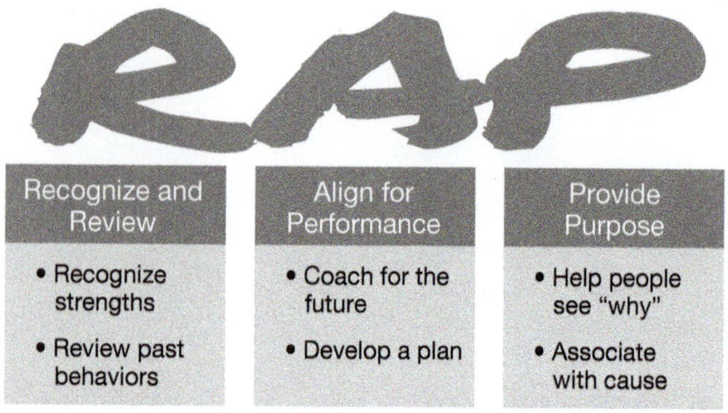

FIGURE 16.8 **RAP framework**

By walking through the RAP framework with potential leaders on a regular basis, managers can develop these employees, enhancing their international experiences and helping them learn from the different challenges they experience in their international roles. Log in to WileyPLUS to watch a video that provides a clear picture of how to implement the RAP framework to develop global leadership competencies in your employees and peers.

WileyPLUS

See Whiteboard Video: RAP Framework

16.4 Building Global Leadership Competencies in Yourself

LEARNING OBJECTIVE

Develop a plan to improve your global leadership skills.

You decide how much you will invest in developing your global leadership skills. While companies should help develop their global leaders, and many try to do so, the most successful global leaders are those who take the initiative themselves. Thus, we highlight here three things you can start doing now to improve your global leadership competencies.

Find Academic Environments That Encourage Global Development

Attending seminars, getting coaching, and reading books about leadership can all be helpful up to a point. However, people learn the most when they do things they haven't done before.[46] You can start that process by getting involved in academic programs that offer opportunities to serve, gain exposure to a foreign language, study abroad, observe cross-cultural business, or study history.

For example, at Northeastern University in Boston, Massachusetts, undergraduate students majoring in international business are required to take a global competency inventory developed by the Kozai Group before their international experience. The international experience consists of one year of coursework in another country, followed by six months of full-time work experience in that country. Upon their return, students retake the assessment to identify their areas of growth. Results of this testing have shown that students significantly improve their overall global leadership ability.[47]

Other schools have students create individualized personal development plans based on global leadership skills. The students are then graded on the implementation of their individual development plan each week, the insights they gain, and the adjustments they make to their plan throughout the semester. At the end they write an in-depth paper reflecting on how well they implemented the development plan and what they will do based on it once they graduate.[48] **Figure 16.9** provides an individual development plan you can use to help develop your own global leadership competencies while still in school.

Seek Opportunities at Work and Ask for Help

In your work experience, look for international assignments. For example, one man working for an oil company commented:

> *I was trained as a geologist and spent the first seven years of my career trying to discover oil. One day when I was heading an exploration assignment, they called me to the headquarters and told me that they wanted me to take over the responsibility for*

1. Identify your passion (Of the eight competencies on which you assessed yourself, identify a global leadership competency you most enjoy applying.)
2. Identify your strengths (Which competencies are your strongest? List two to four.)
3. Design your global career (Describe an ideal global career track. What companies will you work for? Where will you live? What type of work will you do?)
4. Short-term career plan (How can you build skills in global leadership? Which behaviors will you change?)

Goals	Actions	Timing

FIGURE 16.9 **Global leadership development plan**

a troubled department of 40 maintenance engineers on the other side of the world. Geology is the noble elite, and maintenance engineering is somewhere between here-and-hell in the value system. I didn't want the job—in fact my first thought was that they were punishing me for some mistake I had made—and I told them that I knew nothing about maintenance engineering. "We're not sending you there to learn about engineering," they said. "We are sending you there to learn about leadership."

With a lot of doubts, I took the job, and I was there for just over four years. And I learned practically everything I know about management and leadership in that job—all I've done since is refine what I picked up there. Fortunately, they sent me on a management training program during the first three months, and that helped me to understand what was happening and how to adjust—otherwise I might not have survived. Afterwards I returned into a more senior position in oil exploration, but I'd completely changed as a result of that experience with the maintenance engineers.[49]

This man later became CEO of one of the largest multinational corporations in the world.

International assignments aren't offered to just anyone. People are more likely to get such positions when they are willing to reach out to managers and others in their company to find out what is needed to qualify. The first hurdle is letting people know you're interested in multicultural experiences.

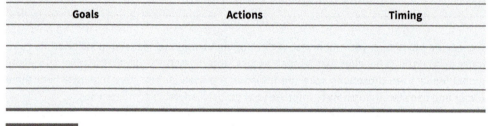

Start by being clear about your ideal, multicultural career path and the types of experiences you seek. A performance review or professional development conversation could be a great time to have these conversations. Your manager can help you clarify your goals and adjust your expectations about what an international assignment entails. That said, don't limit your conversations to these venues. Conduct informal interviews with managers whose geographic areas of focus interest you. Express interest in working with these people. Be enthusiastic, explicit, and open about your goals, and consider the advice and input of others; they may help you realize your goals in ways you hadn't considered.[50]

For example, when approached about a job with a foreign multinational company from South Korea, a U.S. student said, "I'm not interested in living in Korea, but I'd be happy to talk with you more about the position." Then, feeling dishonest, he asked a professor whether he should fly all the way to South Korea for a job he didn't really want. The professor replied that if there was even a 1 percent chance that he wanted the job, he should go. The company flew the student to South Korea for an interview, and after seeing all the opportunities available and learning more about the country, he was convinced this was the place for him to be; he turned down offers from companies in China and the United States to take the job. Since then, the student has said that going to South Korea was one of the best decisions he could have made for his career.[51]

Be Patient and Flexible

The story of the U.S. student taking a job in South Korea shows the importance of identifying opportunities in unlikely places. It also shows the value of being flexible. Even if you have laid the best plans, the greatest opportunities for global leadership development often come in unusual or unexpected ways. Working in a global environment requires much more flexibility than working in a domestic environment. This means being able to choose the trade-offs you are willing to make in achieving your goals.

For example, one U.S. manager at Intel moved to China only because he feared losing his job at home, where many employees were being laid off; he never realized what a career boost the move would be. He enjoyed his time abroad so much that he agreed to take over a new plant being built in Vietnam.[52] Finally, after years of working overseas, he came back to the United States with a secure position in the company as a global leader who understood how to manage Intel's complex global talent pool.

Summary and Case

Summary

LEARNING OBJECTIVE 16.1 Explain the nature and role of global leadership.

In the current economic environment, it is more important than ever to have employees who can think constructively about global issues and operate accordingly. Companies that develop effective global leaders will be nimble in their decision-making and bring value to their shareholders and to society.

LEARNING OBJECTIVE 16.2 Identify specific leadership competencies and their value in a global context.

Competencies that can help ensure success in managing a global company include collaborative synergy, cultural intelligence, contextual resilience, personal integrity, corporate vision, functional excellence, market savvy, and global mind-set.

LEARNING OBJECTIVE 16.3 Describe ways to develop leadership competencies in others.

The RAP framework requires managers to recognize the contributions of their employees, encourage employees to align their actions with personal goals and objectives in ways that support the company and their own goals, and provide employees with a greater purpose or cause.

LEARNING OBJECTIVE 16.4 Develop a plan to improve your global leadership skills.

Anyone interested in developing global skills should find ways to live and work abroad; be patient and flexible, even in adversity; and seek help from managers and mentors.

Case Study

Honeywell Identifies Future Leadership Needs

For the past year, Anshuman had been working as the head of organizational development and learning for the high-growth regions of Honeywell. This assignment required Anshuman to leave his home country of India to live and work in Shanghai, China. Anshuman couldn't help but reflect on his boss's final comment before going home from work the night before: "We can't afford to give profit and loss responsibility to our strategic business group leaders in these high-growth countries. We have too much riding on the future performance of these markets and can't risk someone who doesn't know what they're doing messing it up."

Anshuman thought they needed to give the business unit managers the autonomy necessary to make their own strategic decisions. The problem was, in order to make effective decisions, the business unit managers would need to know how to navigate the local market as well as the Honeywell bureaucracy. It was easy finding one or the other, but finding both seemed a bit daunting. Anshuman and his team began exploring the attributes and competencies needed from future leaders.

Honeywell's HR department has one of the most extensive and thorough archives of data on managers and leaders all over the world. Anshuman and his team started by examining the company's list of twelve behaviors of and six criteria for successful general managers. These factors consisted of things like "makes people better", "takes intelligent risk," and "gets results." After some exploratory analysis to determine which behaviors were most highly correlated with a person being promoted, the team turned to a more predictive model and examined what managers were saying about employees when they promoted them.

What they found was somewhat surprising. The most successful managers were those who spoke up and communicated with the leadership team in New Jersey, the company's headquarters. The most important type of communication revolved around understanding the company's strategy and being able to tie that strategy back to the local environment. This required managers to fly to headquarters and also to invite members from the corporate team to fly to the local subsidiary location.

But communicating with corporate was not enough. Managers needed to have a strong understanding of the movements and shifts in the local environment. For example, if they couldn't negotiate with local suppliers to get the deals the local buyers were getting, then these managers weren't able to succeed in their role. They also needed to be willing to take risks by looking for gaps in the market where customers could be using the product for something different than its original intention.

Anshuman had just presented his findings to the head of HR for Honeywell and was given the green light to develop a specific leadership program for managers in high-growth countries, starting with China as the pilot location. He had designed many leadership programs before, but this time much more was at stake.

Case Discussion Questions

1. What specific leadership traits are most important for Honeywell managers in high-growth regions?
2. How do these global leadership traits differ from domestic leadership traits?
3. How would you create a leadership development program for high-growth region managers using the RAP framework?

Endnotes

[1]P. Ghemawat, "Developing Global Leaders: Companies Must Cultivate Leaders for Global Markets. Dispelling Five Common Myths about Globalization Is a Good Place to Start," *McKinsey Quarterly*, June 2012. http://s3.amazonaws.com/academia.edu.documents/33375465/Ghemawat_2012_Developing_global_leaders.pdf?AWSAccessKeyId=AKIAIWOWYYGZ2Y53UL3A&Expires=1499812288&Signature=ZwE2p7jeFnRTqO73EVMvpKrAe68%3D&response-content-disposition=inline%3B%20filename%3DAs_Developing_global_leaders.pdf.

[2]M. E. Mendenhall, B. S. Reiche, A. Bird, and J. S. Osland, "Defining the 'Global' in Global Leadership," *Journal of World Business* 47, no. 4 (2012): 493–503; M. Mendenhall et al., *Global Leadership: Research, Practice, and Development* (New York: Routledge, 2008).

[3]Mendenhall et al., "Defining the 'Global' in Global Leadership."

[4]S. Ghoshal and D. E. Westney, "Introduction and Overview," in *Organization Theory and the Multinational Corporation*, eds. S. Ghoshal and D. E. Westney, 1–23 (New York: St. Martin's Press, 1993).

[5]J. S. Osland and Allan Bird, "Process Models of Global Leadership Development," in Mendenhall et al., *Global Leadership*, 97–112; A. M. Soederberg and L. Romani,"Boundary Spanning in Global Software Development: A Major Indian Vendor Case," *Academy of Management Proceedings* 2015, no. 1 (January 2014): 11025.

[6]Mendenhall et al. "Defining the 'Global' in Global Leadership."

[7]A. W. Harzing, M. Pudelko, and B. Sebastian Reiche, "The Bridging Role of Expatriates and Inpatriates in Knowledge Transfer in Multinational Corporations," *Human Resource Management 55*, No. 4 (July/August 2016): 679–695.

[8]A. W. Harzing, A. Sorge, and J. Paauwe, "Multinational Companies: A British–German Comparison," in *Challenges for European Management in a Global Context: Experiences from Britain and Germany*, eds. Mike Geppert, Dirk Matten, and Karen Williams (New York: Palgrave Macmillan, 2016), 96.

[9]"Definition of Global Leader," *Financial Times*, http://lexicon.ft.com/Term?term=global-leader (accessed January 2016).

[10]Maruca, Regina Fazio. "The Right Way to Go Global: An interview with Whirlpool CEO David Whitwam." *Harvard Business Review* 72 (1994): 134–134.

[11]Suzanne Snowden, "PwC's 19th Annual Global CEO Survey," PriceWaterhouseCoopers, 2016. https://www.pwc.com/gx/en/ceo-survey/2016/landing-page/pwc-19th-annual-global-ceo-survey.pdf.

[12]GE Look ahead, "The Global Leadership Gap," *Economist*, April 29, 2015, http://gelookahead.economist.com/the-global-leadership-gap/.

[13]P. Ghemawat, "Developing Global Leaders."

[14]M. Javidan and D. Bowen, "The 'Global Mindset' of Managers," *Organizational Dynamics* 42 (2013): 145–55.

[15]Javidan and Bowen, "The 'Global Mindset' of Managers."

[16]L. B. Andersen, A. Bøllingtoft, and C. B. Jacobsen, "Are Leaders Born or Made? Leadership Training Effects on Employee Perceptions of Leadership," in *The 2016 Academy of Management Annual Meeting*, Anaheim, CA, 2016; R. Riggio, "Leaders: Born or Made? The Most Often-Asked Question about Leadership," *Psychology Today*, March 18, 2009.

[17]R. Henson, "Building an Organizational Global Mindset Culture: Implications for Practice," in *Successful Global Leadership* (New York: Palgrave Macmillan, 2016), 261–83.

[18]D. A. Ready and M. E. Peebles, "Developing the Next Generation of Enterprise Leaders," *MIT Sloan Management Review* 57, no. 1 (2015): 43–51.

[19]G. William, K. Palepu, C. Knoop, and M. Preble, "Unilever's Paul Polman: Developing Global Leaders," Harvard Business School case 413-097, May 23, 2013.

[20]Personal conversation with Unilever employee by Shad Morris, May 2017.

[21]Ready and Peebles, "Developing the Next Generation of Enterprise Leaders."

[22]Judy Woodruff, "Who Is H.R. McMaster, Trump's New National Security Adviser?" PBS NewsHour, February 20, 2017. http://www.pbs.org/newshour/bb/h-r-mcmaster-trumps-new-national-security-adviser/.

[23]For reviews of the literature on global leadership competencies, see A. Bird and M. E. Mendenhall, "From Cross-Cultural Management to Global Leadership: Evolution and Adaptation," *Journal of World Business* 51, no. 1 (2016): 115–26; Mark E. Mendenhall, Ming Li, and Joyce S. Osland, "Five Years of Global Leadership Research, 2010–2014: Patterns, Themes, and Future Directions," in *Advances in Global Leadership*, vol. 9, eds. Joyce S. Osland, Ming Li, and Mark E. Mendenhall (Bingley, UK: Emerald Group Publishing, 2016), 401–26; P. Caligiuri and I. Tarique, "Dynamic Cross-Cultural Competencies and Global Leadership Effectiveness," *Journal of World Business* 47, no. 4 (2012): 612–22; A. Bird, "Mapping the Content Domain of Global Leadership Competencies," in Mendenhall et al., *Global Leadership*, 80–96; G. K. Stahl, N. M. Pless, and T. Maak, "Responsible Global Leadership," in Mendenhall et al., *Global Leadership*, 240–59.

[24]S. Morris, S. Snell, and I. Björkman, "An Architectural Framework for Global Talent Management," *Journal of International Business Studies* 47, No. 6 (2016): 723–747; Mendenhall et al., *Global Leadership*.

[25]Louis Fischer, *Gandhi: His Life and Message for the World* (New York: Penguin, 2010).

[26]"Top 28 Greatest Leaders of All Time," TopiBestList, September, 17, 2016, http://topxbestlist.com/greatest-leaders/.

[27]See Chapter 8 on culture for a more detailed discussion of how to build cultural intelligence.

[28]D. Livermore and S. Ang, "Virtual Chaos at WORLDWIDE Rx: How Cultural Intelligence Can Turn Problems into Solutions," *Intercultural Management: A Case-Based Approach to Achieving Complementarity and Synergy*, eds. Christoph Barmeyer and Peter Franklin (New York: Palgrave Macmillan, 2016), 167; S. Ang and L. Van Dyne, *Handbook of Cultural Intelligence* (New York: Routledge, 2015).

[29]W. R. Sieck, L. J. Rasmussen, and J. L. Duran, "Considerations and Best Practices for Developing Cultural Competency Models in Applied Work Domains," in *Critical Issues in Cross Cultural Management*, eds. Jessica L. Wildman, Richard L. Griffith, and Brigitte K. Armon (Switzerland: Springer International, 2016), 33–52.

[30]"Ford Smart Mobility LLC Established to Develop, Invest in Mobility Services; Jim Hackett Named Subsidiary Chairman," Ford Motor Company Mediacenter, March 11, 2016. https://media.ford.com/content/fordmedia/fna/us/en/news/2016/03/11/ford-smart-mobility-llc-established--jim-hackett-named-chairman.html.

[31]Personal interaction with John Larsen, Head of Smart Mobility in Asia, in Shanghai office by Shad Morris, August 2016.

[32]M. Beer, R. Khurana, and J. Weber, "*Hewlett-Packard:* Culture in Changing Times," Harvard Business Case, 2005.

[33]M. K. Linnenluecke, "Resilience in Business and Management Research: A Review of Influential Publications and a Research Agenda," *International Journal of Management Reviews* 19, No. 1 (2015): 4–30.

[34]Steven Snyder, "Why Is Resilience So Hard?" *Harvard Business Review*, November 6, 2013. https://hbr.org/2013/11/why-is-resilience-so-hard.

[35]Martin E. P. Seligman, "Building Resilience," *Harvard Business Review*, April 2011. https://hbr.org/2011/04/building-resilience.

[36]Personal interaction by Shad Morris with Head of ThyssenKrupp in Mumbai, India, 2014.

[37]Colonel Eric Kail, "Leadership Character: The Role of Integrity," *Washington Post*, July 8, 2011. https://www.washingtonpost.com/blogs/guest-insights/post/leadership-character-the-role-of-integrity/2011/04/04/gIQArZL03H_blog.html?utm_term=.de9a4a86b8a1.

[38]J. Keyes, *Implementing the IT Balanced Scorecard: Aligning IT with Corporate Strategy* (Boca Raton, FL: CRC Press, 2016); H. Armitage and C. Scholey, "Using Strategy Maps to Drive Performance," *Management Accounting Guideline,* 2006. http://www.cimaglobal.com/Documents/ImportedDocuments/Tech_MAG_Strategy_Mapping_March07.pdf.

[39]Personal interaction by Shad Morris with Honeywell manager in Shanghai, China, November 2016.

[40]Primary research conducted by the authors, December 2015.

[41]R. Henson, "Building an Organizational Global Mindset Culture: Implications for Practice," in *Successful Global Leadership: Frameworks for Cross-Cultural Managers and Organizations* (New York: Palgrave Macmillan, 2016), 261–83); Javidan and Bowen, "The 'Global Mindset' of Managers."

[42]M. Javidan and D. Bowen, "The Global Mindset: A New Source of Competitive Advantage," *Rotman Management Magazine*, May 1, 2015, 43–47.

[43]V. Pucik, P. Evans, I. Björkman, and S. Morris, *The Global Challenge: International Human Resource Management*, 3rd ed. (Chicago: Chicago Business Press, 2016).

[44]Karie Willyard, "Millennials Want to Be Coached at Work," *Harvard Business Review*, February 27, 2015. https://hbr.org/2015/02/millennials-want-to-be-coached-at-work.

[45]Marcus Buckingham and Ashley Goodall, "Reinventing Performance Management," *Harvard Business Review*, April 2015. https://hbr.org/2015/04/reinventing-performance-management.

[46]P. M. Caligiuri and L. Dragoni, "Global Leadership Development," in *The Routledge Companion to International Human Resource Management* (New York: Routledge, 2014), 226; R. Henson, "The Road Ahead: The Future of Global Leadership and Implications for Research and Practice," in *Successful Global Leadership*, 285–301.

[47]A. Bird, "Start Them Young: Developing Global Leadership Skills in Students," Aperian Global, October 11, 2016. http://www.aperianglobal.com/start-them-young-developing-global-leadership-skills-in-students/.

[48]Bird, "Start Them Young."

[49]Pucik et al., *The Global Challenge*.

[50]Jevan Soo, "Take Control of Your Global Development," *Harvard Business Review*, March 22, 2012. https://hbr.org/2012/03/take-control-of-your-global-development.

[51]Personal experience of Shad Morris.

[52]Personal interaction by Shad Morris with senior HR Manager for Intel in Vietnam, June 2015.

CHAPTER **17**

Global Marketing

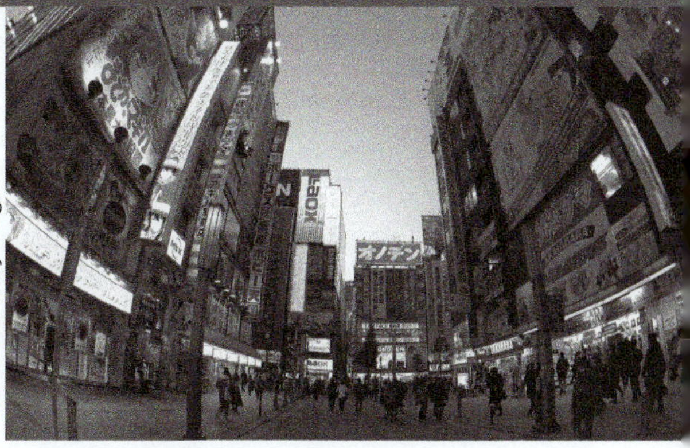

Gavin Hellier/Getty Images

Introduction

Globalization and its rapid spread are facilitated, in part, by the successful marketing strategies of companies around the world. As global competition increases, success depends on firms' ability to effectively adjust their marketing efforts in order to reach and persuade target consumers in different markets across the world.

A natural tension exists between marketers' need to customize products for local markets and their need to standardize products for the sake of efficiencies of scale. An optimal marketing strategy strikes a profitable balance between these two goals. While many companies can gain efficiencies by taking advantage of a global brand, some may be better served by customizing products for local markets and managing several independent brands rather than one global brand. For example, Coca-Cola maintains a global Coke brand but also customizes its marketing message from one culture to the next in order to ensure that people see Coke as specific to their own culture.

LEARNING OBJECTIVES

After you explore this chapter you will be able to:

1. **Explain** how to customize a marketing mix to different countries and cultures
2. **Describe** the advantages and disadvantages of standardizing and differentiating a product
3. **Outline** ways to globally brand a product while maintaining a local feel
4. **Describe** ways to effectively set international pricing and distribution strategies

17.1 Global Market Segmentation

LEARNING OBJECTIVE

Explain how to customize a marketing mix to different countries and cultures.

The goal of marketing is getting the right product in the right place at the right price and at the right time. In other words, to market effectively, companies must create a product that meets a need felt by a particular group of people, then make the product available for sale at a location

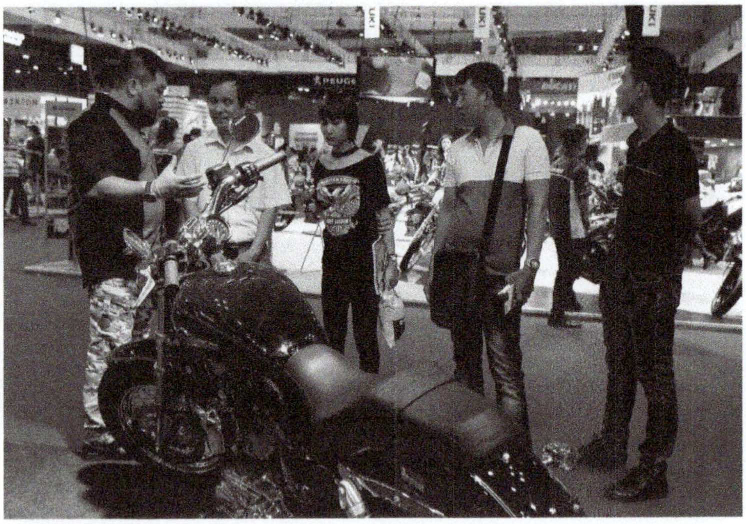

Yan Lerval/Alamy Stock Photo

FIGURE 17.1 **Harley is building a consumer base in Vietnam**

those people can access at a price they can afford.[1] Doing so across multiple global markets is a difficult endeavor.[2] Differences in access, culture, regulations, income, and preferences require global firms to build a **global marketing strategy**. A global marketing strategy is how a firm decides which market segments to operate in, how it will position its offerings, and to what extent products and services will be standardized or differentiated in each market.

global marketing strategy the way in which a firm decides which market segments to operate in, how it will position its offerings, and to what extent products and services will be standardized or differentiated in each market

Consider Harley Davidson. Harley's rough, individualistic image and loyal riders have built a strong brand in the United States. In taking the brand global, however, Harley faces new and different challenges. To succeed, Harley must accurately gauge the size of the new markets, meaning the number of people who are likely to buy one of its motorcycles; identify potential buyers' specific needs; and create a compelling message indicating how its product meets these needs. For instance, in assessing the potential market for Harley Davidson in Vietnam, the company will quickly realize that while many people travel by motorcycle, Harleys are not typical of the cheaper, smaller, more efficient motorcycles common in Vietnam. Because cheaper alternatives are plentiful, marketing strategies for selling Harleys in Vietnam need to be different from those adopted in the United States. Rather than promoting a Harley as an outlet for freedom and self-expression, as in the United States, a better move might be to emphasize the brand as a symbol of wealth or to focus on its greater power and size as a positive differentiating quality. Erik Koehne, an expatriate from California, who now lives in Vietnam, noted, "Buying a Harley in Vietnam is like buying a jet airplane in the U.S."[3] It is expensive. But despite the relative high cost, a growing group of Harley riders, or HOGs, is emerging in Vietnam (**Figure 17.1**).

marketing mix the collection of decisions regarding product, place, price, and promotion that companies make during the process of bringing a product or service to market

market segmentation the process by which companies cluster customers into homogeneous groups

global market segmentation the process of grouping of customer across national markets based on criteria such as level of economic development, cultural characteristics, language, buying patterns, and regulatory environment

A **marketing mix** is the collection of decisions regarding the four P's of marketing: product, place, price, and promotion. These govern the process of bringing a product or service to market. **Market segmentation** is the process by which companies cluster customers into homogeneous groups—be they demographic, geographic, or even psychographic. For instance, Red Bull targets extreme-sports enthusiasts globally. On the other hand, Ford Motor Company builds vehicles on global platforms in order to harness economies of scale; however, rather than sell identical vehicles through identical channels globally, the company customizes its offerings for each country location and markets them in different ways. In one particularly successful marketing effort aimed at first-time car buyers in Vietnam, Ford dealerships offered driving classes to new drivers and salespeople took time to explain how the radio, wipers, lights, thermostat, and other features work.[4] This is a very different approach from that in the United States and Europe, where Ford can safely assume its customers already know the basic concepts behind operating a car.

While effective marketing strategies can create a competitive advantage for companies, even well-known global companies like Facebook, Samsung, and BMW are likely to miss portions of the population who don't connect with their marketing efforts. Rather than spending resources by trying to capture all consumers, even the hard-to-reach ones, global companies are more likely to target more promising customer segments with customized marketing strategies. To do this, international firms often engage in **global market segmentation**, a process of grouping customers across national markets based on criteria such as level of economic development, cultural characteristics, language, buying patterns, and regulatory environment.[5] See Application Exercise: Segmentation. For instance, popular international musicians like Taylor Swift, Kanye West, and Rihanna target a global market segment made up of young adults who love music. Taylor Swift actually shifted her musical style away from country music (which has primarily U.S. fans) toward pop music and its broader global appeal.[6]

Global market segmentation has a key benefit: it enables companies to better position product offerings in the minds of consumers. By understanding consumer behaviors, companies can better match the context in which their products are perceived. For instance, Britain fell in love with Krispy Kreme doughnuts as a result of careful product positioning. Unlike U.S. consumers, the British don't typically eat doughnuts for breakfast. Creating a new marketing plan, Krispy Kreme capitalized on the British tradition of bringing sweet snacks to the workplace, advertising that a box of its doughnuts served as an impressive reward bosses could give to high achievers.[7] To reinforce the message, the company distributed its doughnuts through prestigious retailers like Harrods and Selfridges, further enhancing their appeal as a gift.[8] Thanks to its careful segmentation and targeting, Krispy Kreme became the United Kingdom's number one doughnut brand.[9]

Robert Laberge/Getty Images

FIGURE 17.2 **Porsche** The introduction of the Porsche Cayenne brought the carmaker into a much larger global segment, with Maria Sharapova as spokesperson.

One of the purposes of segmenting global customers is to see how well products meet the needs of different customer segments. For instance, Porsche, the global sports car brand, had traditionally focused on the premium sports car segment. The classic 911, a midsize car; the 718 Boxster, a compact sports car; and the 718 Cayman, a premium sports coupe, all focused on this segment. The company succeeded by focusing on its global target segment—wealthy men in their late 40s. In 2003, the company realized it was missing large global segments and that its core segment was aging. To focus on new segments, Porsche created the Cayenne, the world's first luxury sport utility vehicle (**Figure 17.2**).

This car brought Porsche into a new and larger market segment—that of everyday driving. And with Russian tennis star Maria Sharapova as its spokesperson, sales to women increased from 8 to 15 percent. The Cayenne now represents half of Porsche's profits. The company also introduced the Panamera, a four-door sedan, in 2010 and the Macan, a smaller SUV, in 2014 to further pursue this larger market segment.[10]

17.2 Standardization Versus Differentiation in International Marketing

LEARNING OBJECTIVE

Describe the advantages and disadvantages of standardizing and differentiating a product.

Beyond segmenting global customers, international companies face a challenge balancing their desires for product and marketing standardization with customer's needs for differentiation. Standardizing products and processes can reduce production and advertising costs per unit, improve control over the product, and increase global branding. **Global branding** is a marketing approach in which promotion, product, and price are standardized globally. By adopting global branding, companies like Samsung, McDonald's, and Coca-Cola are able to reap high profits while maintaining a consistent identity for their products. This approach works best when customer segments are global, when customers in different markets desire similar features, and when consumers and businesses have converging product expectations. These advantages are highlighted in **Figure 17.3**.

global branding a marketing approach where promotion, product, and price are standardized globally

However, standardization of a firm's marketing approach isn't always the right choice. Some standardized firms fail when attempting international expansion because they encounter new and different national preferences, living standards, political structures, and legal procedures. With that in mind, when companies discover strong differences between customer segments, they should differentiate their marketing approach by tailoring products and

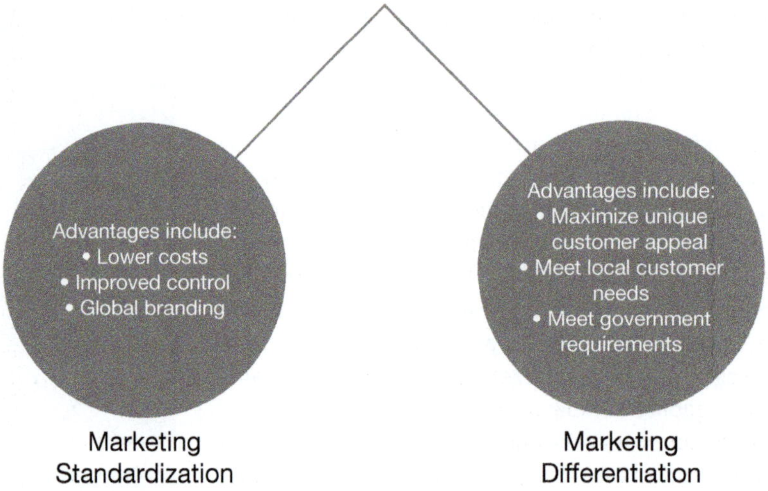

FIGURE 17.3 Advantages of global marketing standardization and differentiation

promotions for each country and each segment. By localizing, companies can better meet customer needs and avoid the complications of being perceived as an outsider. These advantages are identified in Figure 17.3.

When companies choose between standardizing or differentiating a marketing strategy, they first establish whether the new market will respond favorably to the same marketing mix as customers in the domestic market.[11] If the answer is yes, the company can standardize to take advantage of the cost reductions gained through economies of scale. If the answer is no, then the company needs to modify its marketing mix to match the different needs and expectations of the foreign market.

In reality, a company's marketing strategy is generally neither completely standardized nor fully differentiated. Instead, firms are challenged to strike a balance between standardization and differentiation. The most successful firms are those that effectively manage the inevitable trade-offs. They are often said to be using a "glocalization" strategy.

Standardization of the Marketing Mix

Standardization occurs when a firm uses the same mix of marketing strategies in its foreign and domestic markets.[12] Pharmaceuticals, credit card services, computers, luxury watches, and aircraft manufacturing are all industries in which a standardized marketing mix often succeeds. For example, the product features desired by Rolex customers across markets are largely the same: perfect timekeeping and timeless style. With its global marketing approach, Rolex produces only a few styles of watches, such as the Oyster Perpetual Explorer, which it made in honor of the first ascent of Mount Everest in 1953 and updated in 1971.[13] Similarly, Rolex watches are sold primarily in certified high-end stores that focus on pampering customers, and the company works hard to reduce the appeal of online bargain hunting—which often results in the purchase of a fake.[14] Luxury watches are premium priced across all global markets.

Finally, Rolex luxury watches are largely promoted uniformly across markets, focusing on sports stars like the Swiss tennis great Roger Federer (**Figure 17.4**). When Rolex began social marketing online, it was careful to preserve the brand image of Rolex by focusing on quality, not quantity. "Creating buzz is not the intent. We craft our content thoughtfully, privilege quality over quantity, talk only when we have something to say and when we feel it's right," noted the company.[15] The company launched a YouTube channel that focused not on the product but on in-house documentaries of Himalayan expeditions and deep-sea exploration.

Victor Fraile/Corbis/Getty Images

FIGURE 17.4 Tennis great Roger Federer markets the Rolex watch

Differentiation of the Marketing Mix

On the other hand, differences in languages, customs, cultures, and government regulations sometimes require firms to adapt their marketing mix in order to succeed. These differentiation approaches work best in highly localized industries such as legal services, consulting, restaurants, and software. Many global companies are realizing that it takes local influencers to endorse their products and are paying local celebrities to talk about their products on blogs and Twitter accounts.[16]

Differentiation often takes time. When Coca-Cola first introduced Coke to the Japanese market in 1957, it faced several difficulties. First, Coke was unappealing to Japanese customers because the drink resembled soy sauce in color. Second, it faced the obstacle of winning over a health-conscious culture opposed to sugary drinks. To overcome these hurdles, Coca-Cola positioned the product as a drink that accelerates individual performance and group productivity for adults. For Japanese youth, Coke positioned itself as a coming-of-age drink.

These efforts increased the consumption of Coke, but the company had to respond further. It adapted to local tastes and has introduced over 850 different beverages in Japan, 4 of which now earn over $1 billion a year: Georgia coffee, Aquarius sports drink, I Lohas bottled water, and Ayataka green tea. The positioning of Ayataka relies on Japanese chefs claiming it tastes as good as tea from a teapot. The company also differentiated its positioning using a host of vending machines, as shown in **Figure 17.5**. These machines not only offer convenience but also have both the capability to provide hot tea and coffee or cold soda. After Coca-Cola's 60 years of carefully differentiated marketing to Japanese customers, Japan is the company's second-largest market for Coke after the United States, with sales over $10 billion a year.[17]

Francois LE DIASCORN/Gamma-Rapho/Getty Images

FIGURE 17.5 Vending machines These are common in Japan and offer both hot and cold beverages, allowing Coca-Cola to differentiate its Japanese drink products.

Differences in culture plays an important role in determining the degree of standardization or differentiation.[18] For instance, a recent study found that global firms that adapt to country culture in Brazil, Russia, India, and China are 55 percent more effective in managing customer relationships.[19]

On the other hand, examples of firms failing to adapt to cultural differences are plentiful. For instance, Bharti Airtel, an Indian cell phone carrier, sought to advertise across 17 African countries. However, the advertising was not well received because the company used only South African models and had coins in the ads despite the fact that many of the countries don't have coins.[20]

Similarly, Home Depot succeeded in the United States by appealing to the do-it-yourself aspirations of the U.S. middle class. The company then expanded successfully to Canada, Mexico, and even Chile. Riding this wave of success, Home Depot decided to enter the Chinese market and quickly opened 12 stores before realizing a critical flaw in its marketing plan. The primary message of Home Depot does not resonate with Chinese consumers. They don't like to do it themselves; they prefer to have someone do it for them. After six years of constant losses amid uncertainty about how to adapt, Home Depot eventually closed its stores and let its associates go.[21]

Another cautionary tale is the failure of Walmart in Germany. After operating 85 stores in the country for 8 years, Walmart had to reverse course, incurring $1 billion in losses.[22] Most experts agree that Walmart's failure stemmed from its overconfidence and inability to address cultural differences quickly enough.[23] In fact, the U.S. managers Walmart brought in to help the company get started in Germany taught subordinates the same well-intentioned, standardized customer service techniques that work so effectively in the United States, like smiling at customers and offering to bag groceries. They didn't realize that most Germans prefer to bag their own groceries and are uncomfortable with the idea of smiling at strangers.[24] Once the company realized its mistake, it replaced its expatriate managers with Germans. Unfortunately, as James Bacos, the director of retail and consumer goods practice at Mercer Management Consulting in Munich, said, "They found they had some things to learn about the German market, and they did change, but maybe too late."[25]

Glocalization

The tension between standardization and differentiation is often not resolved by international companies just choosing one or the other; rather, they often must determine how to balance them for each product in each market. In fact, for many global corporations, the most successful marketing strategy is a blend of standardization and differentiation. The right blend enables companies to achieve economies of scale by standardizing products as much as possible and creating a brand that is recognizable across continents, while retaining the flexibility to customize products and marketing efforts to the end user based on market preferences. This blended approach is known as **glocalization** (GLObal + loCAL). Glocalization means balancing global integration while still meeting the demands of local culture (see **Figure 17.6**).

glocalization an approach whereby firms achieve global integration while still meeting the demands of local markets

McDonald's is widely considered a master practitioner of glocalization. On any given day, the fast-food chain serves more than 69 million people in over 100 countries. If you were to spend the next few weeks traveling around the world, visiting the golden arches in each of these countries, you would find the goat cheese Le McWrap Chèvre in France, the lamb and Arabic flatbread McTurco in Turkey, and the grilled salmon McLaks in Norway. In addition, you'd find jasmine tea in Singapore, chopsticks in Japan, and a wide variety of vegetarian options in India.[26] While maintaining an internationally unified brand, McDonald's has glocalized to become culturally in touch with all 69 million of its consumers. Through its glocalization strategy the company has standardized its restaurants, its advertising, and its prices while differentiating its product.

McDonald's isn't the only company to maximize market share by glocalizing. During the 1990s, Unilever recognized a demand for ice cream that appealed to consumers in Asia. The

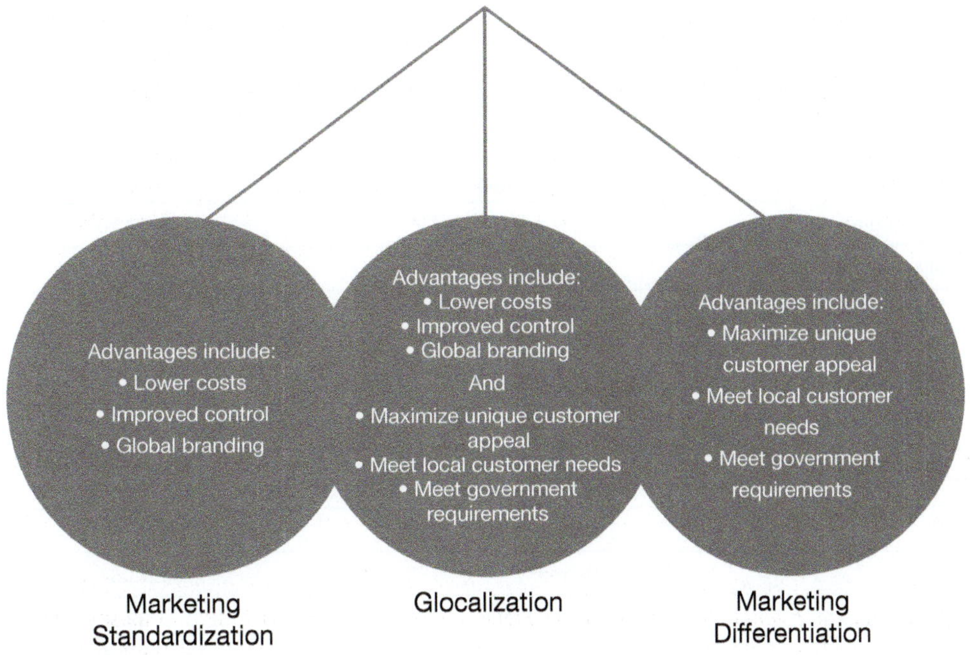

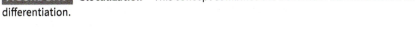

FIGURE 17.6 **Glocalization** This concept combines the benefits of standardization and differentiation.

company was able to make slight changes to its standard ice cream recipe by adding ingredients engineered to appeal to Asian tastes, such as lychee and green tea. As a result, it claimed 41 percent market share by 2000. Disney has also glocalized its theme park franchise by incorporating local architecture, folklore, and cuisine into the design of its parks in Paris, Tokyo, Hong Kong, and Shanghai. In 2012, the Italian company Piaggio, which manufactures the Vespa scooter, released a model specifically designed for the Indian market. The Indian Vespa had better gas mileage, higher ground clearance, and a lower footboard to accommodate Indian women riding sidesaddle on the back.[27]

Adopting a glocalization strategy means making adjustments according to regional consumer needs. By selling products and creating experiences that appeal to local tastes, producers are able to build a level of brand loyalty across borders that would be impossible with a standard, homogenous product. In addition, glocalization allows companies to maintain a level of standardization that lets them build a global image that transcends cultural barriers.

17.3 Global Branding

LEARNING OBJECTIVE

Outline ways to globally brand a product while maintaining a local feel.

Brands are vital in capturing consumer interest. According to the American Marketing Association, a **brand** is the "name, term, design, symbol, or any other feature that identifies one seller's goods or service as distinct from those of other sellers." According to Interbrand, Apple had the world's most valuable brand in 2016, valued at $178 billion. Google, Coca-Cola, Microsoft, and Toyota rounded out the top five. **Table 17.1** shows the world's top 15 global brands, their country of origin, and their value in 2016.

brand the name, term, design, symbol, or any other feature that identifies one seller's goods or service as distinct from those of other sellers

TABLE 17.1 The World's Top 15 Global Brands, 2016

Company	Country	Value in Billions ($)
Apple	United States	178.12
Google	United States	133.25
Coca-Cola	United States	73.10
Microsoft	United States	72.80
Toyota	Japan	53.58
IBM	United States	52.50
Samsung	South Korea	51.81
Amazon	United States	50.34
Mercedes-Benz	Germany	43.49
GE	United States	43.13
BMW	Germany	41.54
McDonald's	United States	39.38
Disney	United States	38.79
Intel	United States	36.95
Facebook	United States	32.59

Adapted from http://interbrand.com/best-brands/best-global-brands/2016/

Global brands enable companies to standardize their efforts to reach customers around the world. Samsung's Galaxy phones are branded the same around the globe. Other companies engage in a global rebranding effort by consolidating national brands into a global brand. For instance, Eveready Battery Company took its national brands UCar, Wonder, and Mazda and combined them into one global brand: Energizer.[28]

International companies often engage in three activities designed to build a strong global brand: building brand awareness, establishing the brand image, and capturing brand loyalty. These activities combine to create brand equity.

Building Brand Awareness

guerilla marketing marketing through unconventional, innovative, low-cost means to generate social buzz and maximum exposure

viral marketing marketing focused on producing a marketing message that people share with their friends by email, reposting, or retweeting

For consumers to develop a well-defined opinion about a brand, they must first be aware of it. Most brands establish awareness through traditional advertising and marketing. Others attempt to build awareness through "guerilla" or "viral" marketing techniques. **Guerilla marketing** makes use of unconventional, innovative, low-cost marketing designed to generate social buzz and maximum exposure. For instance, the Copenhagen Zoo wrapped several city busses with a picture of a giant snake squeezing the bus (**Figure 17.7**). The advertising created a stir and worked so well that some commuters refused to get on the bus.[29] Companies using this tactic engage target audiences directly, making their advertising so entertaining that customers will view it for fun and share it with friends, further exposing themselves and others to the underlying message.

Viral marketing produces a message people share with their friends by sending emails, reposting, or retweeting. Like a virus, these messages spread through self-replication as people see and share them with others. For instance, Dos Equis, a Mexican brand of imported beer, managed to triple its business by launching its "Most Interesting Man in the World" campaign in 2007. Even more impressive is that the boost came at a time when sales of imported beer were declining and sales of craft breweries were on the rise. Dos Equis managed to capture this increase through memorable commercials that appealed to a younger demographic. The beauty products maker Dove launched a recent viral global campaign that cleverly asked women whether they thought they were beautiful. Women chose to walk through a door marked

CB2/ZOB/WENN.com/Newscom

FIGURE 17.7 Guerilla marketing A giant snake squeezes a Copenhagen city bus in the Copenhagen Zoo's guerilla marketing campaign.

"beautiful" or "average," as shown in **Figure 17.8**. The company then asked women what they thought about their experience. The video has been viewed virally nearly 9 million times.

Global companies often choose to build brand awareness using a push or a pull approach. **Push marketing** consists of marketing efforts designed to actively *push* a product through the channel of distribution, starting with the producer, moving through the distribution partners, and finally reaching the consumer. For instance, the global pharmaceutical industry often uses a push strategy by sending out pharmaceutical representatives to convince physicians to prescribe company products to their patients.[30] Push marketing frequently includes price-oriented promotions or initial discounts to create awareness of products.

push marketing marketing efforts designed to actively *push* a product through the channel of distribution, starting with the producer, moving through the distribution partners, and finally reaching the consumer

The opposite of the push strategy is the pull strategy. **Pull marketing** cultivates customer desires and expectations so the customer will demand more product, effectively *pulling* the product through the production and distribution process. Typically, a pull marketing strategy gets customers excited about a product. For example, when Chinese cell phone maker OnePlus launched its new smart phone in the United States, it offered phones by invitation only. The invitations were primarily distributed through contests, such as one that promised

pull marketing marketing efforts designed to cultivate customer desires and expectations so the customer will demand more product, effectively *pulling* the product through the production and distribution process

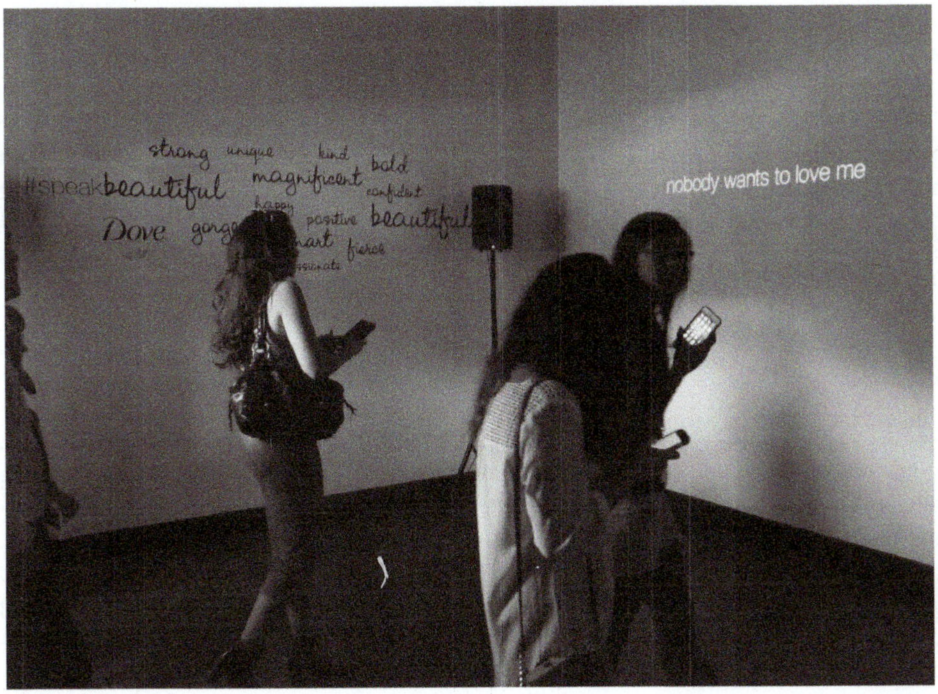

Anna Webber/Getty Images

FIGURE 17.8 Viral marketing Dove asked women to choose whether they thought they were beautiful or average in several global cities.

new phones to 100 customers if they would "smash the past" and destroy their old phones. The "invite-only model" created a huge amount of interest in a smartphone, described as the "flagship killer," that became one of the most talked-about phones of 2014. The phone sold over 1.5 million units, largely in the United States and India. Demand was so great that traffic to the OnePlus website skyrocketed, reaching 25.6 million visits in December 2014, just one year after the phone was launched.[31]

JACQUES DEMARTHON/AFP/Getty Images

FIGURE 17.9 **Ferrari** The prancing black horse on a yellow background is a powerful brand image recognized around the world, even by consumers who will never buy the company's iconic car.

Brand Image

brand image the set of associations in a customer's mind regarding a brand

Once customers become aware of a brand, they begin to form an impression of it, including both good and bad perceptions. **Brand image** is the set of associations in a customer's mind regarding a brand. The image is built from assessments customers make regarding their experiences with and perceptions of a brand. For instance, the country where the company is located may affect the brand image of a company. Consumer feelings about German automobiles, Swiss watches, and Italian food can affect the value they give to Audi, Rolex, and even Olive Garden restaurants. More than just a mental image, brand image also communicates a brand's emotional value. For example, for many consumers, Ferrari products are the pinnacle of high-end sports cars, and owning one makes people feel unique. The brand's association with positive feelings has enabled Ferrari to command high prices yet still enjoy robust sales year after year. While most consumers will never own a Ferrari, its positive brand image has allowed the company to market clothing, watches, and even electronics (**Figure 17.9**).

On the other hand, companies from emerging markets may face a negative brand image in their domestic market and globally because customers may stereotype them; as a result, the companies have a less favorable brand image. To avoid this disadvantage, many global companies from emerging markets use brands names that try to mimic Western brands. These include Clio Coddle, a causal clothing brand in China whose name is an imitation of Crocodile, a Singapore brand that itself mimics Lacoste, and shoe companies like Converse and Puma.[32]

Brand Loyalty

brand loyalty commitment to a brand in the face of competition

As a customer's positive view of a brand develops, it can solidify into brand loyalty. **Brand loyalty** is a commitment to a brand in the face of competition. Customers with brand loyalty typically engage in repeat purchases over time, regardless of convenience or price. Loyal customers often act as unofficial brand ambassadors. To instill brand loyalty, international companies such as Marriott Hotels use marketing strategies like loyalty programs, incentives, and differentiated customer service.

Costco has been very successful in creating brand loyalty, including in new markets like South Korea and Japan, even though it has no formal marketing budget.[33] The retail giant spends little to nothing on advertising; it simply sends out the occasional mailer to prospective and current members. By contrast, other retail companies spend a great deal. One of Costco's competitive strategies is to pay higher wages, believing that happier employees provide a better customer service experience.

Brand Equity

brand equity the additional market share and profits products earn because of the brand's strength compared with that of competing products

After earning brand loyalty from customers, businesses hope to convert it to brand equity. **Brand equity** is the additional market share and profits products earn because of the brand's strength compared with that of competing products. According to research organizations like Millward-Brown and Forbes, brand equity can actually be measured in dollars. In Forbes' 2016 rankings, the top three brands in the world were Apple, Google, and Microsoft. At $154.1 billion, Apple's brand equity actually equals the brand equities of Google and Microsoft combined.[34] This in turn helps explain why Apple's company valuation is so high.

Benefits of a Global Brand

A primary benefit of developing a single global brand is the positive effects of being known as a global company.[35] For instance, local Chinese consumers are more likely to be drawn to Chinese companies that operate in global markets, because they assume these firms are meeting global standards.[36]

In addition, a global brand gives a firm power to negotiate with its global partners. For example, when Samsung entered the U.S. smartphone market, U.S. wireless carriers demanded unique handsets to reduce competition with other carriers and to comply with the technology protocols of the different carriers' networks. As a result, Samsung had to release four different phones—one for AT&T, one for Sprint, one for Verizon, and one for T-Mobile—in order to place a "flagship" phone with each carrier. As the company's brand has grown, however, Samsung has gained more control over the end-user experience, enabling it to release nearly identical Galaxy-branded handsets across all four major wireless carriers. Samsung continued its global leadership despite the Galaxy Note 7 recall. The Galaxy phone is among the world's most popular brands, accounting for nearly 20 percent of the market worldwide.[37]

Downsides of a Global Brand

Despite the economies of scale advantages of having a unified, global brand, it's not always the optimal solution. Sometimes marketing a global brand can cause problems that far outweigh the benefits. For example, different brands may have different meanings in different languages. Coca-Cola has found great success through global marketing, but it ran into problems while marketing Diet Coke in Europe. The company quickly discovered that the word "diet" meant illness in Germany and Italy. Ultimately, Coca-Cola changed the product name to Coca-Cola Light outside the United States. Similarly, Nokia launched its phone called the Lumia; however, to the embarrassment of the company, the name means prostitute in Spanish.[38]

Moreover, creating a global brand strategy that is applicable worldwide is extremely complex. For instance, in the United States, the Honda brand represents quality and reliability. In Japan, however, high-quality cars are expected and therefore quality is not a selling point. As a result, Honda's brand team for Japan has worked to create a brand image of speed, youth, and energy. For these reasons, developing a global brand shouldn't necessarily be a priority for a firm. Developing localized brand messages for markets is sometimes the better option.

17.4 Global Pricing and Distribution

LEARNING OBJECTIVE

Describe ways to effectively set international pricing and distribution strategies.

An important part of international marketing is determining a pricing strategy. In general, global firms adopt one of three pricing strategies: cost-plus, penetration, and skimming.[39]

General Pricing Strategies

Pricing strategies become more complex for international businesses. We look first at cost-plus pricing.

Cost-Plus Pricing Strategy A **cost-plus strategy** prices a product or service at some margin over the seller's cost. If a product costs a company $1 and the company uses a 50 percent margin strategy, the price to customers is $1.50. Cost-plus pricing is common in emerging markets, particularly where competition is low.

cost-plus strategy pricing a product or service at a fixed margin over costs

While cost-plus strategies are fairly straightforward in domestic markets, they can create pricing challenges in global markets. For instance, Tata, an India car company, sells its popular Indica sedan for 5 lakh (~$8,000) in India. If the company operates on a cost-plus basis with a 20 percent margin, the car costs Tata about $6,700 to produce and yields $1,300 in profit. If Tata were to bring the car to the U.S. market, its cost for the Indica would increase to about $7,700 because of the price of transportation, tariffs, and other regulatory costs, such as the need to add labels in other languages. Thus the price would need to be higher—$9,200—to yield the same 20 percent margin for the firm. The downside of the cost-plus strategy for global firms is that foreign customers must be willing to absorb the higher prices of their goods.

Global firms often follow one of two types of cost-plus strategy: a rigid model and a flexible model.

- **Rigid cost-plus pricing:** this method relies on a fixed price for all export markets. In general, firms add a flat percentage to the domestic price, as in the Tata Indica example above, to compensate for the expense of doing international business. The firm combines that percentage with a gross margin to account for manufacturing and intermediary costs. This method is often favored by less-experienced exporters and typically fails to account for buyer demand, income levels, and competition.
- **Flexible cost-plus pricing:** this method adjusts the price depending on the customer, order size, and other competitive influences. For example, Tata may realize that U.S. consumers could be unwilling to absorb the $1,200 difference between the price in India and the price in the United States, and thus accept a lower margin on its exports. Global companies that face intense competition often use a flexible strategy, effectively setting a price range and then settling on a specific price on a per-order basis. Zara uses this strategy for its clothing by adapting prices to accommodate local competition in its global markets.

penetration pricing strategy a strategy where a company sets the price of a product very low to get customers to try it

Penetration Pricing Strategy In contrast to a cost-plus strategy, global firms also use a **penetration pricing strategy** focused on gaining market share. Under a penetration strategy, a company sets the price very low to get customers to try the product. This strategy is often used in highly competitive markets. For instance, Uber often prices rides significantly below those of its competitors in an effort to gain customers.[40] Similarly, when the South Korean carmaker Hyundai entered the U.S. car market, it used a price penetration strategy focused on gaining share. It offered the lowest-priced car in the United States—the KIA Rio. In 2016, Nissan used a penetration strategy in the U.S. car market with its Versa, priced at just $12,825.[41] The advantage of using a penetration strategy is that global companies can quickly gain a share of global markets. However, the strategy is often problematic in that it leads customers to expect low prices, and global firms often have difficulty raising them in the future.

dumping selling a product for a price less than the cost of production to capture market share and force competitors out of the market

International businesses face another challenge in penetration pricing. It is against the provisions of the World Trade Organization to sell products in foreign markets at prices lower than cost. This practice is called **dumping**, a form of predatory pricing or pricing so low that it forces competition out of the market, with the intent to raise prices once the competition is gone. For instance, GM is reported to be losing $9,000 on every Chevy Bolt it sells in the United States in its effort to penetrate the nascent electric car market.[42] But, if the company were to export the car at a price below costs, foreign manufactures could sue GM for dumping and force the firm to raise its price and incur fines and penalties.

skimming a pricing strategy where a company sets a high price for a product and sells to the segment that is willing to pay a premium

Skimming Strategy The final pricing strategy is **skimming**, in which a global company charges a high price to the segment willing to pay a premium and a lower price to attract other customers.[43] This strategy maximizes profits for a company. Sony uses it for its high-end televisions. A 4K 55-inch TV priced at $4,000 in 2013 for early adopters cost just $1,500 for buyers in 2015.[44] This strategy can not only boost an international firm's profits, it can also help define the brand as exclusive. Tesla entered the car market by offering high-end luxury electric cars, and in August of 2017 the company introduced a lower-end model with a base cost of US$35,000.

While price skimming has advantages, one of the downsides is that customers may move to a competitor's cheaper alternative. Apple has used a price skimming strategy to earn margins of over 50 percent on its iPhones.[45] However, many customers have moved to a cheaper phone sold by Samsung or OnePlus. The consequence of this shift is that the Apple iOS holds only a fraction of the current market, as Android has come to dominate it.

Other Factors Affecting Global Pricing

In addition to the pricing strategies of global organizations, other factors that influence international pricing are government intervention, market positioning, fluctuations in currency value, and gray market activity.[46]

Government Intervention One of the most influential factors of price in international business is the degree to which the local government intervenes in the market. Government intervention takes many forms, including tariffs, price floors or ceilings, and antidumping regulations. For instance, many governments levy tariffs on imported goods to protect domestic products, consumers, infant industries, and industries deemed vital to national security. The government of Japan allows 770,000 tons of rice to be imported tariff-free each year.[47] However, rice growing is a critical part of the Japanese economy and composes a major percentage of Japan's agricultural sector. To protect local producers, the government therefore levies a 778 percent tariff on anything over the annual import cap. This huge tariff reduces the profitability of U.S. rice producers that sell to Japan beyond the import cap.

Because tariffs can be a serious burden for companies, firms have learned different strategies to circumvent them. For example, a firm can sometimes ship unassembled components—say, of bicycles—to an importing country and then have the product assembled locally. This often meets requirements for local production and enables the firm to qualify for lower tariffs on the components, rather than paying the higher tariff that would be assessed on the assembled final product.

A firm can sometimes also qualify for lower tariffs by reclassifying its products. For example, some countries have higher tariffs on dolls that represent humans than on dolls that look like mythical creatures. To avoid the higher tariff, a company could simply send mythical-creature dolls to the high-tariff country.[48]

Another option is to move production to another country. This doesn't necessarily avoid a tariff so much as enable the company to benefit from lower manufacturing costs. While this strategy may incur a considerably higher risk because of the need to build new production facilities, companies like Toyota have succeeded by sourcing production outside the home country and offsetting higher tariffs with lower production costs.

Market Positioning While pricing can be influenced by external factors, firms can also use it as a direct signal of product quality. Many luxury products are priced above and beyond any incremental increase in production and distribution costs. In effect, these items become status symbols that indicate a customer's success and wealth.

A product's price can have a powerful emotional effect on the perception of quality. Most consumers assume that more expensive products are also better quality or more desirable for some other reason. For instance, Stella Artois, a Belgian beer, is positioned as a low-cost beer in its home market and holds a mere 6.5 percent market share. However, the product is sold as a premium lager in foreign markets such as in the United States.[49] In Japan, farmers sell a limited quantity of specialized watermelons—including heart-shaped and square ones grown in special molds, as shown in **Figure 17.10**—as luxury

TORU YAMANAKA/AFP/Getty Images

FIGURE 17.10 **Shaped watermelons are popular in Japan**

items for over 20 times the normal price. While a normal watermelon may sell for $10 or less in the United States, these watermelons (which cost over $200 in Japan) are frequently exported to Russia and sold for $800.[50]

For high-end consumers, the price of a product can validate its allure and quality. In other words, if done properly, a company's pricing strategy can be part of its effort to position the product as a highly desirable, luxury item. For example, many consumers would see the Danish company Bang and Olufsen's $6,700 price tag for a 40-inch TV and shy away; a Samsung 40-inch TV at Walmart is a mere $548.[51] But for the technophile, Bang and Olufsen's perfect balance of design—melding aluminum, wood, glass, fabric, and plastic—coupled with superior sound quality and an auto-adjusting picture control that senses surrounding light and automatically adjusts the screen brightness is well worth the price premium (**Figure 17.11**).

Fluctuations in Currency Value When a company expands internationally, constant currency fluctuations make pricing more difficult. In countries where extreme currency fluctuations occur, a firm may need to constantly adjust prices in order to stabilize real earnings. However, frequent price shifts can be unsettling to customers.

Gray Market Activity Government tariffs, distribution channels, premium product positioning, and currency fluctuations can result in significant price differences between domestic and foreign markets. When differences in price occur across borders, arbitration becomes possible. **Gray market activity** is a specific kind of arbitration in which companies or individuals buy in a cheaper market and sell in a more expensive one. Such activity most often occurs with high-margin or luxury items such as pharmaceuticals, electronics, watches, and cosmetic products. It can happen at the company level or at the individual level. For example, it is often cheaper—even including the cost of air travel—for Chinese shoppers to go to Paris to buy high-end fashion. Shopping in Paris allows them to avoid the import duties on luxury goods that can double the price in the Chinese market.[52]

gray market activity a specific type of arbitration whereby companies or individuals buy a product in a cheaper market and sell it in a more expensive market

Global companies can combat gray market activity by designing products with exclusive features, such as nontransferable warranties on electronics that are in effect only when accompanied by legitimate paperwork and proof of purchase, like a dated receipt. A company could even control gray markets by cutting prices in countries that have them, thus eliminating the

Ray Tang/Anadolu Agency/Getty Images

FIGURE 17.11 **Bang and Olufsen's BeoVision 14 Television** The product offers a premium viewing experience at a premium price.

arbitrage opportunity and the reason for the gray market. Finally, firms can publish information about the dangers of purchasing gray market products—voided warranties, contaminated products, limited recourse for defects—and publicize ways to identify gray market vendors.

Transfer Pricing Perhaps one of the biggest pricing challenges that global companies face is not determining the price it will charge customers in different markets but in determining what it will charge different subsidiaries for the goods sold in global markets. Transfer pricing is defined as the price a division charges another division of the same firm for supplies or labor. Transfer prices can have important tax consequences and represent nearly 60 percent of all global goods sold.[53] Governments around the world are increasing pursuing companies that either buy their own good too cheaply or too expensively in an attempt to reduce their tax liability. For instance, Chevron recently lost a case with the Australian government; it now owes the government over US$250 million in avoided taxes stemming from a loan the company made to itself to finance operations in Australia. All loans are supposed to be at "arm's length," meaning fairly priced, but Chevron was charging its Australian operations 9 percent interest on a loan it took out in the United States at a mere 1.2 percent interest. The company was not paying taxes on the difference in either the United States or Australia.[54]

Distribution Strategies

Even if a global company can build a global brand and develop an effective pricing strategy, if customers can't find its product, its marketing strategy has failed. Distribution is thus a final important step in a global marketing strategy. **Distribution** is the process of taking goods from production to consumption. International businesses face several important decisions when managing their distribution activities.

distribution the process of taking goods from production to consumption

WileyPLUS

See Whiteboard Video: Distribution Agents

Distribution Channels The way international businesses distribute products and services is determined by the channels they use. They have many choices. First, some global companies go to market by directly opening stores. This path offers a company the most control but also the most risk. Establishing independent distribution channels in a new market requires significant investment. Where will the company warehouse goods? Which stores will the company sell through? How will the company get access to these stores? What kind of shelf space within the store will the company be able to get? All of these questions must be answered as a firm expands globally into new markets. Those that persist and make the necessary investments can achieve handsome rewards. For instance, Starbucks has 24,000 stores in 70 countries, some of which it owns directly and some of which are owned with franchise partners.[55] Similarly, Amazon.com has invested roughly $5 billion in infrastructure in India to deliver products to consumers across the country.[56]

A second option is to enter a new country through global online markets, catalogues, or other direct channels. This allows a firm to sell into a country with minimal investment, but it requires the firm to be dependent on postal systems or international shipping companies to deliver goods, and in many cases these services may not be reliable. Moreover, many global customers do not expect to make a payment until they receive a product, requiring a company to ship the product before they collect payment.

A third option, and the one most frequently used, is for global companies to use an external distributor to handle distribution within a country. These local distributors act as middlemen, taking products from global producers and getting them into local stores. In many markets, such as South Korea, distributors have a tight lock on the market, and a product's success or failure can hinge on the producer partnering with the right distributor. The same is true of the U.S. market. When Samsung made a big push to increase sales of its refrigerators and washing machines, the company was quick to sign distribution agreements with big distributors like Lowes, Home Depot, and Best Buy. While a global company may benefit by establishing quick entry into a country by using a local distributor, these distributors often offer limited growth. They frequently distribute for multiple companies and thus have more incentive to add a new client to their preexisting distribution infrastructure than to expand their infrastructure.[57]

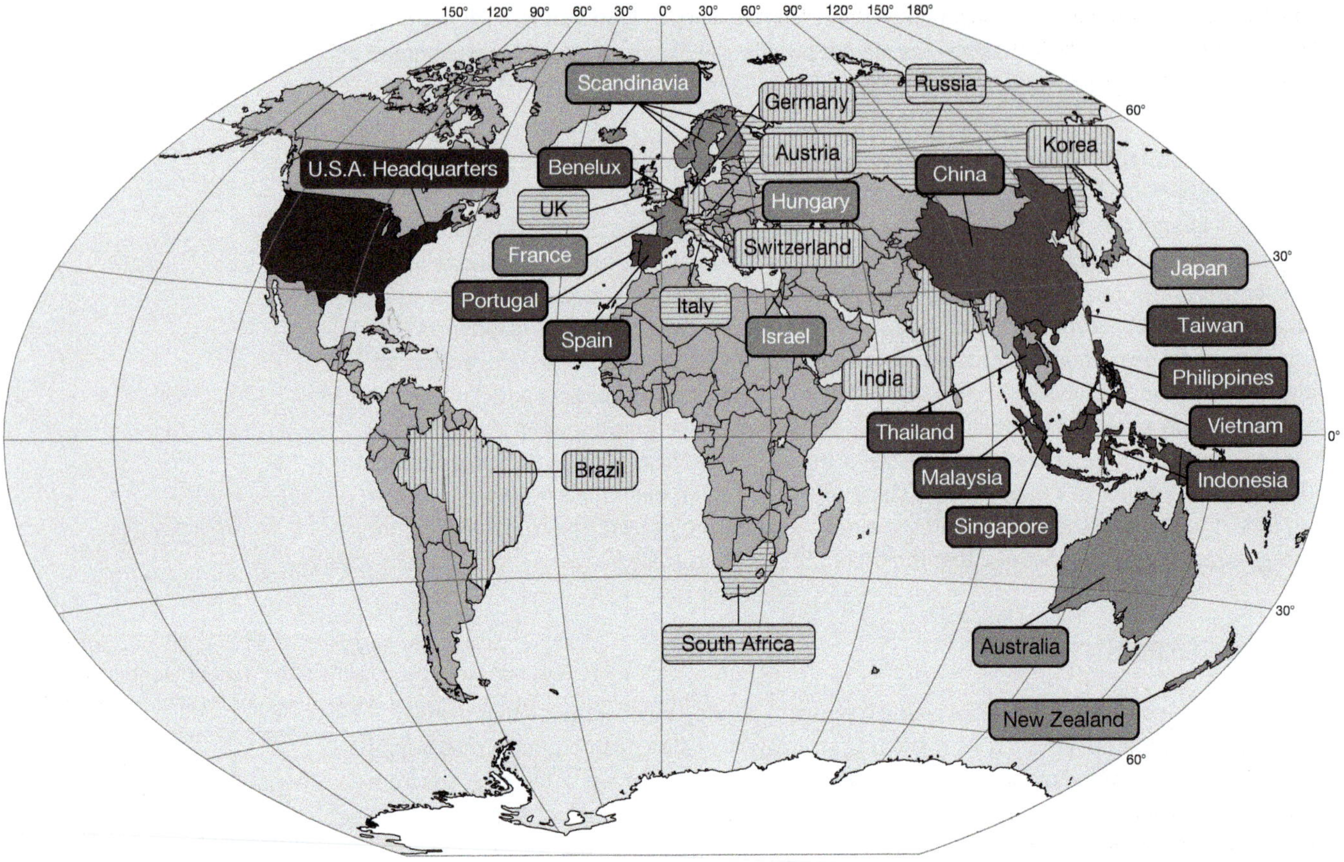

FIGURE 17.12 **Distribution chain** SignalQuest, a company headquartered in New Hampshire, uses distributors to access global markets. **Source:** https://signalquest.com/contact/distributor-finder/

For instance, as **Figure 17.12** demonstrates, the U.S.-based company SignalQuest, a maker of microsensors, uses international distributors to gain access to global markets. Its distributors in local markets help the company quickly enter these markets.

Some companies use a multichannel approach, such as Apple's strategy of building stores in different global markets and using distributors to gain access to other retailers' stores. Similarly, Zara opens its own stores in different markets and offers an online channel in many countries. Key for global companies is the ability to get products to customers.

Summary and Case

Summary

LEARNING OBJECTIVE 17.1 Explain how to customize a marketing mix to different countries and cultures.

Marketing aims to get the right product to the right place at the right price at the right time. By focusing on delivering the right product, place, price, and promotion (known as the four P's), businesses create a marketing mix. Getting this mix right is difficult in domestic markets, but it is even more challenging for global firms. To have the most impact through the marketing mix, firms divide the market into segments based on different customer characteristics, such as location, religion, age, gender, income, and even personality. Market segmentation is especially important when a business is operating in multiple countries, because local cultures, economies, and locations have an effect on market segments, or may even become market segments of their own.

LEARNING OBJECTIVE 17.2 Describe the advantages and disadvantages of standardizing and differentiating a product.

Global firms face tension in standardizing versus differentiating their marketing approach. On one hand, standardization allows firms to reduce costs and build a unified brand. On the other, differentiation allows firms to focus on meeting the needs of unique customers. Some firms use a glocalization approach to achieve the benefits of both standardization and differentiation.

LEARNING OBJECTIVE 17.3 Outline ways to globally brand a product while maintaining a local feel.

Brands include a company's name, logo, image, design, symbol, and any other characteristic that sets the company apart from its competitors. Building a global brand requires firms to build awareness, establish an image, develop customer loyalty, and turn that loyalty into brand equity. Brands can be established globally, but doing so incurs benefits and risks.

LEARNING OBJECTIVE 17.4 Describe ways to effectively set international pricing and distribution strategies.

Global companies face the difficult task of setting product prices in different markets. In general, companies can use a cost-plus strategy that ensures a fixed margin, a skimming strategy that seeks to maximize profits, or a penetration strategy that seeks to maximize market share. Government intervention can seriously affect international businesses through tariffs, price floors and ceilings, and antidumping policies. In addition, companies must build distribution channels to get their products to market.

Case Study

Peaks Sends Kilimanjaro to Brazil

Peaks Corporation, a leading U.S. manufacturer of outdoor gear, wants to begin exporting climbing harnesses to Brazil and needs to determine how to price the product in that market. The company has three options: a cost-plus approach, a penetration strategy, or a skimming strategy. The company plans to export its Kilimanjaro harness, which is a climbing harness that falls into the premium segment in the United States market and retails for $100. Initial research reveals that additional costs of shipping, insurance, and a 10 percent Brazilian tariff will add a total of $15 to the cost of each harness. If the company merely used the U.S. cost plus the additional $15, it would potentially result in a price of $115 in Brazil.

Peaks has the option of using its relationship with a distributor in Brazil, Amazonas Corporation, which will add an additional 10 percent margin to the cost of each imported harness ($11.50 in this case). That would bring the price of each harness to around $126.50 if the company used a cost-plus strategy. This would be the floor price if the company's management did not want the Brazilian margin per unit to drop below that in the United States.

However, the cost-plus strategy may not be the best way to go. Market research on income and competitor prices in the market reveals that Brazilian climbers are willing to pay about 40 percent above typical U.S. prices for high-quality harnesses. Given this information, Peaks management believes Brazil could sustain a skimming strategy; the company could sell the Kilimanjaro harness for about $140—attracting the upper end of the market.

Finally, research also suggests that the market for climbing gear in Brazil is likely to grow quickly in the next 24 months, as several international competitions are scheduled to be held in the country and the publicity is likely to drive more interest. Because of this growth, Peak's leadership is also considering using a penetration strategy and offering the harness for $90 in the market. This would provide low margins but would not be below the firm's costs, so the company could not be accused by local firms of dumping products into the Brazilian market. Some in the company offered strong arguments for this approach because Brazil is an important market, as it tends to be the springboard for global retail firms into other South American markets.

After considering all three potential pricing strategies, Peaks' management remained unsure which strategy would provide the most value to the firm. They have come to you for help in choosing their pricing strategy.

(case source: Though based on factual events, all names and prices have been disguised by the authors)

Case Discussion Questions

1. What are the pros and cons of each strategy?
2. What strategy would you advise the firm to use as it enters the Brazilian market? Why?
3. What implications does the pricing strategy you take in Brazil have for the company's domestic market?

Endnotes

[1]Shaoming Zou and S. Tamer Cavusgil, "The GMS: A Broad Conceptualization of Global Marketing Strategy and Its Effect on Firm Performance," *Journal of Marketing* 66, no. 4 (2002): 40–56.

[2]Bodo B. Schlegelmilch, "Segmenting Targeting and Positioning in Global Markets," in *Global Marketing Strategy: An Executive Digest* (Cham, Switzerland: Springer International Publishing, 2016), 63–82.

[3]Eugene S. Robinson, "Ho Chi Minh Harley," NPR Fast Forward, October 23, 2013, www.ozy.com/fast-forward/ho-chi-minh-harley/3005.

[4]Cathy Chu, "Ford Hopes Free Driver's Ed in Vietnam Leads to Sales," *USA Today*, August 5, 2010, https://usatoday30.usatoday.com/money/autos/2010-08-05-forddriving05_ST_N.htm.

[5]Stephen H. Craft and Salah S. Hassan, "Global Consumer Market Segmentation Strategy Decisions and Managerial Assessment of

Performance," in *Revolution in Marketing: Market Driving Changes: Proceedings of the 2006 Academy of Marketing Science (AMS) Annual Conference*, ed. Harlan E. Spotts (New York: Springer International Publishing, 2015), 26–30.

[6]"Taylor Swift Shake, Shake, Shakes up a Slowing Music Industry," PBS NewsHour, October 31, 2014, www.pbs.org/newshour/bb/taylor-swift-shake-shake-shakes-slowing-music-industry/.

[7]Michael Swenson, David Whitlark, and Gary Rhoads, "Marketing Fundamentals," My Educator, https://www.myeducator.com/reader/web/510/. (accessed September 3, 2015).

[8]Emine Saner, "How Britain Fell in Love with Krispy Kreme Doughnuts," *Guardian*, June 3, 2011, www.theguardian.com/lifeandstyle/2011/jun/04/krispy-kreme-doughnuts-britain.

[9]"No. 1 Food Brand," Krispy Kreme, April 16, 2015, www.krispykreme.co.uk/No1-Food-Brand

[10]Stephen Zoeller, "How to Segment Your Target Market: Porsche Case Study," Stephenzoeller.com, September 30, 2016, www.stephenzoeller.com/targetmarketsegmentporsche/.

[11]Michael Swenson, "Standardization versus Customization," 2015 MyEducator (accessed August 27, 2015).

[12]Swenson, "Standardization versus Customization."

[13]Rolex Oyster Perpetual Explorer. www.rolex.com/watches/baselworld/new-explorer/m214270-0003.html (accessed December 12, 2016).

[14]Marton Radkai, "Swiss Watchmakers Fight Online Against Fakes," The Local ch, April 9, 2013, www.thelocal.ch/20130409/swiss-watchmakers-fight-online-against-counterfeiters.

[15]Eli Epstein, "Rolex: How a 109-Year-Old Brand Thrives in the Digital Age," Mashable, April 17, 2014, http://mashable.com/2014/04/17/rolex-marketing-strategy/#zq7cGxYL7PqB.

[16]Katrina Manson, "'One Size Fits All' Marketing by Global Companies Fails in Africa," *Financial Times*, March 16, 2014, www.ft.com/content/944c7018-a5f2-11e3-b9ed-00144feab7de.

[17]Yuri Kageyama, "Coca-Cola No. 1 in Japan with Drinks Galore, but Not Coke," ABC News, November 28, 2016, http://abcnews.go.com.

[18]Marieke De Mooij, *Global Marketing and Advertising: Understanding Cultural Paradoxes* (Thousand Oaks, CA: Sage Publications, 2013).

[19]Stephen A. Samaha, Joshua T. Beck, and Robert W. Palmatier, "The Role of Culture in International Relationship Marketing," *Journal of Marketing* 78, no. 5 (2014): 78–98.

[20]Manson, "'One Size Fits All' Marketing by Global Companies Fails in Africa."

[21]Laurie Burkitt, "Home Depot Learns Chinese Prefer 'Do-It-for-Me,'" *Wall Street Journal*, September 14, 2012, https://www.wsj.com/articles/SB10000872396390444433504577651072911154602.

[22]David Macaray, "Why Did Walmart Leave Germany?" *Huffington Post*, August 29, 2015, www.huffingtonpost.com/david-macaray/why-did-walmart-leave-ger_b_940542.html; "Our Locations," Walmart, http://corporate.walmart.com/our-story/our-business/locations/ (accessed August 29, 2015).

[23]Macaray, "Why Did Walmart Leave Germany?"

[24]Macaray, "Why Did Walmart Leave Germany?"

[25]Mark Landler, "Wal-Mart Gives up Germany – Business – International Herald Tribune" *New York Times*, July 28, 2006, www.nytimes.com/2006/07/28/business/worldbusiness/28iht-walmart.2325266.html.

[26]Kelly Nataly, "McDonald's Local Strategy, from El McPollo to Le McWrap Chèvre" *Harvard Business Review*, October 8, 2012, https://hbr.org/2012/10/mcdonalds-local-strategy-from

[27]"Glocalization Examples – Think Globally and Act Locally," Case studyinc.com, February 10, 2010, www.casestudyinc.com/glocalization-examples-think-globally-and-act-locally.

[28]Bruce David Keillor, *Marketing in the 21st Century and Beyond: Timeless Strategies for Success* (Santa Barbara, CA: ABC-CLIO, 2013).

[29]Lesley Ciarula Taylor, "Copenhagen Commuters Get a Big, Slithering Surprise," thestar.com, December 2, 2010, www.thestar.com/news/world/2010/12/02/copenhagen_commuters_get_a_big_slithering_surprise.html.

[30]Michael Swenson, "Promotion Strategy," 2015 MyEducator (accessed August 27, 2015).

[31]Angela Doland, "OnePlus: The Startup That Actually Convinced People to Smash Their iPhones," Advertising Age, August 10, 2015, http://adage.com/article/cmo-strategy/oneplus-convinced-people-smash-iphones/299875/.

[32]Dan Levin, "Adidos and Hotwind? In China, Brands Adopt Names to Project Foreign Flair," *New York Times*, December 26, 2014, www.nytimes.com/2014/12/27/business/international/adidos-and-hotwind-in-china-brands-evoke-foreign-names-even-if-theyre-gibberish.html?_r=0.

[33]Andres Cardenal, "3 Strong Companies with Powerful Brands," The Motley Fool, September 22, 2015, www.fool.com/investing/general/2015/09/22/3-strong-companies-with-powerful-brands.aspx.

[34]"The World's Most Valuable Brands," *Forbes*, June 2, 2016, www.forbes.com/powerful-brands/list/#tab:rank.

[35]Warat Winit et al., "Global vs Local Brands: How Home Country Bias and Price Differences Impact Brand Evaluations," *International Marketing Review* 31, no. 2 (2014): 102–28.

[36]Bernhard Swoboda, Karin Pennemann, and Markus Taube, "The Effects of Perceived Brand Globalness and Perceived Brand Localness in China: Empirical Evidence on Western, Asian, and Domestic Retailers," *Journal of International Marketing* 20, no. 4 (2012): 72–95.

[37]"Smartphone Vendor Market Share, 2017 Q1," IDC,(Accessed August 1, 2017), www.idc.com/prodserv/smartphone-market-share.jsp.

[38]Dave Smith, "Lost in Translation: Nokia Lumia, and the 5 Worst Name Oversights," *International Business Times*, October 26, 2011, www.ibtimes.com/lost-translation-nokia-lumia-5-worst-name-oversights-361866.

[39]James Wills, A. Coskun Samli, and Laurence Jacobs, "Developing Global Products and Marketing Strategies: A Construct and a Research Agenda," *Journal of the Academy of Marketing Science* 19, no. 1 (1991): 1–10.

[40]Sara Silverstein, "These Animated Charts Tell You Everything About Uber Prices in 21 Cities," *Business Insider*, October 16, 2014, www.businessinsider.com/uber-vs-taxi-pricing-by-city-2014-10.

[41]Kelsey Mays, "The Cheapest Car in the U.S. for 2017 May Surprise You," Cars.com, August 31, 2016, www.cars.com.

[42]David Welch and John Lippert, "GM's Electric Shock: It Will Lose $12,000 on Each Chevy Bolt," *Australian Financial Review*, December 1, 2016, www.afr.com/business/transport/automobile/gms-electric-shock-it-will-lose-12000-on-each-chevy-bolt-20161130-gt1agt#ixzz4SpX8PkU7.

[43]Martin Spann, Marc Fischer, and Gerard J. Tellis, "Skimming or Penetration? Strategic Dynamic Pricing for New Products," *Marketing Science* 34, no. 2 (2014): 235–49.

[44]Anders Bylund, "How Price Skimming Boosts Modern Pricing Strategies," Fool.com, June 24, 2015, www.fool.com/investing/general/2015/06/24/how-price-skimming-boosts-modern-pricing-strategie.aspx.

[45]Alicia Adamczyk, "The iPhone 7 Costs You 3x More Than It Costs Apple to Make," *Money*, September 26, 2016, http://time.com/money/4508221/iphone-7-mark-up-profit-margins/.

[46]Marios Theodosiou and Constantine S. Katsikeas, "Factors Influencing the Degree of International Pricing Strategy Standardization of

Multinational Corporations," *Journal of International Marketing* 9, no. 3 (2001): 1–18; Bodo B. Schlegelmilch, "Extracting Value from Global Operations," in *Global Marketing Strategy*, (2016): 105–27; Stanford A. Westjohn, Holger Roschk, and Peter Magnusson, "Eastern versus Western Culture Pricing Strategy: Superstition, Lucky Numbers, and Localization," *Journal of International Marketing* (March 2016).

[47]"U.S. Agrees to Let Japanese Tariffs Stand on Rice, Wheat," *Japan Times*, April 17, 2014, www.japantimes.co.jp/news/2014/04/17/business/u-s-agrees-to-let-japanese-tariffs-stand-on-rice-wheat/#.Vfm0-xHBzGc.

[48]"Reduce Your Customs Costs," International Trade www.internationaltrade.co.uk/articles_print.php?CID=13&SCID=&AID=160 (accessed September 23, 2015).

[49]David Marcelis, "Belgians Have a Term for People Who Drink Stella Artois—Tourists," *Wall Street Journal*, September 16, 2016, www.wsj.com/articles/hey-stella-its-getting-really-hard-to-find-belgiums-most-famous-beerin-belgium-1474037470.

[50]Maria Yates, "10 of Japan's Most Expensive Foods," The Richest, May 25, 2014, www.therichest.com/expensive-lifestyle/food/10-of-japans-most-expensive-foods/4/.

[51]Walmart website, www.walmart.com (accessed December 14, 2016); Connor Flynn, "Bang & Olufsen BeoVision 14 TV: A 4K Display with Class," Tehcnabob.com, August 14, 2016,http://technabob.com/blog/2016/08/14/bang-olufsen-beovision-14-tv/.

[52]Jason Chow, "Chinese Luxury Shoppers Speak Euro," *Wall Street Journal*, September 14, 2015, www.wsj.com/articles/chinese-open-luxury-wallets-for-europe-1442261511.

[53]"Transfer Price," *Investopedia,* www.investopedia.com/terms/t/transferprice.asp, (accessed May 15, 2017).

[54]Peter Wells and Vanessa Houlder, "Chevron Loses Landmark Tax Case on Transfer Pricing," *Financial Times*, April 20, 2017, www.ft.com/content/9eaef50e-264f-11e7-a34a-538b4cb30025.

[55]"Starbucks Coffee International," www.starbucks.com/business/international-stores (accessed December 14, 2016).

[56]Itika Sharma Punit, "Amazon Has Just Given a $3-Billion Reason for Flipkart and Snapdeal to Worry," Quartz India, June 8, 2016, http://qz.com/701919/amazon-has-just-given-a-3-billion-reason-for-flipkart-and-snapdeal-to-worry/.

[57]David Arnold, "Seven Rules of International Distribution," *Harvard Business Review*, November–December 2000, https://hbr.org/2000/11/seven-rules-of-international-distribution.

CHAPTER **18**

Global Operations and Supply-Chain Management

simonkr/Getty Images

Introduction

To compete in the global market, companies like Walmart, Lenovo, Boeing, and UPS have each used global operations and supply-chain management to improve their operational efficiencies and deliver superior value to customers. In this chapter, we discuss how to improve the operations and supply chains of international companies.

We begin by exploring a company's "make or buy" decision, and then we explore optimal locations for manufacturing products or outsourcing production to someone else. These decisions affect the supply-chain structure and the best structure for today's global market. Finally, we conclude the chapter by formulating ways to draw upon data analytics to improve operations.

LEARNING OBJECTIVES

After exploring this chapter you will be able to:

1. **Compare** the advantages and disadvantages of global procurement
2. **Evaluate** locations for global production
3. **Explain** benefits of global supply-chain management and modern planning systems
4. **Identify** ways to improve supply chains through the use of data analytics

18.1 Global Procurement

LEARNING OBJECTIVE

Compare the advantages and disadvantages of global procurement.

All businesses sell something. Some sell goods (such as cell phones, gasoline, or heavy machinery), whereas others sell services (for example, haircuts, help with filing taxes, or personal fitness training). Some businesses sell goods *and* services (like a car dealership that sells the car and then performs maintenance services).

In this chapter, we refer to both goods and services as *products*. When the production system is primarily used to create goods, it is called a manufacturing system. When it primarily creates a service, it is called a service system. Production systems are the overall strategy and mechanism for converting inputs—such as raw materials, land, labor, machinery, information, and energy—into a product that brings value to customers. For example, Marriott International, the world's largest hotel company, uses buildings, beds, food, drinks, entertainment, exercise space, and staff in over 110 countries to create a comfortable environment for its guests (**Figure 18.1**). All these factors are components of its production system.

As a field, operations management includes the work of managing all the resources used in the production system of a business organization—keep in mind that production systems are not limited to manufacturing companies. All companies spend significant time acquiring goods and services (the procurement process), producing products to sell (production), moving materials through the production system (logistics), and designing new products (research and development). While on the surface global operations might seem completely different from company to company, experts agree that effective supply-chain management is an invaluable tool all firms can adopt to reduce costs, increase revenues, and ultimately reap profits.

One of the most basic and critical decisions an international business leader has to make is whether to buy production components from external suppliers or make those components in-house. This is sometimes called the "sourcing decision" or the "make-or-buy decision." How a given firm answers this question has a huge influence on what that company will become as it moves forward. For example, the U.S. company Gulfstream Aerospace could manufacture the engines for its business jets or it could buy them from a global supplier such as Rolls Royce, General Electric, or Pratt & Whitney. Both options are viable, but Gulfstream itself will change as a company depending on which option it chooses.

Almost anything in business can be obtained from outside the company, even from international markets. This is also known as **outsourcing**. For example, major pharmaceutical companies can either spend millions of dollars to design, develop, and perform clinical trials for new cancer therapies in-house, or they can survey hundreds of drug ideas and buy the most promising ones from researchers who develop them at medical schools and universities across

outsourcing obtaining a good or service from an external supplier, often in international markets

Michele and Tom Grimm/Alamy Stock Photo

FIGURE 18.1 **Marriott International is the world's largest hospitality company**

the globe. Buying ideas can save years of development time by bypassing the dead ends inevitable in the course of development, but it also cuts into profits because the best ideas often cost millions of dollars, and the price only goes up the closer a drug gets to market. To help offset the costs of making drugs themselves, smaller pharmaceutical companies often partner with universities to help them.[1] Rather than pay for the research upfront, the companies share the costs and share the profits.

As a result, a crucial step in the make-or-buy decision process is to consider the advantages suppliers have in their area of expertise and compare that to the time and money required to develop the same abilities internally. If a pharmaceutical company analyzes its financial capital and human capital and has confidence in its scientists' abilities to design therapies, then it will probably decide to research and develop drugs in-house. If, on the other hand, the company realizes that its core competencies are in fielding clinical trials and marketing therapies to the public, then it will probably purchase ideas instead.

WileyPLUS

See Whiteboard Video: Offshoring Decisions

Once leaders settle the make-or-buy decision, they must also decide whether to make or buy locally or globally. Buying globally is called *global procurement*; producing globally is called *global production*. In some cases, global procurement is actually a necessity because of a lack of locally available natural resources. For example, Singapore has a strong export economy, but it is also highly dependent on imports for natural resources because it is a small island nation. It even imports drinking water to supplement the domestic supply, as illustrated in **Figure 18.2**.[2] In fact, almost all raw materials used in Singapore's vast production chains are procured internationally.

Advantages of Global Procurement

One obvious advantage of global procurement is that it enables a company to take advantage of cheaper costs abroad for components like labor, land, and resources. These cost savings can make a firm more competitive. Procuring rather than producing can also save a company millions of dollars of investment and years of headache—especially if it is procuring high-tech, expensive, or otherwise complex products that are not core to its business.[3] Global procurement also enables a firm to focus on its core capabilities by outsourcing those activities that are not vital to creating value for the customer.[4]

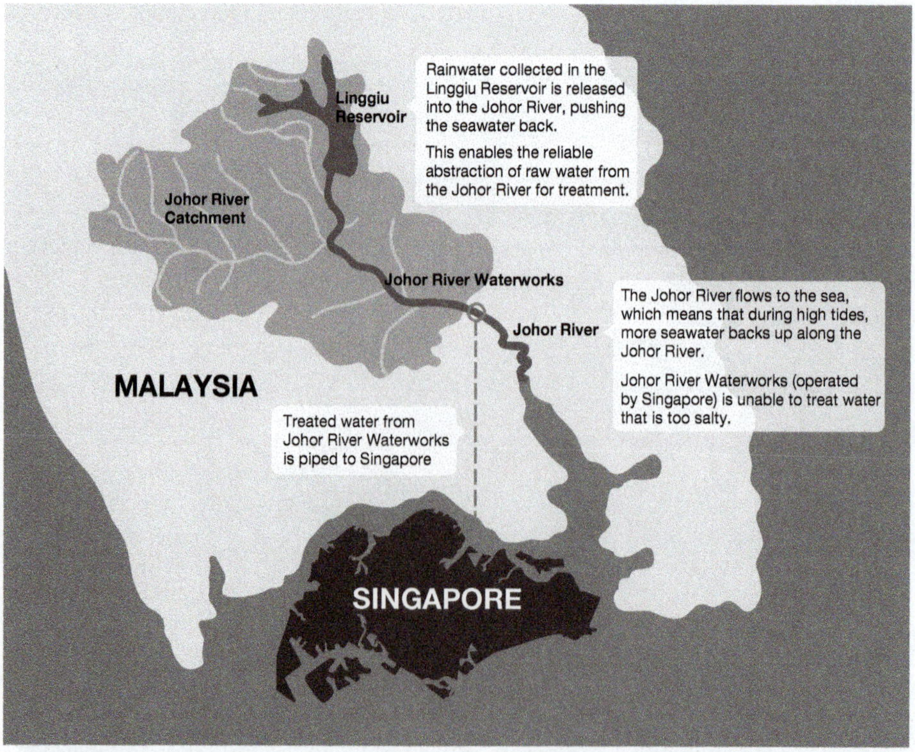

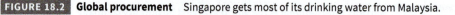

FIGURE 18.2 **Global procurement** Singapore gets most of its drinking water from Malaysia.

Global procurement allows a firm the most flexibility in deciding on which products or inputs to use because it opens up sources to the global market. Firms limited to a single locale can be undone by issues such as governmental turmoil or collapse, currency fluctuations, taxes, tariffs, or even climate.[5] For a company practicing global procurement, these issues all influence the attractiveness of different vendors, but the firm can adjust procurement according to changes in the competitive landscape in order to maintain its own advantages.

Richard Atrero de Guzman/AnadoluAgency/Getty Images

FIGURE 18.3 **The 2016 earthquake in Japan disrupted Japan's just-in-time supply chain**

Disadvantages of Global Procurement

Global procurement is not always the cheapest option, however, and often it is not as cheap as it might seem on paper. Transportation costs for goods and communication challenges between parties can absorb significant time and money, and in the process supply chains often become long and convoluted. As the supply chain lengthens, inventories can become larger and less efficient. **Just-in-time (JIT)** manufacturing is a common method of reclaiming efficiency in the production process. It consists of carefully planning the whole production process from start to finish in order to avoid carrying excess inventory. JIT systems work extremely well under normal conditions, but even the most finely tuned processes can be rendered useless if an event disrupts the supply chain. For example, in 2016 Japan was hit by earthquakes, which temporarily suspended the activities of Toyota's production plants (**Figure 18.3**). This shows how Japanese companies are susceptible to supply-chain disasters, even after many companies made changes after the 2011 earthquake and tsunami that led to over 20,000 deaths and major problems with supply chains, especially those using JIT.[6]

just-in-time (JIT) a method manufacturing that consists of carefully planning the whole production process from start to finish in order to avoid carrying excess inventory

From a strategic standpoint, excess inventory isn't the only problem companies may face when they engage in global procurement. Some firms lose control of their operations when they purchase goods and components around the world because maintaining quality and punctuality standards becomes more difficult. A delay anywhere along the supply chain can quickly escalate and prevent companies from filling orders.

Another potential drawback is that procuring from suppliers may have the unintended consequence of helping suppliers become future competitors. When a business allows external companies to manufacture parts of their products, those companies begin to develop the capabilities necessary to copy and produce the product themselves.[7] For instance, when Dell Inc. was first founded, it manufactured its entire product line in-house. Later, to achieve production efficiencies, it decided to outsource the simpler parts of its computers to ASUSTek, a vendor in Taiwan. Outsourcing brought increased margins and enabled Dell to focus on the most complex portions of the product—where the most value was added. Over time, Dell continued to outsource to ASUSTek more of its end product, such as the whole computer, until Dell was essentially a brand name and the company focused on design and marketing and did no manufacturing at all. It initially chose to outsource because it could cut costs without cutting revenues, increasing profitability over the short term. However, ASUSTek learned everything Dell had to teach it and started putting those new competencies to work. It eventually developed its own products, and now it competes with Dell directly in the United States. By aggressively outsourcing, Dell inadvertently created a new competitor.[8]

Last, a business practice called **offset agreements** may force companies to practice global procurement in a way that reduces their competitiveness. In an offset agreement, a supplier agrees to buy products from the party to which it is selling, in order to win the buyer as a customer and "offset" the buyer's production costs. Usually the seller is a foreign company and the buyer is a government that requires the foreign company to buy products from local companies.[9] For example, if Japan-based All Nippon Airways purchases aircraft from Boeing, the

offset agreement an agreement wherein a supplier agrees to buy products from the party to whom it is selling in order to win the buyer as a customer and "offset" the buyer's production costs

Japanese government may ask Boeing to offset this order by purchasing parts for or assembling portions of the aircraft in Japan. This allows some of the value Boeing will create to directly affect the Japanese economy.

Outsourcing and Offshoring

offshoring moving production outside the home country

If outsourcing is buying production from outside a company, then **offshoring** is moving production to outside a country. If a company offshores, it is not necessarily outsourcing, and vice versa. For example, United Airlines can open its own customer service office in India and hire Indian workers to work there. This is an example of offshoring but not outsourcing. Delta could pay a separate company near its Atlanta, Georgia, headquarters to handle all its customer service calls. This is an example of outsourcing but not offshoring. Of course, the company could outsource to an offshore firm, allowing it to both outsource and offshore.

The decision to outsource and/or offshore some aspect of a firm's operations can have major strategic consequences for the firm. Managers should choose these strategies only after considering the current economic climate, industry trends, and the firm's long-term goals. Outsourcing has grown more common in recent decades, largely because companies need to find the best possible products at the best possible prices from around the globe in order to compete.[10] When outsourcing, a firm and its suppliers sometimes enter into a partnership rather than simply transacting with one another. By partnering, both firms share in the risk and the reward. Some firms, called hollow corporations, outsource and offshore almost everything they do. Dell became an example of this by outsourcing its entire production to ASUSTek in Taiwan.

But outsourcing and offshoring aren't just about production costs. They also introduce transaction costs that come from relying on the market to obtain a product or component rather than making it yourself; see **Figure 18.4** for an example.

operational risk a measure of a firm's inability to document the work remote employees do, describe the different situations they might face, and direct their responses in each scenario

Once a company has considered its goals and other factors related to the industry and the economic climate, it should also consider the two types of risk in outsourcing and offshoring decisions. The first is **operational risk**, which measures how difficult it is to codify and control the production process. When companies can document the work employees do in the production process and stipulate what employees' actions should be, the process can be codified and entails low operational risk. When companies can assess the quality of a process, that process is measurable and also entails low operational risk. Companies must factor in the transaction costs associated with operational risk; these costs accrue from the travel, communication, and coordination associated with managing outsourcing and offshoring.

structural risk a measure of a firm's difficulty when relationships with vendors do not work as expected

The second type of risk is **structural risk**, which comes into play when relationships with service providers or outsourcing vendors become problematic. Companies can assess this type of risk by examining how well they can monitor, or at least trust, their suppliers.[11] When structural risk is present, a company must factor in the transaction costs of guarding against opportunistic behavior by the supply partner. These can include the costs of finding reliable vendors the firm can trust, drafting contracts to prevent those vendors from competing with the company, and enforcing contracts and resolving disagreements. **Figure 18.5** provides further insight into the transaction costs associated with structural and operational risk.

insourcing the practice of using a company's internal employees or other resources to accomplish a task.

Based on the different risks associated with outsourcing, firms may have compelling reasons for wanting to maintain production in-house, or **insourcing**, rather than outsourcing. For instance, Boeing struggled for years to tighten its global production of the 787 Dreamliner. Delays and quality issues plagued the project, and management ultimately decided to insource more of the manufacturing in order to gain greater control.[12] As the project moves forward, the company will probably continue this practice. Boeing is likely to insource more on future products as well, until it is once again confident that outsourcing won't lead to diminished quality and costly delays.

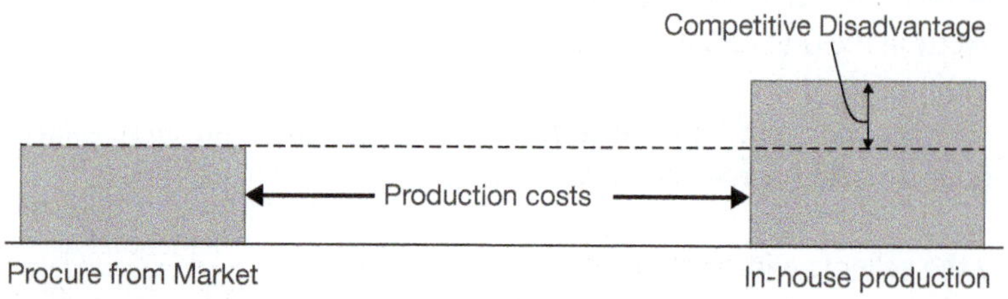

FIGURE 18.4 **Transaction costs associated with outsourcing**

Structural Risks: Resources spent on guarding against opportunistic behaviour by vendor

- Finding reliable vendors
- Drafting contracts
- Enforcing contracts
- Dispute resolution

Operational Risks: Resources spent on managing interactions with a (remote) vendor due to non-codifiability and non-measurability

- Travel
- (Tele) communications
- Coordination mistakes

FIGURE 18.5 **Risks from transaction costs**

WileyPLUS

See Whiteboard Video: Offshoring Tools

18.2 Global Production

LEARNING OBJECTIVE

Evaluate locations for global production.

The decision to produce rather than buy products is complex for global firms because they must decide *where* to produce—domestically or offshore. In this section, we discuss the advantages and disadvantages of making products rather than buying them. We also discuss where to locate production if a firm decides to make its own products.

Advantages of Making

Making components in-house can ensure a steady supply, enable stable price estimates, and maintain control of sensitive knowledge. Making components gives a firm more control over production time frames and deliveries—extremely important characteristics when demand is uncertain. For example, Samsung originally decided to produce most of the batteries for its Galaxy phones in-house to ensure that it could leverage its in-depth knowledge of energy management in electronics and that competitors do not get hold of the technology. In a twist of fate, however, in the fall of 2016, Samsung had to recall all its Galaxy Note7 phones because some of the devices were catching fire because of the battery overheating (**Figure 18.6**). More than 65 percent of the faulty batteries had been produced in-house by a Samsung subsidiary. Ironically, the remainder, supplied by the external vendor TDK of Japan, were not flawed.[13] This caused Samsung to reconsider its decision to make most of the batteries for its phones.

ASSOCIATED PRESS

FIGURE 18.6 **Samsung Galaxy Note7** These phones were banned from airplanes, businesses, and entire governments by the end of 2016 because of the possibility they could catch fire.

Companies like FedEx and UPS have also recognized the advantages of producing inside the company, but with much better results. For example, both companies decided to hire full-time meteorologists to help them alter flight plans in real time at any airport they use.[14] Like the pharmaceutical companies that make their own drugs, UPS and FedEx figured out how beneficial and costly it would be to build a center and staff it with competent meteorologists, compared that analysis with the value of hiring an outsourced

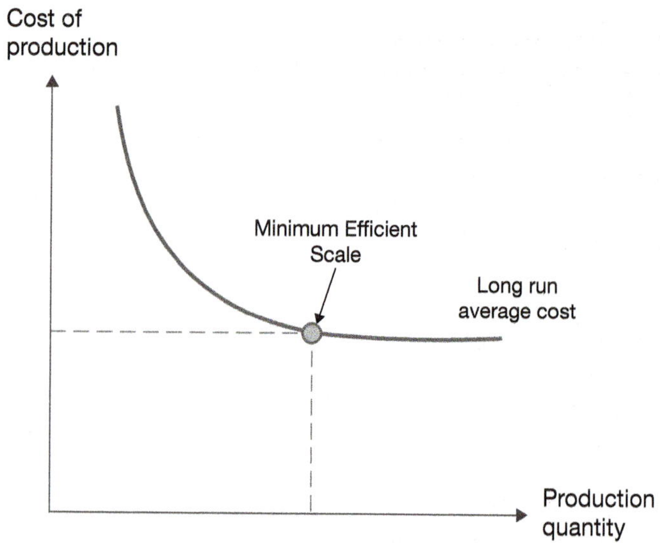

FIGURE 18.7 **Unit cost curve**

weather team, and then acted accordingly. This "make" decision by UPS and FedEx was well worth the cost, as forecasting weather is key to getting packages to people on time.

On the other hand, firms must also consider how much of the product they will produce. To make in-house production worthwhile, a company must make at least the **minimum efficient scale**, the smallest quantity at which long-run, total average cost is minimized. In other words, companies need to consider whether they can produce enough of the product to make an investment in the production process economically worthwhile. The more a product will be purchased by consumers, the more likely that making the product in-house will be a good decision (see **Figure 18.7**).

minimum efficient scale the smallest production quantity at which long-run, total average cost is minimized

Disadvantages of Making

The main disadvantage associated with making products or components is that it requires the company to develop production expertise. This takes considerable time and effort, and it also runs the risk of distracting the firm from its strategy if production is not at the core of what the company does.[15] No matter how many smart or hard-working people a company employs, it will never be able to be great at everything. For that reason, sometimes the best decision is to use the competitive advantages of other firms by buying from them what they produce or provide better than you can.

As we discussed, producing components in-house can make it difficult to achieve economies of scale. When this happens, buying from another company can be more cost-effective. For instance, Zipp, a U.S. manufacturer of bicycle racing wheels, is able to achieve greater efficiency and economy of scale by focusing on just producing wheels and selling them to many different bicycle companies, such as Trek, Specialized, and Felt.[16] By aggregating demand, Zipp is able to achieve economies of scale in wheel manufacturing that none of the bike companies could match on their own.

Moreover, in-house producers often do not have the same incentives as external suppliers to produce high-quality products because internal producers have captive customers. Competition tends to inspire innovation, and in-house production often doesn't face competition. For instance, ACDelco provides parts to General Motors. However, because General Motors owns ACDelco, ACDelco needs to produce products that are merely sufficiently good to win the business, rather than being forced to make products that are world-class.[17]

dual sourcing a source strategy in which firms produce products in-house to ensure quality and availability while also purchasing the same products from suppliers in order to force competition and push innovation within the in-house unit

To combat this apathy, firms sometimes use a strategy of **dual sourcing**, or producing certain products in-house to ensure quality and availability while also purchasing the same products from suppliers in order to force competition and push innovation within the in-house unit. When Samsung's own subsidiary created the faulty battery used in over 65 percent of Samsung phones, Samsung considered adding an additional outside supplier to spur some competition. This strategy motivates internal suppliers to be as efficient as external suppliers.

Last, building up in-house production leads to increased fixed costs for companies. A firm that merely buys what it needs incurs only variable costs because it is obligated to buy only what it needs to fill orders. A firm that makes products in-house has both the fixed costs of any production assets and the variable costs of production. Fixed costs can make it more difficult to *become* profitable, but they can also make it easier to *remain* profitable as the firm moves down the learning curve.

Location

To decide where to locate production, firms must evaluate many factors such as culture, political climate, and economic environment. For instance, China became the world's largest manufacturer because it had cheap and plentiful labor, abundant natural resources, and a government that encouraged growth and modernization. However, the Chinese economy has become so modernized that wages are climbing higher and costs are rising for foreign firms. While China will undoubtedly retain some manufacturing, many firms are shifting production to China's less-developed neighbors, such as Vietnam, Thailand, Malaysia, and Indonesia.[18] (See **Figure 18.8** for a look at the most attractive locations for offshoring production).

In addition to low labor costs, environmental externalities may make a particular country or city more desirable for production. Bangalore, India, has quickly become a technology hotspot and in some ways is beginning to resemble California's Silicon Valley. Several universities are located in the area, and each year they graduate thousands of highly competent students. Venture capital firms such as Innosight Ventures, Accel, IDG Ventures, and Intel Capital are actively funding startups in the area. Moreover, thousands of information technology workers are repatriating to Bangalore from the United States, Canada, and Western Europe. With abundant venture capital, human capital, and skills, Bangalore is an attractive location for technology companies.[19]

Beyond the physical environment, the economic climate can also affect location decisions. Foreign exchange rates are a major factor that makes certain areas more desirable as manufacturing locations. A devalued currency allows products from that country to be sold for a lower price. For example, the euro has recently been a very strong currency, which gives Europeans greater purchasing power when buying imports; however, that strength also makes their exports more expensive. On the other hand, the Vietnamese dong is one of the weakest currencies in the world, helping Vietnam to quickly become one of the largest exporters in the world.

2016 A.T. Kearney Global Services Location Index™ Top 20

+ Moved up − Moved down

Rank	Country	Δ	Value
1.	India	0	6.96
2.	China	0	6.49
3.	Malaysia	0	6.05
4.	Brazil	+4	6.00
5.	Indonesia	0	5.99
6.	Thailand	0	5.92
7.	Philippines	0	5.88
8.	Mexico	−4	5.87
9.	Chile	+4	5.72
10.	Poland	+1	5.68
11.	Vietnam	+1	5.66
12.	Bulgaria	−3	5.60
13.	Romania	+5	5.59
14.	Sri Lanka	+2	5.54
15.	United States	−1	5.51
16.	Egypt	−6	5.45
17.	Russia	+4	5.38
18.	Latvia	+5	5.33
19.	Costa Rica	+5	5.32
20.	Colombia	+23	5.32

■ Financial attractiveness ■ People skills and availability ■ Business environment

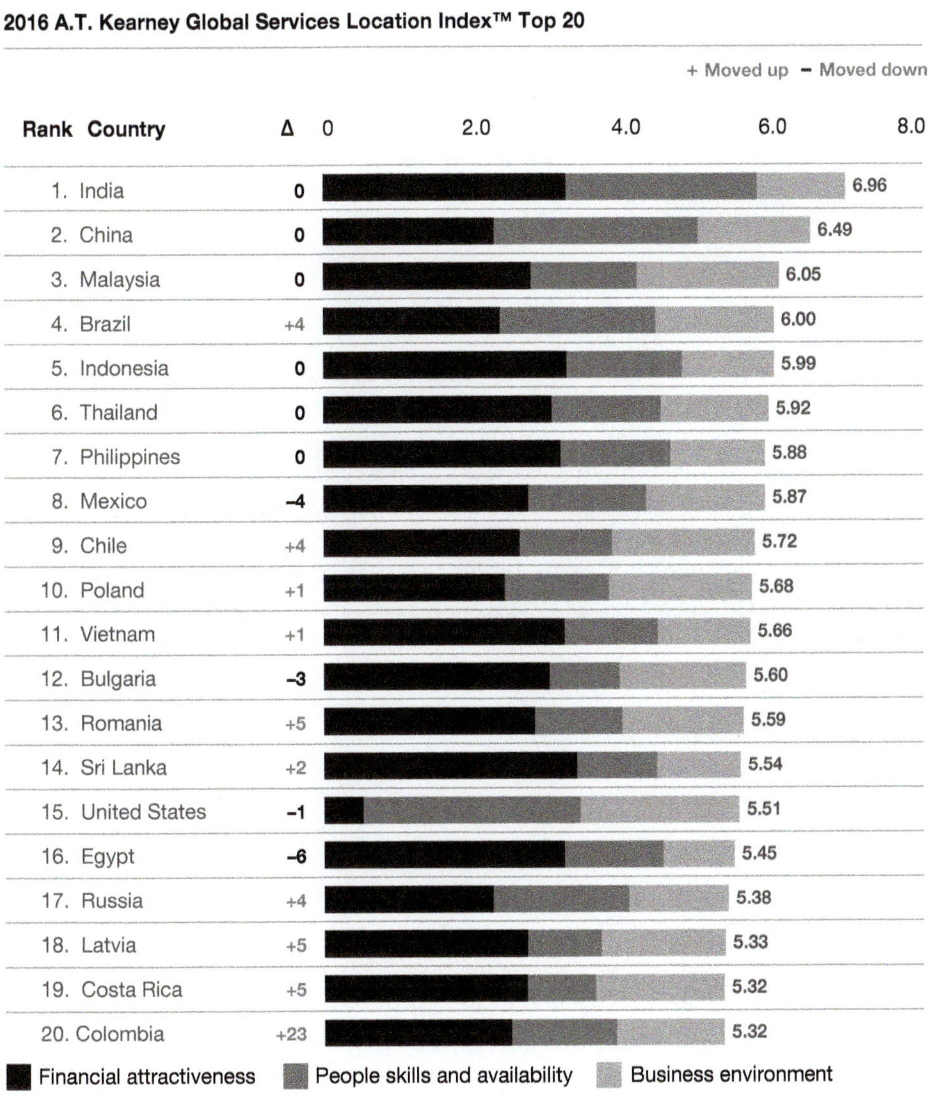

FIGURE 18.8 Global location index **Source:** Adapted from 2016 A.T. Kearney Global Services Location Index Top 20 List, https://www.atkearney.com/strategic-it/global-services-location-index.

The degree to which a product is standardized can also influence the choice of production location. Companies that sell a standardized product worldwide may decide to operate facilities in one country to take advantage of economies of scale; however, a customized product might be better served by having multiple, regional sites for production. Felt Bicycles designs and manufactures bikes exclusively in its Irvine, California, factory because its products are standardized, even though they are sold worldwide.[20]

On the other hand, many companies customize their products for different target markets. In seventy-five countries and territories, vehicles drive on the left side of the road, and vehicles sold there must be designed to meet those drivers' needs.[21] Each country's environmental agency may require different levels of fuel efficiency or other technical specifications. For these reasons, car companies find it advantageous to spread production facilities across various countries in order to sell their vehicles on a global scale. Toyota not only produces vehicles in Japan but has fifty-one other manufacturing facilities across the globe[22] (see **Figure 18.9**).

Another consideration for locating production is the price of the product compared to its weight and volume. Rolex watches and Apple computers have a high value-to-weight ratio, which means they are expensive yet light. This means the cost of shipping is low compared with the revenue the products will eventually bring in, so it is less important for such products to be manufactured geographically close to the end consumer. Raw steel and gasoline, on the other hand, have very low value-to-weight and value-to-volume ratios. These products are expensive to ship relative to their final price, so it is more important to produce close to the final customer. **Table 18.1** compares the value-to-weight ratios for iron and steel with those of coffee, tea, and spices traded between the United States, Canada, and Mexico (the NAFTA countries). In 2015, iron and steel had a value-to-weight ratio of 0.61, while coffee, tea, and spices had a ratio of 4.71. This indicates that coffee, tea, and spices are more likely to be shipped across borders because their value-to-weight ratio is nearly eight times that of iron and steel.[23]

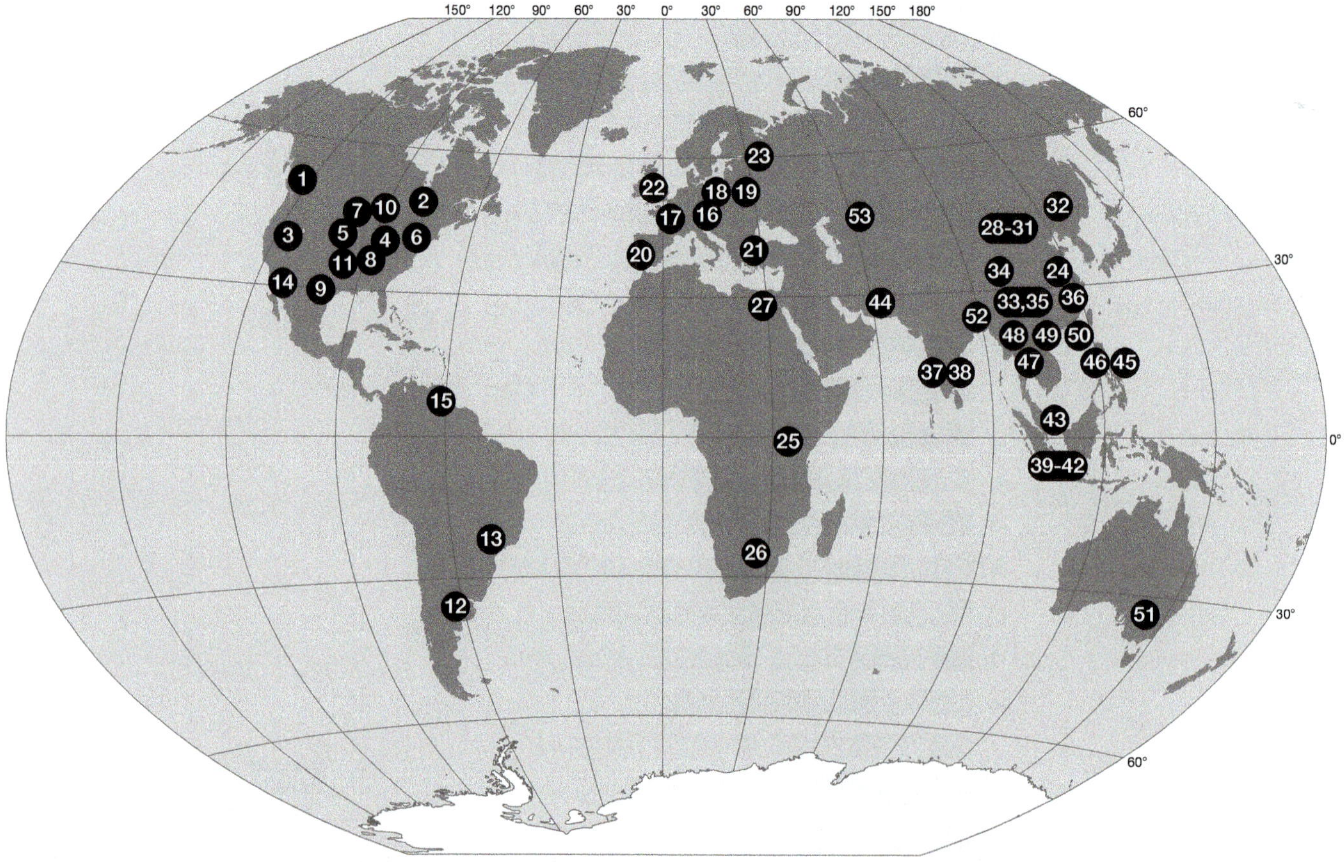

FIGURE 18.9 **Toyota's international manufacturing operations** **Source:** "Worldwide operations," Toyota Newsroom, March 2, 2016, http://newsroom.toyota.co.jp/en/corporate/companyinformation/worldwide.

TABLE 18.1 Value-to-weight ratios of goods traded between NAFTA countries

Yearly Trade Ratios of Value to Weight between USA - NAFTA by Aggregate All Models						
	Iron and Steel			Coffee, Tea and Spices		
Statistical Year	Import Value by All Modes	Import Weight by All Modes	Ratio of Import Value to Import Weight (U.S.$/Kg)	Import Value by All Modes	Import Weight by All Modes	Ratio of Import Value to Import Weight (U.S.$/Kg)
2004	$ 5,574,904,641.00	10,991,886,396	0.51	$ 260,007,105.00	133,278,865	1.95
2005	$ 6,144,559,517.00	11,511,302,870	0.53	$ 302,583,726.00	117,280,552	2.58
2006	$ 6,327,472,996.00	11,635,451,943	0.54	$ 346,976,624.00	140,370,480	2.47
2007	$ 6,625,451,041.00	11,018,648,251	0.6	$ 371,600,993.00	135,831,187	2.74
2008	$ 8,932,838,388.00	11,205,431,166	0.8	$ 425,658,041.00	131,873,185	3.23
2009	$ 4,187,517,443.00	7,327,152,444	0.57	$ 490,427,006.00	154,923,349	3.17
2010	$ 7,039,825,482.00	10,723,087,749	0.66	$ 599,317,258.00	147,741,064	4.06
2011	$ 7,925,885,632.00	10,646,527,750	0.74	$ 994,976,276.00	172,509,958	5.77
2012	$ 7,294,684,844.00	9,704,424,703	0.75	$ 972,546,985.00	193,790,893	5.02
2013	$ 6,971,609,291.00	10,213,841,935	0.68	$ 744,290,220.00	178,233,164	4.18
2014	$ 7,932,232,774.00	11,203,895,901	0.71	$ 760,149,910.00	165,937,525	4.58
2015	$ 5,881,587,802.00	9,583,820,076	0.61	$ 769,136,248.00	163,250,976	4.71
Note: Surface modes are defined as truck, rail and pipeline. For additional detail refer to the metadata.						
SOURCE: U.S. Department of Transportation, Bureau of Transportation Statistics, TransBorder Freight Data.						
Report created: Thu May 26 13:19:26 EDT 2016						

Source: "North American Transborder Freight Data: Value to Weight Ratio Data," Bureau of Transportation Statistics, http://transborder.bts.gov/programs/international/transborder/TBDR_VWR.html (accessed Aug. 1, 2017)

For simplicity in the supply chain, final production facilities for end products are often located as close as possible to the end customer, even when the value-to-weight ratio is high. For instance, Mercedes-Benz opened a state-of-the-art factory in Vance, Alabama, in 1997. Today, the facility produces the popular C-Class sedan, primarily for the United States and Canada, because it makes sense to locate production as close to the end consumer as possible, rather than ship a 3,500-pound vehicle across the Atlantic Ocean. So far, the Alabama-based plant has been an enormous success, and Mercedes-Benz is considering manufacturing more vehicles at the plant in the future.[24]

The last thing to consider when choosing a location is the image of the product and how that image relates to the production location. Certain geographic areas have developed a reputation for producing certain products at a very high quality, so producing products in these areas can enhance the prestige of the brand. Switzerland's image and reputation as a manufacturer of luxury mechanical watches makes it an attractive country for producing hand-crafted watches, even though it is expensive to do so there. Rolex and Patek Philippe, which are both Swiss companies, maintain production facilities in Switzerland despite the cost advantages they would achieve by moving to Eastern Europe or Asia.[25] The prestige of the Swiss watch industry allows these firms to remain profitable even though their production costs are high.

Relocation

Choosing and building a production facility is an expensive proposition, no matter where the facility is located, and it can be one of the most important decisions a firm makes because it is such a major driver of costs over the long-term. Another challenge is that many of the factors that influence costs can change over time. Currencies appreciate and depreciate in value, unemployment rates change, transportation costs fluctuate, new markets open up, and old markets become less lucrative. Sometimes, enough changes may occur to make it worthwhile for a company to relocate its production facilities.

reshored moving production from outside a country back to the home country

Both the business and popular press frequently report news stories about companies building foreign plants and "sending" jobs overseas. However, some manufacturing has actually been **reshored**—or onshored, as it is also called. Reshoring is the act of reintroducing domestic manufacturing to a company's home country. After experiencing extreme transaction costs in foreign markets, some companies have decided to reshore their overseas outsourcing endeavors. When rich-world companies from rich countries began to produce goods abroad, they did so because the costs of materials and labor were lower. However, recent shifts in the global environment, such as increased costs of production in China and India, make the cost of production high enough that when companies factor in the transaction costs from outsourcing and offshoring production, they may opt to reshore.[26] For example, in 2016 General Electric shifted production of a water heater from China to a plant in Louisville, Kentucky. Similarly, Walmart asked General Electric to manufacture high-efficiency light bulbs in its plants in Ohio and Illinois as part of the giant retailer's "Made in the USA" initiative.[27]

18.3 Global Supply Chains

LEARNING OBJECTIVE

Explain benefits of global supply-chain management and modern planning systems.

In today's business world, supply chains and their management are crucial for success. A supply chain includes all the activities related to transforming components into products for the end user, including the transfer of money and information. Supply-chain management refers to the management of all those activities in an effort to minimize costs while maximizing value for end users. If a supply chain is managed effectively, it can be a competitive advantage for a firm.

An effective supply chain matters for producing high-quality, low-cost products and for maintaining a firm's reputation as an ethical organization. Customers often hold companies responsible for activities throughout the supply chain—regardless of whether those activities were under the direct management of the company or of one of its suppliers. Customers are unlikely to return if service is poor or mistakes are made, or if supply-chain members use child labor or inhuman or environmentally costly work practices.

Globalization has opened a world of opportunity for supply-chain managers, giving them the freedom to produce each component of a product in the best location; however, these new opportunities come with new challenges. For instance, A. Schulman, a global plastics manufacturer based in Fairlawn, Ohio, decided to open production facilities in China when some of its business customers began building production facilities there. It was a conscious decision made with the hope of shortening the supply chain and providing better service for its customers that were moving to China. Then, in 2012, a factory explosion at its nylon supplier in Germany made it very difficult for the Chinese plant to acquire the nylon necessary for its products. This could have been a supply-chain disaster, but the company was able to switch quickly to alternate materials that it could access locally in China, without diminishing the quality of its products.[28] The global supply chain of A. Schulman makes production more efficient and competitive, but the coordination of the global supply chain also makes production more complex and risky. As **Figure 18.10** shows, the company has operations across the globe.

The final piece of the globalization puzzle is that everything in the supply chain needs to run smoothly. Otherwise gains in one area may be cancelled out by inefficiency in another. For example, a company could source raw materials from a stable, massive operation in order to

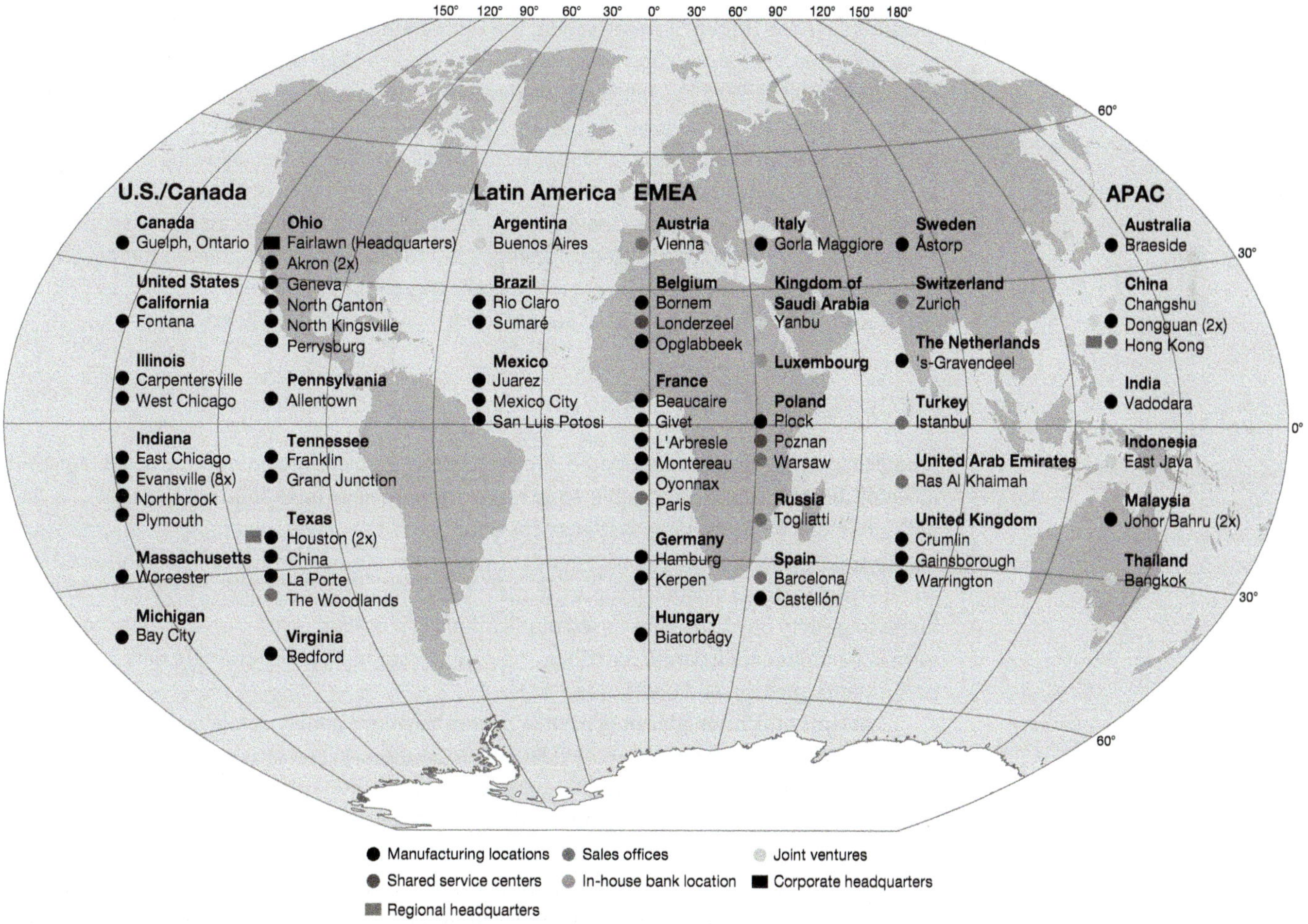

FIGURE 18.10 **A. Schulman's operations span the globe** **Source:** "Form 8-K SCHULMAN A INC For: Sep 03," StreetINsider.com, September 2, 2015, www.streetinsider.com/SEC+Filings/Form+8-K+SCHULMAN+A+INC+For%3A+Sep+03/10865794.html.

gain bulk discounts through economies of scale, but this is less effective if production is not modified to accompany the increase in available materials. The firm would need to either ramp up production or find a place to store the raw materials until they are ready to be used—and storage both costs extra money and slows the production process.

Because all parts of the supply chain are interconnected, before making changes global leaders need to think about how one change will affect all the subsequent steps of the production process. Improved technology and data analytics are becoming critical for supply-chain managers to ensure reliability and keep costs down while simultaneously monitoring the overall operation of the global supply chain. We discuss these next.

Improving Global Supply-Chain Management

When Boeing started its ambitious Dreamliner project, the multinational U.S. manufacturer decided to outsource nearly the entire production process for its new wide-body passenger plane to countless different overseas firms, as **Figure 18.11** highlights.

The hope was to cut total production time from six years to four while saving money on production. Unfortunately, just the opposite occurred. Production has been delayed three years, and maintaining quality has been a challenge. The project has encountered problems with software, lithium-ion batteries, and airframe weaknesses.[29] This example demonstrates the need to always see supply-chain management as a major area for competitive advantage and improvement.

Consumers today are more interested than ever in making sure that the products they consume are produced responsibly and sustainably. This interest becomes a serious point of concern for companies when they tolerate questionable behavior or market a product that could harm the end user's health. For example, Chipotle Mexican Grill—a fast-casual chain with restaurants in the United States, Canada, the United Kingdom, Germany, and France—is dedicated to the ethical production of the pork, beef, and chicken served in its restaurants. This focus on ethical farming has been very well received and has enabled the company to expand rapidly. In early 2015, however, Chipotle's supply-chain auditors discovered that its primary pork supplier was not adhering to Chipotle standards, which included allowing the pigs access to the outdoors instead of forcing them to live in cramped pens their entire lives. The restaurant temporarily removed pork from the menus of most of its restaurants until a new supplier was found. Chipotle has also committed to raising antibiotic-free, grass-fed animals for meat and to using locally sourced produce. Its customers take this commitment very seriously, so Chipotle needs to know the ins and outs of its supply chain in order to satisfy diners.[30]

Information Technologies

An efficient and globally coordinated supply chain is a powerful competitive advantage, but it would be practically impossible to achieve without help from Internet applications and enterprise resource-planning systems. The Internet is the largest example of internetworking, or the linking of multiple, independent networks into one, massive interconnected network. An estimated 3.5 billion people use the Internet for various purposes, and that number is increasing every day.[31] Internet-based applications (also called cloud-based applications) perform any number of disparate functions and enable companies to coordinate data, schedules, performance metrics, and plans in real time.

enterprise resource-planning (ERP) systems technology that helps firms gather all relevant information into a single database, represent all business functions in a module, and provide access to data in real time

Enterprise resource-planning (ERP) systems help firms gather all relevant information into a single database, represent all business functions in a module, and provide access to data in real time. Because of the global nature of the world economy, ERP systems operate across multiple languages, multiple nationalities, and multiple currencies. When using an ERP system, the user selects which language to apply, which nation's accounting standards to follow, and which currency to use. As a result, a company can use the system in the German language, following Swiss accounting standards, and reporting currency in Swiss francs just as easily as using it in French, following Canadian accounting standards, and using Canadian dollars as currency. Today, almost all industries have developed ERP systems, and when these systems are combined with the power of the Internet, they become the structure on which supply chains can be coordinated globally.

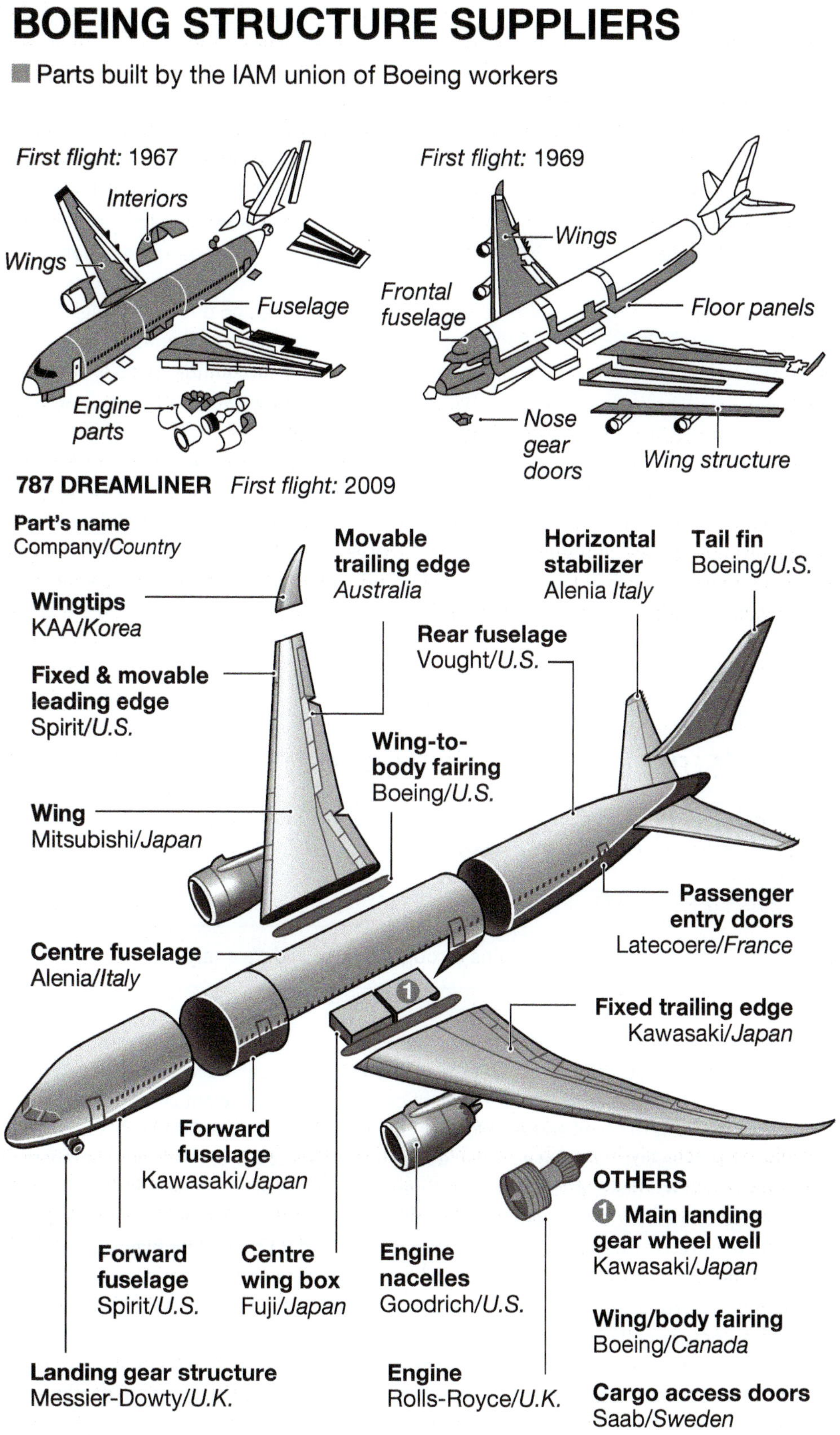

FIGURE 18.11 **Outsourcing** Boeing outsourced production of most of the Dreamliner to companies around the globe. **Source:** Kyle Peterson, "Outsourcing at Boeing: How the Aerospace Giant Looks Abroad for Key Suppliers in Dreamliner," *Huffington Post*, January 20, 2011, www.huffingtonpost.com/2011/01/20/a-wing-and-a-prayer-outso_n_811498.html.

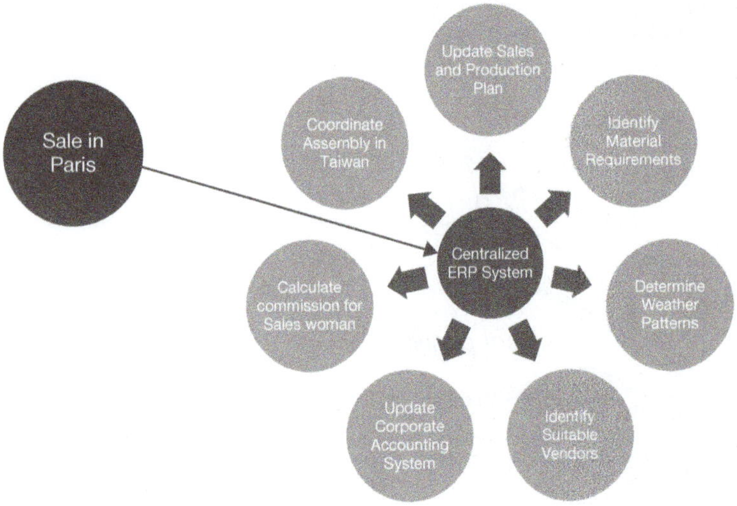

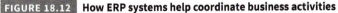

FIGURE 18.12 **How ERP systems help coordinate business activities**

For example, a saleswoman working for a U.S. computer company in Paris can enter basic customer information into the system, which can then automatically verify the customer's credit limit. As soon as the sale closes, the system can take over to update the company's sales and production plan, create a list of material requirements for the order, schedule a shipment date, access weather patterns to identify the best delivery route, order parts from global vendors, coordinate final assembly at a factory in Taiwan, record the commission due to the saleswoman, update the corporate cash accounts in the United States, and update accounts payable, accounts receivable, and profitability on the cash flow statements (see **Figure 18.12**).

An effective ERP system will perform all these transactions automatically throughout the global supply chain and then monitor and update as necessary. The ERP industry—dominated by SAP and Oracle—has grown quickly in the past 15 years, and it continues to gain traction as ERP firms develop new products and functionality to help manage inventory, plan sales and operations, perform cloud computing, and plan work.[32]

18.4 Using Data Analytics to Improve Supply Chains

LEARNING OBJECTIVE

Identify ways to improve supply chains through the use of data analytics.

big data extremely large data sets that users can analyze to uncover statistical patterns, trends, and associations that might otherwise go unnoticed because of the volume of data

Big data describes extremely large data sets that users can analyze to uncover statistical patterns, trends, and associations that might otherwise go unnoticed because of the volume of data. Big data has been used to analyze epidemics, design more efficient cities, predict where crimes are most likely to occur, and even forecast the results of Supreme Court rulings. The 2003 book *Moneyball: The Art of Winning an Unfair Game*, by Michael Lewis, and the movie adaptation of the same name tell the story of Billy Beane, general manager for the Oakland Athletics, and the challenge of building a competitive baseball team without the financial resources of big-city teams (**Figure 18.13**). Beane's solution was to use big data to analyze players. Lewis and baseball writer Bill James postulated that on-base percentage and slugging percentage were much more important indicators of a player's run-scoring potential than batting average, stolen bases, or runs batted in. By focusing on these statistics, they were able to put together a winning team of players who had been overlooked by teams with greater financial resources.[33] Likewise, data analysis has opened new avenues for supply-chain managers to identify areas for improvement in their global operations.

Companies have used data analysis techniques for many years, but the analyses were typically narrow in scope, used in simple situations, and were applied to a limited quantity of data. Today, analysis methods have become very sophisticated. We've reached a point at which big data can play a major role in even routine decision making. Almost all large firms understand the importance of big data analysis and the promise it brings for supply-chain efficiency, but many struggle to implement analytics to drive higher performance. Some do not yet have the capability to perform analytics in-house for its global supply chains, and hiring an analytics

FIGURE 18.13 **Big Data even works for Brad Pitt** In the movie *Moneyball*, Peter Brand (played by Jonah Hill) shows the general manager of the Oakland Athletics, Billy Beane (Brad Pitt), how to recognize value in the stats of undervalued baseball players.

firm can be very expensive. Managers also worry about potential data-security issues, such as corporate espionage or theft by employees, that could result from handing over so much data to an outside party.

Applications of Data Analytics

Further complicating the decision to adopt expensive analytics methodologies are the mixed results implementation seems to bring. Among companies that have made a significant investment in big-data analysis, some have reported significant improvements and some have not. Research by Accenture has shown that developing an enterprise-wide strategy for data use increases the likelihood of success for a firm.[34]

If it is impossible or unrealistic to implement a firm-wide strategy, the next best thing is to implement data analysis within the supply chain. A clear data strategy helps managers decide how to collect and store data, generate insights from it, and act on those insights to achieve positive business outcomes for the global supply chain. Developing a clear strategy does require investments of time, energy, and money. Some firms struggle for years before defining a solid strategy for using data correctly.

In the same study, Accenture found that the most successful companies used analytics to continually collect information from all their global suppliers and put that information to use immediately to make necessary changes in the production process. Some of the benefits include less time from order to delivery, better customer and supplier relationships across borders, quicker reactions to supply-chain issues, and improved understanding of the inventories that exist across countries. Companies with a dedicated analytics team see much better results from their investments. Big-data analysis relies on technology, but investing in the people who will carry out useful analyses is crucial. Ideally, a company's data scientists will have strong backgrounds in statistics, computer science, and econometrics, and will understand the nuances of the industry in which they are operating. For example, CubeMaster is a cargo load-planning program that uses algorithms to help determine the optimal load capacity for trucks, shipping containers, rail cars, and other types of containers[35] (see **Figure 18.14**).

Improving Performance

To make the best use of its global supply chain, companies should develop supply-chain networks that map out a production process from beginning to end, including purchasing,

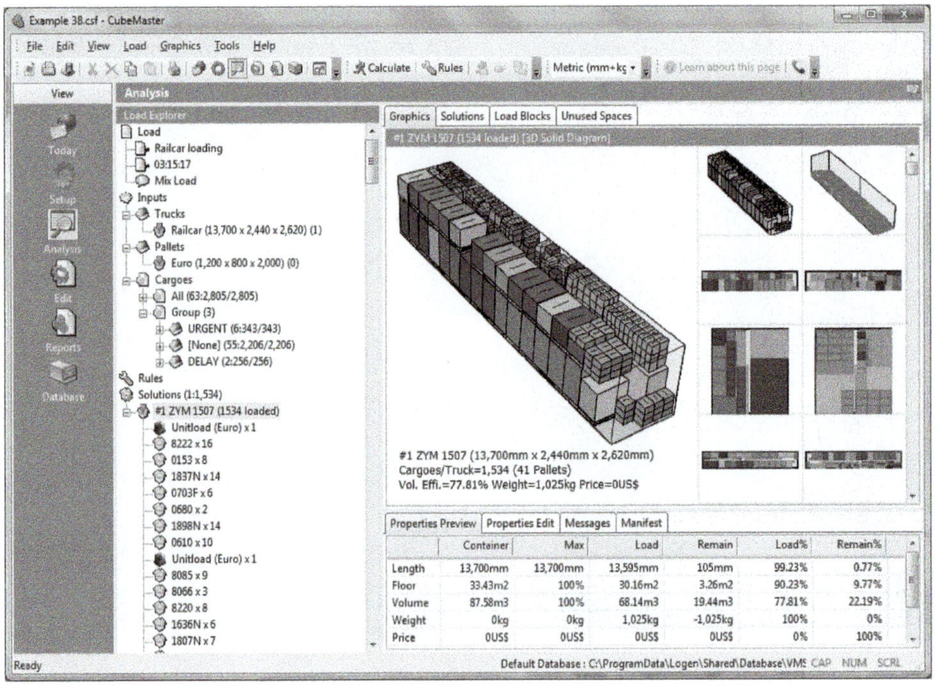

	Container	Max	Load	Remain	Load%	Remain%
Length	13,700mm	13,700mm	13,595mm	105mm	99.23%	0.77%
Floor	33.43m2	100%	30.16m2	3.26m2	90.23%	9.77%
Volume	87.58m3	100%	68.14m3	19.44m3	77.81%	22.19%
Weight	0kg	0kg	1,025kg	-1,025kg	100%	0%
Price	0US$	0US$	0US$	0US$	0%	100%

FIGURE 18.14 CubeMaster
This program provides a software solution that uses algorithms to optimize loads

production, warehousing, transportation, and inventory. They can then apply data analytics to optimize the supply chain by monitoring information about changing tax laws, new suppliers joining the market, foreign exchange rates, the locations of new customers in different countries, and other factors in the global landscape.

For example, Baker Hughes, a U.S. oil and gas equipment manufacturer, might have production facilities in Houston, Texas, that procure steel from mills in Indiana because they offer the lowest price. Then, if the United States and China enter a trade agreement to reduce tariffs against Chinese mills, it might become cheaper to procure steel internationally, even though the materials have to travel across the Pacific Ocean. Data analysis could run simulations that factor in traffic patterns, fuel prices, and the changing tariff situation to determine the most efficient place to procure raw materials. The most efficient method is often a form of conditional solution in which the best choice depends on factors such as time of day, fuel prices, currency exchange rates, prevailing weather patterns, and order size. Data analytics can help a firm implement an exact formula for procuring materials in the most efficient, cost-effective way possible and can update variables in real time to compensate for any changes in conditions.

Another area in which data analytics can prove invaluable is minimizing a firm's exposure to risk. Managers can gain insights about the risks they face by comparing real-time statistics across thousands of similar scenarios, paying special attention to the varying levels of success in those scenarios. For example, the consulting firm Deloitte has developed a prediction tool that helps consultants pinpoint weak links in projects by comparing a set of 28 characteristics drawn from a database of 2,000 projects.[36] The data provided by these cases provide a basic framework from which to analyze the activities of Deloitte's clients, enabling consultants to deliver clear insights on how operations can be improved.[37]

This or a similar tool could have been useful in analyzing the operations of Lululemon Athletica, a Canadian athletic apparel company (**Figure 18.15**). For its global retail operations, Lululemon was overly reliant on a single Taiwanese supplier for a fabric called luon—the primary material used in its branded clothing. Essentially sourcing all its products from one company was a risk that led to serious consequences when the fabric proved too sheer for customers' needs and products had to be recalled. Caught off-guard, investors filed a class-action lawsuit over the millions of dollars of lost revenue and the rapid 12 percent drop in the company's stock price. The right kind of data analysis would have warned Lululemon early enough to identify and reduce the risk it was taking.[38]

Xaume Olleros/Bloomberg/Getty Images

FIGURE 18.15 Lululemon recalls sheer pants Data analytics might have helped Lululemon, a maker of athletic apparel, avoid a product recall caused by overreliance on a single fabric supplier.

While big data attempts to reduce risk, no analysis can remove risk completely. Data scientists use advanced tools to deliver new insights every day, but they are not fortune-tellers. Global supply chains will always experience problems, no matter how much they are optimized. For example, Toyota Motor Company, the largest car manufacturer in the world, is widely emulated for its efficiency as a multinational corporation. However, even Toyota and its world-class production system is not immune to the chaos of random events.[39]

Summary and Case

Summary

LEARNING OBJECTIVE 18.1 Compare the advantages and disadvantages of global procurement.

Global procurement is the act of buying product components in another country or an overseas location. The advantage is that it enables a company to outsource functions to vendors with competitive advantage in those areas so the company can focus on its own core competencies. The major disadvantage is a potential loss of control in the supply chain—which sometimes can lead to the creation of a new competitor.

LEARNING OBJECTIVE 18.2 Evaluate locations for global production.

Global production is the act of making products in-house while using an international supply chain. The major advantage is increased control over the process. Outsourcing adds steps and distance to the production equation but can come with advantages in efficiency and cost. In-house production teams also often suffer from apathy because of their captive customer. Some companies combat this issue through dual sourcing. Typically, facilities are either consolidated to achieve economies of scale or placed regionally to meet the needs of specific customer segments.

LEARNING OBJECTIVE 18.3 Explain benefits of global supply-chain management and modern planning systems.

An efficient, effective supply chain can be a powerful competitive advantage. To maintain greater control over supply chains, companies are taking a more active role in managing supplier operations by integrating systems and processes. Companies are also using tools like the Internet and Internet-based applications coupled with enterprise resource-planning (EPS) systems to streamline and automate supply chains, improving efficiency and quality.

LEARNING OBJECTIVE 18.4 Identify ways to improve supply chains through the use of data analytics.

Big data uses statistical models and computerized algorithms to automatically identify efficiencies based on huge pools of data drawn from past experiences and their outcomes. Data analytics enables companies to identify weak links in their global supply chains and take preventive action to strengthen their positions.

Case Study

Boeing in China

The global market for passenger jets, which are complex and expensive products, is highly competitive. Both Boeing and its chief rival Airbus recognize the need to pursue sales in emerging markets, particularly China. Boeing anticipates that China-based airlines will need 7,120 new airplanes—worth roughly $1 trillion—over the next 20 years, which is about half of all demand from the Asia-Pacific region.[40] As China grows into an economic power, its citizens are beginning to earn relatively high incomes and to demand cheap air travel between metropolitan areas across the country. This has led new low-cost carriers to enter the market and offer this service, as Southwest Airlines and JetBlue Airways have done in the United States and Ryanair has done in Europe.

Low-cost carriers in China will need to purchase many small and medium-sized planes that are efficient and safe in order to accommodate the new demand. Boeing already has the perfect plane to meet these requirements—the 737 series. Several versions are already manufactured with a single aisle and seating for about 200 passengers. The 737 is the most widely produced jetliner ever, with 8,246 planes sold since the late 1960s. On average, a Boeing 737 takes off or lands somewhere in the world every five seconds. It has been incredibly popular with airlines because of its low price, inexpensive maintenance, high reliability, and strong safety record. To capitalize on this new opportunity, Boeing announced on September 23, 2015, that it would build a final assembly plant for the 737 line in China.[41]

This move serves several purposes simultaneously. First, if the majority of new 737s are needed in China, it makes sense to shorten the supply chain by completing final assembly close to the end customer. Second, manufacturing the planes in China is an efficient way to offset costs associated with exporting them there, benefitting all parties involved. Third, the main 737 plant in Renton, Washington, is already experiencing a severe backlog because it cannot keep up with worldwide demand. As of September 2015, the backlog stood at $50 billion worth of orders, and the Renton plant was already turning out fifty completed jets per month. A backlog is particularly inefficient in this industry because orders are typically paid for upon delivery of the completed aircraft, not when the order is placed. With those conditions in mind, it makes sense for Boeing to build an additional factory to satisfy demand for this aircraft.

When the new Boeing factory was announced in China, a sales announcement was also released detailing a 300-jet order worth roughly $38 billion.[42] The commercial aviation industry in China will remain competitive, but Boeing has made the most of it by seizing an opportunity to optimize the supply chain as a strategy to gain an edge moving forward.

Case Discussion Questions

1. What is the reason for the increased demand for airplanes in China?
2. How is this demand being met?
3. Other than building a new plant, what changes could Boeing have made to its supply chain to prevent the backlog in 737 production?

Endnotes

[1] J. Baguley, *Outsourcing Clinical Development: Strategies for Working with CROs and Other Partners* (Boca Raton, FL: CRC Press, 2016).

[2] S. Ming En, "Receding Water Levels at Linggiu Reservoir Expose Singapore's Vulnerability," April 25, 2016, Channel NewsAsia.

[3] Francis Gouillart and Bernard Quancard, "The Five Levels of Competitive Advantage Yielded by Co-Creation for Sales and Procurement," in *The Co-Creation Edge: Harnessing Big Data to Transform Sales and Procurement for Business Innovation* (New York: Palgrave Macmillan, 2016), 173–86.

[4] S. G. Lazzarini, "Strategizing by the Government: Can Industrial Policy Create Firm-Level Competitive Advantage?" *Strategic Management Journal* 36, no. 1 (2015): 97–112.

[5] F. Vargas, "Optimal Sourcing Strategies for Managing Supply Chain Risk for Platinum Group Metals in Automotive Catalytic" (MIT, PhD diss.).

[6] Reuters, "Toyota, Other Major Japanese Firms Hit by Quake Damage, Supply Disruptions," *Fortune*, April 17, 2016, http://www.reuters.com/article/us-japan-quake-toyota-idUSKCN0XE08O.

[7] C. H. Wu and H. H. Wu, "Competitive Remanufacturing Strategy and Take-Back Decision with OEM Remanufacturing," *Computers & Industrial Engineering* 98 (2016): 149–63.

[8] Steve Denning, "Clayton Christensen: How Pursuit of Profits Kills Innovation and the U.S. Economy," Forbes.com (accessed September 25, 2015).

[9] D. J. Brennan and L. S. Amine, "A Longitudinal Study of Offset Agreements in the US Aircraft Industry: 1966–1990," in *Proceedings of the 1991 Academy of Marketing Science (AMS) Annual Conference* (New York, New York: Springer International Publishing, 2015), 119–23.

[10] Benoit A. Aubert and Suzanne Rivard, "A Commentary on: 'The Role of Transaction Cost Economics in Information Technology Outsourcing Research: A Meta-analysis of the Choice of Contract Type,'" *Journal of Strategic Information Systems* 25, no. 1 (March 2016): 64–67.

[11] Kit Sadgrove, *The Complete Guide to Business Risk Management* (New York: Routledge, 2016).

[12] R. Donnellan, "Project failures: Boeing's 787 Dreamliner," BrightWork, May 13, 2016, https://www.brightwork.com/blog/project-failures-boeings-787-dreamliner#.WXJfhYjyvcs.

[13] Eun-Young Jeong, "Samsung's Massive Galaxy Note 7 Recall Brings Battery-Maker into Focus," *Wall Street Journal*, September 5, 2016, www.wsj.com/articles/samsungs-massive-galaxy-note-7-recall-brings-battery-maker-into-focus-1473082175.

[14]Benjamin Zhang, "UPS and FedEx Are Going to Great Lengths to Deliver Holiday Packages on Time—but It May Not Be Enough," *Business Insider*, November 23, 2016, www.businessinsider.com/ups-fedex-holiday-shipping-plan-new-technology-2016-11.

[15]Geoffrey M. Kistruck, Shad S. Morris, Justin W. Webb, and Charles E. Stevens, "The Importance of Client Heterogeneity in Predicting Make-or-Buy Decisions," *Journal of Operations Management* 33–34 (January 2015): 97–110.

[16]Steve, "The Best Wheels for Road Bikes with Disc Brakes – 2016," In the Know Cycling, 2016, https://intheknowcycling.com/2016/02/21/best-wheels-for-disc-brake-road-bikes-2016/.

[17]"All Parts," http://www.acdelco.com/auto-parts/all-parts.html (accessed December 2016).

[18]M. Magnier, "How China Is Changing Its Manufacturing Strategy," *Wall Street Journal*, June 7, 2016, www.wsj.com/articles/how-china-is-changing-its-manufacturing-strategy-1465351382.

[19]S. Bengali, "Why Silicon Valley Is Betting Big on India," *Los Angeles Times*, February 28, 2016, http://www.latimes.com/world/asia/la-fg-india-silicon-valley-20160228-story.html.

[20]Leonard Zinn, "Six Reasons Why Felt Is Making Some of the World's Best Bikes," Velonews, August 5, 2014, www.velonews.com/2014/08/bikes-and-tech/6-reasons-felt-making-worlds-best-bikes_339460.

[21]"List of Left- & Right-Driving Countries," WorldStandards, February 20, 2016.

[22]"Worldwide operations," Toyota Newsroom, March 2, 2016, http://newsroom.toyota.co.jp/en/corporate/companyinformation/worldwide.

[23]"North American Transborder Freight Data: Value to Weight Ratio Data," Bureau of Transportation Statistics, http://transborder.bts.gov/programs/international/transborder/TBDR_VWR.html (accessed December 2016).

[24]Ruben Ramirez, "American-Made Mercedes C-Class Rolls off Production Line in Alabama," Thestreet.com, September 10, 2015.

[25]Ariel Adams, "10 Things Every Rolex Owner Should Know," *Business Insider*, January 30, 2015, www.businessinsider.com/10-things-every-rolex-owner-should-know-2015-1.

[26]D. Carlberg, "Re-shoring—Why U.S. Manufacturers Are Bringing Jobs Back Home," Association for Manufacturing Excellence, March 28, 2016, www.ame.org/target/articles/2016/re-shoring-why-us-manufacturers-are-bringing-jobs-back-home.

[27]M. Sauter and S. Stebbins, "Manufacturers Bringing the Most Jobs Back to America," *USA Today*, April 23, 2016, https://www.usatoday.com/story/money/business/2016/04/23/24-7-wallst-economy-manufacturers-jobs-outsourcing/83406518/; "Coming Home: A Growing Number of American Companies Are Moving Their Manufacturing Back to the United States," *The Economist*, January 19, 2013, https://www.economist.com/news/special-report/21569570-growing-number-american-companies-are-moving-their-manufacturing-back-united.

[28]F. Esposito, "A. Schulman Seeks Compensation for Lucent Product Issues," Rubber & Plastics News, May 8, 2016, http://www.rubbernews.com/article/20160408/NEWS/160409969/a-schulman-seeks-compensation-for-lucent-product-issues.

[29]Ally. Schmidt, "Understanding Boeing's 787 Dreamliner Project," Market Realist, February 18, 2016, http://marketrealist.com/2016/02/understanding-boeings-787-dreamliner-project/; Steve Denning, "The Boeing Debacle: Seven Lessons Every CEO Must Learn," Forbes.com, January 17, 2013.

[30]"Why Did Chipotle Stop Serving Carnitas?" https://www.chipotle.com/pork-details (accessed August 1, 2017).

[31]"Number of Internet Users Worldwide from 2005 to 2016 (in Millions)," Statista www.statista.com/statistics/273018/number-of-internet-users-worldwide/.

[32]Mariko Iwasaki, "Oracle, SAP to Face More Software Challengers as Innovation Trumps Scale," TheStreet, November 11, 2016, www.thestreet.com/story/13887755/1/oracle-sap-to-face-more-software-challengers-as-innovation-trumps-scale.html.

[33]Michael Lewis, *Moneyball: The Art of Winning an Unfair Game* (New York: W. W. Norton, 2004).

[34]"Big Data Analytics in Supply Chain: Hype or Here to Stay?" Accenture Global Operations Megatrends Study, 2014, https://www.accenture.com/t20160106T194441__w__/fi-en/_acnmedia/Accenture/Conversion-Assets/DotCom/Documents/Global/PDF/Digital_1/Accenture-Global-Operations-Megatrends-Study-Big-Data-Analytics-v2.pdf.

[35]CubeMaster Load Plan & Optimization Software. www.logensol.com/cubemaster/cargo_load_plan_optimization_software_overview/ (accessed January 16, 2017).

[36]Kelly Marchese and Jerry O'Dwyer, "From Risk to Resilience: Using Analytics and Visualization to Reduce Supply Chain Vulnerability," Deloitte Review issue 14, Deloitte University Press, January 17, 2014, https://dupress.deloitte.com/dup-us-en/deloitte-review/issue-14/dr14-risk-to-resilience.html.

[37]Kim S Nash, "How Big Data Can Reduce Big Risk," CIO, March 7, 2012, www.cio.com.

[38]Aries Poon and Karen Talley, "Yoga-Pants Supplier Says Lululemon Stretches Truth," *Wall Street Journal*, March 19, 2013, www.wsj.com/articles/SB10001424127887323415304578369812787114262.

[39]Marchese and O'Dwyer, "From Risk to Resilience."

[40]Reuters, "Boeing Says China Is Going to Buy $1 Trillion Worth of Planes," *Fortune*, September 13, 2016, http://fortune.com/2016/09/13/china-buys-planes-boeing/.

[41]Trefis Team, "Why Is a China Plant Important for Boeing?" *Forbes*, September 25, 2015, www.forbes.com/sites/greatspeculations/2015/09/25/why-is-china-plant-important-for-boeing/#183a839265ef.

[42]"Boeing to Open Assembly Plant in China," BBC News, September 23, 2015, www.bbc.com/news/business-34344067.

CHAPTER 19

Global Human Resource Management

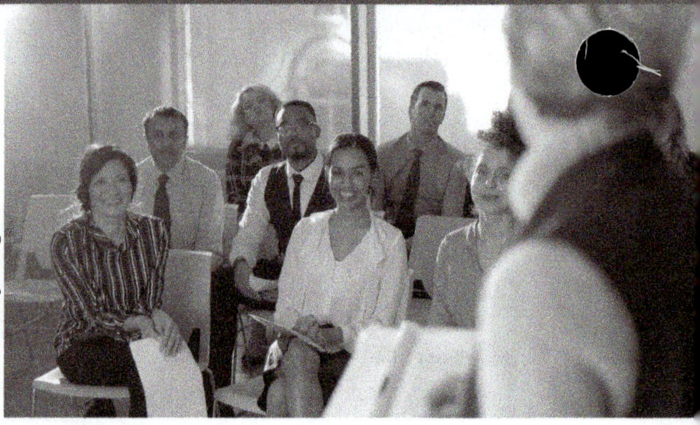
Caiafilm/Getty Images

Introduction

Managing global human resources (HR) is about building a team of the best people to help a company effectively implement its strategy. That in turn requires understanding the company's global strategy. Does that strategy focus on adapting products to local cultures or on creating a global brand unified across all countries?

Once the company has chosen its strategy, it needs to identify the people necessary to implement it. Hiring and developing the right set of employees requires specific HR management practices—practices that will help people make contributions that give a competitive advantage to the company. The HR function works as a strategic partner rather than as an administrative roadblock.

LEARNING OBJECTIVES

After exploring this chapter you will be able to:

1. **Utilize** the global HR wheel to align human capital with a company's strategic objectives
2. **List** the types of human capital needed for company success
3. **Identify** specific HR practices necessary to develop a human capital portfolio
4. **Discuss** the role of the HR function in achieving company success

19.1 The Global HR Wheel

LEARNING OBJECTIVE

Utilize the global HR wheel to align human capital with a company's strategic objectives**.**

organizational capability the power to combine and leverage a company's resources to achieve specific goals

To succeed in its international strategy, a company needs to develop the necessary **organizational capability**, or the power to combine and leverage its resources to achieve specific goals.[1] Toyota's continuous improvement in manufacturing, 3M's long track record in innovation, and the ability of Southwest Airlines to deliver excellent customer service at a low price are all examples of companies using human abilities and resources to accomplish specific company goals.[2]

The strength of a company's organizational capability depends on the quality of its human capital portfolio. Human capital consists of the skills and knowledge company employees possess, which the company relies on to create economic value. For example, many careers require applicants to pass competency tests, such as the bar exam to become a lawyer or the CPA exam to become an accountant. Passing these professional tests demonstrates that an individual has the skills necessary to be a valuable asset to a company. Line workers in an auto plant who assemble a car or airline customer service representatives who help you book a flight also create value for a company.

The collective portfolio of human capital for a given company is developed and managed through HR practices. When executed properly, the company's HR strategy and its organizational capabilities reinforce each other in a cycle called the **global HR wheel**.[3] The idea is that the company's global strategy and its corresponding organizational capabilities (1) should be reflected in the underlying human capital portfolio, which (2) guides the use of specific HR practices, which in turn (3) leads to a set of desired organizational outcomes in keeping with the strategy. **Figure 19.1** provides additional details about the global HR wheel.

global HR wheel a guide to help align employee skills and behaviors with a company's strategic objectives.

Human Capital Portfolios

A unique characteristic of international businesses is that they include people from many different cultures and function in many different locations. Successfully utilizing this diversity is both a challenge and an opportunity. The challenge is that it becomes more difficult to coordinate activities and get people to relate with one another. The opportunity is that people will have different ideas that can lead to new and innovative solutions to common problems. For example, an individual's store of human capital can be useful to a local branch (or subsidiary) of a company, to the global corporation, to the local market and culture, and to the global industry. The company can acquire and develop these different types of human capital to more effectively implement its strategy.

Multinational companies tend to focus on two dimensions of human capital.[4] The first is employees' knowledge about the company itself—its unique culture, routines, and systems. This is known as *company-specific human capital*, and it is developed and maintained within the company. A manager with company-specific human capital knows how to get things done in the organization. He or she understands where to get answers, how to fill out forms, and how to do the work required in the company. This knowledge is not directly applicable to other companies in the industry but is nonetheless critical for efficient operations within that particular company.

The second dimension is *location-specific human capital*, knowledge relevant or applicable to a particular market. This type of knowledge includes familiarity with the unique geographic, cultural, political, or economic landscape of a country and is relevant to any company doing business within that country. A business executive who imports paper products from Thailand to Vietnam has robust location-specific human capital about Vietnam. As a result, he is able to move products through Vietnamese customs quickly and without paying bribes, he can find cheap transportation options, and he understands and responds quickly to customers' changing needs.

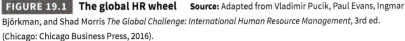

FIGURE 19.1 **The global HR wheel** **Source:** Adapted from Vladimir Pucik, Paul Evans, Ingmar Björkman, and Shad Morris *The Global Challenge: International Human Resource Management*, 3rd ed. (Chicago: Chicago Business Press, 2016).

HR Practices

HR practices tasks focused on attracting, training, motivating, and retaining people

Multinational companies need to align their employee talent with the demands they face in the market. That is, every company has to perform a number of basic yet vitally important HR tasks in order to get the right people to the right place at the right time. These tasks, called **HR practices**, focus on attracting, training, motivating, and retaining people. Organizational performance suffers if HR practices are not executed well. **Table 19.1** provides a simple framework for categorizing key HR practices. Next we explore these categories in detail.

Recruitment and Selection Because of worldwide skill shortages, companies everywhere face the challenge of attracting new employees who possess the desired skills and competencies, who fit the specific vacancy and the company culture, and who demonstrate the potential for future growth. A company cannot simply recruit and hoard brilliant people and still remain profitable. It must recruit the right people, give them opportunities to grow starting from day 1, and develop them into the people it will need in the future. With this in mind, managers of international companies use a variety of selection and assessment methods to review candidates for jobs. These tools have different levels of applicability and legality across cultures, meaning companies need to vary the way they recruit and select people across countries.

For example, if you're recruiting someone from France, it's common to be emotionally expressive and even confrontational with the candidate you're interviewing. Conversely, being emotionally expressive or confrontational with a candidate from the United Kingdom would be insulting and detrimental. At the same time, with someone from Germany, you can be confrontational but should not be emotionally expressive during a recruiting interview. Rather, you should be very even-keeled but willing to push back if the person says something you don't agree with. Like the Germans, the Japanese are also generally less emotionally expressive than the French or even employees from India. However, Japanese are not confrontational and should not be challenged in an interview. Being confrontational is not only considered impolite, it can show a lack of trust in your Japanese recruit.[5]

No selection and development process will be worthwhile unless the company can retain people long enough to profit from the investment it makes to hire and train them. To combat turnover, companies use tactics such as offering an attractive compensation package,

TABLE 19.1 Key HR Practices in Multinationals

Recruitment and Selection	• Workforce planning • Employer branding • Recruitment • Selection • Induction and socialization • Termination and outplacement
Performance Management and Rewards	• Job evaluation • Goal setting • Performance measurement • Appraisal and feedback • Compensation and benefits • Rewards and recognition
Development and Training	• Training (on-the-job and off-the-job) • Talent assessment and reviews • Succession planning • Career management • Coaching and mentoring • Leadership development

cultivating appealing growth opportunities, building sound relationships between leadership and managers, and providing the opportunity to achieve a healthy work-life balance. For example, a company may offer signing bonuses only in the United States, but provide both signing and retention bonuses in the Philippines because employees there are more likely than those in the United States to leave soon after being hired.[6]

Performance Management The performance management process links business objectives to the goals of units, teams, and individuals. That is, it aligns individuals' and groups' goals with those of the overall organization to ensure that all parts of the organization are pulling in the same direction. Then, through periodic performance appraisals and rewards, employees are evaluated on their contributions to the organizational goals. Performance management thus has three successive phases: setting goals and objectives; evaluating and reviewing performance, providing feedback; and linking goal achievement to compensation and development outcomes. However, implementing this process involves a number of challenges for companies.

The ability to set goals effectively depends on healthy two-way communication between the superior and subordinate.[7] For international businesses, cultural differences often complicate this communication. Different cultural attitudes regarding things such as hierarchy and gender differences can profoundly affect communication. As an example, singling out an individual for praise may not be the best reward approach within a collectivist culture. Rather than helping that individual feel valued, it might cause him or her to feel isolated from the collective. Discipline represents challenges, too. In some Eastern cultures, it is very important for individuals to "maintain face" or feel publicly respected, and any public action perceived as disciplinary can cause serious morale problems.

In some countries, legal and social constraints restrict the actions employers can use to address performance issues. For example, implementing individual-based performance management systems in companies operating in Ghana has proven difficult because the society's collectivist norms often supersede the idea that individuals should be evaluated individually, or at least be differentiated from their peers. The other issues with performance management faced by multinationals in Ghana is that men are often rated more highly than women because of the traditional culture's tradition of male dominance.[8]

Development and Training Developing future global leaders is always a high priority for any multinational company, so it is usually one of the major strategic concerns of high-level management. However, once you consider multiple cultural perspectives, "good leadership" no longer has a simple definition. For example, in Sweden good leadership may mean bringing employees in on the strategic decisions being made. In Malaysia it might mean that the leaders make all the difficult decisions and do not place that burden on the employees.[9]

In addition, how can a global company with operations spread throughout the world effectively identify people who have leadership potential when those people often work far from the home office? Multinational companies need to make specific effort to identify and track leaders from different countries (**Figure 19.2**). For example, Honeywell requires its subsidiary managers to create a list of high-potential leaders every year and submit it to corporate headquarters. The potential leaders are then brought in for interviews so top management can get to know them and start helping them develop their leadership skills so they can take on bigger roles in the future.[10]

People develop quickest when they accept difficult assignments and learn from the associated challenges. For international leaders, this means tackling complex assignments outside their comfort zone and/or geographic expertise, which offers a significant opportunity to grow individual talent. But the larger the challenges new or recently promoted people take on, the higher the likelihood they will make mistakes that can be costly for the company. Therefore, companies must ensure that employees are adequately prepared to be successful. Training, coaching, and mentoring should be part of a company's people risk-management strategy. Moreover, companies must be willing to allow people to make mistakes. As Woody Allen once said, "If you're not failing every now and again, it's a sign you're not doing anything innovative."[11]

JUNG YEON-JE/Getty Images

FIGURE 19.2 Samsung's Training Center Samsung's training and development center in Yongin, South Korea, offers a serene mountain setting in which to train its global leaders.

Focusing on Organizational Outcomes

HR practices, guided by the company's human capital portfolio needs, can promote desired organizational outcomes—the final element in the global HR wheel outlined in Figure 19.1. A company's ability to retain its competitiveness over a long period of time is the ultimate outcome of the global HR wheel. Although no "single best way" exists to manage people, evidence suggests that having an established set of HR practices focused on developing desired organizational capabilities helps companies achieve competitive advantage.[12]

competitive advantage a condition that puts a company in a superior business position.

strategic objectives long-term organizational goals that help make a strategy successful

Competitive advantage in a global environment is a condition that puts a company in a favorable or superior business position compared with that of similar businesses both within and across national borders.[13] Competitiveness comes as companies achieve their strategic objectives. **Strategic objectives** are long-term organizational goals that help make a strategy successful. They tell you where to go from a yearly or even quarterly perspective and focus on how the company must position itself to gain a favorable position in its global markets. Take Tesla, for example. Its main strategic objective is to provide clean energy and transportation solutions using advanced technologies. This objective represents a differentiation strategy that will help Tesla gain a favorable or superior position compared with that of its competitors, who are less interested in using only renewable energy sources for their cars[14] (**Figure 19.3**).

critical behaviors the few key areas of activity in which meeting strategic objectives are absolutely necessary

To determine whether it is on its way to meeting this strategic objective, Tesla needs to identify the **critical behaviors** of its employees that would demonstrate they are on the right path. Critical behaviors represent the few key areas of activity in which meeting strategic objectives is absolutely necessary.[15] For instance, the critical behaviors through which Tesla employees provide cutting-edge energy and transportation solutions might be (1) reaching out to different energy companies and universities to learn how their own technology can be improved, (2) observing potential customers to identify what components of Tesla's cars are most important to them, and (3) delivering reliable customer support service to ensure no Tesla owner is ever stranded. A good critical behavior starts with an action verb, such as "deliver," and clearly and concisely conveys the type of behavior that will help the employee and the company reach their strategic objectives.

key performance indicators (KPIs) clear-cut instruments to quantify whether individuals are on the right track to helping a company achieve its strategic objectives

After the managers at Tesla identify the critical behaviors required to reach their objectives, they need to decide how they will measure success. **Key performance indicators (KPIs)** are clear-cut instruments that quantify whether individuals are on the right track to helping the company achieve its strategic objectives.[16] Selecting the right KPIs depends on the industry and which part of the company is being evaluated. These measures should be easy to track,

Bloomberg/Getty Images

FIGURE 19.3 **Tesla Powerwall Home Battery System** Tesla aim to provide an average home 7 days worth of power stored in these battery packs. When combined with solar power these can provide all of a home's energy needs.

collect, and analyze. For Tesla, KPIs for employees on the engineering and design team might be developing a car that (1) can go from 0 to 60 mph in under 3 seconds, (2) costs less than $35,000, and (3) can drive for 400 miles before needing to recharge.

In simple terms, critical behaviors tell you how to achieve the objective, and KPIs tell you whether you are on track to do so. Managers must know what actions employees need to take and must be able to assess whether they are taking them—both are necessary to achieve competitiveness in a global environment.

19.2 Human Capital in the Global Context

LEARNING OBJECTIVE

List the types of human capital portfolio needed for company success.

Returning to our discussion of company specificity and location specificity, recall that four primary types of human capital exist within an international company: local, subsidiary, corporate, and international. The human capital in each of these categories typically develops differently, is managed differently, and contributes differently to the company's strategic objectives (see **Figure 19.4**).

Local Human Capital

Local human capital consists of the knowledge, skills, abilities, and other attributes that make up the location-specific experiences of employees in a particular country or market. These skills include understanding customer needs, cultural traditions, institutional barriers, and political processes, which may differ across countries.[17]

local human capital the knowledge, skills, abilities, and other attributes that make up the location-specific experiences of employees in a particular country or market

Individuals develop local human capital as they spend time working with local customers, learning about the customers' lifestyles and expectations.[18] Companies can either hire people who already have the necessary skills and familiarity, or they can provide training after hiring them—for instance, by encouraging employees to reach outside their offices and talk more with local clients. Interactions create understanding, and the experience makes individual employees more valuable to the company. For example, when the Chinese kitchen appliance maker Haier

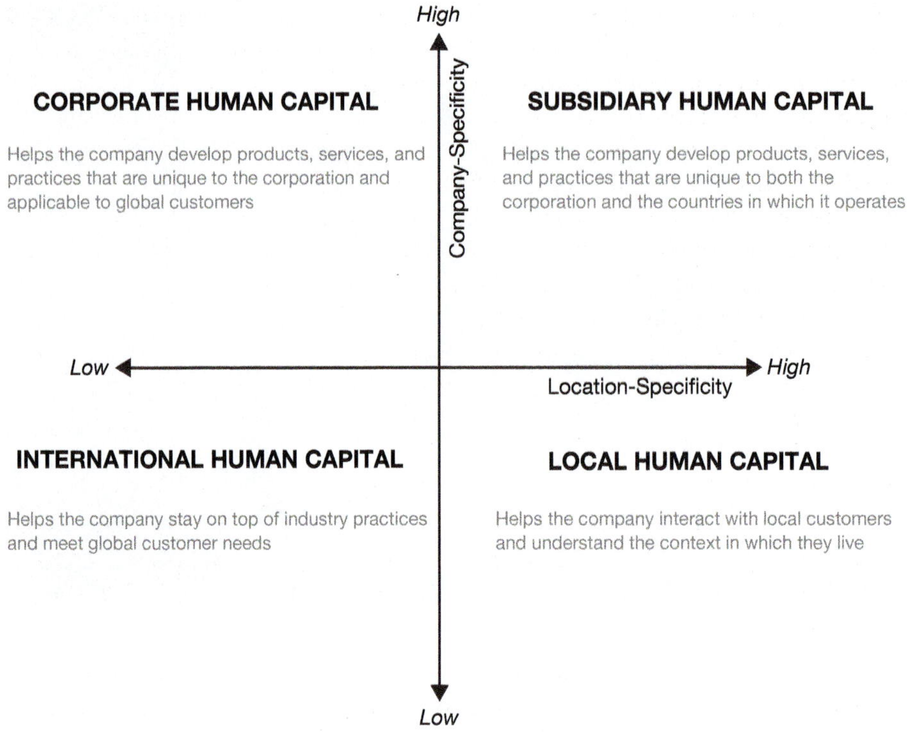
High
CORPORATE HUMAN CAPITAL
Helps the company develop products, services, and practices that are unique to the corporation and applicable to global customers
Company-Specificity
SUBSIDIARY HUMAN CAPITAL
Helps the company develop products, services, and practices that are unique to both the corporation and the countries in which it operates
Low
High
Location-Specificity
INTERNATIONAL HUMAN CAPITAL
Helps the company stay on top of industry practices and meet global customer needs
LOCAL HUMAN CAPITAL
Helps the company interact with local customers and understand the context in which they live
Low

FIGURE 19.4 **Human capital portfolio** Which types of human capital matter most in a global context?

started up a research and development center in the United States, it set up its new operations in Evansville, Indiana. Evansville was the former home of Whirlpool's refrigerator design center, and Haier knew it could hire smart designers who already knew the local tastes of U.S. consumers.[19]

Not surprisingly, local human capital can transfer to competitors within the same local context. For that reason, companies like Haier that enter new regions are often very interested in acquiring employees from competitors because their human capital forms a foundation for the company entering into business there (**Figure 19.5**). In this case, Haier didn't have to poach employees from Whirlpool, because Whirlpool had recently moved its design center to Michigan. On the other hand, local human capital can sometimes be too specialized to be transferable to other countries, but by exerting constant effort to develop local human capital, companies can maintain fruitful relationships with local customers and governments. Some former Whirlpool employees came out of retirement after they heard that Haier was a great place to work.[20]

subsidiary human capital company knowledge within a specific location

Billion Photos/Shutterstock

FIGURE 19.5 **Local Employees** The Chinese company Haier employs local customer service representatives in Saudi Arabia to ensure they understand and relate to the customers there.

Subsidiary Human Capital

When you combine location-specific knowledge with company-specific knowledge, you get employees with **subsidiary human capital**. Subsidiary human capital is company knowledge within a specific location. For example, as the new Haier employees in Indiana learned about the way things are done in the company and how to navigate the Chinese style of efficiency, they were able to combine that knowledge with their knowledge of local tastes to effectively design innovative products for the U.S. market, but at a much lower price point.[21] By combining this local human capital with knowledge of the company and its subsidiary operations, employees develop subsidiary human capital (**Figure 19.6**). Subsidiary human capital helps companies adapt their experience to the local environment in ways that support corporate goals while laying the foundation for further innovation.

Subsidiary human capital does not replace local human capital; the two are complementary company assets. For example, employees who are assigned internationally can develop subsidiary human capital as they develop relationships in both their home and host countries. Combining an understanding of corporate standards and culture with one of individual cultures and locations makes subsidiary human capital a valuable and flexible asset possessed by employees.

Developing subsidiary human capital also helps people devise products, services, and practices that are unique to both the company and the country. For example, engineers at the German company Siemens combine their deep understanding of Siemens products and processes with their understanding of rural markets in Western China. As a result, Siemens has been able to successfully develop and market products that meet the fire- and security-system needs of schools and small companies in the rural Chinese market.[22]

Europa Newswire/Alamy Stock Photo

FIGURE 19.6 **President of Bolivia "Likes" Facebook** Even though Bolivia's President Evo Morales does not work for Facebook, he does know a lot about the company. President Morales has tried to improve his image using social media tools like Facebook. It goes without saying that he knows a lot about business in Bolivia—demonstrating a high level of subsidiary human capital for Facebook in Bolivia.

Corporate Human Capital

Corporate human capital includes company-specific knowledge, skills, and abilities that transcend any particular location within the entire global company, not simply the collective knowledge of the staff at headquarters. Corporate human capital is knowledge about the policies, procedures, and goals that are constant across a company's global operations (**Figure 19.7**).

As individual employees communicate across borders with managers from corporate headquarters and other subsidiary main offices, they often develop corporate human capital. Constant communication with corporate headquarters allows employees to develop knowledge of the corporate mission and vision, and to recognize how their activities and behaviors might more effectively align with corporate objectives. Leadership development programs within multinational companies are often explicitly designed to achieve this kind of corporate human capital.[23]

For example, to develop corporate human capital, Haier invests in rotation programs to give employees different ways of doing things. Through this experience, employees develop knowledge specific to the company that helps them internalize and deliver on the mission and

corporate human capital company-specific knowledge, skills, and abilities that transcend any particular location within the entire global company, not simply the collective knowledge of the staff at headquarters

Paul Kitagaki Jr/ZUMA Press/Newscom

FIGURE 19.7 **Shouldn't Youtube have tube slides?** Did you know that at YouTube headquarters you can either take an elevator, stairs, or a slide to get to the main level? While this kind of corporate knowledge is useless if you work for YouTube outside of the United States, foreign subsidiary employees should know how some things like communication modes or getting around the campus are done at YouTube headquarters.

vision of the company.[24] Rather than dictating protocols through a top-down approach, rotational leadership programs use a bottom-up approach to develop an employee's corporate human capital, which will be informed by local experience yet still relevant to global concerns.

International Human Capital

international human capital knowledge of global best practices, global industry standards, international trade laws, modular systems and processes, cross-border industry networks, and other experience applicable across multiple companies and countries

The last category, **international human capital**, is often overlooked because it has low company specificity and low location specificity.[25] This characteristic makes a person's international human capital highly portable between organizations and key to keeping ahead in global industries. International human capital includes knowledge of global best practices, global industry standards, international trade laws, modular systems and processes, cross-border industry networks, and other experience applicable across multiple companies and countries.

For example, when Haier first entered the U.S. market it hired a U.S. refrigerator seller to manage the new subsidiary. The manager not only possessed strong knowledge of the local context (local human capital); he also had extensive experience working abroad and with companies worldwide. He had a strong sense of industry best practices and had developed a significant network of contacts around the globe.[26] This international human capital enabled the new country manager to help Haier become a global industry player—and not just another Chinese company selling low-cost products in the United States.

People can develop international human capital by engaging with and learning from international experts and professional associations; closely observing global standards and new technologies; and identifying with and keeping abreast of a profession rather than a particular company.[27] In fact, most senior managers acquire strong international human capital because their experience in different locations, subsidiaries, and contexts gives them an understanding of how things work in the broader business environment. These employees can continue to develop when they are provided opportunities for upward mobility that lead to more responsibility and influence. They are then more effective at networking across borders, understanding global business operations,[28] and coming up with innovative solutions for companies.[29] Developing international human capital helps a company stay on top of global best practices and can be a source of competitive advantage.

In summary, local, subsidiary, corporate, and international human capital are all valuable to a global company. The human capital portfolio of any multinational company will include some proportion of all four types. The challenge faced by management and HR is how to strategically balance the four categories in the most beneficial way, given the unique needs of the organization. Each form of human capital is necessary in some measure to achieve success in the global context, and when they are effectively used together, companies are able to achieve and maintain competitive advantage.

WileyPLUS

See Whiteboard Animation: Talent Portfolio

19.3 Meeting Strategic Objectives Through Human Capital

LEARNING OBJECTIVE

Identify specific HR practices necessary to develop a human capital portfolio.

The four types of human capital form the foundation of a company's human capital portfolio, but companies sometimes struggle to invest in all four simultaneously. Each requires different resources, and multinationals must sometimes make trade-offs among the four. As a result, some companies emphasize local and subsidiary human capital, relying on their connections to the local market to drive success. Other companies take the opposite route, preferring to focus on corporate and international human capital, thereby sacrificing local specialization in favor of economies of scale and corporate efficiencies. Still other companies try to balance all four categories to better link local expertise with company-wide knowledge, sacrificing specialization in favor of a more balanced approach.

While any mix can be successful, companies should be explicit about the structure of their human capital portfolio so they can be sure it supports their strategic objectives. This section focuses on three international strategies: multidomestic, meganational, and transnational. We discuss the specific HR practices necessary to develop each type of human capital within the context of each of the three strategies and the ways in which managers can use strategy and HR practices together to create competitive advantage.

The Multidomestic Strategy

Companies that pursue a multidomestic strategy focus on increasing profitability by customizing products, services, and operations so they can respond to the differentiated needs and preferences of customers and employees in each of the countries where they operate. In effect, these companies become a group of locally focused subsidiaries that act independently, like domestic companies, in their various local markets.[30] Based on their heavy emphasis on localization, multidomestic companies are able to easily customize products and services for local clients. This ability to adapt quickly to changing local circumstances generally conveys a competitive advantage.

A multidomestic strategy requires companies to invest heavily in local human capital and subsidiary human capital, and less so in corporate and international human capital (see **Figure 19.8**). Local human capital is critical in each of the different locations in order for the company to generate business opportunities; subsidiary human capital helps employees to understand how to adapt existing products to local customers' needs. Because subsidiaries in a multidomestic organization operate independently, adopting this strategy can fuel local creativity and innovation.

To invest in local and subsidiary human capital, companies should adapt HR practices that help them to meet local needs. Specific HR practices for building local and subsidiary human capital begin with staffing. For example, companies like Haier in the United States should focus on hiring people with strong knowledge of the local refrigerator market. These employees must then be trained to develop a unique knowledge of the Haier way of doing things, which can then be filtered through their existing local human capital.

These HR practices should focus on empowering employees to take action when faced with local challenges to adapt existing Haier products to meet local needs.[31] Incentives can help the company develop a culture that emphasizes creative thinking by encouraging subsidiary

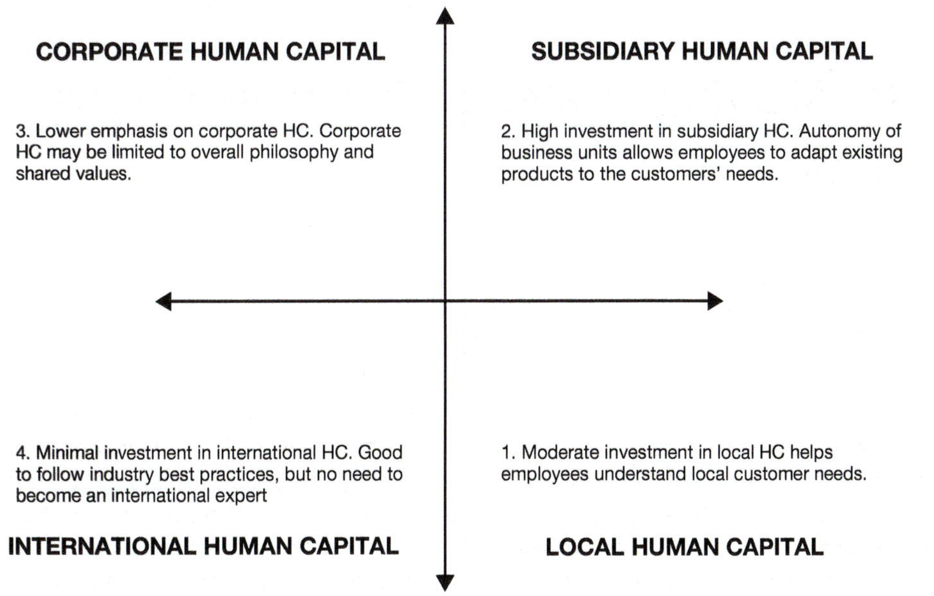

CORPORATE HUMAN CAPITAL
SUBSIDIARY HUMAN CAPITAL
3. Lower emphasis on corporate HC. Corporate HC may be limited to overall philosophy and shared values.
2. High investment in subsidiary HC. Autonomy of business units allows employees to adapt existing products to the customers' needs.
4. Minimal investment in international HC. Good to follow industry best practices, but no need to become an international expert
1. Moderate investment in local HC helps employees understand local customer needs.
INTERNATIONAL HUMAN CAPITAL
LOCAL HUMAN CAPITAL

FIGURE 19.8 Multidomestic strategy and human capital (HC) **Source:** Adapted from S. Morris, S. Snell, and I Björkman, "An Architectural Framework for Global Talent Management," *Journal of International Business Studies* 47 (2016): 723.

employees to create products that better meet the local needs so the company can sell more of them—and earn more money in the process.[32] Outcome-based incentives motivate employees to invest in knowledge that develops their skills for the local context.

Of course, these HR practices must also focus on retaining valued local employees. Otherwise, companies risk having their top talent poached by competitors who want that same local expertise. One way to increase retention is to help local employees feel their role is valuable to the company as a whole. Another way to increase loyalty among local employees is for corporate headquarters to share more resources with the subsidiary and then trust the subsidiary employees to use them effectively.[33] For example, the thermostat maker Honeywell creates centers of excellence in different countries. Their HR analytics group, for example, is headquartered in Shanghai, China, and is led by a manager from Japan. All of the HR analytics decisions throughout the company are approved by the Shanghai office, not headquarters in the United States.

The Meganational Strategy

In contrast to a multidomestic strategy, a meganational strategy emphasizes coordination and integration across business units to provide a common platform for the company (see **Figure 19.9**). Companies that use this strategy are more centrally managed, with the goal of creating consistent standards, processes, products, and services across business units and company locations.[34] This strategy tends to establish the company's competitive position in markets where advantage depends on leveraging economies of scale and scope in order to achieve lower costs and global reach.

Meganational companies invest more heavily in corporate and international human capital; they have little need for local and subsidiary human capital. They gain the benefit of being able to offer a common set of products and services to global customers.[35] Knowledge about international standards, trade laws, and cultures can be valuable in any company's internationalization efforts. Moreover, combining international human capital with corporate human capital enables the company to provide great products and services that are both unique to the company and at the forefront of its industry.[36] For instance, research about call centers has shown that local employees are not necessarily hired for their strong knowledge and skills related to the local environment. Instead, their value lies in their international human capital (their lack of accent, their customer service skills, and their problem-solving abilities).[37]

expatriates employees assigned from headquarters or another location to work in a foreign market

HR practices for a meganational strategy differ widely from those for a multidomestic strategy. Traditionally, companies adopting a meganational strategy have staffed their foreign units with **expatriates**, or people from the company's headquarters who relocate to work in a foreign market.[38] For example, when Icon Health & Fitness, the maker of Nordic Track and Altra running

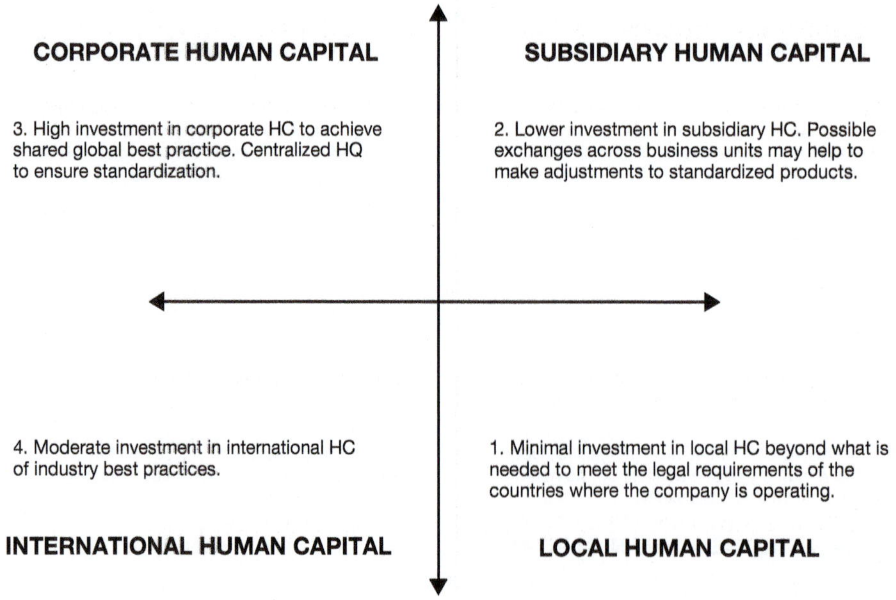

CORPORATE HUMAN CAPITAL
SUBSIDIARY HUMAN CAPITAL
3. High investment in corporate HC to achieve shared global best practice. Centralized HQ to ensure standardization.
2. Lower investment in subsidiary HC. Possible exchanges across business units may help to make adjustments to standardized products.
4. Moderate investment in international HC of industry best practices.
1. Minimal investment in local HC beyond what is needed to meet the legal requirements of the countries where the company is operating.
INTERNATIONAL HUMAN CAPITAL
LOCAL HUMAN CAPITAL

FIGURE 19.9 Meganational strategy and human capital (HC) **Source:** Adapted from S. Morris, S. Snell, and I. Björkman, "An Architectural Framework for Global Talent Management," *Journal of International Business Studies* 47 (2016): 723.

shoes, wanted to ensure its operations in Asia were consistent with those at its headquarters, they sent company insider Kyle Freebairn to live in Asia and run the operations there. Luckily, Kyle is fluent in Mandarin[39] (**Figure 19.10**).

Expatriates can be very costly employees; companies usually pay two to three times their normal salary to cover expenses abroad, such as private schooling for their children, housing, and a higher cost of living.[40] However, companies gain benefits by using expatriates to manage foreign subsidiaries: the company can exhibit greater control over decision making by subsidiaries and can provide a more standardized approach to work.[41] Expatriates are also expected to socialize nationals from the host country within a unified corporate culture.

I AM ICON

Courtesy Kyle Freebairn

FIGURE 19.10 Kyle Freebairn, general manager of Icon Health & Fitness

Another effective HR practice for investing in local and corporate human capital is to focus on helping local employees stay close to corporate and international standards. This orientation increases employees' ability to integrate ideas across borders. It has a major drawback, however: Employees often become more loyal to their professions than to the company.[42] In addition, if corporate policies are perceived as too rigid, local individuals may develop unsanctioned "workarounds" to achieve desired ends in the local market. As a result, loyalty to the profession is often a much stronger force among top local talent than compensation or commitment to a foreign company.[43]

Finally, HR practices such as performance appraisals and compensation may provide individualized solutions to developing corporate and international human capital.[44] For example, General Electric appraises people on their ability to bring cutting-edge international knowledge into the global operations of each division. As a result, many employees at General Electric possess high levels of international human capital and eventually are poached by rival companies.[45]

The Transnational Strategy

The transnational strategy is often considered a hybrid because it combines the benefits of the multinational and meganational strategies. However, it is not simply a compromise between them. Instead, a transnational strategy blends aspects of local responsiveness with aspects of global integration (see **Figure 19.11**). Like the multidomestic approach, it allows subsidiaries the discretion and autonomy to adapt and customize to meet local challenges. Unlike a

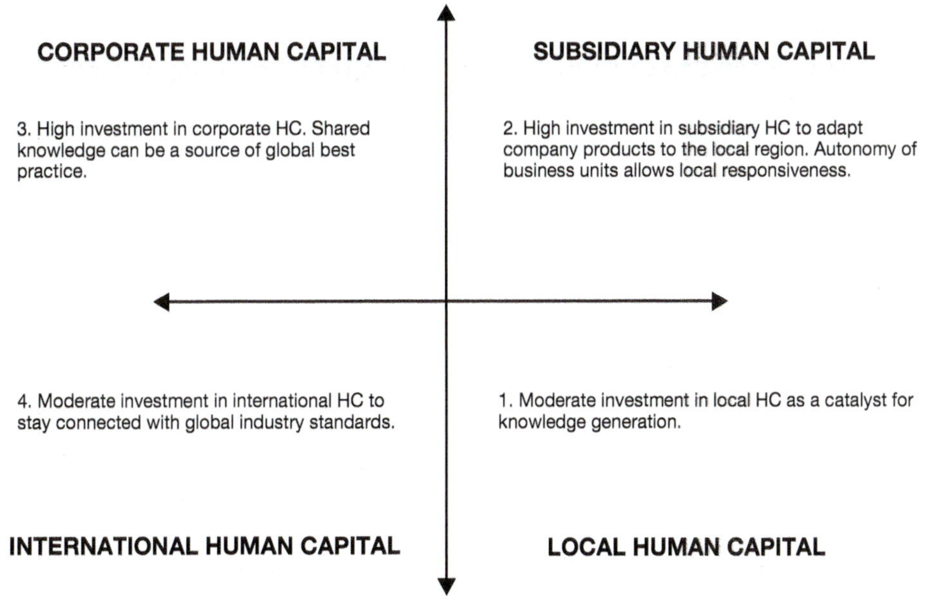
CORPORATE HUMAN CAPITAL
SUBSIDIARY HUMAN CAPITAL
3. High investment in corporate HC. Shared knowledge can be a source of global best practice.
2. High investment in subsidiary HC to adapt company products to the local region. Autonomy of business units allows local responsiveness.
4. Moderate investment in international HC to stay connected with global industry standards.
1. Moderate investment in local HC as a catalyst for knowledge generation.
INTERNATIONAL HUMAN CAPITAL
LOCAL HUMAN CAPITAL

FIGURE 19.11 Transnational strategy and human capital (HC) **Source:** Adapted from S. Morris, S. Snell, and I. Björkman, "An Architectural Framework for Global Talent Management," *Journal of International Business Studies* 47 (2016): 723.

	Multidomestic	Meganational	Transnational
HR Practices	Adapt HR practices to meet local needs. Empower employees to make decisions. Reward employees based on outcomes. Increase individual autonomy.	Align HR practices with HQ. Create process-based incentives to specify the need for integration. Emphasize corporate and industry standards.	Allow for flexibility, but align HR practices enough to ensure common language. Build employee "ambidexterity". Build multiple types of human capital to ensure new ideas are shared and integrated.

FIGURE 19.12 HR practices align with different strategies

meganational strategy, which achieves competitive advantage through centralization and standardization by headquarters, a transnational strategy achieves advantage by taking ideas created all over the organization and integrating them in a way that allows the company to deliver standardized products across countries.[46]

A transnational strategy requires companies to invest heavily in corporate and subsidiary human capital and moderately in local and international human capital. In other words, companies should emphasize all four types of human capital, but in different proportions. HR practices should focus primarily on corporate and subsidiary human capital. Although these two forms of human capital may seem like opposites, successful transnational businesses are able to focus simultaneously on aligning with corporate practice and adapting to local needs.[47] On the other hand, the difficulty of establishing and maintaining this balance is the main reason companies often choose one of the other strategies, either meganational or multidomestic.

Consider the case of Briggs & Stratton, a U.S. company that produces small engines for appliances and outdoor tools. Employees in China developed new engines for the U.S. market that were smaller, less bulky, and more closely aligned with U.S. customers' tastes than the original products specifically designed for China.[48] Because the Chinese employees were able to combine their knowledge of the local market with their knowledge of Briggs & Stratton products and goals, they were able to generate more value for the Chinese subsidiary. This knowledge was then shared across the subsidiary units in different countries, becoming a catalyst for ways to change Briggs & Stratton's standard engines and generating more value for the entire company. A transnational strategy provides autonomy to individual units, giving them freedom to adapt to local conditions while still holding them accountable for sharing and transferring knowledge throughout the global organization.

To replicate this kind of success, companies should consider the global employee market when hiring so that the best people are recruited regardless of their nationality.[49] Companies can cultivate this ability through socialization processes, such as new-employee orientation programs that emphasize both national and corporate cultures as valuable sources of knowledge.

In summary, these three international strategies require different approaches to managing human resources. **Figure 19.12** aligns HR practices with the different corporate strategies.

19.4 Tasks of the Global HR Function

LEARNING OBJECTIVE

Discuss the role of the HR function in achieving company success.

The role of HR within the global environment is threefold, as shown in **Figure 19.13**:

- Contributing to business decisions
- Providing HR expertise
- Delivering HR services

Many international companies organize their HR function to fill these three roles. For example, Unilever, a British-Dutch company that sells personal care products, organizes its HR functional activities into business partners that help to make critical *business decisions, HR expertise* teams that provide specialized knowledge about issues such as performance management or labor relations, and *HR services* that help employees understand their benefits and provide career advice (which it primarily outsources to Accenture, an international consulting firm).[50] Below we provide an overview of the three primary roles of global HR.

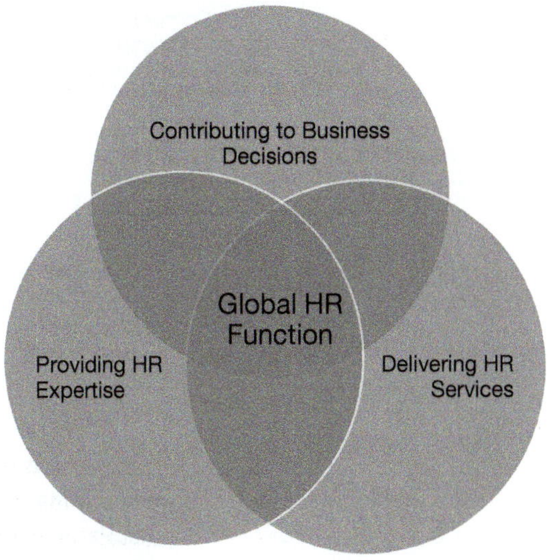

FIGURE 19.13 **The threefold mission of global HR**

Contributing to Business Decision Making

HR professionals who work directly with top managers on strategic challenges play the first role of global HR—contributing to business decisions. HR employees who advise top management on strategic decisions often become a link between foreign business units and the company's centers of expertise, often also bridging the gap to the HR service centers.

However, not all the work in this category is solely strategic. A critical part of the role is to perform some routine HR tasks and to help managers resolve employee issues and concerns. Such tasks might include developing a workforce plan that projects the number of employees needed in the next year or two. Employee issues can be anything from wondering what they should do to meet their supervisor's expectations to negotiating an expatriate compensation package.

Another key decision HR managers must be able to help make consists of how many foreign workers to hire within a country of operation. Foreign workers require a work permit or visa, which is a document issued by a government giving a person permission to work in the country. For example, when we travel to do extensive work in other countries, we must apply for work permits from the government in the host country. If a foreign professional comes to work in the United States, he or she may need an H1B visa. H1B Visas were created to allow for specialized technological and scientific talent that can't be sufficiently recruited from within the United States. HR managers at places like LinkedIn and Snap Inc. found it difficult to recruit the technical talent they needed in 2017, as the U.S. government put additional pressures on companies to hire locally. The problem, however, was that they could not find sufficiently qualified Americans to fill the job openings. As a result, many tech companies like Workfront opened programming in countries like Ukraine and Bulgaria.[51]

Providing HR Expertise

The key goal of those who fill the HR expertise role is to develop a deep level of expertise in an area such as global employee compensation or change management. For example, Ryan Hill is an HR expert who focuses on executive compensation for all the expatriate employees at the Houston-based oil company Baker Hughes. He has over 15 years of experience designing salaries and bonuses for global executives.[52] Professional knowledge of state-of-the-art HR management is a key requirement in this role.

Given the constant pressure to do more with less, organizing the HR management process is a challenging task for any international company. The solution depends on the company's unique structure, but a common approach is to have functional experts at headquarters who are responsible for global tasks such as talent and performance management. These experts need deep international experience and an awareness of how their own home-country perspective can bias their perceptions. Another common practice is to take the opposite approach and decentralize responsibility, giving subsidiaries more control over developing policies, processes, and tools (see **Figure 19.14**).

One particular area of HR—labor relations— requires multiple subsidiary centers of expertise. In many countries, the regulation of labor contracts is profound and unique. Labor unions around the world also differ significantly.

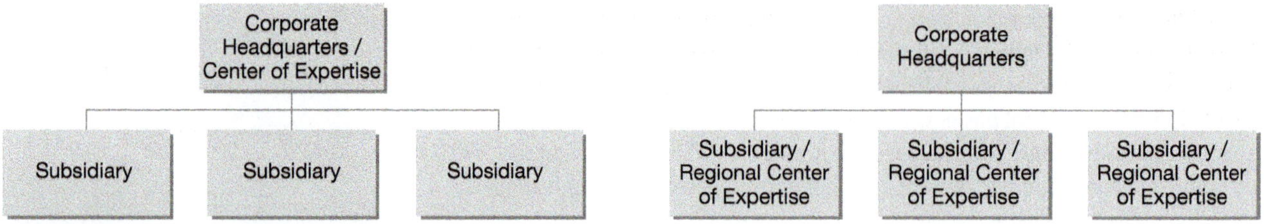

FIGURE 19.14 **Two options for creating centers of expertise**

For example, the European Union prohibits discrimination against workers in unions, but labor unions are illegal in many other countries, including countries in Central America and Asia,. China has only one union, the All-China Federation of Trade Unions (ACFTU), a Communist Party institution that for decades has aligned itself more closely with management than workers. As Walmart discovered, Western firms that want to do business in China have to reach collective bargaining agreements with the ACFTU (**Figure 19.15**). In some countries, only workers at larger firms are allowed to organize.[53]

Union strength depends on many factors, such as the level of employee participation, per capita labor income, mobility between management and labor, homogeneity of labor (race, religion, social class), and unemployment. Nearly all of Sweden's workers are organized, giving the unions in that country considerable strength and autonomy. By contrast, in countries with relatively high unemployment, low pay levels, and no union funds with which to support social welfare systems, unions are driven to ally with other organizations: political parties, churches, or governments. This is in marked contrast to the United States, where the union selected by the majority of employees bargains only with the employer, not with other institutions. The unions in many European countries (such as Sweden), however, have a great deal of political power and are often allied with a particular political party. When employers in these countries deal with unions, they are, in effect, dealing indirectly with governments.

codetermination cooperation between management and workers in decision-making, particularly by the representation of workers on boards of directors.

In many European countries, provisions for employee representation are established by law. An employer may be legally required to allow employee representation on safety and hygiene committees, worker councils, or even boards of directors. While their responsibilities vary from country to country, worker councils basically provide a channel for communication between employers and workers. The legal codes that set forth the functions of worker councils in France are very detailed. Councils are generally concerned with grievances, problems of individual employees, internal regulations, and matters affecting employee welfare.

A higher form of worker participation in management is found in Germany, where representation of labor on the board of directors of a company is required by law. This arrangement is known as **codetermination** and often referred to by its German word, *Mitbestimmung*. While sometimes puzzling to outsiders, the system is fairly simple. Company shareholders and employees are required to be represented in equal numbers on the supervisory boards of large corporations. Power is generally left with the shareholders, and shareholders are generally assured the chairmanship. Other European countries and Japan either have or are considering minority board participation.[54]

Each of these differences makes managing human resources in a global context more

VCG/Getty Images

FIGURE 19.15 **Walmart Employees in China**

challenging. But the crux of the issue in designing HR systems is not choosing one approach that will meet all the demands of international business. Instead, organizations facing global competition must balance multiple approaches and make their policies flexible enough to accommodate differences across national borders.

Delivering HR Services

Delivering HR services in a global context means providing services to managers and employees that will enable them to do their jobs more effectively, be more engaged, and be safe. Some companies, like Honeywell, computerize selected HR services, such as payroll, benefits, and retirement.[55] Still others, such as IBM and Microsoft, choose shared HR service centers that allow employees and managers to serve themselves if possible, allow recruiters to share prospects globally, deliver new approaches to online learning, and make HR data available worldwide.[56]

In companies that have invested in electronic HR solutions, employees can go online for up-to-date and locally adapted answers to questions about holidays, pensions, regulations, and other routine transactions.[57] While investments in standardized, computerized HR processes and information technology systems can be expensive, they also allow companies to use professional talent across borders by letting HR professionals communicate with and coordinate people more easily.[58]

Shared service centers began to emerge as companies realized that many administrative HR tasks could be standardized. One significant new trend has been to locate these service centers in areas that have lower overall costs, such as in Central America, Central and Eastern Europe, and India.[59]

The trend toward outsourcing larger parts of HR has recently continued, often combined with standardizing HR practices across the world.[60] However, even if a company adopts outsourcing as a strategy, it should keep important practices such as leadership development in-house.

Summary and Case

Summary

LEARNING OBJECTIVE 19.1 Utilize the global HR wheel to align human capital with a company's strategic objectives.

The basic categories of HR practices are recruitment and selection, performance management and rewards, and development and training. These practices can all be used to align human capital with anticipated organizational outcomes.

LEARNING OBJECTIVE 19.2 List the types of human capital portfolio needed for company success.

Local human capital refers to knowledge about interacting with customers and challenges in a specific market. Subsidiary human capital blends local knowledge with company-specific protocols and processes, or localizes company standards. Corporate human capital is a knowledge of the general company guidelines that apply to every location, without a need for localization. International human capital refers to industry-wide understanding and best practices that enable companies to keep ahead of their competition.

LEARNING OBJECTIVE 19.3 Identify specific human resource practices necessary to develop a human capital portfolio.

In a multidomestic company, local subsidiaries are given broad leeway and decision-making authority, emphasizing local and subsidiary human capital as their competitive advantage. Meganational companies do opposite, creating a strong corporate framework as a foundation for operations and relying on international and corporate human capital to connect employees under a unified set of policies and structures. Transnational companies focus on innovating at the local level and then transferring that innovation to the corporate level. This strategy focuses on subsidiary human capital to generate local, external networks, and on corporate human capital to create global, internal networks.

LEARNING OBJECTIVE 19.4 Discuss the role of the HR function in achieving company success.

Within a given company, the HR function serves three major supporting roles. First, HR representatives can contribute to business decisions about organizational capabilities and human capital requirements. Second, they can provide expertise regarding HR practices and procedures, operating in a tactical capacity to aid leaders in everyday management. One very important need in this area is managing labor relations across different countries. Third, they can automate and improve HR services to reduce costs and increase efficiencies.

Case Study

Intel's Search for Talent in Vietnam[61]

Intel is today's leading manufacturer of computer microprocessors. Intel's success lies not in technology but in talent. To build a talent pipeline, the company sponsors various science-centered events and competitions, including the Intel Science Talent Search. It also has scholarship and study-abroad programs in addition to a wide array of partnerships with higher-education institutions. However, the company can't recruit what doesn't exist, and that has been a problem in Vietnam and other emerging markets.

Vietnam's Talent Shortage

Vietnam has a large, cost-competitive labor force that is centrally located. These factors make Vietnam very attractive to foreign companies, and the country's government has taken steps to increase that attractiveness by encouraging education.

The number of students in Vietnam continues to grow annually; however, the Vietnamese university system struggles to produce enough graduates with the knowledge and experience required for employment in top engineering companies like Intel. During Intel's initial hiring wave for its new Vietnam facility in 2010, the company tested more than 2,000 graduating students and found that only 90 passed the test; of those, only 40 could speak proficient English. At the same time, companies like Foxconn, Samsung Electronics, and LG all compete for talent from the same tiny pool.

The Diversity Challenge

To overcome the talent scarcity, Intel Vietnam decided to tap into the largely underrepresented population of female workers. In fact, in 2010 only about 10 percent of graduating Vietnamese engineering students were female, and less than 20 percent of all engineers were female.

A primary obstacle in increasing the number of qualified female engineers was the patriarchal nature of Vietnamese society. A woman's primary duty was seen as caring for her husband, children, and aging parents—no matter what else she might pursue in life. Men often made critical decisions regarding a woman's career path—often without her input.

As a result, women in professional positions were expected to be as productive as their male counterparts while still fulfilling all their traditional household duties. And Vietnamese schools and society did very little to encourage women to study engineering—or to obtain higher education at all. If Intel Vietnam wanted to broaden the female segment of the working population, it was going to have to focus on early education and take drastic measures to encourage women to consider engineering programs.

Case Discussion Questions

1. What are the advantages of establishing major operations in markets with large, inexpensive labor pools? The disadvantages?
2. What could Intel Vietnam have done to fill its hiring needs?
3. What can Intel Vietnam do to increase interest in engineering among women?

Endnotes

[1]S. Morris, R. Hammond, and S. Snell, "A Microfoundations Approach to Transnational Capabilities: The Role of Knowledge Search in an Ever-Changing World," *Journal of International Business Studies* 45, no. 4 (2014): 405–27.

[2]V. Pucik, P. Evans, I. Björkman, and S. Morris, *The Global Challenge: International Human Resource Management*, 3rd ed. (Chicago: Chicago Business Press, 2016).

[3]Pucik et al., *The Global Challenge*.

[4]Shad Morris, Scott Snell, and Ingmar Björkman, "An Architectural Framework for Global Talent Management," *Journal of International Business Studies* 47, no. 6 (2016): 723–47.

[5]E. Meyer, "Getting to Si, Ja, Oui, Hai, and Da," *Harvard Business Review*, December 2015.

[6]Amy Remo, "Turnover in PH Firms on the Rise as Employees Seek Better Pay," Inquirer.net, February 25, 2016; Hannah Morgan, "Here's How Recruiters Really Fill Jobs," *U.S. News and World Report*, September 23, 2015, https://money.usnews.com/money/blogs/outside-voices-careers/2015/09/23/heres-how-recruiters-really-fill-jobs.

[7]Lawrence A. Pervin, ed. *Goal Concepts in Personality and Social Psychology* (New York: Psychology Press, 2015).

[8]J. O. Antwi, A. C. Opoku, ASeth, and O. B. Margaret, "Assessing the Human Resource Management Practices of Public Banks from Employees' Perspective: Case Study of Selected Branches of Ghana Commercial Bank, Kumasi," *Global Journal of Human Resource Management* 4, no. 1 (2016): 13–30; F. Louis and K. Ohemeng, "Constraints in the Implementation of Performance Management Systems in Developing Countries," *International Journal of Cross-Cultural Management* 9, no. 1 (2009): 109–32.

[9]Mert Aktas, Michele J. Gelfand, and Paul J. Hanges, "Cultural Tightness-Looseness and Perceptions of Effective Leadership," *Journal of Cross-Cultural Psychology* 47, no. 2 (2015): 294–309.

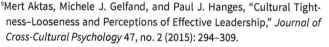

[10]Personal interview with HR leader at Honeywell in China by Shad Morris (November, 2016).

[11]Woody Allen Quotes, BrainyQuote, www.brainyquote.com/quotes/quotes/w/woodyallen121347.html (accessed December 2016).

[12]J. T. Mahoney and Y. Y, Kor, "Advancing the Human Capital Perspective on Value Creation by Joining Capabilities and Governance Approaches," *The Academy of Management Perspectives* 29, no. 3 (2015): 296–308; Morris et al, "An Architectural Framework for Global Talent Management."

[13]N. W. Hatch and C. Howland, "When Does Competitive Advantage Improve Customer Welfare?" *Academy of Management Proceedings* 2015, no. 1 (January 2015): 18091; Academy of Management, Y. Doz, and C. K. Prahalad, "Quality of Management: An Emerging Source of Global Competitive Advantage?" in *Strategies in Global Competition (RLE International Business): Selected Papers from the Prince Bertil Symposium at the Institute of International Business* (New York: Routledge, 2013), 345–68.

[14]Jeff Dyer and Hal Gregersen, "Decoding Tesla's Secret Formula," *Forbes*, September 7, 2015, https://www.forbes.com/sites/innovatorsdna/2015/08/19/teslas-secret-formula/#5bdd1a19653c.

[15]K. McLachlan, et al., "Exploring Critical Success Factors for Effective Collaborative Relationships," in *Learning Through Community Engagement* (Singapore: Springer, 2017), 231–43; R. Klimoski, "Critical Success Factors for Cybersecurity Leaders: Not Just Technical Competence," *People and Strategy* 39, no. 1 (2016): 14.

[16]A. Kylili, P. A. Fokaides, and P. A. L. Jimenez, "Key Performance Indicators (KPIs) Approach in Buildings Renovation for the Sustainability of the Built Environment: A Review," *Renewable and Sustainable Energy Reviews* 56 (2016): 906–15; D. Parmenter, *Key Performance Indicators (KPI): Developing, Implementing and Using Winning KPIs* (New York: John Wiley & Sons, 2007), 3.

[17]Y. L. Doz, and J. F. P. Santos, *On the Management of Knowledge: From the Transparency of Collocation and Cossetting to the Quandary of Dispersion and Differentiation*, mimeo (Fontainebleau, France: INSEAD, 1997).

[18]P. Caligiuri, *Cultural Agility: Building a Pipeline of Successful Global Professionals* (San Francisco: John Wiley & Sons, 2013).

[19]Jesse Powers, "Haier America Opens New Tech Center in Evansville," 14News.com, October 10, 2016, www.14news.com/story/29547290/haier-america-opens-new-tech-center-in-evansville.

[20]Powers, "Haier America Opens New Tech Center in Evansville."

[21]"Haier America Tech Center Finds Home in Evansville," press release, Haier America, April 11, 2016, www.haieramerica.com/release/haier-america-tech-center-finds-home-evansville.

[22]www.siemens.com/entry/cn/en/ (accessed December 2016).

[23]P. Caligiuri and I. Tarique, "Cultural Agility and International Assignees' Effectiveness in Cross-Cultural Interactions," *International Journal of Training and Development* 20, no. 4 (2016): 280–89.

[24]P. Leinwand, C. Mainardi, and A. Kleiner, "Strategy That Works: How Winning Companies Close the Strategy-to-Executive Gap," *Harvard Business Review* (2016).

[25]P. Almeida, "Knowledge Sourcing by Foreign Multinationals: Patent Citation Analysis in the U.S. Semiconductor Industry," *Strategic Management Journal* 17, winter special issue (1996): 155–65.

[26]F. Frank, "Options for Growth: The Case of Haier (A)," European School of Management & Technology, 2010.

[27]P. Cappelli, *Talent on Demand: Managing Talent in an Age of Uncertainty* (Cambridge, MA: Harvard Business Press, 2008).

[28]P. Caligiuri, and V. Di Santo, "Global Competence: What Is It, and Can It Be Developed Through Global Assignments?" *People and Strategy* 24, no. 3 (2001): 27.

[29]S. S. Morris and S. A. Snell, "Intellectual Capital Configurations and Organizational Capability: An Empirical Examination of Human Resource Subunits in the Multinational Enterprise," *Journal of International Business Studies* 42 (2011): 805–27.

[30]C. Bartlett and S. Ghoshal, *Managing Across Borders: The Transnational Solution* (Cambridge, MA: Harvard Business Press, 1989).

[31]S. Kilroy, P. C. Flood, J. Bosak, and D. Chênevert, "Perceptions of High-Involvement Work Practices, Person-Organization Fit, and Burnout: A Time-Lagged Study of Health Care Employees," *Human Resource Management* (August 2016); J. P. Guthrie, "High-Involvement Work Practices, Turnover, and Productivity: Evidence from New Zealand," *Academy of Management Journal* 44, no. 1 (2001): 180–90.

[32]P. Caligiuri, M. Lazarova, and S. Zehetbauer, "Top Managers' National Diversity and Boundary Spanning: Attitudinal Indicators of a Firm's Internationalization," *Journal of Management Development* 23, no. 9 (2004): 848–59.

[33]T. O. Davenport, "Thriving at Work: How Organizational Culture Affects Workplace Fulfillment," *People and Strategy* 38, no. 3 (2015): 38; K. S. Law, L. J. Song, C.-S. Wong, and D. Chen, "The Antecedents and Consequences of Successful Localization," *Journal of International Business Studies* 40, no. 8 (2009): 1359–73.

[34]Pucik et al., *The Global Challenge*.

[35]Bodo B. Schlegelmilch, "Segmenting Targeting and Positioning in Global Markets," in *Global Marketing Strategy: An Executive Digest* (Geneva: Springer International Publishing, 2016), 63–8; J. Cantwell, "Location and the Multinational Enterprise," *Journal of International Business Studies* 40 (2009): 35–41.

[36]Morris et al., "An Architectural Framework for Global Talent Management," 723.

[37]A. Presbitero, "It's Not All About Language Ability: Motivational Cultural Intelligence Matters in Call Center Performance," *International Journal of Human Resource Management* 28, no. 11 (2017): 1547–62.

[38]R. Tung and B. J. Punnett, "Research in International Human Resource Management," *De Gruyter Studies in Organization* (1993): 35–55; M. A. Shaffer, M. L. Kraimer, Y. P. Chen, and M. C. Bolino, "Choices, Challenges, and Career Consequences of Global Work Experiences: A Review and Future Agenda," *Journal of Management* 38 (2012): 1282–327.

[39]Personal interview with Kyle Freebairn in China by Shad Morris, December 2016.

[40]K. G. Tan, K. Y. Tan, R. Yuan, and L. P. A. Nguyen, *2014 Annual Indices for Expatriates and Ordinary Residents on Cost of Living, Wages and Purchasing Power for World's Major Cities* (Singapore: World Scientific Publishing Company, 2016).

[41]Morris et al., "An Architectural Framework for Global Talent Management," 723; S. J. Kobrin, "Expatriate Reduction and Strategic Control in American Multinational Corporations," *Human Resource Management* 27, no. 1 (1988): 63–75.

[42]Cappelli, *Talent on Demand*.

[43]M. Alvesson, D. Kärreman, and K. Sullivan, "Professional Service Firms and Identity," in *The Oxford Handbook of Professional Service Firms* (2015), 403.

[44]I. Björkman, W. Barner-Rasmussen, and L. Li, "Managing Knowledge Transfer in MNCs: The Impact of Headquarters Control Mechanisms," *Journal of International Business Studies* 35, no. 5 (2004): 443–55.

[45]Doz and Prahalad, "Quality of Management," in *Strategies in Global*, (345–68); B. Groysberg, A. N. McLean, and N. Nohria, "Are Leaders Portable?" *Harvard Business Review* 84, no. 5 (2006): 92.

[46]S. Morris, R. Hammond, and S. Snell, "A Microfoundations Approach to Transnational Capabilities: The Role of Knowledge Search in an Ever-changing World," *Journal of International Business Studies* 45, no. 4 (2014): 405–27.

[47]C. B. Gibson and J. Birkinshaw, "The Antecedents, Consequences, and Mediating Role of Organizational Ambidexterity," *Academy of Management Journal* 47, no. 2 (2004): 209–26; S. C. Kang and S. A. Snell, "Intellectual Capital Architectures and Ambidextrous Learning: A Framework for Human Resource Management," *Journal of Management Studies* 46, no. 1 (2009): 65–92.

[48]N. T. Washburn and T. B. Hunsaker, "Finding Great Ideas in Emerging Markets," *Harvard Business Review* 89, no. 9 (2011): 115–20.

[49]P. Suk Kim and A. Kotchegura, "Talent Management in Government in Times of Economic Instability: Selected Cases from the BRICS Countries," *Public Money & Management* 37, no. 1 (2017): 7–14.

[50]"Human Resources," Unilever, www.unilever.com/careers/graduates/uflp/human-resources/ (accessed December 2016).

[51]Personal interview with Scott Johnson, founder of Workfront by Shad Morris, June 2016.

[52]Personal conversation with Ryan Hill, 2016.

[53]Randall S. Schuler, Susan E. Jackson, and Ibraiz Tarique, "Global Talent Management and Global Talent Challenges: Strategic Opportunities for IHRM," *Journal of World Business* 46 (2011): 506–16; Christopher Rhoads, "Germany Faces Storm over Tech Staffing—Labor Groups Are Enraged by Proposal to Import Badly Needed Workers," *The Wall Street Journal*, March 7, 2000, A23; "European Workplaces Tighten Policies as Countries Struggle to Compete Worldwide," *Pittsburgh (Pennsylvania) Post-Gazette* (via Knight-Ridder/Tribune Business News), November 28, 2004.

[54]Herbert Spiro, "Co-Determination in Germany," *The American Political Science Review* 48, no. 4 (December 1954): 1114–27; Yuko Nishimura, "Reconstructing Minority Identities in 21st Century Japan," *Global Ethnographic Journal for Ethnographic Research* (January 23, 2012), http://oicd.net/ge/index.php/reconstructing-minority-identities_yukonishimura/.

[55]Personal conversation with HR managers at Honeywell by Shad Morris, 2016.

[56]"Modernizing HR at Microsoft," IT Insights-Business Case Study, Microsoft, 2015, https://msdn.microsoft.com/en-us/library/mt210440.aspx.

[57]Pucik et al., *The Global Challenge*.

[58]Pucik et al., *The Global Challenge*.

[59]Pucik et al., *The Global Challenge*.

[60]M.J. Schniederjans, A. M. Schniederjans, and D. G. Schniederjans, *Outsourcing and Insourcing in an International Context* (New York: Routledge, 2015).

[61]V. Thong, "Intel Vietnam Confirms Downsizing after Rumors of Closure," VNExpress, September 29, 2016, http://e.vnexpress.net/news/business/intel-vietnam-confirms-downsizing-after-rumors-of-closure-3475745.html; B. Einhorn and O. Kharif, "Intel's Vietnam Engineering Talent Pipeline: Women Dominate Its Final Batch of Scholarships in Portland, Ore.," Bloomberg, June 26, 2014; M. Horn, "Intel Integrates Backward to Improve Vietnamese Education, Society," *Forbes*, March 4, 2014, https://www.forbes.com/sites/michaelhorn/2014/03/04/intel-integrates-backward-to-improve-vietnamese-education-society/#238635ff348a; S. Tibken, "Schooling Vietnam: How Tech Companies Are Training the Next Wave of Workers," CNet, July 22, 2015, https://www.cnet.com/news/schooling-vietnam-how-tech-companies-are-training-the-next-wave-of-workers/; Robert J. House, et al., *Strategic Leadership Across Cultures: GLOBE Study of CEO Leadership Behavior and Effectiveness in 24 Countries* (Thousand Oaks, CA: Sage Publications, 2013).

CHAPTER 20

Global Finance and Accounting

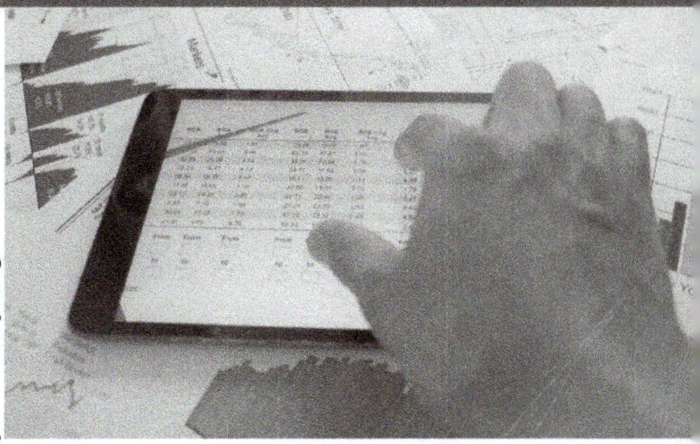

jessikla/Getty Images

Introduction

Did you know more than 150 currencies are in use in the world today? That means that in international business, being able to get your hands on the right kind of money is crucial to success.

Firms need foreign money to pay for goods purchased abroad, to invest in projects in foreign countries, and to invest in foreign stock markets. However, exchanging your money isn't as simple as swapping with someone in another country. Accounting standards ensure that companies meet global benchmarks for reporting and communicating when and how they exchanged or acquired money. These standards also help business leaders properly account for transactions made across countries. For example, the bicycle company Specialized owns manufacturing operations in Taiwan. When Specialized wants to transfer a bike from Taiwan to the United States, the company's U.S. distributor needs to pay Specialized's manufacturing operation in Taiwan for the bike. However, if Specialized reports a profit on the bike in Taiwan *and* in the United States, it stands a chance of being taxed by both countries on the same transaction. Avoiding this kind of costly mistake is one reason business leaders need to learn about global finance and accounting.

LEARNING OBJECTIVES

After exploring this chapter you will be able to

1. **Discuss** how companies raise money for international trade and investment
2. **Apply** net present value analysis to the capital budgeting decision
3. **Describe** international accounting practices
4. **Identify** specific tax issues multinational companies face

20.1 Financing International Trade and Investment

LEARNING OBJECTIVE

Discuss how companies raise money for international trade and investment.

Firms finance their operations and expansion efforts using both short- and long-term strategies. The institutions at the core of international trade and investment are international

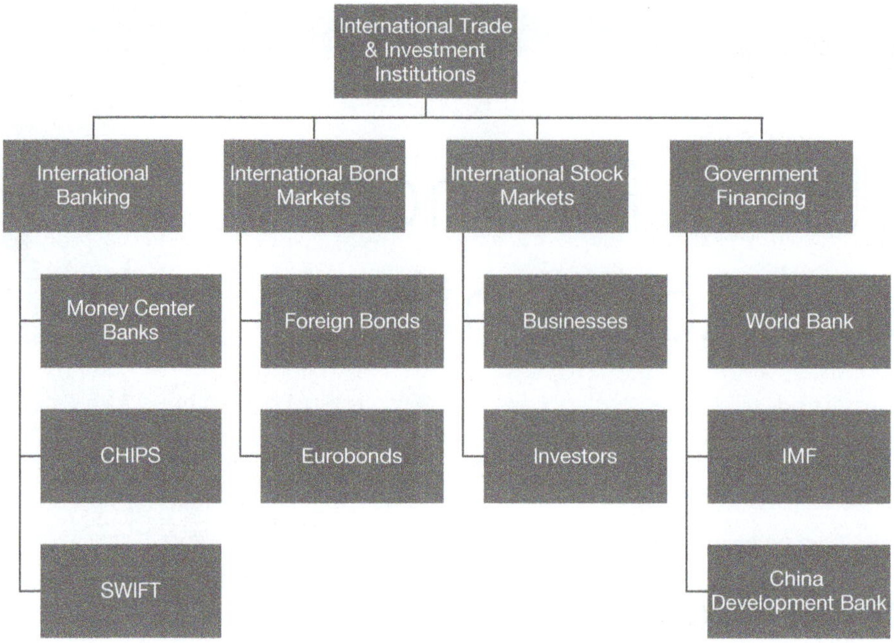

FIGURE 20.1 International trade and investment institutions CHIPS, Clearing House Interbank Payments System; IMF, International Monetary Fund; SWIFT, Society of Worldwide Interbank Financial Telecommunications.

banking, international bond markets, international stock markets, and government financing (see **Figure 20.1**). We'll look at each of these in turn.

International Banking

The daily operations of multinational firms around the world generate trillions of dollars in transactions. However, all those transactions are at risk of default, theft, and mishandling of funds. Naturally, firms and governments of all sizes are very concerned with the safety and reliability of every financial transaction. As governments and multinational corporations (MNCs) have grown, the size and types of organizations that meet the financial needs of large companies have grown too.

Money center banks large banks that borrow from and lend to governments, other banks, and corporations

Money center banks are one of the oldest types of organizations that support the financial operations of large businesses. Unlike conventional banks, which do business primarily with consumers, money center banks borrow from and lend to governments, other banks, and corporations. Today, international banking is dominated by more than 200 money center banks around the world. Some of these banks include household names like Citigroup, JPMorgan Chase, Wells Fargo, and Bank of America.[1]

Clearing House Interbank Payments System (CHIPS) a private company that handles large payments to governments and corporations

Large payments to governments and corporations sometimes are run through money center banks, but many are handled through a private company known as the **Clearing House Interbank Payments System (CHIPS)**, located in New York City. Any bank or financial institution can become a member of CHIPS, which is a bank-owned, privately run electronic payments system that process more than $1.5 trillion worth of international transactions every day.[2] **Figure 20.2** illustrates how CHIPS is used to move money from one company to another in an international location.

Society of Worldwide Interbank Financial Telecommunications (SWIFT) a global telecommunications company that facilitates secure international payment transfers from one bank to another

Also integral to large organizations is the **Society of Worldwide Interbank Financial Telecommunications (SWIFT)**, a global telecommunications company that facilitates secure international payment transfers from one bank to another. The organization neither holds funds nor manages client accounts, it just facilitates the transfer of payments between banks. By 2017 it was handling more than 26 million messages a day across more than 210 countries.[3]

cash in advance a method of payment in which the importer pays to the exporter the full amount due in advance

CHIPS and SWIFT aren't the only ways businesses and governments can perform financial transactions across borders. Organizations use different payment methods depending on the level of risk, security, and expense each party can tolerate; different methods are more favorable to some industries than others. For instance, **cash in advance**, a method of payment where the importer pays the full amount in advance to the exporter, is the safest method for exporters but the least safe for importers. When exporters receive payment in advance, they

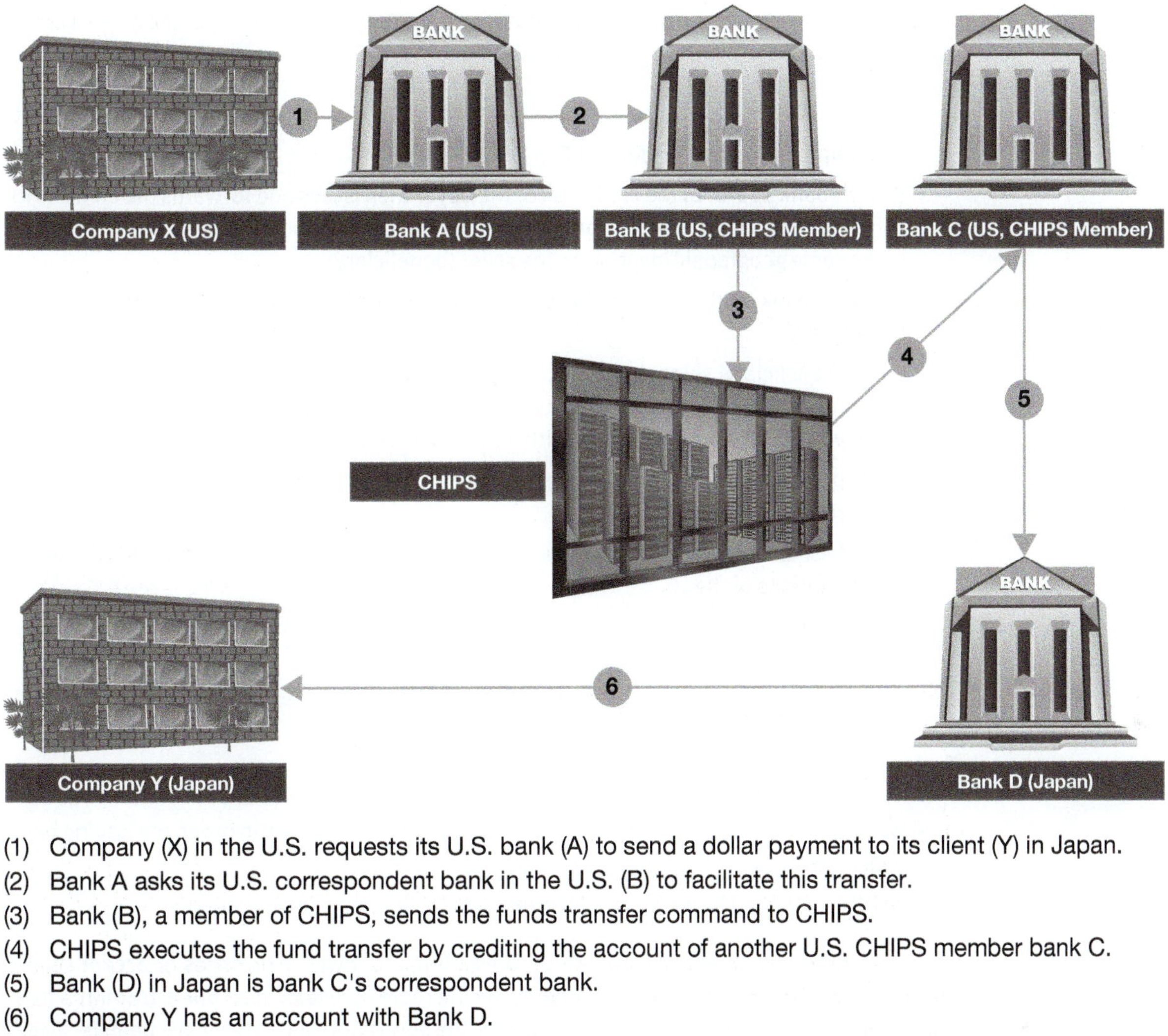

BANK
BANK
BANK
Company X (US)
Bank A (US)
Bank B (US, CHIPS Member)
Bank C (US, CHIPS Member)
1
2
3
4
5
CHIPS
BANK
6
Company Y (Japan)
Bank D (Japan)
(1) Company (X) in the U.S. requests its U.S. bank (A) to send a dollar payment to its client (Y) in Japan.
(2) Bank A asks its U.S. correspondent bank in the U.S. (B) to facilitate this transfer.
(3) Bank (B), a member of CHIPS, sends the funds transfer command to CHIPS.
(4) CHIPS executes the fund transfer by crediting the account of another U.S. CHIPS member bank C.
(5) Bank (D) in Japan is bank C's correspondent bank.
(6) Company Y has an account with Bank D.

FIGURE 20.2 **CHIPS** An example of how cross-border payment works: (1) Company X in the United States requests its U.S. bank (A) to send a dollar payment to its client (Y) in Japan. (2) Bank A asks its U.S. correspondent bank in the United States (B) to facilitate this transfer. (3) Bank B, a member of CHIPS, sends the funds transfer command to CHIPS. (4) CHIPS executes the fund transfer by crediting the account of Bank C, another U.S. CHIPS member. (5) Bank D in Japan is Bank C's correspondent bank. (6) Company Y has an account with Bank D. Adapted from Daniel Cawrey, "Payments Veterans Seek to Unlock Blockchain's Power with Align Commerce," CoinDesk, January 11, 2015, www.coindesk.com/payments-veterans-seek-unlock-blockchains-power-align-commerce/.

avoid credit risk but create an unbalanced value flow. That is, the exporter or seller has been paid, but the importer, or buyer, runs the risk that the goods it paid for will not be sent or will be damaged or lost in transit. Wire transfers, credit cards, and escrow services are the most common methods for paying cash in advance. Consumers who buy items on websites like Amazon, Taobao, or eBay use a form of the cash in advance method.

The allure of cash in advance for a seller is, of course, eliminating what could be a high level of risk. Without getting payment up front, a seller could ship goods, only to find that the buyer is suddenly unable or unwilling to pay the agreed-upon amount.[4] Once goods are sitting in a foreign country with no buyer, the seller has to either find a new buyer in that country or pay to ship the goods somewhere else.

To avoid situations like these, importers and exporters frequently use a highly secure form of payment known as a **commercial letter of credit (LC)**. An LC is a guarantee of payment when goods are delivered as long as all selling conditions have been met. This provides a level of protection to both the exporter/seller and the importer/buyer because the importer's bank assures the seller it will receive payment and helps the buyer get what it paid for. An LC is useful

commercial letter of credit (LC) a highly secure form of payment in which an importer's bank offers a guarantee of payment when goods are delivered as long as all selling conditions have been met

when an exporter trusts the buyer's bank but is unsure about the reliability of the buyer's credit or legal standing. Here are the steps that take place in an LC[5]:

- Buyer and seller agree to conduct business. The seller wants an LC to guarantee payment.
- Buyer applies to the bank for an LC in favor of the seller.
- Buyer's bank approves the credit risk of the buyer then issues and forwards the credit to its correspondent bank (advising or confirming). The correspondent bank is usually located in the same geographic location as the seller (beneficiary).
- Advising bank authenticates the credit and forward the original credit to the seller (beneficiary).
- Seller (beneficiary) ships the goods, then verifies and develops the documentary requirements to support the LC. Documentary requirements may vary greatly depending on the perceived risk involved in dealing with a particular company.
- Seller presents the required documents to the advising or confirming bank to be processed for payment.
- The advising or confirming bank examines the documents for compliance with the terms and conditions of the LC.
- If the documents are correct, the advising or confirming bank claims the funds by
  - debiting the account of the issuing bank.
  - waiting until the issuing bank receives the documents and then remits payment.
  - reimbursing another bank as required in the credit.
- Advising or confirming bank forwards the documents to the issuing bank.
- Issuing bank examines the documents for compliance. If they are in order, the issuing bank debits the buyer's account.
- Issuing bank then forwards the documents to the buyer.

open account a form of payment in which an importer doesn't pay for goods until after they have been received, creating an unfavorable balance of value for the exporter

syndicate a group of banks that work together to offer credit in order to reduce risk

documentary collection (DC) a process in which an exporter's bank is entrusted with collecting payment for goods. This bank sends to the importer's bank any documents necessary to collect the goods. The importer's bank then releases those documents to the buyer only after payment has been received

Sometimes the threat of competition drives firms to lower their prices or accept selling terms that are less than favorable in order to secure more business. In an **open account** agreement, for instance, the importer doesn't pay for the goods until after they have been received, creating an unfavorable balance of value for the exporter. In effect, the exporter becomes a lender to the importer, enabling the importer to purchase goods on credit. In general, open account transactions result in 60- to 90-day waiting periods until payments are due.[6] This gives buyers a two- to three-month window to sell the goods before having to pay for them. Although an open account is a high-risk method for exporters, those unwilling to offer open account terms may lose sales and thus market share. For that reason, some financial analysts believe over 70 percent of all international trade transactions use open account terms.[7]

When large international firms deal with high volumes of goods, they sometimes need access to more credit than a single bank can handle. In these situations, they often obtain credit from a group of banks known as a **syndicate**. A syndicate enables banks to combine their resources and share their risks. A lead bank negotiates the terms of credit between the firm and the syndicate. Because multiple banks each undertake a portion of the credit, however, the risk is spread across the group, minimizing the risk to any individual bank. The syndicate profits from this arrangement by charging the borrower underwriting, commitment, and other related fees. To set interest rates, syndicates use floating international interest rates plus a premium for credit risk. In the United States and Europe, the London interbank offered rate (LIBOR) is a common international interest rate. In the Asian Pacific region, the Singapore interbank offered rate (SIBOR) is often used. As **Figure 20.3** demonstrates, the LIBOR and SIBOR often move in parallel—increases in LIBOR increase the SIBOR. From 2014 to 2016, SIBOR was priced at a premium over LIBOR because of a risk premium. This premium disappeared with the rise in LIBOR rates in early 2017.

When a seller/exporter wants to avoid open account terms but trusts the buyer enough to forgo the safety net and expense of an LC, a **documentary collection (DC)** is an option. In a DC transaction, the exporter's bank is entrusted to collect the payment. This bank sends to the importer's bank any documents necessary for collecting the goods. The importer's bank then releases those documents to the buyer only after payment has been received. DCs do not offer the same level of protection as LCs, so they require a higher level of trust between the parties, but they tend to be less expensive.

The last major method of transacting international business is **consignment**, in which an exporter sends goods to the importer without transferring ownership. Some transactions require that consumers see and test the product before buying, so exporters use consignment to get their goods to potential buyers who would otherwise be unwilling to take the risk that the purchase entails. The importer, on the other hand, doesn't pay the exporter until a third party has bought the goods from the importer. Consignment agreements are attractive to importers because of the lack of risk attached to the transaction: Unsold goods can be returned to the exporter without any extra expenses. Artists and craftspeople often use consignment to let retailers sell on their behalf in exchange for a percentage of the sale.

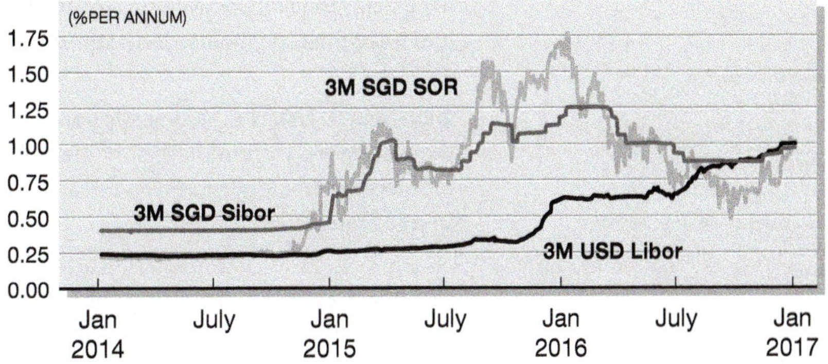

FIGURE 20.3 **LIBOR and SIBOR** 3-Month U.S. dollar LIBOR and Singapore dollar SIBOR rates often are closely related. If one increases, the other moves in parallel. **Source:** Siow Li Sen, "Pressure on Sibor and SOR Continues with Spectre of Fed Hikes," Business Times, January 5, 2017, www.businesstimes.com.sg/banking-finance/pressure-on-sibor-and-sor-continues-with-spectre-of-fed-hikes.

consignment a process in which an exporter sends goods to an importer without transferring ownership

International Bond Markets

Many firms are continually expanding, and that expansion requires regular infusions of capital. The international bond market provides a way for corporations to arrange long-term financing for capital equipment, land, and buildings.

Before we discuss bond markets, however, let's review the definition and purpose of a bond. A **bond** is a debt investment in which the issuer of the bond owes the bondholder a debt. Typically, the issuer is required to pay interest throughout the life of the bond and then repay the entire principal amount at the end of the term. Bonds have three components: the interest rate (called the *coupon*), the amount initially borrowed (the *principal*), and the date the principal is due to be repaid (the *maturity date*). Companies often issue bonds to investors in order to raise money for ongoing projects or to finance new ones. For instance, during World War II the United States issued war bonds to encourage citizens to help fund military operations (**Figure 20.4**). War bonds promised a 2.9 percent return after a 10-year maturity. Although their rate of return was lower than market prices (meaning they had less earning potential than other investment options in the market), the bonds successfully galvanized citizens to support the fight, and at that time, bonds were a popular way for citizens to contribute to the national defense.[8] Japan continues to rely on cheap government bonds sold to citizens at a discount to finance its government debt.

bond a debt investment in which the issuer of the bond owes the bondholder a debt

Now let's consider international bonds. Before the 1990s, large MNCs from developed countries—companies like Coca Cola and Toyota Motor Corporation—were the only entities that issued long-term bonds in international markets. The past 20 years have seen great changes in international markets, though. Events like the fall of the Soviet Union and the creation of the euro have expanded the international bond market by encouraging emerging countries and additional developed countries to open up to foreign investors and issue international bonds. The euro in particular has enabled European companies to invest all across the continent without having to worry about foreign exchange rates or other currency-based complications.

FIGURE 20.4 **War bonds** The United States issued war bonds during World War II to encourage citizens to help fund military operations.

Both domestic and international bonds are typically bought and sold among corporations, banks, governments, and large institutional investors such as hedge funds, insurance companies, pensions, and retirement funds. Bond denominations are usually too high for everyday investors and individuals. Today, bond markets are separated into three main segments: domestic bonds, foreign bonds, and Eurobonds.

Domestic Bonds Domestic bonds are not part of the international bond market. Instead, they are issued by firms in their home countries and in the local currency. For instance, Nike, a U.S.-based company, issues a domestic bond in the United States for investors who live in the United States.

Foreign Bonds Foreign firms issue bonds in (for them) foreign currencies to investors in other countries. For example, Huawei, a Chinese telecommunications company, can issue bonds to U.S. investors denominated in U.S. dollars. Foreign bonds have nicknames based on where they are sold. For instance, foreign bonds sold in New Zealand are called kiwi bonds, whereas foreign bonds sold in the United States are called Yankee bonds.[9] Samurai bonds sell in the Japanese market and Bulldog bonds in the U.K. market. Investors can evaluate these bonds in the familiar terms of their home currency, which makes them somewhat more attractive in stable markets, but it also requires the issuing companies to conduct a foreign currency exchange to bring the capital they raise back to their home markets.

Eurobonds Eurobonds are issued in any country outside the home country but still in the domestic currency. (Despite their name, they don't necessarily have anything to do with Europe or the euro). For instance, if Huawei issues bonds to U.S. investors but they are denominated in the Chinese renminbi, they are Eurobonds. The Eurobond market is particularly attractive because it has fewer regulatory requirements that can add additional fees to the bonds, enabling companies to raise money at lower cost. This market also offers bond buyers a more favorable rate at which the bonds are taxed and more relaxed disclosure requirements than most domestic bond markets. However, certain events—such as a decline in the value of the euro—can lead to less profit for international investors and encourage them to buy foreign bonds, such as U.S. Treasury debt.[10] Eurobonds are easier for companies to evaluate than other bonds because the funds are paid in their home currency; however, the additional risk of foreign currency fluctuations can make them more complicated for overseas investors. For instance, as Figure 20.5 shows, foreign ownership of Eurobonds issued by Southeast Asian firms increased dramatically from 2009 to 2014, and it continues to rise today.

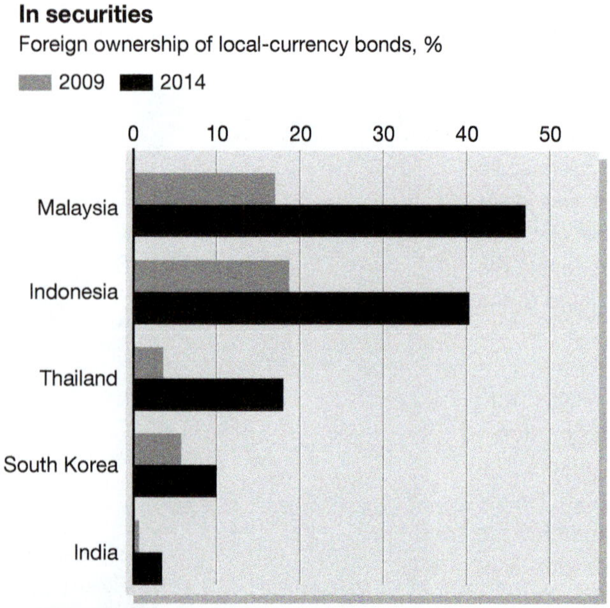

FIGURE 20.5 **Eurobonds** Rapid growth in Southeast Asia's Eurobonds has tied many foreign investors to the fate of local foreign currency markets. **Source:** "The Calm Before the Tantrum," The Economist, May 2, 2015, www.economist.com/news/finance-and-economics/21650121-south-east-asian-bond-markets-have-performed-well-recently-tests-loom-calm.

International Stock Markets

Businesses need to raise equity and obtain long-term capital in order to expand and grow, but it's not a one-sided effort. Global financial integration often benefits customers, too, because growing companies are able to make and deliver better, cheaper products to meet customer needs. Stock markets, in which companies sell *stock*, or shares of ownership in the firm, provide a venue for businesses to reach investors from both developed and emerging markets around the world. What's more, stock markets reward innovative, fast-moving, adaptive companies, providing them with more capital to grow. Conversely, companies that underperform and fail to reach goals suffer when investors turn to more promising firms. Thus stock markets have benefits for both business and investors.

Businesses Stock markets provide a way for businesses to raise capital. The most prominent reasons to raise capital are to make acquisitions, build new infrastructure, and expand. Without selling stock, companies like Honda, Home Depot, and Chevrolet would have struggled to get the capital they needed to build billion-dollar companies. For instance, Walmart lagged behind Kmart for many years until it went "public" (that is, sold shares of stock in the stock market for the first time) in the spring of 1970. Going public generated enough capital for Walmart to pay off short-term debts owed to vendors and banks, and have enough left over to rapidly expand the number of its stores. In the 10 years following Walmart's *initial public offering (IPO)* of its stock, its sales increased from $313 million to $1.2 billion, and it became the United States' number-one retailer in 1990,[11] a position it still holds.[12]

Investors Stock ownership has become a popular form of investment because it offers potentially higher gains than safer options like bonds or savings accounts. This is true despite the inherent risks of investing in stock. If a firm's performance does not live up to expectations, for instance, the value of its stock can fall, sometimes sharply, and its stockholders will experience losses. Stocks are not all equally risky, however. Individuals can invest in more stable stocks (like utilities) or preferred stocks (which promise milder returns for better assurances of gain). But the higher the risk, the higher the potential for significant gains—and losses.

Another option for investors is to buy **exchange-traded funds**, which follow different *stock indexes* like the S&P 500 (which tracks the free-float value of the top 500 major corporations). **Figure 20.6** shows the average returns from the different international stock markets. As you can see, higher returns (and higher losses) usually occur in higher-risk markets.

Investors can also buy **mutual funds**, which pool and repackage shares of various stocks—as well as other assets like bonds, real estate, and commodities—to allow individual investors to buy smaller stakes in more companies. This strategy, called **diversification**, reduces investors' risks by spreading investment capital across a range of possibilities that are likely to react differently to outside events. When the value of one stock or asset class is going down, another will be going up, and the two responses balance out to prevent sudden swings in the mutual fund's valuation. Thus investors can harness overall market growth rather than the individual growth of any given company.

However, because stock markets worldwide have become increasingly interconnected, the effectiveness of diversification has been reduced as markets in different countries have begun reacting similarly, in a phenomenon called **contagion**. For instance, on October 19, 1987, also known as Black Monday, the Hong Kong stock market crashed. Then the crash spread west to

exchange-traded funds trading vehicles that follow different stock indexes, such as the S&P 500

mutual funds pooled and repackaged shares of various stocks—as well as other assets like bonds, real estate, and commodities—that allow individual investors to buy smaller stakes in more companies

diversification an investment strategy to reduce investors' risks by spreading investment capital across a range of possibilities that are likely to react differently to outside events

contagion a pattern in which stock markets have become increasingly interconnected around the world and markets in different countries have begun reacting similarly

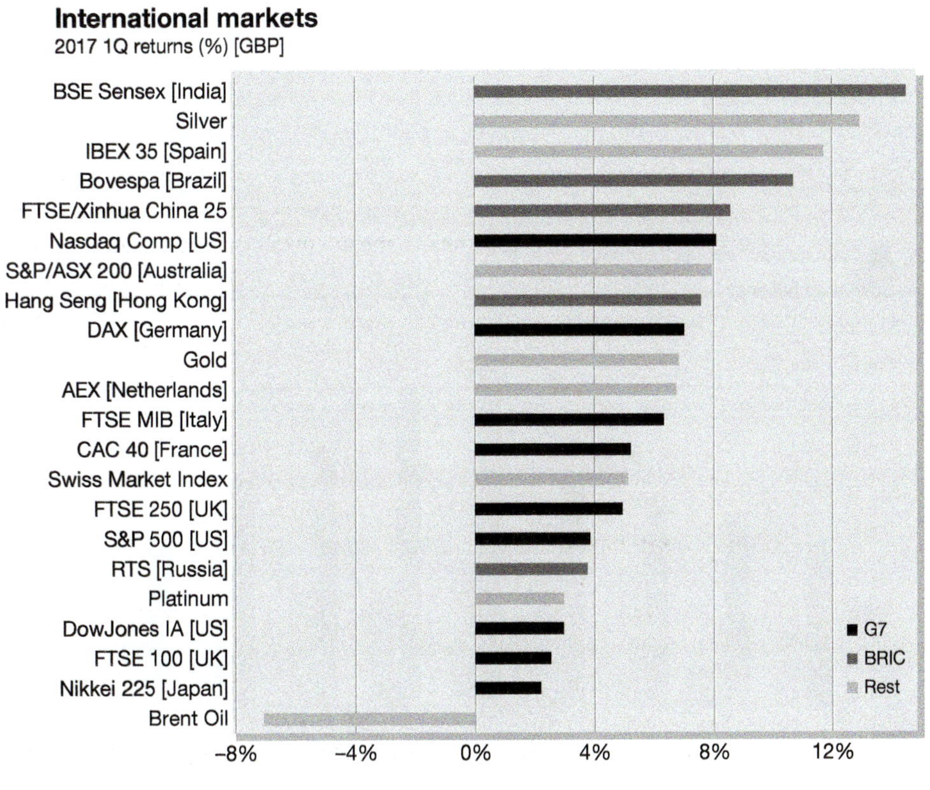

FIGURE 20.6 Exchange-traded funds A list of some of the world's exchange-traded index funds and markets. **Source:** Almanacist, "International Markets 2017 1Q," Harriman Stock Market Almanac, April 4, 2017, http://stockmarketalmanac.co.uk/2017/04/international-markets-2017-1q/.

Europe and eventually the United States, sending these markets down like dominoes. Another example of contagion occurred on September 11, 2001, when terrorists successfully coordinated attacks on U.S. targets. The aftershocks rippled through markets all across the world, setting a record for the biggest one-day loss in stock exchange history.[13] As proof of the wisdom of diversification, however, many investors in the airline, tourism, and insurance industries suffered deep, lasting losses, whereas in other industries, like technology and defense contracting, a temporary drop was followed by a strong increase in share prices.

When global or even local financial crises occur, firms that are essential to their countries' economies can sometimes end up short of cash, investors, or credit. They are forced to scale back by laying off employees and curtailing expansion plans—and forgoing any profits that would have come as a result of growth. Just when investment and capital are most critical to these firms, banks and investors often pull back to shore up their own finances. As a result, other institutions like governments often step in to jump-start the recovery process and reduce damage to the economy.

In addition to national governments, some international organizations are also equipped to help during such crises. Two of these are the International Monetary Fund (IMF) and the World Bank. These organizations can provide valuable financial support to countries in need and help reestablish a more stable global economy. The World Bank focuses on raising the standard of living worldwide and on promoting long-term economic development by offering long-term loans to developing countries. The IMF provides short-term help to member nations in the form of loans, advice, and training.

Many agencies in developed countries also provide government-supported financial aid. The Export-Import Bank of the United States (Ex-Im Bank), the U.S. Small Business Administration, Japan Bank for International Cooperation, Germany's, and Canada's Export Development Corporation are just a few of the governmental agencies around the world engaged in international development. For example, the Ex-Im Bank provides loans and insurance to small businesses selling to customers overseas. However, since 2011 the bank has received criticism for only serving special interests of big companies and not the needs of small businesses. As a result, in 2017, President Donald Trump, as part of his "America First" campaign, pushed to revitalize the bank in an effort to make America more competitive in driving exports (see **Figure 20.7**).[14]

More recently, China created the China Development Bank (CDB). Unlike the Philippines-based Asian Development Bank, which was established in 1966 and is heavily influenced by the United States (its second-largest shareholder), the CDB was established as an alternative to the World Bank and counter U.S. influence in the development of Asia. When the CDB was first proposed, the United States saw it as a political threat to the region and took a hard-line approach, appealing to allies to not join. However, as countries like Great Britain decided to join

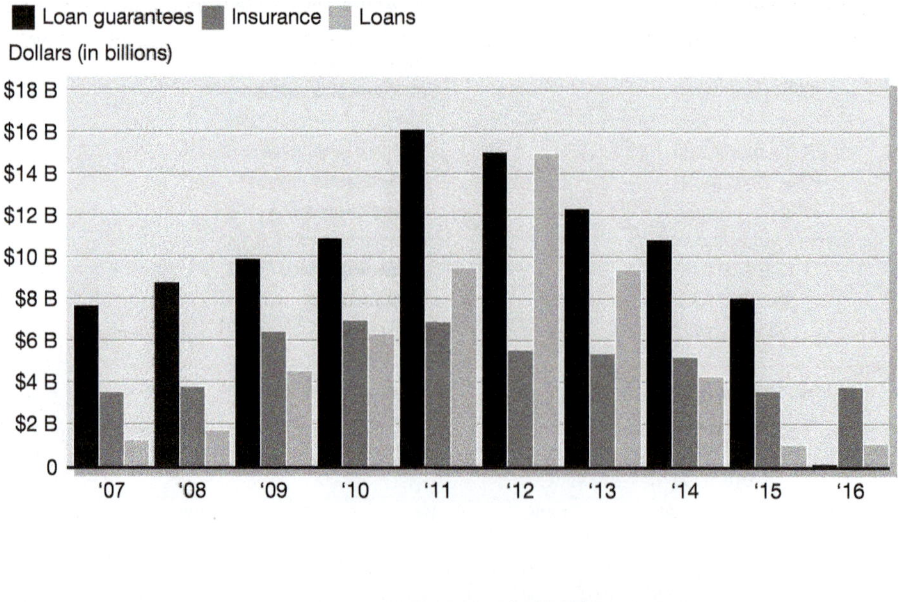

FIGURE 20.7 Decreased use of the Ex-Im Bank The United States' Ex-Im Bank has decreased the loans, insurance, and loan guarantees it issues. **Source:** Export-Import Bank of the United States. https://www.dallasnews.com/news/donald-trump-1/2017/04/27/trump-sends-mixed-messages-ex-bank-loved-exporters-hated-texas-republicans

anyway, many other nations—14 of them with advanced economies, such as Brazil, France, and Germany—also rushed to join by the 2015 deadline.[15]

The CDB has proven instrumental in promoting development in Asia (such as by providing funding for the Three Gorges Dam) and also in Latin America. For example, in 2015, when Brazil's oil company Petrobras faced allegations of corruption for bribing officials, the CDB stepped in and signed a $3.5 billion financing deal with the company.[16] China's involvement in Latin America continues, and since 2005 it has extended more than $100 billion in credit there.

In the United States, small businesses and entrepreneurs are supported by the U.S. Small Business Administration through government-backed loans, counseling, and export-financing assistance. Similarly, Brazil helps small businesses and entrepreneurs through the Brazilian Service of Assistance to Micro and Small Enterprises. Other countries also have agencies designed to help small businesses get started and flourish.

The United States assists larger organizations through its official Export-Import Bank, which helps finance and insure the purchase of U.S. goods by foreign companies when private lenders are not willing to accept the credit risk these buyers might represent. The Ex-Im Bank's efforts to support sales have helped lift U.S. firms to the same level of competitiveness as other nations' government-supported firms. But this assistance doesn't come free; firms receiving assistance from the Ex-Im Bank are often required to sell products of which at least 51 percent are made in the United States.[17]

While government financing and bailouts of companies can be controversial, such assistance has proven very beneficial to companies in the past decade. In 2010 and 2011, several European countries—including Greece, Ireland, and Portugal—were assisted by the IMF. Government intervention in these instances helped restore market confidence and saved businesses from failure.

20.2 Capital Budgeting for Multinational Companies

LEARNING OBJECTIVE

Apply net present value analysis to the capital budgeting decision.

MNCs are in constant need of new ideas to maintain and promote sales, and of the investment capital necessary to bring those new ideas to market. A firm's managers aim to maximize the value of the firm and its shares by efficiently allocating the company's capital. To decide whether to make a given capital investment, managers weigh several factors, including political risk, economic risk, cultural risk, technological risk, and net present value. We discuss net present value in some detail below.

The Parent Firm's Capital Budgeting Decisions

Let's consider whether the pharmaceutical company Eli Lilly, with headquarters in Indiana, should approve certain capital investment projects overseas. Suppose the company owns a holding company or subsidiary company in Brazil and wants to start a new research and development (R&D) initiative there. Like all parent firms, Eli Lilly needs to analyze the investment from the perspective of both the subsidiary and its headquarters in the United States in order to judge whether it makes financial sense to start the R&D initiative in Brazil. For instance, the Brazilian project will be a profitable investment if it has a positive **net present value (NPV)**. NPV is the difference between the present value of cash inflows (money

net present value (NPV) the difference between the present value of cash coming into a company and the present value of cash going out of the company

jetcityimage/iStock Editorial/Getty Images

FIGURE 20.8 Eli Lilly has made significant investments in countries like Brazil However, in 2017 the company announced it would increase investments in the city of Indianapolis, Indiana, because the cost of capital had gone up in the new political climate of the United States.

coming into the company) and the present value of cash outflows (money going out of the company). It is used in capital budgeting to measure the profitability of a potential investment. To measure NPV, the parent company in the United States needs to consider, among other factors, what it will cost to eventually repatriate (bring back) subsidiary profits to the United States in order to pay dividends to its shareholders. Calculating NPV helps the company assess risk from potential negative returns on investment (**Figure 20.8**).

Another risk of such an investment is fluctuating exchange rates. Many MNCs seek to reduce this risk by diversifying their operations across multiple countries or by hedging. Hedging is when an investment is made to reduce the risk of adverse movements in the price of an asset. It's like taking out an insurance policy: to hedge exchange rate movements, firms often use derivative contracts, currency futures, forwards, options, or swap contracts (some of these strategies were discussed in Chapter 6).

sensitivity analysis a method to assess the riskiness of a capital investment by forecasting the most optimistic, the normal, and the most pessimistic outcomes possible under reasonable circumstances

One way firms assess the riskiness of a capital investment when using NPV is through a **sensitivity analysis** that forecasts the most optimistic, the normal, and the most pessimistic outcomes possible under reasonable circumstances. This analysis allows firms to calculate whether political, economic, inflationary, or even tax risks could jeopardize their investment. If the firm estimates a positive NPV even given a pessimistic projection, managers will be more likely to implement and have confidence in a project. Managers tend to favor these projections, even though they present high risk to the company.[18]

The Cost of Capital: Domestic versus Global

cost of capital the rate of return demanded by stock and bond investors

The minimum rate of return demanded by stock and bond investors is called the **cost of capital**, which is what it costs to get a loan or investment. The cost of capital is usually the amount loaned plus a percentage rate of return from the loan or investment. In calculating NPV, companies compare the cost of capital with the expected return on the investment. If the present value of the expected cash outflows is greater than the present value of the expected cash inflows, then NPV < 0. When the potential rate of return on the investment is less than the cost of capital (or the cost of the investment or loan), a firm is unlikely to make the investment. Similarly, if the present value of the expected cash outflows is equal to the present value of the expected cash inflows, then NPV = 0. A company is also unlikely to make the investment under this condition. However, if the present value of cash outflows is less than the present value of the expected cash inflows, then NPV > 0, and the firm will be likely to make the investment (**Table 20.1** shows an example of this using our hypothetical example of Eli Lilly).[19]

weighted average cost of capital (WACC) the interest rate that a company is expected to pay to its investors (stockholders and bondholders) to raise money for its operations or projects

If Eli Lilly, a U.S. company, wants to find the NPV of raising money for its Brazilian projects, then it calculates the **weighted average cost of capital (WACC)**, that is, the interest rate a company is expected to pay to its stock and bond investors to help raise money for its operations or projects. WACC is not a factor companies can control; rather, it is defined by a specific formula that all investors apply to calculate the rate of return they will get on their investment in a company. A firm can compute its WACC using the formula

$$\text{WACC} = \left(\frac{\text{Equity}}{\text{Total Market Value}}\right)\text{COE} + \left(\frac{\text{Debt}}{\text{Total Market Value}}\right)(1 - \text{Tax Rate})\text{BTC},$$

where Equity is the market value of the company's stock (i.e., what all the stock shares on the market are worth); Debt is the market value of the company's debts (money they owe); COE is

TABLE 20.1 Hypothetical Brazilian investment decision for Eli Lilly

IF	Then	Capital Budgeting Decision
NPV < 0	Potential Rate of Return on the Investment < Cost of Capital	Provides losses. Reject the investment from a financial perspective. Other factors like gaining market share in Brazil or positive government relations could be important.
NPV = 0	Potential Rate of Return on the Investment = Cost of Capital	Provides a break-even return. Probably reject from a financial perspective. However, other factors that are important would probably make Eli Lilly want to make the investment in Brazil.
NPV > 0	Potential Rate of Return on the Investment > Cost of Capital	Provides positive returns. This does not necessarily mean Eli Lilly should invest in the Brazilian project. But at least it means the company will probably be safe financially if the transaction costs are not too high.

cost of equity, or the rate of return required by the investors (the interest rate paid to compensate investors for the risk they are taking on); BTC is the before-tax cost of debt or interest rate; Tax Rate is the marginal tax rate of the firm; and Total Market Value represents the amount of equity plus the company's debt.

Notice that a higher tax rate, interest rate, debt level, or equity value could lead to a higher cost of capital and thus a lower NPV. By reducing any of these factors, firms can increase NPV and the amount of possible profit. By reducing the cost of capital, a company's NPV is likely to become more positive and lead to more investments. In this way, governments often try to stimulate corporate investments by lowering interest rates, which increases the NPV of potential projects and makes global companies more willing to invest.

20.3 International Accounting Standards

LEARNING OBJECTIVE

Describe international accounting practices.

Accounting is often called the language of business and has become the universal method by which firms record, summarize, and report the economic activities of their organizations. To ensure transparency and comparability between different companies, several sets of accounting standards have been made law. Two in particular have been adopted to help companies report financial information internally to management and externally to investors and other concerned parties. The first set of standards, known as Generally Accepted Accounting Principles (GAAP), provides guidelines preparing public financial statements in the United States. The second set, the International Financial Reporting Standards (IFRS), was created to enable that same level of comparability across international companies and countries. Let's talk about each set.

Generally Accepted Accounting Principles

The financial statements of publicly traded companies in the United States must be prepared according to the basic accounting principles and guidelines set forth in the **Generally Accepted Accounting Principles (GAAP)**. GAAP are issued and maintained by the Financial Accounting Standards Board (FASB), and to avoid sanctions firms must

Generally Accepted Accounting Principles (GAAP) the set of accounting principles that U.S. public companies must use

follow FASB's GAAP standards. They must also adhere to rules issued by the U.S. Securities and Exchange Commission. Last, public accountants in the United States are required to obtain a license to work in the auditing, tax, or consulting fields. This license, conferred on a Certified Public Accountant (CPA), requires individuals to log a minimum number of hours of instruction and pass a rigorous exam. Other licenses are granted for the role of Certified Internal Auditor (CIA), Certified Fraud Examiner (CFE), and Certified Management Accountant (CMA).

In other countries, businesses use modified forms of GAAP, adapted to their country's cultural environment and issued by their respective version of FASB. Unfortunately, these conflicting accounting standards make it difficult to compare companies across country borders, so the past several decades have seen a push from the industry and from business to create a universal set of accounting standards.

International Accounting Standards Board (IASB) an international organization located in London, England, that sets international accounting standards

International Accounting Standards (IAS) a set of international accounting principles to which companies in many countries must comply

International Financial Reporting Standards (IFRS) a set of international accounting standards detailing how transactions and other events should be reported in financial statements

International Financial Reporting Standards

If companies in different countries interpret what constitutes a liability differently, a firm's overall profit and revenue could vary widely according to where it was reported, and could thereby confuse investors. Some of the main differences we find when comparing U.S. GAAP and the standards of other countries include the types of political and legal systems, level of business complexity, rate of inflation, basis for taxation, culture, history, and methods for reporting sources of capital.

The need to develop an international set of accounting standards led to the creation of the **International Accounting Standards Board (IASB)**, located in London, England. The IASB has issued **International Accounting Standards (IAS)**, which can be used by businesses anywhere around the world. While the IASB is privately funded and may not have the legal authority to enforce its rules, the group's influential nature has encouraged many countries to require companies to comply with IAS.

As of 2016, more than 120 countries and the 28 European Union nations required or encouraged the use of the IASB's **International Financial Reporting Standards (IFRS)**[20], a set of international accounting standards detailing how transactions and other events should be reported in financial statements. The ultimate goal of IFRS is to facilitate comparisons of accounting practices and companies. Cultural and ethnic differences still hamper the immediate acceptance of an international accounting standard; however, the IFRS aims to, in time, eliminate these barriers so that companies, governments, and investors alike can benefit from a simpler, standardized accounting system. **Figure 20.9** provides additional insight into the similarities and differences between IFRS and GAAP.

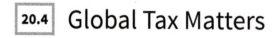

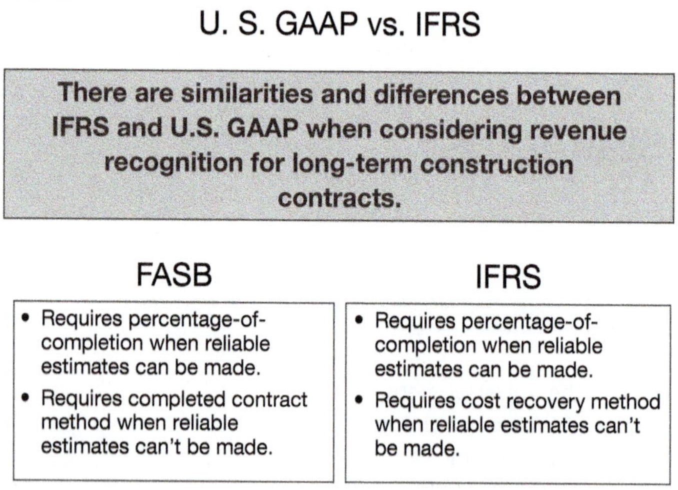

U. S. GAAP vs. IFRS
There are similarities and differences between IFRS and U.S. GAAP when considering revenue recognition for long-term construction contracts.
FASB
• Requires percentage-of-completion when reliable estimates can be made.
• Requires completed contract method when reliable estimates can't be made.
IFRS
• Requires percentage-of-completion when reliable estimates can be made.
• Requires cost recovery method when reliable estimates can't be made.

FIGURE 20.9 **U.S. GAAP versus IFRS** **Source:** Koy Chumnith, "Cash and Receivables," Royal University of Law and Economics. McGraw-Hill/Irwin, 2011).

20.4 Global Tax Matters

LEARNING OBJECTIVE

Identify specific tax issues multinational companies face.

In addition to differing accounting practices, another of the complex challenges MNCs face is working with differing tax systems across regions, countries, and governments. Relevant taxes include sales tax, property tax, payroll tax, goods and services tax, and value-added tax, but probably the most important in governing management and operations is corporate income tax.

Corporate Income Tax

Most countries impose a corporate income tax. In fact, for the U.S. government and many other countries, corporate income tax is the largest source of revenue after income and payroll taxes (see **Figure 20.10**). For instance, corporate income tax makes up about 11 percent of overall U.S. federal tax revenue.[21] Most governments thus have a vested interest in attracting new businesses and creating new economic growth for existing ones. Some countries, however, like the Bahamas, the Cayman Islands, Andorra, and others, collect low or no corporate income taxes. Such countries are called **tax havens**. For example, Apple has kept earnings abroad and borrowed money from its own foreign subsidiaries to pay dividends to its shareholders. Because the interest paid on loans is also deductible, Apple ends up reaping a second tax benefit.[22]

tax havens countries with no or low corporate taxes

While it might be tempting to pay no corporate income tax, companies must recognize that governments still need funding, so countries without this tax usually have higher property, payroll, and sales taxes. For example, the United Arab Emirates has a 55 percent corporate tax, whereas the Cayman Islands has no corporate taxes. The Cayman Islands, however, makes their money through other taxes, including some additional noncorporate taxes corporations have to pay.[23] However, it takes more than low taxes to attract firms to a specific country.[24] Other considerations are factors such as market volatility, political environment and stability, infrastructure, culture, and labor costs—and in some instances these can be more important than tax rates. For example, Japan and the United States have some of the highest corporate tax rates in the world, yet they are also some of the most desirable business locations (see Figure 20.8). Even with taxes as high as 40 percent (Japan), companies still flock there. Why? Because these countries use their tax revenues to promote stable economies, steady government, educated labor forces, reliable infrastructure, strong consumer bases, and fair legal systems.

While a favorable business environment is certainly attractive, a very high corporate tax rate will still drive away business—particularly as markets elsewhere continue to mature and stabilize. Because high tax rates can hurt economic growth, interest groups have formed to promote competitiveness. One international group in particular, the Organisation of Economic Co-operation and Development (OECD), has been working tirelessly to simplify tax codes and

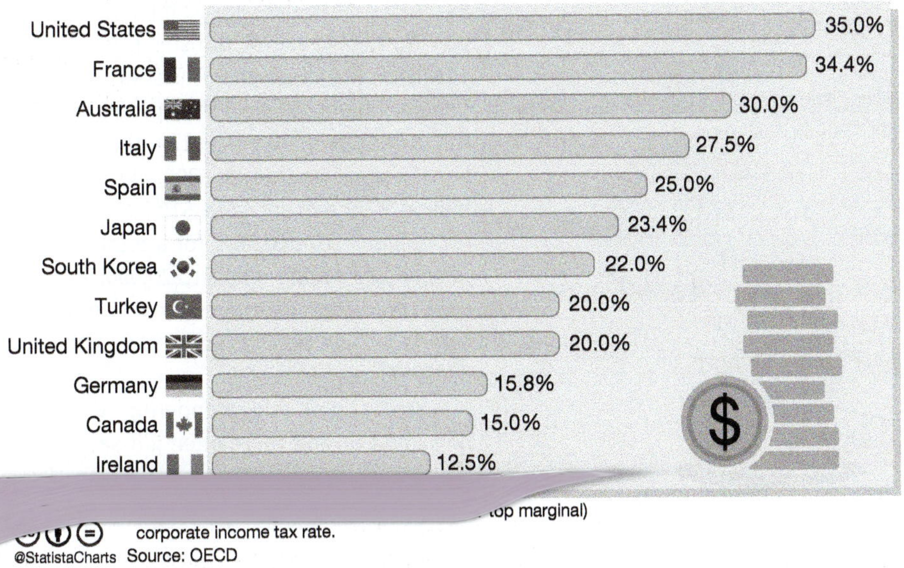

FIGURE 20.10 **Select corporate tax rates, 2016**

make them more competitive, as a way of promoting economic development.[25] Made up of 34 members, the OECD has managed to decrease the average global corporate income tax rate from 47 to 25 percent.

Lower tax rates attract investment in and growth of business, strengthening economies.[26] For example, the standard corporate tax rate in China is 25 percent but lowers to 15 percent for companies in specific industries, such as high technology and circuit production, that the Chinese government has deemed important for the national economy.[27] The United States, with a high corporate tax rate, ranks near the bottom for tax competitiveness. Part of the problem is that profits earned outside the United States are not taxed until they are brought back home. This creates perverse incentives, encouraging companies like Apple to stash their money in tax havens outside the United States. As of 2017, that stash was about $2.6 trillion. If things stay as they are, the United States will see a slow flow of businesses moving headquarters to more favorable countries, undermining the country's economic growth.[28]

Transfer Pricing

transfer pricing the price charged when two parts of the same multinational corporation, often the parent company and a subsidiary in another country, engage in trade with one another

One of the most significant ways a corporation can navigate the world of international tax in order to protect its profits is **transfer pricing**. Transfer pricing occurs when two parts of the same multinational corporation, often the parent company and a subsidiary in another country, engage in trade with one another. It can increase a company's profits by allowing the firm to earn profits in locations with lower tax rates. For example, a Japanese-based subsidiary of Toyota Motor Company buys some parts from a U.S.-based subsidiary. If the Japanese subsidiary pays a higher price for the parts from the United States than it would at home, the U.S. subsidiary will realize a higher profit at that stage of production—and the profit will be taxed at the lower U.S. corporate tax rate.

Transfer pricing can be applied to transactions relating to nearly any good or service, including raw materials, royalties for the use of copyrighted material or intellectual property, component parts, interest on loans, finished goods, and even fees. Consider a hypothetical company, illustrated in **Figure 20.11**, that sells computer software and has its headquarters in Taxistan (a country found in the nether regions of taxpayer hell). Last year the company made $2 million in pretax profits and expects to pay a 39 percent tax rate (or $780,000) in corporate income taxes, keeping only the difference of $1,220,000. One way it might save on taxes is to set up a subsidiary in a country known as Taxhaven, which imposes only a 10 percent tax rate. The parent company can then give its patents, trademarks, and copyrights to the subsidiary and claim that it has to license the use of this intellectual property from the subsidiary in order to sell its software. As a result, the parent company pays the subsidiary a certain amount in licensing fees rather than realizing that amount as direct profits—let's say $1 million, in our example. Now, because of transfer pricing, the parent firm pays the higher Taxistan tax rate of 39 percent on only $1 million of profits, and it pays the lower rate of 10 percent on the other $1 million. Its taxes are thus be $390,000 in Taxistan ($1 million × 39 percent) and $100,000 in Taxhaven ($1 million × 10 percent), for a total of $490,000. Instead of keeping only $1,220,000, as we originally predicted (without transfer pricing), the company now gets to keep $1,510,000—nearly $300,000 more in profits.

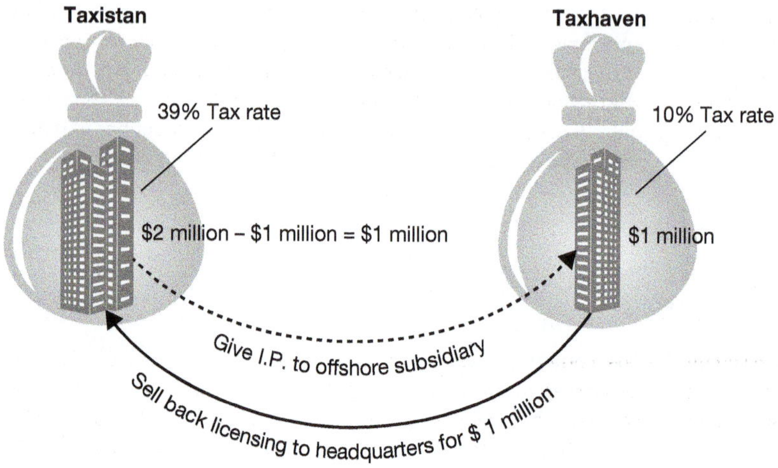

FIGURE 20.11 **Transfer Pricing**

You're probably wondering why companies don't do this more often if it saves so much money. The answer is that they want to. However, there is a real risk in transfer *mis*pricing—that is, in abusing transfer pricing. Transfer pricing isn't normally illegal, but it can *become* illegal if companies distort the transfer price (up or down) in order to evade taxes and shift profits to a tax haven. To avoid violating transfer pricing laws, firms need to match the internal transfer price to what the seller would charge any other entity.

Another reason for caution is that governments have anticipated these types of loopholes and have created legislation to close them by taxing repatriated profits. In other words, companies can still avoid taxes using transfer pricing, but their profits will be taxed anyway when they are brought back into the high-tax country to be used for business growth. In this way, governments have worked to negate the benefits of transfer pricing in order to keep the business playing field level for all companies.

Keep in mind, however, that transfer pricing in and of itself is perfectly legal. Only abuses are illegal. For example, a few years ago Merck was accused of illegal transfer pricing and forced to pay around $5.6 billion in penalties to the United States and Canada.[29] Merck had manipulated its profits by giving critical patents to a subsidiary in Bermuda and then paying the subsidiary a significant amount of money for the use of those patents. Upon investigation, it was determined that Merck was manipulating its profits through the use of transfer pricing, giving an unrealistic picture to investors while simultaneously evading taxes—a serious misstep for any company.

Incidentally, Bermuda and the Cayman Islands are the top tax havens for U.S. companies, and most U.S.-based MNCs have a subsidiary in at least one of those two countries (at least on paper).[30] The widespread use of tax havens has received a lot of attention recently as governments began to crack down on abuses in order to increase corporate income tax receipts. Even companies like Apple have been scrutinized by the U.S. Senate oversight panel for potential transfer pricing abuses. This scrutiny stems from the fact that Apple has avoided paying U.S. corporate income taxes on at least $74 billion by moving intellectual property rights overseas.[31] Many of the top Fortune 500 companies have engaged in similar activities to save on federal taxes.

Summary and Case

Chapter Summary

LEARNING OBJECTIVE 20.1 Discuss how companies raise money for international trade and investment.

The rise of international banking systems has opened up critical sources of credit for large organizations, whereas international markets for stocks and bonds have made corporate maintenance and expansion possible through the use of both long- and short-term financing. Finally, the increasingly interconnected international economy has necessitated the rise of multilateral agencies such as the IMF and World Bank.

LEARNING OBJECTIVE 20.2 Apply net present value analysis to the capital budgeting decision.

To make the right investment decisions, corporations evaluate several crucial factors—such as the net present value (NPV) of capital investments, cost of debt, cost of equity, and weighted average cost of capital (WACC)—through the use of formulas and sensitivity analyses. These in turn help the parent firm make smart decisions about what

LEARNING OBJECTIVE 20.3 Describe international accounting practices.

To facilitate global financial comparison and communication, governments have created accounting standards such as Generally Accepted Accounting Principles (GAAP) (in the United States) and the International Financial Reporting Standards (IFRS) that companies must follow. Without universal standards for accounting, investors would find it impossible to evaluate the financial health of companies with different accounting standards.

LEARNING OBJECTIVE 20.4 Identify specific tax issues multinational companies face.

The corporate income tax rate can range from 0 to 35 percent, depending on the country. Understanding the different rules and rates can help companies increase their after-tax profits through transfer pricing. On the other hand, companies also need to understand what constitutes tax evasion and the risks of being investigated for illegal

Case Study

GlaxoSmithKline: What's the Right Price to Pay?

MNCs have the distinct advantage of using transfer pricing to help shepherd profits into low-tax countries, resulting in higher overall profits. This can lead to an unfair advantage over domestic companies, but it also leads national governments in high-tax countries to feel they have been cheated of tax revenues.

To avoid conflicts relating to transfer pricing-related conflicts, MNCs have typically adopted the concept of an "arm's-length" transaction—meaning subsidiaries of the same parent company treat each other as though they weren't related. Still, the exact distance for an arm's-length transaction is open to interpretation, and companies often find themselves at odds with governments over just how long is long enough.

For instance, GlaxoSmithKline (GSK) got into difficulties over transfer pricing. Between 1990 and 1993, GSK was purchasing ranitidine from a Swiss company, Adechsa S.A., for between C$1,512 and C$1,651 in order to market it as Zantac, one of the most profitable drugs in the world.[32] During the same period, other companies were purchasing a generic form of ranitidine for between C$194 and C$304—one-fifth the price—in order to make generic forms of Zantac.[33]

When the Canadian Revenue Agency (CRA) made the connection, it alleged that GSK was using transfer pricing to avoid paying corporate income taxes in Canada. Why? Because GSK is the Canadian subsidiary of the British pharmaceutical giant Glaxo Group plc (Glaxo), and Adechsa S.A. is a Swiss subsidiary group for Glaxo that holds much of the giant's intellectual property, meaning the two companies are related. As a result, the CRA assessed GSK with an additional C$51 million in taxable income. GSK appealed the decision to the Tax Court of Canada.

A ruling by the Tax Court of Canada in 2008 found that GSK had indeed engaged in illegal transfer pricing. The court ruled that a reasonable, arm's-length price should have been closer to the price that generics were paying, not five times higher. GSK argued in turn that the court wasn't considering all the facts. GSK had a licensing agreement with Glaxo to use its branding and to gain access to Glaxo's product library. GSK stated that those factors needed to be considered in deciding how the proper price was assessed. The Court disagreed and ruled to uphold the CRA's penalty, so GSK appealed the decision again.

The case next went to the Canadian Federal Court of Appeal, which, in July 2010, overturned the Tax Court's decision on the grounds that the Tax Court had failed to adequately consider all the details of the case. The CRA dissented and filed a cross-appeal, taking the case before Canada's Supreme Court.

In a landmark decision in 2012, the Supreme Court of Canada upheld the ruling of the Appeals Court overturning the Tax Court's initial ruling. The Supreme Court declared that the licensing agreement also needed to be considered in determining a correct transfer price.[34]

Case Discussion Questions

1. How can transfer pricing improve a company's profits?
2. When does transfer pricing open the door to tax problems?
3. Was the Canadian subsidiary of GSK paying an excessively high price for ranitidine from its affiliate company in Switzerland? Justify your answer.

Endnotes

[1]Chris Lange, "How the Top US Money Center Banks are Responding to the Brexit," 24/7 Wall St., July 1, 2016, http://247wallst.com/banking-finance/2016/07/01/how-the-top-us-money-center-banks-are-responding-to-the-brexit/.

[2]"CHIPS," The Clearing House, www.theclearinghouse.org/payments/chips (accessed December 2016).

[3]"SWIFT FIN Traffic and Figures," Society for Worldwide Interbank Financial Telecommunications, www.swift.com/about-us/swift-fin-traffic-figures (accessed December 14, 2016).

[4]"How Letter of Credit Can Ease the Stress of Doing Business Overseas" BridgeBank, June 26, 2014, https://www.westernalliancebancorporation.com/bridge-bank-home.

[5]"Understanding and Using Letters of Credit, Part 1," Credit Research Foundation, www.crfonline.org/orc/cro/cro-9-1.html (accessed May 19, 2017).

[6]"Chapter 5 Open Account," in *Trade Finance Guide*, U.S. Department of Commercehttp://trade.gov/media/publications/pdf/trade_finance_guide2007ch5.pdf (accessed July 29, 2015), 11–12.

[7]"Topic 9: Payment Methods & Strategies" Food Export Association of the Midwest USA www.foodexport.org/GettingStarted/content.cfm?ItemNumber=1294 (accessed July 29, 2015).

[8]"U.S. War Bonds," United States History, www.u-s-history.com/pages/h1682.html (accessed July 9, 2015).

[9]"Issuing a Foreign Bond," Financial Pipeline www.finpipe.com/foreign-currency-bonds/ (accessed July 29, 2015).

[10]Min Zeng, "Global Government Bond Yields Tumble on ECB Bond Buying," *Wall Street Journal*, March 10, 2015, www.wsj.com/articles/u-s-europe-government-bond-yields-fall-on-ecb-bond-buying-1425994904.

[11]Evan Carmichael, "Building a Frugal Fortune: The Growth of Wal-Mart," www.evancarmichael.com/Famous-Entrepreneurs/591/Building-a-Frugal-Fortune-The-Growth-of-WalMart.html (accessed July 30, 2015).

[12]Barbara Farfan, "The World's Biggest Retail Chains," The Balance, May 10, 2016, www.thebalance.com/largest-us-retailers-4045123.

[13]Marc Davis, "How September 11 Affected the U.S. Stock Market," Investopedia, May 16, 2017, www.investopedia.com/financial-edge/0911/how-september-11-affected-the-u.s.-stock-market.aspx.

[14]Alan Rappeport, "He Wanted to Close the Export-Import Bank. Now He May Run It," *New York Times*, May 8, 2017, https://www.nytimes.com/2017/05/08/us/politics/he-wanted-to-close-the-export-import-bank-now-he-may-run-it.html?_r=0.

[15]Jane Perlez, "Stampede to Join China's Development Stuns Even Its Founder," *New York Times*, April 2, 2015, www.nytimes.com/2015/04/03/world/asia/china-asian-infrastructure-investment-bank.html.

[16]Will Connors and Luciana Magalhaes, "Brazil's Petrobras Obtains $3.5 Billion in Financing from China Development Bank," *Wall*

Street Journal, April 1, 2015, www.wsj.com/articles/brazils-petrobras-obtains-3-5-billion-financing-from-china-development-bank-1427892756.

[17]"The Facts about EXIM Bank," Export-Import Bank of the United States, www.exim.gov/about/facts-about-ex-im-bank (accessed December 14, 2016).

[18]Kirt C. Butler, Thomas J. O'Brien, and Gwinyai Utete, "A Fresh Look at Cross-Border Valuation and FX Hedging Decisions," *Journal of Applied Finance (formerly Financial Practice and Education)* pgs 1-11, 23, no. 2 (2013).

[19]B. Gold, Vol 19, Issue 2, "The Shaky Foundations of Capital Budgeting," *California Management Review* (Winter): 51–60; Robert H. Hayes and William J. Abernathy, "Managing Our Way to Economic Decline," *Harvard Business Review*, July–August 2007, 138–49 (this is a reprint of their 1980 article, with a retrospect by Hayes on p. 141); Devaun Kite, "Capital Budgeting: Integrating Environmental Impact," *Journal of Cost Management* 9, no. 2 (Summer 1995): 11–14.

[20]IFRS resources.www.ifrs.com/ifrs_faqs.html#ftnt1 (accessed December 16, 2016).

[21]"Policy Basics: Where Do Federal Tax Revenues Come from?" Center on Budget and Policy Priorities, March 4, 2016, https://www.cbpp.org/research/policy-basics-where-do-federal-tax-revenues-come-from; "Top 5 Tax Challenges and Strategies for Multinational Companies," Forteintax, www.forteintax.com/wp-content/uploads/international-taxation-trends-challenges.pdf (accessed July 18, 2015).

[22]Patricia Cohen, "Curb the Use of Overseas Tax Havens? Yes! But How?" *New York Times*, April 26, 2017, https://www.nytimes.com/2017/04/26/business/economy/trump-tax-plan-repatriation.html.

[23]"Corporate Tax Rates Table," KPMG, 2017. https://home.kpmg.com/xx/en/home/services/tax/tax-tools-and-resources/tax-rates-online/corporate-tax-rates-table.html.

[24]Sabine Vollmer, "It Takes More Than Low Taxes to Attract Most Companies," *CGMA Magazine*, March 11, 2013. www.cgma.org/Magazine/News/Pages/20137536.aspx.

[25]"Members and Partners," Organisation for Economic Co-operation and Development www.oecd.org/about/membersandpartners/ (accessed July 31, 2015).

[26]Kyle Pomerleau and Andrew Lundeen, "The U.S. Ranks 32nd Out of 34 OECD Countries in Tax Code Competitiveness" *Forbes*, July 31, 2015, www.forbes.com/sites/realspin/2014/09/22/the-u-s-ranks-32nd-out-of-34-oecd-countries-in-tax-code-competitiveness/.

[27]"Overview of PRC Taxation System," PriceWaterhouseCoopers, www.pwchk.com/home/eng/prctax_corp_overview_taxation.html (accessed December 16, 2016).

[28]R. Rubin and L. Hoffman, "New Rules on Tax Inversions Threaten Pfizer-Allergan Deal," *Wall Street Journal*, April 4, 2016, https://www.wsj.com/articles/u-s-treasury-unveils-new-steps-to-limit-tax-inversions-1459803636.

[29]"Transfer Pricing Fraud," Whistle Blowing Protection www.whistleblowingprotection.org/?q=node/38 (accessed July 21, 2015).

[30]Brian Tumulty, "Bermuda, Cayman Islands Are Top Tax Havens for U.S. Firms," WGRZ.com, June 8, 2014, www.wgrz.com/story/news/2014/06/08/top-tax-havens-for-us-firms-report-finds/10199525/.

[31]Tumulty, "Bermuda, Cayman Islands Are Top Tax Havens for U.S. Firms.

[32]"GlaxoSmithKline Prevails in Canadian Transfer Pricing Case," Dixon Hughes Goodman, February 2013, www2.dhgllp.com/res_pubs/transfer-pricing-glaxosmithkline.pdf (accessed September 30, 2015).

[33]Julius Melnitzer, "Glaxo Case Sets Principle for Dealing with Transfer Pricing," *Law Times News*, September 26, 2010 www.lawtimesnews.com/201009271730/headline-news/glaxo-case-sets-principle-for-dealing-with-transfer-pricing (accessed September 30, 2015).

[34]Julius Melnitzer, "GlaxoSmithKline Transfer Pricing Case Settled," *Financial Post*, January 12, 2015 http://business.financialpost.com/legal-post/glaxosmithkline-transfer-pricing-case-settled (accessed September 30, 2015).

Glossary

10% Presumption the presumption that 10 percent of activity is conducted globally; the other 90 percent of activity is domestic

Absolute advantage the ability of a country to produce a specific good or service more efficiently than any rival

Alliance a contractual relationship between two or more companies

Anarchists extreme individualists who believe all government or organization of society should exist on a voluntary basis only and that individuals should be self-governed

Antidumping actions a class of protective tariffs imposed by a domestic government on foreign imports that are thought to be priced below fair market value

Appreciation when the value of a currency increases relative to that of other currencies

Arbitrage international search for deals on production factors

Arbitration the process of reaching a binding decision by an arbitrator (third party) outside the courts

Assertiveness a measure of how competitive and aggressive a culture is

Association of Southeast Asian Nations (ASEAN) a trade agreement between Indonesia, Singapore, Thailand, and the Philippines

Authoritarian a political system characterized by a leader or small group of leaders with centralized, concentrated power who are not constitutionally responsible to citizens for their actions

Balance of payments the value of exports minus the value of imports and the net amount received from investments

Balance of trade a measure of the difference between exports from and imports into a country

Base of the pyramid (BOP) the largest but poorest socioeconomic group in the global economy

Benefit corporation (B-corp) a legal entity explicitly organized with an additional focus beyond making money

Big data extremely large data sets that users can analyze to uncover statistical patterns, trends, and associations that might otherwise go unnoticed because of the volume of data

Big Mac Index a scale used to determine whether a currency is over- or undervalued; consists of comparing the price of a Big Mac across countries and then comparing that with the actual exchange rates

Bilateral trade agreement a trade agreement between just two countries

Bond a debt investment in which the issuer of the bond owes the bondholder a debt

Born global firms companies that internationalize from the outset or soon after founding

Brand equity the additional market share and profits products earn because of a brand's strength compared with that of competing products

Brand image the set of associations in a customer's mind regarding a brand

Brand loyalty commitment to a brand in the face of competition

Brand the name, term, design, symbol, or any other feature that identifies one seller's goods or services as distinct from those of other sellers

Bureaucratic control control accomplished through rules and routines

Business incubator a company that helps found and grow new business

Capital account an account of a country's transfer of capital to or from other countries

Capitalism an economic system where factors of trade and production are controlled by private owners rather than by the state

Capital a resource that can serve to generate wealth; includes monetary investments in factories, equipment, and technology

Cash in advance a method of payment in which the importer pays to the exporter in advance the full amount due

Civil law a system of law with a comprehensive code of written law that judges translate into legal principles and regulatory statues

Clean economy an economy that produces goods and services with environmental benefit

Clearing House Interbank Payments System (CHIPS) a private company that handles large payments to governments and corporations

Codetermination cooperation between management and workers in decision-making, particularly by the representation of workers on boards of directors

Collaborative synergy the ability to create an environment where people understand that success for one member of the team means success for all members of the team

Collectivism the belief that people should prioritize the good of society above the advancement of the individual

Commercial law law that specifies the rights and duties of individuals in their business dealings, the way businesses are created and organized, and the manner in which business is transacted

Commercial letter of credit (LC) a highly secure form of payment in which an importer's bank offers a guarantee of payment when the goods are delivered as long as all selling conditions have been met

Common law a system of law in which judges interpret law and set precedent for subsequent interpretation and use

Communism a political system characterized by collective ownership of the factors of production and allocation of goods and services to workers according to their needs; argues for revolutionary means to establish a communal society

Company culture the unique combination of a company's vision, values, norms, systems, symbols, language, assumptions, beliefs, and habits

Comparative advantage the ability of a country to produce a specific good or service at a lower opportunity cost than a rival

Complexity operating in multiple countries, dealing with multiple cultures, and, most importantly, recognizing that optimal solutions will vary across different countries

Consignment a process in which an exporter sends good to an importer without transferring ownership

Constitutional law law that sets the bounds of government and governmental procedures

Consumer price index (CPI) an index that tracks the price of a specific set of consumer goods across time to detect general price increases or decreases

Contagion a pattern in which stock markets have become increasingly interconnected around the world and markets in different countries have begun reacting similarly

Content requirements a minimum level of materials, parts, or inputs that must originate in a local country rather than be imported

Contextual resilience a leader's ability to anticipate roadblocks and find better ways of doing things in a complex, cross-border environment

Contract employees outside workers who are hired by a firm to perform specific predetermined tasks for a company and who are paid by the job

Control systems means by which headquarters may force compliance from global subsidiaries

Copyright a form of protection available to authors of literary, dramatic, musical, or artistic intellectual property

Corporate human capital company-specific knowledge, skills, and abilities that transcend any particular location within the entire global company, not simply the collective knowledge of the staff at headquarters

Corporate social responsibility (CSR) a form of corporate self-regulation used to further some social good beyond the requirements of law

Corporate vision Understanding the company's overarching objectives and helping individuals stay focused on these objectives

Corruption the abuse of an official title or office for personal gain; includes bribery, embezzlement, and nepotism

Cost of capital the rate of return demanded by stock and bond investors

Cost-plus strategy pricing a product or service at a fixed margin over costs

Criminal law law that describes laws and punishments including regulations for social conduct, personal protections, and human rights protections

Critical behaviors the few key areas of activity in which meeting strategic objectives are absolutely necessary

Cultural intelligence the knowledge to function effectively across cultural contexts

Culture a society's unique set of values and norms that govern how people live and interact with each other

Currency and trade controls government action to regulate the amount of currency and goods that can be traded or purchased; includes tariffs and taxes, export/import volumes, restrictions on licenses and permits, restrictions on currency exchange, fixed exchange rates, and bans on using foreign currency within the country

Currency exchange the process by which countries and companies swap one nation's currency for that of another

Current account an account of a country's exports and imports of goods, services, and income

Customary law a system of law derived from

behavior that are not morally significant

Decenter to take what one has learned about another's culture and use that knowledge to adapt one's own behavior and thinking

Deflation a general decline in prices in an economy

Democracy a political system characterized by citizen participation in the political process

Depreciation a decrease in the value of a currency relative to that of other currencies

Depression a period of contraction of gross domestic product worldwide that is particularly long-lived or severe in nature

Deregulation the process of removing government regulations, oversight, and involvement in an industry

Differential pricing offering different prices to different customers for the same goods or services

Differentiation strategy a strategy that helps companies succeed by differentiating their product in order to persuade customers to pay more for it

Discount rate the interest rate central banks charge to commercial banks for borrowing money

Distribution the process of taking goods from production to consumption

Diversification an investment strategy to reduce investors' risks by spreading investment capital across a range of possibilities that are likely to react differently to outside events

Divisional structure a structure that organizes a company by units according to the products they make, the customer segments they serve, or the geographic location in which they operate

Documentary collections (DCs) a process in which an exporter's bank is entrusted with collecting payment for goods. This bank sends to the importer's bank any documents necessary to collect the goods. The importer's bank then releases those documents to the buyer only after payment has been received

Dollarization when a country abandons its own currency altogether and adopts U.S. dollars instead

Dual sourcing a source strategy in which firms produce products in-house to ensure quality and availability while also purchasing the same products from suppliers in order to force competition and push innovation within the in-house unit

Dumping selling a product for a price below the cost of production in order to capture market share and force competitors out of the market

this planet

Economic exposure a company's exposure to unexpected change in foreign exchange rates

Economic factors external factors that affect businesses, including the strength or weakness of markets, stability of trade cycles, specific industry conditions, customer preferences, and a government's economic policies

Economies of scale the cost advantages companies achieve as they progress down the learning curve and spread fixed costs over more units of output

Efficiency-enhancing innovations changes to existing products or ideas that make them lower cost

Embargo a quota that limits all forms of trade on entire categories of goods or services

Emerging markets countries moving toward open-trade and free-market policies

Enterprise resource-planning systems (ERPSs) technology that helps firms gather all relevant information into a single database, represent all business functions in a module, and provide access to data in real time

Ethical system a set of moral principles of values to guide and shape behavior

Ethics the moral principles of right and wrong that guide personal and organizational decision making

Ethnocentrism bias a bias indicating that customers prefer local brands over foreign brands and are willing to pay more for local brands even when the quality is inferior

European Union (EU) a politico-economic union made up of 28 countries in Europe

Exchange rate the amount of one currency that is required in order to buy the equivalent purchasing power in a different currency

Exchange-traded funds (ETFs) a trading vehicle that follows different stock indexes, such as the S&P 500

Expatriates employees assigned from a headquarters or another location to work in a foreign market

Exporting sending goods or services out of a company's home country

Expropriation a government's seizure of assets as a result of political action; also called nationalization

Extremism holding extreme political or religious views

Facilitation payments payments made by a business to speed up the actions that government officials

Fair Trade a product certified to support the payment of a fair wage to laborers abroad

Fiat currency currency that is not backed by a physical good and has no intrinsic value

First mover a business that successfully enters a new market first

Fiscal policy government actions, including tax and spending actions, intended to spark or diminish consumption

Float currencies of countries where the government does not explicitly or directly influence the price of the currency

Flow the movement of information and relations across countries and business units

Foreign aid money and programs provided by governments, nongovernmental organizations, or corporations to help alleviate poverty

Forward exchange rate transactions a transaction involving two parties that agree to exchange currency at some future date at a specific rate they agree to at the time of the deal

Franchising permission to use another company's trademarks, patents, copyrights, and expertise according to a strict template setting out the way that company does business

Free trade trade without government intervention or restrictions

Functional excellence The ability to collaborate with different units and functions within the company

Functional structure a structure that organizes a company into units identified by their functional roles, or what they do

Future orientation the degree to which a culture chooses future rather than immediate results

FX swap the simultaneous purchase and sale of a given amount of currency at two different rates

G20 a multilateral organization that aims to coordinate financial and monetary policies to respond to financial crises

General Agreement on Tariffs and Trade (GATT) a treaty whose purpose is to reduce trade barriers and tariffs while eliminating trade preferences and to provide a multilateral forum to resolve trade disputes between member countries

Generally Accepted Accounting Principles (GAAP) a set of accounting principles that U.S. public companies must use

Gini coefficient a measure of a country's wealth distribution

Global branding a marketing approach wherein promotion, product, and price are standardized globally

Global Business School Network a multilateral organization that provides advisory services to business schools in the developing world, helps train corporations and nongovernmental organizations, and measures the results and impact of management training programs

Global convergence the spread of common preferences across country borders

Global HR wheel A guide to help align employee skills and behaviors with a company's strategic objectives

Global integration the process by which a company combines different global activities so the different parts of the corporation use the same methods

Global leadership the process of influencing others to adopt a positive vision in a global context

Global market segmentation the process of grouping customers across national markets based on criteria such as level of economic development, cultural characteristics, language, buying patterns, and regulatory environment

Global marketing strategy the way in which a firm decides which market segments to operate in, how it will position its offerings, and to what extent products and services will be standardized or differentiated in each market

Globalization of production sourcing land, labor, and capital from different nations rather than obtaining everything locally

Globalization the evolution of an integrated and interdependent world economy

Globalized market a large global market created by combining separate national markets

Glocal marketing strategy a marketing approach whereby global companies strike a balance between standardization and differentiation

Glocalization an approach whereby firms achieve global integration while still meeting the demands of local markets

Gold standard the amount of gold a paper currency is worth

Gray market activity a specific type of arbitration whereby companies or individuals buy a product in a cheaper market and sell it in a more expensive market

Green index an index that allows investors to track a company's carbon use

Gross domestic product (GDP) the value of finished goods and services within a country's borders, whether made by domestic or foreign companies

Gross national product (GNP) the value of finished goods and services within a country's borders and net income from foreign assets owned by nationals, excluding net payment outflows to foreign owners; the equation is GNP = GDP + Net income receipts − Net payment outflows

Growth what occurs when a company is able to increase its profits relative to past profits

Guerilla marketing marketing by unconventional, innovative, low-cost means to generate social buzz and maximum exposure

High-context a culture that relies on implicit messaging and contextual elements to convey information

Horizontal coordination the process by which subsidiaries communicate and coordinate work among themselves

Host country a country in which an international business operates

HR practices tasks focused on attracting, training, motivating, and retaining people

Human capital the abilities, skills, experience, and knowledge possessed by individuals

Human Development Index (HDI) a broad measure of well-being developed by the United Nations and focused on health, education, and economics

Importing purchasing goods or services from another country for sale in a company's home market

Individualism a concept that gives preference to individual freedoms, liberties, and rights

Industrialization the process of building businesses and industry on a large scale

Industrialized the process of building businesses and manufacturing on a large scale

Infant industry theory a theory that states that certain emerging industries need to be protected and nurtured for a period of time or they will be unable to compete against established foreign firms

Inflation a general rise in prices in an economy

Innovation combination of new or existing ideas to create marketable value

Innovation life cycle a process designed to help companies drive innovation by going local, reaching out, and uncovering principles

Innovator's imperative the need for individuals to understand local market problems, to reach out to others globally to search for unique solutions to the problem, and to uncover the causal relationships found within that foreign knowledge to ensure it is correctly applied to the local problems

Insourcing The practice of using a company's internal employees or other resources to accomplish a task

Integrated technology platforms common operating systems that can be used across multiple computers connected through the Internet

Intellectual property (IP) any creation of the human mind; consists of patents, trademarks, indications, literary works, films, music, artworks, and architectural designs

International Accounting Standards (IAS) a set of international accounting principles to which companies in many countries must comply

International Accounting Standards Board (IASB) an international organization located in London, England, that sets international accounting standards

International Financial Reporting Standards (IFRS) a set of international accounting standards detailing how transactions and other events should be reported in financial statements

International human capital knowledge of global best practices, global industry standards, international trade laws, modular systems and processes, cross-border industry networks, and other experience applicable across multiple companies and countries

International joint venture a new legal entity created and owned by two or more existing companies from different countries

International laws laws that are agreed upon by and bind groups of nations, superseding their national laws

International Monetary Fund (IMF) a multilateral organization established to rescue countries from financial crises

International product life cycle a theory that suggests that the level of trade in a product at any given time is a function of the current stage in the product's life cycle, which consists of introduction, maturity, standardization, and decline

International strategy actions by which companies manage differences across borders to create advantages over their competitors

Intracultural variation an understanding of differences within a nation and the ability to identify local preferences that are irrelevant for global companies

Invention a new concept or product that derives from ideas or from scientific research

Joint venture two or more companies jointly owning a separate, third company

Just-in-time (JIT) a method of manufacturing that consists of carefully planning the whole production process from start to finish in order to avoid carrying excess inventory

[illegible] on the right track to helping a company achieve its strategic objectives

Law of one price a theory that states that if goods and services could move freely across national borders without trade barriers, transportation costs, or perishability, any given good would carry the same price everywhere

Law of the Sea allows countries to seize and prosecute pirates who commit crimes on international waters

Liability of foreignness a liability foreign firms face as the geographic, economic, cultural, or administrative differences between that foreign market and the domestic market increase

License a contractual agreement between two parties, known as the licensor and the licensee, that grants the licensee certain rights, such as the right to produce or sell the licensor's patented goods, display the licensor's brand name or trademark, or use the licensor's intellectual property

Licensing permission to use another company's trademarks, patents, copyrights, or expertise

Local human capital the knowledge, skills, abilities, and other attributes that make up the location-specific experiences of employees in a particular country or market

Local responsiveness adjusting or creating an approach to meet the differentiated needs of local markets of local customers and stakeholders, such as government officials and employees, and of suppliers and distributors

Location economies the cost advantage of performing each stage in the value chain at the lowest cost for that activity

Low-context a culture that relies on the direct means of conveying messages with little background information

Low-cost strategy a strategy that helps companies succeed through efficiencies and by reducing costs

Macro political risk the possibility of adverse political actions that affect all foreign investments and operations in a host country

Managed float a type of currency policy in which the government doesn't generally interfere in the value of the currency but has plans to explicitly intervene if the currency appreciates or depreciates too much; also called "dirty float"

Market economy an economic system regulated by the market forces of supply and demand; *see also* Capitalism

Market segmentation the process by which companies cluster customers into homogeneous groups

[illegible] mine how much private consumption and investment to make in the economy

Market-creating innovations Products or ideas that meet the needs of a group of potential consumers whose needs have not been met before

Marketing mix the collection of decisions regarding product, place, price, and promotion that companies make during the process of bringing a product or service to market

Matrix structure a structure that organizes a company along multiple dimensions that may include geography, function, and division

Meganational strategy a strategy whereby global firms focus on increasing profitable growth by reaping cost reductions from economies of scale and other advantages of global integration

Mercado Comum do Sol (MERCOSUL)/Mercado Comun del Sur (MERCOSUR) a trade agreement between Argentina, Brazil, Paraguay, Uruguay, and Venezuela

Mercantilism a trade theory that suggests that trade generates wealth for a country with a trade surplus; emphasizes colonization and military conquest

Micro political risk the possibility of adverse political actions that affect only a specific sector, firm, or project

Microfinance a source of financial services for entrepreneurs and small businesses lacking access to banking and entrepreneurial training

Micro-multinational corporations small, web-wired start-ups that are using social media to recruit the best talent from around the world and leverage it for immediate innovation and impact

Minimum efficient scale the smallest production quantity at which long-run, total average cost is minimized

Mixed legal system a system of law that mixes two or more frameworks

Modular design a system in which a process, product, or service is divided into components that can be changed independently and then reintegrated into the system

Monetary measures efforts related to regulating the supply of money

Monetary policy manipulations of interest rates, banking rules, or the volume of currency in a country in an attempt to spark or diminish consumption

Money center banks large banks that borrow from and lend to governments, other banks, and corporations

Moore's law a prediction that processing power will double every 24 months

Most favored nation clause a clause applying [illegible] member countries extends to every other member as well

Multidomestic strategy a strategy whereby global firms respond to differentiated needs and preferences in each local market in which they operate

Multilateral aid agencies collectively owned aid agencies

Multilateral organizations organizations funded and managed by representatives from multiple governments or organizations; they establish and enforce guidelines governing the interactions of individuals, businesses, and governments in a globalized world

Multinational corporation (MNC) a company with operations in more than one country

Mutual funds pooled and repackaged shares of various stocks—as well as other assets like bonds, real estate, and commodities—that allow individual investors to buy smaller stakes in more companies

National treatment the equal treatment of foreign and local goods

Neo-mercantilism a trade theory that suggests that trade generates wealth for a country with a trade surplus, emphasizing rapid economic development

Net present value (NPV) the difference between the present value of cash coming into a company and the present value of cash going out of the company

Network structure a structure that organizes a company by groups that form to work on a project, and then dissolve once the project is complete

Nominal GDP GDP that has not been adjusted to account for inflation

Normative control control that gets subunits to adhere to the values of the organization

Norms the social rules that govern people's interactions

North American Free Trade Agreement (NAFTA) a trade agreement between the United States, Mexico, and Canada

Offset agreement an agreement wherein a supplier agrees to buy products from the party to whom it is selling in order to win the buyer as a customer and "offset" the buyer's production costs

Offshoring moving production to outside the home country

Open account a form of payment in which an importer doesn't pay for goods until after they have been received, creating an unfavorable balance of value for the exporter

Open innovation platform an electronic platform where people from different companies and independent contractors work collaboratively with internal R&D staff to innovate

Open market operations the process of a central bank buying or selling government bonds, corporate bonds, or equities

Operational risk a measure of a firm's inability to document the work remote employees do, describe the different situations they might face, and direct their responses in each scenario

Organization of the Petroleum Exporting Countries (OPEC) a multinational organization with the goal to unify oil producers

Organizational capability the power to combine and leverage a company's resources to achieve specific goals

Output control control that focuses on profitability and/or market share

Outsourcing obtaining a good or service from an external supplier, often in international markets

Ownership-based governance a strategy that requires board members to have both relevant industry experience and a stake in the company

Parliamentary democracies a system of government in which a constitution outlines the separation of political power into branches; ministers are chosen by the parliament (legislative branch)

Patent a form of legal protection provided by a government that excludes anyone other than the patent holder from making, using, or selling the invention for a set period of time

Peg currency that is fixed to a foreign currency, usually a stronger or more stable one

Penetration pricing strategy a strategy where a company sets the price very low to get customers to try the product

Performance-improving innovation improvements to existing products or ideas that meet more of a customers' needs

Personal control the use of frequent human interaction to enforce control

Personal integrity a demonstration of honesty and high ethical standards in work

PEST analysis tool a spreadsheet that allows you to quantify the different PEST threats and opportunities to determine which countries are most attractive

Political factors external factors that affect businesses, including labor laws, property rights, and patent processes

Political ideology a set of principles, ideas, and doctrines used to organize and administer social order

Political risk the risk that host-country political conditions might change, negatively affecting foreign businesses

Political system the principles, laws, and procedures relating to a particular form of government

Porter's Diamond Model a model that assesses the competitive potential of countries

Poverty science a movement by economists, policy researchers, and business researchers to understand what types of activities and interventions might more effectively alleviate poverty

Power distance the degree to which subordinates in an organization accept that power is distributed unequally

Presence degree to which an individual is required to physically move across geographical, cultural, and national boundaries, and not just communicate across them through technology

Presidential democracies a system of government in which a constitution outlines the separation of political power into branches; the president (executive branch) is most often elected directly in a presidential vote

Private international law law that establishes legal jurisdiction and procedures for people and organizations, including businesses

Privatization the transfer or sale of a government-owned property or industry to the private sector

Profitable growth when a company increases revenues in excess of expenses over time

Property rights the rights of companies and individuals to own resources, make decisions about how to use them, and reap the returns or losses of business activities

Protectionist actions actions taken by a country to protect domestic industry

Public international laws laws that govern the interactions of nation states, including governing war, criminal law, refugee law, human rights law, and law of the sea

Pull marketing marketing efforts designed to cultivate customer desires and expectations so customers will demand more product, effectively *pulling* the product through the production and distribution process

Purchasing power parity (PPP) a measure that compares the costs of common products and services in terms of one local currency

Push marketing marketing efforts designed to actively *push* a product through the channel of distribution, starting with the producer, moving through the distribution partners, and finally reaching the consumer

Quota a direct limit on the number of goods that can be imported into or exported from a country

Raw materials the basic materials from which goods are made

Real (inflation-adjusted) quantity any quantity that has been adjusted to account for the effect of inflation on value

Recenter to find or create shared ground between old and new behavior and understanding

Recession a period of GDP contraction worldwide for at least two consecutive quarters of a year

Religion a system of shared beliefs and rituals expressing the way adherents interpret their place in the universe

Representative democracies a system of government in which citizens elect to public office representatives who hold ultimate sovereignty and form a government to implement the will of the people who elected them

Reserve requirement the amount of money a nation's banks must keep on hand as a safety measure

Reshored moving production from outside a country back to the home country

Resource constraints limits on the availability of factors of production that reduce a company's ability to produce goods and services

Reverse innovation the process of taking innovations developed in emerging markets and repackaging them for developed markets

Royalties payments from a licensee to the licenser, consisting of a percentage of what is earned from selling licensed products and services

Rule of law a form of rule in which all individuals are subject to the law regardless of rank, status, or office

Rule of the individual a form of rule in which one individual is the ultimate authority and has discretion to set and enforce laws

Sensitivity analysis a method to assess the riskiness of a capital investment by forecasting the most optimistic, the normal, and the most pessimistic outcomes possible under reasonable circumstances

Shared economy a system in which owners rent out something they are not using, such as room, a car, or even a service, to a stranger through peer-to-peer services

Short-termism an excessive focus on short-term results, even at the expense of long-term interests and objectives

Skills shortage a difficulty in finding people with the right skills to fill vacant positions

Skimming a pricing strategy whereby a company sets a high price for a product and sells to the segment that is willing to pay a premium

Social democracies a socialist or collective system of government achieved by democratic elections

Social mores strict norms that control moral and ethical behavior in a culture

Socialism a collective form of government in which the means of production and the distribution of production are owned collectively by the community as a whole; argues for peaceful means to establish a communal society

Society of Worldwide Interbank Financial Telecommunications (SWIFT) a global telecommunications company that facilitates secure international payment transfers from one bank to another

Sociocultural factors external factors that affect businesses, including method and style of communications, religions, values and ideologies, education standards, and social structure

Sovereign nation a country that governs itself rather than being controlled by a foreign power

Spot exchange rate the rate banks charge each other for currencies

Spread markup on currency

State-owned enterprise (SOE) a legal entity created by a government or governmental representative to directly engage in commercial activities on behalf of the government

Strategic objectives long-term organizational goals that help make a strategy successful

Strategy the actions managers take in pursuit of company objectives for profitable growth

Stretch goals company-level objectives that require employees of a company to do something beyond what one might reasonably expect

Structural risk a measure of a firm's difficulty when relationships with vendors do not work as expected

Subsidiary human capital company knowledge within a specific location

Subsidiary a "child" company to parent company; the parent company owns 100 percent of the subsidiary's operations

Subsidies government support for industries

Supranational law law that limits the rights of sovereign governments

Sustainability a way of doing business that supports the long-term ecological balance of the environment

Syndicate a group of banks

Tariffs taxes on foreign products that discourage imports

Tax haven a country with no or low corporate taxes

Technological factors external factors that affect businesses and that pertain to the technological infrastructure in a country, including intellectual infrastructure and investments, information systems, manufacturing equipment, and consumer access to technology

Terrorist organizations A political group that uses unlawful violence and intimidation as a weapon to achieve its goals

Theocratic government a form of totalitarian government in which leaders rules by a mandate from God by interpreting religious law

Theocratic law a system of law that relies on religious doctrine and belief

Theory of overlapping demand a theory that suggests that trade is the result of customer demand and that customers of similar wealth are likely to demand similar products and services

Total factor productivity (TFP) measures the efficiency with which labor and capital come together

Totalitarianism an extreme form of autocratic political system in which the government regulates every aspect of public and private life

Trade secret any information that provides a business with a competitive advantage but isn't shared openly

Trade surplus the result when a country engaged in trade exports more than it imports; also called positive trade balance

Trademark legal protection of a recognizable brand name, design, or logo; calls a specific product to a consumer's mind

Transaction exposure the extent to which income from foreign transactions is exposed to currency fluctuations before payment is made

Transatlantic Trade and Investment Partnership (TTIP) a proposed trade and investment agreement between the European Union and the United States

Transfer pricing the price charged when two parts of the same multinational corporation, often the parent company and a subsidiary in another country, engage in trade with one other

Translation exposure the impact of exchange-rate fluctuations on a company's financial statements

Transnational strategy a strategy whereby global firms take a hybrid approach that combines the meganational and multidomestic strategies, simultaneously offering the benefits of both global and local advantages

Trans-Pacific Partnership (TPP) a trade agreement between Canada, the United States, Mexico, Peru, Chile, Vietnam, Singapore, Japan, Malaysia, Australia, New Zealand, and Brunei

"Trapped" in poverty the nature of poverty to deprive individuals of key capabilities, keeping them poor and limiting their ability to increase their capabilities

Turnkey project A project ready for immediate use, especially a project in which a company already in a particular country builds a building, plant, or machine for a foreign company

Uncertainty avoidance a business-related aspect of culture that measures how a person deals with an unknown future

Uncommon information information not available to all decision makers

United Nations (UN) a multilateral organization that facilitates countries' ability to resolve differences through diplomacy with the goal of maintaining and promoting global peace

Value capture the process of maximizing the portion of that value a company keeps

Value chain all the value-creating activities undertaken by a company

Value creation the process of maximizing the difference between a customer's willingness to pay and the cost of the product

Values the shared assumptions that identify what a society believes is good, right, and desirable

Viral marketing marketing focused on producing a marketing message that people share with their friends through email, reposting, or retweeting

Virtual organization an organization that enables employees to coordinate and execute activities almost entirely through information technology, rather than by working in the same physical space

Weighted average cost of capital (WACC) the interest rate that a company is expected to pay to its investors (stockholders and bondholders) to raise money for its operations or projects

Wholly owned subsidiary a new legal entity set up for operation in a foreign market that is a separate company in legal terms but that it fully owned by a parent firm

World Bank a multilateral organization that focuses on preventing war by promoting economic development in poor countries; provides heavily subsidized loans to poor governments in an effort to help them build their infrastructure

World Economic Forum (WEF) a multilateral organization with the goal to improve the state of the world through public-private cooperation

World Trade Organization (WTO) a multilateral organization that ensures that international trade runs freely and fairly between countries and that member nations impose the minimal number of restrictions on each other

Index